NORTH CAROLINA
STATE BOARD OF COMMUNITY COLLEGES
LIBRARIES
STANLY TECHNICAL COLLEGE

D1648040

30515

30515

FLIGHT FANTASTIC

THE ILLUSTRATED HISTORY OF AEROBATICS

ANNETTE CARSON

Foulis

Haynes

By the same author (in collaboration with Eric Müller): *Flight Unlimited* (ISBN 0 9509252 0 9)

ISBN 0 85429 490 2

A **Foulis** Aviation Book

First published 1986
© Annette Carson and Haynes Publishing Group 1986
All rights reserved. No part of this book may be reproduced or transmitted in any form or by any means, electronic or mechanical, including photocopying, recording or by any information storage or retrieval system, without permission of the publisher.
Published by
Haynes Publishing Group,
Sparkford, Near Yeovil, Somerset
BA22 7JJ, England

Haynes Publications Inc.
861 Lawrence Drive, Newbury
Park, California 91320 USA

British Library Cataloguing in Publication

Carson, Annette
    Flight fantastic: the illustrated history of aerobatics.
    1. Stunt flying—History
    1. Title
    797.5'4   TL711.S8
    ISBN 0-5429-490-2

Library of Congress catalog card number 86-80522

Editor: Mansur Darlington
Page Layout: Tim Rose

Photo pages 2 & 3: Christen Eagle II (courtesy Christen Industries)

Printed in England, by:
J. H. Haynes & Co. Ltd

Contents

Foreword

by George C. Larson,
Editor of the Smithsonian Institution's *Air & Space* Magazine

When mankind took its inspiration from bird flight, people could only guess what went on in the birds' minds as they wheeled about the sky, free as ... well, birds. But one cannot watch a bird going about its day without imagining that its existence must be joyful, even if briefer than ours. Birds seldom comport themselves in a way that suggests the Protestant work ethic, and though they cannot smile with their rather inflexible lips, we hardly think of them as the dour, utilitarian sort. In fact, even when birds are apparently at work, they seem to be playing.

Playing is one part of bird flight *we* have almost forgotten. The air is there for us to use, and use it we do. We've become quite serious and stern about it, lifting vast quantities of people and cargo over incredible distances in a rather routine way, and none of that has much fun left in it anymore. But there are a few among us throughout the world who have preserved the right to play in the air with our flying machines, and who have developed the art of aerobatics.

This book is about them and their art. It is long overdue, and for all I have seen, it is the only book of its kind in that it tells the whole of their history between two covers. That it does so playfully is altogether fitting.

George C. Larson

Introduction

The world of aerobatics is always breathtaking – sometimes heart-stopping – and is infinite in its variety and excitement. It combines some of the highest elements of human achievement, from consummate artistry to hair's-breadth accuracy to technical wizardry. It demands the physical training of an athlete, the total concentration of an equilibrist, and the split-second reflexes of a racing driver. And always there is that indefinable symbiosis of pilot and machine which transcends the merely human and merely mechanical, breathing into that tiny whirling, dancing aircraft a mind and spirit that guides its intricate ballet in the sky.

This book is an essentially personal view of how aerobatics came to be, and how it developed through the years. The subject is an ephemeral one: there are few written records, and those that survive – especially from the early days – are fragmentary and imprecise. It is, in any case, a forever growing and changing art; few traditions exist, and very few are the outstanding names from the past who are remembered outside their own country. A major part of my aim has been to bring the greatest of those names, set in relief against their national background, to a wider audience who will appreciate their work. Some have lived and profited by it, others have died and sometimes sacrificed themselves that others might live.

Lack of space dictates that only the leaders of any one era can be recorded here, together with their aeroplanes and the manoeuvres they flew. That there are important characters who will be passed over is inevitable and regrettable, but a 'history', however meticulous, can never hope to be comprehensive: at best it is still only selective hindsight. And during the process of selection I have had to exclude many aspects of the subject.

Sadly I could not attempt to do proper justice to glider aerobatics, to formation aerobatics, or to jet aerobatics. Though they are not totally overlooked, to those readers who are disappointed by their minimal coverage I can only offer my apologies: it was better to bypass these subjects rather than treat them inadequately.

Even though confined to individually-performed powered aerobatics, this fascinating study has produced enough material to fill three books, and all too much has had to be sacrificed. It seemed important, nonetheless, to take time to explain exactly how the principal manoeuvres are performed, and how competititions are – and were – judged. And if the final chapters of the book are more concerned with World Championship aerobatics than with the kind of aerobatics you will see in airshows, the reason is that here the frontiers are being forever pushed back and excitingly innovative aircraft designs are being produced. It is still essentially a story of individual people. When the pilot performs he performs alone, and it is his own personal ideal of perfection that he tries to satisfy.

What do we mean by aerobatics, anyway? In the earliest days it was called *stunting*, not with the dismissive connotations that the word has today, but with a considerable amount of admiration for the skills (and risks) involved. Pilots daring enough to take their aircraft and themselves to the very limits were fêted and paid enormous sums of money, even by today's standards, to exhibit their prowess to an enraptured public.

It was when the daring began to outweigh the skill that stunting became synonymous with foolhardy and irrespon-

Flight Fantastic

sible flying. In official circles the view sometimes still persists; although the more enlightened soon realized that a mastery of the aircraft in all flight conditions was a key to confidence and safety in the air. *Aerial acrobatics*, later *aerobatics*, then became the accepted term in aviation for that kind of flying in which the aircraft was made to perform unconventional and sometimes spectacular evolutions, while always remaining within the control of the pilot.

Today's definition has gained an extra dimension, thanks to developments in the sport of competition aerobatics. For this the term *precision aerobatics* is often used. Certainly, the participants still perform the same loops and rolls, but in precision aerobatics they submit themselves to the most excruciating standards of *exactly geometrical* execution of those loops and rolls; something which sets it quite apart from the mainstream of aerobatics performed for display or simply for personal pleasure.

All these aspects of the art have a place in its history. So, with these guide-lines in mind, I have tackled the subject both chronologically and geographically: starting from its earliest beginnings, when the pioneers of aviation first grappled with how to control their flying machines; recording the aerobatic skills so quickly learnt by their pilots and so recklessly squandered in the theatres of war and of peace; and taking the reader onward through a period of eighty years during which manoeuvres were invented (and sometimes re-invented), aeroplanes were designed, improved and modified, reputations were made and often sadly forgotten, and the art evolved to the state of excellence which can be seen today all over the world.

My hope is that with this historical survey, and with the explanations it contains, the special and wonderful world of aerobatics may be better understood. And that its great exponents may never be forgotten.

Annette Carson
1 October 1985

Acknowledgements

This work would never have been possible without the help and encouragement of friends and enthusiasts all over the world, who willingly gave time, energy and material help without any reward other than to know that the book would be all the richer for their input.

Many had no specific connection with aerobatics, but were concerned to see this hitherto sparsely-documented subject given a full and accurate treatment. At the head of this list is the Musée de l'Air at Le Bourget, Paris, whose staff – in particular historian Stéphane Nicolaou – spared no effort to provide research materials, facilities, advice and illustrations. For as long as aviation history is in the hands of such as these, we need have no fears for its safe custody.

Three marvellous people read, criticised and advised on the manuscript of the book: my heartfelt thanks to Lynn Williams, Hal Groombridge and Pete Jarvis. Other dear and valued friends from overseas undertook research on their country's aerobatic history for me. For this I am grateful to Andrzej Abłamowicz, Don Berliner, Luis Cabre, Gabor Fekecs, Gerhard Fieseler, Werner Garitz, Klaus Habermann, Gianna Hagander, Nils and Erik Hagander, Henry Harlé, Jan Krumbach, Marie-France Leire, Scully Levin, Chuck Mann, Kasum Nazhmudinov, Frank Price, Jan F. Šára, Arnold Wagner, Walter Wolfrum.

At home the list of helpers is massive and only a few can be mentioned: special thanks go to Jean Alexander, John Bagley, John Barfoot, Tony Bianchi, James Black, John Blake, Frank Cheesman, Christopher Clarkson, Richard Goode, Mike Hooks, Mike Jerram, Michael Jones, Frank Kendall, Tony Lloyd, Arnold Naylor, Peter Phillips, Ranald Porteous, 'Sandy' Powell, Claire and Jeffrey Quill, Iona Radice.

And finally, among those who raided photographic collections and freely loaned precious illustrations, the following names must be added to those already mentioned: Lewis Benjamin, Chaz Bowyer, Alex Henshaw, Hermann Liese, Bob Lyjak, Maurice Marsh, Edmond Petit, Nick Pocock, Bruce Robertson, John Underwood, 'Wes' Schmid; and in particular Mike Heuer of the International Aerobatic Club and Jean Sorg of *Sport Aerobatics*, who generously allowed me full access to their archives and photographic material.

To these and all the other helpers whom space does not allow me to name individually, I hope the end product justifies their faith in me and their kind efforts on my behalf.

1

Wing~warping, ailerons and joysticks

Aerobatic flight is no new thing: the birds had it figured out a long time ago. I once saw a bald eagle fly a perfect horizontal roll, and Wing Commander Norman Macmillan reported seeing buzzards perform not only a full roll but a roll-off-the-top, this latter manoeuvre – half-roll at the top of a half-loop – not being invented by earthbound man until the late years of World War I.

In fact the performance of aerobatic flight, whether human or avian, depends fundamentally on the equipment available to the flyer. And an essential of that equipment is full control in all three dimensions of pitch, yaw and roll. Here, therefore, is the starting point of this book: the achievement of that control.

But when men came to work on the problems of mechanical flight, this idea of three-axis control was something they found exceedingly difficult to grasp. Many distinguished and courageous pioneers at the turn of the century, principally those in Europe, stood in the way of their own progress by looking no further than the two-dimensional control philosophy of the airship: up-and-down (pitch) and side-to-side (yaw). To sail along like an ocean liner was definitely the thing. Banking the wings was a far too risky business, grossly dangerous and wholly unnecessary!

Charles H Gibbs-Smith of the London Science Museum drew a particularly vivid contrast between the then-prevailing European school of thought – that of the 'chauffeur' – and the philosophy epitomized by Wilbur and Orville Wright, over 6,000 kilometres away in Dayton, Ohio – that of the 'airman'. In Europe in the early 1900s, the flying machine was still viewed as an airborne motor car (a view which persists, to the detriment of flying safety, throughout the world even today). But the two Americans, studying the wheeling flight of the buzzards, had latched on to the vitally significant principle of three-dimensional manoeuvring.

Obsessed by the idea of manned flight, and reading every text they could find on the subject, Wilbur and Orville made a decision to go out on a limb and flout the doctrine of the *inherently stable* aeroplane: this stated that the very construction of the airframe should if possible resist any force tending to unbalance it, and should tend to return to an 'even keel' if disturbed in any axis.

It was the genius of the Wright brothers that they dared to build *inherently unstable* machines which would wholly depend on the pilot's skill in handling the controls. As Wilbur said, "We would arrange the machine so that it would not tend to right itself". Hitherto, any control surfaces incorporated by other pioneers (rudders, elevators, ailerons and the like) had been intended to nudge the apparatus into the desired attitude and direction of flight with the minimum of disturbance from straight and level. Obviously, such machines could only be successfully flown in conditions of flat calm. The Wrights, however, intended to fly in wind – even gusty wind.

Wilbur and Orville had no illusions about the difficult and dangerous path they were taking. In an early letter (May, 1900) Wilbur wrote: "For some years I have been afflicted with the belief that flight is possible to man. My disease has increased in severity and I feel that it will soon cost me an increased amount of money, if not my life." In fact neither brother was called upon to make the supreme sacrifice, and both were eventually to die in their beds. But they took a serious, even dedicated view of their work. By mutual agreement they never married: Wilbur's view, that neither had the means "to support a wife and a flying machine, too", foreshadowed that of many a later aviator!

Wilbur was aged 35 and Orville 31 when the breakthrough came in late 1902 while they were still working with gliders. They had already mastered the fairly straightforward matters

The Wright brothers in France, 1908, adjusting the launching rail of their Model A biplane: Wilbur at left, kneeling, and Orville standing on extreme right. (via Musée de l'Air)

Wright No 3 glider in its modified form, showing the rear rudder (Orville piloting). (via Musée de l'Air)

of pitch control (by means of forward elevators) and yaw control (with rear rudders), but now at last they perfected an integrated three-axis system including successful roll control which gave them mastery over all the aeroplane's movements, both expected and unexpected.

"The basic idea was the adjustment of the wings to the right and left sides to different angles, so as to secure different lifts on the opposite wings." This was achieved by means of a torsion of the wing-tips (which they had observed in the buzzards), using wing-twisting cables which were operated by movements of the pilot's hip-harness as he lay prone on the lower wing. In fact, 'twisting' was the Wrights' preferred and more accurate term for this process; but the world came to call it 'wing-warping' and the brothers bowed to the common use of the phrase.

Now, for the first time in a practical machine, they applied the dual principle of an adjustable rudder combined with this wing-warping as a system of effecting lateral control. They had always known that they must 'roll' the wings in order to manoeuvre efficiently, but the combined rudder movement was the secret of doing this safely and controllably. The idea of varying the aerofoil to achieve different wing-lifts was not unique to the Wrights; but never before had it been used in this way.

It was on the Glider No. 3 design in September 1902 that their system was first installed: they decided to modify the fixed rear 'vane' or double fin to become an adjustable rudder, and hit on the idea of linking it to the wing-twisting cables. This was in order to counteract the drag that always

came into play on the up-going wing as it was banked, caused by the warped trailing-edge being lowered into the relative airflow. In modern parlance this is known as adverse yaw: the drag on the wing has the effect of yawing or slewing it back at the same time as it rises. The result being a sideslip which could get the unwary pilot into trouble – especially at the very low heights at which flight was carried out in 1902!

So now, whenever the wings were warped, the rudder was

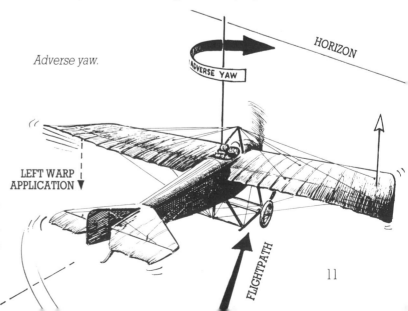

Adverse yaw.

HORIZON

ADVERSE YAW

LEFT WARP APPLICATION

FLIGHTPATH

11

Flight Fantastic

simultaneously adjusted to deflect toward the side *opposite* the lagging wing, thereby yawing the wing forward: the co-ordinated turn was born.

Wilbur and Orville were the very first to combine lateral and directional (rolling and yawing) flight controls for the purpose of banking the aircraft. From that moment on, gusty winds and the possibility of 'losing one's balance' in the air were no longer a threat.

Yet even after the publication of their successful system, it seems astonishing to the present-day reader that other contemporary pioneers failed to recognize its significance. In France, for example, although several copies of Wright gliders were built, the wing-warping system was rejected – some even said it was too dangerous! And though in some early designs there were occasional aileron-type devices to be seen (Santos-Dumont, Blériot, etc), still they were strictly for use as a corrective balancing device, not for the danger-ous pursuit of banking the wings.

absence of the strong winds and low temperatures of Kitty Hawk. It was from here with the Flyer II that they achieved the triumph of the first full **360 degree banked turn** in history, lasting 1½ minutes, on 20 September 1904.

The distinction should be noted, however, that this rudder/wing-warping system was an automatic linkage. With the Flyer III of a year later, September 1905, the Wright brothers came up with the winning combination. They separated the wing-warping controls from the rudder and thus permitted their independent or combined operation in any desired

Wright Flyer III, incorporating the Wrights' own design of 12hp, four cylinder, water cooled, fuel-injected gasolene engine driving two geared-down pusher propellers (also of their own design) situated about 10ft (3m) apart and revolving in opposite directions.

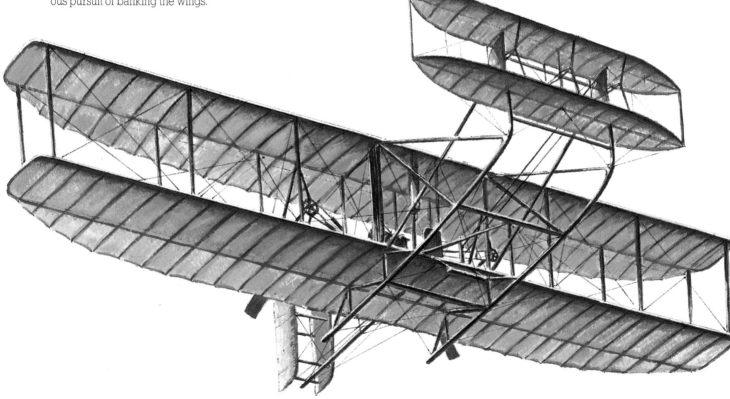

But so far they had only worked with gliders. Transferring these principles to powered flight, the Wrights' next step was to add engine and propellers of their own design and construction: more evidence of an inventive genius that almost defies description. Eventually, with the Flyer I which took to the air on 17 December 1903, they achieved the first powered, sustained and – most important – *controlled* flights in history in a heavier-than-air machine. Their design was a braced pusher biplane on a skid undercarriage, with a biplane elevator jutting out at the front for pitch control, and a double rudder at the rear linked to the wing-warping system.

With a sense of relief the brothers at last felt able to return home with their invention. Transferring their operation to a local field near Dayton, they made a further change by erecting a catapult device to assist their take-offs in the

degree. Now the pilot was wholly in charge of the handling of the machine, and an unstable machine at that: he must apply control inputs to initiate manoeuvres – banked turns, circles, figures of eight – and he must learn the corrective control actions to keep the aircraft behaving as he wished it to. The art of piloting had been born, and with it the beginnings of aerobatics.

Both Wilbur and Orville taught themselves to become first-rate pilots on the Flyer III. Crashes, of course, were a routine by-product of any attempt at manoeuvrability. They had to be especially alert for the dreaded sideslip, and quite early on they invented a home-made 'slip indicator' – a short piece of string tied to the crossbar beneath the front elevator – which when it started moving to one side in the relative airflow gave warning of an incipient sideslip.

Wing~warping, ailerons and joysticks

They also solved the perennial problem of the stall in a tight turn, which had bothered them for quite some time and led to numerous crashes. Their explanation was that the limited engine power available under the increased *g* loads in the turn was insufficient to maintain flying speed', and their remedy for this was to pitch the nose forward.

The application of the term 'stall' to aeronautics also appears to stem initially from the Wrights, referring to that loss of lift when the machine was allowed to 'turn up' too much. Unfortunately, as well as giving us the term, they also gave us the concept of linking the stall with speed (or loss of it): they associated pitching the nose down with regaining 'flying speed', rather than with restoring a correct angle of attack*. It was the right remedy, but the wrong diagnosis. In fact the misleading phrases 'stalling speed' and 'loss of flying speed' soon became common aviation parlance, and still recur even to the present day.

Such misconceptions about the stall hindered the progress of aviation for longer than we perhaps nowadays realize: as late as 1934, for example, Professor B Melvill Jones stated in his Wright Memorial Lecture:

... until the stall is thoroughly understood and its attendant dangers pushed out of the way, aviation will not be free to play the great rôle which it is undoubtedly destined to play in the civilization of the world...

In the year 1905 the Wright brothers felt that they now had a safe and controllable flying machine, and were ready at last to put it on the market. But they were bitterly disappointed to find there was no market yet ready for them. Mostly they were faced by incredulity, quite often by sheer apathy. They had placed their faith on obtaining military orders, but when their overtures to their own and other governments came to nothing, they simply withdrew from active flying and went into a self-imposed retirement. For 2½ years from October 1905 they remained grounded, concentrating instead on improving their engines and perfecting their machines, until they had produced the standard Wright Model A biplane design of 1907 onwards.

One part of the problem was their natural reticence, combined with a reluctance to offer their prized invention to public examination until it was fully protected by patents (which took years to be granted). Then a tendency to stagnation set in, which was eventually to cost them their lead in the world of aviation. They stayed with the skid undercarriage and catapult-assisted launch for too long, and clung to their patented wing-warping system even in the face of developments that were soon to catch up and then to overtake them: for the more successful aileron system was about to be born.

While the Wrights were toiling away in complete anonymity, in another part of America the quest for manned flight continued at full tilt with the Aerial Experiment Association, which was born on 1 October 1907, under the leadership of Dr Alexander Graham Bell (of telephone fame). The other AEA members, who comprised a group of American and Canadian enthusiasts, included a 29-year-old motorcycle designer and racer by the name of Glenn H Curtiss.

Curtiss had made quite a name for himself by setting a world motorcycle speed record with his own 40 hp air-cooled V-8 engine, and had already begun designing engines for airships when he was invited to join the AEA as Director of Experiments. From that moment onward his

Glenn Curtiss.   *(Musée de l'Air)*

interests quickly extended from the power plants to the aeroplanes themselves.

The Association's first two efforts were passably successful pusher biplanes, which encouraged them to press onward. Next they produced the much improved White Wing, and then in June 1908 the very successful June Bug emerged, mainly under Curtiss's own direction. The remarkable thing about these last two designs was that they pioneered an entirely new system of interconnected triangular ailerons set in frames at the wingtips, working in conjunction with each other for lateral stability – an idea recommended by the inventive Dr Bell.

The aileron system was much easier to operate than wing-warping, and, more important, it permitted stronger, more rigid wing construction: this in turn allowed the aircraft to achieve significantly greater speeds than were possible with the wing-warp designs. (In addition to such structural considerations, well-designed ailerons also have the advantage that, placed as they are outboard of the wing, they do not have the wing-warpers' tendency, near the stall, of inducing a stall in the very wing one wants to lift.)

Ahead even of the AEA ailerons, however, were those of Dr William W Christmas of Washington, DC, who built (and allegedly flew) a 40 hp pusher biplane of his own design at Fairfax City, Virginia, in March of 1908, about the same time that the White Wing was being constructed. He, too, had hit on the idea of the wingtip aileron, but the significant thing here is that Dr Christmas's cross-controlled inset ailerons were a hinged portion of the wingtip just like the modern variety. While Glenn Curtiss was to suffer endless lawsuits for his use of the aileron, being accused of infringement of the

---

*The angle of attack is the angle at which the wing meets the relative airflow. At certain angles – speaking very generally, up to about 15 degrees or so – efficient lift is produced. At angles of attack greater than this, the wing begins to lose lift and will tend to stall unless the pilot reduces the angle by lowering the nose of the aircraft.

Flight Fantastic

Wright wing-warping patents, Dr Christmas quietly registered his invention and received a US patent in May 1914.

Christmas was a doctor of medicine who lacked any sound engineering basis for his various harebrained aircraft designs, and there is no corroboration as to how far they actually 'flew' before crashing and killing their unfortunate pilots. Though since generally recognized as a charlatan, he never seemed short of backers at the time; and indeed in 1923, influential friends in Congress put through a bill paying him compensation to the tune of $100,000, since the US government had used the trailing-edge aileron on all their aircraft manufacured during World War I!

Christmas Bullet with trailing edge ailerons.

Meanwhile, so successful was the June Bug design that Curtiss entered and won the *Scientific American* air trophy contest for the first public flight of 1 kilometre in a straight line, held in a carnival atmosphere on the Fourth of July, 1908, with press and public in attendance. It was not until the end of August, however, that he managed a complete 360 degree turn (which the Wrights had achieved four years earlier), taking 2 minutes 28 seconds. The rudimentary wingtip panels obviously were not efficient enough, and Glenn Curtiss improved on the concept in his subsequent designs by setting these control surfaces half-way between the wings, mounted on the interplane struts.

Curtiss Golden Flier (1908).   *(Smithsonian Institution)*

Next, and last, of the Association's models was the Silver Dart, a very fine machine with which in February 1909 its designer, John McCurdy, flew the first heavier-than-air flight in Canada. The AEA had now achieved its goal of building a practical, man-carrying aeroplane, and its members decided to call it a day; a decision no doubt accelerated by their Director of Experiments having already struck out on his own, for by now Glenn Curtiss had accepted a private commission to build an aeroplane for the Aeronautic Society of New York.

For this commission Curtiss shortly produced a fast, sturdy biplane, using mid-gap ailerons, which was christened the Golden Flier. The design was so successful that, taking it as his prototype, he now felt confident to enter for a newly announced air race that was due to take place later that year. This was the Gordon Bennett Speed Trophy, to be held during the world's first great aerial meeting at Reims, in France, during the month of August 1909. The new Curtiss machine was to be the Reims Racer.

Before we move on to that historic event, however, let us examine the state of progress in European aircraft design up to mid-1908, which was the date that Wilbur Wright emerged from retirement and demonstrated his aeroplane in France.

During the first flurry of interest in Wright glider types, a young French architectural school graduate by the name of Gabriel Voisin had tried his hand at construction, and soon afterwards established the famous firm of Voisin Frères with his brother Charles. But the Voisin machines, in keeping with the pursuit of inherent stability, totally ignored the question of lateral control: no European machine had yet been designed to perform banking or rolling actions. The only way to make a turn was to yaw the aircraft around and then, when one set of wings rose and the other fell, yaw it back the other way again!

Such was the state of the art in France when Henri Farman, a one-time cyclist and recent convert to the cause of mechanical flight, acquired for himself a Voisin 'box kite' in October 1907 and thus became the first British pilot.

Despite his French sounding name, Henri was the son of an English journalist who was domiciled in Paris; he was chris-

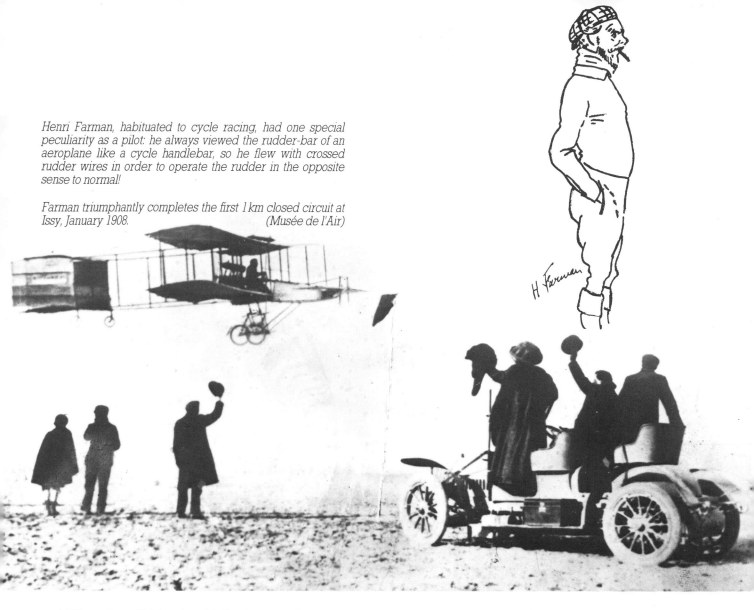

Henri Farman, habituated to cycle racing, had one special peculiarity as a pilot: he always viewed the rudder-bar of an aeroplane like a cycle handlebar, so he flew with crossed rudder wires in order to operate the rudder in the opposite sense to normal!

Farman triumphantly completes the first 1km closed circuit at Issy, January 1908. (Musée de l'Air)

tened Harry, but with French as his first language he generally called himself by the French version of his name. With his Voisin-Farman I, in November 1907, Henri managed the first flight in Europe of more than one minute's duration, and thus encouraged he soon decided to make an attempt on the Deutsch-Archdeacon Prize of 50,000 francs which had been offered for a 1km closed circuit flight. This he arranged to take place at the military parade grounds at Issy-les-Moulineaux on the left bank of the Seine – Europe's first real aerodrome – where the public was now beginning to be attracted to the aeronautical goings-on at this easily accessible spot on the outskirts of Paris.

The circuit which Farman successfully negotiated on 13 January 1908, consisted of a 500 m leg followed by a wide turn and another 500 m leg back to the start again; the tricky part being the execution of a fairly steeply banked turn at the half-way point (probably 40–45 degrees of bank) necessitated by the terrain at Issy. He achieved this with a modification which entailed the removal of the stabilizing vertical end-panels from between the biplane wings of the machine. A blow had been struck for instability at last!

Progress was slow, but it was steady. From late 1907 onwards, French pilots began to achieve more and more success with their 'two-dimensional' craft, gradually working up to flying durations of 20 minutes at a time, though naturally in conditions of total, flat calm. The test of flying conditions

was the simple 'cigarette test': if the smoke from a lighted cigarette went straight on up, the weather was flyable; if not, it was a tempest, a hurricane, a tornado – no flying today!

But there was one vitally important area in which the Europeans soon led the world in the field of aeronautics, and that was in engine design.

The engine was a major consideration in early powered flight, for lightness of structure was all-important and aero engines therefore had to be expressly designed with this in mind. Although the Wrights, working in splendid isolation, had managed to design their own power plant, most early experimenters bought their engines off the shelf, and it was to France that they invariably turned. Following hard on the heels of in-line engines such as the Antoinette came the rotary Gnôme of 1909, designed by Laurent and Louis Séguin, which was soon to become the most popular and (for those days) reliable power plant on both sides of the Atlantic.

And in one other invention, or combination of inventions, the French also led the way in those early years: the classic monoplane with stick and rudder controls. For this we have the redoubtable Louis Blériot to thank.

Blériot started as a well-to-do manufacturer of automobile accessories with money to spend on his hobby – which soon became an obsession – of designing and constructing aeroplanes. After a short-lived partnership with Gabriel Voisin on biplanes, Blériot decided in 1906, amid a tumult of im-

Louis Blériot.
(via Musée de l'Air)

Blériot VIII-bis with revolving wing-tips. (Musée de l'Air)

passioned argument, to pursue his revolutionary monoplane projects on his own. Selling his business, he staked everything on a series of monoplane designs in which he experimented with a bewildering variety of configurations and control surfaces; but his empirical experiments eventually produced the world's first successful true monoplane in June 1908 with his model VIII. In its subsequent version the VIII-*bis* he achieved respectable flights of over eight minutes the following month. Here he perfected the now familiar cruciform shape which we all take so much for granted, with a 50 hp engine positioned in front of the mainplanes and a fuselage extending to a tail at the rear.

It had pivoting end-panels at the wingtips, to preserve lateral balance (though not to initiate rolling actions), and twin horizontal elevators on the tail. Its clean and simple lines were the forerunner of our most popular present-day light aeroplane configurations.

But perhaps Blériot's greatest contribution to aviation during this period was his ingenious *cloche* system by which

Blériot's cloche *control system.*

the control column simultaneously operated both the lateral and pitch controls. As its name implies it was a bell-shaped unit, which was mounted on a universal joint, with wires from the rim which led to the elevators and to the lateral surfaces. Rudder movements were controlled separately by the feet operating a rudder bar. This was a true stick-and-rudder combination, and Blériot's *cloche* system was the direct precursor of the modern joystick used by aerobatic pilots today.

Nothing, of course, was standardized. Many different control systems remained in use side by side for years, and the Blériot-type stick and rudder did not become universal until World War I. One thing was generally true, however: the theory of proper lateral control had not yet been adopted in Europe when Wilbur Wright appeared in France on 8 August 1908. Invited by the French, he proceeded to demonstrate his 30 hp Model A biplane, and the little audience at Le Mans

Wilbur flying the Wright Model A at Le Mans, France. Note that the pilot sits upright, with hand levers replacing the original wing warping hip-cradle. (via Musée de l'Air)

A WARP

A₁ WARP

B ELEVATOR

C ELEVATOR

could scarcely believe its eyes. Spectators marvelled at its manoeuvrability and dexterity of performance. They were amazed by the ease and precision of its landings, even in gusty winds. The Paris *Herald* reported that it "rose to a height of 8 to 10 metres, circled twice, took turns with ease at almost terrifying angles, and alighted like a bird".

Daily Mail reporter Harry Harper retained an indelible impression of the occasion:

For one thing it was the first time I had ever seen anything like a real aeroplane flying ... Wilbur began to take it up in a smooth, steady climb till he was several hundred feet above our heads. After which he proceeded to give us an aerial display which held us breathless as we stood there beside his shed, gazing up into a tranquil evening sky. Climbing, diving, banking, circling this way and that, he handled his machine with an absolute certainty and precision which had to be seen to be believed.

What I remember, more perhaps than anything else, is the superb skill he displayed in sending that biplane round in a series of turning movements. It was in carrying out such a manoeuvre that Wilbur took full advantage of the way in which the warping of his wing-tips, for lateral control, was interconnected with the operation of his twin rudders. The effect of this was that, as the airman banked over his machine, quite easily and gently, it seemed just to slide round on its correct angle on the turn, reminding one of the way in which a fast car adapts itself to the banking of a track.

What a contrast to the tentative efforts seen hitherto, and how different were these turns from the yawing, skidding motions of the non-warpers!

Of course, such a challenge to the inherent stability doctrine could not go unrefuted. Critics were quick to charge that 'only an acrobat' could fly the Wright machine; but this was amply disproved by the ease with which total novices mastered its controls after only a few lessons. Louis Blériot took the wiser course of profiting from his observations, and promptly set about constructing his next model, the celebrated Model XI, with stick and rudder and an efficient Wright-type wing-warping system, in which he made the unforgettable first Channel crossing on 25 July, 1909.

Allen Wheeler, recounting the experiences of a modern pilot flying the aircraft of that period, described as most noticeable –

... the very considerable feeling of insecurity ... mainly due to the general flexibility of the whole structure which, in greater or lesser degree, according to the type flown, gives the impression that one is trying to fly a blancmange. Added to this unsteadiness is the fact that in most of the types one is sitting out in the open, almost on top of the blancmange. A third and not unimportant disturbing feature is that response to movement of the lateral controls is sluggish, sometimes to the point of non-existence.

... the whole flight is essentially a friendly arrangement between the pilot and the aeroplane: the former cannot tell the latter what to do, he can only arrange a situation wherein the latter will probably do what the former wants. Skill and tact are needed in this friendly arrangement, and if both are applied resourcefully it is (almost) certain that each flight will be satisfactory.

(*Building Aeroplanes for 'Those Magnificent Men'*, G T Foulis, 1965)

The Channel-crossing prize money just about saved Blériot, for he had spent everything he had on experiments with aeroplanes. And to complete his joy, within two days of the crossing he had received over 100 orders for the machine. 'The waistcoat-pocket monoplane' the British called it, and it was powered in those days by a 3-cylinder air-cooled Anzani fan-shaped radial, which aspired to all of 25 hp, driving a 2 m (6.6 ft) diameter laminated-walnut Chauvière propeller.

Later versions of the Model XI incorporated the French Gnôme rotary engines of 50 hp and more, and sold in their hundreds; and with its admirable handling qualities, the machine had a distinguished career ahead of it for several years to come. We shall meet the Blériot XI again in 1913 in the talented hands of Adolphe Pégoud, the first Frenchman to 'loop-the-loop'.

Blériot XI Channel-crossing machine.   *(Musée de l'Air)*

2

Air meetings and air shows

Within a month of Louis Blériot's triumphant flight across the Channel, the ancient French city of Reims staged a 'Grande Semaine d'Aviation' from 22 to 28 August 1909 – the world's first grand-scale Aviation Meeting.

Some 300,000 spectators thronged to Bétheny plains, immortalized in the fifteenth century by Joan of Arc, where enclosures, a covered grandstand and huge public scoreboard had now been erected. There were sideshows, a fairground, reporters, photographers. All Paris society was there – not to mention thousands of visitors from abroad, including Britain and the US – all dressed in style, with formal hats and parasols, as if for a race meeting at the height of the season.

With 200,000 francs on offer in prize money, practically everyone in the European aviation community was either flying or spectating. There were prizes for passenger flights, altitude, speed and endurance, and the high-spot of the week was the eagerly-awaited *Coupe Internationale d'Aviation* for the big speed race. A magnificent silver trophy had been donated in honour of the occasion by the flamboyant James Gordon Bennett, publisher of the Paris *New York Herald*, already a liberal patron of aviation and of yachting, automobile and balloon contests.

Under the rules of the Fédération Aéronautique Internationale, set up in 1905 as the official body to ratify aviation record-taking, a team of three was allowed from each member nation for the race. For the French entrants this necessitated a series of eliminators, flown in the worst possible weather during the early days of the meeting: the skies opened, rain decended in sheets, and the field was thoroughly flooded.

The original poster for Reims week, the 'Champagne Air Meeting'.   *(via Musée de l'Air)*

The grandstands at Reims, August 1909.
(Smithsonian Institution)

At the end of the trials – some aspirants being forced down with engine trouble, some being unable to get airborne at all – the French team places were awarded to Louis Blériot with his Blériot XI, now a Chevalier of the Légion d'Honneur; Hubert Latham, famous for his fearless handling of the graceful Antoinette monoplane; and modest, quiet-spoken Eugène Lefebvre, engineer and chief pilot with the Wright company in France, flying a cut-down French built Wright model.

During the course of the meeting, 27-year-old Lefebvre made an unforgettable impression with his antics in the air, obviously going all out to thrill the crowd and drawing rapturous applause for his exuberant performances. Among his daring manoeuvres were sharp double-turns and figures-of-eight in front of the grandstand; sometimes he would bear down until it looked as though he would surely crash, then at the last moment put his aircraft into an unbelievably steep bank, with one wing-tip just skimming the grass, and zoom away in a climb. In fact he ended up with a fine for being rather over-daring, an effect well illustrated by this nice grab-shot of a photographer throwing himself to the ground in the path of Lefebvre's machine!

Lefebvre was entirely self-taught and had acquired his first

A frightened photographer throws himself to the ground as Lefebvre makes a low pass. *(Flight)*

(Inset) A spectacularly low, banked turn from Eugène Lefebvre as he rounds a pylon in his Astra Wright (a machine of the Ariel Company, owners of the French rights in Wright aeroplanes). *(via Musée de l'Air)*

Eugène Lefebvre, the first 'aerobatic' exhibition pilot.
(via Musée de l'Air)

machine only a month before in Holland; it had not taken long for a skilled pilot to make full use of those effective Wright controls. Harry Harper, the *Daily Mail* reporter who witnessed the whole event, believed him to be "the first flyer in the world to give in public an exhibition of anything like what we came afterwards to call 'aerobatics'".

How tragic that such a promising career was then suddenly cut short only a couple of weeks later, on 7 September, while he was testing a Wright machine fitted for the first time with wheels: the aircraft went into a dive – probably due to jammed controls – and Eugène Lefebvre died in the crash.

The roll of names at Reims, almost all of them French, reads like an aviation Hall of Fame. The pilots were novices; their aircraft for the most part underpowered, unreliable and precarious; but what a show they put on for the public! Here

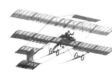

was Henri Farman with his own design of biplane; Louis Paulhan, soon to make a name for himself internationally; Léon Delagrange, Farman's great friend and rival; and Capt Ferber, Roger Sommer, Count Charles de Lambert, Paul Tissandier; the list goes on and on.

A story – no doubt apocryphal – is told of an exchange between Hubert Latham, darling of the Paris salons, and President Armand Fallières, during that august gentleman's tour of the hangars. Observing the distant airborne progress of a dirigible, Fallières turned to Latham and, looking askance at the slender lines of the Antoinette, asked:

"But . . . where do you put the gas?"

Latham, unperturbed, slipped another cigarette into the famous cigarette-holder:

"*Monsieur le Président*, it's the exhaust gases that inflate the fuselage!"

Farman, on the strength of his Deutsch-Archdeacon Prize winnings, had been able to set up an aeroplane factory himself, and in October 1908 produced the Voisin-Farman I-*bis*, based on the original Voisin box kite but generally lightened and now incorporating an idea of his own: four large ailerons hinged to the outboard trailing edges of each wing. They had no balance cables and were designed to hang limp until the airflow lifted them into the flying attitude once the aircraft was moving; then one or the other could be angled downwards by the pilot to achieve additional lift on that side. He captured a respectable number of records and prizes with these machines, and some years later the British Army ordered well over 1,000 to equip the embryonic RFC.

Biplanes vied with monoplanes for top honours during the week-long meeting, and knowledgeable spectators by now were animatedly debating the relative merits of four wings versus two wings, a debate still familiar in the world of aerobatics today! Among the original field of 38 entrants – though not all of them started – were five biplane types (Breguet, Curtiss, Farman, Voisin, Wright) and five monoplane types (Antoinette, REP, and Blériots XI, XII and XIII).

Thankfully, the final day dawned warm, sunny and clear for the Gordon Bennett Trophy. It was generally acknowledged to be a two-horse race anyway, between Glenn Curtiss – the 'unknown quantity', newly arrived from the United States with his one precious machine which he dared not risk in any of the preliminary events – and the home favourite Louis Blériot, who had a brand-new Model XII which he was keeping under wraps for the big event. This advanced, two-seat, aileron-equipped high-wing monoplane sported a 60 hp water-cooled ENV engine and was the most powerful machine at the Reims Meeting.

Certainly it was a formidable rival for Curtiss's Reims Racer, a clipped-wing version of the Golden Flier with a fast, efficient aerofoil shape, featuring ailerons between the wings, double front elevator, tailplane with rudder at the rear, and tricycle landing gear. Mounted above and behind the pilot was Curtiss's own 50 hp 8-cylinder water-cooled Vee-engine which he had finished barely in time to sail for Europe; even then, he and his mount had reached the Meeting only hours before the required qualifying rounds.

First to fly in the race itself, Curtiss climbed as high as possible in order to have the extra speed from a gradual descent, and put his ailerons to good use cutting the corners

Henri Farman biplane design showing flap-type trailing edge ailerons.
(Musée de l'Air)

Curtiss Reims Racer. Frequently misnamed Golden Flier, the Racer was actually a close copy of the Aeronautical Society's machine, the original having been left in America with Charles F Willard who took it on a series of exhibition dates while Curtiss was in France. The Reims machine still had ailerons hinged to the forward interplane struts but they were rendered more efficient by the reduced upper and lower wingspans. The aircraft also had a slightly different aerofoil, designed for speed. It was covered in grey coloured rubber silk, and was built in the remarkable time of less than four weeks. Great secrecy surrounded the specially designed engine, which was crated and shipped before Curtiss could even test it in the aeroplane. (Musée de l'Air)

as close as he dared and banking the machine outrageously on the turns. He finished at an average speed of 75.7 km/h (47 mph). Blériot followed, with the crowd on their feet cheering him on; but, although completing one of his laps in a faster time than Curtiss, he managed to finish 6 seconds slower on average. The American had snatched the coveted trophy from under the noses of the French.

The importance of the Reims Meeting can scarcely be exaggerated. The aircraft on view there represented the very latest in technological development both in airframe and power plant, and no less than six different types were for sale with prices varying between 10,000 and 30,000 francs. All at once the frontiers of mechanical flight were thrown wide open: records were made one day and broken the next. Aviation as a sport and as entertainment had well and truly arrived.

During the ensuing twelve months more than 20 aviation meetings were held in Europe (Italy, France, Britain, Germany, Belgium, etc.), and a dozen or so in the USA. The stars of Reims were in demand for all of them, and many more aerial performers quickly emerged who had the talent to please the public with daring and skilful exhibitions.

After their respective triumphs in Europe, the Wrights and Curtiss at last received the recognition they deserved at home, and were showered with awards and medals. With Wilbur receiving the princely sum of $15,000 in September 1909 for a single exhibition flight during the Hudson-Fulton celebrations, the Wrights quickly realized that here was a vital source of income to be exploited; and they wisely set about training an exhibition team – the Wright Flyers – to take on the work of demonstrating Wright machines.

Walter Brookins, a keen 21-year-old who had hung around the Wright shop as a boy, was their first recruit. He was trained simultaneously as both pilot and instructor, and soloed after $2\frac{1}{2}$ hours dual in their latest side-by-side two-seat training model, which featured dual elevator controls and a wing-warping/rudder control lever set between the seats.

Next to be taught was 26-year-old Arch Hoxsey, a one-time motor mechanic and auto racer who wore *pince-nez* and got hooked on flying in January 1910. Brookins and Hoxsey were natural flyers and soon became almost legendary exhibition figures, along with later team member Ralph Johnstone, a former trick-cyclist from Kansas City. The team's first outing was in June 1910 at Indianapolis, where Brookins immediately set a new altitude record.

But the newspapers were not impressed with mere demonstrations of adroit handling: they found the event tame. In contrast to the Europeans, who were captivated by flying as a sport in itself, the American press and public were hungry for thrills. So, naturally enough, the pilots began thinking up

*Wright exhibition team. Left to right;
Frank Coffyn, Ralph Johnstone, Wilbur Wright, Orville Wright and Walter Brookins.* (Smithsonian Institution)

Flight Fantastic

Walter Brookins.   (Smithsonian Institution)

more exciting feats to capture the audience's interest and acclaim. Walter Brookins was among the first to start pulling in the crowds with his **spiral dives** and steep turns: in June 1910 he set a world record for fast turning in 5½ seconds with a 90 degree bank (outside the exhibition circuit, banking in a turn still continued for some years to be viewed with grave misgivings, and many considered it highly dangerous!).

Hoxsey and Johnstone, billed as 'The Heavenly Twins', soon acquired a reputation for daredevilry. The Wrights grew increasingly unhappy about such risk-taking, and even grounded Arch Hoxsey at one time, but they were powerless to restrain their pilots' audacity when spurred on by the public. Johnstone himself said:

I fly to live. If I didn't have to, I wouldn't. I am a fatalist ... Let me tell you, the people who go to see us want thrills. And, if we fall, do they think of us and go away weeping? Not by a long shot. They're too busy watching the next man and wondering if he will repeat the performance.

Egging them on at the same time, of course, was the fact that the Wrights' arch-rival Glenn Curtiss also had his own team competing for public acclaim.

He had already exhibited his prizewinning Reims Racer at the first aerial meeting in the United States, held at Dominguez Field, Los Angeles, from 10–20 January 1910. Afterwards, the aeroplane's flying career continued in the hands of the madcap Charles K Hamilton, a one-time stunt parachutist who had learned to fly in the newly-opened Curtiss Flying School; he toured it in a series of exhibitions, but in the spring of the year it soon went the way of all Hamilton's machines when he wrecked it in a crash landing. CK, who suffered from tuberculosis and doubtless reckoned that his days were numbered anyway, was unbelievably daring and reckless and soon became one of the stars of the Curtiss squad, despite – or because of – his constant crashes. Reports described him in landing competitions pointing the nose straight down from about 200 ft (60 m), just like a power dive, then at about 5 ft (1½ m) from the ground he would straighten

Lincoln Beachey.   (Smithsonian Institution)

Curtiss 'Headless'. The price of the original 'D' model started at $4,500, depending on engine power. The 'Headless' became standard from 1912 at a price of $5,000. Powered by a 90 hp OX-5 V-8 engine, this faithful replica, Silver Streak, is built and flown by Dale Crites, former manager of the Waukesha Airport, Wisconsin. (Dale Crites)

up and stop right on the line in front of the grandstand. Heady stuff indeed, in 1910!

Although not so beautifully harmonized as the Blériot stick-and-rudder system, the Curtiss biplane's controls in the standard D-III models were not difficult to handle. They consisted of a tall lever with a wheel on top, situated between the pilot's legs, and a shoulder yoke which controlled the small ailerons between the wings. The wheel was pulled or pushed to raise or lower the nose; turning the wheel to right or left turned the vertical rudder at the tail, and while this was done the pilot banked by leaning into the turn.

With these controls it was even possible to fly 'hands off' (with the steering lever gripped between the knees), which is exactly the stunt pulled by the young Lincoln Beachey, later known as the greatest aerial daredevil of them all, who joined the Curtiss team in 1911.

At the close of his act, Beachey would start his **vertical dive** (or 'death dip') from 5,000 ft (1,500 m) with the motor cut, and at the last moment pull out so close to the ground that spectators rose to their feet in horror. Sometimes he would allow the aircraft to straighten out by itself, both arms flung wide as he passed the grandstands. His hair-raising low passes and short landings were known to make people swoon: he had the knack of flying in and out of the tiniest landing strips, zipping underneath telegraph wires and the branches of trees.

A stunt has been defined as something which is difficult to do, and not worth doing when it is done. The 24-year-old Beachey, who started out barnstorming with balloons and dirigibles, was a stunt flyer *par excellence*. He probably flew more shows in 1911/12 than any other pilot in America: a little fellow with a pugnacious jaw, he customarily flew his shows attired in an expensively-tailored business suit with a high starched collar, a 2-carat diamond stickpin in his tie, and a chequered golfing cap jauntily worn backwards to keep it from blowing away. And he always seemed to have a girl in every town.

It was Beachey who, in June 1911, flew over Niagara Falls and underneath the nearby suspension bridge in front of 150,000 spectators. He was game for anything just so long as it would keep the public rolling in. One day while flying at a show in Springfield, Illinois, he accidentally hit a fence on landing and destroyed the front controls of his Curtiss D-III;

but he nonchalantly continued his performance quite undeterred by the absence of a large piece of aeroplane. According to Beckwith Havens, Beachey was 'pleasantly surprised' to find that it performed better than before, and did some wonderful flying with the machine foreshortened in this way. Havens immediately followed suit with his own D-III, the modification was quickly adopted by Curtiss, and within a short time all existing exhibition machines were 'headless'!

Despite his extravagant aerial feats, Beachey was a somewhat enigmatic figure, usually disappearing after a show to avoid the crowds of fans. In contrast to his team-mate Hamilton, Beachey took little alcohol as it seemed to affect him more readily than most. But this did not prevent him making good friends among his contemporaries and fellow flyers.

Meanwhile, the business of pilots vying to outdo one another had wound up to alarming proportions, not only between the various exhibition teams, but between individuals everywhere. Unscrupulous promoters booked pilots into venues where conditions were unsuitable and landing fields were often dangerous: and the public themselves sometimes constituted an even greater threat if weather or other problems delayed the start of a performance. They were known to attack pilots and wreck their aeroplanes if there were signs of the expected show failing to materialize as advertised.

The following vivid report, which appeared in the New York *American*, describing the Asbury Park air show of August, 1910, gives a taste of the aerial jockeying carried on for the benefit of the spectators:

The rivalry existing between Archie Hoxsey and Ralph Johnstone, two of the Wright aviators, manifested itself today in a thrilling aerial duel with their biplanes ... they went through a series of hair-raising evolutions which made today's exhibition one of the greatest demonstrations of eccentric aeroplane riding ever seen in America. They

Flight Fantastic

twisted, spiralled and steeplechased over the course while the 10,000 spectators wildly applauded...

Johnstone's machine ... tossed and tumbled on the turns like a leaf in a wind eddy. Curving at the corners with the sharp perpendicular turns which brought Brookins to grief yesterday,* Johnstone caused many spectators concern.

Then Hoxsey went up. Not content with sidewise slanting turns, he soared higher and set out to cut figure eights. Then he commenced a series of wild dips, toboggan slides and curves that distinguished him even from Hamilton. With unerring judgment, the young man coasted from a height of 600 ft at an angle of 55 degrees, his motor running full power. As the crowd stood on its toes ... he daintily raised the front planes and bounded cleanly and beautifully over the invisible hurdle on the ground. But he had scarcely switchbacked 25 ft in the air when he put his craft over another of those imaginary hurdles. The aerial steeplechase continued almost around the entire field...

Now it was Johnstone's turn to be airborne again, and he started with a climb to 1,200 ft (365 m):

Then he came coasting down. Plunging from this height to a scant 25 ft above the ground, he began a series of evolutions that for daring have scarcely been equalled in the air. Skipping, sliding, twisting, turning, dipping twice, thrice and even four times in succession, he plunged over the field in a manner that plainly indicated he wished to do everything that Hoxsey had done.

He played leapfrog and he coasted at angles that seemed but a hair line removed from a complete somersault. In one wild, final bacchanalian swoop he dropped his goggles and finally finished his orgy of flying with a wild flourish of corkscrew spirals around the field.

This put Hoxsey on his mettle. He was soon in the air and boring upward to a height of at least 2,000 ft. Then he came coasting down in a long, curving sweep and repeated his earlier performance of steeplechasing with new embellishments. At one time the machine whizzed through the grass scarcely 8 inches off the ground. He finished his startling performance by landing in the center of a marked square 190 ft wide.

Of course, the greater the show put on by any individual pilot, the harder it was for others to satisfy the crowds, and there were far too many fatalities caused by pilots pushing themselves and their aeroplanes beyond their limits.

Johnstone's stunting cost him his life at the age of 30, on 17 November 1910, when he overstressed his Wright biplane while performing the high-spot of his act, which he called a 'spiral glide'. For this manoeuvre he would nose down in a steep dive with engine on, and then pull up a few feet from

'The Heavenly Twins', Arch Hoxsey and Ralph Johnstone.
(Smithsonian Institution)

1909 Demoiselle being landed by Santos-Dumont on the lawn of a friend's château. This tiny high-wing machine weighed in at 143 kg (315 lb), with the seat of the pilot's pants no more than 10 cm (4 in) above the ground. There was a foot throttle, and the control surfaces were operated by levers in the left and right hands respectively for rudder and elevator, and by a leather harness fixed to the pilot's back for wing-warping, operated by moving from side to side.   (Musée de l'Air)

the ground, bank hard, and climb away in a sharp spiral. This time the airframe collapsed as he entered the bank and the machine crashed. Within six weeks of his team-mate's death, Arch Hoxsey suffered the same fate when pulling out of a steep power dive at a show in Los Angeles; and on the very same day, 31 December, John B Moisant, the leader of Moisant's International Aviators, also died in an aerial accident in New Orleans.

Moisant's 'Aviators' were a truly impressive international line-up recruited from the October Belmont Park meeting where the second Gordon Bennett Speed Trophy had just been run, and his flying circus – the first of its kind – was in the middle of a tour of 17 cities throughout the USA, Mexico and Cuba in true barnstorming fashion. Among those who learned the art of exhibition flying during that memorable tour were the Frenchman Roland Garros and the Swiss Edmond Audemars, exponents of the ultra-light Santos-Dumont Demoiselle, who were both later to become top-ranking aerobatic flyers. The popular Garros was a leading feature of the tour, billed as 'The Cloud Kisser'; Audemars, who hailed from Geneva, was a small, dapper, little man with a toothbrush moustache and quickly became known as 'Tiny' – and the Demoiselle was advertised as 'the smallest and most dangerous aeroplane in the world'.

More and more venturesome feats had come to be expected – and attempted – and Beachey in particular as the greatest stunter of them all found himself blamed for the mounting toll of deaths. Some newspapers cynically referred to 'pulling a Beachey' when there was a fatal accident. Terribly distressed by this, and by the death of his friend and fellow team-member Eugene Ely and the accusations of Ely's distraught widow, Lincoln Beachey decided in late 1912 that it was time to quit.

He was under no illusions about his devoted public: "They call me Master Birdman, but they pay to see me die," was his bitter comment. In fact his retirement was to last less than a year; but in 1912/13 a year was a long time in aviation terms.

*This was an undeserved slur on Brookins. He had deliberately crash-landed his Wright aircraft during the previous day's show, in order to avoid causing injury to a throng of press photographers who – despite repeated warnings – insisted on crowding into the path of the machine where it would touch down. Brookins landed short by diving in from 50 ft (15 m), and spent 6 days in hospital with injuries that included a broken ankle. The aircraft was completely wrecked.

3

Three~dimensional freedom

Slow starters the Europeans may have been, but by 1911 great strides were being made in France with new models such as the Morane-Saulnier, Deperdussin and Nieuport which now began to leave the rest of the world standing. The British, later in joining the lists, did not produce a truly successful home-grown design until A V Roe's neat little triplane of 1909. Indeed, such was the disdain in which aviation was held in England, that Roe was about to be prosecuted for disturbing the peace (still a sadly familiar ring to this, even 70-odd years later!) when Louis Blériot suddenly became an international hero with his Channel crossing, and the case was hastily dropped.

Having pioneered the use of Brooklands race-track for aviation, AV was to be seen there from the year 1907 onwards making short hops with a number of promising designs. In August 1908 – nearly at the end of his resources – he was so determined to see Wilbur Wright fly in France that he rode all the way to Le Mans by bicycle. Hearing of this, Wilbur gave generously of his time and advice, which certainly contributed greatly to AV's aircraft design successes in the years that followed.

It was in the early Avro biplanes that the first successful recoveries from inadvertent **spins** were recorded. The term 'spin' or 'spinning nose-dive' did not come into general use until World War I, so pre-1914 terminology is rather vague and generally speaks of such occurrences as a 'spiral dive' (as distinct from the 'spiral descent' or 'spiral glide' which a proficient aviator might use as an approach to land in those days). It was on 21 September 1911 that Avro test pilot Fred Raynham got into what he called a 'spiral dive' at 1,500 ft (457 m), and was thoroughly frightened by the machine going into an almost vertical dive, in which position it described two complete revolutions, finally straightening out at 500 ft (152 m). Raynham had no idea what he had done to recover

from the situation, but was certainly glad to be the first pilot in recorded history to survive it and tell the tale.

Although Raynham's experience has passed into aviation lore as the earliest successful spin recovery, when the facts of the case are considered it begins to appear unlikely that it *was* actually a spin. For a start, he had the power on all the time and never mentioned stalling into the dive; furthermore, two turns of a spin in an early Avro biplane would be unlikely to lose 300 m of altitude.

Much more significant was the experience of Lt Wilfred Parke, RN, on 25 August 1912, when he fell into a left-hand spin in his Avro G cabin biplane during the military trials at Salisbury Plain. Parke managed to recover, and moreover recorded his recovery actions. Here is an extract from the eyewitness account which was published in *Flight* under the heading 'Parke's Dive':

... The machine at once started a spiral nose-dive. At the point C, Parke opened the throttle full out, in the hope that the propeller might pull the nose up, for he was aware ... that the machine was slightly nose-heavy with the throttle closed. The engine responded instantly, but failed to produce the desired effect on the machine; it may or may not have accelerated the descent, but the fall was already so rapid that the maximum engine speed was unlikely even to be equal to it.

Also at the point C, he drew the elevator lever hard back against his chest and put the rudder hard over to the left with his foot so as to turn the machine inwards, this latter being the principle of action that is accepted as proper in cases of incipient side-slip and, therefore, naturally to be tried in an emergency such as this. The warp was normal, i.e. balanced with the control wheel neutral. These operations failed utterly to improve the conditions.

... According to Parke, the angle was very steep, but certainly not vertical; he noticed no particular strain on his legs, with which he still kept the rudder about half over to the left (about as much as is ordinarily used for a turn), nor on his chest, across which he was strapped by a wide belt to his seat. His right hand he had already

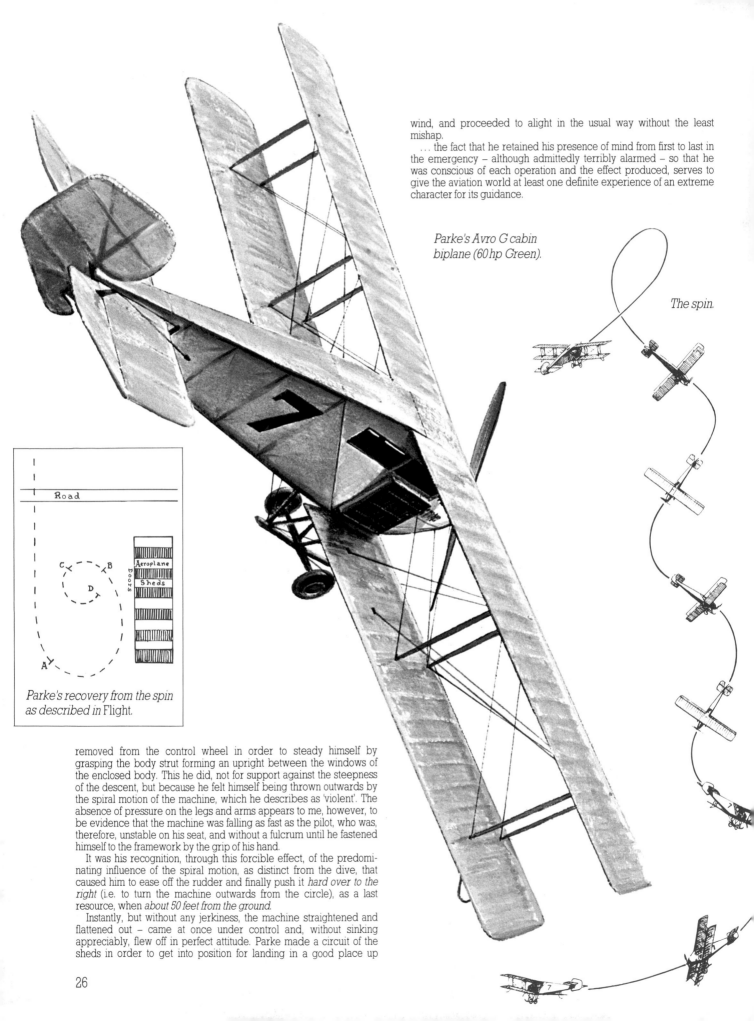

wind, and proceeded to alight in the usual way without the least mishap.

... the fact that he retained his presence of mind from first to last in the emergency – although admittedly terribly alarmed – so that he was conscious of each operation and the effect produced, serves to give the aviation world at least one definite experience of an extreme character for its guidance.

Parke's Avro G cabin biplane (60 hp Green).

The spin.

Parke's recovery from the spin as described in Flight.

removed from the control wheel in order to steady himself by grasping the body strut forming an upright between the windows of the enclosed body. This he did, not for support against the steepness of the descent, but because he felt himself being thrown outwards by the spiral motion of the machine, which he describes as 'violent'. The absence of pressure on the legs and arms appears to me, however, to be evidence that the machine was falling as fast as the pilot, who was, therefore, unstable on his seat, and without a fulcrum until he fastened himself to the framework by the grip of his hand.

It was his recognition, through this forcible effect, of the predominating influence of the spiral motion, as distinct from the dive, that caused him to ease off the rudder and finally push it *hard over to the right* (i.e. to turn the machine outwards from the circle), as a last resource, when *about 50 feet from the ground.*

Instantly, but without any jerkiness, the machine straightened and flattened out – came at once under control and, without sinking appreciably, flew off in perfect attitude. Parke made a circuit of the sheds in order to get into position for landing in a good place up

Lt Wilfred Parke, R.N.
(via John Blake)

Three-dimensional freedom

Geoffrey de Havilland was one of those present who witnessed the event and, in a quickly convened on-the-spot discussion with Parke, he and *Flight*'s technical reporter undertook a thorough analysis of the mishap and its successful outcome. Fundamentally, they differentiated between sideslip recovery (ruddering inwards) and spin recovery (ruddering outwards), noting that Parke's use of rudder had counteracted the heart of the problem – the spiralling movement – thereby regaining an even keel from which normal flight was easily attained. This opposite rudder technique was published for all to read.

Lt Parke's subsequent report to the Royal Aero Club Committee prompted them to suggest further experimentation: a first ever attempt to investigate the phenomenon of the spin. However, as *Flight* magazine commented, "No-one is going to risk voluntarily losing control of his machine in mid-air for the sake of demonstrating the facts". It was not until 1916 that serious spin research took place, and then only after it had become a widely-used manoeuvre.

And, ever since, the spin has been the cause of more dissent in aeronautical circles than any other single aspect of aircraft handling!

Notwithstanding the facts – that it is a condition not infrequently encountered and, thanks to modern manufacturing standards, from which recovery is straightforward once the technique is learnt (given sufficient altitude, of course), and that for 70 years adept pilots have routinely used it to get out of trouble, or simply for a quick descent from altitude – there seems to be a universal paranoia about the spin which has persisted to this day and has even led backward-looking aviation authorities in several countries to *remove it from the flight training syllabus* on grounds of 'safety': thereby contriving to perpetuate that mindless fear of spinning which ought to have been extinguished by so many years of familiarity.

We have talked so far of recovery from inadvertent spins; but the art of aerobatics lies in complete control of the aeroplane, and the next vital stage in spinning was its deliberate initiation once recovery was assured. Strangely enough, the life-saving technique discovered by Parke remained a curiosity which seemed to be known only to a very few, and never featured in such 'flying manuals' as were written during the years preceding World War I. Parke himself tragically died in a crash soon afterwards due to the age-old predicament of attempting a turn at low altitude with a failing engine; he was thus unable personally to spread the gospel that might have saved so many lives.

With his talent for analytical thinking, Wilfred Parke had distinguished himself as the first test pilot ever to employ the technique of writing up performance notes on the aircraft types he flew, in a period when the normal technique was simply a matter of jumping into the aircraft, making a number of empirical tests, then discussing and later implementing the pilot's findings in the workshop. Sadly few written records survive, and even the log books of such great test pilots as Harry Hawker and Geoffrey de Havilland were not meticulously kept as they would be today.

When it comes to researching the earliest deliberate spinning, therefore, one is greatly hindered by lack of corroborative evidence. Certainly pilots were reluctant to try it, even including Orville Wright, who in November 1912, concerned by several recent accidents, himself took an aeroplane up to 100 m to test the effects of stalling in practice; but he did not go so far as to investigate spinning. We shall have to wait two more years before the first voluntary spins were made.

Meanwhile, one very important event during this time was the opening of the new London Aerodrome at Hendon. The great British pioneer Claude Grahame-White, having

Claude Grahame-White.   *(via John Blake)*

Flight Fantastic

returned in triumph from the United States with the Gordon Bennett Trophy of 1910, bought up 207 acres (about 84 hectares) of flat pasture-land on the North side of London and proceeded to transform it into a flying field which remained a great international centre for aviation for nearly 50 years (it was reported to have changed hands at over half a million pounds when he sold it eventually to the British Government in 1925!).

Grahame-White, a charismatic figure endowed with urbane charm and good looks, came from a well-to-do country family and might have been considered something of a playboy had it not been for his extraordinary flair and energy. At 16 he apprenticed himself to an engineering company; next he got interested in bicycles and became a champion racer; then he went into the car business and founded the Royal Automobile Club. After that he turned to balloon ascents and finally, after seeing Wilbur Wright, he tried his hand at aviation.

He learned to fly on a Blériot monoplane at Pau, where he qualified as the first Englishman to earn the internationally-recognized FAI *brevet de pilote-aviateur* in December 1909. This licence was now required for anyone wishing to give public demonstrations and take part in FAI-sanctioned competitions, and its requirements were as follows: three figure-of-eight turns, then a climb to 150 m, followed by a descent and landing, with touchdown no more than 3 m off a specified mark on the ground.

Thereafter, Grahame-White's exploits in speed and distance races and his later books on aviation made him internationally famous. Once his London Aerodrome was opened in October 1910 it became a veritable Mecca for practitioners and public alike, embracing every conceivable type of aerial activity including flight instruction, air racing, passenger flights and aerial displays, both civil and military. On its acquisition by the British Government, Hendon became the site of the world-renowned RAF Pageants every summer.

Similar flying fields were already in existence elsewhere in Europe, and one of the most popular was Juvisy-Port-Aviation, near the site of present-day Orly airport. It was here on 8 June 1913 that the world's very first aerobatic competition was planned to be held, with the celebrated French pilot Roland Garros pitted against the Swiss Edmond Audemars, his great friend from as early as 1910 when they had shared spills and setbacks learning to fly their Demoiselles at Issy, later touring America together with the Moisant flying circus. They had agreed on a contest in three parts: speed, rapid climbing, and 'fantastic and dexterous flight'. Both had a huge following and a well-earned reputation as daring exhibition pilots, Garros also having a particularly brilliant career in long distance flying and record-taking events.

Roland Garros described his first impression of Audemars, three years earlier, as a small, spare, neat little man, with hands that were delicate and sensitive; his clothes were tasteful and elegantly cut, while "in one minuscule, gloved hand he held a flying helmet".

Born in 1882 and a one-time racing motorcyclist, Audemars first caught the public's interest as a Demoiselle pilot in the Bournemouth Meeting of July 1910, where he performed "many amusing tricks with his tiny machine, such as pirouetting round on one wheel and bowing to the applause of the spectators by elevating the tail". The aeroplane's habit of

Roland Garros.   *(Musée de l'Air)*

pitching along with a curiously hurried sort of gait with its tail in the air, as if it were always rushing downhill, earned it the title of 'the infuriated grasshopper' and sometimes 'the angry wasp'. Then in the Gordon Bennett race three months later at Belmont Park, USA, yet another insect was called to mind by the diminutive aircraft and its equally diminutive pilot: "I'll swear he looked like a butterfly!" said Ross Browne. After barnstorming in the Americas, Audemars went on to make record-breaking flights – Paris-Berlin in 1912 and Berlin-Paris in 1913 – in Morane-Saulnier monoplanes.

Although there was tremendous interest in the Garros-Audemars match, with a prize of 10,000 francs (£400) riding on the result, the French Aero Club and one or two influential columnists led a campaign to have the aerobatic event banned on grounds of safety, and unfortunately had their way because it was eventually decided to replace it by a spot landing contest. Disappointment in aviation circles was great, for both men were safe and experienced pilots, and the match would have been the first of its kind ever held. On the day itself Audemars won all three events, probably aided by the fact that Garros was still under the weather after a bronchitis attack. Both were using 80 hp Gnôme-engined Morane-Saulniers.

During the great craze for looping exhibitions that later swept France the two friends were often to be seen on the same bill, and indeed the match itself was revived the following year in somewhat different guise at Angers, where they now proudly claim it as the first aerobatic contest ever held. In fact it took the form of an 'aerial combat', Garros performing the rôle of the attacker and Audemars taking avoiding action. In this friendly demonstration the two men

Edmond Audemars (Inset) and Audemars flying Morane-Saulnier, 1913. (Musée de l'Air)

enacted many of the actual tactics that were all too soon to be used in earnest.

By 1912–13 the stage had long been set in Europe for an exploration of the ultimate frontiers of free flight. Pilots of the nimble French Blériot and Morane monoplanes, with their rotary engines*, were in an ideal position to experiment with any amount of aerial acrobatics: now they had begun to think

of perhaps flying upside down, or even backwards…

The first recorded attempt at deliberately flying backwards, in what became known as a ***tail-slide***, was by the wealthy young Englishman Will Rhodes Moorhouse (later to earn the Victoria Cross with No 2 Squadron RFC and die a hero's death in 1915), who at Brooklands in the spring of 1912 conducted an experiment intended to test the ultimate safety of his Blériot-type Radley & Moorhouse monoplane (50 hp Gnôme). It was reported that he purposely forced the nose up as far as it would go, then cut the motor. The machine

W B Rhodes Moorhouse at the wheel of his personal aircraft transporter. (via Chaz Bowyer)

*This type of engine had the advantage that it would not cut out from fuel starvation so long as fuel was fed to the crankshaft and thence directly to the rotating cylinders. Later, with fairly simple modifications to the fuel supply, the engine would continue to perform no matter what attitude the aircraft assumed.

Flight Fantastic

Marcus Manton.

(via John Blake)

"stood still on end, then rolled slightly over sideways and dived, descending without damage".

A yawing pivot at the top of a vertical climb later became an established manoeuvre known as the **stall turn**, and young Moorhouse must have inadvertently performed something akin to this figure; we cannot, however, credit him with its intentional invention, and its origins actually lay in the later 'cartwheel' which featured in exhibition programmes from 1913 onwards.

By the following year, the tail-slide itself had become a regular exhibition manoeuvre after Adolphe Pégoud had pioneered its scientific execution as part of the Blériot test-

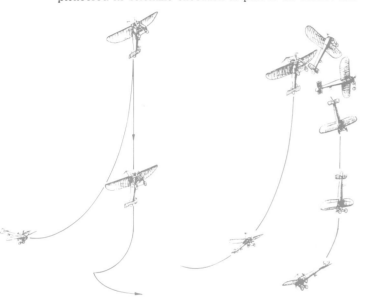

(L) Tail-slide and (R) stall turn. The tail-slide involves a slide backwards in the vertical attitude before diving, whereas the stall turn pivots nose-downwards at the top of the climb. (The name 'stall turn' is itself a misnomer, since at no point is a stall involved).

flight programme. In an edition of *Flight* magazine in 1914, regular Hendon performer Marcus Manton wrote of his tail-sliding experiences in a 50 hp Blériot:

I climbed till the machine was standing on its tail. Then, to my consternation, the motor started to splutter, and the next instant had ceased to work. For a fraction of a second the monoplane remained poised in the air absolutely stationary. Then it commenced to fall backwards, tail first. The noise it started to make is almost indescribable. The wires vibrated and screamed and whistled. Each wing seemed to flap and rattle like a flag in a stiff breeze – this, of course, being due to the wind getting hold of the thin and flexible trailing edge – the metal engine cowl joined in the chorus of noise in a lower key, and for a few seconds it certainly seemed as though the machine was going to break up.

Having plenty of altitude, I did not make any desperate efforts to get the machine back to its proper position. I just let her do what she liked. Down, down we came, the speed increasing with every second until the rattling and roaring were simply deafening. All this time I kept my control lever pulled back ... This would mean that the elevator was up, and in the ordinary way should have had the effect of bringing up the tail and levelling out the machine. But the tail-slide continued, so I thought I would make a little experiment. I pushed the lever forward until it was in a neutral position ... To my great surprise

the fall was immediately checked, then with a hefty kick the machine made a forward plunge, slightly sideways, and then nosedived, after which I got level once again.

Though not by any means my only tail-slide on the Blériot, it is the first time that I have experimented with moving the elevator ... athough the machine underwent a very severe straining, there were no signs of weakness when I came to examine it after landing.

Manton had even got close to the classic modern tail-slide, in which the aeroplane is made to fall through nose first after sliding vertically downwards tail first. Keeping in a geometrically precise axis, the fall-through is made either forward or backward depending on the direction, of stick movement by the pilot. But the especially attractive feature of the present-day figure is the pendulum-movement of the aircraft's nose after falling through, as it travels *past* vertical and then back into a diving attitude. This is why the French name for the figure is *cloche*, since it resembles the 'ding-dong' of a bell's motion. In Germany the tail-slide is called *Männchen*, or 'little man', for no very obvious reason except perhaps that the aeroplane is made to 'sit up and beg' in the air, like a dog performing a trick, for which the phrase in German is *Männchen machen*.

Of course, in 1912 it was very venturesome indeed to try putting one's machine into these extreme attitudes. Such sophistication as we currently see was slowly and painfully achieved over the years, as pilots began to acquire experience and confidence in the capabilities of their machines. Indeed, in 1928, in that gem of a book *Aerobatics*, Oliver Stewart stated "Tail-slides rarely occur in actual practice," and went on to say, "So many observers confuse a steep stall with a tail-slide that I should like first-hand evidence of tail-sliding before I wholly believe in it." He mentioned a wartime example of Oliver Sutton (of harness fame) tail-sliding a Sopwith Pup and damaging the fin and rudder in the process, and sagely concluded, "At any rate, it is probably unwise to try it on any standard aeroplane."

But in the manoeuvrable Blériot, with its rotary Gnôme engine, not only the tail-slide but even **inverted flight** was possible in those heady pre-war days of the *Belle Epoque*. Certain aviators, among them Captain Aubry of the French Air Service and Captains Hamilton and Reynolds of the RFC, had already (between the years 1911 and 1913) reported themselves accidentally overturned by turbulence with the most unnerving results – Reynolds's Bristol biplane even performing a kind of inverted Falling Leaf (a series of incipient spins, checked at the stalling point, first on one side and then the other – see page 61), while he clung to the undersurface of the top wing!

True inverted flight, however, in safety and under the control of the pilot, was a matter which had never been scientifically examined until now; and at this point in our story we are privileged to meet, in the summer of 1913, the greatest of all innovators of early aerobatics: Adolphe Pégoud.

4

The loopers

Europe

Born on 13 June 1889 at Montferrat, in the now fashionable ski resort of Val d'Isère near Mont Blanc, Célestin Adolphe Pégoud was the true precursor of modern aerobatic pilots. He differed from those experimenters who preceded him – brave and gifted though they were – by bringing a scientific approach to flight in all its possible attitudes and by recording and sharing his experiences with others; in consequence he had a profound influence on the progress of aviation.

It was in October 1911, while doing his military service, that Adolphe Pégoud had his first unforgettable taste of flight in a Robert Esnault-Pelterie REP monoplane. He had already seen action in North Africa and had received his cavalry training at the world-famous cavalry camp of Saumur, when a former comrade, Capt Carlin, now a pilot and stationed at Satory, invited him up for a flight. The effect was intoxicating: Pégoud found himself totally captivated and could hardly wait to get his transfer to Satory where he became Carlin's mechanic and contrived to fly with him on every possible occasion. Recognizing Pégoud's very special aptitude, it was Carlin who gave him his initial flight training; and there he remained until his discharge in February 1913.

Aged 23 and bent on a career in aviation, the first thing Pégoud then needed was his civil pilot's licence. For this he enrolled at the Bron (Lyon) school of flying, and in a matter of weeks, on 7 March, he was awarded brevet number 1243. On 13 March he joined Louis Blériot's staff at Buc, where the famous monoplanes were constructed, on the southern outskirts of Paris. Starting as a mechanic, he very soon became an instructor and test pilot for Blériot, and his first recorded· exhibition took place on 13 May 1913, when he was chosen to fly for the visiting monarch Alphonse XIII of Spain.

Described as small and slim in stature, and with a light, upcurled moustache, Pégoud had twinkling blue eyes and was seldom seen (or photographed) without an irrepressible grin on his face. One can almost see the moustache-ends twitching in anticipation as he climbs into his machine and gives his familiar cheery wave before taking off on yet another voyage of discovery.

Happily, he and Louis Blériot shared the same appetite for innovation and empirical research, and in late August 1913 Pégoud readily embarked on a series of flight safety experiments which he and Blériot concocted together. Among the tests he had already made on Blériot's behalf were trials of take-off and landing devices for use on aircraft carriers, and trials of a parachute (previously attempted only from a balloon) invented by G. Bonnet: under Blériot's auspices he was the first pilot, on August 19 of that eventful year of 1913, to leave an aeroplane in flight by using such a parachute – much against the wishes of the French authorities who had tried to forbid the jump on the grounds that it was too dangerous! *The Times* reported:

Pégoud was flying at a height of about 650 feet when he tested the parachute. He turned the machine downwards and released the parachute from its cover, whereupon it at once spread out and drifted slowly to the ground with its passenger. His aeroplane, the motor of which had been stopped, went through a series of fantastic movements before coming to earth, which it did without damage.

This 'series of fantastic movements' was briefly noted in Pégoud's diary as a dive, followed by a vertical climb, a sideslip, and several more dives and recoveries. Other observers recorded a steep climb followed by a stall and a tail-slide; then variously described the aircraft as becoming inverted and righting itself, and alternatively as performing a

'kind of loop'. Whatever they were, these evolutions confirmed Adolphe Pégoud in an idea that had been forming in his mind for some time: that of attempting to fly upside down.

As early as 21 August he announced this intention in the newspaper *Le Temps*. In collaboration with Blériot, a revolutionary programme of experiments with the Blériot XI monoplane was drawn up which included (1) inversion of the aircraft and recovery; (2) sideslip and recovery; (3) tail-slide and recovery; and (4) flight for a given period with hands off the controls. Practising on August 26, Pégoud was seen to perform a number of tight, steep turns and a dive which took him beyond the vertical. The following day he had himself strapped into the machine while it was suspended inverted in a hangar, to accustom himself to handling the controls in this position, for Pégoud realized that, when manoeuvring inverted, both stick and rudder would need to be operated in a different sense from normal.

His first public exhibition of upside-down flying, on 1 September 1913, caused a sensation. But whether this was Pégoud's very first inverted flight is not sure. Ludovic Trotton, a contemporary of his and a Demoiselle pilot, has written a very vivid first-hand account of what he describes as Pégoud's first inverted flight on 28 June 1913, at the Aérodrome de Juvisy-Port-Aviation. Unfortunately, a date as early as June is wildly improbable, and Trotton's account contains other errors of chronology that together lead one to discount its accuracy as to the date, written as it was in 1964 when his memory was probably failing. Nevertheless, it is valuable for its atmospheric description of what must have been a truly momentous event, and this author would like to venture the opinion (based on other references in Trotton's narrative) that 28 August, rather than June, might have been the date in question. Here is a translation, starting at the point where Pégoud and Blériot arrive at daybreak to perform a trial run with a 50 hp Gnôme-engined Blériot XI which has been hangared at Juvisy overnight:

The monoplane that was removed from the hangar, which at first glance seemed nothing special, in fact carried an entirely new arrangement of large belts and shoulder-harness with which Pégoud

Adolphe Pégoud preparing for the parachute trial, August 1913. (via Musée de l'Air)

The harness system installed in Pégoud's aircraft. Previously pilots often sat out in the open as if on horseback, or perhaps used a seat-belt over the lap. C G Grey of The Aeroplane *recognized the importance of Blériot's innovation: "Remove M. Pégoud's straps," he observed, "and you remove M. Pégoud."* (Musée de l'Air)

proceeded to strap himself in his seat ... then with the motor turning at full power, and the machine restrained by the usual method of the tail being held down, he raised his hand to signal its release and cried: *'A la grâce de Dieu!'* ('By the grace of God!')

At this, the one thought among us was: what is going to happen? ... Then, towards 1,200 metres, the machine started banking more and more to the left over Viry-Chatillon, until it ended up with its wheels in the air.

Certainly, if we had not already seen the special harness, and if it had not been for the presence of M. Blériot standing calmly watching with his companions, our first reaction would have been to rush for the ambulance and fire services; but the apparent tranquillity of the constructor, which undoubtedly must have masked feelings of great excitement, clearly indicated that the whole thing was planned, and prevented any of us from showing the least sign of panic, as, in this inverted position, the Blériot proceeded to fly over the surrounding area for about a minute, while rapidly losing height all the time.

The closer he came towards the ground, the stronger grew the uncomfortable impression that he could not right himself; but then, by means of a harmonious *retournement inverse* he returned to normal flight and after a number of vertically-banked turns came in gently to land. The first aerobatic manoeuvre had been born – the half-roll – which was to be followed by many others that remain classical figures to this day.

However, a final surprise awaited [the mechanic] Gasté when he helped Pégoud out of his machine. The pilot was drenched with fuel, not only his flying suit but his mouth, his nose, his eyes, everything; and we trembled to think not just of the fire risk, but of the incredible courage of this man who had just dared to perform a dangerous and untried manoeuvre in a state of semi-blindness.

Gasté had to lend him a change of overalls, in his room over by the café, and in return he received from Pégoud a postcard depicting him

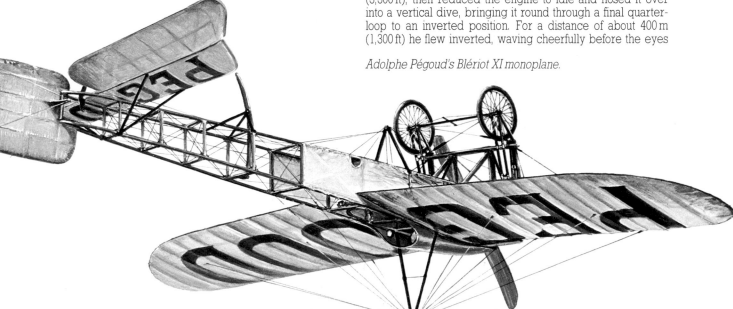

with his Bonnet parachute, bearing the following message: 'To M. Gasté, in memory of my first *loupin télop* (sic), at Juvisy.' This obviously means that, although he had not performed it on that particular occasion, this looping-the-loop was already planned and indeed was to be realized shortly afterwards, in emulation of a current circus act which was going the rounds of the music-halls. Pégoud had distorted the phrase *en route*, proving that one does not need to be a polyglot to be a great and daring aviator!

M. Trotton's comment about the circular **loop** being part of the overall plan is actually correct. But it should be remembered that aeronautical language of the time was in its infancy, and in French newspapers and magazines it was quite common to use the word 'looping' for any flight manoeuvre which involved the pilot in a head-downward position (e.g. Chevillard's *'looping hélicoidal'* – see below). It is perfectly feasible that in the elation of the moment, after turning upside-down for the first time, Pégoud simply used the phrase in vogue: *"Mon premier 'loupin télop'!"* he had written with a flourish, perhaps also with a tremor of excitement at the recollection of inverted flight.

In case you have ever wondered, as I did, how the expression 'looping-the-loop' came about, it all started at the turn of the century in America with the fairground hucksters'

publicly announced his intention to do the same thing with an aeroplane in 1910. But Johnstone had sadly died before realizing his ambition. Looping-the-loop was all the rage in America at that time, and a handsome cash prize had been offered for the first aviator to achieve the same feat in the air.

For Adolphe Pégoud, however, this was not stunt flying but a thorough investigation of the aircraft's flight characteristics in the hands of a skilled pilot. The 50 hp Gnôme-engined Blériot XI, whose fuel-flow problems were soon properly regulated, was specially strengthened with doubled flying and landing wires of stranded cable, and rigged with a central bracing pylon that was 30 cm (12 in) taller and placed 15 cm (6 in) farther forward than usual. It was also reported that the tail had been replaced by that of the two-seat model which, having a larger elevator, gave a greater measure of control. And of course he used the double safety harness installed for him by Louis Blériot himself. Such careful preparations are the mark of the true aerobatic pilot.

It was to Juvisy, on the evening of 31 August, that Pégoud took his machine (his 'cuckoo', as he called it) in readiness for a trial the following morning. There he unveiled his first public aerobatics in the early hours of 1 September 1913, in front of half a dozen or so invited friends. In his demonstration he first climbed the Blériot to an altitude of 1,000 m (3,300 ft), then reduced the engine to idle and nosed it over into a vertical dive, bringing it round through a final quarter-loop to an inverted position. For a distance of about 400 m (1,300 ft) he flew inverted, waving cheerfully before the eyes

Adolphe Pégoud's Blériot XI monoplane.

exhortation to "loop-the-loop!" on the switchback – a centrifugal railway with a circular track or loop in the vertical plane, along the upper portion of which the passengers travelled head downwards. This phrase was soon taken up by various acrobatic and circus acts; and it made its appearance in aviation writing as early as 1908 when speculation about the heady possibilities of three-dimensional freedom first began. 'Looping' is still a common term in French and in German for the manoeuvre which is properly known in those languages as, respectively, *boucle* and *Überschlag*.

It was already well known in France that the Wright exhibition pilot Ralph Johnstone (see page 23), who had looped-the-loop with the bicycle in the United States, had

of the stupefied observers, then dived again into a half-loop and levelled out erect. The first public performance of inverted flight had been given.

Now, when we read the contemporary accounts, we have to bear in mind the relative inefficiency of the Blériot's wing-warping system and the aircraft's limited structural strength (even with reinforced bracing). We should not get carried away with the idea that he entered inverted flight by means of an outside (negative) half-loop, which is an advanced manoeuvre even by modern standards – pushing continuously downwards under negative *g* in a curve during which centrifugal force tends to propel the pilot out of his seat – a figure which later became known as the **bunt**. Pégoud's contemporary, Gustav Hamel, quoted him as follows in his book *Flying – Some Practical Experiences* (Longmans, Green & Co, 1914): "I simply start coming down, stop the engine, and push the steering pillar right forward until the machine has turned over on its back." The *Daily Mirror* had him "dropping from mid-air at right angles": a vertical dive without power, probably initiated by a carefully controlled stall.

He admitted that he had been trying to 'capsize' the Blériot by means of wing-warping, but generally found he could only get to a vertical bank and sideslip followed by a dive and push-through. This may possibly be what Trotton saw in the distance over Viry-Chatillon. On the other hand he may have witnessed one of Pégoud's successful **half-roll** trials, because Pégoud obviously knew that a half-roll was possible (as witness his next exhibition three weeks later). But this manoeuvre took longer to perfect, so the idea of nosing over into a dive was quite likely chosen as simply a better and more elegant way of getting upside-down. An enormous feat of courage and airmanship, when you consider that he was exploring uncharted territory and at the same time subjecting himself to experiences that many pilots even today still find thoroughly unnerving!

And to say that he performed a downward **vertical S** as we now know it would also be stretching the point too far, even though Pégoud's flightpath did roughly describe a downward S shape. The Vertical S figure begins with a half negative loop which is followed immediately by a half positive loop; whereas Pégoud's 20-second inverted pass effectively divided his performance into three distinct parts, showing that his main idea was the exhibition of inverted flight.

The whole underlying purpose, quite aside from Pégoud's own thirst for experiment, was to demonstrate how safe the Blériot aeroplane was in any attitude. That such a public relations exercise was necessary can be traced back to the nervous reactions of the French and British governments in grounding monoplanes in 1912, when a flurry of accidents, many of them with monoplane types, led to official investigations by boards of enquiry. In Britain, an undeserved slur was cast on the monoplane that was to delay its progress in that country for decades.

On 2 and 3 September Pégoud repeated his performance for experts from the military and the press on the Blériot field

at Buc, and once more we hear Pégoud's acrobatics described as 'looping-the-loop'; whereas in fact the world was still waiting to see this particular figure. For Pégoud, of course, the technique of looping in a complete circle must have fallen into place very quickly after his experience so far: in fact it was no more difficult a manoeuvre to perform than those he had already mastered and displayed. But somehow there is something uniquely satisfying about the full circle of the aerobatic loop that captures the imagination and makes it special, and even today people still delight in arguing about who was the first person to loop, and when.

Pégoud's own first public demonstration of the loop took place on 21 September 1913, at Buc – though this was not the first loop in history. *Aeronautics* reported that he "dived a

short distance with engine off, raised the nose and let his momentum carry him vertically upwards; then the engine was switched on again to carry him over the summit." In this exhibition he really put the Blériot through its paces in a sequence which also included the now-famous S-dive, side-slips of 200 metres or so, tight spirals left and right, and the first intentional tail-slides, in which "the machine just stands on its tail and stops dead." It then slid down partially backwards and partially sideways, followed by a swing, pendulum-like, into a nose down position, with the swing repeating itself several times before resumption of normal flight.

Evidently it was considerably less difficult to half-roll the machine from inverted to erect than vice versa, for an additional manoeuvre performed on the 21st was a half-roll recovery from the inverted position after entering via his usual dive and push-through. In these rolling experiments Pégoud was hoping to perform what he called a 'figure S sideways' (i.e. two consecutive half-rolls with inverted flight in the middle), but French eyewitness accounts say that after three or four abortive attempts he landed, saying that the machine was too stable. His later experiments were carried out on a machine with a much enhanced range of wing-warp as well as greater elevator and rudder travel, and with this he eventually achieved a full roll. Gustav Hamel described it thus:

He permitted the machine to lose speed until it had become what is known as 'stalled' – that momentary pause before the aeroplane turns over on its side or nose and falls – but while getting into that position he had warped the wings to the utmost possible extent so that when it began to turn over sideways it came round to the upside-down position and then to the normal flight position again, diving to obtain the velocity necessary for the controls to have effect.

Pégoud by now enjoyed the doubtful pleasure of being a public hero, attended by scenes of adulation whenever he was spotted. On one occasion in a Paris theatre the curtain was held while he was summoned from the audience to give an account of his flying feats!

Pégoud's original S-dive.

The aviation world was, predictably, cautious in endorsing such unorthodox procedures, and when shortly afterwards the young Corporal le Vicomte Guy des Luynes d'Autroche was killed while performing steep dives in a Farman biplane, the French war ministry at once slapped an embargo on 'acrobatic and dangerous feats of flying'. This was gleefully reported by C G Grey, editor of the British magazine *The Aeroplane* and an implacable opponent of aerial acrobatics, who remarked: "'Pégouding' is not to become fashionable in the French Army. It is clearly so much cheaper and wiser to waste a few needless civilians on this sort of work."

Unfortunately, the waters were then considerably muddied when the rival magazine *Flight* published a description of Pégoud's exhibition which was wrongly illustrated: instead of the ordinary positive loop upwards, the magazine printed a drawing of a *full* **outside [negative] loop** *downwards* which the Blériot could never have performed, and it is hardly surprising that controversy continued to rage as to the integrity of Pégoud's performances. While *Flight* called it, "the most scientific flying exhibition that has ever been made," *The Aeroplane* shrilly insisted that upside-down flying and looping were mere music hall performances.

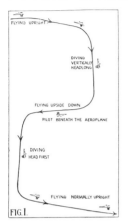

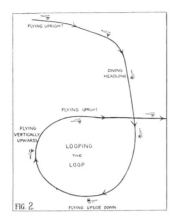

Diagrams from Flight *illustrating Pégoud's manoeuvres. Note that Fig. 2 erroneously shows a* negative *loop!*

The influential French magazine *L'Aérophile* coined the graceful phrase '*Le Pilotage de Haute Ecole*', borrowing a term from the classical art of equestrianism; from this concept eventually derived the French name for aerobatics, *la voltige aérienne*, which again comes from the language of horsemanship.

All unaware of events 2,000 kilometres away in France, 26-year-old Lt Petr Nikolaevich Nesterov of the Imperial Russian Air Service had meanwhile carved for himself an immortal place in aviation history by performing the first ever com-

Nesterov with his Nieuport IV.   *(via Kasum Nazhmudinov)*

plete loop on 9 September 1913, a mere twelve days before Pégoud*. At 6 o'clock on a pleasant Tuesday evening, in front of a small crowd of onlookers, Nesterov took his Dux-built Nieuport IV monoplane (70 hp Gnôme) and calmly looped-the-loop over Syretzk Aerodrome where he was stationed, near Kiev. His intention, he said, was to prove a personal theory about how an aircraft's control surfaces should operate. His method was to climb to about 1,000 m (3,300 ft), stop the motor, and dive vertically to about 600 m (2,000 ft); then he pulled into a climb, restarted the engine, and kept on pulling up and over until the horizon appeared overhead, whereupon he cut the motor again and glided in to land.

Looping diagram taken from Nesterov's diary.

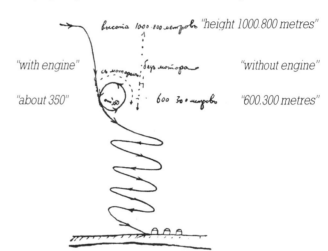

"height 1000.800 metres"

"with engine"   "without engine"

"about 350"   "600.300 metres"

His immediate reward was ten days close arrest for having taken 'undue risk with a machine, the property of his Government'! This was quickly forgotten, however, and within a few days he was promoted to Staff-Captain; later he was awarded a Russian Aero Club medal, and today he is commemorated by the handsome Nesterov Cup, awarded to the winning team in World Aerobatic Championships (see page 225).

*Confusion is sometimes caused by the fact that there was a difference of 13 days between the Gregorian calendar used by most of Europe and the Russian Julian calendar, which gave the dte of August 27 for this occasion. All dates in this book are given in the Gregorian calendar.

Flight Fantastic

Nesterov was born in February 1887, at present-day Gorki, and after a military education his passion for aviation took him to an officers' flying school in October of 1911, where he tried his hand at designing a Taube-type monoplane. He won his wings on 25 September 1912, and transferred to Kiev on 9 May 1913, to take command of the XI Corps Air Squadron. A year after his looping episode, at the outbreak of World War I, he found himself stationed near Sholkiv in Galicia: his war service was to last scarcely more than a month, however, and was destined to add even greater lustre to the name of Nesterov when he became Imperial Russia's first air war hero.

There are many versions of what happened on 8 September 1914, but the most reliable facts seem to run as follows. A two-seater Albatros piloted by the Austrian Lt Baron von Rosenthal was sighted overhead the airfield (whether on a bombing mission or strafing Russian troops is not certain). Nesterov's fertile imagination had already been at work devising various methods of air attack, such as trailing a weight to shatter an opponent's propeller, or descending physically on top of an enemy aircraft to damage it with the undercarriage, and this offered a heaven-sent opportunity to try his luck. Jumping hot-blooded into a Morane type M monoplane, and armed with no other weapon than the aeroplane itself, Nesterov deliberately closed with the two-seater and attempted to destroy its wing surfaces with his landing gear. But he miscalculated, and instead rammed the aircraft with his propeller. Rosenthal's Albatros was destroyed, and Nesterov – who had not paused to strap himself in – was thrown out of the Morane as it plunged out of control to the ground. All three men were killed.

Petr Nesterov, one of the first fighter pilot heroes in history, was buried by the Tsarists with full military honours in the tomb of the ancient Russian Prince Askold – appropriately enough, at Kiev. In December 1951 the Soviets renamed the town of Sholkiv (Lvov district) 'Nesterov' in his honour.

In the autumn of 1913 Pégoud had taken the rest of Europe by storm with his aerial acrobatics, and first among his myriad imitators was Pierre Chanteloup, a pilot for the Caudron company. According to his own account, on 4 September, at Douai, shortly before his release from military service, Chanteloup decided to try an experiment in sideslipping his Caudron G3 biplane (60 hp Le Rhône) – but immediately incurred the wrath of the military authorities! In civilian life a few days later he lost no time in taking up an aeroplane from Juvisy aerodrome, and successfully emulated Pégoud's S-dive over Paris in the still of an autumn evening. Both these incidents were later publicized as 'looping-the-loop', thanks to the very free use of the term at the time, and for a while there were claims that Chanteloup had looped before Pégoud – or even Nesterov!

However, the contemporary interview quoted above makes it clear, from descriptions of the manoeuvres, that neither of his two early performances took the form of a circular loop. Indeed Chanteloup himself, writing in the magazine *Pionniers* in 1974, claimed only to have been *the first to loop a biplane*, but this was not until two months later.

On the same weekend of 20/21 September that Pégoud was successfully demonstrating his half-roll recovery from inverted, Chanteloup turned his Caudron over on its side at Douai and after side-slipping for some distance eventually got it upside down, later recovering by means of a dive – thereby performing the reverse of Pégoud's manoeuvre. It was on 9 November at Juvisy that he performed his first loop, and the first ever with a biplane. Next he repeated the feat with a difference on 21 November when, in front of a huge crowd, he half-rolled to fly an inverted pass and then dived from inverted right around and back up again to his original altitude, immediately continuing with a further series of complete loops: these were the first loops ever started downwards from inverted.

Chanteloup also executed a whirling spiral descent at the end of his exhibition which some French columnists named a spin (*vrille*), but this was in fact his version of a regular showpiece known as the 'corkscrew twist' or 'tourbillon dive'. Gustav Hamel says that the true corkscrew descent was a tight spiral "of no greater diameter than twice the machine's length". Sir Philip Joubert, discussing the origins of deliberate spinning, has stated that a number of pilots including himself performed a 'spiral nose-dive' in those days, but it was not an autorotation. During a turn they pulled the stick back and applied top rudder (*opposite* to the rudder input required for spinning), thereby descending in a tight spiral which, given the light wing loading of their aircraft, had a very small radius.

Seen at Hendon in December 1913, Chanteloup's manoeuvre was described thus:

He goes up to 1,500–2,000 feet, stands the machine vertically on its nose, and then drops to within 100 feet of the ground, turning round and round as he drops, so that the engine is practically vertical over the same spot, while the wings perform a kind of double corkscrew around it. (*Car Illustrated*)

Chanteloup had another variation on his corkscrew descent which was even more spectacular, however. In January 1914, *Flight* reported: "At Le Crotoy, on the 22nd inst., Chanteloup on his Caudron made 11 successive loops, flew upside down, and finished with a corkscrew tail-slide."

We shall come across a reference to another manoeuvre, the 'spinning tail-slide', in 1918 (page 55), equally tantalizing in that the manoeuvre is named but not described. Was it a **torque roll**, the figure which Charlie Hillard performed (for the first time, as we then thought!) at the World Aerobatic Championships in 1972? Best described as a rolling tail-slide, the torque roll starts with a climbing vertical roll, executed at speed, with the aircraft continuing to roll upwards while it decelerates. Eventually it loses all airspeed until it literally hangs on the propeller. Then while the ensuing downward slide is in progress, that initial rolling motion is perpetuated, helped by the engine torque, until the nose falls through in a diving recovery (see page 255).

Another sixteen years later, this figure crops up for a third time in 1934 (page 106), again without description of how it was executed, but this time quite deliberately described as a 'spin' rather than a 'tail-slide'. Oh to have been there and witnessed at first hand the marvels these aerobatic pioneers were performing!

Pégoud meanwhile embarked on a European tour during which neither wind nor rain would prevent his giving a performance. He visited Brooklands Racetrack, England;

Aspern Aerodrome, Vienna; Johannisthal Aerodrome, Berlin, as well as Frankfurt, Hanover and Dresden; Ghent in Belgium; Turin in Italy; and Romania, Holland, Norway and Russia. At a conference in Moscow he endeared himself to everybody present by leaving the platform to call up Nesterov from the audience and present him as his honoured predecessor. He was earning as much as £2,000 a day for his exhibitions and enjoying an unaccustomed luxury: some stories have him consuming a whole roast chicken together with a bottle of his favourite champagne before taking off to give a display!

It was during 25 to 27 September 1913 that he appeared in Britain, at Brooklands, where he was rapturously received. The Englishman Bentfield C Hucks, one-time pilot for the Blackburn company, witnessed Pégoud's performances and immediately determined to be the first British pilot to emulate him; so he betook himself to the Blériot school at Buc for lessons, where on 13 November Hucks performed the S-dive, flew inverted, and looped several times. Shortly afterwards he returned home and started thrilling British audiences with his aerobatic shows.

He became a specialist in low-level displays of looping and inverted flight with his personally modified 70 hp Gnôme-engined Blériot XI, painted with coloured roundels on the upper wing surfaces which were visible to the crowd when he was upside down; it featured a considerably larger elevator than usual and wing-warping nearly four times as effective as on the standard machine, together with his own inverted fuel supply system. He wrote that it was fairly easy to get the Blériot inverted, but that it was noticeably unstable once in that position: "It requires extreme care in balancing, as it were, because the moment it is allowed to get only slightly out of the level, it will sideslip and turn the right way up." The same thing would happen if one tried to climb or simply maintain altitude, even with full power; he said that the maximum length of inverted flight he had managed was 2 minutes 5 seconds, allowing it to plane downwards the whole time.

In 1914 Hucks engaged Marcus D Manton (see page 3) to give looping demonstrations and deputize for him in his country-wide tours with a Blériot two-seater. But all this came to an end, of course, at the outbreak of war when he joined the Royal Flying Corps. After being invalided home he worked for a while as chief test pilot for Geoffrey de Havilland, but succumbed to illness before the war's end. He is still remembered for the Hucks Starter, a convenient method of mechanically turning the propeller-boss to start an aircraft engine in place of hand-swinging the prop.

Next looper on the French aerobatic scene was Maurice Chevillard, a Farman test-pilot and instructor at Etampes who was already internationally famous for his thrilling exhibitions including corkscrew dives and vertically-banked turns, and for a manoeuvre which he called the *chute de côté* ('side dip'), a near-vertical sideslip on the left wing which he then yawed round into a vertical dive: "converting a deadly sideslip into a fatal dive and continuing to exist" as one reporter described it! Sometimes he would start the figure by first pulling up into a zoom; another variation was to bank the machine suddenly to 85 degrees, standing it absolutely on its nose, doing a spiral dive for anything over 30 m (100 ft), and flattening out as low as 15 m (50 ft) above the ground.

Chevillard was fond of issuing challenges to Pégoud to the effect that he would outdo that gentleman's flying feats on any date he cared to name; but he appeared only once with

Pégoud, on 12 October 1913 in front of 200,000 spectators at Buc, where Pégoud on this occasion went to 1,000 m (3,300 ft), half-rolled, flew for 1½ minutes inverted with the engine running, and then performed four inverted turns with his hands off the controls, thus completing further stages in the Blériot test programme. All this was in addition to his now regular looping and half-rolling demonstrations. The newspapers did not report, however, that he was 'outdone' in any way by Chevillard!

Later, on 6 November at Buc and 8–10 November at Juvisy, Chevillard came into his own with a series of exhibitions on a Henri Farman biplane (80 hp Gnôme) in which he managed to turn a complete revolution sideways – the first ever recorded **slow roll** – "thus succeeding in a feat," according to *The Aeroplane* magazine, "of which M. Pégoud himself is not master". He also introduced for his audiences a speciality which he called a *looping hélicoïdal*, which was a maximum rate climbing turn during which the aeroplane traced the path of a rising half-loop whilst executing a banked turn through 180 degrees. We can thus credit Chevillard as the originator of this manoeuvre, which Max Immelmann later made famous (see page 51), and which is often nowadays called a **chandelle**. But for students of early aerobatics, perhaps it should be noted here that in France at that time – indeed until many years later – the term 'chandelle' (candle) meant something far more generalized than this: simply a zoom, or a pull-up into a vertical climb.

Gustav Hamel was the second Englishman to loop-the-loop, and certainly the most dashing and debonair. English born, of Danish stock, he was a Morane pilot who took his brevet at Pau in February 1911 at the age of 21. Rapidly

Gustav Hamel. (via John Blake)

becoming a top celebrity on the British scene, he inaugurated the first airmail post from Hendon to Windsor later that same year, making his delivery despite spectacularly bad weather. He was slight of build, clean-shaven, fair haired and blue-eyed, with engagingly youthful good looks, and was inordinately fond of taking up passengers – particularly attractive young ladies – in his clipped-wing Morane-Saulnier G (80 hp Gnôme engine) which he had especially built for racing and exhibitions. In March-April of 1913 he was booked to give weekly exhibitions of 'acrobatics' at Brooklands, and in 1914 he gave aerial command performances for King George V at

Chanteloup's Caudron.   (Musée de l'Air)

Pierre Chanteloup. (Musée de l'Air)

Flight Fantastic

Windsor. One of his more famous looping passengers was Winston Churchill. He was a past master of the steep spiral descent and daringly low manoeuvres: one favourite story says he knocked a policeman's hat off during a particularly low-level pass at Hendon!

After starting with Pégoud-type performances, Hamel worked up a number of original figures of his own. One, which he named the Apple Turnover, was the first example of the manoeuvre later known as the **split-S**. A friendly rivalry had inevitably sprung up among the European loopers, and on three days over Christmas of 1913, Hamel and visiting French celebrity Pierre Chanteloup delighted the crowds at Hendon, performing their own specialities and trying out each other's.

On Christmas Day, at one point Chanteloup found himself in a predicament which demanded some pretty quick thinking: on pulling up into the start of a loop, all of a sudden his engine decided to quit and the little blue Caudron remained in a vertical attitude while it performed an inadvertent tailslide for 3–400 ft (100–130 m). By way of recovery he quickly made a 'cartwheel turn', i.e. a yawing pivot to nose down, and glided safely back to the aerodrome. The next day he made another cartwheel, intentionally this time, and three more on the following Saturday: the earliest version of today's stall turn had been invented (see page 30).

Chanteloup was noted for using an absolutely standard military type single-seater Caudron with which he needed no preliminary dive for speed before looping. He was still regularly performing his downward loops started from inverted, and his upward loops were so nimble that they resembled nothing so much as 'a performing dog turning a somersault'! Hamel, however, had perfected a different version of the loop, and when he performed three of these in succession followed by a complete loop and a dive, he had traced the shape of a four-leaf clover – complete with stalk – three dimensionally in the sky. The technique of his **Clover Leaf** loop was to roll 90 degrees sideways after passing the top of the loop, so that when he reached horizontal and pulled up into another loop its vertical plane was at right-angles to the previous loop, and so on. Variations on the Clover Leaf theme are still popular in aerobatics today.

Chanteloup went up on the 27th and tried the same thing. According to *Flight*, 'he turned over sideways when at the top of the loop", but with the wing-warping Caudron we may safely assume that this was not, as has been suggested, a **roll-off-the-top** (half roll at the top of a half loop), but a 90 degree roll sideways on the downward path *à la* Hamel. Of the same day's flying the *Daily Telegraph* reported that he also rolled his machine completely over sidways twice in rapid succession: "He simply warps his planes to their fullest extent,

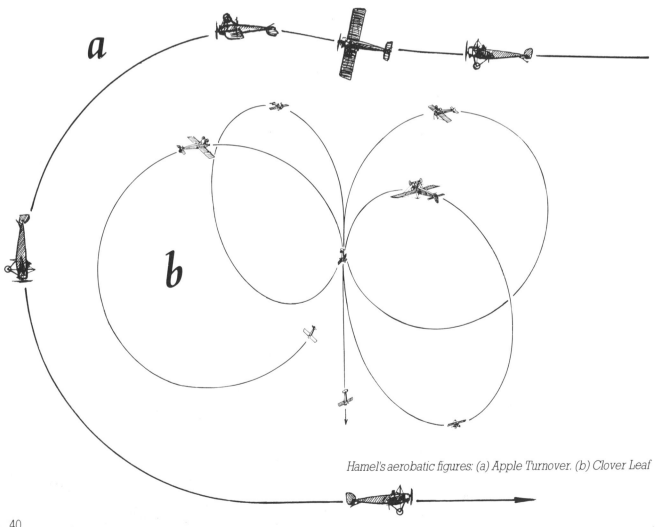

Hamel's aerobatic figures: (a) Apple Turnover. (b) Clover Leaf

keeps the warp full on, and allows the machine to do the rest."

At this very same time, quietly and almost unnoticed, it seems, the word 'aerobatics' entered the English language. A certain Mr E L Gunston wrote the following amusing letter to *The Aeroplane*, which was published in its edition of 1 January 1914:

Since boucling the boucle is a feat which has come to stay and which apparently is as common as sane flying, these feats performed by Pégoud, Chevillard, and certain other scientific gentlemen, will have to be called by a distinguishing name. Why not 'aerobatics'?

Nice one, Mr Gunston!

Gustav Hamel was a tireless cross-country and cross-Channel flyer, and on 17 April 1914, set off on a marathon flight of nearly 400 km (240 miles) nonstop from Dover to Cologne in West Germany. It took him less than $4\frac{1}{2}$ hours – carrying a passenger, as usual – in a two-seat military type Blériot (80 hp Gnôme engine). Earlier, on 22 February, he had the pleasure of meeting Roland Garros at Juvisy aerodrome in one of the challenge matches which they both so loved, earning the highest personal regard from the French pilot as well as an equal respect for his flying. When Garros won the first two out of three speed tests they decided to chalk it up as a win to him, and instead of the third event substituted a splendid concerted display of aerobatic flying. Both used identical Morane-Saulniers with 80 hp Gnôme engines, Hamel having borrowed Edmond Audemars's machine which had its undersurfaces painted black, while Garros's Morane was all white. The 20-minute display started with both aeroplanes approaching the enclosures side by side and looping in unison. Although not intended as an aerobatic contest *The Aeroplane* magazine in comparing the two virtuosi declared "There was nothing to choose between them, victory could not fall to either in the matter of fantastic flying".

It was on 23 May 1914, after going to Paris the previous evening to collect his new 80 hp racing Morane, that Hamel tragically disappeared somewhere over the Channel, braving a thick mist and strong headwind in an attempt to arrive home in time for an air race. He had made 17 Channel-crossings before this one, and the news seemed impossible to believe. Britain had lost one of her brightest young aviators.

A sad footnote to this story is the fact that a year after his death, rumours started to the effect that Gustav Hamel was still alive and was flying for the Germans. No doubt the anti-German hysteria of the time can be blamed, for he was then (and often is today) believed to have been of German descent. His grieving family was obliged to print a rebuttal in *The Times*, pointing out that his body had been found in the sea on 1 July 1914, and identified from his clothing. His father – a fashionable London surgeon – was in fact a naturalized British subject, of Danish extraction born in Hamburg (then a free and independent town), and educated in Sweden and Switzerland. Gustav himself was brought up in England and educated at Westminster School and Cambridge. Ironically enough, along with others such as Claude Grahame-White he had campaigned ceaselessly to awaken England from her lethargy in the face of a growing aerial threat from across the water, and had undertaken his epic flight to Cologne purely to emphasize how distances between the two great powers had ominously shrunk.

In happier days, Hamel and Hucks had been guests of honour at a crazy 'Upside-Down Dinner' thrown by the Hendon Aviators under the chairmanship of Claude Grahame-White in January 1914. The excellent meal, given at London's Royal Automobile Club, was served in reverse order – starting with coffee and liqueurs, ending with soup. An inverted Blériot was suspended above inverted tables, with entertainment provided by a popular music-hall comedian who sang whilst standing on his head. Among the culinary delights on the menu were *Soufflé à la Hucks*, *Vol au Vent à la Hendon*, and *Looping Lobster*. When it came to Hucks to give his speech, he started with the words 'and finally', gradually working backwards via thirdly, second and firstly to 'Good evening'!

Upside-Down Dinner, 1914.   *(via RAF Museum)*

Flight Fantastic

The USA

It was fellow exhibition pilot Beckwith Havens who first brought news to Lincoln Beachey of the momentous happenings in Europe during September 1913, showing him the misleading magazine illustration of Pégoud's supposed negative loop (page 35). Thinking the Frenchman had performed a 'forward somersault', Beachey at once resolved to come out of retirement (which he was finding tedious in the extreme) and go one better: he would perform a 'backward somersault' – a conventional loop, in other words!

He got Glenn Curtiss to build him another aircraft, smaller than the standard Curtiss biplane and with a powerful 90–100 hp Curtiss OX engine, specially braced and nearly twice as strong as the conventional Curtiss D Headless model; he had shoulder straps installed as well as a safety belt. With all that extra weight and drag, however, Beachey had problems handling the Curtiss Special Looper on its maiden flight on 8 October, and a tragedy resulted when he came in on his approach and struck the top of a tent: a young woman who had climbed up for a better view was killed outright and her companion was injured. The aircraft was totally wrecked.

Lincoln Beachey himself was unhurt, saved by the safety harness. Undeterred, he immediately set about having the machine redesigned and rebuilt and, on 25 November 1913, at San Diego's North Island Air Station, became the first to loop-the-loop in America. Then the following day he publicly repeated the feat several times near Coronado Island. Perfecting a new repertoire of sensations to offer his avid public,

Beachey's Little Looper, 1914. (Smithsonian Institution)

he now set off on a second career as America's foremost exhibition pilot; within a year he was to become a legend among aviators.

Unfortunately it is not known exactly how Beachey performed many of his more original manoeuvres. His mechanic Art Mix described the Beachey Bore, for example, conceived in that same month of November 1913, as a 'wing over wing'; and his brother Hillary Beachey said, "... I've also seen him make a vertical spiral coming down, the first roll of this kind ever made". At this stage of his career this manoeuvre of Beachey's was likely to have been the tight spiral 'corkscrew' descent popular in Europe.

There were reports of Beachey executing spins, however, which cannot, alas, be verified. He was also said to have performed **barrel rolls** (the early name for the type of autorotational roll that we nowadays call a ***flick roll***) – but it is highly unlikely that his beefed-up, high-drag 1913 machine would have been capable. For this sort of manoeuvre a different and more advanced type of aircraft was needed, and this very idea now became Beachey's next obsession.

At the beginning of 1914, Lincoln and Hillary Beachey got together with designer Warren Eaton and mechanics Art Mix and Al Hofer to construct what was probably the best high-performance aeroplane yet built in the United States. The famous Little Looper had a wingspan of a little more than 25 ft (7.65 m) and weighed just 775 lb (352 kg) with Beachey aboard, compared with the 901 lb (410 kg) weight of his first Special Looper. It was built for quick take-offs, fast climbing (1125 ft/343 m per minute), and speeds of up to 85 mph (137 km/h). In April he travelled to France and back to

purchase two 80 hp Gnôme rotary engines, which did not suffer the problems of fuel starvation experienced with the Curtiss 8-cylinder vee-type when inverted ... for the tiny aircraft with the big rotary was designed to be flown upside down.

Adding the Pégoud-style S-dive to his repertoire, Beachey became the first American to fly inverted and live to tell the tale. The well known aircraft designer and exhibition pilot E M 'Matty' Laird averred that by the latter part of 1914 Beachey was also performing aileron rolls (slow rolls): he is described as half-rolling at 500 ft (150 m) for an inverted pass along the front of the grandstand, regaining normal flight afterwards by means of another half-roll.

According to pilot Billy Parker, who for fifty years gave regular airshows in a 1916 model similar to Beachey's Little Looper, the rotary-engined Curtiss-type pusher "would spin beautifully and recovered quickly". There seems no reason, therefore, to totally discount the possibility of Beachey spinning with this later machine ... but was Beachey actually performing spins? He left no record.

His greatest dream was one day to have an aeroplane capable of going straight up vertically. One can just imagine how he would have loved today's competition machines! Certainly he was constantly experimenting with improvements to the structure and controls of his aircraft, and one modification to the Little Looper shows it with upper wing extensions and trailing edge ailerons. From his tests with different types of aileron he doubtless achieved a degree of lateral control unheard-of with wing warping and probably a good deal more effective than with the standard Curtiss mid-gap aileron system.

As king of the loopers Beachey reigned supreme. By the end of 1914 it was reckoned that he had looped-the-loop 1,000 times before 17 million people in 126 cities. He charged by the loop: $500 for the first and $200 for each subsequent loop. During that busy year he became a very rich young man indeed, frequently earning upwards of $4,000 a week.

Now he perfected another extraordinary manoeuvre which he introduced at Indianapolis in the summer of 1914; this was described by Art Mix as the Triple Reverse, starting with a normal upward loop, going into a *downward outside loop*, and then back to horizontal for another normal loop again. It is known that he could perform successions of loops one after another with the Little Looper, all the time actually gaining altitude where any other machine would be losing height, and it seems that the aeroplane really might have been capable of performing the Triple Reverse as described. This being so, Beachey seems to have been the first pilot in history to perform the outside (negative) loop, that most testing of manoeuvres both psychologically for the pilot and structurally for the machine. Billy Parker recalls seeing it several times. We must remember, of course, that it was quite normal in these pre-war days for an S-dive or a loop to be performed quite disjointedly, with the pilot nosing over into the dive rather than holding a negative *g* curve; the half-way point consisting of an extended horizontal pass (or, in the case of a positive loop, perhaps a flop over the top). We are not talking here about the circular figures of constant radius that characterize today's loops.

Meanwhile Beachey was experimenting again with ideas for a new machine; the best yet. Back in his home town of San Francisco he continued giving airshows while he and Warren Eaton busied themselves with the new aircraft, scheduled to

be unveiled at the Panama-Pacific International Exposition in February of 1915. When it was rolled out for preliminary tests it created quite a stir, for it proved to be a sleek, racy-looking monoplane of exceedingly advanced design with tricycle undercarriage; but then, after a few test flights, the machine was dismantled and stored away, giving rise to much speculation that Beachey had detected flaws in the revolutionary design.

On 21 February he opened the Exposition with a looping show in his Little Looper biplane, which he proceeded to repeat daily after that. Officials from the event had heard of the new monoplane, however, and were so insistent on seeing it perform that he was at last persuaded. On Sunday 14 March 1915, with the sun shining brightly, a crowd of 50,000 turned out to see Beachey's display in the new machine; instead they witnessed the last tragic flight of a great performer.

After climbing to 5–6,000 ft (1,500–1,800 m) and throwing several "graceful, effortless-looking loops", he started into his

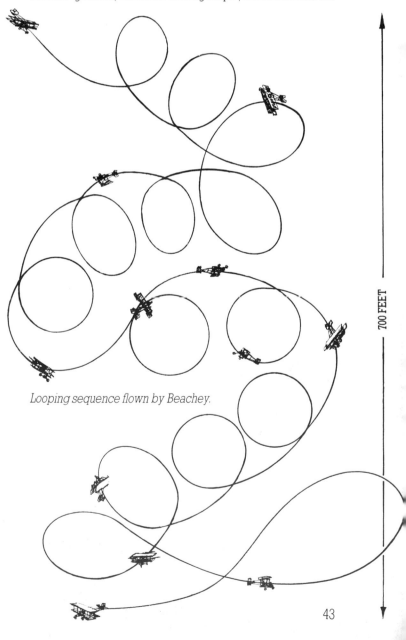

Looping sequence flown by Beachey.

700 FEET

Flight Fantastic

The Beachey monoplane.   (Smithsonian Institution)

S-dive over San Francisco Bay. All went well until he pulled down from inverted into the second half-loop, when suddenly the monoplane went into a screaming dive in which it hit a speed approaching 200 mph (320 km/h), according to estimates made at the ensuing investigation. The Vne (velocity never to be exceeded) of the aircraft was 103 mph (165 km/h), and Beachey had evidently underestimated the rate of acceleration of his slippery new monoplane. He then made the fatal mistake of over-stressing the airframe by hauling back on the stick to try to pull out of the dive, and there was an almighty crack as both the left and right wings snapped and folded upward around the fuselage. A plume of water rose as the stricken aircraft hit the Bay and was swallowed up immediately. As Beachey's body was raised and taken ashore, the crowd watched bare-headed and in stunned silence. And even to this day there are those who quietly honour his memory on the anniversary of the event by casting a wreath into the waters where he died: "The greatest aviator of them all," in the words of Orville Wright.

Beachey's place was soon taken by others. DeLloyd Thompson had already made his name as the second Ameri-

Charles F Niles with Moisant-Blériot. (Smithsonian Institution)

can to loop-the-loop, and joined Beachey in April 1914 on the exhibition circuit. Thompson flew a Day LM biplane with a 90 hp Gyro rotary engine, the first successful American tractor biplane. With it he was able to accomplish a dive and push under to the horizontally inverted position, which he would maintain in a long inverted flight of some half-mile, followed by a push-up into a vertical climb and another push to reach normal flight again at the top. Not what one could call a complete outside loop, to be sure! But nonetheless this was a daring exhibition of flight involving negative *g*, and also an indication of how these 'outside' figures would have been executed in those days.

Next came Charles F Niles ('Do-Anything Niles') from Rochester, NY, who was one of the original Moisant troupe and flew a two-seater Moisant-Blériot especially built by Harold Kantner. He was considered Beachey's closest rival, and by spring of 1914 had performed complete rolls (variously described as 'side flops', 'lateral loops' or 'cartwheels'). He is credited with being the first American to be able to reach inverted flight by means of a half-roll, which was always more difficult for a wing-warping monoplane than for a biplane.

One more famous looper deserves mention before we leave the peaceful skies of America for war-torn Europe, and that is Art Smith, 'The Boy Looper', who is said to have taken over where Lincoln Beachey left off: he certainly did so at the 1915 San Francisco Exposition, since he completed the air display engagement that Beachey could no longer fulfil. He had taught himself to fly on a home-made biplane at the age of 17, and at the age of 20 was not only looping along with the best of them but also performing complete rolls, spins and Split-Ss in his Little Looper-type biplane (90 hp OX engine) which, like its famous predecessor, featured upper wing extensions and trailing-edge ailerons. Taking his aerobatic exhibitions a stage further, Smith inroduced a night-time entertainment of looping with smoke trails and fireworks which set a trend that has lasted ever since in America as a favourite airshow attraction.

Art Smith, 'The Boy Looper'. Smith went on to a later career flying the mails.   (Smithsonian Institution)

5

'Stunt or die'

By the year 1911 Germany had caught up with the heavier-than-air aviation movement and its great centre of activity had become the aerodrome of Johannisthal, near Berlin. It was here that a 21-year-old Dutch lad by the name of Anthony H G Fokker came to seek his fortune, and started earning himself a reputation for the skill and verve of his flying. The original monoplane design which he brought with him was a very primitive affair, and until they saw young Fokker's flying demonstrations the other Johan-

nisthal regulars were inclined to scoff at his outdated ideas. But soon they began to sit up and take notice when he showed himself clearly the best pilot there.

What particularly impressed the established German favourites such as the crack Russian stunt flyer Wssewolod Abramovitch, leading Wright pilot at Johannisthal, was

Anthony H G Fokker with pupil Mme Galanchikoff in the Spin *monoplane, 1913.* (*via Musée de l'Air*)

Flight Fantastic

Fokker's daringly low flying, especially his turns and pirouettes executed so close to the ground that he seemed to invite disaster. Stuttgart engineer Kurt Rosenstein, chief pilot on the Rumpler Taube, was celebrated for his thrilling exhibitions of low dives, steep zooms, and eye-level passes with both hands off the controls; but to young Fokker's immense satisfaction he admitted after watching him that he had met his match.

Even in those days, Anthony Fokker was a designer with fixed notions who did not readily change his ideas; but during the year 1913 he saw a few things that made him stop and think. First there was the Morane, in particular the Morane-Saulnier H which Edmond Audemars had delivered to Johannisthal for assembly at the LVG sheds under the eye of compatriot Franz Schneider, in readiness for his forthcoming Berlin-Paris record taking flight. So impressed was Fokker with the French monoplane that he spirited himself and a companion with a sketch-pad into the LVG premises to make a closer assessment of the design (only to be ejected by the toe of Schneider's boot on being discovered!).

Then in the autumn another Johannisthal designer, Bruno Hanuschke, turned up with his own exciting new monoplane which was virtually a direct Morane copy; and the clincher came in October when Fokker witnessed the great Pégoud giving an aerobatic display at Johannisthal in another French monoplane, the Blériot. He determined immediately to emulate these feats with a new aircraft design of his own based on the Morane. The result was the Fokker model M5, which appeared in May 1914 in two versions – the M5L for aerobatics, and the M5K intended as a high speed military scout. Now he proceeded to teach himself to give performances like Pégoud.

In Fokker's autobiography he states, "I was actually the first in Germany to loop"; but this claim, like several others in the same work, originates more in Fokker's rather colourful recollection of events than in historical truth. The first in Germany to loop, in any case, was Adolphe Pégoud! The first German to loop, according to *Flight* magazine, was Gustav Tweer – he of the upside-down undercarriage (see illustration) – who was reported to have looped on 1 April 1914 at Johannisthal. Coincidentally the French magazine *L'Aérophile* edition of 1 April, which was obviously typeset during March, noted in its list of those who had looped to date that not a single German appeared among the names. Counter-claims have been made on behalf of Breitbeil, Cüppers, Hoehndorf, Jahn, Roth and Scherff; but if any of these did loop before Tweer, he must have done so during March – two months before Anthony Fokker.

At any rate, high fees were to be made giving aerobatic exhibitions, and young Anthony enthusiastically embarked on a series of dates in spring 1914, which included four days at his old haunt, Johannisthal, where he flew a continuous sequence of daring and carefully planned manoeuvres. His steep turns, previously vaunted as 'over the vertical' with his *Spin* (Spider) model (but which have since been established as only about 45 degrees), now genuinely reached a thrilling vertical bank with the aid of the new monoplane's wing-warping controls; and his loops, in true Fokker style, were performed at dangerously low altitude to please the crowds. He brought the machine down 'in parachute-like descents in a semi-stalled state', and demonstrated the shortest of take-offs and landings. Soon his exhibitions were acknowledged to be among the most accomplished in Germany, and he, of course, was delighted with the opportunity they afforded to promote his new M5 design.

Germany's military build-up was by now expanding into the aeroplane as well as the airship field. Aided by a passionate

Grade monoplane of exhibiiton pilot Gustav Tweer, especially built for upside-down landing! *(via Werner Garitz)*

46

Span	11 m (36 ft 1 in)
Length	6.9 m (22 ft 8 in)
Max speed	127 km/h (78 mph)
Rate of climb	1,000 m (3,300 ft) in
	2 minutes 4 seconds

Fokker M5.
The M5K ('kurtz') had a short wingspan, the M5L ('lang') was longer and similar to the Morane two-seater used by Garros and Hamel. The larger wing also compensated for the greater weight of the design with its 80 hp Oberursel (Gnôme type) rotary. It introduced the famous comma-shaped rudder for greater efficiency, and the improved stick-type control system instead of the regulation military wheel. An advertisement in Flugsport *claimed that it "combined aerobatic capability with military usefulness".*

(Musée de l'Air)

devotion to aviation and an equally passionate belief in himself, Fokker had already managed to secure a number of orders for his first *Spin* monoplane from the German military authorities, after the Dutch, British and Italians had – quite wisely – turned it down. Now once again the German Air Service authorities were sufficiently impressed to order the new machines from Fokker for urgent delivery. Preparations for war in Europe reached white-hot intensity, until the month of August arrived and the seething volcano finally erupted.

Ironically – yet predictably – it was the development of the aeroplane for use in the Great War of 1914–18 that marked its final metamorphosis from the 'airborne motor-car' to the most powerful and exciting multi-dimensional vehicle yet invented. Peacetime reporting of aviation in the popular press had always smacked of skill and daring, and it was natural now for the war-stricken nations to fasten on to the aeroplane in a unique way as the epitome of modern military technology, and to its pilots, especially its later fighter pilots, as symbols of heroic man-to-man conflict.

It was, indeed, a uniquely different kind of warfare that they waged in the sky. No wretched, stumbling, faceless masses going over the top to meet thousands of other similarly faceless masses: in the Air Services it was the individuals, the doomed young pilots and observers, some no more than eighteen or nineteen years of age, who daily fought a duel to the death in the airy vastnesses of the sky. Transported on frail man-made wings, they relied on technical skill, marksmanship and sheer reckless audacity as their weapons. Small wonder that a mythology grew up around them, and that 'ace' pilots became national heroes in a war that was inhuman, senseless and pathetically inglorious. The tradition that quickly grew up among flyers of respect for a skilled adversary in the aerial war, whether German, French or British, was certainly not mere fiction, though somewhat overplayed in later years by popular writers and film-makers.

It soon became customary to measure the greatness of the fighter pilots by the number of victories they logged. But these totals were, in fact, notoriously unreliable. Often the experienced pilot had other priorities than totting up his kills, or was content that a companion should deal the final *coup de grâce*. Or an aircraft seen to crash might simply have shot its own propeller off (as in the case of Max Immelmann), or have been broken up in the air by its own pilot, or even shot down by ground fire (as almost certainly happened to Manfred von Richthofen). Relevant, too, were factors such as the period of the war, the particular Front involved, and whether the aircraft types and pilots brought down were relatively defenceless or were fighters of comparable performance to the victor. Whilst recognizing the great achievements of the high-scoring aces, it should be remembered that they were not necessarily the most accomplished pilots of the period.

The first VC to be awarded for air combat did, however, go to an outstanding flyer, Captain (later Major) Lanoe G Hawker, who in a patrol in his Bristol Scout – armed with a single-shot carbine – bested three German aeroplanes all armed with machine-guns. This was on 25 July 1915, one of the earliest offensive patrols to be flown by a Royal Flying Corps officer in a single-seater. Hawker himself was legendary both as a marksman and as a pilot, and in 1916 commanded the first single-seat fighter squadron ever to be formed, equipped with the DH2 pusher biplane (100 hp Gnôme Monosoupape).

Hawker was certainly a pioneer of battle aerobatics: in his delicate handling of controls and throttle, using such ploys as sideslipping out of range during the frantic twists and turns of combat, the manoeuvrability of the sturdy but sensitive little fighter kept him out of trouble long after the British machine had been desperately outclassed by the arrival of the German Albatros D types, until in November 1916 he fell to the lethal combination of the Albatros and Manfred von Richthofen:

... It was a matter of great pride to learn that the Englishman I shot down on November 23 was the equivalent of our great Immelmann. I did not know who he was during the fight, of course, but I knew from his masterly handling of his machine and from his courage that this fellow was a wonderful fighter.

The sideslip had long since lost its fears for the more accomplished of airmen, for whom it was a height-losing technique particularly useful on approach; and it had been regularly employed, of course, by pre-war exhibition pilots. But the ordinary flyer of the period regarded sideslipping with trepidation as the customary prelude to a crash; and in the early days of World War I, aerobatics were generally left severely alone and were certainly not taught by the RFC to its recruits. There was scant chance of learning them, anyway, in the outdated and cumbersome trainers available. Many schools of thought still regarded banking in a turn as highly suspect. A students' booklet of 1914 contained the information: "The ailerons are used to keep you on a level keel while turning."

Ernst Udet, one of the greatest aerobatic pilots to emerge from the war, was clapped in the guardhouse for seven days in late 1915 when, as an eager young volunteer, he stalled and spun in after over-banking in a heavily loaded two-seater: banked turns were forbidden in the German Air Service. Like all the other early pilots, Udet had to teach himself aerobatics the hard way. The first **wing-over** of his life (a steeply banked climb-and-dive turn) was performed in a frantic effort to dislodge a bomb which his observer had managed to wedge in the undercarriage!

The concept of the fighter aeroplane, as opposed to the army cooperation or reconnaissance machine carrying an armed observer, owed a great deal to the vision of the great French pilot Roland Garros, whom we have already met (pages 24 and 28). In March 1915 Garros reported back to his unit after a short spell away from the Front during which he had worked on a new invention: he had a Hotchkiss machine-gun fixed to his Morane-Saulnier N monoplane, which had been mounted by Raymond Saulnier so as to fire forward through the disc of the propeller. On the blades were bolted armour plates to deflect any bullets which hit them instead of

passing in between. Saulnier had been trying for some time to devise an interrupter gear, something which several pioneers had experimented with before the war; but this was the first practical and successful use of deflection plates, and Garros soon proved that an aircraft armed with a fixed, forward-firing machine gun was a formidable weapon of war. Firing now was simply a matter of aiming the whole machine at the target: the aeroplane became a flying gun.

Morane-Saulnier armoured airscrew.
Knowing of Raymond Saulnier's pre-war experiments with interrupter gear, Roland Garros obtained leave to try the device on his own aeroplane, but it could not be made operational in time. However, Saulnier's armoured propeller plates, fitted to deflect the hang-fire bullets that so plagued the tests, were found to be extremely effective. (It has been said that the disconnected interrupter gear itself was still in place when Fokker examined the captured aircraft.)
(Musée de l'Air)

In less than three weeks, between 1 and 16 April, Garros brought down the astonishing total of four enemy machines and became France's first air war hero. The Paris papers immediately dubbed him *as* (ace), a word greatly in vogue to describe any outstanding sportsman of the day; quickly taken up by other newspapers, the term soon became widespread among all the combatant nations, and eventually all top-scoring pilots were known as aces (the German word was *Kanone*).

Forced down on 19 April after a brief but telling career, Garros's attempts to set fire to his aircraft failed and it was captured by the Germans and immediately shown to Anthony Fokker. Within an incredible 48 hours the Dutchman's team had fitted a much improved version to a factory M5K, rejecting the armoured airscrew in favour of an interrupter mechanism by which a knob on the propeller blade operated a cam-and-rod linkage to the machine gun's hammer, so that it fired only when the blades were safely out of the way. The system was suspiciously similar to that patented in 1913 by Fokker's Johannisthal neighbour, the Swiss designer Franz Schneider of LVG, whose original idea had been rejected by

Replica Fokker E-III Eindecker, built by Doug Bianchi and used in the film Aces High. *Note modern ailerons and horizontal stabilizers/elevators. Power unit is a 90 hp Continental C90.* (Bianchi Aviation Film Services)

the German Army. But in this business the prize belonged to whoever was in the right place at the right time and had the ear of the military – which Fokker certainly had.

At the time, although his 80 hp monoplane was the only fighter type in use with the Germans, it had never achieved any real popularity; until, that is, in the summer of 1915, armed with the forward-firing machine-gun, it became the legendary Fokker Eindecker (Fok. E-I).

Yet even in its 100 hp Oberursel versions (E-II and E-III), the machine was underpowered and was never considered an outstanding aircraft: it was not 'handy', and could be out-manoeuvred quite easily. Nevertheless, with this new armament and flown by such masters as Oswald Boelcke and Max Immelmann, making full use of the tactics of surprise, it soon took a high toll of Allied aircraft. By autumn and winter the 'Fokker scourge' was in full force.

Oswald Boelcke has been called the father of aerial warfare. An ace with forty victories, his was the greatest reputation of any German airman in the opening years of World War 1, both as a pilot and as a man. He was a great tactician and leader, loved and revered by his comrades. Known among the Allies for his chivalry in combat and for his generosity to captured flyers, he would make sure they were entertained royally in the mess and then load them up with wine and cigarettes before they were carted off to prison camp.

The French ace Paul Tarascon described an engagement with Boelcke during which he ran out of ammunition and had to break off: Boelcke simply raised an arm in salute, then

Oswald Boelcke, seated in Fokker D-III in which he scored his twentieth victory. (via Musée de l'Air)

circled for a while and finally went on his way. By the time of Boelcke's death in October 1916, in a tragic air collision with one of his own men, he had become a legend at the age of 25: a laurel wreath was parachuted behind the German lines by the Royal Flying Corps with the inscription, "To the memory of Captain Boelcke, our brave and chivalrous foe".

In the same *Feldfliegerabteilung* as Boelcke (Nr 62), and his great admirer and rival, was Max Immelmann; they were among the very first pilots to take delivery of the Fok. E-I, and on his first encounter with the aircraft Immelmann wrote: "We have just got two small one-seater fighters from the Fokker factory ... Fokker and a Leutnant Parschau gave demonstration flights ... and fired at ground targets from the air. Fokker amazed us with his ability."

Perhaps less of an aggressive fighter than his great contemporary, Immelmann was nevertheless a superb pilot and an imaginative innovator. He lost no time in gaining complete mastery of the new machine, even without the obligatory 'Eindecker training' that was considered essential before conversion to the tricky little monoplane. He used many new techniques of air combat which later became standard, such as finding an opponent's blind spot and attacking out of the sun, as well as using aerobatics for escape and evasion. He soon became well known for a 'hit-and-run' kind of attack which involved diving on an unsuspecting enemy from behind, swooping up and firing under his tail, then completing the upward zoom in a climbing, steeply banked turn of 180 degrees which swiftly took him back the way he had come.

This manoeuvre immediately became known as the **Immelmann Turn**, Immelmann himself being thereby immortalized in the world of aerobatics, whilst at the same time becoming an innocent cause of much controversy even to this day. The problem is an interesting one, and illustrates to what extent the task of tracing the origins of aerobatic manoeuvres is complicated by inconsistencies in contemporary as well as later documentation.

Today the title 'Immelmann Turn' is used in many countries (Britain being one of the few exceptions) to mean an aerobatic figure starting with an ascending half-loop which is followed immediately by a half-roll bringing the aircraft back to erect, level flight again. In British aerobatics the name for this figure is a roll-off-the-top.

In the interests of accuracy, let it first be emphasized that Max Immelmann's wing-warping Fokker E-III could never have performed a roll-off-the-top. Here is what World War 1 fighter and test pilot Frank L Courtney says in an American publication *Flight Path* (William Kimber, 1972):

... it would be a long time after Immelmann's death before a plane existed with enough speed and control for that maneuver. In any case

Flight Fantastic

Immelmann was too clever a fighter to use a stunt that would leave him suspended upside down, with almost inert controls, for enough seconds to make him a limp target for an enemy gunner.

The 'turn' that Immelmann actually used for his getaway (and I saw him use it often enough) was simply a very steeply banked climbing turn, requiring much skill in those days when stalling was greatly feared.

It was an impressive feature of stunt flying before the war; ... Immelmann, however, was certainly the first to make combat use of it.

Max Immelmann standing by the wreckage of a BE2c which he has shot down. (Imperial War Museum)

The figure described by Courtney is, of course, that same figure invented by Maurice Chevillard back in 1913 which he had called the *'looping hélicoidal'*; in later years it became known in English-speaking countries as the chandelle.

Perhaps the next best authority after the eye-witness Courtney is Franz Immelmann, Max's brother, who described the turn as a short climb *in combination with* a half-roll. Both

pretty clearly the same figure. Immelmann developed it, he said, as being effective against 'a certain English type of biplane' – the BE observation biplane as described by Courtney – which had its rearward line of fire restricted by the tail surfaces.

In manuals of World War I battle tactics, however, both contemporaneous and post-war, one finds endlessly varying descriptions of the manoeuvre – this adds further confusion. In the book *Aerobatics* by H Barber (McBride, Nast & Co., 1918) the Immelmann Turn is described – and illustrated – as a height-gaining, vertically-banked turn of fully 360 degrees!

Then in a USAAS training syllabus diagram we see the 'Immelmann Turn' clearly illustrated as a steep wing-over, and versions similar to this were evidently in popular post-war military circles:

The movement starts with a hard climb but steep bank is applied and then hard rudder with engine off. The aeroplane does a sharp turn and dives in the reverse direction. (A E Sims, 1932)

A substantial school of thought holds the view that a wing-over would have been a far more intelligent avoiding action for Immelmann to take at the time. Ending a 180 degree turn with height gain may have been useful; but it also left the machine with diminished energy and poised as a potential target for any enemy whose line of fire was unrestricted. In fact, there is no reason to suppose that Immelmann always performed precisely the same kind of turn anyway, given the variety of circumstances he would have encountered in aerial combat, and the probability is that the original hit-and-run chandelle observed by Frank Courtney became a wing-over or any other kind of *Kampfkurve* (combat turn) as occasion dictated.

The place where Boelcke and Immelmann rose to fame was Verdun, where on the French side was ranged against them the world's first large-scale fighter unit, the élite *Cigognes* among whose ranks were numbered such immortals as Georges Guynemer and René Fonck. By early summer 1916 the fighting aircraft available to the Allies had undergone a transformation, and now included the manoeuvrable little Nieuports and Spads capable of hitherto impossible aerobatic performance. Fonck, with 75 victories champion ace not only of the French but of the entire Allied air force, was unrivalled in his handling of the Spad and went on to a post-war career as an aerobatic and demonstration pilot, flying a special Spad S.29 with the registration F-ONCK.

His great contemporary Charles Nungesser was another superb exponent of the Nieuport; not to be outdone, Nungesser had his postwar aerobatic mounts registered F-NUNG and F-NUNB, and went on barnstorming tours in the United States in the early 1920s, where he also starred in the autobiographical film *The Sky Raider*. As a war pilot he was the antithesis of Fonck: daring, reckless, undisciplined, his first act upon being posted to Escadrille N 65 on fighters was to give a dazzling display of low-level aerobatics over Nancy which brought the immediate reprimand from his squadron commander – "If you *must* perform aerobatics, go and do them over the enemy!"

As soon as his CO was out of the way, Nungesser accordingly refuelled his Nieuport and took off for the nearest enemy aerodrome, where he gave a repeat performance of his low-level aerobatics, reporting on his return that he had carried out his commander's orders! His entire career smacked of the same audacity and indomitable self-will;

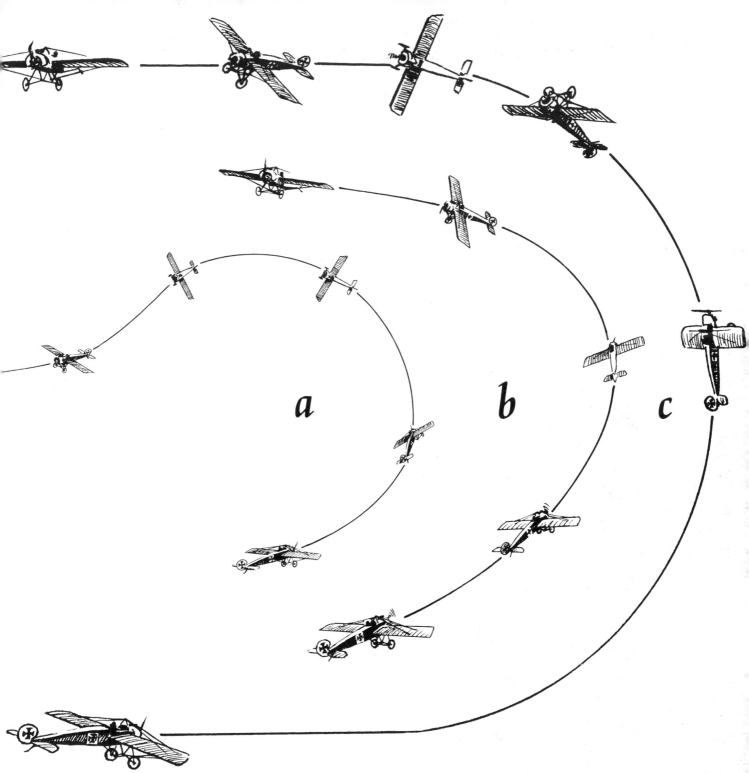

Various combat turns ascribed to Max Immelmann. (a) Wing-over. (b) The original 'chandelle' turn. (c) The modern half-loop/half-roll 'Immelmann Turn'.

racked by a string of injuries that would have kept another man out of the war, there were times when he could no longer walk and had to be carried to his aircraft.

Nungesser applied one invariable test each time he emerged from his many hospitalizations: if he could roast off in a machine and go through one of his bravura aerobatic displays, then he was fit enough for the Front.

Meanwhile, on 31 August 1915, the sands of time had run out for Adolphe Pégoud. Already an ace with six confirmed victories and awarded the Cross of the Légion d'Honneur, he was struck in the heart by an enemy bullet in his last aerial combat and crashed to the ground in his Nieuport at Petit-Croix, near Belfort. The following day, exactly two years after his first demonstration of inverted flight had revolutionized flying for evermore, a wreath was dropped at the site of his crash 'in honour of the aviator Pégoud, fallen in battle for his country, from his adversary'.

By 1917 the aerial war had taken on a terrible intensity and combat machines on both sides matched and then bettered each other in firepower and performance. The German Albatros D types and the Sopwiths which opposed them brought a new level of sophistication and demanded high skills of the pilot; in return they provided him with machines of unparalleled flexibility and responsiveness. Now the full

Charles Nungesser's Morane-Saulnier A1, F-NUNB.
(Musée de l'Air)

René Fonck's Spad S.29 registered F-ONCK.

Charles Nungesser. *(via Musée de l'Air)*

range of aerobatics became not just a desirable but an essential tool for survival.

Major W A (Billy) Bishop said:

To be able to fight well, a pilot must be able to have absolute control over his machine. He must know by the 'feel' of it exactly how the machine is, what position it is in, and how it is flying, so that he may manoeuvre rapidly, and at the same time watch his opponent or opponents. He must be able to loop, turn his machine over on its back, and do various other flying 'stunts'.

The loop and half-loop were established tricks by now, and the half-roll was especially useful in the squirming, jinking, tail-chasing mêlée of the dog-fight; any manoeuvre providing a quick reversal of direction, such as Immelman's turn, was invaluable to keep the enemy off-balance. The 'half-roll' of World War I was actually what later became known as (to use the polite version) the Split-S: half-roll and pull down in a half loop to erect flight going the opposite way.

Here is Captain James McCudden, VC, writing in 1917 of an encounter with a black-and-purple Albatros Scout:

I got behind him at fair range, and he immediately dived and then zoomed. I did the same and, firing both guns whilst zooming, saw my tracers passing to the right of his fuselage. He now half-rolled and I followed and, passing a few feet above him, saw the German pilot look upwards; and it struck me that he did not seem the least perturbed, as I should have expected him to be ... That Hun was a good one, for every time I got behind him he turned upside-down and passed out underneath me. I well remember looking at him too. He seemed only a boy.

In another account, Billy Bishop describes using a tail-slide as a combat manoeuvre (although in *Bring Down Your Hun!* – 1918 notes on aerial fighting – use of the tail-slide is 'not recommended' because of possible strain on the control surfaces):

I pulled back as if to loop, sending the nose of my machine straight up into the air. As I did so the enemy scout shot by underneath me. I stood on my tail for a moment or two, then let the machine drop back, put her nose down, and dived after the Hun, opening fire straight behind him at very close range.

And the stall turn had also come into common use by now, also known variously as 'stalling to one side', 'stalled turn' or 'stalling turn' (though no stall is actually involved in this manoeuvre, which has already been illustrated on page 30). Pilots tell of zooming up under an enemy's tail to attack his blind spot, then ruddering into a dive at the moment of losing all forward speed. It, too, appears in the offical publication *Bring Down Your Hun!*, where the text exhibits the then-current association of the stall with 'loss of flying speed', which explains how this manoeuvre acquired its misleading name:

In order to do a quick turn without losing height, a useful manoeuvre is to pull the control back till the machine is flying vertically upwards. Put on rudder to one side or other and the nose of the machine will fall to that side. The rudder must be put on before the machine loses flying speed, otherwise one gets no control, and the machine will hang in the air. As soon as the nose is pointing downwards the control may be pulled back, and the machine will fly on a course parallel to the original course, about one machine's length away, and in the opposite direction.

On the German side, Werner Voss emerges clearly as the most respected pilot – on 'Albatri' and later on the Fokker triplane – for his handling skills combined with a reckless courage and élan not frequently encountered in the Teutonic temperament. From Jimmy McCudden comes perhaps the greatest tribute to a fellow-pilot's skill, in the following account of what was believed to be Werner Voss's last fight (although recent research suggests that he may have survived this to fight and die in a subsequent engagement):

… we saw ahead of us, just above Poelcappelle, an SE half spinning down closely pursued by a silvery blue German triplane at very close range.

The Hun triplane was practically underneath our formation now, and so down we dived at a colossal speed … The German pilot saw us and turned in a most disconcertingly quick manner, not a climbing nor Immelmann turn, but a sort of flat half spin. By now the German triplane was in the middle of our formation and its handling was wonderful to behold … As he flashed by me I caught a glimpse of a black head in the triplane with no hat on at all.

The triplane was still circling round in the midst of six SEs, who were all firing at it as opportunity offered, and at one time I noted the triplane in the apex of a cone of tracer bullets from at least five machines simultaneously, and each machine had two guns … When I next saw him he was very low, still being engaged by an SE marked 1, the pilot being Rhys-Davids. I noticed that the triplane's movements were very erratic, and then I saw him go into a fairly steep dive, … then saw the triplane hit the ground and disappear into a thousand fragments.

… As long as I live I shall never forget my admiration for that German pilot, who single-handed fought seven of us for ten minutes, and also put some bullets through all of our machines. His flying was wonderful, his courage magnificent, and in my opinion he is the bravest German airman whom it has been my privilege to see fight.

The dead pilot was found wearing the Boelcke collar and his name was Werner Voss. He had the 'Ordre Pour le Mérite', Rhys-Davids came in for a shower of congratulations, … but as the boy himself said to me, 'Oh, if I could only have brought him down alive,' and his remark was in agreement with my own thoughts.

Werner Voss was 20 years old when he died on 23 September 1917; James McCudden was 22.

The 'flat half spin' mentioned by McCudden was an example of the flat, skidding turn known as 'viffing', which Voss is

Werner Voss standing by his Fokker Dr.I triplane with 'totem-pole' face caricatured on the cowling. (via Chaz Bowyer)

Flight Fantastic

credited with inventing. Joseph Jacobs, fifth ranking German ace (Voss was fourth) described it as a 'slip-turn': "a turn solely with rudder. The wing doesn't go up and those behind don't realize you're turning ... in the slip-turn you're skidding around a turn, level, and it's difficult to detect, and the bullets meant for you miss on the outside." (*Fighter Tactics and Strategy, 1914–1970*, E H Sims, Cassell, 1972.)

One of the most interesting revelations of World War I pilot tactics is in their quite nonchalant use of autorotations:

Joystick right back, full right rudder, a twist of a spin, dive and zoom, and suddenly I realised that the sky was crowded with aeroplanes, all Albatroses, all thirsting for our blood. I had a maniacal two minutes, skidding to left, to right, diving, zooming, and generally throwing the poor old Pup around like a drunk on skates.

(*No Parachute*, Arthur Gould Lee, Jarrolds 1968)

In addition to the flick roll, from mid-1916 the spin became a regular standby, used to elude a pursuer or sometimes as a ruse to break off combat under the pretext of being disabled.

Still there was no official training in the techniques of aerobatics, and pilots of all nations were left to acquire these essential skills (if they lived long enough) in the battlefield. This applied equally to the technique of spin recovery, which although known since 1912 and practised since 1914, was never officially part of pilot training until 1917[*].

France set up its 'school of acrobatics' for service pilots in Pau in late 1916, and America introduced its one-week training course in combat 'acrobacy' in September of 1917; but first of the Air Services to remedy the sad deficiencies in flying training with the introduction of a forward-looking and systematic course of instruction including aerobatics was the Royal Flying Corps, thanks to the almost single-handed efforts of Major R R Smith-Barry.

Smith-Barry was a product of the illustrious Central Flying School, an exceptional pilot himself and a man with the vision to see that to prepare a pilot for war flying demanded a very special type of instruction. But to teach such advanced and potentially dangerous techniques demanded instructors who were totally and superbly the master of their craft. From his posting in command of a Scout Squadron on the Western Front, Smith-Barry sent letters back to England at the end of 1916 outlining a revolutionary training scheme; and he was swiftly brought back to put his ideas into practice with a Reserve Squadron stationed at Gosport.

His philosophy was that dual control was of paramount importance. In addition, advanced pilots were encouraged to fly exactly as they chose, their experiments being limited only by the state of their own nerve. All known aerobatics were investigated, taught, perfected – including spin recovery, which Smith-Barry had himself first learned in France in the summer of 1916. Instead of cumbersome and obsolete trainers he insisted on using the remarkable little Avro 504J (100 hp Gnôme Monosoupape): manoeuvrable and responsive, it was also controllable throughout its large speed range and forgiving of inexpert treatment.

The first batch of graduates vindicated overwhelmingly, by their skill and confidence, the unorthodox methods of the new school. In August 1917, acceding to Smith-Barry's cherished wish, Gosport was converted into the School of Special Flying and became the first school to instruct instructors how to instruct pupils. The Gosport technique was adopted throughout the United Kingdom and Colonies, and its influence was felt world wide.

*The development of spin recovery technique is traced in Chapter 6.

Frank Courtney gives the following impression of Gosport training:

A Gosport Instructor was not supposed to waste his time in the simplicities of ordinary flying; every takeoff and landing, and as much as possible of his regular flying, was supposed to simulate some difficulty or emergency: use of minimum space for landing and takeoff on good or poor surfaces, coping with sudden engine failure at low altitude, dodging obstacles on or near the ground, operating the plane with one or more controls damaged, discovering new maneuvers or new ways of doing old ones, making quick recoveries from unusual attitudes, and a hundred other points that could be more readily passed on to students if the instructor could make them appear to be casual procedures in routine flying.

I long ago gave up trying to describe the extreme degree of precision that we developed in doing everything with airplanes that could possibly then be done – hardly anyone believes me. Yet I will claim that flying, regarded as the fine art of handling airplanes, reached a peak of glorious efficiency in the Gosport of those days that has never been surpassed. In fact, it has never been allowed to – today, ten minutes of the old Gosport flying would cause any pilot to lose his licence . . .

This was revolution indeed. The Admiralty had been discouraging 'unnecessary stunts' among RNAS personnel

(Left) Major R R Smith-Barry, founder of the Gosport Instructors' School.
(Frank Cheesman)

Avro 504J of the Smith-Barry School of Special Flying at Gosport ('A' Flight).
This tandem two-seat trainer featured a central 'toothpick' undercarriage skid and was powered by a Gnôme rotary engine. It was astonishingly strong for its light weight.
(Frank Cheesman)

since 1915, and the RFC took the same line: aerobatic flying had been virtually prohibited in the skies over Britain until Smith-Barry came along and placed proper emphasis on its value.

The result was that the young pilots arriving at the Front were now infinitely better equipped to handle their craft. John McGavock Grider, a British-trained US airman about to leave for France in 1918, recorded in his diary for 14 May: "I gave my new plane [SE5a, 180 hp Viper] a work-out in the air today. It flies hands off; I put it level just off the ground and it did 130. Then I went up high and did a spinning tail-slide. Nothing broke so I have perfect confidence in it."

This astonishing manoeuvre sounds very much like the 'corkscrew tail-slide' performed by Chanteloup in 1914 (see page 36); difficult though it is to believe, both seem to be early versions of today's torque roll which involves putting the aircraft into a rolling vertical climb and then maintaining that roll as the airspeed stops and the machine tail-slides backwards. We shall see later that French and Italian pilots of the 1930s were also experimenting with 'tail-sliding spins' (Chapter 8).

Smith-Barry's methods took time to disseminate, however, and not all the young Americans (nor, for that matter, the British) were as well tutored as Grider. And even he steered well clear of flying that notorious aeroplane the Sopwith Camel, which had entered general RFC service in the middle of 1917. The machine was proving exceptionally tricky to master, even for experienced pilots, and by the spring of 1918 had been responsible for an alarming rate of accidents among trainees. Grider recorded on 12 March that three out of a group of six US Naval pilots had been 'washed out' on Camel training; after which two more American pilots spun in

Flight Fantastic

– one an instructor who had 300 hours on Curtisses back home – and then two Englishmen: three flunked and four killed in a matter of days, all on Camels. Grider continued:

Col. Rees is in charge here and he tried to put pep in the boys by giving a stunting exhibition below five hundred feet. He certainly did fight the tree tops and he wouldn't come out of a spin above fifty feet. Then he made all the instructors go up in Camels and do the same thing. It was a wonderful exhibition and then he made us a little speech and told us there was nothing to worry about, to go to it. Several of the boys were so encouraged that they took off in Camels and tried to do the same thing. Only one was killed.

In the debate as to whether speed, ceiling or manoeuvrability should be paramount in a fighter, the rotary-engined Camel went all out for manoeuvrability with all three masses of engine, armament and pilot concentrated in one area. Major W G Moore, OBE, DSC, described the Camel as:

… totally unstable in all directions and very sensitive fore and aft, and much influenced by engine torque … a death-trap for an inexperienced pilot. A skilled pilot could not wish for a better mount. To him it was like having a pair of wings strapped on to his shoulderblades … They were wonderful in a dogfight because they could make the quickest change of direction of any machine that flew in the war. Its peculiarities made it the most manoeuvrable fighter ever built and the best all-round performer. (*Early Bird*, Putnam, 1963.)

In the 'Biggles' stories of Capt W E Johns (who had himself flown Camels as an instructor) are to be found some particularly authentic descriptions of World War I dogfights with the Camel. In *Biggles of the Camel Squadron* we have a classic demonstration of the World War I roll as the pilot pulls the control-stick back into his right side, kicking out his right foot at the same time. "The Camel swung up in a swift barrel-roll," the narration continues – which was the name given to the manoeuvre at that time. In *Bring Down Your Hun!* the advice for execution of a roll is: "With the engine on, pull back the control, and pull it to one side as far as it will go. At the same time put on full rudder on the same side."

Oliver Stewart, whose intimate knowledge of aerobatics spanned 50 years, wrote in 1967 that the normal World War I roll and half-roll was what we nowadays call a flick roll (snap roll in the US). At that period it was also variously known as a barrel roll, quick roll, whip roll or horizontal spin. Like the spin it is an autorotative manoeuvre, but unlike the spin it is performed at speed, with an abrupt change to the stalling angle of attack combined with simultaneous application of ailerons and rudder to initiate the roll.

Curiously enough, despite Stewart's first-hand knowledge of the Camel, it is over this particular aircraft that opinions among present-day pilots tend to disagree when it comes to the question of flick rolls. Although I have yet to meet a pilot who has rolled a rotary Camel, there are those who contend that its design envelope would never tolerate a properly stalled flick entry, and that the Camel's quick rolls were simply gyroscopically induced. Perhaps it was an exception in this particular detail, but nevertheless in fighters of the period, such as the SE5a, the standard rolling manoeuvre was a flick roll (quite logically, when you think about it!). Bear this in mind while reading the following extract, taken from the 3 May entry in Grider's diary which was later published under the title *War Birds – Diary of an Unknown Aviator* by Elliott White Springs:

The idea was that each man should do the stunt of the preceding man and then set another one for the next man. Cal did Mac's [loop] and then half rolled at the top of the loop. Springs was next and his stunt was a full roll at the top of the loop. Of course he was up above a thousand feet.

I was next and I put my nose down to about two hundred after I did my full roll, and as soon as I started up for my zoom I kicked on full right rudder and pulled the stick back into the right-hand corner. I don't know what I was doing but I sure did it. I whirled around a couples of times with my nose up and then I whirled around with my nose down and ended up stalled upside down. The motor stopped and I just did get in the field with a dead prop.

Mac said what I did was an upward spin followed by an outside spin, whatever that is. I told Thompson how I did it and he went up and started into it with terrific speed. The propeller shaft broke and his prop flew off, just nicking the leading edge of the wing … That ended the afternoon performance. Mac and Cal certainly can fly.

That 'upward spin' was obviously a two-turn upward flick roll, which must have been pretty near the vertical: quite an achievement in "an old two-twenty SE"! The 'outside spin', however, presents more of a problem. Some commentators have suggested he performed a **negative flick**, but Grider would have needed a decisive change of stick input to achieve this – or indeed to achieve a **negative spin**, which has also been suggested – both of which would demand the stick to be *pushed smartly forward* to change the angle of attack from positive to negative. Significantly, he doesn't describe moving the stick (or anything else) during the manoeuvre. So, assuming the very minimum of control input other than aft right-hand stick, a more likely answer is that after holding the machine in the autorotation until it ran out of energy after a couple of turns, Grider then found himself sliding off on a wing into a downward spiral. Starting with the fuselage axis tilted backwards, this would leave him head-downwards for a while (though not in fact stalled), until his rotation brought him upright again in a shallow dive.

Another argument against Grider's performing a negative spin is that at this period the manoeuvre was still unconquered, and indeed greatly feared; thus he would certainly have recorded his triumph in recovering from an upside-down spin had he succeeded in doing so! It was not until later that this and other negative manoeuvres came under scientific study at Farnborough, and the story of research into negative as well as positive spinning is traced in the next chapter.

Flick roll (known as 'barrel roll' during World War I).

The normal spin, of course, had become an ordinary part of combat flying. Even in the Camel the spin could be quickly stopped once the technique was mastered, although it required judgment to a nicety; indeed, when spin recovery techniques first began to be set down in textbook form, the tendency of such unstable and 'flicky' aircraft as the Camel to go into a spin in the opposite direction, if over-corrected with rudder, influenced a change in the standard technique at this time from Parke's original *opposite rudder* to the new recovery technique of *centralize all controls* – "and then the elevator may be pushed slightly forward so as to help the machine to get into a nose dive".

Probably the greatest wartime exponent of the formidable Camel was RFC/RAF Captain D'Urban Victor Armstrong, DFC, who tamed the fierce little beast to perform aerobatics with split-second accuracy. Oliver Stewart said of him "the fellow had the hands of a surgeon". An eyewitness account of Armstrong in action runs as follows:

The machine approaches the tarmac, flying parallel with the hangars, and suddenly with a rapidity that makes one blink it flicks over in a roll. Now, this is no 'old pilot's tale'; that evolution was done at no more than fifteen feet from the ground. We caught a glimpse of the greasy belly of the Camel's fuselage, saw the wing tips miss the ground by a matter of twelve inches, gaped as the little kite swung round the right way up again, and, as one man, we let out a blasphemous ejaculation as we watched it sweep up and away in a terrific climbing turn.

… And then he came by again. The sun glinted on the spinning disc of his propeller as he roared towards us; we could hear the wail of Rafwires as the Camel gathered speed. A rabbit ran in terror as the low-flying plane whipped the grass into fluttering agitation. And then again – that flick roll.

So for a quarter of an hour that Camel held our attention. Three times the pilot pulled a loop so low that, as he swept inverted above our heads, we could see for a few fleeting moments intimate details within the cockpit – the instruments glinting in the sun, the green canvas belt, the wings on the fellow's tunic, black, sleek hair and a hand gripping the stick. Meanwhile the Rhône was running at full bore, its note falling and rising, falling and rising, as the machine climbed and dived three times…

And then he would slip away, leaving a faint smoke trail while we stood and watched, shook our heads and laughed…

Despite his consummate skill, D V Armstrong was a charming and unassuming character who was much loved and esteemed by his contemporaries. South African by nationality, he had taken his British licence at the age of 18 in February 1916, after transferring from the South African Defence Corps, and saw action on the Western Front before returning to a Home Defence posting in England in late 1917. It was here that he made his happy acquaintance with the Sopwith Camel, the machine with which his name is forever synonymous.

Armstrong was not the 'display type' even though he quickly became famous for his prodigious skill and judgment in low-level aerobatics: the shows he gave were simply out of sheer *joie de vivre* and for the pleasure of fellow-pilots, without any hint of trying to make a name for himself.

Stationed at Sutton's Farm, and later at Hainault, Armstrong's occasional visits to neighbouring airfields in his distinctive all-red Camel always attracted an appreciative audience. One superlative stunt was landing off a flick roll, for which he started at about 80 mph (130 km/h), bringing on full power as the aircraft went over, which gave him just enough thrust to hold the machine up as it came out so that he could land in a stalled condition. His loops from ground level may have seemed suicidal, but he maintained he always had a method of sideslipping out safely in case of trouble.

Relating his first experience of Captain Armstrong "giving his Camel an airing", Oliver Stewart "received a shock such as no exhibition of aerobatics has ever given me before or since…"

He flew across the aerodrome, the wheels of his machine skimming the grass. Suddenly, yet without any jerk, the machine reared up, turned completely upside down without raising itself above the level of the shed roofs, and flattened out with the wheels again skimming the grass. Had there been the slightest error of judgment, the machine would have struck the ground.

Within a short while, however, Stewart was emulating Armstrong's low-level performances and similarly working out recovery measures that he considered safe in case anything went wrong.

John Grider saw Armstrong flying at Hounslow in May 1918 and described him as a wonderful pilot: "He runs his wheels on the ground and then pulls up in a loop and if he sees he hasn't got room enough, he just half rolls at the top. I saw him land from a full roll, and he glides and does S turns upside down."

This half-roll at the top of a loop (roll-off-the-top) was a figure of which the powerful and agile Camel was capable even though the Fokker Eindecker of two years previously was not, and it was soon copied by other pilots including Grider and his friends.

An interesting article on this manoeuvre of Armstrong's was written in 1963 by Lieutenant Temple N Joyce, who claimed (erroneously) to be the first American pilot to perform the figure after seeing it done by D V Armstrong in the summer of 1918, when Armstrong was loaned to the US training centre at Issoudun. Attempting to reproduce the manoeuvre, and thinking (of course) in terms of a flick roll, Joyce managed to fall into ten or eleven inverted spins – and incidentally teach himself to recover from them – before the truth dawned on him that you just had to "fly it through" (exactly as Armstrong had told him in the first place!). Adding his voice to the many others who consider that 'Immelmann Turn' is a misnomer for this figure, Joyce in his article suggested calling it after its inventor, D V Armstrong, "in memory of the finest acrobatic pilot that I have ever seen".

Sadly, Captain Armstrong was fated not to survive his RAF service. Posted to France with No 151 squadron, he brought his total of confirmed victories to three in the very arduous Night Fighter theatre of operations, and was awarded the DFC for his consistently brilliant work. Yet it was in a flying accident that he died.

Being a pilot of such legendary repute, it is not surprising that stories grew up about Armstrong's flying, many of them apocryphal, such as the myth that he was given to rolling through hangars. There are also several versions of the way he met his death, but the following is the true account as confirmed by his friends and contemporaries. Visiting a neighbouring French airfield in the exuberant days following the armistice, Armstrong had been begged to 'give the boys a bit of a show' as he left. Climbing into C6713 – now painted the regulation dark night-fighter colours – DVA waved his goodbyes, took off, and obligingly went into one of his spectacular low-level routines. But this time, during the course of either a loop or, more likely, a flick roll*, his Camel

---

*The flick roll seems more likely, due to the aircraft's considerable sideways displacement during the manoeuvre.

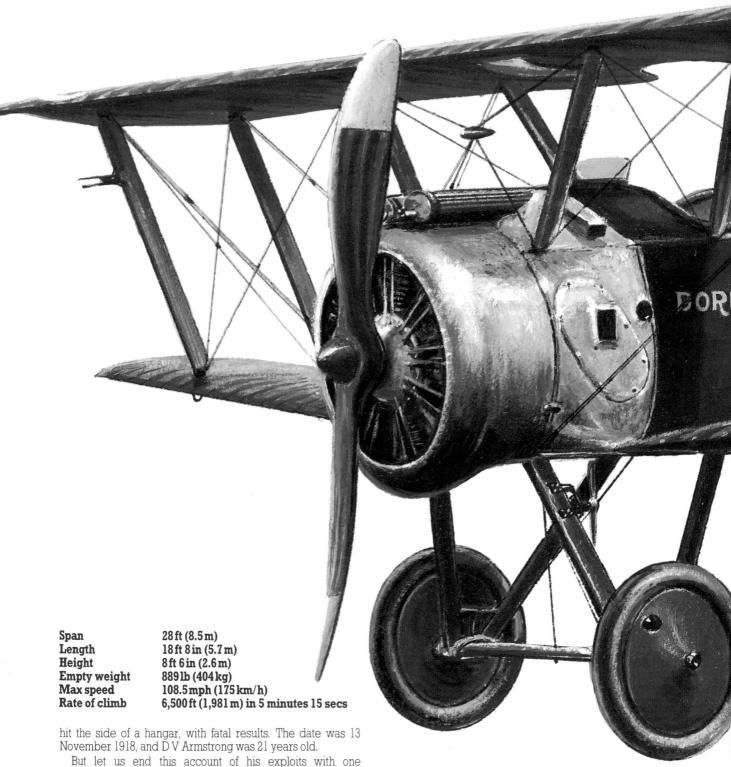

Span	28 ft (8.5 m)
Length	18 ft 8 in (5.7 m)
Height	8 ft 6 in (2.6 m)
Empty weight	889 lb (404 kg)
Max speed	108.5 mph (175 km/h)
Rate of climb	6,500 ft (1,981 m) in 5 minutes 15 secs

hit the side of a hangar, with fatal results. The date was 13 November 1918, and D V Armstrong was 21 years old.

But let us end this account of his exploits with one particular story which most vividly illustrates the man's hairs-breadth judgment. It is related by a close personal friend and fellow pilot, and refers to a certain visit that Armstrong paid him at Sutton's Farm. "His normal method of arrival was always spectacular," says the narrator, "but this beat all".

Parked out at right-angles to the hangars was a row of some half dozen Camels in the middle of which was a gap left by the removal of one. As he approached, Armstrong noticed this gap, put his nose right down and went through it at some 150 mph with his wheels nearly on the ground. He then pulled up into a loop which he completed by passing through the gap again and equally close to the ground.

This was a deadly accurate piece of flying done on the spur of the moment and terrifying to watch. I was standing near enough at the time to be able to see the large amount of left rudder he applied progressively as he went up into his loop.

After reproving him for scaring me to death *I had the gap measured* and found that in the course of his remarkable performance he had taken a 28 ft wing span Camel through a 39 ft gap.

D'Urban Armstrong's Camel C6713 (110hp Le Rhône).
In addition to its extreme sensitivity in all axes, the Sopwith Camel's powerful rotary engine held even worse problems for the unwary due to gyroscopic precession and engine torque. Famous for its lightning right-hand turn, it required left rudder input in this as well as in left-hand turns!

(Below right) Captain D V Armstrong, No 78 Squadron, Sutton's Farm. (via Frank Cheesman)

(Below left) Armstrong (2nd from right, in helmet) chats to (L–R) J H Summers, J L Wingate, J T Collier, C J Marchant and Charles C Banks during a visit to Hainault, 1918; in the foreground his Camel C6713 is having a new tail-skid fitted.
(via Frank Cheesman)

6

Research and discovery

By the end of World War I, aerobatics – through a baptism of fire – had acquired a *raison d'être*. No longer the butt of official disapproval and reproof, aerobatic skills had been honed and perfected, techniques codified. Moreover, aeroplanes themselves had become not only beautiful to look at, but manoeuvrable, interesting and responsive to fly.

Research had been stimulated, but, like so much else during the war years, had followed an erratic course; sometimes carried out officially, sometimes strictly unofficially – for fun, for practice, or more often simply for survival. Of the latter variety, sadly few records remain.

Oliver Stewart had the advantage of a home posting to the experimental base at Orfordness, after an active tour flying Sopwith Pups, where on becoming chief test pilot he found himself in the enviable position of being able to combine both official and unofficial research. Whilst there, during 1918, he had a 110 hp Le Rhône-powered Camel which he flew for his own amusement, and soon developed an obsession for aerobatics; this, together with an equal obsession for analyzing the fundamentals of aircraft handling, led him to propound some of the very earliest theories of aerobatic technique.

... I decided to extend my Farnborough 'universal pilotage' ideas and to learn how to do it *in principle*, so that I would be able to make an accurate loop with any aircraft that was handed to me that was capable of doing the manoeuvre. And this was where the pattern of learning came in, for my thinking on the subject made it plain to me that the critical factor in this as in other aerobatic manoeuvres was the *preservation of a controlled orientation*.

Some young pilots – I have a suspicion that it still happens – did their first loop by flying the aircraft at the prescribed air speed and then pulling the stick back and waiting until the earth came in sight again. For a large part of a loop done in this way the pilot has no check on the orientation of his aircraft. He is looking at a featureless blue sky. Yet if that orientation check is absent for so much as a fraction of a second the chances are that the loop will be defective ... The skilled aerobatic pilot could not be satisfied with this sort of hit and miss performance.

I started my work on looping by learning to orient my aircraft all the way round by looking along the wing towards the horizon and watching the horizon as it seemed to tumble round. At first this did not give me the required information; but it was only a matter of learning how to interpret what was seen, I then found that I could watch my aircraft's heading all the way round – though indirectly – and apply minimal corrections so that the course was pure, smooth and accurate.

(*Words and Music for a Mechanical Man*, Faber & Faber, 1967.)

Stewart was well ahead of his time. In fact it was not until sixty-five years later that these important principles of self-orientation were formulated into a system for aerobatic students by Swiss champion Eric Müller, in *Flight Unlimited* (Müller & Carson, 1983), where he advocated specific sight-lines for maximum visual information.

Next Oliver Stewart followed Armstrong's lead in bringing his manoeuvres down to ground level, working out what he considered a reliable method of extricating himself from any predicament that might arise due to sudden engine failure in any particular figure. Safety in low-level aerobatics, he believed, depended on the pilot's proficiency and skill, not on arbitrary height minima. No doubt this is why every illustration in his celebrated book on the subject has the aeroplane performing at twenty metres above the ground!

Finally he turned to inverted flying. In his service at the Front he had already found it useful to dive *inverted* from above on to an enemy machine that was flying an opposite course, because in this way he could survey his opponent constantly until precisely the right moment came to half-loop

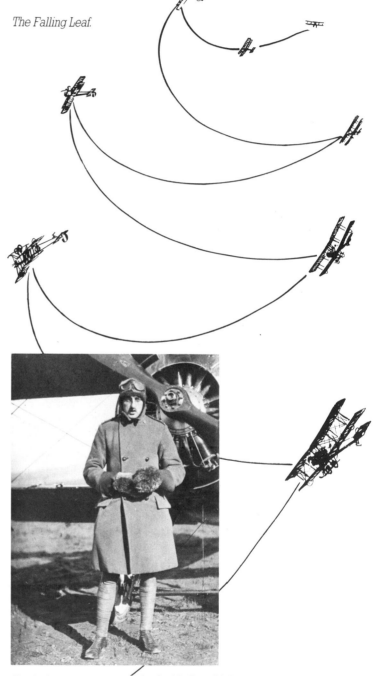

war, though of course one cannot be sure that it was precisely this same Falling Leaf as described by Courtney. Certainly it must have been very similar. And, nearer home, *Daily Mail* writer Harry Harper recounts in *Lords of the Air* (Lutterworth Press, 1940) how BC Hucks invited him to

Lt Oliver Stewart, MC, AFC (No 54 Sqdn, RFC/RAF).
(Frank Cheesman)

The Falling Leaf.

the right way up and at the same time launch his attack. "Whether I was the first to do this I do not know," he said; but during his time at Orfordness he took his inverted experiments a stage further and made himself master of the machine in this position. And here again the eyes were the key to orientation: "the semi-circular canals fail miserably". He learned to half-roll or half-loop to the inverted attitude and spin from it, go into a **Falling Leaf** or make steeply banked turns (inverted and right way up) with assurance and without risk of losing touch with the aircraft's orientation.

To digress slightly at this point, Frank Courtney has some interesting things to say about aerobatic manoeuvres of the period, and claims for himself the invention of the Falling Leaf in late 1917 at Gosport. "Pottering around on a Camel at several hundred metres," Courtney says he began wondering what would happen if he stalled, started to spin and checked the spin, but was too low to check the stall. So he stalled and allowed the right wing to drop in an incipient spin, checked it at once, and immediately the Camel switched sharply over to the left; he repeated the same checking of the incipient spin to the other side, and found that the Camel switched smartly back to the right again; and so on. The resultant series of manoeuvres, descending from side to side, had his Gosport colleagues fooled for a week or so before they worked it out.

One cannot be too sure about his claim to have invented it, however. In fact a stunt by the name of *feuille morte* (dead leaf) had been performed by Pégoud and others before the

Frank Courtney photographed with Sopwith Pup at Shoreham, 1918.
(Frank Cheesman)

Flight Fantastic

Hendon one day in the late war years "to watch a piece of acrobatics he was then practising" in a DH4 biplane, which was "his famous 'falling leaf' trick". "I have seen others do this," Harper goes on to say, "but none of them with quite the artistry which Benny managed to impart to it."

An interesting comment offered by Frank Courtney is that the first initiation of the flick roll could scarcely have come about by accident, and it would be extremely interesting to know when, where, how and by whom this manoeuvre was first discovered! All we now know is that it was, as Oliver Stewart confirms, universally practised during the 1914–18 war. Stewart himself only discovered the slow roll shortly before writing his book *Aerobatics* in 1928, and even went so far as to say that it had not been developed by 1918. But we know that is not the case, because Chevillard, Pégoud and Chanteloup were already flying complete sideways rotations in 1913.

Stewart was an unusual pilot: a thinker, a philosopher even, who had first met aerobatics at Hendon in 1913 as a seventeen-year-old and followed its development through the war years to bring the art to a peak of perfection in 1918. On reflection, he admitted:

… there were … some figures I ought to have discovered but did not, among them the inverted spin. This was, I suppose, within the capability of the Camel, but the idea of its possibility did not occur to me. Had it done so I would have tried it.

Whether the Camel could have done the 'pushed' flick roll I do not know, but I think it might. It could not have done the 'spectacles' (or *noeud de Savoie*) in which an inverted pair of loops is joined in the middle by a twist, because it had insufficient engine thrust.

Stewart knew the Camel well, but he had not taken it beyond the 'known' limits of his day. Leaving military service at the end of 1918, he then missed the thrust of further research during the years 1919–1922, when a team of test pilots at the Royal Aircraft Establishment, Farnborough, undertook a thorough investigation of inverted flight and negative manoeuvres, including that inverted spin and negative flick roll which strangely it never occurred to Stewart to try.

We shall be meeting Oliver Stewart again later, for he maintained a close association with aerobatics throughout his life. A one-time flautist, he was sidetracked away from his early career in music by the lure of flight, to which he eventually succumbed entirely; he became a well known aviation journalist, founding the monthly *Aeronautics* in 1939, and for 30 years he commentated at airshows including the famous Farnborough displays. From 1955 to 1962 he acted as Chairman of the Judges at the Lockheed International Aerobatic Contests which are featured in Chapter 13.

The phenomenon of the spin, in its various guises, was a subject of much intermittent interest at Farnborough. Tracing back to the origins of spin research, however, it is surprising how little attention was paid to the matter by the RAE (then the Royal Aircraft Factory) before the year 1916.

We have seen how Wilfred Parke recovered from his accidental spin in the military trials of 1912, and how his recovery method was set out for all to see in the British magazine *Flight*. Yet after that date there were still many instances of spin accidents, even among those who had taken

due note of the Parke recovery method. For example, Geoffrey de Havilland himself fell into an accidental spin in March 1913 from which he failed to recover; but fortunately the spin went flat, and when the aircraft hit the ground in this attitude he was able to walk away from the crash. It was all very well to know the theory, but putting it into practice was another matter altogether!

Who, then, can we credit with the earliest deliberate spinning and recovery? It is a question which has caused considerable debate in aeronautical journals and among members of such august bodies as Britain's Royal Aeronautical Society, but which I submit has never before been satisfactorily answered, even by the thorough investigation which Wing Commander Norman Macmillan undertook for the magazine *Aeronautics* in 1960–62.

Macmillan's research revealed that during 1915 several RFC and RNAS pilots became adept at spinning: J C Brooke, Vernon Brown, Kennedy-Cochran-Patrick, 'Nobby' Clark and R Balcombe Browne were known exponents. But there were two alleged instances of deliberate spinning a year earlier, in 1914, and it is to these two cases that we now direct our attention. The first involves Harry Hawker, and the second Geoffrey de Havilland.

Macmillan had picked up a reference to Harry Hawker in a report of the Advisory Committee for Aeronautics, published in June 1919, in which Hermann Glauert said: "It is believed that the method of coming out of a spin was evolved first by Mr H G Hawker on a Sopwith aeroplane." Given that the subject of the report is 'The Investigation of the Spin of an Aeroplane', Glauert's statement certainly carries weight, even though he seems unaware of Parke's prior findings (as indeed many people were). If the phrase "it is believed" seems to cast doubt, bear in mind that Glauert is not merely stating that Hawker evolved a recovery method, but that he was *the first* to do so – about which aspect he was quite right to be circumspect, because he could not know what was happening elsewhere in the world.

Already a racing and exhibition pilot, Hawker was one of the earliest to loop in England, his Sunday afternoon displays at Brooklands once being described as 'the finest ever seen'. And as Sopwith's chief test pilot he soon acquired a brilliant reputation for aerobatic skills which earned respect – and inspired emulation – by a whole generation of wartime fighter pilots.

Macmillan, however, dismissed the case for Hawker, being unable to uncover any information beyond the widely reported fact that he had accidentally spun and crashed a Sopwith Tabloid at Brooklands in June 1914; Sir Thomas Sopwith had been unable to add anything either, and the investigation was not pursued.

The case for de Havilland entered Macmillan's series of spin articles a year after they had started, when he published the following observation: "I have since discovered that Sir Geoffrey de Havilland had previously [i.e. before the autumn of 1915] spun intentionally knowing he could recover. He was mounted on a BE2, possibly (but not certainly) a BE2c."

Although he had been insistent throughout the series on eyewitness confirmation before accepting any reports of early spinning, Macmillan astonishingly gave no corroboration for the de Havilland claim and was so vague as to date it somewhere between April and November 1914. DH's own autobiography, published shortly afterwards, made no mention of the supposed spinning episode which had lately

Geoffrey de Havilland in his BE2 design.

(Imperial War Museum)

caused so much interest in the aviation press; indeed the book contains several statements that sound quite contradictory to the theory. Despite efforts by myself and other researchers, nothing has yet been uncovered to substantiate the de Havilland story.

For test pilot Harry Hawker, however, there are eyewitnesses. On 27 June 1914, after an argument with a naval officer about the probable spin recovery characteristics of his Sopwith Tabloid (100 hp Gnôme Monosoupape) Hawker took the machine up and fell into a spin out of the top of a dead-stick loop. Applying sideslip recovery inputs, he was unable to stop the spin and crashed (fortunately damaging only the aeroplane). This is the incident that was reported in *Flight* and *The Aeroplane*.

Two separate eyewitnesses then state that he took the machine up later and spun it deliberately. Howard Pixton says he did this "the next day", and Horrie Miller, a co-worker with Hawker at Sopwith's, says that he first worked on the damaged machine "for the next few days"; but, despite these discrepancies over the exact date, both agree that Hawker deliberately spun and deliberately recovered. Miller expands on the story by saying that Hawker "became completely absorbed in this problem". After his initial crash, Miller has Hawker saying, "I know what I should have done . . . I'll go up and prove my theory". (*Early Birds*, H C Miller, Angus & Robertson 1968).

Though the Miller book errs on certain factual matters here and there, his errors generally are on subjects that were not first-hand knowledge to him. There seems no reason to doubt his personal recollection of events in which he actively participated, and indeed he goes into considerable detail about the spinning episode, giving the name of the tendentious naval pilot as Spencer Gray.

And Schneider Trophy winner Howard Pixton, surely, is an

Harry Hawker with Sopwith Scout, 1914.   *(RAF Museum)*

Flight Fantastic

impeccable witness: he describes Hawker's deliberate spinning as "just about the bravest thing I ever saw".

> I tried to dissuade him, told him it was plain suicide; others used their influence, but he took no notice.
>
> The next day he took up the machine, on what I expected was his last flight. He stalled, got into a spin, and after several turns, the spin stopped and became a straight dive. He had conquered the spin simply by centralizing his controls. Aviation owes Harry Hawker a debt of gratitude."
>
> (*The Brooklands Story*, C Howard Pixton, A V Roe & Co 1955)

On the available evidence, therefore, it seems that to the young Australian Harry Hawker must go the distinction of first deliberately spinning and recovering an aircraft, some time at the end of June 1914. That he left no written evidence is not altogether surprising, since the profession of test pilot in those days carried no such responsibilities, and Hawker himself found both reading and writing laborious in the extreme. He was a man of action, quick and keen, but with a talent for analysis which made him an invaluable member of the Sopwith design team.* It was largely due to his magnificent work, and especially because he was so alive to the importance of aerobatic capabilty in his aircraft, that so many successful wartime Sopwith machines were produced. In 1919, on King George V's recommendation, he became the first civilian to be awarded the Air Force Cross.

It was not until two years after Harry Hawker's pioneer spinning that test pilots Frank Courtney and Frank Goodden carried out the first Farnborough spin tests in FE8s, Courtney having surprised himself by initiating an accidental spin during some routine research into the aircraft's aileron yaw characteristics, and managing to recover thanks to a fleeting recollection of the Parke method. This stimulated a series of tests which were carried out by Goodden in August 1916. His recommended method of recovery was to switch off the engine, put the stick central and forward, and centralize rudder. Shortly afterwards a scientific evaluation of the aerodynamics of spinning was undertaken at Farnborough by Dr F A Lindemann in 1916–17, but by then (by August 1916, in fact) it had become a recognized manoeuvre in air fighting and was quite commonplace.

Gerhard Fieseler writes that the first premeditated spins in Germany were performed in early 1916, and in France Major C Draper saw an unidentified French pilot spin and recover a Nieuport 17 in August 1916 at Issy-les-Moulineaux; but the Imperial Russian Navy can boast of yet earlier intentional spinning on the part of Lt-Commander V V Dybovski (inventor of the Scarff-Dybovski gun-gear) in a Morane G in July of 1915.

In America, Harold T ('Slim') Lewis was instructing in spin recovery in the early summer of 1917, at a time when stunting was prohibited in the Air Service, but the ban was eventually rescinded and aerobatics, including spinning, became part of the advanced service training course in September of 1917. Gil Budwig, who had learnt with Lewis, then became an instructor in the aerobatics course at Rockwell Field, together with buddies Eddie Hubbard and Mike Brown: all three, fortunately for the USAAS, had been keeping up their aerobatic skills on the quiet during the ban! The one-week course in 'Basic Battle Acrobacy and Trick Flying' comprised stalls on Monday, spins on Tuesday, loops on Wednesday, chandelles on Thursday and barrel rolls on Friday. Eddie Stinson, brother of the famous Stinson sisters, was another of the expert flyers on hand to instruct the young US Army pilots of the time and was remembered vividly for his breathtaking precision with the JN-4A: he could pop a row of burned-out light bulbs on the ground without dragging a wing (he could even pop a light bulb fixed to the top of a pole!). Sometimes he would do a series of rolls on finals, coming over the fence inverted, and as he rolled back erect his wingtip would sweep the tall grass on the ground.

With normal spinning now understood and universally taught, service pilots were thoroughly well equipped to

FE8 with controls set in the spinning position; composite photograph taken at Farnborough during the 1916 spin research.   (*Imperial War Museum*)

*When the Sopwith Company was dissolved after the war, TOM Sopwith chose to name its successor the H G Hawker Engineering Company, which later became famous as Hawker Aircraft Ltd.

Eddie Stinson, unruly brother of Katherine and Marjorie, was an instructor from 1916 and was among the first to teach spin recovery in the United States, in 1917. (Smithsonian Institution)

handle their craft and get themselves out of any kind of trouble in the air ... or were they? Returning to *Bring Down Your Hun!* of unknown authorship (1918), under 'Stunt Flying' we find the following piece of advice:

To come out of a loop quickly, directly the machine is upside-down, push the control forward as though one were trying to push the nose of the machine up. The machine will stall at once, the nose swinging down very quickly, giving one control in a very short distance.

Or, in fact, giving one an inverted spin – 'Bring Down Your Camel'! – from which it was not generally known how to recover. Inverted flight being possible only for short periods at a time, and being of no particular use in combat anyway, the condition had not been seriously investigated during the war years nor its implications fully realized. Pilots were becoming more adventurous at the tail-end of the war (witness John McGavock Grider's famous diary), but they were also opening themselves up to hitherto unresolved problems.

Prompted by a spate of Camel accidents from which ten out of thirteen had involved inverted (negative) spins, it was realized that the manoeuvres of inverted flight – flight during which the aircraft's wings met the relative airflow at a *negative* angle of attack, instead of the *positive* angle of ordinary, erect flight – were insufficiently understood. In 1919, Squadron Leader Roderic Hill was placed in charge of a team of test pilots at the RAE whose job it would be to make a thorough investigation. His report, produced three years later, stated in the Introduction:

Flying opinion was so divergent that even those who had made a habitual practice of flying inverted had failed to crystallise definite ideas on the subject. Such general lack of knowledge and the accompanying inability to distinguish real from imaginary risk resulted in a loss of perspective that was injurious to flying morale.

The aircraft used in the tests were, in addition to the ill-famed Camel, the Snipe, BAT Bantam and SE5a. Although none had inverted fuel systems, they could be held inverted for several seconds, the Camel (Clerget engine) holding out for over half a minute and the Snipe (210 hp Bentley Rotary BR2) for a longer period still, even at full throttle, during which it was actually possible to climb.

The investigation of the negative spin was rather embarrassingly delayed, however, by the team's inability to initiate the manoeuvre successfully! This was solved by the arrival of Teddie Gerrard on the scene, in the autumn of 1920. Gerrard had first fallen into a negative spin by accident in 1917, after half-rolling inverted in a Camel, inadvertently holding on his rudder together with full forward stick. It was later discovered that giving opposite aileron at the same time was even more efficient. On that first traumatic occasion Gerrard had been held in only by a lap-strap, and had managed to recover by grabbing the stick with his right hand and pulling as he passed 800 ft (250 m) going rapidly downwards. His left hand was busy at the time; he was hanging on to the seat for dear life!

Taking the precaution of first installing shoulder-straps, Gerrard had then proceeded to carry out negative spins 'frequently' and was believed, on joining the RAE Experimental Flying Department, to be the only pilot who had done so up to that time. With his help, a thorough exploration of the negative spin and its recovery was soon possible.

During this historic research into negative flight conditions, several more discoveries (or rediscoveries) came to light, which marked the further widening of horizons in the realms of aerobatics; the first of which was the slow roll. In the way of manoeuvres for initiating inverted flight, Roderic Hill's team found that there were two alternatives: the half loop or the half roll. The latter, of course, was customarily a flick roll stopped at the halfway point; but Hill recommended that the pilot might also use "a very slow half roll, in the process of which he must, if he is to avoid a rather severe sideslip, turn slightly off his course".

With his usual thoroughness Hill researched and reported on the control inputs necessary for this 'new' manoeuvre*, concluding also with a recommendation how to perform the complete roll with a synthesis of its two halves blending perfectly into a continuous whole. Gerrard again proved the expert in these matters, for it was he who insisted on the necessity of selecting a point on the horizon about which to orientate oneself; he also employed the technique of using rudder to control the aircraft's pitch when elevator and rudder control surfaces exchanged functions during the course of the manoeuvre (a technique already known to

Negative angle of attack in inverted flight.
For the sake of clarity in this book, figures performed with a negative angle of attack are described consistently as 'negative' rather than 'inverted' or 'outside', which can be misleading.

FUSELAGE REFERENCE LINE

RELATIVE AIRFLOW

*The manoeuvre was in fact known, but seldom employed: *Bring Down Your Hun!* states: "The machine can easily be turned over on its back by making a slow half roll or by going straight on after the top of a loop. This manoeuvre has not been used practically in any fight."

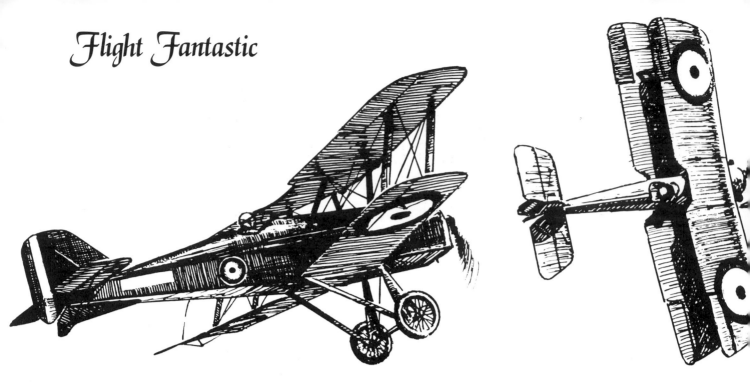

During the slow roll, rudder and elevator exchange functions as the aircraft passes through the vertically banked position.

Gustav Hamel and the other pre-war exponents of vertically banked turns and spirals – see illustration above).

The need to use the half slow roll instead of the normal half flick roll was noted particularly when attempting to return from inverted to erect flight. With flick-rolling, the technique involved forcing the wings beyond the critical (positive) angle of attack by pulling the stick sharply back, in other words by initiating a positive stall: fine when you are in an upright attitude. In inverted flight, by contrast, with the stick well forward and the wings at a negative angle of attack, a smooth aileron roll was obviously easier and gentler on the machine.

In fact, the only reasonable kind of flick roll to have used under those circumstances would be the *negative flick roll*, which the report however gave no sign of recognizing as a distinct manoeuvre (what Stewart calls the 'pushed flick roll'). Nevertheless, without special remark, its use was recorded in their experiments in the BAT Bantam – the machine which demonstrated the best negative performance of all the aircraft under test. Starting from inverted, "... to induce the quick half roll the control stick is pushed quickly forward, simultaneously with the application of rudder. A rapid whirling motion sets in, similar to that of the roll from normal flight."

Finally the Farnborough team attempted to investigate the negative loop. The aircraft used in these tests were the BAT Bantam, flown by P W S 'George' Bulman and T A Langford Sainsbury, and the Sopwith Camel flown by Hill. The second half of the figure, a rising half-loop from inverted to erect, was attempted several times in the Bantam without success; either the wings must have stalled out on the push from inverted, or the 170 hp Wasp Radial lacked sufficient thrust to push up and round – aggravated by its tendency to cease firing almost immediately upon becoming inverted. Roderic Hill felt that maybe the Bantam might have been made to perform the complete loop if the engine had been modified to run inverted, but with no known design limits for negative stresses on the airframe, was reluctant to subject it to excessive loads (minus 1.7 g had already been measured during the negative spin).

The first half, however, was accomplished: the push downwards in a curving half-loop from erect flight to finish horizontally inverted. This new manoeuvre, under constant negative g, we must carefully differentiate from the vertical dive and push-through as hitherto practised, which is not at all the same thing. On later being performed in public it was christened the 'bunt', courtesy of R L R Atcherley (see below), and was often popularly known as the 'English bunt'.

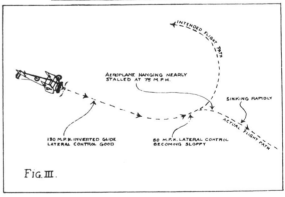

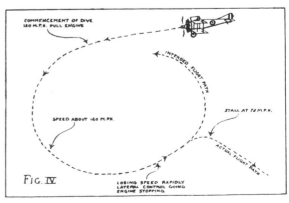

Diagrams accompanying Farnborough report on negative loop experiments, 1922. Fig. IV illustrates the bunt.

The full-blooded bunt was certainly not a manoeuvre that Hill was prepared to perform with the Farnborough Camel. He was himself aware of Adolphe Pégoud's pioneering S-dives, and, in nursing the Camel carefully through the downward path to inverted, faithfully reproduced (and recorded) the same method of entry to inverted flight as that used by his great predecessor:

I produced the manoeuvre in the most gentle way possible, by stalling the aeroplane sharply in normal flight, allowing the nose to drop and pushing the control stick quickly forward, thereby hoping to swing the aeroplane round before the speed rose excessively. This I was successful in doing...

(a) Sutton harness (four piece). Straps were adjustable by slotting over a central cone and pin fastening, designed so that it could be undone even when the pilot was upside down with his weight on the straps.
(b) Zlin Trener harness (five piece, including negative g strap). The central attachment is again secured by a spring clip for quick release.

This description is very helpful in drawing the essential distinction between the two techniques.

From a position of uncertainty and alarm among service pilots about negative spinning (many believing that the aerodynamic condition itself was not recoverable, others that the physiological stresses on the pilot were not survivable!) Hill's R & M report in September 1922 clearly showed (1) that steady inverted flight was possible on all the aircraft types at their disposal; (2) that there was no inherent resistance to recovery from inverted flight; (3) "that provided the pilot appreciates the correct control movements to make, recovery from the inverted spin presents no insurmountable difficulties"; and (4) that an adequate harness was "of supreme importance".

The Sutton harness, with shoulder straps as well as lap straps, all fitting into a quick-release system that worked well under negative as well as positive *g*, had been invented by Oliver Sutton in 1917 and came into limited use during the war, as did other shoulder-strap harnesses. They were not, however, universally used for some years to come. The RAE

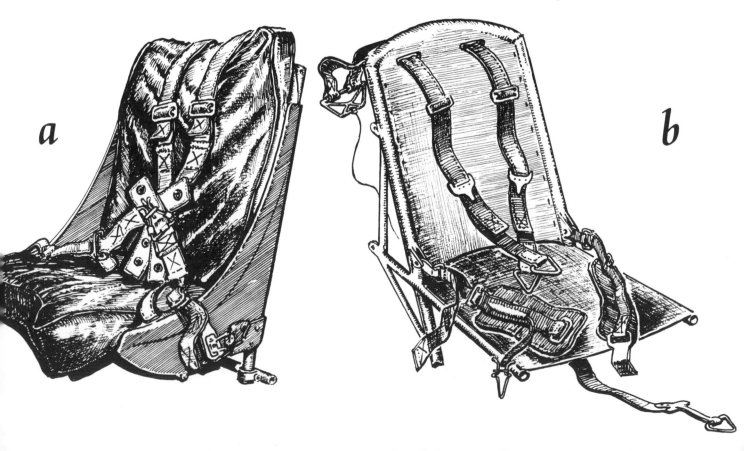

a *b*

Flight Fantastic

team strongly recommended that future aircraft design should take negative manoeuvres into account and hence forth make provision for them in stress calculations; and that with this in mind the pilot must be adequately strapped into his seat.

The necessity for proper aerobatic harness may seem obvious to us today, just as the use of the parachute seems nowadays a fundamental safety measure, yet neither became normal equipment until the mid-1920s. If shoulder-harness had only been standard in the Sopwith Camel, untold numbers of accidents and deaths would undoubtedly have been prevented, especially among trainees: the aeroplane's extreme sensitivity in pitch being such that pilots were often thrown unexpectedly forward after pushing a little too eagerly to initiate a dive, with the result that centrifugal force parted them unceremoniously from their seat, and in such circumstances the aircraft might go to the ground out of control before they could apply corrective action.

Allen Wheeler's account of learning to fly in the RAF during 1925 reveals that only lap straps were installed in the Avro 504 (*Flying Between the Wars*, GT Foulis, 1972). The normal aerobatic training repertoire then included stalls, spins, loops, stall turns, horizontal flick rolls, slow rolls (except on those types, such as the Avro, which would not perform them), and the Falling Leaf. Very sensibly, before going on their first solo all students were taught to spin and recover – standard recovery in RAF Training Manuals having by then reverted to the original *opposite rudder* technique, with 'in some aircraft' forward stick recommended. Inverted flying was carried out where permitted (and, naturally, attempted where not permitted), especially with the Sopwith Snipe in which quite a number of negative manoeuvres could be performed.

In the early winter of 1925 Wheeler records seeing the first upside-down Falling Leaf beautifully demonstrated at the hands of Pilot Officer 'Scruffy' Purvis, a pilot of great talent who, had he not come to grief the following year, "would undoubtedly have been one of the great aerobatic pilots of the Air Force". He also witnessed some brilliant flying by the remarkable R L R 'Batchy' Atcherley at the Royal Air Force Hendon Pageant of 1926, when he performed what he called an upward spin, i.e. a vertical flick roll, after which he flew off horizontally. Wheeler was mightily impressed, although *The Aeroplane*'s reporter noted rather loftily: "One has seen an American pilot do two upward spins in that way ... but one gathered that it was not standard practice even in America."

Wheeler was himself called upon to give a solo display at the 1927 Hendon Pageant with the Siskin IIIA, and, believing that the aircraft had sufficient power to weight ratio to duplicate Atcherley's manoeuvre, worked up to it gradually by starting with horizontal flick rolls and then performing them at more and more of an upward angle. Eventually he was able to do $2\frac{1}{2}$ vertical flicks!

After two and a half turns of upward spin things became a little confused and I found it best to centralize the controls and leave the Siskin to sort itself out which it always did. I then went into the next manoeuvre pretending that I had had the Siskin under control all the time.

In addition, he found that the little fighter could perform a full upward slow roll – the first **vertical roll** that this author has been able to trace. Like the upward flick, which he entered at 180 mph (290 km/h), this manoeuvre depended on

Hendon Pageant programme, 1927.

building up a lot of speed with a preliminary dive, and quickly ran out of energy afterwards:

As in the upward spin I let the Siskin fall out of the manoeuvre at the top and the result was just as exciting to me as to anyone watching, since on some occasions the Siskin would do a tail slide, having stopped completely in the air still pointing upwards. It was thus advisable to hold the stick firmly back just at the end so that if a tail slide ensued the Siskin would finally fall forwards and remain the right way up: if it fell backwards recovery from the inverted dive would take a little longer.

Featured in R L R Atcherley's Hendon display of 1926 with the Gloster Gamecock (420 hp Bristol Jupiter), but unfortunately missed by many observers, was the first public performance in Britain of the negative half-loop originally pioneered by Roderic Hill's Experimental Flight at Farnborough. Batchy named it the 'double bunt', after a verse in the celebrated ditty *Eskimo Nell*, which he disarmingly described as 'our classic guest-night song' ("She tried the bunts and double bunts and other stunts well known ..."). The following year at Hendon he incorporated the bunt – as well as a three-turn formation spin – into the five-ship formation display given by the Genet Moths of the Central Flying School.

According to Allen Wheeler the manoeuvre worked very well with the Lynx Avro (Avro 504N, 215 hp). He recorded that there were still the two different approaches to executing the bunt, either the Roderic Hill (Camel) method of stalling into a dive, which we may also call the Pégoud method; or to push over steadily after starting level at a speed well above the stall, which is of course the geometrically accurate half-loop method. Wheeler never could decide which of the two "gave one least anxiety and discomfort," although fortunately shoulder-harness was installed in the open-cockpit fighters by then! "In both cases there seemed to be an unconscionably long time diving upside down almost straight at the ground before the welcome sight of the horizon appeared in front..."

The RAF Pageants at Hendon took place every year between 1920 and 1937 and were immensely popular, drawing crowds of 150,000. They featured 'crazy flying' and both solo and formation aerobatics, the latter frequently enhanced by smoke trails, adopted by the RAF from Major J C Savage, who had invented skywriting shortly after the war with a team of ex-service pilots flying a handful of SE5as. Later he devised a method of tinting the smoke to produce coloured trails. What an impact that coloured smoke does make as it follows the aeroplane's flightpath through the sky – and where would our modern aerobatic displays be without it?

At the Hendon Pageant on 30 June 1928, Flying Officers Richard Atcherley and Dermot Boyle, both Central Flying School instructors, gave a dazzling display with D H Moths (75 hp Armstrong Siddeley Genet) fitted with extra tanks for inverted flight. It included the first public performance in Britain of the full negative or 'outside' loop, a remarkable achievement for both these pilots and their machines; by then, however – in fact twelve months before – the manoeuvre had already been pioneered independently, and

R L R (later Air Marshal Sir Richard) Archerley, inverted in a Genet Moth at the Hendon Pageant, 1928. *(RAF Museum)*

almost simultaneously, by two other pilots about whom the reader will shortly hear. A couple of months afterwards, Atcherley found himself under arrest in Paris for performing precisely the same trick ... but on this occasion he had given an entirely gratuitous (and illegal) solo airshow to enliven a light aircraft event at Orly which he found a little dull for his taste. "The crowd seemed very appreciative," he said, "the gendarmerie very hostile".

Batchy's disregard for convention and decorum was as famous as his prowess in aerobatics and speed flying, which led to memorable appearances in the American National Air Races of the 1930s. As a student pilot at the RAF College, Cranwell, he qualified for the clandestine 'League of Intrepid Airmen' by performing a suitably audacious feat: two half-rolls and a loop on his first solo. In later years, as Commandant of that same College, he endeared himself to the cadets by inventing a novel kind of parade inspection: with everyone at attention, expecting his arrival by staff car, instead he would appear at rooftop level in a Vampire, perform a swift double roll and disappear ("just to let them know that there was something at the end of it all worth parading for").

It was at about the time of Atcherley's Hendon displays that Oliver Stewart's book *Aerobatics* (Pitman, 1928) was first published in Britain. It had originated in article form in the periodical *Airways* and in some respects appeared rather less up-to-date with current aerobatics than its date of publication (and later revision in 1930) would suggest, as witness the remarks on the tail-slide already quoted (page 30); the only person Stewart had so far encountered who had done this manoeuvre was Oliver Sutton (of harness fame)

Flight Fantastic

although he had heard 'recently' of a famous foreign pilot giving exhibitions of tail sliding (not, one hopes, unaccompanied by other evolutions of more variety and interest!).

Although he knows of the existence of the inverted spin, he gives no advice as to its execution and recovery; likewise the **flat spin**, which he says a French pilot has done for exhibition purposes, but from which the method of extrication is "not definitely known". He describes the double bunt as diving "steeper and steeper until the vertical point is passed and the machine flattens out upside-down". And the negative ('outward') loop is known to him, but again he does not suggest how to do it beyond limiting it to machines which have inverted fuel systems. The climbing Vertical S is envisaged when aircraft have the more powerful engines needed to perform it, but the downward Vertical S is suggested as a possibilty with current machines, though Stewart has obviously not himself tried it. A combination of the two would then produce a **vertical 8**, he says.

On the subject of figures which Stewart has not himself performed, it is interesting to note that he has evidently discussed with Allen Wheeler the performance of vertical rolls and vertical flicks, but in his writing unfortunately fails to distinguish between them. Be not in doubt however: the two distinct types had both been practised and seen publicly at the Hendon RAF Pageants.

Following on the heels of *Aerobatics* came *Stunt Flying* by Captain Richard Duncan, MC (Crosby, Lockwood & Son, 1930), an American who had been trained as a Gosport instructor. He had obviously read Stewart's book, and from it confused the two types of vertical roll under the heading 'Vertical Spin'. Likewise his comments on the tail-slide and flat spin exactly reflected Stewart's own, although he was much more forthcoming about the negative loop. Duncan's book also included the 'aileron roll' and 'wing-over' for the first time under those names, and introduced the 'vertical reversement' and 'lazy 8' which are American terms for steeply banked turning manoeuvres.

The aviation scene in the USA had gone through some remarkable developments in the ten years since the end of the war, when many thousands of trained pilots (some 2,000 of whom had actually seen active service) found themselves suddenly on the scrap-heap with skills that nobody wanted to employ and with an ingrained hunger for flight that no factory or desk job could eradicate. Glenn Curtiss's business had boomed thanks to the war effort, and his model J and JN trainers had been turned out at fever-pitch to teach these eager boys their now-redundant flying skills. With thousands of these war surplus 'Jennies' going for a song, some for as little as $300 apiece, and with thousands of ex-service pilots falling over themselves to get back into the air, small wonder that America soon became the land of the itinerant flyer and barnstormer where every cow-pasture was a potential landing strip.

For these purveyors of joyrides at $5 for 5 minutes, aerobatics were just a means of attracting their rural customers, and with a modicum of skill – at a low enough altitude – a pilot could put on a passable show that would bring the customers running: buzz the local townsfolk, give a quick exhibition of stunting (a few loops, some steep turns and a roll or two) then fuel up and wait for the punters to arrive

clutching their precious dollars and cents. Technique and precision were not a major consideration!

The JN-4D was not the only Curtiss trainer used, and indeed Curtisses were not the only popular barnstorming models, but somehow the flavour of the period is captured in the phrase 'The Jenny Era', and the aeroplane's wide wing-span with its maze of wires, struts, kingposts and wing skids gave aerial wing walkers and acrobats the ideal cat's-cradle around which to clamber to their heart's content.

With its huge and overweight Curtiss water-cooled engine (90 hp OX-5) the Jenny's performance was modest even at the best of times, when the airframe was in good condition and the engine working as planned. But the fabric weakened and wood rotted from being tied down outside in all weathers, the wires pulled out and bolts became rusty. The OX engine was a notoriously unreliable powerplant ('a failure looking for somewhere to happen'), and its design – especially the water-cooling system – simply invited trouble. Either it overheated in warm weather and leaked through the water jacket, fouling the ignition system, or in winter the drips froze on the carburettor, stopping up vents and sticking valves. And of course you were guaranteed to get water in the fuel, from the position of the leaky pump overhead the carburettor. There was no upper lubrication, so each day all the upper moving parts had to be lubricated with a squirt-can.

On the other hand, both engine and airframe were easy to repair once you got the hang of it, and on several battered Jennies the lower wing panels, always in short supply due to universally rough usage and ungentle landings, were replaced altogether by a set of upper panels with the strut fittings reversed! Smaller mishaps were quickly rectified with the aid of an ever-present supply of fabric and dope, and broken flying wires replaced from a nearby farmer's fence.

Soon the barnstormers teamed up in pairs and small groups, and started dreaming up more exciting entertainments: the Aerial Circuses were born. But enough has been written elsewhere about this magical era and of the legendary performers who graced it. Reluctantly we must leave the wing walkers and aerial trapeze artists on one side, for here the paths begin to divide between 'stunting', in the sense of circus, and 'aerobatics', in the sense of piloting skills: we shall be following this second path. The 'stunters' will not be ignored, however. Many of the great US airshow stars were also outstanding aerobatic pilots, and we shall be meeting them soon in Chapter 9 – America's Golden Age.

Immediately following the war there was a craze for setting up looping records, and after Eddie Stinson had set up the first world record with 150 consecutive loops in 1918, fellow-American Temple N Joyce set about breaking it in January 1919 with 300 loops in a Morane-Saulner A-1. Joyce had already gained fame as a wartime test pilot in France, giving exhibitions of Camelbatics to visiting brass-hats – a speciality being his roll-off-the-top learned from the great D V Armstrong. Within a month the looping record had been raised to 318 by another serving American, Belvin W Maynard (the 'flying parson'), in a Nieuport 28. Not to be outdone, the French pilots took up the challenge and Alfred Fronval carried away all honours with scores of 629 in 1919, 960 in 1920, and an incredible 1,111 in February 1928 in a little under five hours of solid looping. But even that figure was later beaten by American 'Speed' Holman with a score of 1,433!

Maynard must have been quite a character, for during his brief career as an exhibition pilot from 1919 to his death at an

airshow in 1922 he conceived the 'Skyrocket Roll', which was 2½ upward flick rolls (in what aircraft we unfortunately do not know). This was five years ahead of Allen Wheeler's 2¼ vertical flicks at Hendon, though all we know about Maynard's manoeuvre is that it was 'upward', not whether it was vertical.

At about this time, barnstormer Earl Daugherty developed a stunt with the faithful Jenny which would not reappear in the aerobatic repertoire until ten years later, with machines many times more powerful. During the performance of a loop, at the top of the figure he would throw a complete flick roll – starting and ending it upside down – and then return to normal again by finishing the second half of the loop. He needed a terrific speed in order to flick at the top, and his method of entering the manoeuvre was to dive the Jenny to the unheard-of speed of 120 mph (195 km/h), which allowed him 60 mph (95 km/h) entry speed for the roll; ending on the verge of a stall, he relied on the weight of the engine to pull him through the final half-loop. (*Baling Wire, Chewing Gum and Guts*, Bill Rhode, Kennikat Press, 1970.) One hears that he needed the persuasion of a handsome fee to perform the feat at all! [Later, in the 1950s, it acquired the name **avalanche** – see Chapter 13.]

In Hollywood the moviemakers were not slow to capitalize on the air heroes of World War I; flying had been featured in films as early as 1915, when Glenn Martin starred as an aviator in the Mary Pickford film *The Girl of Yesterday*. Now the movies about wartime airmen gave opportunities to ex-service pilots and barnstormers like Ormer Locklear, perhaps the greatest aerial daredevil of the silent screen; and one of the most successful of all World War I films was the Academy Award winning *Wings*, directed by William Wellman from a storyline by John Monk Saunders, both former comrades from the famous Escadrille Lafayette of US volunteers who flew for the French.

With the great new market for movie stunts offering jobs – flying jobs – to any pilots who would take them on, a group of flyers and drivers formed the Thirteen Black Cats association to regulate the rates of pay: a midair fight on the wing of an aircraft was worth $225 (one man falling off); a crash into a tree or house, or a crash from a spin, was $1,200; and a midair explosion with the pilot baling out earned $1,500!

But while this orgy of stunting and barnstorming and joyriding was going on in the Land of the Free, a young Army Air Service pilot was gaining a name for himself that would soon become a byword for aerobatic wizardry, and would later become legendary in his own lifetime. That pilot was Jimmy Doolittle.

Small of stature, Doolittle learned early on in life how to take care of himself, becoming an agile gymnast and a competitive boxer. He had a childhood dream of flying (which he attempted in various 'aircraft' of his own construction) and a burning desire to be forever up and doing, which led him to sign on in 1917, hoping for combat duty in France. All he got, however, was an assignment to Rockwell Field, San Diego, as an instructor of cadets in advanced flying training. But if he was to be an instructor, he reasoned, he would be the best darned instructor in the Air Service!

Accordingly he spent hours and days of conscientious practice on the Curtiss 'Jenny' trainers and Thomas-Morse S-4C single-seaters, perfecting all the aerobatic manoeuvres then known and working out all the new ones as soon as he heard of them from airmen returning from France. To relieve

moments of boredom, he also engaged in (strictly forbidden) stunts such as wing-walking and handstanding on the undercarriage cross-axles! Then he suggested to fellow-instructors at Rockwell Field the idea of trying their aerobatics in formation, and after a period of quiet practice together, they put on what was probably the first formation aerobatic display on record. Doolittle very soon acquired a reputation for his prowess and had great pleasure in living up to it.

His enforced absence from the war in Europe at least preserved him for a career of unparalleled distinction in peacetime, the arrival of which he celebrated in characteristic fashion in November 1918 with his formation aerobatics, leading a five-man team of Army flyers at the Rockwell Field Victory Air Display. Selection for the show was hotly contested, and the team put in eight hours practice a day. In reporting the occasion, the Los Angeles *Times* waxed lyrical:

… the five acrobats … swooped, dived, looped and spun in as perfect unison as though they had been operated by a single hand.

… the antics and evolutions of the five stunt men increased until finally the skies cleared and the acrobats held the center of the heavens alone, supreme in the mad glory of their thrilling feats.

Jimmy Doolittle.   *(Smithsonian Institution)*

Doolittle stayed with the Air Service using every opportunity to improve on both his flying and his practical engineering knowledge; then, with official encouragement, he proceeded to the Massachusetts Institute of Technology where he took his Master of Science degree in aeronautical engineering and began studying for his doctorate. With such talent on hand, however, the Army suddenly decided to take full advantage of Doolittle's rare combination of skills, and

Flight Fantastic

recalled him to McCook Field in March 1924: they had a special assignment for him, test-flying a Fokker PW-7 pursuit aircraft to determine its structural limits. During this intensive and arduous testing – for which he received his second DFC – his job was to stress the Fokker to the ultimate in power dives and pull-outs and high-*g* manoeuvres. As the official report stated,

… a recording accelerometer was mounted in the airplane and the accelerations taken for the following maneuvers: loops at various air speeds, single and multiple barrel rolls, power spirals, tail spins, power on and power off, half loop, half roll, and Immelmann turn; inverted flight; pulling out of dive at various air speeds; flying the airplane on a level course with considerable angle of bank; and flying in bumpy air.

At the same time as examining the effects of high *g* and centrifugal force on the aircraft, Doolittle's report 'Accelerations in Flight' also addressed the question of their effects on the human frame. He purposely subjected himself to the 'blacking out' effect on vision caused by the loss of normal blood supply, and he pulled up to as much as 7.8 *g*. Using his specialist engineering knowledge together with his flying expertise, he produced a revolutionary document that created intense interest both at home and internationally, setting many new aeronautical engineering and research standards.

Eighteen months later, in October 1925, he dazzled New Yorkers with his hotshot aerobatics at an Army display at Mitchel Field, culminating in an inverted pass across the field just a few metres above eye-level. Already famous to the public for his endurance and cross-country records, notably his coast-to-coast record (Florida to California) in September of 1922, now Jimmy Doolittle went on to win the Schneider Cup for the Army Air Service and set a world seaplane record. Success brought him even more fame and a top job in experimental flight testing; then, a year later, the Curtiss company asked permission to send the Army's star pilot to South America where they wished him to demonstrate their brand new P-1 fighter (435 hp Curtiss D-12): permission was granted, and Jimmy and the P-1 were duly shipped to Chile.

There followed one of Doolittle's most extraordinary adventures, which epitomizes the sheer madcap exuberance of the man coupled with that true grit which together go to make up the indefinable 'right stuff' of aviation pioneering. Finding that he was up against strong competition from the

Curtiss JN-4 'Jenny' trainer (90 hp OX-5).
Designed by B Douglas Thomas from Sopwiths in Britain (who later went on to found the Thomas Morse Company), it combined the best features of the Model J and Model N, together with stick-and-rudder controls. This beautiful machine belongs to Wally Olson who still performs air displays with a wing-walking act by Mary McIlvain (both of them are grandparents!). (Tracy Weir photo)

Curtiss P-1B Hawk in a negative-g turn. (Smithsonian Institution)

Avalanche – flick roll at the top of a loop.

Flight Fantastic

Italians, Germans and British, Jimmy allowed himself to get wound up at a pre-demonstration party given by his Chilean officer hosts. The drinks were flowing freely, and talk had got around to the amazing screen stunts of movie star Douglas Fairbanks. This gave him an irresistible opportunity to demonstrate a little American one-upmanship: before he knew it, Jimmy Doolittle found himself performing back somersaults and walking around on his hands – simple tricks for one trained from an early age in gymnastics. "But Fairbanks does those tricks on balconies and balustrades," they protested, "sometimes on window ledges . . ."

"That's nothing," Doolittle rejoined, "any American kid can do those things," and without further ado he performed a handstanding act on a 2 ft (60 cm) ledge overlooking a courtyard below. Encouraged by his cheering audience, he went into another gymnastic act – child's play to him, of course – but he had omitted to test the strength of the stone ledge, and this time it crumbled away under him. He ended up six metres below with a pair of broken ankles.

Doolittle was mortified, and furious with himself for his foolishness. Whatever happened, he was not going to let down the Curtiss company and the Air Corps when they were relying on him to bring back orders for the American machine: somehow, even with his legs in casts, he must fly the P-1. From his hospital bed he figured out a way to have a pair of clips made up that would clamp his plaster-encased feet to the rudder-bar and enable them to operate the control, though it would cost him excruciating pain with every movement.

On the appointed day, with the demonstrations already under way and everyone expecting him to be still in hospital, Doolittle arrived at the last minute in an ambulance and had himself hoisted into the cockpit and the clips attached. Seeing the German machine in action – a new 260 hp Dornier, which was reputed to be his closest rival – he decided on impulse to take off and join its pilot, wartime ace Carl August von Schoenebeck, in a mock dogfight. The German caught on to the idea and within seconds they were diving and zooming, Doolittle and the responsive little P-1 always managing somehow to get on to the other's tail, literally running rings around the Dornier. The qualities of the Curtiss had been graphically demonstrated, and as the Chileans cheered their approval, Doolittle half-rolled inverted and treated them to a long, low pass as only he knew how. The tour was a success after all.

His subsequent recovery needed over six months hospitalization to repair the damage, but during that frustrating time he occupied his mind turning over various aeronautical problems, one of which gradually formed and solidified and grew into an obsession: the negative (outside) loop. Over the invervening dozen or so years, Lincoln Beachey's pre-war exploits had been either forgotten or simply discounted; and with the growth of technical knowledge about aerodynamics had come a new respect for the limitations of engines and airframes. The negative loop had come to be regarded as 'impossible', too much to ask of an aeroplane. Doolittle's own researches cautioned respect also for the human frame; although he knew he could calculate and make provision for the negative loads on the machine and harness, he realized that any investigation into adverse effects on the blood-vessels and vital organs would of necessity have to be empirical – with himself as the guinea-pig!

Later, in dead-pan riposte to the questioning of a reporter, Jimmy said that he thought he would try it 'just on the spur of the moment'; but nothing could have been further from the truth. After satisfying himself that the 435 hp Curtiss P-1B could withstand the manoeuvre, and after getting back into good physical shape again after his months in hospital, he started taking the little fighter up to the safety of 16,000 ft (5,000 m) and practising negative flight. First extended periods of flying and climbing inverted, then push-ups into the curve of a partial negative loop, each landing followed by an analysis of the negative stresses and an examination to see how the machine and he were standing up to it. Beyond the red-out effect well known now in negative flight, caused by the concentration of blood in the region of the head, he found himself with no appreciable ill-effects and no burst blood-vessels. The experiments proceeded, now with pushes down to a dive and under to the upside-down position, taking a careful step further with each flight. True to his own famous philosophy, Doolittle was prepared to take risks, but only calculated risks.

At last, on 25 May 1927, he felt ready to try the complete loop; mentioning it only to a few fellow pilots at McCook Field, Dayton, he preflight-checked his machine and harness, took off and climbed to 10,000 ft (3,000 m) where he dived vertically, reaching the Curtiss's Vne of 350 mph (563 km/h). He then pushed and kept on pushing until he rounded out inverted at 280 (450), fighting the effects of sustained negative *g* and hoping to get up the other side of the figure to the top again. After what seemed an interminable length of time pushing forward on the stick, suddenly he saw the horizon ahead again and he was there: he had done it!

Congratulations showered on Jimmy Doolittle's head and he was in the headlines yet again. His method had been to enter in a power dive rather than a downward curve or bunt, so the really round, loop-shaped negative loop had still not been accomplished – but by proving it to be possible, Doolittle had pioneered the way forward and opened up new vistas of negative flight for the aerobatic pilots who followed him.

7

Deutschland über alles

One thing the continents of Europe and America had in common was the post-war frenzy on the part of their wartime pilots to keep on flying. Airshows, mock dog-fights, banner-towing, joyrides; anything would do. And in defeated Germany, suffering from economic disaster as well as from the exigencies of the Versailles Treaty, flying most of all seemed an impossible dream.

Young Ernst Udet, at the age of 22, emerged from the war as Germany's greatest surviving ace. Aviation had been his passion since as a boy of eleven he had built his first model aeroplane, and two years later – in the year of Blériot's Channel-crossing – he had founded the 'Munich Aero Club 1909'. Together with other youthful aeromodellists he would hold competitions down on the river-bank: Erni's models were always ugly, bedraggled little sparrows, but somehow they always seemed to fly farthest.

Too young for flying training at the outset of war, he went to a civilian flying school at his own expense, and by 1915 was serving as an instructor. As a novice two-seater pilot, he must have shown exceptional promise: his sentence of only seven days in the guardhouse when he spun in from a (strictly prohibited) over-banked turn was an extremely lenient one; and within hours of his release he was promoted to the coveted position of fighter pilot on the Fokker Eindecker. In his autobiography, Udet tells of his initial inability to fire on a hostile aircraft, a revulsion which he forcibly overcame on finding himself the only defending pilot at readiness when a 22-ship bombing raid attacked his area. He took them on single-handed and chalked up his first victory by downing the biggest bomber he could get in his sights.

His ability as a pilot soon became renowned, and he devoted hours to teaching the men under his command the life-saving techniques of tight-turning, spinning and sideslipping in combat. "In those days," he says, "flying skill was all-

Ernst Udet in 1918. (Musée de l'Air)

Flight Fantastic

important. A proficient aerobat earned the immediate respect of the enemy". On one occasion in a duel with Guynemer when his guns jammed, the French ace, observing this, broke off the combat with a wave of his hand. Although there might have been any number of other reasons for Guynemer's action, Udet always believed that it was out of mutual respect for a skilled opponent. He maintained the same philosophy as that of his one-time commanding officer Heinrich Gontermann: "We fight an honourable foe with honourable weapons".

He was soon talent-spotted by Manfred von Richthofen, and by February 1918 was in command of Jasta II in the famous Jagdgeschwader I. The 'Jageri' was constantly battle-ready, taking off to attack whenever enemy aircraft were sighted, sometimes three, four or five times a day, no matter what the weather or the condition of their nerves. It was at this time, in early 1918, that Udet's health first began to break down: he suffered an agonizing middle-ear infection which temporarily grounded him and was to return again to trouble him in later life. During his sick leave in April he learned, within the space of a few short days, the most glorious and also the most shattering news of his young life: first, that he had been awarded Germany's highest military honour, the *Pour le Mérite* (the famous 'Blue Max'); and next, that his commanding officer, the Red Baron, whose extraordinary success seemed somehow a symbol of German invincibility, had been posted missing in action.

Returning to the Front he threw himself into the oblivion of daily combat, as more and more old comrades failed to return. By the end of the war he had totalled 62 victories, a score second only to von Richthofen's 80. He lived to fly: he was a national hero, the ace of aces. Then, like so many other pilots, he found himself suddenly aimless in a defeated Germany.

Udet had a certain kind of amazing luck – almost a charmed life – which saw him through the war and, perhaps to his ultimate disservice, opened new doors as if by magic whenever an old one closed. In 1919, he and his wartime comrade Robert Ritter von Greim managed to get their hands on a number of ex-service Fokkers, against all regulations, and immediately started out on a series of exhibitions in aid of prisoners-of-war, performing aerobatics and mock dog-fights overhead local fields to ecstatic audiences.

A captured Fokker D.VII being looped in the United States by Lt Eugene Barksdale in 1919. In mock dogfights, Ritter von Greim flew a silver-grey D.VII while Udet flew a flame-red D.VIII Parasol. (*via John Underwood*)

With new fame added to his already glittering reputation, Udet found that opportunities were not lacking even in post-war Germany. Although the Versailles Treaty prohibited all German aircraft production until 1922 (and placed severe restrictions on maximum permissible power and endurance right up until 1926), Udet was one of a small number of enthusiasts who clandestinely worked on designs for sport aeroplanes even during the ban. In the long run, in fact, Germany's rapid rise to the forefront of aviation between the wars owed much to this very repression: prohibitions always foster a hardening of the human spirit, a strengthening of resolve to surmount them, and with skill and enterprise added to an ineradicable love of flying, Germany's aviators began to excel in new designs for light aircraft suitable for pleasure-flying and aerobatics.

An offer of financial backing fell into Udet's lap like manna from heaven, and he found himself able to start his own aircraft construction business. By 1924 the company was doing well with the aerobatic U-12 Flamingo, and Udet used this as the springboard to take himself off with his own machine and start the happiest and most successful phase of his entire life: the career of a wandering, freewheeling airshow pilot.

The little Flamingo – a two-seater biplane – proved an enormously popular design at a cost of about £1,300: light, responsive, robust, and built specifically with aerobatics in mind. Udet gave his first aerobatic show with the new aircraft on 12 April 1925, and the type swiftly became a favourite with other airshow pilots such as Paul Bäumer and Thea Rasche. The following year he acquired his most famous Flamingo, D-822, with a Siemens Sh11 radial engine and striking red and silver paint scheme. He flew '822 from 1926 to 1934, earning a dazzling reputation in Germany and throughout the world, not only for his unique brand of low-level precision aerobatics but also in spectacular films such as *The Miracle of Flight* and *Storms over Mont Blanc*, which included some breathtaking mountain-flying sequences. In *The White Hell of Piz Palü* Udet performed stunts of such audacity that critics refused to believe they were not trick photography!

He was a master of entertainment, of daredevilry to please the crowd: he knew that his low powered little biplane could not thrill with startling zooms and high-performance aerobatics, so he concentrated on ground-floor precision stunts such as his most famous trick of all, picking up a handkerchief from the ground or from a car roof with a hook fixed to his wingtip. As well as the full repertoire of known aerobatics – loops, flick-rolls, spins, vertical dives, half-rolls to inverted just before landing – his air displays would include balloon-bursting, hedgehopping or 'steeplechasing', and crazy flying; later he introduced an uproarious 'Absent-Minded Professor' act complete with beard, top hat and umbrella. As a pilot he knew his capabilities down to the minutest detail; his performances were impeccable, ever more daring, colourful and varied.

Udet lived up to and beyond his means, always the centre of attention, the practical joker, the mimic, the cartoonist, the darling of the ladies and one of the few rays of sheer sunshine brightness in Germany's time of depression and mass unemployment. He was a bird of passage: as long as he could fly, all was right with the world.

In 1931 he was signed up to perform at the National Air Races in Cleveland, astounding even the Americans with his low-level aerobatics. The *Daily News* reported: "Udet was

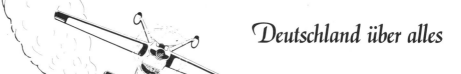

the most brilliant and unsurpassed of a team of four foreign pilots... He performed aerobatics near the ground with a perfection that has never before been witnessed. All the most famous veterans of the sporting aviation world agreed." He was re-engaged in July 1933 at Los Angeles, when his repertoire included three low level dead-stick loops and a spot landing on the exact place from which he had taken off. Life was at its sweetest. He was fêted in Hollywood, was invited to be technical adviser on flying movies, and for a bet picked up Mary Pickford's handkerchief with his wingtip.

It was during the 1931 visit that Ernst Udet had his fateful encounter with the Curtiss F6C Hawk. The faithful Flamingo was now six years old and the Hawk was a new breed of aircraft, designed as a dive-bomber, speed and power written all over it. On returning to Germany his mind was filled with nothing else: he must have the Hawk for his new airshow season; but the price was $14,000, (60,000 Rentenmarks), and Udet didn't have money like that. Once again his proverbial luck stepped in when his ex-Squadron Commander Hermann Goering, now a high-ranking Nazi, unexpectedly offered him the means of bringing over two of the coveted aircraft. The *quid pro quo* seemed simple enough: he must demonstrate the powerful new dive-bomber to Nazi military chiefs. But it was the bait to lure him into the party machine.

Suddenly all his old friends were back in uniform, while he was pursuing a life of pleasure, his earnings in the region of 200,000 RM a year. They reproached him, exhorted him,. An immense new enthusiasm for flying was being nurtured,

Udet's Curtiss Hawk II (export version of the US Navy's F11C). Repeated dive-bombing demonstrations in the aircraft aggravated Udet's middle-ear trouble. (Chaz Bowyer)

especially among the young, and Udet was their hero: surely he must see what he owed to the fatherland.... Goering and the Nazi party would not rest until they had fixed his bright star in their own firmament.

But the star, once transfixed, was gradually extinguished. Udet found himself dragged into an alien world of uniforms, ranks and power-politics as he took on responsibilities for aircraft supply and technical development.

In time there came orders to cease aerobatics. For a while he was still allowed to test new aircraft types, but then even this freedom came to an end and Ernst Udet – now General Udet – found himself tied to an office desk amid the petty jealousies of a Berlin ministry. So innocent was he of Nazi designs that foreign emissaries took his simple, personal goodwill as proof that Germany was not anticipating a war. On the invasion of Poland he was shattered, utterly unprepared.

Holding down one of the hottest jobs in Hitler's regime, lacking the essential materials for production and subjected to a constant stream of impossible demands and political manoeuvrings, it was all too much for him. By the end of 1941 he was broken in health and spirit, could not carry on but was not permitted to resign. He saw Hitler leading his nation to total destruction. On the morning of November 17, alone in his Berlin apartment, he took a revolver and ended his own life.

But Ernst Udet was not the only great aerobatic pilot to rise like a phoenix from the ashes of Germany's defeat in 1918. Totally opposite in style, in background and personality,

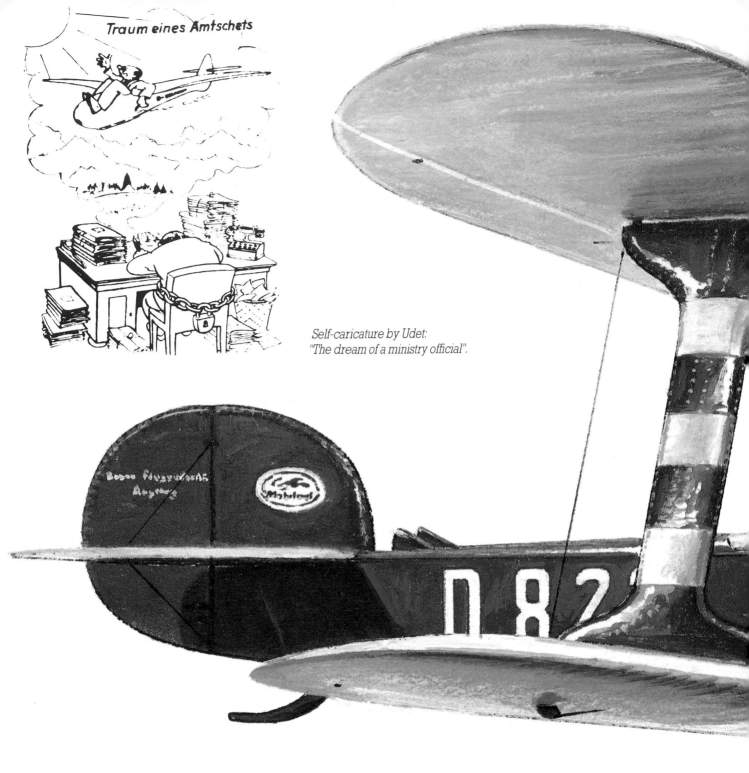

Self-caricature by Udet:
"The dream of a ministry official".

blessed far less by nature's grace and good fortune, Udet's contemporary Gerhard Fieseler raised aerobatics to the level of a science and achieved for himself an everlasting distinction as the true father of modern competition aerobatics.

His birth in April 1896 was separated only by days from that of Udet. From an obscure childhood young Gerhard had to move heaven and earth to obtain flying training in the German Air Service, and was then posted to equal obscurity on the Macedonian Front where there was no Richthofen Circus, no glamour, no heroics. His score of over 20 victories was phenomenal for that theatre of operation, and he soon became known as the 'Tiger of Macedonia', the most dangerous German pilot of the sector.

Making his way in the grim world of post-war Germany was a struggle for Fieseler, and thoughts of returning to the enticing skies were impossible until he had established himself and his young family with a small printing business. Then in the mid-20s, seeing airshows by pilots such as Ernst Udet and Paul Bäumer, he was suddenly bitten again by that bug which never quite leaves a flying man in peace, and resolved to try his fortune in the world of aviation. He joined Raab-Katzenstein in 1926.

Antonius Raab and Kurt Katzenstein had enviable reputations as pilots and were constant rivals in the informal aerobatic competitions which had become popular features of the airshows and meetings of the time. Raab had won

contests in 1924 in Prague and 1925 in Munich, and had come second to Udet in 1926 in Frankfurt, all the time with Katzenstein close behind him. Both flew the Dietrich-Gobiet DPIIa (70 hp Siemens Sh 5) until they joined forces in Kassel to produce their own very successful Schwalbe (Swallow).

Fieseler found himself at home as ever in the cockpit; his old gifts had not deserted him, and he added instructing to his other activities with the company. But there was a different dimension to Gerhard Fieseler, an extra edge that made him a dedicated competitor: not only in business, where he became such an outstanding success as an aircraft designer and constructor, but also in flying – and especially in aerobatics. He knew his own capabilities, knew he was at

Udet's Flamingo D-822. Equipped with 84 hp Siemens Sh 11 in 1928, 95 hp Sh 14 in 1930.

Span	10 m (32 ft 10 in)
Length	7.5 m (24 ft 7½ in)
Height	2.8 m (9 ft 2 in)
Empty weight	525 kg (1,157 lb)
Max speed	134 km/h (83 mph)
Rate of climb	1,000 m (3,300 ft) in 10 minutes

Ernst Udet with Gerhard Fiesler.   (Fiesler/Bertelsmann)

Antonius Raab and Kurt Katzenstein. Katzenstein eventually emigrated to South Africa where he continued to fly aerobatics; he presently lives in Johannesburg under the name of Kurt Kaye.   (via Musée de l'Air)

least as good as those stars who were attracting all the headlines. And he was right. When he staged his first commercial airshow for Raab-Katzenstein at Kassel, over the Easter holiday of 1927, he decided to have the audience judge who gave the best performance – Raab, Katzenstein, Untucht or Fieseler. Needless to say, Fieseler was the winner!

Encouraged by this propitious start, he took himself off to Essen where an aerobatic contest was taking place during a big Whitsun Air Meeting. Udet was there, together with Bäumer and five other contestants, each having to fly one compulsory and one free programme within a predetermined time limit. There were no other criteria for judging or scoring – the panel of judges consisted of ex-wartime pilots whose decision was on the basis of personal taste.

In his free programme Fieseler astounded the judges, flying a borrowed Raab-Katzenstein Schwalbe, with a selection of new figures that were unique to him: they included an inverted spiral glide from 1,000 m (3,300 ft) down to 200 m (650 ft) above ground level, a negative half-loop downwards (or bunt), and a revolutionary new figure which was soon to become his trademark, to which he gave the name of *Schraube* – which in German doubles as the word for a 'twist' in athletics or 'airscrew' in aviation – three successive horizontal slow rolls, straight as a die and without losing a metre of altitude. His performance was so impressive that he won by a unanimous decision: Udet and Bäumer had been toppled from their pedestals!

Enjoying a fast-growing reputation, Gerhard Fieseler now found himself on the invitation list in April 1927 when the

Swiss announced an International Flying Meeting at Zurich (Dübendorf) on 17–21 August, which was to include the world's first large-scale International Aerobatic Competition. The Germans, still the outcasts of Europe, had never yet been invited to an international event of this kind, and their aircraft were unknown outside their own country. France was the current leader in aviation: the clear favourites were Alfred Fronval, chief test pilot for Morane, with a Morane A1 (130 hp Clerget); and Marcel Doret, the 'King of the Skies' and Dewoitine chief pilot (Dewoitine DI CI, 300 hp Hispano Suiza). If Fieseler were to put up an effective fight against them, he must think up a string of new figures … and for that he needed a new aeroplane. He had started already to explore negative flight, and he realized that this must be the way forward from now on.

The Farnborough research of five years earlier was known to him, and he had already successfully reproduced the bunt. Fieseler had himself conceived the idea during wartime that a forward (negative) half-loop followed by a half-roll would give a fighter superiority in both attack and defence; but the machines available to him at the time had not been strong enough to try it. He knew that pilots since 1913 had experimented with inverted flight, but no consistent standard of performance in negative figures had ever been attained, for the simple reason that no aero engine yet had the capability of sustained inverted flight, and no sport aircraft had been built with the necessary strength of airframe.

Despite the prevailing scepticism about the negative (outside) loop, he felt sure that it was possible; but he was working from scratch and at the same time aiming for new standards of smoothness, continuity and precision which placed different demands on both pilot and aircraft from those which previous pilots had set for themselves. By an amazing coincidence, but with vastly different aims in view, Gerhard Fieseler was all unknowingly working on the negative loop at precisely the same moment as Jimmy Doolittle.

Fieseler took a Schwalbe airframe and proceeded to equip it with a 120 hp Siemens Sh 12 engine with a specially designed oil system for inverted flight. Tanks for an inverted fuel supply were no great problem, but in the modern static engines the question of carburation whilst inverted was a poser. Siemens could not come up with a solution, and in desperation Fieseler turned to the carburettor manufacturer Sum, who gave him the only help he could: a once-tested fuel injection system that had been rejected as unworkable. Sheer dogged trial and error on the part of Fieseler and his dauntless engineer Welle eventually got the thing going, and in June 1927 they celebrated a great achievement: the first ever sustained inverted flight using a purpose-built inverted system. Aerobatics would never be the same again.

Now Fieseler was ready to work at an outside – negative – loop, but he took it gradually and in stages, for he (like Doolittle) knew that unusual stresses would be placed on both the airframe of the machine and the blood-circulation of the pilot. He intended to perform the negative loop by starting *downwards* from erect flight, but initially he had to practise the second half of the loop, a *push up* from inverted in a semicircular path to erect. Would the wings and control surfaces hold up under the stress, and would the aerofoil shape be efficient enough under a negative angle of attack? All these unknowns – as well as the possibility of pilot blackout – had to be faced and their effects overcome. Only recently Plauth, chief test pilot for Junkers, had lost his life attempting the very same thing.

Fieseler's systematic approach paid off, and after many days of effort he had mastered the upward push to arrive at the top with the desired attitude and speed. Now he had to work at adding the first half of the loop, pushing the nose down to vertical and past vertical to inverted, his head on the outside of the curve, getting the speed and the radius of the loop just right to be able to push up again in a perfect circle; for the great difference between his and Doolittle's down-

ward start to the figure was that he did not dive or flop into it from a stall but flew the aeroplane down in a steady curve from a starting speed of around 60–75 mph (100–125 km/h). Satisfied at last with the combination of the two halves, Fieseler accomplished his negative loop in June 1927. And the time-honoured method of learning the two halves separately is still the standard approach to this figure in student training.

By the date of the Zurich meeting, only a few weeks away, he managed to perfect no less than six original figures with his new aircraft: the negative loop, the *Schraube* (his three arrow-straight slow rolls), the *Steuerwechselkreis* (a steeply banked horizontal circle performed upside down) the *Steuerwechselacht* (a steep figure-of-eight turn in inverted flight), the Vertical 8 (a positive loop upwards placed above a negative loop downwards), and the Horizontal 8 (another pair of positive-negative loops, later popularly known as the 'spectacles'). His programme was meticulously worked out so as to be flyable in any weather conditions.

On arrival in Dübendorf Fieseler found 30 competitors from countries including Czechoslovakia, France, Italy, Poland, Yugoslavia and Switzerland. In addition to Fronval and Doret of France, there were Swiss pilots Bärtsch, Burkhard and Hertzig, and the Czech champion Malkovský. (Full results appear on page 93). Although Udet was considered a hot favourite, he did not put in an appearance; perhaps because his good friend Bäumer, test pilot for Rohrbach and seventh ranking ace in the war, had tragically spun in during trials of a new monoplane the month before.

Right from the start it was obviously a three-way contest between Fieseler, Doret and Fronval. The 8-minute compulsory consisted of two loops; left-hand and right-hand rolls, steep turns and spins; and a spot landing. This, together with

RKK1 1c Schwalbe D-1212 with special inverted system, used by Fieseler in Zurich 1927. *(via John Underwood)*

Span	7.95 m (26 ft 10 in)
Length	6.2 m (20 ft 4 in)
Height	2.6 m (8 ft 6 in)
Empty weight	470 kg (1,034 lb)
Max speed	145 km/h (90 mph)
Rate of climb	1,000 m (3,300 ft) in 3 minutes

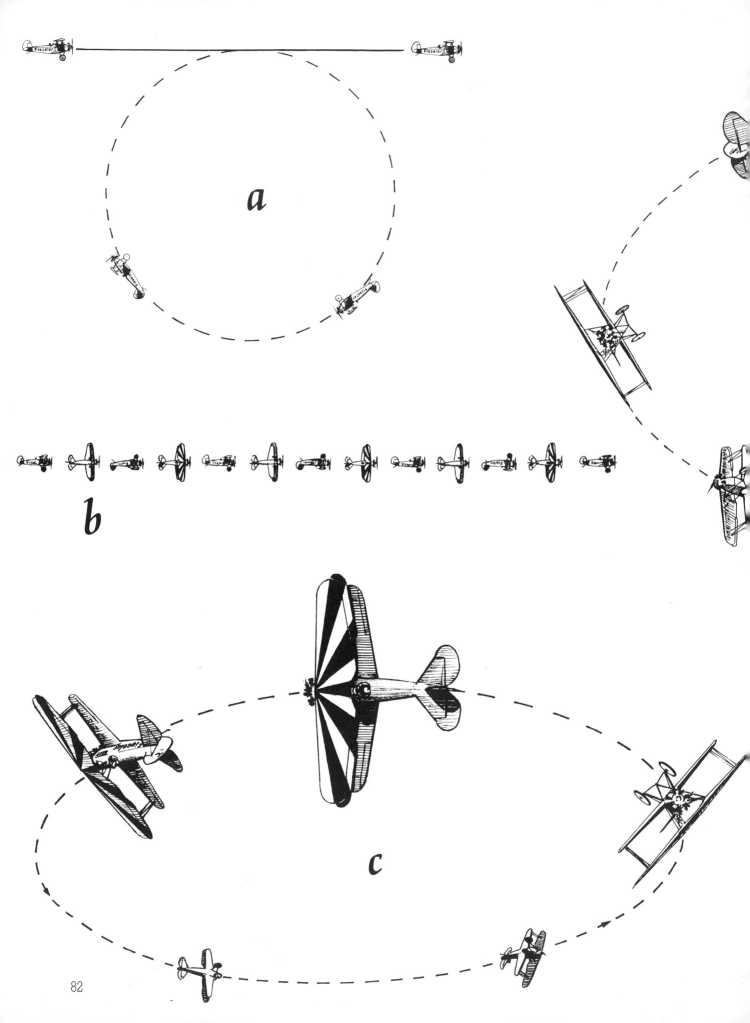

a

b

c

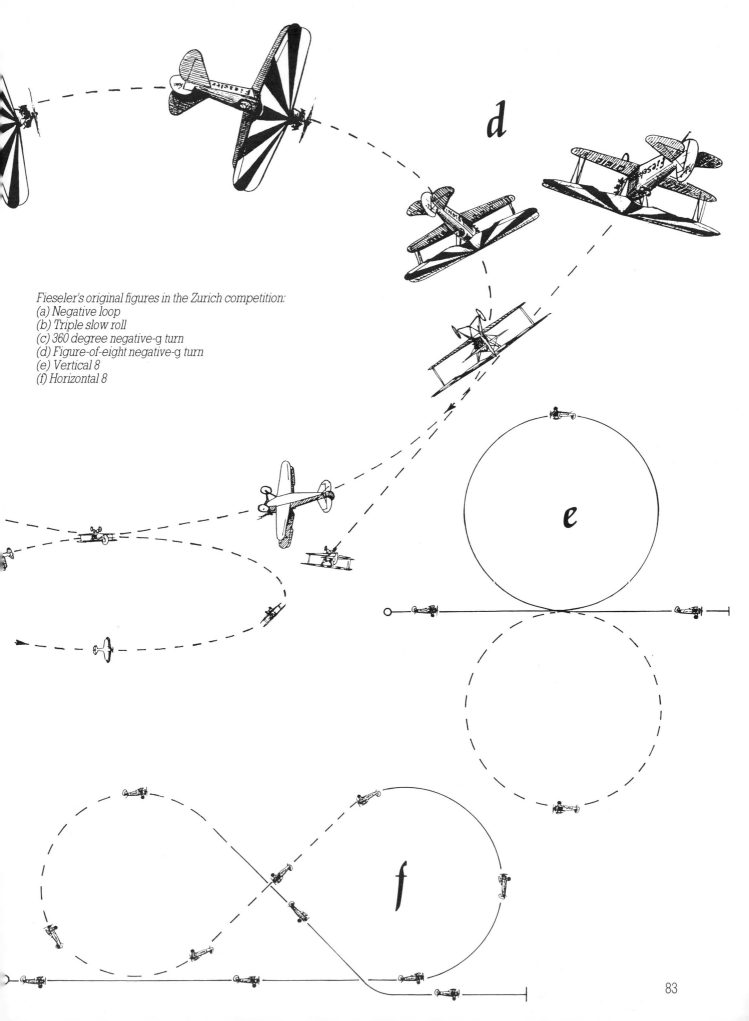

Fieseler's original figures in the Zurich competition:
(a) Negative loop
(b) Triple slow roll
(c) 360 degree negative-g turn
(d) Figure-of-eight negative-g turn
(e) Vertical 8
(f) Horizontal 8

d

e

f

the pilot's own 10-minute free programme, comprised the eliminators, and the five judging criteria (20 points each) were accuracy, precision, difficulty and diversity, elegance, and overall impression.

On 19 August five pilots flew their freestyle programmes in the finals: the three favourites together with Bärtsch and Burkhard. Doret performed some impressive hands-off-flying together with loops from ground level, but did not seem on top form. Fronval's programme frequently traversed from one end of the airfield to the other with five loops, five flick rolls or slow rolls or one super-slow roll, and included knife-edge flight after a three-quarter roll, finally landing off a Falling Leaf. And the Swiss pilots presented vertical rolls and inverted spins with great precision. Fieseler, however, drew universal acclaim for the originality of his programme, containing as it did such a wealth of new material exploiting his aircraft's inverted capability, and including geometrically accurate tail-slides on to his back: a performance described in *Flight* as "entirely different from the others".

In his autobiography Fieseler relates how, after flying his free programme without fault, he was sure he must have beaten the French pilots, but that to his disgust – a feeling shared by several participants and observers – the panel of judges placed Fronval first (93.25), Fieseler second (92.25) and Doret third (90.75). He claims to this day that it was a political decision, and in German newspapers he was proclaimed the moral victor. Years later he described meeting the judge who had represented Switzerland on the panel and challenging him about the judging. Yes, he had admitted, the other judges did award Fieseler highest marks, but the political feeling of the time made it simply impossible to give first prize to a German. The 'neutral' Swiss had laid the foundations for political bias in competition aerobatics.

After the contest Fieseler immediately invited the two French pilots to a return match, and to eliminate the great disparity between the power and performance of their various aerobatic aircraft, proposed including one round in which they would exchange machines. Fronval, being in the position of champion already, understandably declined; but the likeable Doret, renowned as a good sportsman, immediately accepted and in fact won the duel which took place a few months later in Berlin. Later, in his memoirs, he wrote amusingly of his experiences in Germany, and expressed his appreciation of the way the huge Berlin crowd enthusiastically applauded his victory. He also told of an incident at the Fieseler household when he mistook for an *hors d'oeuvre* the cold cuts of meat offered to him, and, having taken only a modest helping, spent the rest of the evening hungry.... Learning from his mistake, he tucked into a good plateful of *charcuterie* at the airfield next day, and then saw to his horror that there were at least three more courses to follow!

On 1 July 1928, the German Aero Club held its first National Aerobatic Championship in Düsseldorf. With no generally accepted criteria of difficulty for aerobatic figures, and not even an existing list of known manoeuvres, Gerhard Fieseler was assigned the formidable task of devising an evaluation system for competition aerobatics. The current requirements emphasized precision, versatility, exacting performance standards; to this Fieseler contributed the first ever system of coefficients depending on the difficulty and complexity of each manoeuvre. If a figure was valued at, say, a coefficient of 8, the judges would give it a mark from 1 to 8 depending on the pilot's performance. This was something progressive and

Gerhard Fieseler, seen here with Marcel Doret at the time of their Berlin 'match' in 1927.   *(via Musée de l'Air)*

different, and the system was quickly adopted throughout the rest of Europe.

Out of ten contestants, Gerhard Fieseler won the German

championship with the silver Schwalbe; Udet came second, flying his Flamingo, D-822, fitted with a special carburettor and fuel tank for inverted flying; and Willi Stör, a DVS (Deutsche Verkehrsfliegerschule) instructor, came third flying a DVS Flamingo.

Fieseler's prominence was now unassailable. Demand for his presence at airshows was so great that he commanded the highest airshow fees in the world: 3,000–5,000 RM in Germany, up to 10,000 RM abroad. He won the German title five times altogether, in 1928, '29, '30, '32 and '33. Udet did not contest the championships again after his first attempt: his free, improvisational style of airshow performance did not suit the stringent demands of the new rules.

Willi Stör, for the first time introducing the graceful low-wing monoplane to aerobatics, won second place in 1929 with his new Messerschmitt M 23b (95 hp Siemens Sh 13); and it was young Gerd Achgelis who interrupted Fieseler's string of wins by claiming the championship in 1931 with another new aerobatic machine, the Focke-Wulf S-24 Kiebitz (Peewit) (80 hp Siemens Sh 13), after previously setting a record by flying for a total of 37 minutes inverted. For a while, records for inverted flying promised to become as popular as those for multiple looping in the 1920s: a British record for 7 minutes had been officially beaten by Gerhard Fieseler, at the Zurich meeting, with 10 minutes 56.8 secs, and a certain RAF F/O George Stainforth (who had taught 'Batchy' Atcherley to slow roll in 1924) had achieved 11 minutes 42 secs in a Mono-Avro 'Y' type in 1927. Fieseler had subsequently increased the record to 16 minutes, but 37 minutes now became a serious proposition indeed. We shall see in the next chapter how Italian and American pilots took the endurance for inverted flight to its very ultimate in 1933.

It was in 1928/9 that Fieseler evolved his new Tiger-Schwalbe model. The original Lynx-powered prototype had crashed on test, due to a fault in construction, and his famous machine D-1616 was a modified RK226 with a 230 hp Walter Castor engine and an airframe strengthened to an ultimate load factor of ±12 g. He continued inventing new figures, especially variations on the slow roll theme, and among them the first **rolling circle** can be traced to Fieseler in the 1929 German Championships. In this extremely difficult figure the pilot performs four complete slow rolls during the course of a horizontal 360 degree turn, each roll taking up one quadrant of the turn. Four-point **hesitation rolls** were being performed by then, as well, in which the pilot stops the roll momentarily after each quarter – first in knife-edge, then inverted, then in knife-edge again, and finally back in horizontal flight.

During the next six years Fieseler took part in contests all over Europe and collected most of the major trophies. The five-yearly Swiss International Meeting was held in Zurich again in 1932, and this time his win was decisive: other German pilots swept the board, too, with Gullmann second, Achgelis third, and two outstanding women pilots, Liesel Bach and Vera von Bissing, fourth and sixth respectively. A lone Swiss, Victor Glardon, came in fifth place with an RK Schwalbe.

By now Fieseler had his own aircraft company and was flying his new design the F2 Tiger (400 hp Walter Pollux) with

Gerd Achgelis and Focke-Wulf S-24 Kiebitz with which he made his inverted flight record in 1929.

(via Musée de l'Air)

Span	8.9 m (29 ft 2 in)
Length	6.25 m (20 ft 6 in)
Height	2.25 m (7 ft 5 in)
Empty weight	350 kg (770 lb)
Max speed	140 km/h (87 mph)
Rate of climb	1,000 m (3,300 ft) in 10 minutes

Span (upper wing)	9 m (29 ft 6 in)	
(lower wing)	8.16 m (26 ft 9 in)	
Length	6.8 m (22 ft 3 in)	
Height	2.73 m (8 ft 11 in)	
Empty weight	810 kg (1,782 lb)	
Max speed	240 km/h (149 mph)	
Rate of climb	1,000 m (3,300 ft) in 1.5 minutes	

Fieseler F2 Tiger.
Fieseler named the Tiger F2, reserving the mark F1 as a retrospective designation for his Tiger-Schwalbe design (which was later produced in various European countries as the RK26 Tigerschwalbe).
(Gerhard Fieseler, courtesy of Bertelsmann Verlag)

symmetrical aerofoil*; it was ready in the month of April 1932. But it was so sensitive in all three axes, with the masses of pilot, motor and fuel tanks concentrated in one area, that he reckoned it took him six weeks before he had the mastery of the machine. He was proud of the Tiger, but always felt it suffered from being rather too heavy, which was a handicap in the free choice programme.

There was a new figure, however, which these very features of the Tiger now enabled Fieseler to perfect: he named it the *Fächerturn* ('fan turn'), and it was his own version of the stall turn. Pulling up into the vertical, he would wait until the machine reached a stop and stood completely still in its upward facing attitude, whereupon he could kick on full rudder and pivot the machine abruptly and swiftly around its centre of gravity to face downwards again. Herr Fieseler has assured the writer that never before, and never since, has he seen an aircraft capable of performing this *Fächerturn* with its absolute stop in mid-air.

Not unnaturally, pilots throughout Europe began to call it the Fieseler Fächer – but Fieseler himself was taken quite by surprise when in conversation one day a top Italian pilot referred to it by this name! It is still a popular name for the stall turn to this day, both in Italy and elsewhere.

Meanwhile Doret's ascendancy in France had been superseded by the new young star Michel Détroyat, chief pilot for Morane-Saulnier. The promoters lost no time in setting up a contest between him and Fieseler, and after their first match was declared a draw, Détroyat even managed to get the better of the German star in late 1933, later beating Doret in early 1934. This man was now Fieseler's closest rival.

There was great speculation when a World Cup competition for aerobatics was announced in early 1934, to take place at Vincennes, Paris, on 9–10 June. Although he was seriously cutting back on aerobatics by 1934 – preferring to concentrate his energies in the field of aircraft design –

Fieseler could not refuse the French Aero Club's invitation to this first ever World Championship with total prize money of 275,000 francs on offer (about £3,600). The winner would receive 100,000 francs.

It was an enormous event, a high-spot of the Paris society season, with 150,000 spectators crowded into the military parade-ground at Vincennes which had been converted expressly for the occasion, with grandstands specially erected. Nine competitors took part, drawn from six nations: Ambruž and Novák from Czechoslovakia, Cavalli and Détroyat from France, Achgelis and Fieseler from Germany, Christopher Clarkson from Great Britain, Ambrogio Colombo from Italy and Placido d'Abreu from Portugal.

The initial compulsory programme required a list of figures to be performed within a time limit of eight minutes, including a right-hand and a left-hand spin, a bunt, a negative loop forward and upward, and an inverted 360 degree turn. On the Sunday, each contestant flew his free programme, for which he had ten minutes: his sequence was submitted in advance to the Jury, and each manoeuvre was assigned a difficulty coefficient already set out in the rules; new figures were also awarded appropriate coefficients, but most were to be found already in the current catalogue of 87 manoeuvres. The task of the judges was to assign each figure a mark between 1 and 5 for quality of performance, with a zero mark for figures not executed. These were then multiplied by the difficulty coefficients, the totals of all the judges were added together, then they were divided to arrive at an average.

For most figures in the catalogue a generally accepted criterion of proper performance had become established, such as the requirement that there must be no horizontal line between the two halves of a Vertical 8; and the secret of success in the free programme was to cram in as many manoeuvres as possible within the time limit. Détroyat himself said that one would get a better score by performing 25 figures averagely well than by performing 23 figures perfectly.

On the second day, Sunday, after the morning's air display, Fieseler had the harrowing experience of watching a French pilot crash to his death on landing right next to him shortly before the contest resumed. The atmosphere became charged, but this was only a foretaste of later events: the

*The symmetrical aerofoil introduced a design concept which rendered the wing almost as efficient inverted as in erect flight. It has now become a standard wing design on the majority of modern aerobatic aircraft, and we owe its inception to Gerhard Fieseler.

"Eyes up!" The panel of judges scrutinizes a contestant's flight at Vincennes, 1934.   *(Musée de l'Air)*

fourth competitor of the afternoon, the Portugese Captain d'Abreu, mishandled his controls during a half-roll from inverted and got into a spin at very low altitude; his aircraft speared into the middle of the field and burned ... pandemonium reigned. Two men dead in the space of an hour.

The organisers were at a loss; should the competition be stopped? Many felt that it should. Gerhard Fieseler stepped forward and assumed the rôle of spokesman for his fellow-pilots: "Each man among us knows that he may meet his fate at any time. We are prepared for that. What if the early pioneers had given up when one of their number lost his life to aviation? I believe we will best honour our comrade by continuing to fly."

The contest was resumed, and immediately afterwards another mishap occurred: the Italian Ambrogio Colombo, flying a newly-built aircraft from the Breda factory in Milan, started a spin without enough height and collided with the top of a tree. He retired with a branch embedded in his landing gear. On a later take-off, with the machine repaired, he had an engine failure and crash-landed the aeroplane rather than risk coming down in the public enclosures; the aircraft was destroyed, though he himself escaped without serious injury. The crowd remained calm.

The afternoon wore on: Cavalli, Novák, Ambruž, Achgelis, Détroyat; Fieseler flew last. He had spent five weeks practising his free programme, which contained 38 extremely complicated and taxing figures, among them super-slow rolls which carried very high marks if performed precisely. Suddenly, four minutes before the end, he felt his shoulder-harness come loose. This was his main security during manoeuvres under negative g, and it had happened at the worst possible moment: immediately before a negative loop. His only solution was to make a much bigger circle – widen the diameter of the loop – so as to reduce the amount of negative g he would have to sustain. But in doing this he consumed vital seconds from his time limit, and at the end of the sequence he had over-run by three whole manoeuvres. Surely this must dash his hopes of the title.

When the results were announced, however, Fieseler had a lead over Détroyat by 23 points despite the over-run; he was the first World Aerobatic Champion in history. Michel Détroyat finished second, Gerd Achgelis third. Fieseler now took the decision to retire from the sport at the pinnacle of his success. His Tiger was put at the disposal of the Air Ministry, who were sponsoring aspiring young aerobatic pilots at the time, but none of them could handle the tricky machine. Eventually it was displayed in a place of honour at the Berlin Air Museum, until sadly destroyed by Allied bombing in World War II.

Gerhard Fieseler himself had a distinguished career in aircraft design and manufacture, perhaps his best known (and still frequently seen) design being the 1936 Storch with its outstanding STOL qualities. He is a valued patron of sport aerobatics to this day, and thanks to his generosity the Fieseler Trophy contest is one of the most prestigious international events in the modern competition calendar.

Now, in the absence of the master, the new generation of young German pilots, actively supported by Hitler's Luft-sport-Verband, battled for supremacy between themselves. Monoplane pilot Willi Stör succeeded as German Aerobatic Champion in 1935–6 flying the M 35 (150 hp Siemens Sh 14a), with Gerd Achgelis, Rudolf Lochner, Graf von Hagenburg and Albert Falderbaum hotly contesting the many competitions which fostered Germany's reawakened sense of national pride during the 1930s.

Perhaps the most splendid aviation events in pre-World War II Germany were those held in connection with the 1936 Olympic Games, though only the glider events featured as Olympic contests. There was an Olympic Air Display at Berlin Tempelhof aerodrome, a balloon race, two air rallies, and on 29–31 July an International Aerobatic Competition consisting of a compulsory and a freestyle programme. Pilots from Germany and Czechoslovakia dominated the results, with a striking difference in placings between the two programmes: Willi Stör, winner of the compulsory programme, came only sixth in the overall results; while young Otto von Hagenburg, overall winner (and master of the eye-level inverted pass!), achieved only eighth place in the compulsory. He owed his eventual success to a freestyle programme of unparalleled brilliance with the Focke-Wulf Fw 44 Stieglitz (Goldfinch).

Meanwhile, conceived originally for the Luftwaffe in the 80 hp category, there came into being one of the all-time

Messerschmitt M35 flown by Willi Stör, one of the early instructors at the Schleissheim flying training base in the 1920s. Vera von Bissing was another M35 pilot and won the International Women's Championship at Berlin-Rangsdorf in 1936; it was also a favourite aerobatic mount of Hitler's wayward deputy, Rudolf Hess. (Note that the post-war censor has eradicated the swastika emblem on fin and rudder.)

(via Musée de l'Air)

Span	11.57 m (38 ft)
Length	7.48 m (24 ft 6 in)
Height	2.75 m (9 ft 3 in)
Empty weight	500 kg (1,100 lb)
Max speed	230 km/h (143 mph)
Rate of climb	1,000 m (3,300 ft) in 3.3 minutes

great aerobatic trainers. The German Carl Clemens Bücker and brilliant young Swedish designer Anders J Andersson had formed an aircraft manufacturing company in 1933, and their first product was the Bü 131 Jungmann which had its

150 hp Siemens Focke-Wulf Fw 44 Stieglitz, successor to the Kiebitz. D2409, in inverted flight, is here flown by Gerd Achgelis in 1933.

(via Musée de l'Air)

Span	9 m (29 ft 6 in)
Length	7.28 m (23 ft 11 in)
Height	2.72 m (8 ft 11 in)
Empty weight	530 kg (1,166 lb)
Max speed	190 km/h (118 mph)
Rate of climb	1,000 m (3,300 ft) in 6.5 minutes

maiden flight in April 1934. With welded steel-tube fuselage and tail assembly, it had all-wood wings and fabric covering (apart from the sheet-metal engine and cockpit housings), and the upper and lower wings were interchangeable with ailerons fitted to both.

Robust and highly manoeuvrable, the merits of the Jungmann for primary aerobatic training soon won export orders, with greater success attending the Bü 131B version (105 hp Hirth HM 504) which was first bought in quantity by Switzerland, Dornier-Werke AG having secured rights to manufacture the aircraft at Altenrhein. Spain's adoption of the Jungmann led to licensed production at Cadiz under the designation CASA 1.131. By 1939 the aeroplane was a bestseller in countries all over the world for both military and private use.

Although the German defeat of 1945 meant that the German Jungmanns ceased to exist, many of the foreign-built machines kept right on flying especially in Spain (where they continued to be built right up until 1960) and in Czechoslovakia and Switzerland. Still much loved for training and for primary aerobatics to the present day, the Jungmann was given a face-lift by the enterprising Swiss in the 1960s, when with a new wing and modern 180 hp Lycoming engine it was renamed the Lerche (Lark) (see page 210). It continued in front-line competition as late as the year 1970.

Hard on the heels of the Jungmann (Young Man) came the single-seat Bü 133 Jungmeister (Young Champion) of everlasting fame, considered by many to be the best aerobatic machine available between the middle thirties and middle sixties. Such claims are, of course, hotly challenged by pilots who point to its reluctance in outside (negative) manoeuvres and poor vertical penetration; but when the prototype was granted its Certificate of Airworthiness in early 1936, its superb performance and handling qualities took Europe and America by storm. Mike Murphy was the first American to own a Jungmeister (see page 132), and he said: "You don't fly it – you wear it. It fits you. Now, thirty years later, it's still the nicest airplane to do aerobatics in. It never resists you. It's smiling all the time. The airplane will snap roll at 70 mph or 170."

Its arrival eclipsed the sweeter but less high-performance Jungmann; of similar construction, it had stubbier wings and a

Graf Otto von Hagenburg in 1938.   *(via Musée de l'Air)*

shorter fuselage which was built up to increase the area of lift in knife-edge flight. The Bü 133C version, which became standard, had a Siemens-Bramo 160 hp Sh 14A4 radial engine.

Stars of the Jungmeister became a flourishing breed, and Graf Otto von Hagenburg delighted spectators in Switzerland with his astounding performance in the machine in 1937, when he won the International Aerobatic Competition in Zurich in Category A (engines under 10 litres). In this category the first nine places were all won by Jungmeister pilots, as were the first six places in the 1937 German Championships.

The legendary Romanian pilot Captain Alexandru Papana secured one of the very first pre-production aircraft which he introduced to the USA in the 1936 National Air Races in Los Angeles, having transported the aeroplane in the airship *Hindenburg*. The following year, Otto von Hagenburg joined him at the NARs in Cleveland and the two pilots vied with each other in virtuoso displays with their respective machines. Papana's Jungmeister was famous throughout the

Alex Papana hooks a handkerchief with one wing of his Jungmeister YR-PAX.   *(John Underwood)*

Flight Fantastic

Poster from the World Championship held at Vincennes, 1934.
(Musée de l'Air)

This CASA 1-131 Jungmann (125 hp ENMA Tigre G-IV-A) was still delighting airshow audiences in 1977. G-BECX is pictured here during the memorable last display given by its owner Neil Williams, who finished his act with a Cantacuzino-style flick roll on landing (see Chapter 14) (Lynn Williams)

Span	7.4m (24ft 3in)
Length	6.62m (21ft 9in)
Height	2.25m (7ft 5in)
Empty weight	380kg (836 lb)
Max speed	183km/h (114mph)
Rate of climb	1,000m (3,300ft) in 5.2 minutes

USA as YR-PAX until one sad day at Chicago it was involved in a collision with a Boeing P-12 and just about two-thirds destroyed. The remains were purchased and rebuilt, as NC15696, by Mike Murphy who flew it with great success (he was never beaten in a competition with the machine) until he sold it to fellow-American Bevo Howard in 1948. Howard then piloted it until he and his beloved Jungmeister both died together in 1971: he crashed after his wingtip hit a tree in an inverted pass during an airshow. The aeroplane, restored to its former glory, is currently on display as part of the National Air and Space Museum's collection in Washington.

After the war another celebrated Romanian, Prince Cantacuzino, flew a Spanish Bü 133C registered EC-AEX on the display circuit, later adopting a 275 hp Lycoming engined model in the mid-1950s, EC-AMO, probably the most powerful Jungmeister to have flown (see Chapter 14). A few years later an attempt was even made by American enthusiasts to restart Jungmeister production in Germany, and four machines were indeed built; but cost and other problems put an end to the venture in 1969. Since then, a more successful venture by Frank Price of Texas has Jungmeister plans available for homebuilders, and he has recently turned to marketing kits as well – all of fifty years after the prototype D-EVEO made its first flight at Berlin-Rangsdorf.

This Bü 133 Jungmeister (160hp Siemens Sh 14A-4) has been restored to resemble pre-war configuration. NB: The prototype originally flew with 140hp Hirth HM506 in-line engine. (via Mike Hooks)

Span	6.6m (21ft 8in)
Length	5.9m (19ft 4in)
Height	2.25m (7ft 5in)
Empty weight	420kg (924lb)
Max speed	314km/h (195mph)
Rate of climb	1,000m (3,300ft) in 2.8 minutes

8

Europe between the wars

Although Germany was so soon to take the lead in aerobatics, it was actually in post-war France and Switzerland that the first friendly competitions took place during the course of air displays. They started in France as early as 1920; and in 1922 Switzerland inaugurated the first of its celebrated five-yearly Zurich Aviation Meetings which featured large-scale international aerobatic contests as well as air shows and rallies. The 1922 winner was the Swiss flight instructor first lieutenant Robert Ackermann, flying a Nieuport Bébé 607 (160 hp Le Rhône), and interestingly a contemporary magazine reported inverted spins as a feature of his programme. The rules were simple enough: each contestant flew a sequence of freely chosen manoeuvres, which he listed in a sealed envelope given to the jury in advance, and marks were accorded for the content of this programme. Then, after deductions for any faults in performance, the two highest scoring pilots were awarded prizes of 3,000 and 1,000 Swiss francs respectively.

Soon to capture the spotlight as France's premier aerobatic pilot was Alfred Fronval, whom we have already met in Chapter 7. Fronval had undergone French Air Service training in 1917 but was prevented from serving at the Front, being considered more valuable in his rôle as instructor at the *Centre d'Entraînement de la Chasse* at Pau. This, of course, gave him the opportunity to develop his piloting technique to perfection, a technique at the same time daring and carefully thought-out, which set the standard for French aerobatic flying of the 1920s. His sound knowledge of engineering combined with technical skill and an innate sense of style created a unique synthesis between man and machine: one almost had the sense of the aeroplane flying itself through those complex yet fluid manoeuvres.

Invited by Robert Morane to join Morane-Saulnier at the end of the war as a test and exhibition pilot, Fronval was to

Alfred Fronval, winner of the Zurich aerobatic contest, with Morane-Saulnier A1. (Musée de l'Air)

stay with the firm for ten years, all the while flying his orange and blue MS A1, F-ABAD (130 hp Clerget), in which he chalked up the looping records already mentioned – culminating in 1,111 successive loops in 1928.

His first competition success was as early as July 1920, when at Anvers he won a *concours de virtuosité* against all the foremost World War I aces. But his greatest triumph was undoubtedly at the second Zurich International Aviation Meeting of 1927, in the famous battle of the three giants – Fieseler, Doret and himself – in which Fronval eventually snatched victory by a mere 1 point!

It has proved impossible so far to find a complete list of entrants and results of this contest, but the following is the most detailed information that the writer can track down:

1.	Alfred Fronval (Morane-Saulnier A1)	French	93.25
2.	Gerhard Fieseler (RK K1 1c)	German	92.25
3.	Marcel Doret (Dewoitine D1 C1)	French	90.75
4.	W. Burkhard (Nieuport Bébé)	Swiss	89.50
5.	Bärtsch (Nieuport Bébé)	Swiss	85.00

Other contestants included Oblt Herzig, who had just won the Swiss National Aerobatic Championship; the Czech pilot František Malkovský, who came seventh in an Avia BH 22; Nardini from Italy; and three Yugoslavian pilots, Markitschevitch, Roubtschich and Uzelatz.

Alfred Fronval was among the first, in a long and illustrious line of aerobatic champions, to express the view that no pilot has really mastered the aeroplane until he has mastered aerobatics and thereby achieved the safety and self-confidence imparted by a command of the machine in every attitude. As an instructor and exhibition pilot he was greatly respected, even loved, and when he met his death in July 1928 all French aviation mourned him deeply. It was a sad and needless death, caused by another pilot in a Breguet who collided on take-off with Fronval's taxiing Morane. Shortly afterwards Robert Morane donated F-ABAD, Fronval's famous exhibition machine, to the *Musée de l'Air* in Paris.

Marcel Doret was successor to Fronval as France's great aerobatic star, and a wartime pupil of his at Pau – where Doret distinguished himself early on by soloing after a mere 1 hour 42 minutes of instruction!

After the war Doret became chief pilot for Emile Dewoitine's aircraft company, and his staunch loyalty to the firm remained unshaken even in the face of other offers when Dewoitine went into liquidation shortly after he joined them: he had faith that the company would revive, as indeed it soon did by dint of starting up production in Switzerland. Doret was proud to say in his autobiography, *Trait d'Union avec le Ciel*, that after twenty-seven years he was still flying the Dewoitine D 27 (500 hp Hispano-Suiza) which had entered its first competition in 1927, and for which he did the original test flights.

His machine up to that date, with which he had competed in Zurich, was the 300 hp Dewoitine DI CI, an aircraft which was adequate for aerobatics but not really competitive. This was the machine with which Fieseler sportingly exchanged his own special Tiger-Schwalbe during their duel in Berlin, which Doret won. After this it soon became a regular feature for pilots to exchange aeroplanes, not just for fun, as nowadays, but to perform at least one competition programme on an opponent's machine, for which the stringency of the marking was reduced accordingly. These duels – known as

Doret waves from the cockpit of his D 27.   (via Musée de l'Air)

Alfred Fronval's Morane-Saulnier A1 (130 hp Clerget).
(Musée de l'Air)

Span	8.71 m (28 ft 7 in)
Length	5.77 m (18 ft 11 in)
Height	2.45 m (8 ft 5 in)
Empty weight	420 kg (924 lb)
Max speed	225 km/h (140 mph)
Rate of climb	2,000 m (6,600 ft) in 4 minutes 25 sec

'matches' and 'tournaments' – between the various European aces became a regular alternative to the ordinary national and international competitions.

When Doret proudly took his D 27 to the US for the National Air Races of 1930, the Americans were much taken with its smooth stressed-skin all metal construction (although metal monocoque construction was by no means new in the USA at the time). Like all the Dewoitine designs, the D 27 was primarily a fighter and not fully aerobatic in comparison with other contemporary machines; but Doret never wavered in his loyalty to Dewoitine aircraft.

Marcel Doret's interests were not confined to the realm of aerobatics: altogether he captured no less than 18 world records, principally in speed, distance and endurance. Perhaps best known was his 10,372 km closed circuit distance record in 70 hours, gained with the D 33 *Trait d'Union* in 1931. During his long career with Dewoitine he was test pilot on a total of 43 different aircraft types. Always delighted by any new flying experience, he was captivated in 1937 by Hanna Reitsch's exhibition of the German Habicht glider and acquired one immediately. Within two years he had won the World Glider Aerobatic Championships!

His career as an air display pilot spanned more than thirty years, both before and after World War II: he even made a return visit to the NARs in 1948, electing to go as a glider pilot while Fred Nicole accompanied him to perform power

aerobatics with a Stampe. During the war, after the French armistice, Doret fought as a member of the small team which organized the first Free French fighter group, and participated with distinction in fighter operations until the liberation. He was still flying airshows right up to June 1955, two months before his death from an illness at the age of 59.

But in the world of 1930s competition aerobatics, where each nation and each aircraft factory strenuously promoted its own stars of the genre, Marcel Doret was rapidly overtaken and then outclassed by the new young French pilot Michel Détroyat.

During that period, aerobatics had become a high prestige activity in which almost every European country participated. The competitions were thought of less as a sporting event than as a trial between the various masters of the art and their aeroplanes, and were usually arranged as grand public spectacles with the usual attendant airshow attractions, parachute jumps, etc. It was the heyday of the professional test

Marcel Doret's Dewoitine D27 (500 hp Hispano-Suiza).
(Musée de l'Air)

Span	9.8 m (32 ft 2 in)
Length	6.5 m (21 ft 4 in)
Height	2.9 m (9 ft 6 in)
Empty weight	930 kg (2,046 lb)
Max speed	310 km/h (193 mph)
Rate of climb	5,000 m (16,500 ft) in $8\frac{1}{2}$ minutes

Flight Fantastic

pilots who had the advantage of the very latest purpose-built aerobatic machines supplied and maintained by the major companies.

Negative manoeuvres called for properly stressed aircraft structures and specialized power plants, and virtually the only sources of competitive top line machines outside of the military services were the factories themselves. With the advent of more and more powerful engine installations, rising to as much as 500 and 600 hp, it reached a pitch where amateur pilots simply could not compete in the same league as the professionals. Indeed in 1937, in the fourth Zurich International Aerobatic Competition, the organizers found it necessary to separate the competing aircraft into three categories according to engine capacity.

Michel Détroyat, as Alfred Fronval's successor at Morane-Saulnier, was one of the first to benefit from the new breed of aerobatic machine. Born in 1905, he belonged to a new generation of flyers who had learned their technique at the hands of the great masters and were carving out their own style of refined, precise and disciplined performance. Like Pégoud, Nungesser, and many others, Détroyat was an accomplished horseman who perpetuated the French 'equestrian' way of thinking about aerobatics.

Marcel Doret had a reputation for flying hard and pulling hard, which was the best way to achieve an entertaining performance within the limitations of his Dewoitine; whereas Détroyat followed the view of Fronval and favoured a smooth, slow and supple performance; from his way of thinking originated the idea of 'drawing pictures in the sky' which reached its apotheosis in the Lockheed Competitions of the 1950s and 60s. A methodical execution was not good enough now, the pilot must combine artistry with precision and sureness of touch to design his trajectories in space and time.

Détroyat had risen through the French Air Service, taking his licence at the Military Flying School of Istres in 1924; in the same year he distinguished himslf as the first (post-war) French pilot to fly the slow roll. He soon became an instructor for the Air Service, but did not catch the public eye until 1927, when by pure chance he happened to be at Le Bourget on the day of Lindbergh's historic flight across the Atlantic, and was sent up to provide a little aerobatic entertainment for the vast and impatient crowd. Lindbergh, an aerobatics exponent and ex-barnstormer, asked permission to try Détroyat's military Nieuport 29, and from that moment the two became fast friends.

Later that same year Détroyat joined Morane-Saulnier, becoming chief pilot on Fronval's death and testing all the new prototypes including the excellent Morane 230, which became the standard trainer at the famous Istres military school and a much-loved aerobatic mount. He was the first Frenchman to perform the negative loop pioneered by Fieseler, and to develop engines and fuel systems for inverted flight.

Détroyat codified aerobatics for the French at a time when it was achieving ever higher levels of sophistication, founding the concept of the *Haute Ecole Aérienne*, the advanced class of aerobatics. In *l'Acrobatie Classique*, basic aerobatic technique, he listed seven classic manoeuvres which were fundamental to the art: *looping* (loop), *vrille* (spin), *tonneau* (flick roll), *glissade* (sideslip), *renversement* (stall turn), *retournement* (climbing half-roll followed by descending half-loop)*, *Immelmann* (horizontal half-roll at the top of a half-loop)*.

The accompanying illustrations show that in French aviation of the 1930s this name of 'Immelmann' was given to what we currently call a roll-off-the-top. But in Germany the 'Immelmann-Turn' was a steep wing-over; they described the French version as *ein halber Überschlag, eine halbe Rolle* – half loop half roll.

Once these seven basics were mastered, the *Haute Ecole* involved the performance of inverted and negative manoeuvres, for which a special engine and fuel system were of course necessary; starting with the slow roll and bunt, and taking in all the variations of positive and negative loops, the repertoire was thus expanded to include virtually all the aerobatic figures in use today, and a few more that are not.

With catalogues starting to be introduced for the purpose of listing appropriate marks for the difficulty of each figure, one saw the humble sideslip, banked turn and zoom credited with 1 point each, the bunt, slow roll and vertical roll with 2, 3 and 4 respectively, and marks of 4–5–6 generally attributed to figures performed in sustained negative flight. The negative (outside) loop performed downwards was worth 4, and performed upwards from an inverted attitude it was worth 5. Thereafter, the marks of 7, 8 and more were reserved for the Horizontal 8s and Vertical 8s where a negative and a positive loop were juxtaposed, either side-by-side or one above the other.

One of Détroyat's most famous inventions was a figure which he called the '5 loopings' (see *d* opposite), in which he performed two Vertical 8s linked by a half loop, exemplifying during the course of the figure every one of the four possible types of circular loop. Other specialities of his included vertically climbing flick rolls, and the classic Vertical S pushing downwards from horizontal flight.

In 1934, when the French Aero Club announced a prestigious World Aerobatic Championship to take place on 9–10 June, it was decided to select its own two-man team by means of the first ever French National Championships: Michel Détroyat was the winner, Jérôme Cavalli coming second. In the *Coupe Mondiale* itself, however, it was Germany's Gerhard Fieseler who gained the world title, with Détroyat in second place flying his powerful orange, black and white Morane-Saulnier MS 225 Cl single-seater fighter (500 hp Gnôme-Rhône K9).

Jérôme Cavalli was another product of the Istres flying school, where all military pilots underwent a ten-hour course in aerobatics as part of their standard training. In 1931 he became test pilot of the Gourdou-Leseurre aircraft company, and flew one of their special aerobatic machines to achieve fifth place for France in the 1934 World Championship. From 1934 to 1939 he was a celebrated air display performer with the Gourdou-Leseurre LGL B6 (350 hp Hispano Suiza). His precision with the Gourdou was much admired, but the machine itself was rather unattractive with its squared-off wings, and hardly manoeuvrable enough for top-level aerobatics.

A sure sign of international fame in the 1930s was to be invited to the US National Air Races, of which the reader will find more in the following chapter. Michel Détroyat was invited in 1934 and 1935 for the aerobatic shows which always provided the incidental entertainment, but the races themselves made such an impression on him that he determined to return and challenge the Americans with the best of French racing machines. When he did return with a Caudron C-460 in 1936, he carried off not one but two of the most important

*Twenty-five years later, when he wrote his treatise on aerobatics *Polite d'Acrobatie*, Détroyat was calling this roll-off-the-top a *rétablissement*, and by contrast illustrating the *Immelmann* as a half-roll performed during the climbing curve of a half-loop. All very confusing!

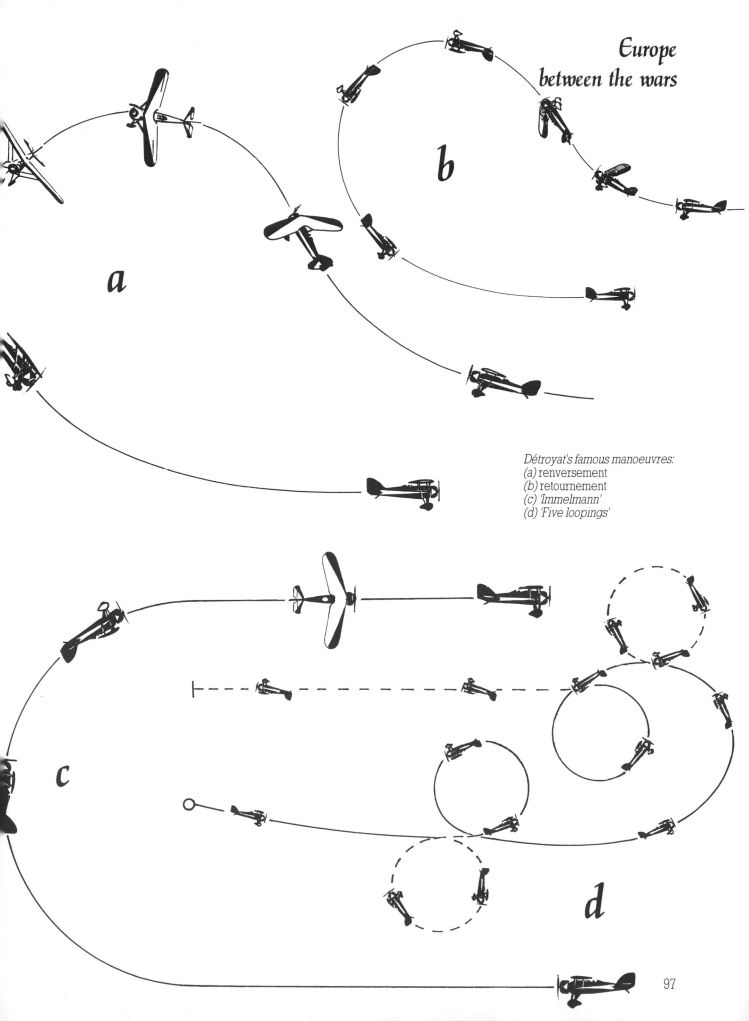

a

b

Détroyat's famous manoeuvres:
(a) renversement
(b) retournement
(c) 'Immelmann'
(d) 'Five loopings'

c

d

97

Fieseler-Détroyat match, Le Bourget 1933.   *(Musée de l'Air)*

prizes – the Thompson and Greve Trophies – as well as enrapturing the crowd with yet more stunning aerobatic displays!

Perhaps best known of all Détroyat's aeroplanes was his red and black special MS 234, a variant of the 230 but with the original 230 hp Salmson replaced by a 300 hp Hispano-Suiza with special inverted carburation and fuel systems. With the aid of this machine he devised, in April 1937, a public contest between four of the great French aerobatic pilots of the day: Marcel Doret, Jérôme Cavalli, Louis Massotte and René

Jérôme Cavalli and Gourdou-Leseurre.
Cavalli's Gourdou had certain disadvantages as an aerobatic mount, not least of which being the square-cut wingtips which immediately accentuated even the smallest error of geometry or axial alignment.   *(via Musée de l'Air)*

Michel Détroyat's red and black Morane-Saulnier 234 (300 hp Hispano-Suiza). *(via Musée de l'Air)*

The Four Aces practising at Villacoublay, 21 April 1937. L to R: Massotte, Doret, Cavalli, Paulhan. *(via Musée de l'Air)*

Flight Fantastic

Paulhan*. It was known as the battle of the Four Aces, and it took very much the form of what we would nowadays call a Masters Competition, in front of the largest audience that had ever attended an aviation event in France.

Détroyat on this occasion took the rôle of judge, with his Morane 234 placed at the disposal of all four pilots. The contest was arranged in two separate parts. In the first round it was to be a strict competition event, introducing a new idea of total anonymity for the four participants, achieved by clothing them in identical flying suits and having them all perform their sequences on the same machine. René Paulhan was the winner of this event. Then in the second round each pilot returned to his own individual aeroplane, and it was left to the audience to adjudicate between their performances: here the public vote went to the ever-popular Marcel Doret.

Doret later expressed his mounting conviction that the repetitive flights of competition aerobatics must surely be terribly boring to uninitiated spectators, each pilot performing the same programme one after another, with the accent on technical expertise rather than entertainment for the public.

By now, with sophisticated cataloguing and marking of competition aerobatics, performances were already being judged almost as minutely as in present-day contests, with marks lost for tiny errors where the geometry of the figure did not conform to the accepted criteria. The loop, for example, must be perfectly round; the slow roll must last for a minimum of ten seconds, the flick roll less than 4 seconds; and the Vertical S must consist of two half-loops without a horizontal line between them. Such niceties of performance were clearly visible to experts, and necessary for the difficult task of distinguishing between a number of pilots of almost equal excellence. But it is easy to see the division steadily growing up between aerobatics to please the judges and aerobatics to please the crowd!

Although the factory pilots had all the advantages in the competition world, there were still plenty of enthusiastic non-professionals going the rounds of the airshow circuits, and a fair number of them were women. Most famous were the Germans: Liesel Bach, the outstanding woman pilot of her day, Vera von Bissing (a pupil of Fieseler's), Hanna Reitsch (who started as a glider pilot) and the swashbuckling Thea Rasche, who turned down an advantageous marriage to lead the life of an itinerant air display pilot. Among the French were Hélène Boucher (Détroyat's pupil) and Maryse Hilsz, both of whom flew Moranes. There were even a number of all-female aerobatic contests, including a *Coupe Feminin* organized by the French prior to the *Coupe Mondiale* in 1934, won by Liesel Bach, and a special women's event at the 1936 Olympic Celebration Competition which was won by Vera von Bissing. Bach was also proclaimed female champion at the 1937 Zurich meeting.

Also seen at these international events of the thirties were isolated representatives from the smaller European nations; but the worlds of display and competition aerobatics were gradually diverging, and pilots with the highest reputations in their home countries were often outclassed in competition – especially in the matter of their machines – by the specialists of France and Germany. Among the more notable competition pilots from other parts of Europe were Victor Glardon of Switzerland who flew the Raab-Katzenstein Schwalbe to fifth place in the 1932 Zurich meeting, and Placido d'Abreu of Portugal (Avro Tutor) whose death in the 1934 World Cup has

Swiss pilot Victor Glardon with K11C Schwalbe.
(Musée de l'Air)

already been recounted.

Poland produced Capt Boleslaw Orliński, exponent of the manoeuvrable little PZL (Państwowe Zakłady Lotnicze, or National Aviation Establishment) fighters, especially the PZL 6 (700 hp Gnôme-Rhône), later to fly Mosquitos with the RAF in World War II; and Col Jerzy Kossowski, who together with Orliński made the PZLs famous on both sides of the Atlantic.

Another favourite Polish aerobat was Lt Józef Orłowski, especially famed for his air displays with the PWS 12 (Podlasian Aeroplane Company) of which a civil registered version, SP-AKE, appeared in 1933. Powered by a 220 hp Wright/Skoda J5 9-cylinder radial engine, it incorporated a number of modifications for advanced aerobatics and inverted flying, including a gravity fuel tank, and was rated an outstanding aerobatic performer. On a 1933 tour, Orłowski's staggering display in Sofia, Bulgaria, caused a sensation: it consisted of 55 minutes of non-stop aerobatics including every manoeuvre in the book, eight minutes of which were spent inverted.

During the inter-war years, Poland's thriving aircraft industry produced not only these very successful fighters and trainers, but a considerable number of sport aeroplanes such as the RWD 6 and 9, famous for their prizewinning results in international contests for touring aircraft. The RWD 10 (110 hp PZ Inż Junior) was a single-seat parasol monoplane built for aerobatics, with delightful handling qualities which were amply displayed in a brilliant performance by test pilot Kazimierz Chorzewski when it went for certification: he included 28 consecutive loops in his demonstration (almost blacking out in the process!) to disprove the allegation that

*All four were test pilots – Doret for Dewoitine, Cavalli for Gourdou-Leseurre, Rene Paulhan for Caudron and Louis Massotte for Blériot: both Paulhan and Massotte were eventually to meet their deaths in the course of their work, Paulham only the following month while flying a new Caudron fighter.

Boleslaw Orliński from Poland, with the first pre-production PZL 5 SP-ACW (85–100 hp Gipsy I). (via Musée de l'Air)

the aircraft could not be looped. The later RWD 17 (130 hp PZ Inż Major) was a two-seat trainer of rather more docile characteristics, later used as a military trainer.

But gliding and glider aerobatics have always occupied the major place in Polish sport aviation, and their specialist designs – from the CW-7 and Sokol to today's IS-4 Jastrzab and SZD-21 Kobuz – have constantly been at the forefront of this sport. Jerzy Makula, World Glider Aerobatics Champion in 1985, combines the two sports and is one of Poland's best known power-aerobatics champions; while Andrzej Abłamowicz, perhaps Poland's foremost post-war authority on aerobatics, has written several books on both sailplane and power-flying and until his untimely death in 1985 was a leading figure in the international organization of both types of aerobatics.

Józef Orlowski's PWS 12, specially modified for aerobatics and famous throughout Europe. Its ultimate military development, the PWS 26, gave outstanding aerobatic performances at displays in the late 1930s. (Jerzy B Cynk)

Great Britain in particular was conspicuous by her absence from the European aerobatic scene in the 1920s and 30s,

The RWD10, used by Polish aviation clubs as an aerobatic trainer, was looped 28 times for its flight certification test.
(Jerzy B Cynk)

when aerobatics were almost exclusively the domain of the RAF. Indeed they still play a significant rôle, being a basic requirement for all pilots under training, no matter in what type of aircraft they may ultimately serve.

Although civilian sport flying enjoyed a certain amount of popularity, the country as a whole needed whipping up into a state of 'air-mindedness' before even basic facilities such as civic aerodromes were thought of as desirable.

Sir Alan Cobham, knighted for his record-breaking flight to Australia, set out almost single-handedly to stimulate progress in civil aviation with his National Aviation Day displays between 1932 and 1935: a touring airshow which set up, performed and hit the road again within the space of 24 hours, offering aerobatics, inverted flying, wing-walking, pylon racing and, of course, joyrides for the public. National Aviation Day stars included Charles ('Toc-H') Turner Hughes (later chief test pilot with Armstrong Whitworth) and his successor Geoffrey Tyson, who duplicated Ernst Udet's trick of picking up a handkerchief with his wingtip. Tyson, later a test pilot for Short Brothers and Saunders-Roe, made a speciality of inverted flying in air displays both before and after the war, and both men later became regular judges at the Lockheed Aerobatic Competitions of the 1950s.

In the Royal Air Force, true to irrepressible Smith-Barry tradition, the star exponents of the art were always the Central Flying School instructors, who appeared each year at the Hendon Pageant and exhibited solo and formation aerobatics and crazy-flying. This annual airshow also gave rise to keen competition among the squadrons for the right to provide additional aerobatic demonstrations at Hendon.

Flight Lieutenant Christopher Clarkson had been a devotee of aerobatics since joining the service in 1924, but was scarcely able to indulge his enthusiasm until posted to CFS at Wittering, where he served as an instructor on Avro 504Ks from 1927 to 1929. Prior to that time only a limited amount of aerobatics was performed there apart from the spinning and spin recovery which featured in the standard course of instruction, and the occasional loop and flick roll for fun or to give the students a thrill. Lack of shoulder-harness precluded anything more serious. Then in 1927 Clarkson and fellow instructor George Stainforth – who had been teaching the slow roll since 1924 and was a keen 'upside-down' flyer – obtained for themselves two sets of harness from a friend in a

Christopher Clarkson, pictured while at Central Flying School in 1928. *(Christopher Clarkson)*

fighter squadron, where it was fitted as standard. This meant that the full range of positive and negative manoeuvres was at least possible for them.

Whether by coincidence or as a result of their efforts, shoulder harness became standard on the CFS Avros shortly afterwards; and instructors like Clarkson and Stainforth, Boyle, Atcherley and Waghorn built a complete course of aerobatics into the syllabus of the famous school, laying emphasis on precision of flying to achieve the perfect, smooth, accurate manoeuvre. Christopher Clarkson himself, on his departure in 1929, presented a Cup which was to be awarded to the best aerobatic pilot on each course in an

open competition. The Clarkson Aerobatics Trophy, oldest of the school's many awards, is still presented to the student whose aerobatic performance on the current trainer attains a sufficient degree of excellence.

On leaving the RAF he did a certain amount of demonstration work, and in 1932 went into partnership to form the British D H Moth agency, stepping up his airshow activities considerably in the process. With Gipsy Moth G-ABBX fixed up for inverted flight he was regularly to be seen giving aerobatic displays at nearly all the aviation meetings.

The Air Ministry had meanwhile issued warnings against flick rolls and negative manoeuvres because of the strain they put on aircraft structures, and in 1937 outside looping and bunting were outlawed in the RAF; a ban on the flick roll followed. This brought to a sad halt that quest for progress and development which had started with the Farnborough research and had been carried resolutely forward by such as Allen Wheeler, R L R Atcherley and the Central Flying School instructors.

In the 1939 Flying Training Manual a new entry appeared under the name **barrel roll**, "a continuous uniform smooth motion in roll and loop, with practically no sideslip". This described an already well known positive-*g* rolling manoeuvre which was not a true horizontal roll – involving negative *g* – but a roll around a looping trajectory (see diagram on page 120). It had been in use for a long time although not dignified by any generally accepted name, and indeed was rather looked down on as only for those who did not want to face the problems of negative *g*. Not considered an aerobatic manoeuvre, it did not figure in any aerobatic catalogues of the period. With the autorotative roll now firmly known as the flick roll, somebody evidently decided to bring its old name of barrel roll out of retirement, and applied it to this innocuous style of rolling which now met with Air Ministry approval.

During the early 1930s Christopher Clarkson was virtually the only standard-bearer for British aerobatics in the international arena, and was often called upon to display the DH82 Tiger Moth (130 hp Gipsy Major) in European aerobatic events. Of those meetings he attended where any kind of serious competition took place, his first was in 1932 in Estoril, Portugal, which he modestly describes as an easy victory over a much depleted field of entries.

When the 1934 World Championships were announced to take place in Paris, Christopher Clarkson looked forward to competing in a borrowed Armstrong Whitworth AW16 fighter, but, in his words,

… they couldn't do it at the last minute and I had to scratch around for an aeroplane of some sort. Finally DH lent me a Tiger Moth which was on its way back to London from points Far East, and I picked it up at Le Bourget. It was a pretty tired workhorse and had a large extra tank in the front seat; not only did it weigh a lot, it had no inverted flying engine modification!

He was desperately handicapped by the meagre power/weight ratio of the aircraft, and its inability to perform negative manoeuvres severely limited his repertoire of figures in the competition. But, having entered, he was sporting enough to want to see it through; and though not by any means disgracing himself, he predictably came in last. The French newspapers, aware of the quality of his flying under normal circumstances, described Clarkson as a brilliant pilot who had simply been let down by his aircraft.

World Aerobatic Championships, Paris 1934

1.	Gerhard Fieseler (F2 Tiger)	German	645.5
2.	Michel Détroyat (MS 225)	French	622.9
3.	Gerd Achgelis (FW Stieglitz)	German	537.6
4.	František Novák (Avia B.122)	Czech	451.8
5.	Jérôme Cavalli (Gourdou-Leseurre)	French	361.0
6.	Ambrogio Colombo (Breda 28)	Italian	344.8
7.	Placido d'Abreu (Avro Tutor)	Portugese	337.3
8.	Jan Ambruž (Avia B.122)	Czech	309.2
9.	Christopher Clarkson (Tiger Moth)	British	144.0

Another country with its own strong military tradition was Italy, where individual and formation aerobatics dated back to the 1920s; though it was perhaps better known for its successes in speed races, notably the Schneider Cup. Mario de Bernardi, Schneider Trophy winner when the event was staged in the USA in 1926, was an ex-World War I pilot who collected several speed and height records in a long career which included outstanding successes in the aerobatics field as well. Commemorating his famous cornering technique around the pylons of the great water-speed race, the Italians gave the name 'Schneider' to the steeply-banked turn in aerobatics.*

Mario de Bernardi, pictured after his Schneider Trophy win in 1926.
(via Musée de l'Air)

De Bernardi was a collaborator with Count Caproni in pioneering an autopilot system in the mid-1930s, and in 1940 made the initial test flight of the Caproni-Campini N.1, the first Italian aircraft to be propelled by a jet engine. For this he gave all his time and effort to his friend Caproni quite freely,

*Cornering technique was exhaustively researched by the RAF's High Speed Flight for their 1929 Schneider attempt, in an effort to decide the most efficient turn. After measuring acceleration, speed and climb they calculated that the perfect turn should be vertically banked, between 4 and 6*g*, and as level as possible, with the stick pulled back but not too hard'. They learned, too, that a smooth and even use of the controls in cornering reduced the severity of the visual blacking out caused by loss of blood-supply during high *g*.

Flight Fantastic

without payment or reward. In the mid-1950s he was still pioneering with an 'aeroscooter', the Libellule, which he toured happily around the airshows giving aerobatic exhibitions and doing his best to resuscitate post-war Italian aviation.

He had a reputation as a serious, conscientious and sensible pilot, careful and unruffled in competition. In 1930 at Taliedo he even managed a win over the great Gerhard Fieseler; but his progress in aerobatics was handicapped by the absence of a suitable machine until in 1931 Caproni produced his high-performance CA 113 (240 hp Walter). With this aeroplane de Bernardi triumphantly represented Italy at the international aerobatic displays accompanying the 1931 NARs in Cleveland, where the Americans were quick to appreciate the elegance and precision of his flying.

Truth to tell, however, formation flying was of much greater interest to the Italians than solo aerobatics, especially since flying in Italy was predominantly concentrated in the Italian Air Force. Great competition grew up among the many military teams, and those of Mario de Bernardi and Arturo Ferrarin were arch-rivals during the 1920s.

Within the discipline of Italian military flying several more worthy successors to de Bernardi soon appeared, foremost among them being Pietro Colombo. Destined for evermore to be confused with his equally famous contemporary Ambrogio Colombo, Pietro was an open-hearted and outgoing character, a Breda pilot with the military rank of Maresciallo. So far as we know he had no family relationship to Ambrogio. To his unbounded delight, Pietro – or Pierino as he was known – was chosen to appear in the 1930 NARs by means of a nationwide (military) aerobatic competition in which he clearly excelled. Flying the BA 19 with style and panache, he was such a hit with the warmly welcoming Chicago audience that it was difficult to say whether he made a greater impression on America or America a greater impression on him!

Pierino continued representing his country in formation aerobatics, and was one of the nine-man team which won top honours at the Zurich Aviation Meeting of 1932, under the leadership of Tenente Andrea Zotti. In the same year it was Zotti's turn to carry the flag to the American National Air Races in Cleveland, Ohio, where Italian military-style aerobatics again made an indelible impression on the spellbound audience.

By now the regular Italian presence each year at the NARs was something of an institution, and 1933 saw the turn of diminutive Lt Tito Falconi to cross the Atlantic with his CA 117; in his absence Sgt Andrea Citi represented Italy in solo aerobatic events and came second to Fieseler – beating Détroyat and Cavalli – in a championship held at Lyon.

Pietro Colombo, 1938.   *(via Musée de l'Air)*

In the early months of 1933 it had become quite the fashion in Italy to set up records for inverted flight, and at the time of Falconi's departure the duration record, held by a certain Lt Willy Bocola, stood at 1 hour 5 minutes 5 seconds. On arrival, Tito found that the American Milo Burcham had just beaten that with an inverted flight of 1 hour 9 minutes in a Fleet aircraft, so the Italian decided to have a try himself and on 16 July, after the Races had finished, he established a new record with 1 hour 15 minutes 20 seconds.

This then sparked off a crazy duel between the two pilots as each gradually pushed up the duration record to 2 hours, 2 hours 8 minutes, 2 hours 20 minutes, until finally the ultimate laurels went to Tito Falconi with a marathon 3 hours 6 minutes 39 seconds, which he achieved by flying the entire 260 mile (420 km) distance between St Louis and Chicago inverted.* Ironically, he is remembered now more for his inverted flying than for his considerable aerobatic skills.

Meanwhile, back home in Italy, the reptuation of test pilot Ambrogio Colombo was growing steadily. Ambrogio was a civilian, a qualified engineer and chief test pilot for the Breda company of Milan which produced the standard trainers used by the Italian Air Force. After taking his licence in 1918 – too late for war service – he spent 1919–21 as an instructor in Japan, Argentina and Brazil, and then joined Breda and built up considerable international fame as an exhibition pilot. Even he could not escape being caught up in the military formation flying craze, however, and in 1932 he was 'enlisted' with a temporary Captain's commission in order that he might lead Italy's *Nucleo di Alta Acrobazia* formation team!

Ambrogio Colombo with Gerhard Fieseler.

(via Musée de l'Air)

Colombo's Breda 28 at Vincennes, 1934. (Musée de l'Air)

Span	10 m (32 ft 10 in)
Length	7.8 m (25 ft 7 in)
Height	3.37 m (11 ft 7 in)
Empty weight	960 kg (2,112 lb)
Max speed	240 km/h (150 mph)
Rate of climb	5,000 m (16,500 ft) in 16 minutes

At last in 1934 Breda produced a really top line aerobatic machine, better and stronger than the Caproni CA113, with which Ambrogio Colombo could compete internationally on equal terms. Although he was classed very much as an outsider, in the press reports leading up to the World Aerobatic Championships of that year there was great interest in Colombo's extremely strong and manoeuvrable Breda

*Subsequent inverted flight records continued to be set, of course, both by Burcham and by others in many different countries.

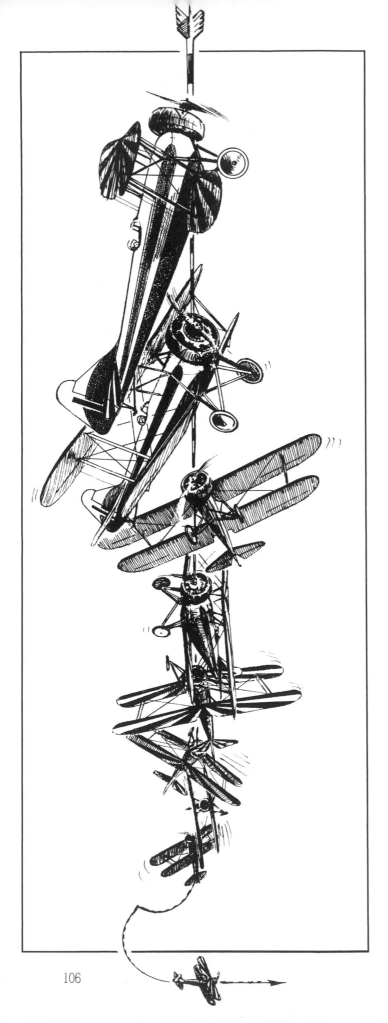

Colombo's spinning tail-slide.

28, the new Italian trainer built solely for aerobatics, which had been developed from the Breda 25 and 26 machines. It sported a 380 hp Piaggio engine with fully inverted fuel, oil and carburation systems.

Although the machine promised much, Ambrogio suffered the disadvantage of unfamiliarity with the brand new aircraft which had been rushed through its final stages to be ready in time for the Championships. This, together with the nervous strain only natural on such an occasion, combined to cause Colombo a too-late spin recovery in his free programme, the aircraft's undercarriage coming so low as to foul the tops of a clump of trees bordering the airfield. Although he had featured some remarkable flying in his sequence, including his own invention of a Horizontal 8 made up of two *negative* loops, this mishap with the spin put an end to his chances in the contest and he did well to come in sixth.

Another manoeuvre pioneered by Ambrogio Colombo, which deserves special mention in the history of aerobatic development, is that mixture of spin and tail-slide, versions of which we first encountered in 1914 performed by Pierre Chanteloup and in 1918 by John McGavock Grider – pages 36 and 55. It is by no means clear how Chanteloup or Grider executed the figure, and unfortunately we have no better information how Colombo did it either; but in the first two cases it seems reasonable to regard the figure as an early form of torque roll, probably quite a hit and miss affair at that.

In 1934, however, there was nothing at all hit and miss about aerobatics; competition successes sold aeroplanes, and aircraft sales, particularly sales of military trainers, were big business in Europe. It was the job of the professional test pilots to perfect their technique and win contests – and this involved constantly striving after elusive new figures.

Just such an elusive figure was the spinning tail-slide – or perhaps tail-sliding spin would be a better description – a manoeuvre which only the most foolhardy or the supremely confident pilot would even dare to attempt. Indeed, one would be tempted to discount the possibility of anyone trying the manoeuvre were it not for the fact that it was reported, and illustrated, in the reputable aviation paper *Les Ailes* by Edmond Blanc, himself a pilot, judge and writer on the subject of aerobatics.

In an article describing the aerobatic catalogue of 87 figures used in the 1934 World Championships, Blanc says:

> The catalogue lists all lines and trajectories of flight that have been conceived up till now, basic and advanced, whether performed already or simply imagined as possible. Note, however, the solitary exception of the flat spin, which does not appear since it is considered too dangerous by most top aerobatic pilots.
> Among the list of figures not yet performed, we illustrate the tail-sliding spin [*vrille sur la queue*], for which a minimum of three rotations is demanded. It appears that Colombo has succeeded in accomplishing one rotation, but in his estimation to perform it better he would need a machine with the centre of gravity located further aft.

Presumably Ambrogio had already had enough of dodging treetops without trying anything so imprudent as tinkering with his C of G in a spin, for there were no more reports of further experimentation with the figure.

Was this another attempt at a torque roll, ie a rolling tail-slide? Flat spins may have been eschewed in 1934, but tail-slides and vertical rolls were a normal part of the aerobatic repertoire, so the combination of the two is perhaps not altogether surprising – especially for a test pilot who has a parachute strapped to his back, a factory machine to play with, and carte blanche to work out the best prizewinning routines he can devise.

But what is surprising is that our knowledgeable French commentator employs the word 'spin' [*vrille*] to define the manoeuvre, knowing full well that a spin is an autorotation which is entered from a condition of stall. When Blanc defines Colombo's manoeuvre in what must have been the current parlance of the day – literally 'spin on the tail' – and illustrates the aircraft in a nose-up attitude with the tail tracing the familiar helical rotation of the spin as it descends, one begins to wonder just what those factory test pilots actually got up to in the heady pre-war days of experiment with the ultimate boundaries of flight...

Finally, to end this section devoted to the growth of aerobatics in pre-World War II Europe, the long aerobatic tradition of Czechoslovakia merits a specially close examination.

The Aeroclub of Czechoslovakia traces its origins back to the year 1913, that same year when Adolphe Pégoud, during his extensive European tour, stopped off in Prague to give flying exhibitions there at the end of the Christmas holidays. After the war, in 1918, the Czechoslovak Republic came into existence together with an independent Air Force which included aerobatics in its pilot training. As early as 1920, Josef Novák won a prize for his aerobatic display in a Prague Air Rally. Later, during the craze for looping records, he executed 244 consecutive loops while carrying a passenger aboard a Czech-built Aero biplane.

Right from the very first international competitions in the 1920s, Czechoslovakian pilots – both military and civilian – took part with considerable success. Light aeroplanes for aerobatics, mostly military trainers, were being built in large quantities by the Letov and Avia factories. Most notable among these were the Avia machines such as the BH 22 (180 hp Hispano Suiza), a single-seat fighter trainer built in 1925 with which the celebrated aerobatic pilot František Malkovský, the darling of the Czech airshow audiences, gained seventh place at the 1927 Zurich International Flying Meeting. He continued to have great success with the subsequent BH 33E (450 hp Walter-Jupiter) in which he thrilled the French public in 1929 with negative loops which were previously considered the special prerogative of the German pilot Fieseler; but Malkovský was tragically killed in a flying accident in 1930.

Successor to Capt Malkovský's crown as king of Czechoslovakian aerobatics was Lt František Novák, a young military pilot who made a name for himself in the early thirties with the Avia B 22 aerobatic trainer, winning an International Air Contest in Warsaw in 1933. The following year he achieved fourth place in the first World Aerobatic Championships at Vincennes, Paris. For this contest he and his fellow-competitor Jan Ambruž had a brand new Avia machine, the B.122 (260 hp Walter Castor II), which soon became an international favourite, being sold as a trainer to the USSR, Romania and Bulgaria. Novák, most popular of all the pre-World War II Czech pilots, is regarded today as founder of the school of

1924 poster of Czechoslovakian Air Display.

(via Musée de l'Air)

formation flying for which Czechoslovakia is justly famous. A speciality of his three-ship team was the performance of formation aerobatics while tied together with cords.

Novák was winner of the first Czech National Aerobatic Championship in 1935, but did not compete in subsequent years, preferring instead to act as judge together with fellow team member Petr Široký. Then in 1936 Široký joined Novák and Ambruž in the Berlin Olympic Games competition, all three flying the little yellow and red Ba122 which had now been equipped with the more efficient 350–380 hp Avia Rk-17 engine. Široký and Novák achieved second and third places after the winner Graf von Hagenburg, against a very strong field of top pilots (mostly military trained) from six European countries. The overall results were as follows:

Olympic Games, Berlin 1936

1. Otto von Hagenburg (Fw Stieglitz)	German	658.83
2. Petr Široký (Avia Ba122)	Czech	651.41
3. František Novák (Avia Ba122)	Czech	641.66
4. Pierre Fleurquin (MS 225)	French	639.99
5. Gerd Achgelis (Fw Stösser)	German	631.41
6. Willi Stör (BFW M55)	German	628.66
7. Hörning (Bü Jungmeister)	Swiss	619.33
8. Jan Ambruž (Avia Ba122)	Czech	597.08
9. Ercolano Ercolani (Breda 28)	Italian	544.50
10. Mario Viola (Breda 28)	Italian	516.82
11. Guido Carestiato (Breda 28)	Italian	487.33
12. Alexandru Papana (Bü Jungmeister)	Romanian	435.00
13. Jérôme Cavalli (Gourdou-Leseurre)	French	418.46
14. Edmond Blanc (Morane)	French	409.25

František Malkowský with his red-painted Avia BH 21, serial no. 96 (300 hp Skoda Hispano Suiza) nicknamed 'Red Devil'. It was stressed to 12.5 g. (Jan Krumbach)

Avia BH 22, the first Czech aeroplane specifically for aerobatics and stressed to a maximum 16 g (180 hp Hispano-Suiza 8.Aa). (Jan Krumbach)

Papana's fellow-countryman Prince Cantacuzino, also a Jungmeister pilot (see Chapter 14), had entered as a contestant in the Olympic celebrations but was prevented at the last minute when he damaged his aeroplane. This was a great pity: it would have been extremely interesting to compare the two famous Romanians in a large-scale international event.

Novák, however, was on top form for the contest and introduced a number of original figures in his free programme which left the opposition gaping. Following Fieseler's lead, rolling turns and circles of every kind were now being performed, with any number of rolls in any direction (including alternate rolls to left and right). Rolls were also being added to loops of every kind, and one of Novák's figures was a Vertical 8 started in the middle and featuring four half-rolls. Another was a downward (positive) loop integrated with four complete rolls.

But his really outstanding invention was a figure featuring the revolutionary use of flat spins, which most of the aerobatic stars of the thirties left very severely alone! His complex figure-of-eight illustrated here started with a half-loop from erect to inverted, falling into a negative flat spin at the top and then slow-rolling diagonally (from inverted to inverted) back to his starting altitude, whereupon he commenced a second half-loop from inverted to erect, falling into a positive flat spin, out of which he slow-rolled diagonally to finish erect at his starting point again. The whole figure earned him the maximum 12 points for difficulty.

Even greater successes were awaiting the Czech pilots the following year, when they swept the board with their placings in the 1937 Zurich International Aviation Meeting. They used two types of 350/360 hp Ba122, one having the Avia Rk-17 and the other the Walter Pollux motor, competing in the 'B'

Avia Ba 122, 360 hp Walter Pollux version, for the Berlin Olympics 1936.   *(Jan Krumbach)*

category and 'C' category respectively (see table of results below). In both categories the phenomenal František Novák took first place, with his compatriots close behind. The following year at Saint-Germain-en-Laye, Paris, Novák flew the modified Avia machine B 422 to second place behind von Hagenburg. This was destined to be his last competition before the Nazi invasion of Czechoslovakia brutally put a stop to the gentle art of aerobatics.

Zurich Aviation Meeting, 1937

Category 'A' (under 10 litres)

1. Graf von Hagenburg (Bü Jungmeister)	German	158.05
2. Oblt Kuhn (Bü Jungmeister)	Swiss	119.50
3. Oblt Hörning (Bü Jungmeister)	Swiss	116.32

Category 'B' (10–20 litres)

1. František Novák (Avia Ba122/Rk-17)	Czech	164.55
2. Gerd Achgelis (Fw Stösser)	German	143.85
3. Petr Široký (Avia Ba122/Rk-17)	Czech	139.875
4. Josef Hubáček (Avia Ba122/Rk-17)	Czech	139.675

Category 'C' (over 20 litres)

1. František Novák (Avia Ba122/Walter)	Czech	145.50
2. Petr Široký (Avia Ba122/Walter)	Czech	135.50
3. František Výborný (Avia Ba122/Walter)	Czech	99.12

During this period of growth in the Czech aircraft industry several other firms started up in business, building sport aeroplanes and basic trainers, among them ČKD-Praga with the popular Air Baby, Beneš & Mrás with the Beta series, and Tatra with a short run of licence-built Bücker 131s. Then, in 1934, a small-scale aircraft production outfit was set up in Moravia under the unlikely aegis of the Bata shoe company, and began to produce small, cheap and popular aeroplanes. Their initial Z-XII two-seat monoplane was the first of what was destined to become a long and distinguished line of light trainers, leading to the most outstandingly successful aerobatic designs of the post-war years: the Zlin monoplanes. But the Zlin story we shall leave for another chapter.

František Novák with Avia B.422 (360 hp Avia Rk-17) at Saint Germain en Laye, 1938, for the match with Jérôme Cavalli and Otto von Hagenburg. The biplane's upper wing was modified to improve the pilot's field of vision in inverted flight.

(Jan Krumbach)

František Novák (centre) with Široký (left) and Hubáček (right). Novák died during World War II after escaping to fight in France. (Jan Krumbach)

Novák's Horizontal 8 figure with flat spins, as flown in the 1936 Olympic Celebration Competition.

9
America's golden age

It is time now to pick up the American story from where we left off in Chapter 6, with Jimmy Doolittle's negative ('outside') loop on 25 May 1927.

Doolittle's tally of aviation achievements from that date onward began to mount up steadily: 24 September 1929, first experiment in blind flying in a Consolidated Training aircraft at Mitchel Field, Long Island, Doolittle taking off, flying under the hood for 15 minutes and landing entirely on instruments; 4 September 1931, winner of the Bendix transcontinental race in the Laird 'Super Solution' (also setting a new time of 11 hours 16 minutes coast to coast, exactly nine years after he had himself set up the first record); September 1932, winner of the Thompson Trophy speed race in the Gee Bee R.1 racer, setting a world landplane speed record of 296.3 mph (475 km/h); and many more speed, distance and endurance flights all of which were milestones in aviation progress, blazing the trail for later airmail and passenger transport routes.

By the year 1930, he had decided to quit the US Army Air Corps: though by far their best and most highly-qualified pilot, Jimmy still had not progressed beyond the rank of Lieutenant, and the Shell Oil Company had made him an offer too good to refuse. The job involved a tour of 21 European countries demonstrating four different aeroplanes. Whilst in Germany he noted with foreboding their preoccupation with building up the speed of their aircraft, which he rightly saw as part of an overall military design. But America preferred to remain blind and deaf to all warnings, and it was for this reason that Doolittle now embarked on a racing career that was to span three years, helping to push back the frontiers of speed and endurance in an attempt to keep America at the forefront of aviation development.

It was after his 1932 world landplane record in the Gee Bee that he announced his retirement from racing. "We have learned a lot about engines and airplanes through racing," he said, "the time has come to give attention to safety and reliability."

True to pioneering form, Doolittle pushed Shell to develop 100 octane fuel for engines of greater horsepower, which came on to the market in 1934; then during the later thirties he continued to tour the world demonstrating the Curtiss Hawk. In Japan his impressions of their airline expansion and pilot training policies were as ominous as those he had received in Germany, and like General Billy Mitchell he tried in vain to speak out against the United States falling behind in aviation progress – especially military aviation. Making no headway, he requested a return to active duty in 1940.

Entering service as a major, he was promoted brigadier general in 1942, then major general, then lieutenant general in 1944. He commanded the Twelfth Air Force in North Africa, the Northwest Africa Strategic Air Force, then the Fifteenth and Eighth Air Forces. The highlight of Jimmy Doolittle's heroic World War II flying career, now a very proud part of American history, was his historic Tokyo Raid in April 1942: leading sixteen B-25 medium bombers, his squadron made pinpoint bomb drops on vital targets in Tokyo and other Japanese cities.

Doolittle's negative loop was not long in being reproduced by his equally famous Naval counterpart, Lieutenant Alford J (Al) Williams, a New Yorker who grew up in the Bronx. Al was in his second year as an ace pitcher with the New York Giants baseball club when America entered World War I and he enlisted as a Naval aviator. His merits both in flying and in analytical thinking were soon recognized and, like Doolittle, he was kept back from the Front to serve instead as a combat tactics instructor, later a research test pilot for the US Navy.

Jimmy Doolittle wins the Bendix with Laird Super Solution in 1931.   *(Smithsonian Institution)*

After the war he managed to combine his naval career with an evening course reading law at Georgetown University, and was admitted to the bar in 1926.

In 1919 Williams became interested in inverted flight, and with a Curtiss N-9 seaplane undertook research similar to that going on at the same time at the Royal Aircraft Establishment in England; by 1922 he had moved on to spin research and high speed flying at Hampton Roads, Virginia, and by 1923 had won the Pulitzer Trophy Air Race for the Navy in a Curtiss R3C-1.

On learning of Doolittle's negative loop, Al Williams immediately decided to reproduce the feat himself – but the other way around. Installing double seat belts in a standard 410 hp Wasp-powered F6C-4 Hawk (the naval version of the P-1B), Williams started his loop at the bottom instead of at the top, half-rolling from erect to inverted at 3,500 ft (1,070 m) and pushing up and over until he came back down again to his starting point. He reported no ill effects apart from a slight nosebleed and some loss of vision as the blood rushed to his head under the impetus of centrifugal force. Soon he was performing Vertical Ss and Vertical 8s under negative *g*, as well as negative (inverted) spins.

In pursuance of a NACA (National Advisory Committee for Aeronautics) research programme which mirrored Jimmy Doolittle's work, and for which he, too, was awarded the

DFC, Williams proceeded to carry out valuable investigations into the airframe loads imposed by aerobatic manoeuvres of all kinds, using recording instruments installed in a standard fighter.

Realizing that other pilots would be impatient to follow Al's lead as soon as word got out about his research, the Navy chiefs quickly slapped an embargo on negative manoeuvres among service flyers, and progress was effectively stultified. The same thing had happened in the Army Air Corps, too: in their 1930 Advanced Flying School Handbook (Pursuit Section) appears an entry in which the outside loop is 'prohibited by order of the Chief of Air Corps'. It was thus in the America of the 1930s that the pattern began to emerge which now pervades practically all aerobatic flying in the Western world: civilian pilots gradually took over what had formerly been the domain of military and factory test pilots.

Williams, like Doolittle, became a civilian in the year 1930. With their careers paralleling each other in so many ways, there was undeniably a certain rivalry between the two men; but one thing in which they were united was in their outcry for proper development of military aviation in the light of rapid and warlike expansion abroad, which their own armed forces seemed determined to ignore.

Experiencing the same degree of career frustration, Al resigned and embarked upon a round of exhibition flying. He had already won tremendous acclaim at the National Air Races of 1929, with his beautifully controlled ultra-slow rolls and prolonged inverted flying, making an inverted glide

113

Flight Fantastic

approach as if to land upside-down and rolling out at the very last moment for a smooth three-point landing. Jimmy had made a big impact, too, when his Hawk P-1 fighter shed its wings during a practice flight. He simply bailed out, climbed into another Hawk, and coolly completed his aerobatic routine!

In the 1930 NARs at Curtiss-Reynolds Airport, Chicago, Al – now out of uniform – was awarded a trophy for the most meritorious flying with his newly acquired Curtiss Hawk 1A demonstrator NR982V, which had its original Conqueror engine replaced by a 575 hp Bliss Jupiter radial and was especially rigged for inverted flight. From that year onwards he made it his job to organize the famous aerobatic events which were flown in conjunction with the annual NARs, bringing over to America the cream of European aerobatic talent. Not only did this help make the Races just about the most exciting and prestigious event in American aviation, it also introduced the latest in European machines and state-of-the-art aerobatics. This of course had a profound influence, as we shall see later in the chapter.

Joining the Gulf Refining Company's Aviation Department in 1933 (again counterpointing the career of Jimmy Doolittle, who had joined Shell) Al Williams renamed his orange and blue Hawk the *Gulfhawk* and replaced the Jupiter engine with a 710 hp Wright Cyclone F. The aircraft underwent many modifications during its time with Gulf, the fuselage was rounded out all the way to the tail and metal skinned, and several different cowlings were tried, including narrow Townend rings and the full NACA cowl. One of his airshow specialities was steep dive-bombing attacks with the Hawk at ground targets set up in front of the stands, levelling out at a bare 50–70 feet.

Veteran airshow promoter and commentator Bill Sweet gave a memorable description of Williams's art in his book *They Call Me Mr Airshow* (Ken Cook Transnational, 1972):

Al seemed to play the engine noise like a mighty celestial organ. The Hawk did the most beautiful aerobatic ballet I ever saw, and with almost no imagination at all you could see the plane swoop, wheel and pirouette through the sky in a wide, sweeping aerial dance. Every maneuver gave the engine a different sound and Al orchestrated his act with motor sounds. Others have tried this but none of them have the big engines capable of making the organ tones. Too many of the new engines sound like angry hornets, while the huge old Cyclones had a resonance you can't match today. Al flew a plane as if he was riding a big bird, flying the wings rather than the engine.

In 1936 Gulf bought Al Williams a civil version of the Navy Grumman F3F fighter, into which they transferred the Cyclone from the Curtiss, and the new machine was christened the *Gulfhawk 2*. The original airframe of the Curtiss was later bought by movie pilot Frank Tallman in 1958, who re-engined it with a 450 hp Pratt and Whitney Wasp; since restored with its 'Gulfhawk' livery, the aeroplane is now at the National Air and Space Museum's Silver Hill facility, Washington DC.

The short-span Grumman F3F modified for inverted flight was known as the G-22, and it later acquired a 1000 hp Wright Cyclone engine: Al flew it until 1948, taking it to Europe with him in 1938 to give displays in England and Germany. This

Al Williams's four Gulfhawks.
(a) Gulfhawk 1, *Curtiss Hawk 1A*   (Mike Jerram)
(b) Gulfhawk 2, *Grumman G-22*   (Mike Jerram)
(c) Gulfhawk 3, *Grumman G-32A*   (Smithsonian Institution)
(d) Gulfhawk 4, *Grumman G-58A Bearcat*   (Mike Jerram)

Flight Fantastic

historic aeroplane (NR1050) also can be seen on view to the public at the National Air and Space Museum.

There was also a third 'Gulfhawk' NC1051, a stretched two-seater version of the Grumman called a G-32A, in which Williams was able to travel with his engineer in the back.

Finally, from 1948 onwards Al's *Gulfhawk 4* was a Grumman G-58A, a version of the F8F-1 Bearcat, the first civilianized Bearcat to be licensed. It bore the registration NL3025.

Al held the post of Manager in Gulf's Aviation Department until 1951, but during the war years he spent all his leave from the company touring the United States as a technial consultant to the Army Air Forces, teaching and demonstrating combat technique just as he had done 25 years earlier in World War I, and refusing all payment.

The name of Al Williams remains forever synonymous with the National Air Races, and we shall shortly come to a survey of these famous aviation events which the great man helped to make uniquely memorable. Meanwhile, with the early days of the NARs in 1928, this is where the great Freddie Lund comes in.

Freddie was a one-time Hollywood stunt flyer and wing-walker for the Gates Flying Circus during the 1920s, where his billing was 'The Man Without Nerves'. He was known throughout the US as the best commercial stunt flyer in the country when in 1928 he joined the Advance Aircraft Company as test pilot for their Waco sport biplanes. In those first NARs of September 1928, held in Los Angeles, standard Taperwing Waco aeroplanes powered by Wright J-4B en-

Freddie Lund, Waco test pilot, here stands in front of a line of Taperwing Wacos. (Smithsonian Institution)

gines swept the board. Freddie literally stole the show with his aerobatics, while three other Taperwing Wacos finished second, third and fourth in the 75 mile closed course race and also placed first, third and fifth in the New York to Los Angeles race of over 2,500 miles.

Advance Aircraft had been making Waco biplanes since 1921 using welded steel tube for the fuselage which was far more rugged than the prevalent plywood structures. In a long line of successful designs, the Model Ten of 1927 outsold all its rivals and was already a proven market leader when, in 1928, the old OX-5 powered version was supplanted by a revised model using the more powerful 220 hp Wright Whirlwind J-5 nine cylinder radial.

Test pilot Charlie Meyers had meanwhile suggested the radical new departure of a set of tapered wings with a new aerofoil (the NACA M-6) which would make the model faster and sportier, and after tests a Taperwing Model Ten was brought out in 1928 as an alternative to the Straightwing. An extra bonus conferred by the wing design was outstanding aerobatic performance, which, coupled with the virtues of high speed, quick take-off and rapid rate of climb, soon made it the favourite American aerobatic mount of the 1930s. In particular, the machine's rate of roll was vastly improved not only by the reduced wingspan, but also by the tapered planform which reduced the rolling inertia by moving the centre of the wing mass inboard. Although other, smaller and lighter aerobatic designs might later come along to challenge its excellent manoeuvrability, the Waco Taperwing still had the edge on good vertical penetration thanks to its powerful engine.

Several versions were made, using a range of different

power plants, but the most popular always remained the Waco ATO: the 220 hp Wright J-5 Taperwing Model Ten.

After his triumph at the Races, Freddie determined to be the first civilian to emulate the famed negative looping performances of Jimmy Doolittle and Al Williams, using his Waco Taperwing. Over and over he tried, but somehow the aeroplane lacked sufficient speed reserves to get him up through the push from inverted. At last he figured that a special propeller would do the trick.

Now, propeller installed, he was ready to try again in front of the press. It was announced that he would give a 'special test performance' of the J-5 Taperwing X5673 overhead the Waco Airport at Troy, Ohio. The date was 20 October 1928. The employees had been let out early and flocked to watch the demonstration: they were not disappointed. Climbing to an altitude of 2,600 ft (800 m), Freddie started a long power dive and then half-rolled inverted, pushing up into a complete negative loop the way Al Williams had performed it – from the bottom up. He was so elated that he promptly followed the feat with a triple vertical flick roll, easily surpassing the 2 and 2½ rolls so far recorded up to that date! Then he ended by running through his entire repertoire of aerobatics, to the delight of the watching spectators.

After that, Freddie Lund and his smoke-equipped, red, white and blue Taperwing Waco became a legend of the 1930s, performing his outside loops at every airshow and aerial meet worthy of the name. And he featured other highly sophisticated aerobatic figures in his routine, including inverted spins, multiple snap (flick) rolls, a roll during the top segment of a positive loop – sometimes called a **Chinese loop** – and an 'inverted whip-stall', which we would nowadays

call a stick forward tail-slide. In this manoeuvre he would enter and exit the figure with an erect horizontal line, but after pulling up to the highest point of his vertical zoom and allowing the machine to slide back tail first, he would then push the stick smartly *forward*, thereby enabling his reversed elevator effect* to tip him over *backwards*, head first, into the final dive.

On 18 June, Freddie married the remarkable Bettie Elkins, who proved herself not only a wonderful marriage partner but also an excellent flying partner under his tuition: soon she captured several women's aviation records in her own right, as well as joining his air display act. The day after first going solo, she set a women's world record by performing 67 barrel rolls, straight off, in 28 minutes.

It is worth a moment's pause here to discuss the modern barrel roll, which appears for the first time in the 1930s under that name (a new usage of the term that was previously applied to the flick- or snap-roll in World War I).

The earliest European reference found by this author is an entry in the RAF's Flying Training Manual for 1937 which describes it as 'a slightly exaggerated form of the slow roll' (see Chapter 8); but in fact the two rolls could scarcely be more different. Whereas the slow roll revolves around its longitudinal axis whilst maintaining level flight and a constant heading, the barrel roll diverges off axis both laterally and vertically whilst combining a looping or arching trajectory with a rolling motion. And whereas the slow roll involves a

---

*Down-elevator from a forward stick movement will tip the aircraft's nose forward when the relative airflow is coming from the normal direction; but when the airflow comes from behind in a tail-slide, the effects of all the aeroplane's control surfaces are reversed.

Span   30 ft 5 in (9.27 m)
Length   22 ft 6 in (6.858 m)
Height   9 ft (2.74 m)
Empty weight 1,585 lb (720 kg)
Max speed   135 mph (217 km/h)
Rate of climb 900 fpm (4.5 m/sec)

Span   30 ft 5 in (9.27 m)
Length   22 ft 6 in (6.858 m)
Height   9 ft (2.74 m)
Empty weight 1,585 lb (720 kg)
Max speed   135 mph (217 km/h)
Rate of climb 900 fpm (4.5 m/sec)

This magnificent Taperwing Waco belongs to American airshow pilot Bob Lyjak (350 hp Wright R760). His astounding routine in the classic 1930 machine features a double flick roll on take-off, plus two spectacular figures all his own: the 'Cobra Roll' is a quasi-lomcovák started from positive with a vertically climbing flick roll which he then allows to somersault into a cascade of rolls; and the 'Polish Centrifuge' begins with a near-vertical positive half flick, whereupon the controls are fully reversed with negative flick inputs, stopping in the vertical attitude and continuing to move laterally with the accumulated inertia; it goes finally into a nose-down recovery.

(Larry Davis)

Flight Fantastic

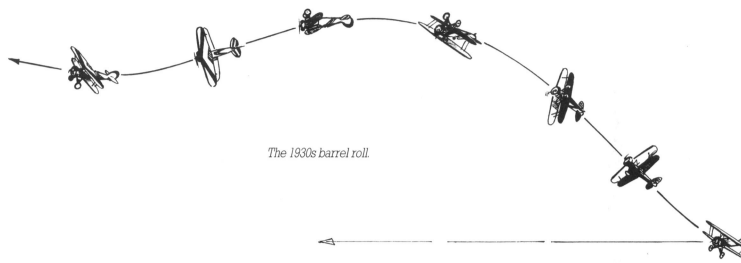

The 1930s barrel roll.

temporary transition through negative g in the inverted position, the barrel roll retains positive g throughout and is a very gentle manoeuvre on both pilot and aircraft.

The only significant thing about the positive-g barrel roll, in fact, is this strange duplication of the name for the flick roll! Nobody can remember when it actually got its name, but Jimmy Doolittle assures the writer, "It is true that, in the old days, we did two types of barrel roll: the snap-roll, in which the plane was stalled, and the other in which it was 'flown' through the roll. The snap-roll was first".

Being scarcely an aerobatic manoeuvre, it was quite popular then, as now, with the more inexperienced pilots. Press reporters used the term freely to refer to almost any kind of roll, so care needs to be exercised to ascertain which kind of manoeuvre they had in mind. In those Depression Years, anyone was doing anything that might attract attention and earn a buck or two, so barrel-rolling records began to be added to inverted flight, looping and outside looping marathons. After Bettie Elkins Lund set her record of 67 (having presumably learned the manoeuvre from Freddie), Laura Ingalls set the ultimate record in August 1930 with 714 barrel rolls in 3 hours 39 minutes in a 100 hp Gipsy Moth, beating a previous record of 417 by Dale Jackson.

It was only two months after the wedding, in August 1929, that disaster nearly struck as Freddie was about to perform his outside loop for a show at Cincinnati, Ohio: after half rolling and starting the push-up, his seat belt suddenly snapped. He was immediately catapulted right out of the cockpit, and was halted only by his shoulder coming into contact with the top wing! Hooking his feet inside the edge of the cockpit, he held on grimly while the aircraft rolled over in a (positive) loop and started down in a screaming dive, throttle wide open. While this was happening, he somehow fought his way back down into the cockpit again, climbed inside, and chopped the motor. Then, hauling back on the stick, he managed to pull out of the dive at 500 ft (150 m) and landed safely.

But though he had cheated death on this occasion, he lived only two more years before fate caught up with him in the form of a midair collision on 3 October 1931. During a race at Lexington, Kentucky, he rounded the home pylon just a little too close to a Monocoupe that was also cornering at about 100 ft (30 m) above the ground. The Waco's tail was sliced completely through by the Monocoupe's prop, and although he jumped, Freddie was far too low for his chute to open.

While the aviation world grieved at the loss of their foremost aerobatic pilot, his young widow Bettie bought herself a Taperwing and proceeded to fulfil every one of his airshow bookings that season. Then to commemorate his memory, the city of Miami established the Freddie Lund Trophy, the first annual trophy for precision aerobatics in America, which ran for ten years from its inaugural year, 1932.

But we shall come to the Lund Trophy in a little while. First let us look at some of the other great Waco pilots of the era.

Foremost on the list must surely be Joe Mackey, star of the Linco Flying Aces airshow team, whose exploits are described so evocatively in Bill Sweet's book quoted above.

Joe learned to fly in 1926 and soon decided that aviation was the career for him; by 1929 he was an instructor and exhibition pilot with the Curtiss-Wright Flying Service, and by

Joe Mackey, star of the Linco Aces airshow team. In 1953 he opened up Mackey Airlines in Fort Lauderdale, Florida, where he was later joined by Len Povey.

(Smithsonian Institution)

1930 he had branched out with a flying school and airshows on his own account. At the end of that year the Ohio Oil Company (Linco gas and oil) offered to sponsor Mackey and his team if they would advertise their products exclusively – which meant basing themselves at Findlay, Ohio, and carrying out a non-stop round of air displays, airport dedications, sky-writing and publicity stunts, using a sometimes hair-raising band of acro pilots, wingwalkers and sky-divers.

Among their equipment they featured a Curtiss-Wright Fledgling – a big, slow biplane trainer – which they rigged up with the words 'LINCO GAS' and 'LINCO OIL' in neon lights on the wing undersides. There was a big generator in the front cockpit and the pilot lit up the signs with a hand switch while he flew at night overhead fairs, fêtes and jamborees, with nothing more than a compass and a sharp lookout to get him into and out of unlit country fields.

Joe Mackey's Waco Taperwing, NR13918, was probably the most famous Waco ever. It was bought as an ATO in 1935 from the CAA with the registration NS25, and re-engined with a 330 hp Wright J6-9E which gave it a lot more power for sky-writing and aerobatics, thus transforming it to a CTO. Over the winter of 1935–6 the Linco team then decided to have the aircraft totally reworked: the fuselage was rounded out and metal covered by Hill's Streamline Company of Cincinnati, wheel spats (pants) were fitted to the main and tail wheels, and a new NACA cowling complete with streamline bumps for the rocker boxes replaced the original Townend ring which had broken off in flight and injured Mackey at the Dayton Air Olympics a few months before.

Meanwhile, Sweet and his engineer Fatso DeBolt rebuilt and recovered the wings, and chromium plated the struts, flying wires and exhaust collector ring. The whole aircraft was finished in white with red trim: it was magnificent.

In *They Call Me Mr Airshow*, Bill Sweet tells the irresistible story of how they came to pay John Hill for the job, who was one of the old school and – knowing the financial precariousness of aerial circuses – "wanted his cash right on the barrelhead". Mackey had therefore entrusted Sweet with $12,000 in dollar bills.

Since it made a wad big enough to choke an elephant, I didn't know how to carry it. I finally dug out an old gym bag I had, stashed the twelve thou in the bottom and covered it with some old socks and dirty underwear. Hill's office was typically dark and dingy, with a single bulb hanging in the center and the walls crowded with pictures of his previous jobs.... All the time we were loading the Taperwing fuselage, Hill kept fussing about the money, because he hadn't seen me bring in anything that looked like a money bag. When we went to lunch with him in his Lincoln Zephyr, I left the old gym bag sitting on his desk.

'I've got to have cash, Bill,' he again reminded me. 'If you haven't got cash you'll have to call Joe Mackey and arrange for a bank note!' He had parked the Zephyr so we couldn't move the truck!

I let him rant on while Taylor and I went through the motions of preparing to leave, as if we weren't really hearing him. When it looked as if Hill was about to call the sheriff to prevent our leaving, I finally told him to throw me that old gym bag. He tossed it at me like it was so much junk, then regarded me with a jaundiced eye while I pulled out the old socks and dirty underwear, one piece at a time. When I finally got to tossing greenbacks on the table, Hill almost went through the ceiling.

'You mean all that money was sitting on the desk while we went to lunch?' he asked. 'I didn't even lock the office!' The whole episode made him so nervous he had to pop into the anteroom and empty his bladder.

As soon as he came back, he again looked at me suspiciously. 'That's true money isn't it! That's not counterfeit, is it?' he said. His final comment, after I assured him it was genuine, was: 'You didn't touch that money while I was in the john, did you?' 'Count it,' I said, as Jimmy and I went out the door.

Mackey's immaculate customized Taperwing, NR13918.
(via John Underwood)

Milo Burcham with Boeing 100. Burcham later became chief test pilot for Lockheed.　　*(via John Underwood)*

1936 was a big year for Joe Mackey. During the month-long Kentucky Derby that spring, while the Linco Aces were doing their regular airshows and aerial advertising, a telephone call came through from the French Embassy in New York inviting Mackey to take part in a grand International Meeting in Paris. Without more ado he packed up and shipped the Waco to France aboard the USS *Washington*, arriving in time for the big show on 17 May at the famous Saint-Germain-en-Laye airfield. Only two American pilots had been invited, so it was a great honour for Joe Mackey. to be offered the all-expenses-paid trip along with fellow-countryman Milo Burcham. They were to fly in company with the French stars Michel Détroyat, Marcel Doret and Louis Massotte.

Although the event has sometimes been described as a contest, in fact there was no element of competition – except, of course, in a personal sense as between some of the world's top aerobatic aces. The Parisians loved the blond, cigar-chewing Mackey ('Mickey' as he was known to the crowd), and he came away with a fee of $8,000 for an eight-minute show, on top of full transportation and expenses, which was top money in 1936.

Milo Burcham, too, had been on the airshow circuit for several years, his speciality being upside-down flying in his 500 hp Pratt and Whitney Boeing 100 (P-12A). In his air circus days he was a past master of the 'lost wheel' gag in a Kinner engined Bird biplane, where at some strategic point in the afternoon he would 'lose' a wheel on take-off in full view of the crowd, and the commentator would ham up the drama of signalling frantically to the worried pilot. With tension at its highest and emergency services standing by, Burcham would cut the engine and come in to land, ground-looping (slewing around on the good wheel) to a halt and being bundled away to the first-aid tent, only to emerge a while later smiling and waving to terrific applause.

Of course, the trick was that he had the tiny tail wheel of a Monocoupe aircraft attached to the main gear axle inboard of the wheel that came off, and although it was only half an inch larger than the brake drum, it was enough for the aircraft to land quite safely – the ground-loop being initiated by Burcham for effect.

It was Milo Burcham who started off the *tour de force* of inverted flying at the 1933 NARs which ended as a duel between himself and visiting Italian pilot Tito Falconi (see Chapter 8). Although Falconi went home the winner in August 1933, with a record duration of 3 hours 6 minutes 39 seconds upside down, Burcham later topped this total with a world-beating 4 hours 5 minutes 22 seconds, in a specially rigged aircraft where the radial engine was actually installed upside down so that it would run the right way up when he flew inverted!

Another ingenious, as well as talented, pilot was Len Povey, famous as the inventor of the **Cuban 8**. He had started his aviation career as a mechanic in the USAAS in 1922, and, although an enlisted man, got himself transferred to flying training by special permission of General Billy Mitchell. On leaving the military he barnstormed all over America, joining the American Air Aces Show in 1933 flying Waco J-5 Taper-wing NC6711. In 1933/34 at the top of his form he won both the Freddie Lund Trophy and the International Aerobatic Competition at St Louis, Missouri; then during a show at the 1934 Miami Air Races he was spotted by a talent scout for the Cuban President Fulgencio Batista, and thus began a most extraordinary career.

Batista was looking for somebody to reorganize, build up and train pilots for his Cuban Air Force, and had sent a scout to Miami with orders to bring back the right man for the job. Povey was flying a special night-time act in the show,

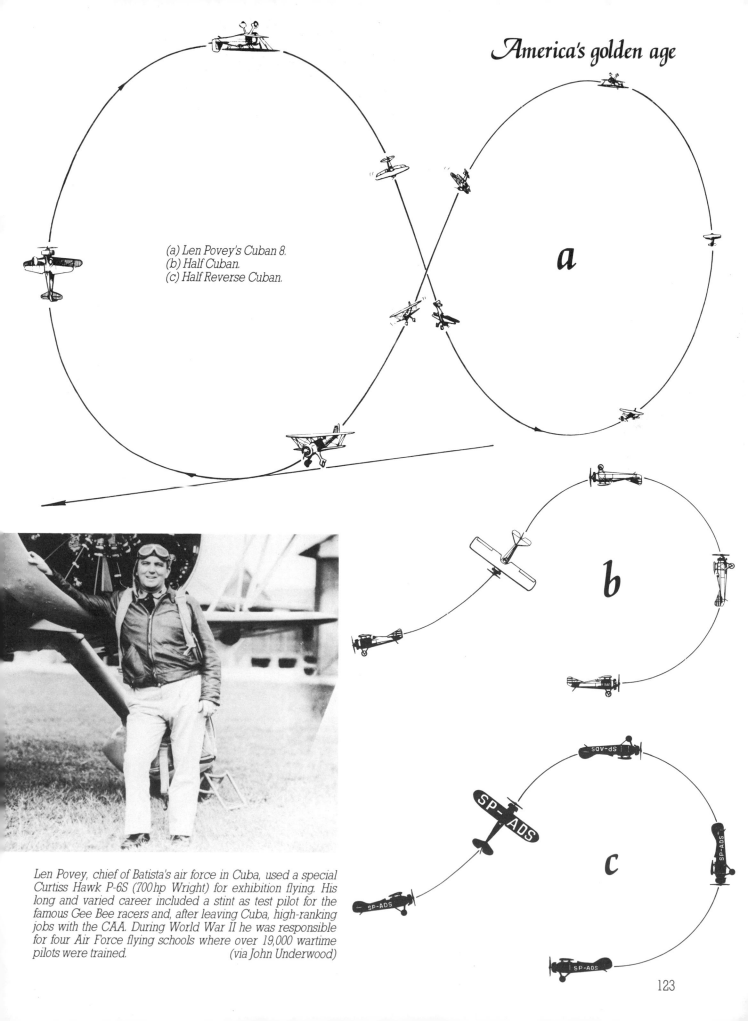

(a) Len Povey's Cuban 8.
(b) Half Cuban.
(c) Half Reverse Cuban.

a

b

c

Len Povey, chief of Batista's air force in Cuba, used a special
Curtiss Hawk P-6S (700hp Wright) for exhibition flying. His
long and varied career included a stint as test pilot for the
famous Gee Bee racers and, after leaving Cuba, high-ranking
jobs with the CAA. During World War II he was responsible
for four Air Force flying schools where over 19,000 wartime
pilots were trained.   (via John Underwood)

Flight Fantastic

featuring fireworks attached to his wings, which were pretty effective against the night sky. Len himself said later: "Cubans are emotional people and when he saw all the Roman candles and rockets exploding, he thought I must be the greatest pilot in the world." He was taken to Havana and engaged immediately, remaining for four years as head of the Air Force and as Batista's personal pilot.

It was during this time that he attended another of the Miami All-American Air Race Meetings in 1936, flying a multicoloured Cuban Air Force Curtiss Hawk (750 hp Wright), and once again entered for the Freddie Lund Trophy competition. During the freestyle event, when he had intended to perform a triple snap (flick) roll on top of a loop, Len recalled: "... somehow or other I got that Hawk up real clean and saw I had 140 mph indicated, which I knew was too much speed for the snaps, so I rode it on over and as I came down the other side I said to myself, 'Hell, I'll just put another end on this one'." (*Curtiss Hawks*, Page Shamburger and Joe Christy, Wolverine Press, 1972.)

What he did was to go into a Horizontal 8, but he jazzed it up a little by inserting a half-roll during the inverted downline after the first half of the 'spectacles', and then inserted a matching half-roll in the inverted downline after the second half, which made a very pretty figure indeed and one that seemed quite new to the onlookers.

When Povey landed, the question was on everyone's lips: "What figure was that, Len?" Thinking quickly, Povey answered, "That? Oh, that's a Cuban Figure Eight!" – and the name has stuck ever since. It even came to be used, at one time, as a generic name for any figure-of-eight manoeuvre, whether vertical or horizontal, plain or embellished with rolls. But its proper application is only to that Horizontal 8 with two half-rolls described above.

The figure now lends its name to other variations, one being the Half Cuban, which consists of the first half only of the 'spectacles', returning to a horizontal line instead of pulling up into the second loop; another being the Half Reverse Cuban, which sounds more complicated but in fact is again simply half the figure-of-eight, but this time performed from the end backwards and stopped once more on the horizontal line before the second loop is entered (see diagrams).

We should note, in passing, that Povey's original intention was to perform a triple flick roll at the top of a loop, an impressive figure which not many contemporary aeroplanes other than the high-powered Hawk could have handled. We have already seen in Chapter 6 how barnstormer Earl Daugherty was one of the first to perform the flick at the top of a loop with his Curtiss Jenny, though only with a single flick, of course, and then only just managing to get through it. Things had come a long way since then. Nowadays we would call the figure an avalanche, and the story of how this name was invented is told in Chapter 13.

Returning to the subject of famous Waco pilots, Freddie Lund's three-man 'Taperwing Stunt Team' helped bring to fame two more excellent pilots, Tex Rankin and Phil Love. Tex had taught himself to fly aerobatics after accidentally getting into an inverted spin with a Jenny, an oversight which he thought he should quickly rectify! He soon made a speciality of the negative loop, and started out on a series of record looping performances beginning with 19 consecutive 'outside' loops in 1930. A committee set up for the purpose decided that the criteria for Tex's loops to be counted should not only be the completion of loops without stalling or falling off to one side, but should also require the exit line to be not more than 30 degrees off the original heading. It was for reasons of an off-heading finish that 15 out of the total of 34 loops he flew on that occasion were disallowed.

In an article for *Popular Aviation* dated September 1930, Tex and Phil described 'How to do an Outside Loop' for the benefit of armchair aviationists. Phil Love, who had been first to perform the manoeuvre with a passenger (in a Taperwing Waco) recommended a start at about 100 mph (160 km/h) with the Taperwing, building up to 140 (225) at the bottom: this resulted in a loop diameter of some 1,000 ft (300 m), with very little height loss.

Tex, who was more closely identified with the Great Lakes biplane for most of his career, reckoned on starting the loop from level flight "with the stabilizer set clear down to make the ship nose heavy, with the engine wide open, and making

John G 'Tex' Rankin's Great Lakes, one of the earliest machines to display the pilot's name upside down on the fuselage   *(Smithsonian Institution)*

Large-tail Great Lakes belonging to Dr Dale Drummond, with Warner radial engine. (Dale Drummond, via IAC)

Original 25-1A specifications (with 90 hp American Cirrus III) were:

Span	26 ft 8 in (8.14 m)
Length	20 ft 4 in (6.20 m)
Height	7 ft 11 in (2.4 m)
Empty weight	1,102 lb (500 kg)
Max speed	106 mph (171 km/h)

a dive of 3,000 ft (900 m) around an arc of 1,500 ft (450 m)". This resulted in a net height loss of around 500 ft (150 m).

He later set the all-time record for outside loops by performing 131 of them in 131 minutes in a 90 hp Great Lakes. He was also a winner of the coveted Freddie Lund Trophy, and of the International Aerobatic Championships at St Louis in 1937, which he described in a magazine article shortly afterwards. Evidently there was a ten minutes time limit for the display, and with a catalogue of 87 manoeuvres to choose from, the art was to put together the maximum number of figures carrying the maximum difficulty coefficients. These coefficients ranged from 1 (for a spin, flick roll, etc) to 10 for the very difficult combination figures (such as any kind of Vertical or Horizontal 8 in negative flight, some with up to six or eight added rolls!). Rankin went through 20 alternate programmes before settling on one with an average difficulty value of 28.3 points per minute.

His most famous machine was probably NX315Y, a Great Lakes Special with 150 hp Menasco engine and ailerons on all four wings, whose performance was compared favourably to that of a Jungmeister. Another of his Great Lakes was fitted with the even more powerful 185 hp Continental, which sported Cessna gear and modified Aeronca Champion tail. This machine met its end many years later along with its eventual owner, Paul Maguire, who collapsed both right-hand wings in front of NBC television cameras as he pulled too hard into a square (four-point) loop.

Various types of hesitation loop can be formed in place of the ordinary circular loop (see diagram), but the square loop is probably the most popular. Airshow promoter Bill Sweet credits its invention to famous aerobatic pilot 'Squeek' Burnett. Unfortunately the description 'square' can be misleading: no aeroplane is able to perform square corners, and in attempting to do so more pilots than just Maguire have overstressed and destroyed their machines.

Before leaving Tex Rankin, we must first briefly examine the Great Lakes aerobatic biplane, which first saw the light of day in 1929 as the 2T-1 with straight wings, and later appeared as the 2T-1A (90 hp Cirrus III) or 2T-1E (95 hp inverted Cirrus Hi-Drive) with the upper wing swept back 9 degrees. It was a small – unusually small – two-seater constructed from welded steel tube with fabric covering, and achieved enormous popularity in the United States for its aerobatic manoeuvrability. Hit by the great Depression, it only remained in production for 3 to 4 years, during which time various factory models were produced with changes in the tail, the fuselage width, the cowling, and the dihedral of the upper wing. The model with larger vertical tail surfaces was not given a separate designation, but was simply referred to as the 'Large Tail' as opposed to the 'Small Tail'.

As with the Bücker Jungmeister, the popularity of the design survived World War II and many Great Lakes were re-engined with Lycomings, or – a very happy arrangement – with 160 hp seven-cylinder Warner Scarab radials. The wide

Flight Fantastic

a

b

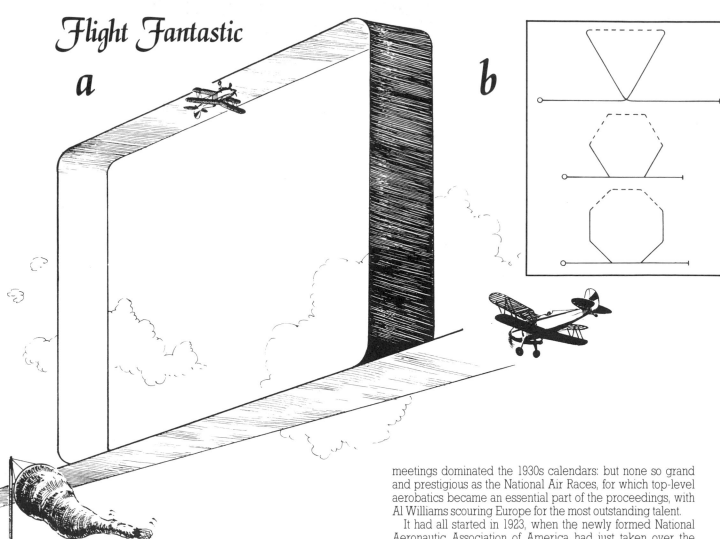

(a) Square loop. After starting with the basic circular loop, other geometrical shapes can be flown by the technique of 'hesitating' – showing a brief line – between the various cardinal points. Thus the square loop is better described as a four-point loop, especially since square corners are impossible in an aeroplane (as Paul Maguire and many more like him have tragically proved).
(b) Three-point, six-point and eight-point loops.

fuselage of the 'Large Tail' fairs neatly into a Fairchild 24 cowling around the Scarab.

Even more remarkable is the fact that with such a demand for these classic little open-cockpit aerobatic craft, an enterprising company went out and acquired the manufacturing rights in 1972 and set itself up as the Great Lakes Aircraft Company, which now produces a fully certificated Lycoming engine version. Or you can build your own from plans.

There were so many outstanding aerobatic stars of the 1930s in America that of necessity only a few can be included here. Most of them started out barnstorming and most of them also enjoyed air-races, whether the big cross-country events, the thrilling closed-circuit pylon chases, or the relatively low-key races staged between members of the same flying circus during the course of an airshow. Air-racing was enormously popular with the crowds as well, and several annual race

meetings dominated the 1930s calendars: but none so grand and prestigious as the National Air Races, for which top-level aerobatics became an essential part of the proceedings, with Al Williams scouring Europe for the most outstanding talent.

It had all started in 1923, when the newly formed National Aeronautic Association of America had just taken over the conduct of all air racing. During the first week of October at Bridgetown Airport, St Louis, the 'International Air Races' took place, with Al Williams winning the Pulitzer Trophy, and entertainment being provided by the legendary Gates Flying Circus. One of their acts, Cloyd P Clevenger, had a show-stopping finale where he dived to within a few feet of the runway, cut the engine, and zoomed up almost vertically into a tail-slide without power. After hanging momentarily nose-upwards, he would slam the stick back to bring the nose down again and drop lazily into a three-point landing! (Inevitably, of course, a time had to come when it would go wrong: attempting to recover from a height of about 10 feet one day, Clevenger dropped like a pancake and the aeroplane crashed and folded up. He walked away unhurt.)

The first 'National Air Races' were from 2 to 4 October 1924 at Dayton, Ohio, and the following year they were held at Mitchel Field (8–12 October 1925), when the great Pulitzer Trophy series came to an end after its sixth year. On the latter occasion, the Gates pilots 'attacked' New York with their brightly painted biplanes, looping, rolling, diving and spinning down to within a couple of hundred feet of Broadway, Times Square and Central Park!

In 1926, from 4 to 11 September at Model Farms Field, Philadelphia, there were nineteen race events in the NARs with 215 entrants participating, besides contests for other aerial sports including parachute jumping. The following year, on 19–25 September, 1927, the races were held at Spokane, Washington. Entertainment continued to be provided by the Gates Flying Circus, the longest-running aerial circus outfit of them all.

Speed Holman with Laird LC-R Speedwing Mailplane (220 hp Wright), which he used for racing and aerobatics. Holman was a great aerial circus star from the early twenties and won a 'stunt flying' contest at the first ever NARs in 1923. He broke the world's looping record in February 1928 with 1,433 continuous loops performed in the space of 5 hours at St Paul, Minnesota. (Smithsonian Institution)

By 1928 the event had grown much bigger and was held at Mines Field, Los Angeles. This was where the new Taperwing Waco aeroplanes stole the show, not only with outstanding race victories but also in the masterly aerobatic displays given by their new test pilot Freddie Lund. The daily shows also featured formation aerobatics performed by an Army team of Boeing PW-9Ds, 'The Three Musketeers', and the Navy's 'Three Sea Hawks' in Boeing F2B-1s. The Navy flyers had a sensational routine of close-formation manoeuvres, often inverted and at heights below 100 feet; this encouraged the Army team to bring their own show down lower, but the attempt led to death when their leader, Lt J J Williams, hit the ground in an inverted dive across the airport. His place was ably taken for the rest of the week by Army Reservist Charles 'Slim' Lindbergh, who the previous year had rocketed to fame as the first pilot to cross the Atlantic single-handed.

In 1929 (24 August–2 September) the NARs moved to Cleveland, Ohio, which ever afterwards became synonymous with the event. Over half a million paid to watch, and countless thousands more saw the flying from vantage points outside. By now there were nine cross-country derbies and 27 closed-circuit races for aircraft of every conceivable type. In the five-lap free-for-all race a civilian machine, the sleek Travel Air Mystery Ship, won immortality by beating Army and Navy opposition for the first time.

This year's display saw formation aerobatics from Freddie Lund's three-man Taperwing Stunt Team, and triple-engined aerobatics from Charles 'Speed' Holman in the massive Ford Trimotor, who had the crowd rubbing their eyes as he flew low-level loops – including outside (negative) loops – and then an inverted pass in the huge passenger carrier. It was this year also that Al Williams first graced the NARs with his beautiful and artistic aerobatics – while Jimmy Doolittle, in marked contrast, pulled the wings off his Hawk in a practice flight! During all this, a certain race pilot by the name of R W 'Bert' Mackie got so excited by it all that he roasted off into the sky to give an impromptu (and strictly unauthorized) exhibition of outside looping with a borrowed Taperwing.

Accounts varied as to how many loops he completed, but Mackie himself claimed eight in a row, after an initial practice loop away from the field, thereby beating Al Williams's previous record of six. He then turned the whole thing into a publicity stunt for Taperwing aeroplanes which the Waco manufacturers were quick to put to good account!

The 1930 event was even bigger, with the NARs held from 23 August to 1 September at Chicago. The previous year had introduced a women's long-distance race, and now for the first time women's closed course events were also included. Winner of no less than five races, with pylon-shaving vertical turns, was an unknown young airmail pilot who had brought along his own tiny low-wing homebuilt which he called 'Pete'. This was the phenomenal Ben O Howard, who even flew his 90 hp little sparrow to third place in the inaugural Thompson Trophy unlimited race. Marine Captain Arthur Page appeared to have the race in the bag with his powerful new parasol-design 700 hp Hawk, but crashed fatally in the seventeenth lap after being overcome by carbon monoxide fumes; Speed Holman became the first Thompson Trophy winner in Matty Laird's first purely racing machine, the 470 hp Laird Solution biplane. Holman was to die tragically in a crash the following year when his seat-belt came undone during a low inverted pass in front of thousands of spectators. The Speed Holman Aerobatic Trophy was established in his memory.

The 1930 aerobatic displays, too, were the greatest ever: Williams and Doolittle put on their usual superb shows, and from Europe Al Williams had brought over Fritz Loose from Germany, Pietro Colombo with his Breda 19, and French star Marcel Doret with his all-metal Dewoitine D 27. From England came Flight Lieutenant 'Batchy' Atcherley with the new Blackburn Lincock biplane fighter, and all the visiting pilots found themselves travelling together on the ocean liner *Leviathan*. On arrival they were given places of honour in a two-mile long procession through the streets of Chicago, with confetti, streamers, flowers, aeroplanes buzzing overhead and no less than five bands playing!

In 1931 the Thompson Trophy was joined by the new Bendix free-for-all cross country race from California to Cleveland, where the NARs took place from 29 August to 7 September. Jimmy Doolittle won the Bendix Trophy and at the same time set a new coast-to-coast record averaging 217 mph (350 km/h) in Matty Laird's new souped-up Super Solution. In the Thompson event the great 1930s purpose-built racing ships began to appear, the Gee Bees, the Wedell-Williams, the Lockheed Altair and, of course, Ben Howard's 'Pete'. All were monoplanes (except for three Laird

The international aerobatic pilots at the 1932 NARs. (L to R): Richard Atcherley (UK), Placido d'Abreu (Portugal), Jerzy Kossowski (Poland), Andrea Zotti (Italy), Emil Kropf (Germany), Jean Assolant (France).   (Smithsonian Institution)

machines), and the winner was Lowell Bayles flying the black and yellow Gee Bee Super Sportster, powered by the ever popular Wasp Jnr engine.

Once more, a galaxy of European stars came over at Al William's behest for the air displays: Orliński from Poland, Kubita from Czechoslovakia, de Bernardi the Schneider Trophy winner from Italy, and the great Udet from Germany, specialist in stunning ground-floor aerobatics which the crowd adored. Invited back for a second time, Atcherley from Great Britain sailed for America with Ernst Udet and they cemented a lasting friendship.

When Atcherley's Lincock was assembled on arrival, the omission of an important bolt from the undercarriage resulted in one leg of the aircraft coming completely adrift and, inevitably, a crash. Batchy later hazily recalled himself falling out and staggering away from the machine, then turning to join the milling throng which had soon gathered, all searching fruitlessly for 'the body'. "I was so dazed myself that I did not know what we were looking for, but was keen to join in. Eventually someone on whom I inadvertently bled gripped my arm, and I was soon in an ambulance en route for the local 'blood box'!"

Not to be left out of the show, Atcherley was soon airborne again in a borrowed Curtiss Fledgling and performing an outrageous 'crazy flying' act, bouncing like a grasshopper and splashing in puddles with his wingtips as he darted, twisted and sideslipped to the delight of the crowd.

Back in Cleveland again, from 27 August to 5 September, the 1932 National Air Races brought out both new and tried designs from the Gee Bee, Wedell-Williams and Ben Howard stables to combat for the Bendix and Thompson Trophies. Jimmy Haizlip won the Bendix in a new Wedell-Williams and in the process set more speed records, beating Doolittle's coast-to-coast time by 57 minutes. In the Thompson Trophy the Bob Hall designs (Gee Bee R-1, R-2 and Hall Bulldog) for the first time featured variable pitch propellers whose advantages (see page 135) were immediately apparent as they pulled rapidly away. Jimmy Doolittle, flying the even more powerful new R-1 Super-Sportster, romped home in a record Thompson Trophy time of 252.7 mph which remained unbeaten for four years.

A new event was the White Eagle Trophy for a 'mile-high' vertical race, which was won by ex-World War I pilot Art Davis, a famous airshow performer and exponent of the Taperwing Waco. One airshow act of his was to hook a flag with his wingtip from the wing of another aircraft as the two of them flew low in front of the crowd. Art climbed his 300 hp 'Question Mark' to a height of one mile and then dived almost vertically to the finish line, located at a height of 40 ft (12 m) right in front of the panel of judges, who timed his entire climb-and-dive operation at 3 minutes 11.85 seconds. Whether the Trophy was ever contested again I do not know, but I doubt whether any judge officiated twice!

The international aerobatic line-up for 1932 featured the popular young Placido d'Abreu from Portugal (later to die in the 1934 World Championships in Paris) and the Italian pilot

Trophy at his third attempt, flying a 900 hp Wedell-Williams. Wedell-Wiliams models practically swept the board in 1933, with Jimmy Wedell capturing the Thompson Trophy as well, after Turner had been disqualified for pylon-cutting.

In the aerobatics arena, Ernst Udet again mesmerized the crowd with his low-level show which, although not exhibiting the power and pzazz of the high-performance American

1932 National Air Races programme. (Smithsonain Institution)

Andrea Zotti (Breda 19) whose remarkable inverted flying included negative spins and low-altitude Immelmanns. Col Jerzy Kossowski, famous as an aerobatics and formation flying expert, came from Poland; racing pilot Jean Assolant represented France; and Emil Kropf came from Germany. The ever-popular Batchy Atcherley was demanded once more, and this time dreamed up a new stunt with the Curtiss Fledgling which involved fixing a saddle to the fuselage behind the cockpit, and riding the aircraft from this position complete with costume of hunting pink! Working the rudder cables outside the fuselage with his stirrups, and with the aid of an extension built on to the joystick, he was able to put on a fantastic display not only of straight and level flying but of aerobatics too – though of course he had to be tied on, and ended up extremely saddle-sore!

The 1933 NARs at Los Angeles were totally revamped, shortened to four days (1–4 July) and restricted to free-for-all events for purpose-built racers only. The enormously popular Roscoe Turner, airshow star *par excellence* who sported a natty uniform and waxed moustache, won the Bendix

machines, nevertheless brought his marvellously skilled manoeuvrings right down to eye-level for the grandstand audience. The Italian Tito Falconi displayed his skill in inverted flight – and embarked on a running battle with Milo Burcham for inverted endurance records – and film stunt pilots Frank Clark, Paul Mantz and Jack Rand, the 'Hollywood Trio', produced some extremely tight formation work in their red, white and blue Travel Air biplanes. Clark thrilled the crowd by spinning down from only 600 ft (180 m), pulling out just in time to run his wheels on the ground before zooming upwards again.

In 1934 the NARs again returned to Cleveland for the four days 31 August–3 September. Doug Davis, 1929 free-for-all winner, won the Bendix in Jimmy Wedell's Wedell-Williams 44, Thompson Trophy winner of the previous year. Jimmy himself had earlier lost his life in a training crash, and soon Doug would tragically join him as a result of a handling accident – no-one knew why – in the eighth lap of the Thompson race. It was won by the ever-popular Roscoe Turner, the first of Roscoe's three Thompson Trophy victories.

Aerobatics entertainment was supplied by the Army's

Flight Fantastic

formation trio 'The Men on the Flying Trapeze', voted the best airshow act, with Milo Burcham as runner-up with his elegant and precise performance in the Boeing 100. Burcham was one of the few American aces who extended his operations to Europe, where he was highly regarded both in display and competition. To add to the fun, Batchy Atcherley appeared masquerading as 'Professor Charles Beresford-Smythe of Oxford University' who had worked out 'a new theory of flight' and insisted on taking off complete with top hat and morning dress to put his ideas into practice – falling all over the place, of course, and thrilling the crowd with near-disasters of every kind. From France came Michel Détroyat with his Morane-Saulnier, and from Germany young Gerd Achgelis with the Focke-Wulf Stieglitz. And these, the cream of the world's aerobatic stars, were mere *hors d'oeuvres*, remember, to the great racing bill of fare!

Again in Cleveland, 30 August–2 September, the 1935 NARs went down in history as the 'Benny Howard NARs' – he captured both the Bendix and the Thompson Trophies with his four-place high-wing cabin monoplane 'Mr Mulligan' and the Greve Trophy with the smaller, three-year-old 'Mike' (these last two races piloted by Harold Neumann, a keen aerobatic pilot who still flies in competitions to the present day).

Another star-studded aerobatics bill included more North American acts this time, with WWI ace Dick Granere from Canada joining Americans Milo Burcham, Harold Johnson with the Ford Trimotor, and Al Williams with his Gulfhawk. Williams pulled a new figure out of the hat which was described in *National Aeronautics* as an 'inverted snap barrel roll', and this seems to have been the first public demonstration of a negative flick roll. It is such a pity that we do not know how it featured in his routine.

From Europe once more came Gerd Achgelis, and Michel Détroyat again entertained with his smooth, fluid style of aerobatics; but he came away with his heart set on returning next year to contest the racing events....

... And in 1936, as good as his word, Détroyat returned to America for the NARs in Los Angeles, 4–7 September, winning both the Thompson and Greve Trophies with his Caudron C-460 (340 hp Renault), the same aeroplane which had set a world landplane speed record of 314.2 mph in 1934. Louise Thaden and co-pilot Blanche Noyes cruised home to an easy win in the Bendix race with their 420 hp Wright-engined Beechcraft. Film pilots Frank Clarke and Paul Mantz (the 'Hollywood Duo') demonstated the first 'mirror formation', but with a difference – they attempted to touch wheels in flight! Mantz flew his Boeing 100 inverted while Clarke flew upright in a Travel Air D-4000 painted with camouflage to represent a World War I Nieuport.

Gerd Achgelis was back again, this time with D-IKNI, his Focke-Wulf Fw 56 Stösser (Falcon Hawk) with 240 hp Argus, and Détroyat with his Morane joined him in the daily aerobatic demonstrations; but the scene-stealer of 1936 was without doubt the new little German aerobatic biplane, the Bücker Jungmeister. Romanian pilot Alex Papana had brought the machine over on the airship *Hindenburg* for the occasion, and enjoyed himself so much that he decided to stay.

The Jungmeister made such an impact in America that it would be not far from the truth to say that every aerobatic pilot who saw the machine immediately desired one for himself. Its performance was fast and responsive, its controls beautifully harmonized, it was stable and controllable and

Alex Papana introduced the Jungmeister to America along with many new aerobatic manoeuvres including the 4-point and 8-point hesitation rolls. (John Underwood)

perfectly-behaved on take-off and landing. Above all, with its short span swept-back wings and double ailerons it was highly manoeuvrable and had an outstanding flick-roll performance.

Papana was back again at the 1937 NARs in Cleveland (3–6 September), where Frank Fuller won the Bendix in a 1000 hp Seversky P-35 and Rudy Kling won the Thompson and Greve Trophies in his Menasco-engined Folkerts. By now another famous Jungmeister pilot, Count Otto von Hagenburg, had crossed the Atlantic to join Papana at the Races, and the two of them enacted a fantastic aerial rivalry which the media played up for all it was worth. Bill Sweet describes the scene in *They Call me Mr Airshow*.

Papana triggered his ship into an explosive series of snap-flick rolls and the first 'point' or sectional rolls seen in this country. The German would then counter with bold and daring low-level, grass-clipping passes with vertical climbing four-point sectional rolls*, capped off with a hair raising inverted spin recovery at race-pylon altitudes.

You would expect this kind of duel to end with one or the other finally pushing it too far, so it wasn't a great surprise when von Hagenburg finally tried too low an inverted pass and came to grief. Flying inverted right on the grass, the Count pushed his stick forward slightly and dug his tail into the ground. His rudder and vertical fin dug a deep furrow in the soil, which stalled the aircraft and it settled to the turf, sliding along on its upper wing panels, engulfed in a cloud of dust. As proof of the Jungmeister's structural integrity, von Hagenburg suffered only a few minor head cuts and about a half-hour later he was paraded before the crowd from the back seat of a white Cord convertible, his head swathed in a turban-like bandage.

The Jungmeister, D-EEHO, rolled itself into a ball, but von Hagenburg calmly borrowed Papana's machine and went on to complete his act! Back home the following year, the German ace won an international competition at Saint-Germain-en-Laye, Paris, against the Czech champion Novák and the Frenchman Cavalli.

Alex Papana was a great sportsman and had been captain of the Romanian winter sports team, a record-holder in cycle and auto racing, and national tennis champion. He won many hearts and appeared at countless air displays in the United States with the Bücker before the machine was sadly involved in a collision on the ground in 1940, at Chicago Midway, with a US Marine Boeing P-12. Papana was just taxiing out to the runway when the Boeing hit him from behind, and although he managed to leap out in time, YR-PAX was two-thirds destroyed by the impact.

Papana continued to fly in the US with a Taperwing, while the remains of the coveted aeroplane were bought by star aerobatic pilot Mike Murphy, who meticulously rebuilt the machine (see below).

Only two more NARs were flown before World War II, both taking place in Cleveland during the first week of September. Jacqueline Cochran won the Bendix in 1938 and Frank Fuller in 1939, both flying Seversky P-35s, and the Greve Trophies went to Tony LeVier ('Firecracker') and Art Chester ('Goon') respectively. Tony was another ex-airshow performer who turned to racing, later to test-piloting, and we shall meet him again later in connection with each of these two activities.

Also in 1938–9 Roscoe Turner made history by winning the Thompson Trophy twice in succession with his Turner Special design, which featured a mid wing and symmetrical aerofoil: this made him a three-times winner. Resplendent in powder-blue uniform, Sam Browne belt and riding boots, and

Three times Lund Trophy winner Mike Murphy, with the Bücker Jungmeister that once belonged to Alex Papana.
(Smithsonian Institution)

always accompanied by his pet lion Gilmore, Roscoe had had a long career as World War I pilot, barnstormer, movie stunt-man and exhibition pilot, and wisely decided to retire from his favourite activity – air racing – while he was still on top. He opened a flight training school at Indianapolis Airport.

Al Williams had been spending a lot of time in Europe, especially Germany, and the aerobatic shows in 1938 had a heavily German orientation. They included von Hagenburg and Papana again on Jungmeisters, Emil Kropf displaying the extraordinary STOL qualities of the Fieseler Storch liaison aircraft, and test-pilot Hanna Reitsch who gave impressive displays with the new Habicht glider, including negative loops and flick rolls. From America Tex Rankin performed beautiful aerobatics with his Menasco Great Lakes, enhanced by a smoke system pouring out pink smoke. And Harold Johnson appeared with his six-ton 'Tin Goose' Ford Trimotor (220 hp Wrights) and outdid Speed Holman's displays of 1929–30 by looping, spinning and flick-rolling the 14-place passenger airliner, which he would then bring in to land on one wheel, dragging a wingtip! Bill Sweet describes him at the NARs doing "hammerhead stalls, Cuban 8s, spins from a starting altitude of 1,000 feet, snap rolls at 350 feet, then three consecutive loops, the last one starting at 25 feet above the

---

*Sweet's memory is at fault here. Count von Hagenburg could never have performed four-point vertical rolls in the Jungmeister, although he can certainly be credited with the first knife-edge to knife-edge 360 degree (horizontal) flick rolls.

Flight Fantastic

ground!" He says millionaire Henry Ford once paid Johnson $10,000 for a 30 minute private performance.

Also at the 1938 NARs as one of the featured performers was a giant of American aerobatics who remained associated with the sport for more than thirty years: Mike Murphy. 'Kokomo Mike' from Indiana started flying in 1927 and soon began earning his living as an instructor; then in 1930 he revived the abandoned Kokomo Airport and used it as a base for his barnstorming, exhibition and aerial advertising activities. When Joe Mackey went to France in 1936 Mike filled his place with the Linco Flying Aces, and eventually took over the outfit altogether in 1938.

He had already worked up some great aerial stunts during his barnstorming years, one of them being an upside-down aeroplane, built to fly and land that way, with main gear under the cockpit and tail gear a matter of inches below the tip of the fin. For effect, another set of undercarriage wheels was also installed pointing upwards in the 'normal' position!

Mike Murphy's 'Cheek to Cheek' aeroplane, built to fly and land upside down!   (Smithsonian Institution)

wheel into the wheel well of the 'car-top airport' and lock the brake, keeping the tail high, then aileron the other wheel in and lock it, finally closing the throttle on both car and aeroplane and letting the tail come down gradually with the deceleration.

Like many pilots Mike developed his aerobatic skills as an attraction to pull in the customers for aerial circus shows, but he became so adept that he soon started entering competitions and carrying off the prizes. His greatest successes came with the Bücker Jungmeister, an aeroplane in which he was never beaten: first he competed in Alex Papana's YR-PAX, loaned to him by the Romanian pilot; then in 1940 he became owner of the machine, which he bought as a heap of wreckage after the Chicago accident, whereupon it became NC15696. The same machine was eventually bought by Bevo Howard, and comes back into our story in Chapter 18.

In the late 1930s, competitions for precision aerobatics started to get more formalized in the US, and the foremost event of its day was the Freddie Lund Trophy held at the Miami All-American Air Maneuvers in December or January each year. This was an invitation contest for professional

His show at the Races included two well-established favourites: taking-off and landing on the runway with a twin-pontoon seaplane Cub, and 'The World's Smallest Airport', which involved flying a (wheeled) Piper Cub from a wooden landing rack bolted on to the top of a moving car. Not too tricky, perhaps – but landing it back there afterwards demanded quite some skill! Once the speed of car and aircraft were synchronized, the technique was to land one

exhibition pilots only, and as in most other American aviation events it formed only one small part of the general format of competitions, air shows and races. There was no set compulsory routine as existed in the European contests with their strict marking systems and judging criteria: in this competition every pilot flew his own individual programme, with smoke if he wished, and there were handsome cash prizes for the winners. Bill Sweet was in at the start of the event and bought the first Lund Trophy in a local Miami shop! Later on, of course, the whole thing became a lot more elaborate and was broadcast all over America on the nationwide NBC radio network.

There were ten such annual competitions, from winter 1931/32 to winter 1940/41, and the line-up of winners included R L 'Pete' Brooks (Monocoupe), Len Povey (Taperwing Waco CTO), Roger Don Rae (Taperwing Waco), Joe Mackey (Taperwing Wago), Vincent 'Squeek' Burnet (Travel Air), and Mike Murphy (Jungmeister) who won in 1937/38, 1939/40 and 1940/41.

After his third win, Mike Murphy took permanent possession of the Lund Trophy and a new award had to be thought up to replace it. At the 1941/1942 Air Maneuvers, scheduled for 9 January 1942, this was to have been the Peterson Aerobatic Trophy, named after Leonard 'Pete' Peterson, but unfortunately America's entry into World War II prevented the event from taking place, and Peterson was never commemorated as intended.

Bill Sweet described Leonard Roosevelt Peterson as "one of the first high-speed precision akro aces", making a clear

tored his performance by means of instruments – rate of climb, altimeter, etc. – while keeping a constant check with visual sightlines. He was master of all the aerobatic figures in the repertoire, and used to do the lowest outside loops imaginable. It was this predilection for low-level manoeuvres that eventually killed him, in a favourite trick that was uniquely his: he would perform a series of loops off the ground all along the runway, rolling the Monocoupe's wheels on the ground in between each loop. This called for an accuracy that left no room for error, and one day in 1940 at Richmond, Virginia, a slight miscalculation resulted in Peterson hitting the runway too low and the gear was wiped off, cartwheeling the aeroplane and killing the pilot immediately.

With the advent of World War II, men with aviation skills were at a premium, and Peterson, had he lived, might have had a career as glittering as that of a Jimmy Doolittle or a Mike Murphy. Murphy entered military service in 1942 and one of his tasks was in the planning of the Normandy invasion. He trained glider officers in Europe and personally led them on D-Day, when he was seriously injured and hospitalized for six months. On retiring from the service in

Leonard 'Pete' Peterson. Pete gave up being a Seventh Day Adventist minister to join the aerial circuses, flying this clipped-wing Dart G (145hp Warner). Later he flew a Warner-powered Monocoupe 110 Special.

(via John Underwood)

distinction between his scientific approach to the art and the aerobatic showmanship of pilots such as Mackey, Rankin, Burcham and others. Pete would meticulously work out the exact mathematics of all his manoeuvres, and carefully moni-

1945 he had among his many awards the Legion of Merit, Purple Heart and Air Medal.

He took a leading interest in post-war aerobatics both at home and internationally, becoming a delegate to the FAI's International Aerobatics Commission (CIVA) and an international judge at World Aerobatic Championships. He died at the age of 74 in April 1981, after having held the office of President of CIVA and being awarded the Gold Medal of the FAI, their highest award for contributions to international aviation.

10

Fighting another war

From the hotly-contested air racing of the inter-war years, one thing emerged conspicuously: the superiority in speed of the aerodynamically clean monoplane. Now the storm clouds were gathering once again: Spain was undergoing a civil war; Germany, Italy and Japan were re-arming and re-equipping; and the peaceful nations of the world were reluctantly – oh so reluctantly – being forced to reconsider their air defences.

With the experience of World War I their only guide, the existing air services had for the most part continued to use fabric-covered biplanes in the fighter and trainer rôle, content with aircraft that were little more than updated and up-engined versions of those flown in that first aerial war. But whereas then the watchword had been manoeuvrability, backed up with the best parameters of speed and ceiling that available technology could afford, from the early 1930s onward it became apparent that speeds of well over 300 mph (500 km/h) would be *de rigueur* in future fighter aircraft performance, which entailed a vastly different type of machine. With modern engines approaching the 1,000 hp range, and with modern airframe construction methods, there was a shift in emphasis from nimble, lightweight little harriers to powerful, all-metal gun platforms, moving at speeds that would run rings around the slower biplanes. Manoeuvrability counted for little if your opponent could always gun you down by simply outpacing you.

Hitler's Germany, arming a brand new Luftwaffe, had no legacy of left-over equipment and outmoded philosophy to hinder the search for better fighting machines. Under the Nazi regime, pilot training was carried out both at home and in one or two accommodating neighbour countries, at first in secret but later flaunted blatantly. The training of Lufthansa pilots at the German Air Transport School was used to cover bomber-pilot training on an enormous scale, for current

military theory decreed that the next war would be won by massive bombing. At Ernst Udet's urging, the Junkers firm started production of the Ju 87 Stuka dive-bombers in imitation of the Curtiss Helldivers. And fighters were needed as formation escorts for the bomber fleets.

In 1936, in response to rebel leader General Franco's request for aid, Goering's newly emergent Luftwaffe was able to use the Spanish theatre of war as a valuable test-bed for both tactics and equipment. Adolf Galland and Werner Mölders, two of Germany's greatest World War II aces, learned about combat technique and strategy with the Condor Legion and passed this knowledge on to their contemporaries. But the greatest lesson learned in Spain was the obsolescence of the biplane fighter. The German He 51s proved no match for monoplanes like the Russian built I-16 Rata fighting on the Republican side, one of whose pilots was the Spanish test-pilot and later aerobatic ace José Luis Aresti, whom we shall meet in Chapter 14.

Willy Messerschmitt had for some time been producing sleek monoplanes for sport flying and aerobatics, whose premier exponent was German Aerobatic Champion Willi Stör; and in response to Hitler's re-equipping programme his *Bayerische Flugzeugwerke* Company (bought from Ernst Udet) had begun work on an all-metal monoplane fighter, the Bf 109.*

There is a widely told and retold story of Udet's conservative reaction when he first climbed into the Bf 109 prototype: "... but my dear Messerschmitt, this will never do as a fighter – the pilot has to have an open cockpit, to feel the airflow – and you need another set of wings above, with struts between, and bracing wires...!" But on seeing the aircraft perform in comparative trials with other fighters, Udet to his eternal credit recognized a master-work when he saw it, and ordered production immediately. Supplies arrived in time to

*Though the aircraft is commonly referred to as the Me 109, historians decree that the 'Bf' prefix is correct, since 'Me' was not introduced until the company changed its name to Messerschmitt AG in 1938.

transform the German offensive in Spain; Galland had left by then, but when Mölders returned home he was an ace with fourteen victories.

Despite the untrammelled success of the various Junkers cantilever monoplanes even before World War I, the unbraced wing had always suffered from mistrust of its strength. Fokker's fabulous 1917 Dr1 triplane, which was also of cantilever construction, had interplane struts added to reduce both the vibration and the unnerving visible flexure of the wings when manoeuvring. Messerschmitt had long been a pioneer of high aspect ratio cantilever wings and light-weight construction, and his design for the 109 (based on the very successful 108 tourer wing) was thin, single-spar, and with a high wing-loading. Moreover, to increase the speed range and thus provide reasonable approach and landing speed, the wing incorporated an unprecedented amount of gadgetry – leading-edge slats, for example – which again unsettled the traditionalists. The whole design was built small, light and efficient, to suit the available (700 hp Jumo 210D) engine of the time, and it was very fast, as well as outstandingly aerobatic, with a turning radius of 750 feet (230 m).

Al Williams, who tried the Bf 109 on a visit to Europe in 1938, declared it to be the fastest and most manoeuvrable production fighter, and the only one he would exchange for his Gulfhawk. "I have seen the English Hurricane and Spitfire," he said, "but would choose the 109 every time." There are two points to be borne in mind here, however. First, Williams had not *flown* either of the British machines, and could scarcely have seen very much of them in his recent visit to England: indeed, he expressed the view that the Spitfire was "decidedly limited in manoeuvrability"!

And second, the wily Germans had given him the initial version of the Messerschmitt, which had never been designed for wing armament. By the time the subsequent Bf 109E entered the Battle of Britain, the wings had been modified to carry a 20 mm Oerlikon cannon installation. True, the more powerful Daimler-Benz engine of the 109E was an enormous improvement, but it also necessitated the addition of ducted radiators as another modification to the wings: all these changes altered their original aerodynamically clean concept, and further eroded confidence in their strength. Although the Messerschmitt had a tighter turning circle and faster dive speed than its opponents, in practice this was often counteracted by fears of losing the wings. Its pilots avoided high *g* in vertically banked turns and in pull-outs from steep dives, some pilots dispensing with the pull-out by continuing the dive under into a negative-*g* half-loop or bunt, half-rolling to normal flight after reaching horizontal.

Every fighter had its drawbacks, however, and the Bf 109 was an otherwise superb machine. The design concept was very advanced, for example the way in which it could be swiftly dismantled for maintenance; and it featured the very latest in airscrew technology with a constant-speed propeller – a British invention which had first been tried in a Gloster Grebe in 1927 (the Gloster-Hele-Shaw-Beacham VP system), but which did not catch on in Britain until its merits were realized in wartime, whereupon it was hurriedly retro-fitted to the fixed-pitch Hurricanes and Spitfires!

Varying the pitch (blade angle) of a propeller makes more efficient use of the power unit by presenting the blades' best angle of attack to the relative airflow, between coarse at the one extreme and fine at the other, to suit either high-speed/cruising or take-off/landing regimes. The constant-speed unit

permits an automatic blade adjustment to any pitch variation between these two extremes, thus providing the optimum blade angle to suit any given flight condition.

By means of a control in the cockpit, the pilot can use this variation of pitch to maintain pre-set propeller rpm which, within certain parameters, will remain fairly constant despite variations in power settings and airspeeds. Increases in power, for example, are rendered more efficient by the blades' adopting a coarser pitch rather than by rpm being raised. Increase in airspeed will produce the same blade reaction, thus helping to give the engine vital protection from overspeeding in the headlong power dives of combat.

Needless to say, in later days the constant-speed unit was to find its way into top-level aerobatics where aero engines are also made to work extremely hard. Although there is a certain sacrifice to be made in accepting the weight of the unit, with a CS propeller the pilot is able to use the throttle more as a power lever, without forever monitoring the engine rpm, while at the same time obtaining a quicker response and – most importantly – getting maximum performance from the power plant.

Another very great advantage of the Messerschmitt was that its excellent DB 601 engine, being fuel-injected, had the enviable capability of continuing to function under negative *g*. One favourite German trick when hard pressed in combat was to pull up into a normal half-loop and then, on reaching the inverted stage, to ease the stick forward and continue with an inverted climb under full power: no standard carburettor-fed fighter could follow on its tail beyond the top of the half-loop. This engine advantage also gave a snappier dive entry than the Merlins of the British, which would tend to miss as the nose was pushed down from horizontal. Here is the sensation of a negative push evoked by Hurricane pilot Peter Townsend:

… keep on pressing on the [gun] button until you think you're going to collide – then stick hard forward. Under the shock of negative *g* your stomach jumps into your mouth, dust and muck fly up from the cockpit floor into your eyes, and your head cracks on the roof as you break away below …

(*Duel of Eagles*, Weidenfeld and Nicolson 1970.)

Losing the engine at the start of the dive wasted precious moments for RAF pilots, until Rolls-Royce later solved the problem with the introduction of the Bendix-Stromberg carburettor. But the Merlin engine for which the Hurricane and Spitfire were expressly designed was unrivalled in its day and phenomenally reliable for the work demanded of it.

The Hurricane was the brainchild of Sydney Camm of the Hawker company. Tough, headstrong and brilliant, he had long been aware of the crying need to match the pace of German progress in aviation and had been experimenting with fighter designs. When working within Air Ministry requirements proved simply too stultifying, he had decided to write his own specifications and produce the best monoplane he could, using the best engine available: the Rolls-Royce PV-12.

The resulting prototype first flew on 6 November 1935. Its test pilot was George Bulman, one of the test pilots who with Roderic Hill at Farnborough had carried out inverted spin investigations fifteen years before. The new aircraft used Fred Sigrist's primary fuselage construction of bolted metal tubes with fabric over wooden stringers and fabric-covered

Bf109G fighter (1,475 hp DB605B1), displayed by aerobatic and test pilot Hermann Liese; the only 109 flying today with original Daimler-Benz motor.

At the Luftwaffe fighter trials, Messerschmitt's test-pilot confounded the pessimists, who were predicting that the prototype BF109 would spin flat once its spin became developed, by performing 17 turns to the left and 21 to the right, instead of the 10 required. He then executed a terminal velocity dive from more than 24,000 feet (7,315 m), pulling out almost at ground level!

(Messerschmitt-Bölkow-Blohm, via Hermann Liese)

metal wings. The fabric on the wings was replaced by stressed metal skin in early 1939, and a ventral fin added for better spin recovery; but by then it had already been in RAF service since December 1937.

Inferior in climb and speed to the Bf109E, the MkI Hurricane was much larger, with a 40 ft (12.2 m) wingspan against the Messerschmitt's 32 ft 6 in (9.9 m); but it was the more manoeuvrable aircraft, aided by the inward-folding landing gear and the wing armament grouped as close together and as far inboard as possible, which concentrated the masses in one centralized area. By reason of its braced wood construction, it could also withstand a great deal of battle damage and still limp home to fight another day – a virtue which endeared it to its many devotees.

It was light, easy to fly, and, as a gun platform, steady as a rock. It had a wide undercarriage (far more forgiving than either Spitfire or Messerschmitt) and an extremely short take-off distance: throttle open, tail up and you were airborne. The landing roll was a couple of hundred yards.

One spectacular method of approach and landing with the Hurricane entailed a half-roll to inverted as low as 800 ft (244 m) while you crossed the field downwind – mixture rich and pump the Ki-gas primer to keep the engine running – then put the undercarriage down (up!), propeller fully fine, throttle back and let the nose drop down to and through the vertical; now dump the flaps; and finally pull through to end the split-S with a flare out and landing that was guaranteed to

raise the hairs on the back of your neck. Naturally there was keen competition among those who practised this stunt as to who could make the lowest inverted approach, and some learned the answer the hard way. Thus, trial and occasional error showed the best approach height for the Spitfire as 1,000 ft (300 m), but with the Hurricane you could do it 200 ft (60 m) lower. Of course, the drawback (if you survived) was a sound ticking-off at the hands of officialdom, and maybe even a grounding for the next few days...

However, this split-S landing was a game played with the later and more powerful Marks. In the Battle of Britain period the early Hurricanes were powered by the 1,030 hp Merlin II or III upright-V in-line liquid-cooled engine (which also powered the Spitfires). The Hurricanes may have lacked some of the limelight given to the more glamorous Spitfires, but in the summer of 1940 they destroyed more aircraft during the Battle of Britain than all other fighters and anti-aircraft guns put together. To compare production numbers, altogether 14,230 Hurricanes were produced, compared with 22,759 Spitfires and Seafires, and some 36,000 ft Bf 109s.

Reginald Mitchell, the man who designed the Spitfire for Supermarine, had been a long-time advocate of the mono-plane concept and had designed the 1931 Schneider Trophy-winning S.6B seaplane in which Flight Lieutenant George Stainforth set a world speed record of 407 mph (654.8 km/h). Mitchell's genius was so obvious that the firm of Vickers bought up the Supermarine company just to obtain its chief designer's services.

After the Schneider Trophy triumph of his S.6B design, which won the trophy outright for Britain and put an end to the races, Mitchell turned his hand to trying out embryonic ideas for monoplane fighters, but he was already a sick man with the cancer that was eventually to kill him, and in 1933 was persuaded to take a holiday in Austria for the sake of his health. Introspective and deeply aware, Mitchell took note of the aggressive militancy that pervaded the youthful *Deutscher Luftsportverband* members, and was indelibly struck with a premonition of war: from that moment onwards he worked with feverish dedication, ignoring all exhortations

Hawker Hurricane prototype K5083 goes through its paces in service trials at Martlesham Heath, February 1936.

(Chaz Bowyer)

to rest, compelled by an overwhelming sense of urgency to build Britain a top-performance fighter with which to defend herself from the Nazi menace.

A little later to fly than the Hurricane, the Spitfire prototype first took wing on 5 March 1936 and RAF orders followed only three months later. Reginald Mitchell lived long enough to see the Spitfire fly, and to realize that he had built the successful fighter he had set his heart on. Despite his failing health he continued to collaborate closely with test pilot Jeffrey Quill during the initial testing; but he died in 1937, at the age of 42, without having the chance to see his Spitfire coming off the production line. It entered squadron service in June 1938.

Looking at the machines used in the Battle of Britain, there are equally sound claims for both the Messerschmitt and the Spitfire that each could out-manoeuvre the other, and the truth of the matter is probably that all else being equal they were pretty evenly matched in manoeuvrability. The Mes-

serschmitt was superior in the climb and the dive, and had the advantage of altitude as well. But the Spitfire was rated slightly faster on the level, with a top speed for the Mk I of 365 mph (587 km/h).

Continual modifications to engines and airframes produced ever higher performance values, of course, as the war progressed. It was not long before fighters of both sides, carrying a full warload with guns, ammunition, etc., were flying at faster speeds than the finest air racers the world could produce in peacetime only a few short years before.

Interestingly, the Spitfire's distinctive elliptical wing was a design change adopted by Mitchell only after the RAF specification had increased the wing armament from two to four guns on each side. It was his solution to the problem of keeping the breeches in line and at the same time making space for the outward-retracting wheels. The Mitchell wing was even thinner than Willy Messerschmitt's, but its large area made for lower wing loading, and the long chord (leading edge to trailing edge) gave it greater strength at the wing root.

The Spitfire was equipped with two sets of rudder pedals: the lower set was for convenience in normal flying, the upper

Battle of Britain Hurricane I fighter of 32 Squadron (1,030 hp Rolls-Royce Merlin III), returns from combat to land at Biggin Hill in August 1940.

(Chaz Bowyer)

Span	40 ft (12.2 m)
Length	31 ft 5 in (9.58 m)
Height	13 ft 3 in (4.04 m)
Empty weight	4,670 lb (2,120 kg)
Max speed	335 mph (539 km/h)
Rate of climb	5,000 ft (1,524 m) in 2.1 minutes

The superb lines of the Spitfire Mk I fighter (1,030 hp Rolls-Royce Merlin III), described by Henshaw as "a sheer dream; controls beautifully harmonized; positive and quick response; like a true thoroughbred, not a vice in the whole machine".

(Chaz Bowyer)

Span	36 ft 10 in (11.23 m)
Length	29 ft 11 in (9.12 m)
Height	11 ft 5 in (3.5 m)
Empty weight	4,332 lb (1,887 kg)
Max speed	387 mph (620 km/h) at 18,500 ft (5,600 m)
Rate of climb	2,300 fpm (11.6 m/sec)

The late Patrick Lindsay's Spitfire Mk 1A (retro-fitted with 4-blade propeller) pictured in its ideal setting on a grass airfield in France. In the cockpit is British Aerobatic Team member Tony Bianchi, the only Spitfire display pilot ever to perform Aresti style manoeuvres in the classic Battle of Britain machine. (Tony Bianchi)

set was designed for use in dogfighting so that the pilot's body was bunched up more in the cockpit against the effects of high *g*. 'Stirrups' or toe-straps helped anchor the feet against slipping during hectic manoeuvring, a feature that seemed to be found only in European machines. Though they seem small details in themselves, all these and many more refinements that were originally developed for combat flying have had a bearing on top-level aerobatics in later years, especially the question of seating position for greater *g* tolerance.

One aircraft type which may seem an unlikely influence at first glance is the Ju 87 Stuka dive-bomber. Nevertheless, we should spare it some attention in passing.

The special technique of dive-bombing entailed a near-vertical dive straight on to the target, in which not only the speed and accuracy of the dive but also its attitude were of critical importance. To enable the pilot to judge his attitude while diving, reference lines like those of a protractor were marked on the canopy at eye level, and the angle formed between these lines and the horizon gave the pilot his necessary attitude information.

In modern precision aerobatics, attitude is equally important to the pilot – though for very different reasons – and you will see just such reference lines taped to the canopy on a profusion of aerobatic aircraft. In some Ju 87s there was also a clear-view panel in the floor for better sighting, and this is another feature that has found its way into universal aerobatic usage. I am sure that today's pilots will be interested to know that these ideas began with the Stuka dive-bomber.

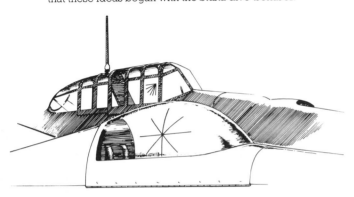

Protractor-style reference lines on Ju 87 Stuka canopy (background) compared with taped sighting guides on modern aerobatic machine.

Though the Messerschmitts, Hurricanes and Spitfires were all superb machines for aerobatics, the urgent requirement was for speed and maximum power during combat and this ruled out the kind of aerobatic manoeuvrings that were used during the previous aerial war. An RAF Handbook on fighter tactics advised: "Don't do stall turns and copybook aerobatics as evasive action. When your speed drops you are a sitter. Remember, skid and slip are good evasive tactics – but of course they ruin your own shooting, so use them properly and at the right time." Another piece of RAF advice suggested that a 'barrelled aileron turn' was very effective. 'Aileron turn' was a phrase which had newly arrived in aerobatics, and remained current only until about 1960. It referred to a descending slow roll in the vertical plane.

While discussing the aircraft and tactics of the RAF pilots, perhaps something should be added about the quality of the men themselves, and in this respect Peter Wykeham's words in *Fighter Command* (Putnam, 1960) can scarcely be bettered:

Air fighting is a personal business, and unless the pilot has the will to get to grips with the enemy the battle is more likely to elude him than he the battle.... The country was perhaps more fortunate than it deserved. The temper of the pilots, who seemed to laugh alike at conventional discipline and even at serious efficiency, proved equal to everything and was unimpaired at the end. The most professional of military corps, it was their conceit to pretend to appear as amateurs, and in fact their own Auxiliaries were indistinguishable from the regulars. In the words of the Official Short History 'they were the gayest company who ever fired their guns in anger'.

Beneath this casual pose lay a first-class training, excellent equipment, the tradition of the rebellious spirits who had first sought their fortunes in the air, and the discipline of comradeship, which is the strongest discipline of all.

Classic aerobatic technique continued to be a basic stock-in-trade of the fighter pilot, and the military trainers of the thirties had been designed very much with this in mind. But once the war was on in earnest, aerobatics were generally relegated to an occasional expression of high spirits in private, away from the pressures of battle. It was foolhardy, in any case, to stunt a machine which had just returned from combat (though sadly a few learned this lesson the hard way); and once the aircraft had been checked out and damage made good, your next sortie was more than likely another scramble and high-speed chase after enemy raiders.

In the test pilot's work, however, aerobatting was still a vital technique as it always had been since the days of Harry Hawker and before; not only for systematically testing the range of an aeroplane's performance, but also for the skills and quick reactions that would sort out a midair problem and perhaps save a valuable prototype without resorting to the parachute. And, of course, it was also his job to give demonstrations of the machine – the more impressive, the better!

The name of Jeffrey Quill will always be synonymous with the Spitfire, although Mutt Summers was the initial test pilot on the prototype, K.5054. It was to young Quill, Supermarine's gifted 'new boy' who had been plucked from RAF service, that all the years of experimental and development work then fell, from the prototype in 1936 to all subsequent Marks throughout the duration of the war. Even afterwards, he aerobatted 'AB 910 QJJ' around the airshows until as late as 1966 (when it was handed over to the Battle of Britain Flight), establishing a thirty years relationship between man and machine that must surely be unique in aviation.

Not merely a fine aerobatic performer, Quill has been called the finest pilot of his generation. Affectionately known as 'Mr Spitfire', he was the acknowledged master of displaying the machine itself, rather than showing off his own particular skills. His demonstrations were famous for their smoothness, polish and pinpoint precision. Afterwards, he wrote:

… flying the Spitfire was the greatest possible fun and I have seldom enjoyed anything so much as the two years during which we flew K.5054, whilst awaiting the emergence of the first production machine in May, 1938.

Writing about the Spitfire's first spinning test, he told how it had shown up badly in the spinning calculations made by the RAE, and there was thus "a certain amount of gloom" about its prospects of recovery; therefore one of the earliest anti-spin parachutes had accordingly been installed for the occasion. He entered the spin at 20,000 ft (6,000 m) "from a strangely silent stall with the big two-bladed wooden airscrew ticking over very, very slowly" – ready to use the emergency parachute if necessary – but happily the machine exhibited delightfully ladylike recovery behaviour and came out of the spin after two and a half turns. "The only difficulty we had with the prototype was persuading the RAE that the spin recovery characteristics were, in fact, perfect. It seemed they had no business to be."

Quill was surprised, however, by the Spitfire's longitudinal pitching during the spin itself, with the nose pointing almost vertically downwards at one point in the rotation and at another point rearing up above the level of the horizon. The rate of rotation also varied from fast to slow in the course of each turn, producing a series of 'convulsive flicks'. But, after personally carrying out the initial spinning trials on every Mark of Spitfire and Seafire thereafter, he reported that there was never a case of any production Mark machine failing to recover from a spin, despite making a great fuss about it all while the spin was actually in progress. (*Spitfire: A Test Pilot's Story*, John Murray 1983).

Though technically too vital as a test pilot to be spared for active service, Quill was convinced that if he was to recommend development of the aircraft, he must experience at first hand its use in squadron service. At last he managed to wangle a posting to 65 Squadron during the Battle of Britain, and claimed three Bf 109s. Later he flew with the Fleet Air Arm when the Spitfire was set to become the Seafire. As one of the 'fighter boys' himself, and speaking their language, he was Supermarine's best troubleshooter and must take credit for the constant improvements which kept the Spitfire in useful action throughout the war years.

In 1940 he reported thus on the machine's performance and the way in which it was used operationally during the Battle of Britain:

The Spitfire is being used very largely for engagements with enemy escort fighters.... That is to say, it is required to be a high altitude 'dog-fighter'.

In manoeuvrability the Spitfire is definitely superior to the Me 109 ... this owing to its small turning circle and low wing loading. Also the good lateral stability at the stall is a very great asset; in fighter engagements inadvertent stalls in steep turns are very frequent, and the fact that the Spitfire gives good warning and maintains good lateral stability in the most adverse circumstances is a very great advantage. The Messerschmitt pilots appear to be frightened of stalling and their usual evasive action is a half roll and dive away – the Me 109s being able to travel faster than a Spitfire in a dive.

The heaviness of the Spitfire ailerons in a dive is the major disadvantage of the aircraft and must be regarded as extremely serious. Immediate steps to remedy this should be taken as the importance of it, and its bad effect on both offensive and evasive action, cannot be over-estimated.

The aileron problem was not unique to the Spitfire, but was greatly alleviated when the fabric covered control surfaces were replaced by metal skinning. The aircraft had originally been designed for a maximum dive speed of 380 mph (611 km/h), and the aileron problem first appeared when the production models emerged with a stiffer wing and a maximum dive speed increased to 470 mph (756 km/h). Quill had the opportunity of testing a captured Bf 109E in October 1940 and was relieved to find the ailerons every bit as bad, if not worse. Also, with no rudder trimmer the foot-load in the Messerschmitt at high speed became very heavy. The official RAF report stated:

The flying controls have excellent response and feel at low speeds but are far too heavy for manoeuvring at high speeds. The extreme heaviness of the ailerons makes rolling almost impossible at speeds above 400 mph.

Another feature of the Spitfire which simply required mastering by the pilot was its marginal pitch stability, something with which pilots of modern specialist aerobatic machines are familiar. Inherent stability – the tendency for a craft to right itself once deflected from an 'even keel' – is obviously undesirable in a machine intended to be thrown into unusual attitudes and maintained there on purpose, so the preferred characteristic for greatest manoeuvrability is

one tending to neutral stability; this means the aircraft has to be 'flown' all the time, which needs getting used to. With this borderline stability the Spitfire's centre of gravity was therefore critical, and any loading or modification that affected it needed careful monitoring.

Later, test pilot and aerobatic champion Neil Williams described the ailerons as crisp, powerful and smooth, although in the dive they became stiff and heavy; the elevator was very sensitive and powerful, with more control than he had ever seen on any aeroplane before. "Looping is easy, but requires a light touch on the stick, too much back pressure and she shudders on the edge of a stall. Over the top she insists on fast accurate footwork to keep straight." The slow roll was really slow – except, as a wartime veteran had once told him – "You can't do a really 'slow' roll in a Spitfire, because the fuel endurance is only an hour and a half!" (*Airborne*, Airlife 1977.)

Alex Henshaw, a civilian pilot and well known air-racing record holder, joined the Supermarine company as a test pilot shortly after the outbreak of war. He was then sent to Eastleigh to join George Pickering and Jeffrey Quill, where

Spitfire development test pilot Jeffrey Quill, right, with George Pickering at Supermarine, Eastleigh, 1938.
(Jeffrey Quill, courtesy of John Murray)

he was introduced to the Spitfire and its testing. Then in 1940, when the great shadow factory at Castle Bromwich got under way, Henshaw was sent to take charge of production testing there while Jeffrey Quill remained at the main Supermarine Works at Eastleigh to concentrate on research and development.

From the beginning, Henshaw's approach was totally

Flight Fantastic

unorthodox and his nonchalant performance of aerobatics at the very minimum limits of altitude and visibility sometimes shook even Quill, but he recognized that Henshaw was 'a sort of aeronautical phenomenon' and came to regard him with amazement and respect. Especially he paid tribute to Henshaw's flight testing of the huge output of production Spitfires, often in dreadful weather, and of course with no let-down aids, radar or direction finding equipment.

Alex Henshaw was frequently called upon to demonstrate his aerobatic skills for the entertainment of visitors to Castle Bromwich, so let us leave him to take us through his display routine himself:

These demonstrations over the years varied according to the audience and the conditions. . . . As a rule the drill was to take off and not climb but pause with the wheels coming up and the machine just clear of the ground, and at 150–160 IAS* pull up slowly but firmly into a half loop finishing with a half roll at the top. I never really liked this as one cough from the engine and I should have been in real trouble; at the roll stage I was in any case holding the machine by maximum engine power well below the normal stall and the slightest coarse handling on the controls would cause the machine to flick out.

I would continue this in maybe another couple of half loops and rolls until I was over 4,000 ft and then placing myself in the correct position over the aerodrome, half roll again and go into an absolutely vertical dive with full engine and maximum revs to pull out a few feet from the ground and go into a vertical roll to the left, a vertical roll to the right and a half roll to the left with a half loop, then pull out to repeat the manoeuvre in the opposite direction. Pulling out in another half loop in the other direction, the throttle would be snapped back,

Alex Henshaw, right, pictured here with Czech RAF pilot Venda (Václav) Jicha.   *(Alex Henshaw)*

and plummeting down vertically one could get in two complete aileron turns to pull out again and open the throttle to do the same thing in the other direction.

Having now used up most of my height and speed, I would pull up vertically to about 1,000 ft and in a tight half loop at the right moment flick the machine into a full flick roll. This I always felt was a tricky one. It took a lot of judging to do it accurately, because very often the manoeuvre was so sudden and vicious that on checking the machine it would be sometimes slightly out of line and I knew it could look untidy. I could usually get one-and-a-half to two full flicks of a roll on the horizontal but for the sake of control and tidiness I usually settled for one, which I knew I could judge to a nicety. In practise I could get in about the same with the vertical flick rolls, but I found these almost impossible for me to judge when to check and to come out clean.

I have never seen anyone flick-roll a Spitfire and I must say that I always found it a little frightening to abuse a machine and have it flash out of your control, if only for a few seconds, like a young spirited blood-horse.

On the pull-out from the flick-roll, sometimes I would open the engine flat out in another vertical climb and at approximately 1,200 ft push the nose over forward and with the engine closed complete the half of an outside loop, usually in those days called a 'bunt'. I never really liked this manoeuvre either; it was easy but required heavy pressure forward on the control column and you could not afford to misjudge at 1,200 ft: with the nose going over down towards the ground the speed built up at such an alarming rate that it left no room to change your mind until it was too late. At the bottom of the inverted dive I would usually 'round off' to a few feet above the ground and then with as much pressure as I dare use on the control column – I say 'dare' because I found it more disconcerting and frightening to 'black-out' from excessive negative *g* than I did from high loads in the positive position – I would push the machine into an almost vertical climb and then as it lost momentum from the negative *g* position, pull the control gently over to form a half-loop, hoping as I did that the

*IAS = Indicated Air Speed as shown on the pilot's airspeed indicator. Relying as it does on outside air pressure for readings, this instrument can frequently give an underestimation of True Air Speed (TAS).

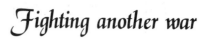

engine would burst into life as I opened the throttle. This it usually did with a spectacular sheet of flame pluming from the exhaust stubs, caused by unused fuel which had accumulated during the inverted manoeuvres. With the engine now on full power I would do a series of very low rolls left and right in front of the audience at below hangar height finishing in the inverted position, from which I would 'raise' the undercarriage, pull into a tight, fast engine-off turn, and lower the flaps as I touched down for the landing.

(Sigh for a Merlin, John Murray 1979)

Henshaw says in his book that these entertainments were something of a chore and tended to hold up the real work, although he was especially pleased to be able to fly for visitors such as Prime Minister Winston Churchill and, on one occasion, Michel Détroyat from France. Significantly, he notes that "ten minutes concentrated aerobatics was as taxing to my system as a whole day's normal test flying." Bearing in mind the fast and slippery performance of the factory-fresh Spitfire, as well as the spirited nature of his demonstrations – and their extremely low altitude – it is not hard to see why!

Sadly, none of us today will ever see a Spitfire flown like that. According to Henshaw, while he and Jeffrey Quill were flying together at Eastleigh it was more than common, especially at the end of a good day's work, for them to beat up the airfield below rooftop height, half-roll to inverted, lower the gear in this position, and then half-roll, flaps down and land, all in one smooth action.

On another occasion he described tail-sliding his Spitfire to shake off his pursuer during the course of a friendly 'dogfight', responding to a challenge from RAF pilot Venda Jicha, a top aerobatic pilot of the Czech Air Force who had made his way to England to fight the Germans. Jicha had bounced him and then remained stubbornly glued to his tail, so Henshaw pulled up vertically with full power, waited for his forward speed to fall to zero, chopped the throttle, and slid backwards with the propeller stationary before at last diving vertically down again – thoroughly unnerving Jicha, who was forced to the abrupt conclusion that following Henshaw's rear end was suddenly a most undesirable pastime!

We started this chapter with three classic aeroplanes which could never, of course, be omitted in any chronicle of aerobatic history. And to round off the list of favourite aerobatic warbirds, the North American P-51 Mustang must not be overlooked, together with its running-mate the Republic P-47 Thunderbolt.

The P-51 started life as a design created at the behest of the Royal Air Force, who were impressed with the North American AT-6 Texan and wanted a fighter from the same outfit. The initial proposal was for P-40s to be produced under licence, but James H Kindelberger, head of North American, already had ideas for his own new design of fighter and was able to persuade his customers to sign up for what eventually became the P-51 Mustang.

Myths grow up easily around famous aeroplanes, and the story has become current that the P-51 prototype was designed and built in 117 days. However good a story, it is of course nonsense: rather like the widespread belief that Mutt Summers's* remark on first flying the Spitfire – "I don't want anything changed" – meant that the aircraft was perfect from the day it was born! Although the P-51 contract was agreed in April 1940 and the aircraft ready by September, 'Dutch'

Kindelberger's team had already been working on the project for several months and even had a mock-up ready during their negotiations with the British Air Purchasing Commission.

The concept of the new fighter was a revolutionary one, employing for the first time the (as yet untried) theory of the laminar-flow wing. Efficiency, minimal drag and suitability for mass-production were the design criteria, and North American took advantage of research by the National Advisory Committee for Aeronautics (NACA) being carried out on an aerofoil to produce optimum reduction of drag. The perfect laminar-flow aerofoil would entail a perfectly contoured, perfectly smooth surface without any vibration, surface flaws, rivets, etc., that might disturb the smooth flow of layers of air 'laminated' on top of each other. This was obviously an idealized concept, but the idea was adapted for the Mustang to produce a wing section which, while not truly laminar, employed a maximum thickness about two-thirds back from the leading edge, whose effect was to shift towards the rear of the wing the onset of turbulent airflow and its attendant drag. All other design features worked towards the same end: the rear-located radiator/air scoop which left the forward part of the aircraft and its wings clear of appendages, and the precisely-calculated outlines which were faithfully reproduced in metal.

It was an all-metal stressed skin airframe, sleek and speedy. The initial Allison engine installation was not a success, especially at altitude, but tests with the 1,705 hp Merlin 65, with two-stage supercharger and Bendix-Stromberg fuel injector, achieved an exceptional maximum speed of 433 mph (697 km/h) at 22,000 ft (6,705 m), with a rate of climb of 3,440 fpm (17.5 m/sec). A deal was concluded for Rolls-Royce engines to be built under licence in the USA to equip the Mustangs, and the first P-51B and C versions were powered by Packard-built V1650-3 engines adapted from the Merlin 61 (take-off rating 1,380 hp, war emergency rating 1,620 hp). A true airspeed of 441 mph (706 km/h) was recorded on the prototype XP-51B.

With the B-17 Flying Fortress, the concept of the strategic bomber that could supposedly defend itself had come seriously unstuck in Europe, and by late 1943 the fighter escort became official American Air Force doctrine. But as long as fighters were forced to fly in close formation at reduced throttle they were acutely vulnerable to enemy attack. It was the arrival of General Jimmy Doolittle to take command of the 8th Air Force that put an end to all that, and from the beginning of 1944 the Mustangs were ordered to take the war to the enemy. German ace Adolf Galland said that the day the Allied fighters went from defensive to offensive was when Germany lost the air war.

Endurance became the deciding factor in an escort fighter, and it was here that the Mustang scored highest. Best version of all was the P-51D (Mark IV) with Packard-built Merlin rated at 1,490 hp at take-off, having a top speed of 438 mph (700 km/h) at 25,000 feet and a rate of climb of 3,500 fpm (17.5 m/sec). It was marginally slower due to the bubble canopy and cut-down rear fuselage, a modification to improve the visibility problems of earlier models. But its long range was its outstanding aspect, and this version could cover more than 2,000 miles (over 3,000 km) with the aid of external wing tanks. You could ride escort for a bombing attack all the way to the target, seek and destroy enemy fighters, spend an hour dog-fighting, and still have fuel to get home safely. The Mes-

---

*Mutt Summers was the Supermarine test pilot who made the initial test flights.

Focke-Wulf Fw190A-4 of 1/JG54, ready to start patrol on the Russian front during the winter of 1942/43.   (Chaz Bowyer)

serschmitt 109 and Focke-Wulf 190 had no more than about 500 miles endurance (about 800 km).

There were some aspects of the P-51 to watch out for, and they included the low- and high-speed stalls which were characterized by an entry which was sharp and made without warning. Both rudder and elevator needed retrimming with every speed change, which kept the pilot pretty busy in the circuit, and sometimes you almost had to stand on a rudder pedal until the trim was cranked in. The spin was a violent affair, and the aircraft used up a lot of altitude before it recovered; then sometimes it would suddenly snap and spin in the opposite direction!

With the long-range rear fuselage tank there was always a problem with the centre of gravity, and the standing recommendation was to burn off fuel from this tank from the start of a mission to bring it back into limits as early as possible. When full, it moved the C of G dangerously rearward, and in a tight turn or a pull-out from a dive the machine could become uncontrollable. A graphic illustration of what could happen occurred one day when a squadron pilot ferried his newly-acquired Mustang back to base with the tank full, having failed to check the manual first. To give vent to his delight with the machine, he first buzzed low over the base, and then pulled up into a steep climb capped off with a roll . . . only he never completed the roll. Instead the aircraft went into an inverted flat spin, resisted all attempts at recovery, and ended up a smoking wreck on the ground. The pilot had meanwhile taken to his parachute, ruefully contemplating his short-lived acquaintance with the prized machine.

Glenn Eagleston, 354th Group ace, preferred to keep his fuselage fuel for extra range and get rid of the drop-tanks first. He learned to lead into a turn using forward stick, and as the manoeuvre progressed this was automatically counteracted by the nose-upward pitching moment induced by the full tank. His ultimate escape ploy if caught with full fuselage fuel was to whip into a right-hand turn and stall at high speed, then snap inverted back to the left, a manoeuvre so fast that it usually shook off pursuit.

When the Rolls-Royce engine installation first came out in the P-51B and C, a marked decrease in directional stability resulted. If the pilot did not handle his rudder input correctly, the aircraft would tend to flick violently, which placed a high unbalanced load on the tailplane: structural failures began to occur. Since these failures were most frequently encountered when performing slow rolls, it was then prohibited to slow roll the Mustang. Later a dorsal fin was added, and the trim tab was rerigged to give opposite boost. Meanwhile some Mustang pilots had discovered a use for this directional instability:

The first well-described use came about when a P-51 combat pilot following an enemy airplane down in a steep dive glanced in his rear view mirror and mistook his wingman (who was following along as a good wingman should) for an Me-109. Since evasive action was apparently mandatory, the pilot proceeded to push all the controls into the northeast corner of the cockpit, and the consequent series of inverted snap rolls, entered at over 450 indicated, separated subject P-51B pilot from his target, his wingman, and almost from his airplane. The fact that the stabilizer fell off in the hands of the crew chief during inspection after the airplane had flown to its home base did not deter other pilots from using the same tactics, when necessary. . . .

(Report No 8679 by Lewis S Wait, Administrative Test Pilot, North American Aviation, Inc.)

A heavier aeroplane than the Spitfires and Hurricanes discussed earlier, the 'Spam Can' was more stable in all axes and did not match them for rate of roll, turning circle, etc. It was quick and clean and not so tolerant of inept handling. Fast as it was straight and level, it really showed its heels in the dive – beating the Germans at their own game, though they still had the advantage on rate of climb. It could manoeuvre as nimbly as the opposition, and even out-zoom the German fighters, and its acceleration from slow cruise to maximum performance was excellent.

In comparisons between the Mustang III (P-51B/C) and the

Stephen Gray's P-51D Mustang (Packard Merlin 1650) carries the authentic markings of 362 Fighter Squadron, 357 Fighter Group, who were stationed at Leeston during World War II.
(Richard Winslade)

Span	37 ft 0¼ in (11.28 m)
Length	32 ft 2½ in (9.82 m)
Height	12 ft 2 in (3.71 m)
Empty weight (equipped)	7,125 lb (3,232 kg)
Max speed	438 mph (700 km/h)
Rate of climb	3,500 fpm (17.5 m/sec)

Focke-Wulf 190 with BMW 801D engine, it had a speed advantage of at least 50 mph (80 km/h) level, and could always out-dive the German machine. The turning circle was very similar, as was the rate of climb, though the Mustang was considerably faster in a zoom climb. In rate of roll, however, "not even a Mustang III approaches the Fw 190".

The Focke-Wulf was probably the greatest opponent of the Mustang in 1944-5, though its performance began to suffer greatly from deployment in a defensive rôle when covered with armour plate and hung about with assorted weaponry. During the latter part of the war the Fw 190 in all its variants was one of the few Axis fighters capable of meeting the P-51 on anything like equal terms. Larger than the Messerschmitt, it was the best fighter that the Luftwaffe had in mass production, but fortunately for the Allies there were too few, too late. Though most were powered by BMW radials, the D-9 had a liquid-cooled Junkers Jumo 213A-1, 12-cylinder inverted-V engine rated at 2,240 hp with MW [Methanol/ Water] 50 boost, and was particularly fast in the dive and the climb; its controls remained light and permitted good aileron rolls and tight turns. Dogfighting with the Fw 190 was "not altogether recommended" to the Mustang pilot, and evasion tactics were preferred.

Although the P-51 was greeted as a great step forward in fighter design, fighter pilots who have flown both it and the P-47 Republic Thunderbolt are quick to point out the P-47's good points, and claim that there were advantages to each aircraft in its different way. Current aerobatic pilot and judge Chuck Mann has commented to the effect that a lightly-loaded P-51 was *initially* easier to handle in basic formation flying and tail-chase aerobatics at low altitudes, and with its faster roll rate, lower wing loading and 40 per cent less mass, the Mustang would 'wax' the P-47 if the pilots involved had similar training and experience of somewhere around 60 hours.

But once beyond the initial stage, the P-47 pilot with a couple of hundred hours would have learned the strengths of his machine, and the contest would more likely be equal at low altitudes and even in favour of the Thunderbolt at 15,000–30,000 ft (4,500–9,000 m). The big, powerful Pratt and Whitney radial up front served well in upward zooms; and in tight turns the large frontal area and weight provided an effective brake which could be used in 'scissor-turn' manoeuvres, where the P-47 pilot would pull up to near stalling point, let the nose drop, then pull up again and in this way tighten his turning circle to stay within that of his opponent.

It was a big, heavy aeroplane, affectionately known by a multitude of nicknames such as the Jug, Thunder Mug or Cast Iron Beast; the manufacturers were generally referred to as the 'Republic Locomotive Works and Iron Foundry'. Evasive action in the Thunderbolt, they said, was when the pilot got up and ran around the cockpit. But it was a beautiful aircraft to fly in combat, tough and reasonably manoeuvrable, and above all reliable. You could hang any armament on her, ask her to do any job from fighter sweeps and bomber escorts to dive-bombing and strafing, and she would execute the mission, survive the flak, and bring you safely home.

Chuck Mann recalls a vivid memory of an early training film

Republic P-47D Thunderbolt, 20 August 1944 (Pratt and Whitney double Wasp, take-off rating 2,300 hp).

(USAF photo, via Mike Jerram)

which depicted a P-47 doing a split-S from cruise speed at 14,000 ft (about 4,250 m) and ploughing a furrow into the ground as it pulled through: the moral of the story being that the aircraft's high diving speed precluded using that type of manoeuvre as an evasion tactic. Several years later, he found himself alone under a 3,500 ft (1,000 m) overcast chasing and firing on a long-nose Fw 190, when suddenly the German decided to roll over and pull it through.

Of course, my personal estimate of my ability left no doubt that I was nearly invincible, so I thought to myself 'If he can do it, so can I!' As I had the throttle through Emergency War Power I used both hands to pull on the stick and clearly recall vapour streamers coming off the entire wing, canopy and cowling due to the high angle of attack with subsequent turbulences in moist air.

As I was still on him while going through the 90 degree diving position my mind flashed back to the P-47 in the training film ploughing in from 14,000 ft, yet here I was below 2,000 ft. That tends to heat your blood a bit. When the Fw 190 levelled we were both below the rooftops going down the main street of a town, with my eight 50-calibres tracing a pattern all over him . . .

One more example of performance beyond prediction came when Chuck's squadron was preparing a number of newly-arrived replacement pilots on training machines which were, true to hallowed tradition, war-weary P-47s which the experienced combat veterans would not touch. One afternoon in 1945, while most of the 'hot fighter jockeys' were sunbathing on the field and watching the raw newcomers carry out their training detail, suddenly they saw one of the most unlikely and most un-military replacement pilots dive over the field, buzz the runway and pull up into a perfect 'double Immelmann' – one roll-off-the-top immediately followed by a second, to form an upward S shape.

Our jaws popped because no-one had seen a P-47 do that before, in fact we would all have bet that it *couldn't* be done in that machine. An immediate mass exodus to the flight line followed as we suited up and proceeded to burn hunreds of gallons of fuel trying to duplicate what that exceptional recruit had done. Few succeeded!

Although fame inevitably went to the widely used Allied and German aircraft, there was one quite exceptional fighter of Soviet design which appeared towards the end of the war and immediately achieved an outstanding reputation for speed and manoeuvrability: the Yak-3.

Alexander Yakovlev had successfully pioneered the monoplane configuration with his UT-1 and UT-2 aerobatic trainers in the 1930s (see Chapter 16), and when war came he produced a succession of excellent fighters in great quantity, from the Yak-1 to the Yak-9, which were the mainstay of the Soviet air force.

Intended originally for the 1,650 hp M-107A engine, teething troubles with this power plant resulted in the initial Yak-3s being equipped with the less powerful M-105PF (1,300 hp at 800 m). But the design was conceived as a lightweight battlefield air-superiority fighter and low-level interceptor of clean and simple lines, and with its typical laden weight of 2,660 kg (5900 lb) it still had a power loading of 2.19 kg/hp even with its lower rated engine. During flight trials the prototype Yak-3 (Yak-1M modified) was clocked at a speedy 680 km/h (422 mph) at 3,700 m (12,000 ft); and when the first Yak-3s started reaching the squadrons in late 1943 the Soviet pilots were delighted with its performance, which was clearly superior to the opposing fighters of the Luftwaffe.

At a height of 1,000 m (3,300 ft) the machine could complete a full 360 degree combat turn in 18.5 seconds *while gaining 1,200 m (3,900 ft) in altitude*. Many a Bf 109G and Fw 190A stalled and crashed while attempting to follow the Yak-3 in a tight turn. It was exceptionally light on the ailerons and had a remarkable rate of roll. Like all the Yak fighters it was delightfully crisp and precise to handle; light stick pressure produced fast and accurate flick rolls, and it was the ideal fighter for close-in, high *g* manoeuvring combat.

Equipped at last with the M-107A engine in 1944, the Yak-3U emerged too late, unfortunately, to see action in World War II. It was externally very similar to the Yak-3, though the cockpit was moved further aft to help compensate for the increase in engine weight. In State Acceptance trials during early 1945 it turned in spectacular speeds of up to 720 km/h (450 mph) at 5,750 m (18,900 ft), with a climb to 5,000 m (16,400 ft) in 3.9 minutes. At that altitude it was some 100 km/h (60 mph) faster than the standard Bf 109G-2 or Fw 190A-4, as well as out-performing the P-51 Mustang! The official report of the trials assessed it as having the best performance of all indigenous and known foreign fighters, being superior in speed, rate of climb and manoeuvrability.

The reputation of the Yak-3 was such that the Luftwaffe issued orders to all pilots on the Eastern Front not to engage in combat with 'the Yak lacking the nose oil-cooler' (a salient recognition feature). With its superior handling and performance, it was the ultimate dogfighter and one of the most effective piston-engined aircraft of the war.

In the summer of 1944, the Free French *Normandie-Niemen* fighter unit operating with the Soviets received its first Yak-3s at Mikountani in Lithuania, and immediately racked up a phenomenal success rate: during the course of a ten-day period that October, they were credited with no less than 119 of the 273 victories claimed in total by this group after nearly 2½ years of fighting with the Soviet air force.

They liked the Yak so much that at the end of the war they took forty-one of them back to France, performing an exuberant multi mirror-formation beat-up over Allied airfields on the way back to Le Bourget, including inside/outside formation loops, with full-throttle speeds of well over 650 km/h (400 mph) on the deck!

To the Soviet people, the name 'Yak' by the end of the war had the same emotional ring as 'Spitfire' to the British or 'Mustang' to the Americans; it was synonymous with

Yakovlev's UT-2 trainers, designed in 1935.   (Jean Alexander)

Yak-3s of Normandie-Niemen unit, celebrating their return to France in 1945.

Flight Fantastic

'Defender', 'Avenger', 'Spirit of Stalingrad': winged guardian of a vast continent.

Like Willy Messerschmitt and Focke-Wulf's Kurt Tank, Alexander Yakovlev exemplified that breed of early designer whose first love was sporting and aerobatic aircraft. And from this beginning he went on to create the outstanding 'Yak line' of fighters and trainers that continues to this day in the field of advanced aerobatics; unique not only in its longevity, but also in its honourable perpetuation of a name that has passed into Russian folk-history as the machine that saved a nation in its hour of need.

Meanwhile, the concept of the long-range fighter had been developed by the Luftwaffe with the Bf 110, which was twin-engined and had sufficient fuel capacity to fly escort on long-range bombing missions. It was being developed hand in hand with the Bf 109 when Al Williams visited Germany in 1938, and he was particularly interested in the degree of manoeuvrability that the German designers could achieve in this type, for without it the machine would be useless as a fighter (in the event it was far from being the success everyone expected it to be).

In undisguised admiration he reported an impromptu aerobatic demonstration that he witnessed by chance while driving along a road neighbouring an airport. The 110 pilot exhibited every manoeuvre that Williams had ever done himself, or seen done, in a single-engined machine, including a roll-off-the-top started from 20 ft (6 m), a slow barrel roll executed at 300 ft (90 m) with the throttle wide open, and a 1,000 ft (300 m) dive followed by a pull-up into a steep climbing roll which he continued for 2–3,000 ft (600–900 m), all performed with great verve and accuracy. Not content with this, the unknown pilot then proceeded to cut one engine and feather the prop, then go through the whole routine all over again! To Williams the exhibition was, "the most remarkable performance flight I have ever seen".

But there was already in his own country a young pilot who could easily match the unknown German with a similar twin-engined machine. Innumerable veterans of the American barnstorming and airshow circuit were putting in valuable time with the US forces, whether on active service like Mike Murphy and Jimmy Doolittle, or spending their best energies on training the younger recruits in essential flying and combat skills. One such ex-barnstormer, racing pilot and aerobatic specialist was Tony LeVier, who had been thrilling audiences since 1932 when, at the age of 19, he had rigged a borrowed Fleet with shoulder-harness and performed a bunt (still a daring manoeuvre) at an airshow in California. We have already met him as winner of the Greve Trophy Race in 1938 with 'Firecracker'.

Later he joined the firm of Lockheed as an engineering test pilot, working on the twin-engine, twin-boom P-38 Lightning, a machine in which he became so expert that he could fly inverted and do single-engine slow rolls as low as 50 feet.

During the P-38 transition training some of the more inexperienced US pilots had been killed in the Lightning performing the classic split-S manoeuvre – the half-roll to inverted and pull-through – which had been a standard combat device since the first aerial war. The fighter was tricky to fly and accelerated rapidly in the dive, and an anxious wrench at the stick in the pull-out could easily overstress the tail group.

The addition of dive brakes soon remedied the problem, but confidence in the aircraft was not restored until LeVier personally went over to Europe in 1944 and toured the fighter bases in England, performing his special brand of single-engine aerobatics.

Afterwards, during the immediate post-war years of 1946–48, he continued giving aerobatic demonstrations in his own specially fitted racing P-38 (1,325 hp Allisons). A high-spot of his daily show at the Cleveland Air Races of 1946 was his final dead-stick act: after climbing to a height of 15,000 ft (4,500 m) he would start into a straight-down vertical dive, both engines dead and propellers feathered, reaching compressibility (the speed of sound) on the way down. When he reached the field he would pull out and whoosh across at about 525 mph (845 km/h), then do a complete aerobatic routine totally without power.

Tony was still chief pilot with Lockheed at the time, and the company did not exactly encourage his private enterprise P-38 displays. In 1948 he decided to retire altogether from racing and airshows, but he has never stopped taking an active interest in all forms of piloting skills and, in particular, safety. Tony LeVier's name is probably best remembered nowadays in connection with air racing and, as we shall see in a later chapter, the design of the Formula One 'Cosmic Wind' racers. But many young American flyers of the war years had cause to be grateful – and may even owe their lives – to his morale-boosting aerobatics.

Tony LeVier with Lockheed P-38 Lightning (two 1,325 hp Allisons) used for his famous aerobatic demonstrations.

(Smithsonian Institution)

11

France and the Stampe

For thirty years France had been intoxicated with aviation, and enjoyed a position at the forefront of aeronautical design and achievement. Then in the mid-1930s the Socialist government made a move which really brought flying within the reach of ordinary youngsters: the *aviation populaire* system of subsidy ws introduced. State-owned aeroplanes and State-paid instructors were available if you were willing, in return, to play your part in the maintenance of the equipment and the running of the aero-clubs. A positive spirit of air-mindedness was generated; moreover, pilots were being trained and thus were ready to be called upon in time of need.

But what happened when they *were* called upon? Already the air force was overstocked with obsolescent aircraft which, with characteristic French bureaucracy, must be 'off the books' before quantities of new machines could replace them. There was no mass-production in the old fashioned, ill-equipped factories, where morale was low and industrial unrest was rife. Brilliant experimental designs were produced but left to stagnate at the prototype stage. Crippled by strikes, the remnants of France's once great aircraft industry declined into the paralysis of nationalisation. The French Chief of Air Staff, on an official visit to Berlin in 1937, was stunned by the German equipment and readiness for war: "If it came to a showdown with Germany," he reported confidentially, "we should be knocked out within a fortnight."

Alas, when the wolf at the door at last forced the provision of modern, high-performance fighters and bombers, the pilots in the squadrons fell victim to official ineptitude, hold-ups in aircraft supply, muddled orders and inadequate equipment. The result, despite some fine machines and men, was the inevitable débâcle of June 1940 and four terrible years of Nazi occupation.

A strong foundation had been established, however, and quite aside from the French civil aviation movement there was a proud military tradition which dated back to World War I. Aerobatics, originally taught at the *Ecole d'Acrobatie* at Pau, where such as Fronval and Doret had their beginnings, continued in the French Air Service to keep pace with the swift progress of the 1920s and 30s, with ten hours of aerobatics forming a compulsory basis for every pilot's training. At this time the great military schools reached the peak of their reputation, among them the Instructor Training Establishment at Salon de Provence, and the Advanced Flying Training School of Etampes.

The *Patrouille d'Etampes*, the first French military formation team, had made its debut on 10 May 1931. Until then, formation flying – especially formation aerobatics – was frowned upon as exceedingly dangerous stuff; but Etampes laid a strong emphasis on aerobatics, and three of the Etampes instructors, Amouroux, Carlier and Dumas, took it into their own heads to form a team with their Morane-Saulnier MS 230 trainers (230 hp Salmson radials). Their success, particularly under their subsequent leader Colonel Pierre Fleurquin, was outstanding. The name of Etampes became synonymous with precision aerobatics.

Fleurquin, who was later Commandant of the Instructors' School at Salon in 1939–40, and commanded the élite *Cigognes* group from 1941 to 1944, was a tireless advocate of the vital rôle that aerobatics must play in proper pilot training. In 1938 he wrote an impassioned article, 'The Educational Value of Aerobatics', in the French Air Service Review, a text which was widely quoted both at home and abroad. In it, he spoke of aerobatics giving the pilot a special feeling for his aeroplane and for the medium of the air in which it moved, thanks to his thorough exploration of all positions and conditions of flight – even to the very worst possibilities that might befall.

Flight Fantastic

The secret of pilotage lay in the ability to analyse and understand every phenomenon of flight and its implications, to practise an economy of control input without abrupt or excessive movement, in short the pilot's rôle was to persuade the machine to perform only those things which he knew to be within its capabilities.

The aerobatic pilot enters into an intimate relationship with his machine, progressively, without jar or discord, and in return he finds that all its secrets are opened up to him, all its virtues and vices. With deftness of touch he tactfully arouses an eager response, catering to its whims and caprices, until at last he obtains his full desire in every movement. From this union of harmony between man and machine are born figures of the utmost perfection.

Fleurquin's mood exactly reflected that of his great compatriots like Michel Détroyat and Alfred Fronval, for whom aerobatics represented not just a skill but a veritable art form. Small wonder that the spirit which suffused the time, undimmed by years of war and deprivation, was to produce in France some of the greatest and most lyrical exponents of that art.

But before we move on to consider the great post-war pilots, let us first look at that unassuming wood-and-fabric biplane – born, incongruously enough, in Belgium – which became synonymous with the best in French aerobatics for many years: the Stampe.

Jean Stampe was a Belgian ex-World War I flyer and test pilot who, after the war, became personal pilot to King Albert I of the Belgians. In 1923, Stampe and fellow ex-fighter pilot

turned financier Maurice Vertongen formed the *Société Stampe et Vertongen* together with engineer Alfred Renard, running a pilot training school and maintenance facility. Renard produced two military trainer designs for the embryo company, which were bought by the Belgian Flying Corps, before moving on to start his own outfit in 1930.

Stampe had known Geoffrey de Havilland since the war, and in 1927 had become the Belgian agent for the popular DH60 Moth biplane; so when he asked Renard's successor Georges Ivanow to come up with a new trainer/tourer design, a model was produced which clearly showed Moth influences. This was the SV.3 of 1932, an open cockpit unstaggered biplane with 120 hp Gipsy III engine; it had ailerons on both upper and lower wings and was stressed for aerobatics. A modified version – the SV.4 – quickly followed when it was realized that the instructor in the front cockpit needed a lot more room for entry, and particularly for exit, when encumbered with full flying kit and parachute. Accordingly the centre-section and cabane struts were shifted forward clear of the cockpit, the upper mainplane being moved forward and swept back and the ailerons removed. Unlike the Tiger Moth, which was also doctored similarly (see Chapter 13), the lower wing was left as it was. Altogether six of these wire-braced, fabric covered biplanes were built and used for flight training at Stampe's flying school.

Over the next three years the Stampe et Vertongen company produced a few workmanlike military designs, though without conspicuous success, until in 1935 it was overtaken by tragedy when both Georges Ivanow and Jean's 24-year-old son, Léon Stampe, were killed during a test flight. Following the disaster Stampe had not the heart to press on with new ideas, until he was approached by an ex-student, Elza Leysen, in search of a Belgian-designed aerobatic aircraft. Eventually she persuaded Jean Stampe and his new engineer Demidoff to develop a special version of the SV.4 for her use.

Leysen was delighted with her SV.4B, which carried the original two sets of ailerons, a new empennage, and an improved aerofoil for aerobatics. Even before delivery in 1937 it revealed its potential by winning a government competition for trainer aircraft, although winning the competition unfortunately did not mean winning orders for Stampe's struggling little design company. A further redesign then followed, during which the upper and lower wing outlines were matched and both swept back to an optimum angle as determined in exhaustive tests by Jean Stampe himself; this resulted in the configuration as we know it today.

Meanwhile, belatedly realizing the necessity for an up-to-date trainer in place of the Morane 230, the French Air Service had announced a competition at Villacoublay in July 1939 to choose a replacement machine; Jean Stampe hopefully took along his new SV.4B model. At the trials it was flown by him and by Michel Détroyat for the French Armée de l'Air, whose praise was unstinting: 'Overall flying qualities perfect. Aerobatic capability remarkable,' was the official assessment (what pilot would disagree with those words?) – and Stampe had struck gold at last!

Already the Belgian Air Service had ordered thirty machines, and Stampe was hopeful of a similar order from the French. When the letter of intent finally arrived, however, he was positively stupefied by the quantity demanded by the by-now frantic Armée de l'Air: *three hundred aircraft*! This was more than his little set-up in Antwerp-Deurne could handle,

Jean Stampe (in background DH60X 00-ADG). (Tony Lloyd)

and a search was undertaken to find a French factory to produce them under licence, equipped with Renault engines. Scarcely had he concluded a manufacturing deal with the Farman company than another French order arrived for 600 more machines! But his luck was too good to hold. Only the first ten had been delivered when the Nazis overran France.

Three days after the Germans invaded the Low Countries, Jean Stampe, airborne in an SV.4B, spotted a column of French troops toiling southward out of Holland ahead of Hitler's relentless *Panzers*. Circling overhead at 150 m (500 ft), suddenly out of the corner of his eye he espied three Messerschmitt Bf 109s streaking in for a strafing run, raking the withdrawing troops with machine-gun fire. As they turned to reposition for another attack, Stampe assessed the situation with an old warrior's quick reactions and, flitting unseen close to his native terrain, sneaked up and suddenly appeared in their midst; it was a desperate attempt to distract their attention and so allow the troops to scramble for cover. Confident in the manoeuvrability of his little biplane, he harried and buzzed in the path of the 109s: too elusive to catch, yet annoying and impudent enough to lead the Germans into a fruitless chase.

Not only did he succeed in his aim of distracting the attackers, he led them such a merry dance that before they realized it they had wasted their last litres of fuel and had to break off. The cheering French troops below him were safe to resume their weary retreat.

Construction of the Stampe aeroplanes did not recommence until 1945, but then a new French Armée de l'Air order for SV.4Cs (140 hp Renault 4-Pei) started to roll off factory assembly lines in France and Algeria, with over 850 being produced between 1945 and 1949. At the same time, Jean Stampe's own factory was building an order for the Belgian air force with 145 hp Gipsy Major X engines. So the impossible dream did come true eventually, and the little Stampe trainer became the first ever commercially successful Belgian-designed aeroplane.

With the return to peace in France, the Communist air minister for the de Gaulle coalition government made a great effort to revitalize French civil aviation by recreating the State-subsidized aeroclubs, and by setting up three National Centres for flying: Saint-Yan, Carcasonne and Chelles-les-Eaux. Altogether 500 Stampes were distributed (at a nominal cost of one franc each!) between the centres and the aeroclubs throughout the country, where they became the ultimate all-purpose flying machine of the day. And who could resist the Stampe's gentle invitation to aerobatics?

Professional British display pilot Brian Lecomber, who includes a Gipsy Major Stampe SV.4B in his line-up of machines, is a devotee of the aeroplane and recommends it as an excellent teacher: "It shows up one's tiny errors in gentle slow motion, is usually fairly forgiving about things when you make a monumental *faux pas* – and when you do get it right, performs with the most satisfying classical grace."

He describes the elevator as light and sweet, and the rudder as "powerful, but definitely on the heavy side". The ailerons, otherwise effective and efficient, are, however, let down by their system of interconnection which transmits stick inputs by relay from the lower to the upper set and consequently inhibits a crisp roll entry: "half the ailerons are

getting the message by second-class post". But the rate of roll – seven seconds or so for 360 degrees – is respectable enough in a 45-year-old biplane.

The Stampe will perform practically any aerobatic manoeuvre you care to name, including flick rolls, fractions of vertical rolls, and negative manoeuvres; but in the latter, performance is much enhanced if the front cockpit is covered over and its windscreen removed to improve the aerodynamics. Being a fairly substantial, draggy biplane – though with light wing-loading – the Stampe demands a high level of finesse from its pilot if he is to achieve good, well-sustained and nicely rounded figures without running out of energy. This means he must take care at the outset to establish the machine in the right attitude, in a slow roll for example, otherwise corrective control inputs may cause it to sag most inelegantly out of the nice straight line he is striving for. In vertical rolls this necessity is even more critical:

If you do not, you will find that firstly you do not have time for corkscrewing corrections on the way up, and secondly if you *do* try to sort it out with all kinds of crossed controls the whole thing will come to a shuddering halt anyway because of the extra drag. From the learning point of view this is actually no bad thing; the comparatively slow rate of roll gives you time to identify your errors, while the nature of the beast will not take kindly to rescuing inaccuracies which should not have been there in the first place. Ergo, you have little choice *but* to get it right. Eventually....

Overall, the secret of Stampe aerobatics is rhythm and flow. If you try for lots of *g* and complication in a sequence the aeroplane will look untidy and run out of energy; but if you are smooth and gentle you can keep going all day and the result will be beautiful to watch.

(First published in *Pilot*, March 1984, and reproduced with permission.)

During the late 1940s the celebrated French *Patrouille d'Etampes*, now under the leadership of Capitaine Perrier,

Capitaine Perrier, leader of the Patrouille d'Etampes in the 1940s, flies a spectacularly low pass at Villacoublay in the unique Mathis-engined SV.4D (175 hp Mathis G7R, about 1947).
(John Underwood)

The graceful lines of Brian Lecomber's Stampe SV.4B (145 hp Gipsy Major X) are displayed over the English countryside.
(Brian Lecomber)

was reformed and equipped with special Stampes; first a 175 hp Mathis radial-engined SV.4D model was tried, but after repeated engine problems with the Mathis, a special inverted version of the Renault 4P was preferred. Stampes thus fitted out, with ash-reinforced airframes, became SV.4As. Perrier himself was famous for his daring aerobatics and often flew down the runway inverted with his head a scant two metres above the tarmac! Under Perrier the team soon revived the former glories of Etampes, becoming renowned for the brilliantly executed formation outside loop which they included in their routine.

One of the earliest French Stampe exponents, Fred Nicole, was charged in 1946 with the opening of the first of the National Centres for aviation, and by way of preparation went off to work with Perrier on a special aerobatics training course. This first establishment was the *Centre National de Saint-Yan*, which opened in January 1948. Here the immediate task was to train instructors who would then carry the Saint-Yan method – soon to become a byword for the ultimate in piloting technique – to all the aeroclubs throughout France.

Nicole was a beneficiary of Pierre Fleurquin's philosophies at the pre-war Instructor Training Establishment, Salon de Provence, and lived to pass them on to his fellow-flyers after the war. He had taken his licence in 1931, and by 1937 was Chief Flying Instructor for an *aviation populaire* group at

Avranches; two years later he was sent on special detachment to Salon, and so impressed Fleurquin that the colonel immediately invited him to remain there as an instructor himself, which he did until the war's end. Thereafter his special gifts of showmanship singled him out, and he became a sort of flying ambassador at air displays and meetings throughout France in the cause of popularizing aviation: he flew both powered aeroplanes and gliders and, later, helicopters.

In 1948 he accompanied Marcel Doret to the newly revived National Air Races in Cleveland, USA, Doret preferring to give exhibitions of glider aerobatics while Nicole displayed the Stampe, to his surprise receiving a handsome 'World Cup' for the outstanding aerobatic performance of the event.

The following year Fred Nicole joined the firm of Breguet as test pilot, while still continuing unabated his constant round of air display flying both at home, in Europe and overseas. He also participated in a medical research project into the effects of negative *g*, which involved inverted flying for an hour and five minutes around a closed circuit course. "The first forty minutes are quite easy," he said, "it's the next quarter of an hour that really makes you grit your teeth; after that, it's no problem!"

It was in a later and less serious inverted flight at an airshow that Nicole made history, and amazed even the veteran Marcel Doret, who gave an eye-witness account of the younger man's exploit. This occurred at Cannes on 9 September 1951.

It seems that the organizers of the big National Air Show at

Cannes had decided to stage the event over the waters of the bay rather than the traditional aerodrome setting, and accordingly a vast crowd had gathered along the Croisette in the kind of beautiful weather that only the South of France can offer. Flying over the bay naturally allowed the performers to come much lower and closer than otherwise, and on the night before the event, after the airshow 'breefing', Doret had overheard Nicole talking to his friend Louis Notteghem about how he couldn't let the occasion go by without producing something a little out of the ordinary. . . .

Marcel Doret sensed a certain tinge of daredevilry in Nicole's tone, but he knew the two pilots extremely well and could not imagine how Nicole thought he could steal a march on the other. He also knew Fred Nicole to be a safe and experienced flyer: surely he did not intend to do anything risky, just to put one over on Notteghem?

Naturally, when Nicole's turn came to fly you can be sure that Doret was well primed to watch the stunt, whatever it might be. Imagine his reaction when he saw Nicole half-roll inverted and fly a passage so low, right in front of the famous Carlton Hotel surrounded by an expectant and tightly packed crowd, that the tip of his tail-fin actually cut a furrow in the surface of the water, leaving a trail of foam in its wake!

Michel Détroyat, when he heard about it, paid tribute to the incredible 'hands' of the man, and his ability to judge the

Below right. Fred Nicole, famous for his airshows in the Bücker Jungmeister; in 1952 he was involved as a passenger in a serious car accident which left him in a coma for 28 days. Fighting back to health against all odds, he recommenced flying in 1958, not merely as a practitioner but also as an instructor. (Musée de l'Air)

Below. Aerobatics below sea level! Fred Nicole here seen cutting the waves with his fin in the Bay of Cannes, September 1951. He repeated the feat many times afterwards with perfect accuracy. (Musée de l'Air)

aircraft's position to such a nicety. He also vowed that he would never dare attempt it himself.

After the event, Nicole explained that he had already practised this over the Lake of Geneva before trying it at Cannes; but that on the day itself he had found the effect of the sea water, with its constantly moving surface, altogether different from the smooth waters of the lake. Nevertheless, he had performed the feat, and proudly showed the water's traces on his tail to prove it!

Nicole's friend Louis Notteghem also merited special recognition from Détroyat in his book *Pilote d'Acrobatie*, published in 1957, for by now Notteghem had taken over from French Aerobatic Champion Michel Berlin as head of the National Centre of Saint-Yan, whose fame had spread far and wide. Not only was every instructor and examiner in France obliged to undergo a course there before he received his licence, but more particularly it had become one of the world's greatest training places for advanced aerobatics. Here the mastery of the Stampe reached its ultimate perfection, and the *Patrouille de Saint-Yan*, the formation team created in 1956 after the dissolution of the Etampes team 2½ years previously, represented the outward manifestation of a system that worked, studied, planned, practised and perfected aerobatics with a dedication never before witnessed.

Notteghem was well known throughout Europe as a supreme master of the art, and under his guidance a new *haute école* of aerobatics had now grown up. It was his boast that any young pilot could be brought up to the Saint-Yan standard in thirty hours of flying, provided that his initial flight training itself was correct, although of course a pilot with the wrong foundation would need much longer. Notteghem's view of aerobatics was that it taught the pilot in two ways: first, it taught the utmost control – self-control – of the pilot's own reflexes; and second, it taught the ultimate in practical handling of the aeroplane. It gave the pilot who had mastered it a competence because his reflexes had been adjusted to all

Close formation by Stampes of the Centre Nationale de Saint-Yan, crucible in which the immaculate French aerobatic technique of the 1940s/50s was perfected. In 1963, when the Centre went over to training airline pilots, its team leader Passadori joined Gérard Verette at Carcasonne where they worked together to perfect an aerobatics training programme to take over where Saint-Yan had left off.   (via Musée de l'Air)

situations, and because he had lost the old habits which derived from the sensory perceptions of pedestrian man. Indeed, he went so far as to state that any pilot who had not taken a course in aerobatics was not a thoroughly trained pilot.

Détroyat spoke with admiration of these young pilot instructors who had picked up the baton and run with it farther than had ever been done in his day, with a new vocabulary of manoeuvres and a scientific system of teaching and executing them. All work was done over a visible axis such as a runway, and good positioning was of the utmost importance, both in framing the performance as a whole and in maintaining the aircraft on axis at the start and finish of each figure. Marks were deducted for gains and losses in altitude as well as for imperfections in the manoeuvres themselves.

All 'this will strike a familiar note to modern aerobatic pilots, for these criteria are exactly the same as those presently used. The method of judging was also the same, though the values of marks were on a different scale: all manoeuvres were codified and assigned a difficulty coefficient between 1 and 8, in a catalogue containing 85 manoeuvres, and at a competition the judges were allowed to

mark each individual manoeuvre from 0 to 5, which mark was then multiplied by the manoeuvre's coefficient.

In wind correction the theory was different from today, however: if there was wind, the axial correction was to be made between figures, not during the manoeuvres themselves. Today, wind corrections must not be visible during an aerobatic sequence, a rule which makes life almost as hard for the judge as for the pilot!

In their championships, each pilot was required to execute a free programme of fourteen figures in not more than ten minutes including take-off and landing: this list of figures he would write out and hand in to the judges in advance, and a great premium was placed on smooth flow from one to the next, using the exit from the previous figure to lead into the start of the following one, which of course required much forethought about matching exit and entry speeds. Conserving time was also important, and conserving altitude was a means of avoiding unnecessary breaks between figures to regain lost height.

For Détroyat, the ultimate aircraft on which to perfect this skill was the faithful Stampe, a slow aeroplane, not easy to fly, and one that revealed to the watching eye every tiny error that its pilot committed. For the goal was perfection, and on this machine nothing short of total mastery could achieve the ideal of an impeccable performance.

Saint-Yan remained at the forefront of aerobatics until the late 1950s, when gradually the second National Centre, Carcasonne, which had opened in 1951, started concentrating on advanced courses in piloting technique, while Saint-Yan veered towards the training of airline pilots. The third

France
and the Stampe

Centre was opened at Chelles-les-Eaux in 1953, and in due course both these latter establishments took over the civilian training in aerobatics, using Stampes right up until the 1970s when they were at last exchanged for Zlin monoplanes.

Synonymous with the Centre at Carcasonne was the much-loved Gérard Verette, a regular member of the French contingent at the British Lockheed competitions in the 1950s and 60s (see Chapter 13) and a devoted instructor who was tirelessly helpful with guidance and advice on aerobatics.

At about this time when all was being set down and codified, a young pilot by the name of François d'Huc Dressler was working on a system of aerobatic notation which allowed all the various manoeuvres in a sequence to be written down in a readily understandable shorthand form. It was first published in the magazine *Aviasport* for April 1955, together with numerous examples not only of the individual hieroglyphics, but also of various aerobatic programmes with the symbols linked together to form a continuous sequence. These, of course, could then be written on a card and fixed to the instrument panel as an *aide-mémoire*.

He explained that his system was only in its early stages, but that he had been prompted by many interested friends to

Gérard Verette. Out of the eight Lockheed Competitions in which he entered, Verette only once failed to make the Finals; his placings included a second, a third and a fourth. He went on to become a regular French Team member in the FAI World Championships until his death in January 1967 in a test flight of the CP.100, prototype of the CAP 10B.   (Nick Pocock)

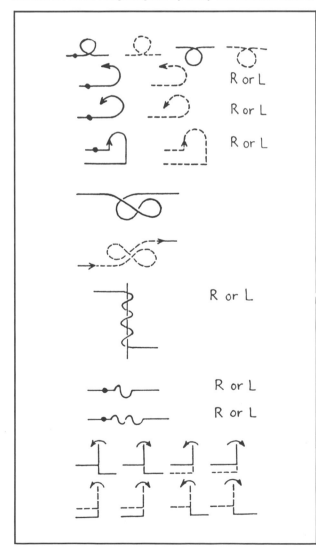

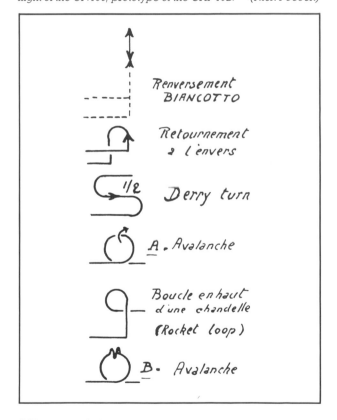

D'Huc Dressler's aerocryptographic notation system as published in Aviasport *and* Aeronautics *in 1955/56.*
(Left) Slow rolls are indicated by arrowheads. The symbol in the 7th line is that for the spin, in the 8th and 9th lines are the single and double flick roll, and the final two lines of symbols indicate tail-slides.
(Above) The stall turn (renversement) is here indicated with added climbing and descending half-rolls in a variation made famous by Léon Biancotto; the remaining signs speak for themselves.

155

Flight Fantastic

publish it nevertheless, in view of the complete absence of written records of any kind if the serious student wished to study past achievements of the great aerobatic pilots. Not only was it impossible to obtain the documentation one would like of the pre-war contests and the programmes flown in those days, one could not even find a reliable account of the Italian contest that Louis Notteghem had won only the other day: aerobatics seemed to rely totally, until that date, on an oral tradition.*

D'Huc Dressler, himself a top-level aerobatic pilot, had been taking part in contests for some time, culminating in the newly-established international Lockheed Trophy Competitions which started in 1955 in England. Using his system, he had built up quite a library of displays that he had witnessed, at the same time improving the notation itself and perfecting his technique of using it. He had, for example, originally thought to start drawing his sequence charts from the bottom upwards, but had eventually settled in favour of starting at the top.

Looking at these symbols, it is easy to read their meaning: solid lines and curves for positive flight, broken lines for negative; an arrow on a line indicates a slow roll, and an arrowhead at the top of a vertical line indicates a stall turn. All these symbols are practically the same in present-day aero-cryptograms. One can see that the symbols for flick rolls and spins are somewhat unwieldy, and certainly less neat than those for slow rolls: today they have been replaced by small triangles of different shapes and sizes (see page 198). But otherwise the whole vocabulary was there with which to build single and combination figures and eventually whole sequences, either to note the programmes of others or to devise and perfect programmes of one's own. It was a great service that François d'Huc Dressler did for aerobatics, and it has been too little recognized.

Another service rendered by his notation system was to help standardize the nomenclature of various manoeuvres which had previously meant different things to different people. After participating at the Lockheed, he clearly differentiated between the names chandelle, Immelmann and roll-off-the-top. By now, a chandelle in France was no longer what we would simply call a 'zoom' or vertical climb: it was a rapid (banked) 180 degree reversal of direction with height gain, finished at a speed close to the minimum. This is also today's classic chandelle. From pilots of other nationalities, however, d'Huc Dressler described wing-overs of varying steepness for which he did not have a separate name, but classed them also as chandelles. He correctly made the distinction that these figures, which were also banked 180 degree reversals of direction – Aresti's angle of bank (Jungmeister) being about 30–45 degrees, and Wheldon's (Provost) about 60 degrees – entailed diving down to starting height again instead of gaining altitude at the end.

Evidently the term Immelmann was still occasionally employed in Britain, even though Lockheed Judge Oliver Stewart dismissed it as 'disused for some time in English-speaking countries': appropriately, it was reserved for the chandelle described by d'Huc Dressler. The French *rétablissment*, half roll at the top of a half loop, in Britain was named 'roll-off-the-top'.

The wing-overs described by d'Huc Dressler, especially the steep ones, approached closely to the French *renversement* or stall turn, which throws an interesting light on how stall turns were performed at that time: gone were the Fieseler-style pivots around the centre of gravity at zero airspeed as if impaled on a pin at the top of a vertical climb. Instead there was a climb and descent at something noticeably less than the vertical, and from contemporaneous drawings it appears that the 180 degree yaw at the top was less of a pivot than a tight turn.

The French were specialists at these *renversements*, and one of their celebrated inventions was the 'French M' which linked two stall turns together: having climbed, pivoted and

The French 'M' figure – two stall turns linked together.

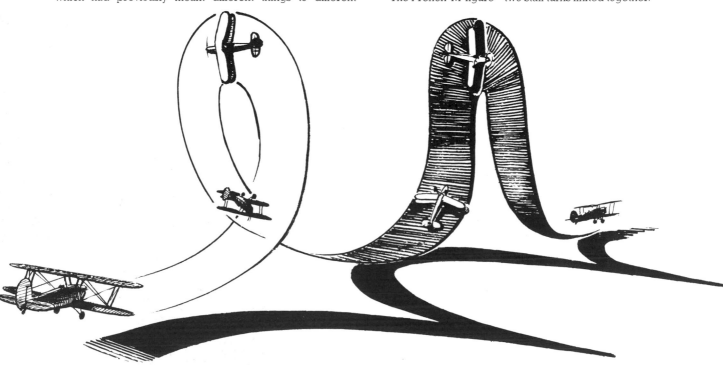

*The author can readily identify with d'Huc Dressler's lament: research into the subject is considerbly hindered by the absence of reliable written records!

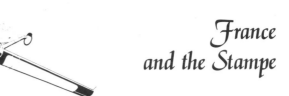

dived a short distance during the first stall turn, an inverted exit was made and the aircraft was then immediately pushed up into a second, nicely symmetrical stall turn to form the 'M' shape. D'Huc Dressler made quite an impression with this figure in the 1956 Lockheed, as well as with a rolling 360 degree circle punctuated by four flick rolls.

Both François d'Huc Dressler and fellow Lockheed competitor Alain Hisler were ex-students of Notteghem's National Centre at Saint-Yan, Hisler being retained there as an instructor. And another ex-student turned instructor was the immortal Léon Biancotto.

Born in 1929, Biancotto lived near the Paris airport of Le Bourget as a boy and loved to watch the aircraft movements, dreaming of one day becoming a pilot himself. Like most small boys besotted with aviation he spent all his spare time and pocket-money building model aeroplanes, but by the age of sixteen he had graduated to lessons in gliding. His early attempts, however, scarcely augured well for the career he had set his heart on: "You're wasting your time, you know," advised his instructor after his third flight. "You would do well to give up your place on the course to someone else!"

Fortunately for aerobatics, young Léon refused to be discouraged and went on to gain his glider *brevet* in 1947. He took his powered-aircraft licence the following year. Then, after becoming a glider instructor, he qualified to instruct on

Léon Biancotto (centre), greatest of the great French aerobatic pilots; with him are François D'Huc Dressler (left) and fellow Lockheed competitor Alain Hisler. (Flight)

light aircraft with a course which included aerobatics under Michel Berlin at Saint-Yan in 1952. Obviously a very gifted pilot, he was invited to stay on as an instructor and member of the *Equipe de Voltige Aérienne* (aerobatic team), which placed him at the very heart of the aerobatics movement in France.

Twenty years after the first French Championship in 1934, France set up a second championship in 1954 in which Michel Berlin took first place, with Biancotto second and Louis Notteghem third. Then in 1956 a 'European Championship' was held in Epinal, which was won by Alain Hisler. Second in this international event was Swiss pilot Francis Liardon, and third was Spaniard José Luis Aresti.

Most of Biancotto's greatest successes were achieved outside his homeland. Starting in 1955, he visited the British Lockheed Aerobatic Trophy competitions every year for the rest of his short life – which made a total of six contests in all – winning the Trophy three times outright and on the other occasions coming 2nd, 3rd and 4th. By 1957 he was undisputedly leader of France's aerobatic pilots, and that year virtually swept the board of all the national prizes: Coupe Jean Claret, Coupe Marcel Doret, Coupe du Poitou.

Biancotto's individual performances in the Lockheed Trophy, considered as the World Championship of its day, are covered year by year in Chapter 13. It is sufficient, as an indication of his consummate artistry, to quote here the judges' summing-up on the occasion of his second win in 1956: they said that his flying 'approached closely to perfection'. Such a tribute is quite simply unique in aerobatics.

Flight Fantastic

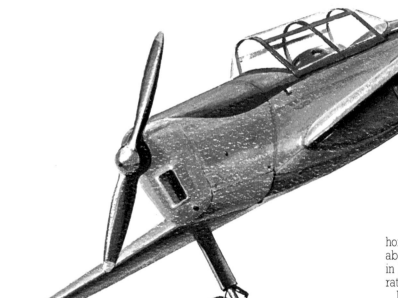

Span	9.44 m (31 ft)
Length	7.28 m (23 ft 11 in)
Height	2.2 m (7 ft 3 in)
Empty weight	930 kg (2,046 lb)
Max speed	230 km/h (143 mph)
Rate of climb	1,000 m (3,300 ft) in 4 min 50 sec

Even ten years later, Lockheed Judge Oliver Stewart maintained the same opinion:

Apart from Pégoud, who pioneered it all, the finest aerobatic pilot the world has known was Léon Biancotto, three times winner of the Lockheed International Trophy. The Chevalier d'Orgeix, who also won the Trophy on two occasions, ran him close in some respects, notably the fluidity with which he linked the most difficult figures together and the smoothness with which he initiated and ended his manoeuvres. But d'Orgeix was not, I think, as great an aerobatic pilot as Biancotto.

One thing was remarkable about his Lockheed appearances, and that was the variety of aircraft on which he opted to perform. Only his first attempt was on the classic Stampe SV.4A; the following two years he arrived at Coventry with a totally different aeroplane, the Stampe et Renard SR.7B Monitor, a low wing monoplane trainer with removable canopy which could be flown open cockpit if desired. The

Stampe et Renard SR-7B Monitor (180 hp Cirrus Bombardier), flown by Léon Biancotto in the Lockheed Trophy, 1957.

motor was a powerful 180 hp Cirrus Bombardier. This newly designed two-seat trainer was on loan to him by the manufacturers, Stampe et Renard – Jean Stampe having teamed up with his former engineer/designer Alfred Renard to form a new company in 1947. The design made use of the fuselage and empennage of the SV.4C of which there was no shortage in the enormous spare parts inventories. Its performance was said to be not unlike the D H Chipmunk, which it rather resembled, but it was not really up to competition standard and it never went into production. Only three prototypes were built.

Then in 1958 Biancotto appeared with a Zlin Trener 6, the latest design of aerobatic aircraft from Czechoslovakia which had taken Europe by storm and which suddenly all the top pilots were flying or hoping to fly. Once again he carried

home the coveted Trophy, amid much amused comment about a French pilot winning the world's top championship, in England, flying a Czech aeroplane with a Belgian registration!

In his last two Lockheeds Léon Biancotto surprised many onlookers by his choice of machine, but there were many more who paid homage to the man who, having won three times, was not too proud to treat the event lightly and experiment with an aircraft that was clearly not a match for the top-level machines he was up against. This applied particularly to the 1959 event, when his entry was the British Tiger Moth, a biplane dating from 1932 which could never measure up to the world's top aerobatic giants. This was the occasion of his lowest placing, fourth, out of a field of sixteen pilots.

In 1960 Biancotto's mount was the Nord 3202, the new standard trainer which was re-equipping the French military; a cumbersome machine indeed, especially compared with the nimble and elegant Stampe. Third place was the best he could achieve with this aeroplane in the July 1960 Lockheed, and it was the same machine that he would also fly the following month in Czechoslovakia, as head of the French team entered for the first FAI official World Aerobatic Championship.

But he was destined never to compete for this greatest of all titles. On 29 August, during his practice flight over the airfield at Bratislava, his machine was seen to go out of control and crash, killing him instantly. It happened during

the $2\frac{1}{2}$ turn inverted spin in the compulsory sequence, from which he was unable to recover.

Many times the question has been asked why the accident happened to so excellent a pilot, and here is the answer given by Michel Berlin himself, who was one of those closest to the events concerned: in his opinion, the Nord was simply not enough aeroplane for the job in hand. He and Louis Notteghem had put it through its initial aerobatic tests at Bourges and had reported that it was fine for primary instruction, but simply unthinkable for advanced competition work. Biancotto knew this, but had taken the machine because he wanted, at this the first World Championship, to represent France flying a French machine.

Biancotto lived for aerobatics, and his wife Lucienne was there by his side all the way, watching on the ground, timing him with a stopwatch, noting and critiquing everything he did. With thoughts turning to a test pilot's career, Biancotto had trained at Brétigny in 1958 and qualified the following year; at the time of his death he was working on the design of a new light aeroplane. In January 1961 he was made a Chevalier of

the Légion d'Honneur, a great tribute not only to Biancotto the man, but also to the art and sport of aerobatics which he loved.

But this is not to suggest that aerobatics died in France with Léon Biancotto, nor even that Biancotto himself is forever gone. I have used the word 'immortal' to describe him, and he is indeed immortal – not only in living memory but in the best type of commemoration that could possibly have been chosen, an international aerobatics competition of the very highest level. This competition began as the Biancotto Trophy in 1965, and developed into the FAI European Championships, held each year when a World Championship does not take place.

Biancotto's fellow-competitor in the Lockheed contests, Jean d'Orgeix, has already been mentioned, and together they reigned supreme at the forefront of French aerobatics of the late 1950s. In truth, for artistry and élan there was not

Biancotto's programme in the 1960 Lockheed (Nord 3202) is easy to follow with the Dresser notation.

One-and-a-half flick rolls

Inverted loop from the inverted position

Upward half roll and inverted pull-out

Inverted stall turn

Half roll and stall turn

Roll off the top of a loop

Slow roll on a 30 degrees descent

Double flick, half roll and pull-out

Stall turn preceded and followed by a quarter roll

Half flick roll from the top of a loop

Avalanche

Half roll and change direction pull-out

Spectacles

90 degrees to the judges' stand { Stall turn / Half slow roll / and pull-out

Half flick roll and pull-out

Eight stage roll

Flick roll from the top of a loop on a 45 degrees descent

Slow roll

Flick roll

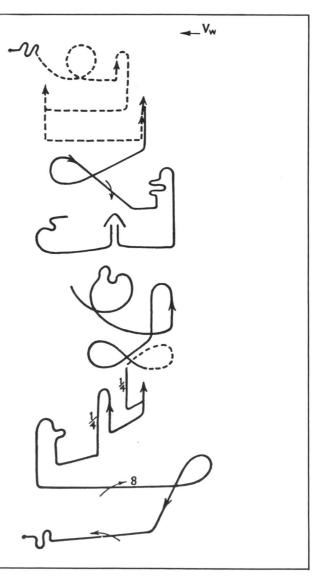

Flight Fantastic

Span	9.5 m (31 ft 2 in)
Length	8.12 m (26 ft 8 in)
Height	3.2 m (10 ft 6 in)
Empty weight	870 kg (1,914 lb)
Max speed	264 km/h (164 mph)
Rate of climb	6.4 m/sec (1,260 fpm)

Biancotto in Nord 3202 (260 hp Potez) during summer 1960, training for the first FAI World Championships in Bratislava.
(via Musée de l'Air)

much to choose between the two pilots. During a 1930s-style duel in 1959, consisting of five matches between the two of them, the result was two rounds each and one drawn!

Scion of an old and aristocratic family, with the title of Chevalier, d'Orgeix was eight years older than Biancotto and had led a life as richly varied as one could hope for, or indeed imagine. Starting out first as an actor, he quickly achieved success with a total of 34 stage rôles and some thirty films, using the pseudonym Jean Paqui. Next, discovering a new enthusiasm for horsemanship, he carried off no less than 108 international victories and a bronze medal in the 1948 Olympics.

For a touch of excitement, however, his fancy turned in the 1950s to stock car racing and he became – of course – a star of this sport as well. Finally, having taken his pilot's licence in 1951, the lure of flight caught him in its spell and he won the amateur Championship of France in 1954. This was enough to spur him on, and he was soon entering the world-class Lockheed Trophy contests in England. Gradually working up

to the top, he was placed third for two successive years, 1957–8, then second in 1959, and finally won the Trophy in 1960 and 1962.

Actor-director of a Paris theatre, organizer of safaris and game-hunting expeditions in Africa, d'Orgeix was a man of rare gifts and a true individualist. He also brightened up the sometimes less than sun-kissed ambience of Coventry with the bevy of young starlets from his Paris theatre who arrived to cheer him on!

From 1956 to 1964, the Chevalier d'Orgeix participated in every Lockheed bar the first and the last, and each time with the Stampe. Fluidity and smoothness were not his only accomplishments, for his flying was complimented on every occasion for its variety, artistry, and pin-point positioning in front of the judges. 'Stylish' and 'a joy to watch' are phrases that stand out over and over again in the reports of his displays. The epitome of the urbane and cultured Frenchman, Jean d'Orgeix will probably be best remembered as the supreme master of the Stampe SV.4: the biplane trainer which started life virtually as an afterthought in 1937, which was still holding its own in world class competition in the 1960s, and which today has its passionate devotees who would almost rather fly the Stampe than anything else with wings.

12

Czech points

Czechoslovakia's pre-eminence in the art of aerobatics has lasted for over half a century, and looks set fair to last a good while longer yet.

Positioned at the heart of Europe, an elongated tract of land stretching from the borders of Germany in the west to the borders of the USSR in the east, she has been vulnerable to countless often-conflicting influences from opposite directions. Small wonder that the territory of today's Czech and Slovak Socialist Republics in fact comprises three distinct regions, once united under the Moravian Empire in the ninth century, but often separated during the ensuing 1,000 years by religious, political and geographical pressures.

The area of Bohemia in the west, jutting out into Germany and bordered by Austria to the south, formed strong links with its germanic neighbours and, together with the central Moravian area, became increasingly entangled with them. The area of Slovakia in the east, meanwhile, was strongly subjected to Byzantine influences and developed a language of its own using the Cyrillic alphabet. Over centuries of religious and political upheaval in Europe, the varying fortunes of the German Empire, the Holy Roman Empire and the Hapsburg Empire all forced changes of allegiance and divisions among the Czech people, until the watershed of the 1914–18 war allowed a Czech national feeling to rise and find a new unification in support of the Allied forces.

The jewel city of Prague, capital of Bohemia, constantly fluctuated in power and fortune: at various times centre of the Holy Roman Empire, home of the first University in Central Europe, prominent centre of the arts and music, it was Prague in the eighteenth century that accorded Mozart his greatest public acclaim and some of his few really happy moments. At the turn of this century, home of Franz Kafka and Max Brod, it was the centre of Bohemianism in the Parisian sense.

But Prague is situated in the extreme west, and character-izes only one small aspect of Czechoslovakia. When independence was declared on 28 October 1918, a genuine attempt had been made to unite the Czech and Slovak elements of west and east in a democratic republic, which gave promise of working for a while; but with sectional differences springing up again it became easy for Nazi Germany to exploit them and encourage unrest among the minority German community in Czechoslovakia, and finally in 1938 to annex the Sudetenland in which they lived. Abandoned in spite of alliances with France and the Soviet Union, betrayed by Britain and the League of Nations, the rest of Czechoslovakia's brave new republic fell to Hitler's invading forces in March of 1939.

Those Czech pilots who managed to escape joined up with the Allies against the Nazis, and three Czech squadrons flew with the RAF in the Battle of Britain. No mention of Czech wartime pilots can go by without especially remembering Josef František, who was Czechoslovakia's outstanding fighter ace in the Battle of Britain. Always the lone wolf, and unable to adapt to the discipline of formation operations, he eventually ended up flying as a 'guest' with 303 (Polish) Squadron, and fighting the war in his own way – chasing Germans. It proved the right policy. With 17 victories to his credit, he was one of the most successful Battle of Britain aces. František died during the Battle of Britain, and 510 other Czech pilots also fell during service abroad; a further 1,000 were executed or tortured for resistance at home. The Czechs eloquently call it 'the era of broken wings'.

Aviation had become a glorious preoccupation in pre-war Czechoslvakia, and she was one of the leading aviation countries of the world, both industrially and militarily. Czech aerobatic pilots and machines, like František Novák and the Avia B 122, were among the best in Europe, constantly among the top international prizewinners. In 1937 at the

Trio of Avia Ba 122s (360 hp RK-17) flown by the team Hubáček, Novák and Široký in 1936. The machine was used in the USSR, Bulgaria and Romania. (Jan Krumbach)

Zurich competition, Czech pilots swept the board in both aircraft categories for which they were eligible. A great tradition had been started which was to grow, flourish, and eventually revolutionize the aerobatic world.

The start of the revolution had humble enough origins, in September 1934, when a shoe company called Bata started a small aeroplane manufacturing concern at Otrokovice in Moravia. About six miles distant was the town of Zlin, and this became their trade name. Twenty years later the name Z-l-i-n spelled m-a-g-i-c.

At first, two powered light aeroplane prototypes were designed, of which the first (Zlin XI) came to nothing. But the second, the Zlin XII monoplane, soon became the most popular light aircraft in pre-war Czechoslovakia; sales ran to over 300 before the Nazi occupation closed down production and instead demanded manufacture of Klemm 35B and Bücker 181 Bestmann trainers for the Luftwaffe. The Bestmann was the latest in the line of extremely fine Bücker aircraft, a monoplane design which came into service in 1940; the Zlin factory produced 783 of them between 1942 and 1945.

After the liberation in 1945 production of the Bestmann continued, to equip the new Czech Air Force, under the designations Z-181 (105 hp Hirth), Z-281 (106 hp Toma), and Z-381 (105 hp Walter-Minor). Designated C-6 by the Czech Air Force, 464 of these Bestmann versions were built between 1945 and 1948, and were used in the aero clubs as well as for military basic trainers. The factory also went on to manufacture excellent gliders and the first post-war sport and semi-aerobatic aeroplane, the three-seat Z-22 Junak, which was widely exported. Aviation in Czechoslovakia was soon back on its feet again.

Thanks to the already proud tradition of Czech aerobatics and to its active encouragement under the new Communist regime, there was always opportunity – and the right aircraft provided – for civilian as well as military aerobatic training. Unique among modern Civil Aviation Authorities, the Czechs required candidates for private pilots' licences to master basic aerobatics as part of the syllabus, taking the enlightened view that it promoted a better sense of orientation in space together with a mastery of the aircraft in the most varied of attitudes and circumstances.

To encourage aerobatics both as an aid to better flying and as a sport in its own right, the efficiently organized aero clubs throughout the country were grouped under Regional Centres each with its own training facility and equipment, and instructor training was carried out at the Central Aviation School along with advanced courses in special subjects, including aerobatics. Thus there existed a framework within which the Czech aircraft industry, and Zlin in particular, were able to concentrate on production-line manufacture of exclusively aerobatic machines, when the rest of the world's aircraft manufacturers would have thrown up their hands in horror at the prospect.

The year 1947 saw the first flight of the new aerobatic trainer prototype designed by Karel Tomáš in welded steel-tube construction, fabric-covered, with wings made of wood, and designated Z-26 or C-5 Trener (Trainer). The aircraft visibly resembled its predecessor the Bestmann, although abandoning the side-by-side seating in favour of a tandem arrangement. It had dual controls and was flown from the rear seat. This and the later Z-126 Trener 2 version with metal wing and tail surfaces (flown from the front seat this time) sold a total of 329 examples all over the world between 1949 and 1956. The power plant was a 105 hp Walter-Minor 4-III.

But it was with the more powerful Z-226 design series with 160 hp Walter-Minor 6-III engines that 'Zlin fever' really began internationally. Chief designer František Zámečnik's first big hit was the 1956 Z-226T Trener 6 model, a total of 283 being produced between 1956 and 1959 with buyers including Germany, Romania, England, Egypt and the USSR. With the extra power of the 6-cylinder engine, the aircraft's performance, even with additional dual controls in the front cockpit, surpassed earlier models and made it suitable for the most advanced aerobatics of the day. The Trener 6 made a triumphant impression on its first visit abroad when Jiří Bláha, the first Czech to enter the British-based International Lockheed Competition, won second place in 1956.

With the success of the 226 trainer, the Zlin designers thought they would prepare a solo version expressly for top aerobatic competition. The Z-226A Akrobat was developed and five were produced in 1956–7 for the Czech market. With the disappearance of the front seat and the canopy shortened

accordingly, this machine enjoyed a significant weight reduction and an increase in top speed from 235 to 245 km/h. In 1957, as if to prove its superiority, Czech pilot Vilém Krysta flew the Z-226A to overall victory in the Lockheed Trophy.

Next in 1957 the Z-326 Trener Master appeared, basically a

The first of the fabulous aerobatic Zlins, Z-226 Trener 6, 1956 (160 hp Walter Minor).   *(Author's collection)*

Span	10.28 m (33 ft 9 in)
Length	7.83 m (25 ft 8 in)
Height	2.06 m (6 ft 9 in)
Empty weight	570 kg (1,254 lb)
Max speed	235 km/h (146 mph)
Rate of climb	4.8 m/sec (945 fpm)

version of the Z-226T with retractable undercarriage, which all the Zlin models featured from now onwards. The wingspan of 10.28 m (33 ft 6 in) which had been standard since the Z-126 was now increased to 10.58 m (34 ft 6 in), and tip tanks were provided. The main pilot position again shifted to the front seat instead of the back, and the canopy was modified to improve visibility. The Walter-Minor engine remained as before, but with the advantage of retracted gear a maximum 245 km/h (152 mph) was possible even though it was a two-seat trainer; this model proved easily the most popular yet, with a total of 421 produced between 1959 and 1964 and with sales all over the world, particularly in Europe. The first Trener Master seen at a Lockheed Competition was that owned in 1963–4 by the British pilot Neville Browning, hitherto a renowned Tiger Moth exponent.

Flight Fantastic

In response to popular demand, a Z-326A Akrobat single-seater version with retractable gear was brought out in 1960, with a shortened canopy this time opening at the side instead of sliding back. Its rate of climb was nearly 1,000 ft (300 m) per minute. Fifteen of these models were produced and were sold primarily in the Soviet Union and Spain.

By now some 2,000 Zlin aircraft had been built, a unique achievement for a series of sport aerobatic machines. And in 1965 the factory received a very special accolade from the FAI in the form of a Diploma of Honour for its achievements in the manufacture of training and aerobatic aircraft.

Meanwhile, in 1963 a small series of four Z-226AS (Akrobat Special) models had been produced featuring wheel spats and – a significant advance – an Avia V 503 constant-speed propeller. They were used by the Czech team in the 1964 World Championships in Spain.

Having seen the excellent results achieved with the con-

aerobatics, which allows him to monitor the amount of positive or negative g to which the airframe is being subjected. Now, with the weight of the constant-speed unit in front, the main pilot seat needed to be moved back to the rear position again: pilots generally found this an advantage because their sideways vision was lined up with the wing trailing edge and they had a sightline vertically downwards to check their position relative to the ground. The prototype machine, registered OK-SND, was flown by 33-year-old engineer Ladislav Bezák to third place in the 1965 Lockheed Competition.

With more efficient use of engine output thanks to the constant-speed unit, the 526 was the first of the Zlin Treners able to fly virtually all known aerobatic manoeuvres without loss of altitude, an important consideration in competitions and in airshows, where interludes between figures spent regaining altitude were a waste of valuable time. The wing

Z-326 Trener Master (160 hp Walter Minor).   (Ian Hodge)

Span	10.58 m (34 ft 9 in)
Length	7.82 m (25 ft 8 in)
Height	2.06 m (6 ft 9 in)
Empty weight	642 kg (1,412 lb)
Max speed	245 km/h (152 mph)
Rate of climb	4.4 m/sec (866 fpm)

stant-speed prop, the Zlin designers now decided to incorporate it in a new model. The result was the new Z-526 Trener Master which went into production from 1965 onwards: the fuselage and cowling designs were altered and a larger instrument panel installed, complete with accelerometer (g-meter), an important instrument to the pilot of advanced

had a thick, rounded aerofoil with very little dihedral but with quite a marked degree of sweepback, and a large aileron area which extended to about half the span. The controls were beautifully harmonized and a delight to handle, although with those large ailerons there was quite a lot of adverse yaw when bank was applied. An elevator servo-tab was incorporated, as in the Z-326 Akrobat, but even so it required quite a lot of muscle power to handle the pitch control.

The stall was a miracle of stability with no tendency to wallow or drop a wing. The propwash over the generous rear controls maintained their effectiveness and a clean exit could be made from a vertically climbing manoeuvre even when all energy had been lost at the top, when in another aircraft one might expect it to fall away from the horizontal

and perhaps spin. The rate of roll – 360 degrees in 6 seconds – would of course be considered very slow by modern standards. It was about the same as the Bücker Jungmann. But of course it must be remembered that the Zlin was a big, graceful monoplane with a 10½ metre wingspan, in which even a flick roll was more of a balletic pirouette than a snap!

Sixty-one of the Z-526 Trener Masters were produced from 1965 to 1967, but now a whole succession of variations on the 526 theme appeared, each with a slightly different market in mind:

– the Z-526A Akrobat version (20 produced in 1966) left the basic Trener model intact but converted the cockpit into a single-seater;

– the Z-526AS Akrobat Special (5 examples sold only in Czechoslovakia, 1969–73) was built to the specifications of the Czech aerobatic pilots and was considerably lightened, with the flaps removed and the side-opening canopy

which sported a 200 hp Lycoming AIO-360 engine but was still suitable for both solo and dual aerobatics;

– then came three models incorporating a change of motor to the 180 hp Avia M 137A and all bearing the suffix 'F', starting with the Z-526F of 1970 (118 examples produced and widely bought abroad) which introduced a more powerful motor with fuel injection and modified fuel and oil systems;

– later the same year a Z-526AF Akrobat version inevitably followed (15 built), embodying all the design features specified by the Czech team pilots for the Z-526AS plus constant-speed propeller;

– and finally the most radical modification of all, the Z-526AFS was produced in 1971/2 and sold 30 models. In an effort to increase the roll rate and the effectiveness of the control surfaces, and at the same time to reduce the bending moment which in modern contests was placing ever

Z-526 AFS with curtailed wings, 1972 (180hp Avia M 137A).
(John Blake)

Span	8.84 m (29 ft)
Length	7.806 m (25 ft 6 in)
Height	1.9 m (6 ft 3 in)
Empty weight	605 kg (1,331 lb)
Max speed	252 km/h (157 mph)
Rate of climb	7 m/sec (1,378 fpm)
Limit load	+ 7, − 4.5 g

replaced with a sliding version. Most important, the forward fuselage and engine bearers were strengthened so that the maximum *g* loading could be increased.

– the Z-526L aimed for the export market (7 models, 1970–72),

greater *g* loads on the long, graceful wings, they were cropped by no less than 1.74 m (5 ft 8½ in) resulting in a wingspan of 8.846 m (29 ft). The ailerons were enlarged and divided into a main aileron and an inboard mini-aileron for better diving roll performance, and a wing fillet (wing root fairing) was inserted to further improve the aerodynamics in vertical manoeuvres.

British Champion Neil Williams's comment on the AFS was that the shortened span only served to increase the induced drag out of all proportion, resulting in a large speed loss when high *g* was pulled; also that the machine could not be flown cleanly away from a stalled condition, which of course had been one of the 526's great virtues. In fact he and a number of his contemporaries lamented the passing of the old 226 model of ten years previously.

British team Zlins, 1970: Z-526 Trener (above) piloted by Carl Schofield, Z-526 Akrobat (foreground) piloted by James Black. (Peter Hewit, via Tony Bianchi)

Although the long line of Treners was further developed in 1973 to produce the Z-726 Universal, with span increased from the AFS to 9.875 m (32 ft 5 in), and later the Z-726K, it was plain by now that a total rethink was necessary to remain competitive against the aerobatic aircraft being produced elsewhere in the world – and this is where the Zlin 50 arrives in our story.

But we are getting ahead of ourselves. The Zlin 50 we shall meet in its proper place later on in our book: it was a different aircraft, designed for the different requirements of a different age of high-power aerobatics.

Tracing the fascinating lineage of the Zlin family has taken us through more than twenty years in as many minutes, but we must return now to review the exploits of the Czech pilots in the 1950s, and for this a swift change of scene is necessary from Czechoslovakia to the British Isles.

In 1955 in Great Britain the Lockheed Hydraulic Brake Company had founded a series of annual aerobatic competitions which were open to solo pilots and aircraft of any nationality. A handsome trophy was provided together with prize money that attracted the world's best from as far afield as Israel, Argentina and America, as well as from all over Europe. The contests were an enormously popular feature of the regular air display held at Coventry Civic Aerodrome, Baginton, and lasted until 1965.

Each pilot flew a five-minute programme of his own composition in an eliminating round, and the best of these then went through to fly a second time, in the finals, from which the winners were chosen. The judges expected to see not only technical precision but a veritable picture traced in the sky, embodying artistry and originality as well as accuracy.

The British, with their reputation for sporting fairness, were popular hosts, and it was not long before Czech pilots were a regular and welcome feature of the event. In the following chapter the eleven Lockheed competitions are covered in more detail with complete lists of results, but for the moment let us content ourselves with an overview of how the Czech pilots fared.

Since the war's end the large number of 'Sunday pilots' flying aerobatics in all parts of Czechoslovakia had led to some diversity in style and approach, and with the advent of the specialized Z-226 machines a definite schism appeared between what is best defined as the graceful, fluid style of the 'Classical School' and the innovative, fast and 'flicky' approach of the 'Dynamic School'. Whereas exponents of the former style would tend towards loops, vertical rolls, figures-of-8 and Ss, the latter favoured plenty of autorotations like flick rolls and spins (notably the flat spin), and invented new figures or new versions of manoeuvres which attempted to explore all possible planes of flight. Inevitably, there also existed a 'Mixed' school of aerobatics which combined the two styles.

Amid such a rich breeding ground, various leagues of

competition and local formation teams grew up, among them the Moravian Team, the Slovak Team, and the Czech Dynamic Aerobatic Team which was headed by Ladislav Bezák, founder of the Dynamic School.

It was MiG.15 test pilot Jiří Bláha (Classical school) who first revealed the potential of the Zlin 226 Trener 6 to an enraptured Lockheed Trophy audience in July 1956, and his solo

Jiří Bláha, solo Czech entrant in the 1956 Lockheed Trophy.
(Nick Pocock)

appearance in Coventry soon led to an ever larger turn-out of Czech competitors in the ensuing years. His sparkling performance was remarkable for an abundance of negative manoeuvres – outside loops and inverted flying predominated – together with a split-second precision in checking his flick manoeuvres exactly on line. It was noted, too, that he was the only competitor who did not have to alter his programme to suit the restrictive weather of the following day's finals. Everyone found the Zlin a most impressive machine.

But Bláha was up against the Frenchman Léon Biancotto in this competition, and Biancotto's skill and artistry were formidable. It has often been said – as it was on this occasion – that Biancotto's flying approached perfection. With his SR.7B Monitor, a low-wing aeroplane by Jean Stampe, Biancotto took the Trophy for the second year running and Jiří Bláha was awarded second place. His turn to win would come later.

The following year, in a field of eighteen competitors, four Czech pilots arrived in England to contest the coveted Trophy: Jiří Bláha once more, Miroslav Přikryl, Karel Krenč and Vilém Krysta. They brought with them three of the new Z-226 Akrobats, and all except Krenč reached the finals. Bláha performed some distinctly unusual manoeuvres, including a Vertical 8 started from the bottom, and knife-flight featuring a flick roll from one knife-edge to the other – a very impressive figure – but he was judged to be a little off his best form when he flew second time around, and on this occasion managed only fourth place, with Přikryl behind him in fifth.

The really exceptional performance of the 1957 contest was that given by Czech coal-miner Vilém Krysta, including outside and inside vertical and horizontal figure eights, laced with flick, slow and hesitation rolls. The Zlin's ability to withstand quite heavy *g* forces was demonstrated by Krysta's backward 'hammer stall' (trail-slide) followed by a two-turn inverted spin. This 32-year-old part-time flying instructor from the Ostrava Flying Club outclassed even the great Biancotto, and carried the Trophy home with him to Czechoslovakia.

The 1958 Lockheed saw a showing of three Czech pilots in Coventry: they were Vilém Krysta again, this time flying a Zlin 226 Akrobat, with Jaromír Hůlka and Zdeněk Beseda who flew Z-226 Trener 6s. By now the Zlin had become a very desirable asset for top class competition, a fact which was proved by Léon Biancotto's change from his Stampe to a Trener 6 with Belgian registration. Unfortunately for the Czechs, Biancotto displayed his usual mastery and turned in a fine performance aided by a fine machine. It was his third win.

Zdeněk Beseda was adjudged second, and his programme was notable for the inclusion of positive and negative flicks, negative stall turns, and a spectacular tail-slide. Vilém Krysta (fourth) also gave an impressive tail-slide, with the airscrew almost stopped, followed by an outside loop; he appeared to use less sky and had more rapid continuity than any other contestant. Jaromír Hůlka tied in sixth place.

That same year of 1958 the Czech National Championships had been inaugurated, and it was Vilém Krysta who took the first-ever title from runners-up Přikryl and Krenč. Sadly, he was not to live to defend the championship: Krysta was killed in a flying accident the following year. But his memory is still perpetuated in a way in which surely every aerobatic pilot would wish to be remembered, which is by a figure that he invented: the **Krysta Loop**.

This 'loop' is actually two half-loops, one upward and then one downward, joined by a flick roll at the top which changes the heading of the aircraft by 90 degrees: if the first half-loop were started on the main x-axis, for example, after the flick roll rotation at the top the next (downward) half-loop would be on the y-axis. Even nicer is to continue on with another Krysta Loop afterwards, by which you have then drawn all four possible half-loops around the cardinal points of a three-dimensional sphere – the whole effect is rather like quartering an orange.

Krysta never told anyone the secret of how he performed the deft change of axis by means of a flick roll at the top of the half-loop: being an autorotation, the flick could be stopped half or threequarters of the way through but could not be 'steered' 90 degrees on to a different axis, so how was it done? With the help of another Czech, Vladimir Pohořelý, members of the Swiss national team managed to work it out more than ten years afterwards. The method was to start a positive flick roll on reaching the top of the figure (to the right, let us say), which displaced you off axis to the left; and then at the half-way point without correcting that displacement you smoothly went into a half negative flick in the same direction, which displaced the aircraft still further to the left and brought you out inverted on the correct axis to pull down into the second half-loop. It was a very original idea, and a very neat use of the displacement that inevitably attends flick-roll manoeuvres.

In 1959 the Czechoslovak pilots did not compete in

Flight Fantastic

Coventry. But in the National Championships the winner was Beseda from Bláha and Hůlka, while in fourth place appeared for the first time that pilot who was to become a great driving force in Czech aerobatics, Ladislav Bezák.

Meanwhile, the Czech representatives at the Fédération Aéronautique Internationale had proposed a motion at the General Conference in May 1959 to establish a World

Vilém Krysta, first of the Czech pilots to win the Lockheed Trophy (1957). *(Flight)*

Championship in Aerobatics. With competition aerobatics already so well organized in their own country, they had come up with a scheme of regulations for the event and proposed that it should take place in Czechoslovakia in the month of August that year.

As so often happens in these international associations, however, the Czech suggestion had not been received in time to be circulated to all the other National Aero Clubs who would need to translate the proposal and give it advance study, so an event in 1959 was out of the question. It was agreed, nevertheless, that the first FAI World Aerobatic Championships would take place in 1960, and the location was to be Bratislava.

Subsequently an FAI *Commission Internationale de Voltige Aérienne* (International Aerobatics Commission) was constituted under the Presidency of the Swiss delegate Fred Forrer, later succeeded by the Czech delegate Jaroslaw Kohoutek. One of its first decisions was that the World Championships would take place biennially. This Commission, known as CIVA, is still the governing body that runs international aerobatic championships under FAI rules, which are agreed at regular meetings between all the countries concerned.

The Czech contingent at the 1960 Lockheed contest was even larger this year, with five pilots represented: Beseda for the second time, and first-timers Juraj Šouc, Antonín Klimenda, Jiřina Lockerová and Eva Krenčová. These last two were the first women to compete in the Lockheed, and were youngsters aged 20 and 21 respectively. Both from the Olomouc Aero Club, they had done well to qualify for the Czech World Championship team, and more than held their own at Coventry by getting through to the final, where they were placed respectively fifth and seventh. Klimenda made

an unfortunate timing error which eliminated him, but flying instructor Juraj Šouc in the Z-226 Trener 6 turned in a highly original performance full of complex and spectacular figures which earned him second place overall. Beseda's fast, crisp, well co-ordinated programme showed plenty of verve and was signed off with an inverted wing-rock, taking fourth place in the finals. The French Chevalier d'Orgeix managed to beat them all to the Lockheed Trophy, however, flying a Stampe SV.4A in a performance of unrivalled artistry.

With a World Championship in the offing, the team selections at the Czech National Championships of 1960 had been hotly contested by 13 pilots: Jiří Bláha was the new champion, with Ladislav Bezák second, and by now Bezák's Dynamic School of aerobatics had really caught hold of the entire aerobatic scene.

It is important to understand just how revolutionary were these new 'dynamic' ideas, and how stunning were the whirling, tumbling figures which followed one after the other in breathless succession. To appreciate them one must look at the innovations which were introduced to aerobatics by Ladi Bezák and his colleagues.

First there was the **flat spin** – a manoeuvre well known for decades but quite consistently avoided for fear that the aeroplane might fail to recover. In fact the flat spin is nothing more than a well developed spin during which the aircraft's nose rises to an angle much closer to the horizon than the usual nose-down angle at the beginning of an ordinary spin. An exaggerated 'flat' angle may be achieved by control and power inputs by the pilot if he wishes to increase the effect, and the dizzying rate of rotation is very spectacular.

The main difference in recovery from an accelerated spin of this sort is that it is likely to take longer to bring to a halt, in exactly the same way that stopping a car from 150 km/h will take longer than from 75 km/h; pilots used to be unhappy about the delayed response and about the extremely fast rate of rotation which might create nausea in even the most experienced aerobat. But, of course, these days we have our standardized tests for aircraft designs which require certain prescribed characteristics in the spin, and there is no need for apprehension as there doubtless was in the less regimented days before the war.

Bezák writes that he flew the first (intentional) flat spin in the 1960 World Championships. "Since the judges did not know how to recognize a flat spin from a normal one, following a few simple explanations they drew on their sheets an elevator pointing down, noted full power during the rotation, and specified that the demonstration had to be below 500 metres to be visible". So Bezák performed his flat spin, of five complete turns and then some, between the heights of 500 and 150 m (about 1,650 and 500 ft). It must have been quite impressive!

The flat spin, however, was not Bezák's only innovation*. We also have him to thank for the invention of an entirely new figure – when one would have thought by the 1950s there were no more new figures to invent – and that figure is what the Czechs call the **lomcovák** (pronounced lom-tzo-vák).

By constant experiment and practice he had evolved a type of gyroscopic figure which, started from a rapid negative flick roll towards the direction in which the torque of the airscrew aids the rotation, could then be induced to revolve the aeroplane rapidly around its own axis in various ways, one of them (the 'main' lomcovák) being a full forward autorotating somersault. It took the aerobatic world by storm. This was

*Although it was an innovation to perform a flat spin as a figure on its own, the figure had previously been used – though rarely – as an element in combination with other manoeuvres. See Novák's figure in the 1936 Berlin Olympic Contest, pages 110, 111.

Z-226A Akrobats (160 hp Walter Minor) flown by the victorious Czech team in the 1960 World Championships.
(John Underwood)

something that pilots had long speculated about but which had previously been considered impossible.

Only the combination of the brilliant Czech pilots and their purpose built, high-performance aeroplanes could come up with a whole new type of manoeuvre which was not just a different combination of existing evolutions, but a radically new concept of allowing gyroscopic forces to work on an autorotation and develop it into an unprecedented series of whirls and pirouettes. Bezák's first public performance of the 'main' lomcovák and 'conic' lomcovák was in 1957 in an airshow at Kladno Airport.

The story of how the figure acquired its name is an amusing one. It happened the following year, 1958, when Bezák was giving a display at Brno, the principal city of the Moravian region of Czechoslovakia, where the Zlin factory is situated. His mechanic was standing on the airfield talking with another

Ladislav Bezák, World Aerobatic Champion 1960.
(Author's collection)

Czech pilot, František Skácelík, when a journalist approached them and asked what it was that Bezák was doing?

"That?" they said, feigning an air of mild surprise, as if anyone who knew anything at all would certainly recognize *that*. "But surely you know what a lomcovák is!" The poor man was mystified, of course, the more so because the word 'lomcovák' is a slang word in the Moravian dialect, referring to the after-effects of rather too much 'slivovitz', the traditional Czechoslovakian alcohol! Since then it has often been misinterpreted as meaning the hangover/headache variety of after-effect, but in reality it means the sort of Chaplin-esque reeling, swaying gait of one who has imbibed a little over the odds. . . .

The whole thing was a pilot's joke that only a Moravian could understand, and Bezák himself swears that he never gave the manoeuvre its name; but somehow the public liked to call it a lomcovák, and the word does have a nice, expressive feel to it.

There are several varieties of lomcovák, of which some are figures with a definite geometric shape, or recognizable outline, and some are the result of setting up the aeroplane in a given set of parameters and then riding through the resultant gyrations. The aerobatic world is fiercely divided between those who consider this second variety to be a valid figure, and those who disagree on the grounds that it is 'uncontrolled'. Be that as it may, the lomcovák has been with us for over twenty-five years and very few indeed must be the number of top pilots who have not featured it in their repertoire. I once saw it included in the possible list of compulsory figures for an international contest, although on the day it wasn't chosen. But that's another story, and you can find it in Chapter 21.

So the Czechs hosted the first World Aerobatic Championship in Bratislava from 27 August to 4 September 1960, and 20 contestants from nine countries took part. Each pilot had to fly two compulsory sequences and one freestyle in the eliminating round, and then the nine finalists again flew the same three sequences in the finals. Contrary to present-day arrangements, the overall results of the two rounds were not added together: had they been, the outcome would have been substantially different! Instead the scores in the final round were the definitive results from which the winners were decided, and Ladislav Bezák emerged as the first World Champion.

There were many other aspects which also differed from today's World Championships. The Czechs fielded ten con-

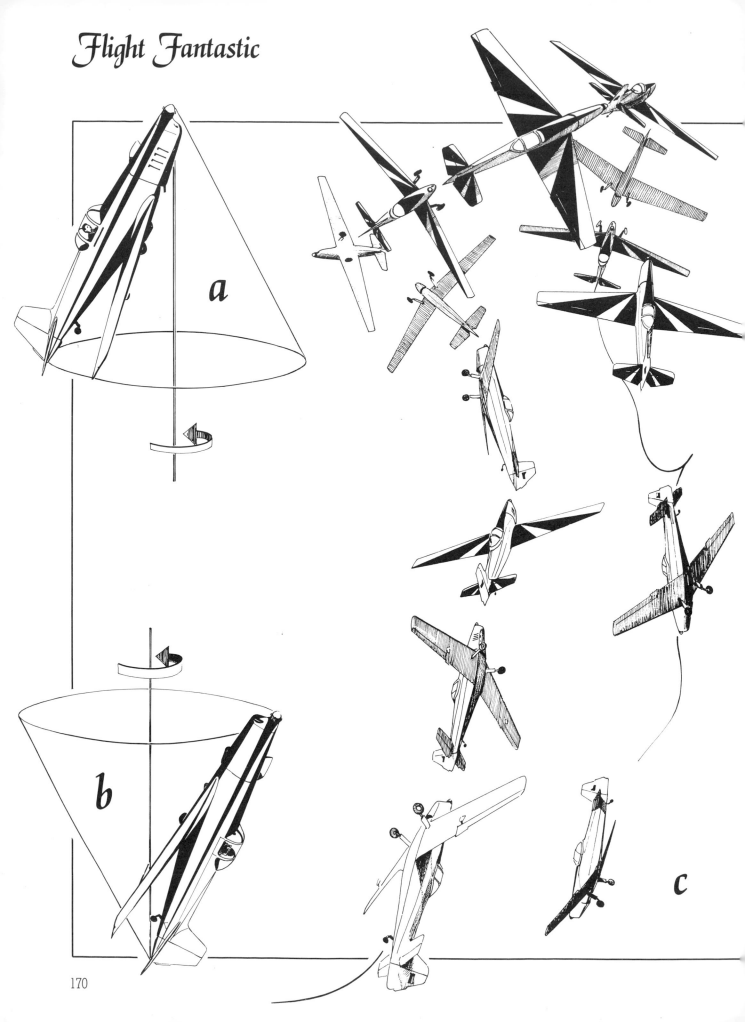

a

b

c

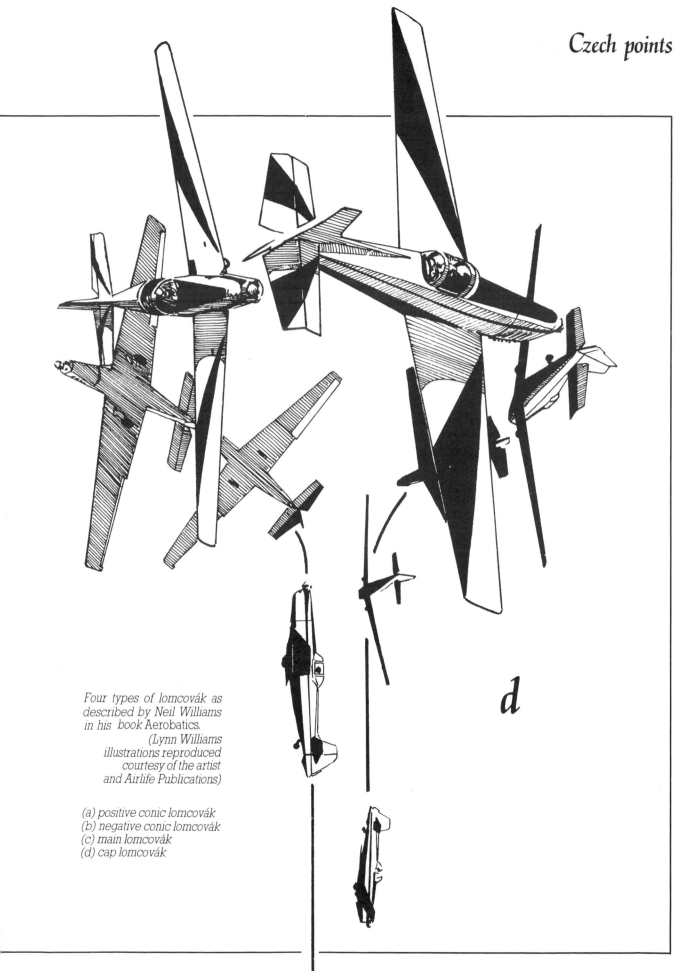

d

Four types of lomcovák as described by Neil Williams in his book Aerobatics.
(Lynn Williams illustrations reproduced courtesy of the artist and Airlife Publications)

(a) positive conic lomcovák
(b) negative conic lomcovák
(c) main lomcovák
(d) cap lomcovák

171

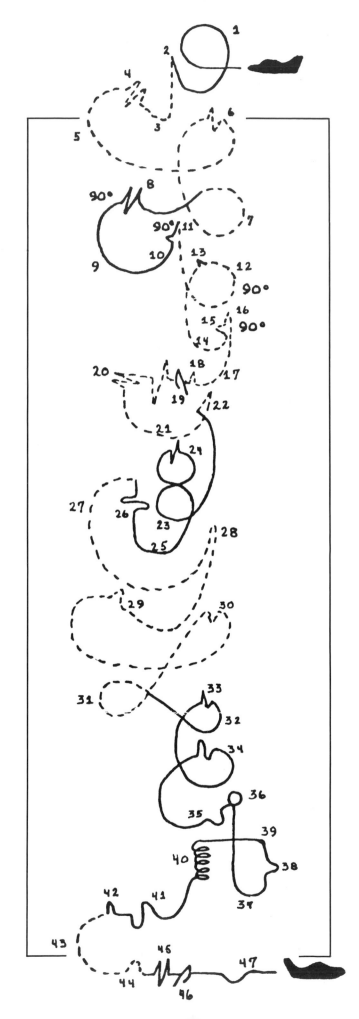

Ladi Bezák's freestyle programme as flown in WAC 1960: first introduction of a flat spin and two lomcováks in international competition. (Krysta Loop fig 12-13, main lomcovák fig 20, conic lomcovák fig 36, flat spin fig 40).

testants, including two women whose scores were listed in with all the other pilots: present rules allow a maximum of five male and five female pilots only, and the female contestants – given that there are sufficient numbers – have a separate championship league of their own (though I still wonder why). The seven judges came from Czechoslovakia, France and the USSR; today not more than one judge of each nationality is permitted.

It is amusing now to look back on the heated controversy that surrounded the rules for these first championships. The British, having what they considered to be a tried and tested formula for a successful competition, hotly protested that with the proposed number of programmes the whole thing would take too long. Why, with 15 competitors, they said – about the number normally expected at the Lockheed – it might take six or seven hours to run! Today's World Championships last a fortnight.

Each compulsory programme consisted of eight figures for which the maximum time allowed was five minutes. They included a 2½ turn negative spin, a stick forward tail-slide from an inverted entry, and a 360 degree inverted turn. The Czechs wanted a circumscribed performance zone 1,000 metres wide and 600 metres deep (3,300 × 2,000 ft), within which all the figures must be executed. The maximum height would be 800 m (2,600 ft) and the lower limit would be 100 m (330 ft). This again was contested, with the result that the 'box' was eventually retained for the compulsory programmes only; the free programmes, of 6 minutes duration, were allowed to be flown free of spatial restrictions.

Of the aeroplanes in use, Zlins predominated everywhere – a total of 18, all of them Z-226 types except for the Z-326s from the Soviet Union. This led to speculation as to whether future World Championships should not be held with all pilots performing on the same aircraft type, as the disparity between the Zlins and the other machines was so pronounced. Since 1960 there have indeed been aerobatic competitions in various countries of the world where a single type of aircraft has been used, but so far this procedure has not been adopted by the FAI.

As to the performances, of course everybody went home talking about the Czechs. Ladi Bezák's comment just about sums up their style of flying: "My aim is to display 'dynamic' aerobatics executed within the smallest posible space and in the rapidest possible succession." To this end it is worth examining his freestyle programme reproduced here, which contains no fewer than 47 different elements according to Bezák's calculations, 59 according to the Czech organizers (using a system whereby a 1½ flick roll is counted as two manoeuvres and an outside Horizontal 8 with half-roll is counted as three). Translated into today's terms, where a combination figure containing more than one element is only counted as one figure, the total in his programme would be 30: still an enormously high number within a 6 minute time-scale!

There were a few unhappy notes during the proceedings, the first of which was the one and only serious accident that has ever happened in an FAI World Aerobatic Championship, and it occurred during the practice day on 29 August.

Jiří Bláha, Lockheed Trophy winner 1961, with his mechanic Vlček. (via Lynn Williams)

That afternoon the wonderful French pilot Léon Biancotto, flying his Nord 3202, went out of control during the recovery from the inverted spin. He died in the crash (see page 159).

A strong wind plagued the contestants on several days, and delayed the flying on one occasion, but otherwise the weather, though not perfect, did not interfere. Even in this first of all World Championships there were protests about unfair judging, which has sadly been a recurrent theme throughout the ensuing years, and requests to inspect the judges' score sheets were refused. Fortunately we allow no such prohibitions nowadays, and all pilots have the right to examine their marks. Of the nine finalists (30 per cent of the total entry) eight were Czechs, and the general opinion agreed that they richly deserved their placings. The ninth finalist was the only Soviet pilot to fly the Yak 18P, Boris Vasenko, whose final score placed him fifth overall. Otherwise the Czechs swept the board of all the medals, with Bezák first in the Trener 6, Bláha second, Skácelík third and Hůlka fourth, all flying the Z-226 Akrobat. Beseda, Stoklasa, Trebatický and Šouc took sixth to ninth places. They even managed to take home one of the 'extra' awards as well – that for the youngest pilot, Ladislav Trebatický.

Ladislav Trebatický – youngest pilot at the 1960 World Championships. (Nick Pocock)

After their World Championship triumphs, Bláha, Hůlka and Trebatický took their Zlins to Coventry in 1961, with the happy result that Jiří Bláha, who had been the first and only Czech representative in 1956, now won the Trophy at his third attempt. Young Ladislav Trebatický also scored highly and achieved third place. In Bláha's programme with the Z-226 Akrobat he featured a seldom seen sixteen-point hesitation roll – a difficult figure from many points of view, not only hard to execute cleanly and evenly, but also, with such quick and tiny facets, difficult to demonstrate visibly and clearly to the judges. That he succeeded despite these impediments is amply shown by the judges' report, which described Bláha's manoeuvre as one that 'must rank among the great aerobatic performances of all time'.

Bláha had already won the 1960 Czechoslovakian Championships, and indeed would have won the World Aerobatic Championships by 26 points had the total scores been added

together in 1960 as they were in all subsequent WACs; but they were not, and he came second. Now in 1961 he again took the Czech national title and then decided to rest on his laurels, for he was never afterwards seen in international competitions.

In 1962 there was all-out preparation for the second World Championship in Hungary, therefore no National Championship or Lockheed Trophy participation. A pattern began to emerge with the home team usually having a distinct advantage in WACs, and accordingly the Hungarians succeeded in fielding the 1962 Gold Medallist in the person of József Tóth, an 'outsider' who had very limited powered-aerobatics experience although he was a past master at the very difficult art with gliders. Hungary also won the newly donated Nesterov Cup for the highest placed team, presented by the USSR in commemoration of Petr Nesterov who performed the first loop in September 1913. Czech pilots Jaromír Hůlka and Ladi Bezák came third and fourth overall, with Hůlka winning Programme 3*.

It was a fact then, as it is now, that the degrees of excellence are so close in top-level aerobatics that anyone achieving the top five, often the top ten, is capable of being a world champion. Hence the balance is often tipped by the home team's familiarity with the terrain, language, ambience, etc., which goes a long way towards combating nervous tension. The Hungarians had equipped themselves with the latest Zlin aircraft, and they based their style of flying on that employed by the 'Mixed' school of technique in neighbouring Czechoslovakia: this proved the winning formula in an international context.

As before, the free choice programme carried a much higher total of potential marks than either of the compulsory sequences, and pilots were asked to present their written programmes in advance to the judges, using an aerobatic notation which the French pilots had developed and which had been published by François d'Huc Dressler in 1955 (see Chapter 11). This time, in Budapest, reference was made to a

Flight Fantastic

catalogue of 180 manoeuvres with given difficulty coefficients, the coefficient for each manoeuvre in the pilot's programme being marked out of 10 for correctness and precision, and out of a further 10 for flexibility and elegance.

Height limits of 1,000 m (3,300 ft) and 100 m (330 ft) were enforced by means of barographs installed in the aeroplanes, but this year the 'box' of $1,000 \times 600$ m ($3,300 \times 2,000$ ft) was scrapped; contestants were simply required to centre their performances in front of the judges and overhead a marked axis. The competitor had five minutes to complete his flight. On the overall effect the judges could award a maximum 250 for harmony and originality, 250 for rhythm, and 250 for efficient use of the performance zone. By some strange quirk there also appeared a bonus of up to 50 points for 'safety' – perhaps in view of all those lomcovácking Czechs whose propellers had been known, on occasion, to part company with their parent aircraft during the more extreme gyrations. Still, 50 points would seem fairly irrelevant either as penalty or reward when you come to think of it.

By now there was some controversy about the highest marks being gained by those who could cram the greatest number of high-scoring manoeuvres into their free programme – quantity to the detriment of quality – and the British writer John Blake analysed the potential of various aircraft types, concluding that the finalists were coming up with totals of 850 marks and more for their free programmes, whereas the British Stampe could manage only half that number of points. Later, at the suggestion of the French, a limit was placed on the maximum points permissible in this programme. Meanwhile, in the following World Championship (in Spain) a maximum of 25 manoeuvres was set.

Bezák's entire philosophy was based, of course, on a plethora of high-scoring manoeuvres in a maximum performance aeroplane. To this end he had been working with several modifications to the Z-226, but as a consequence had several run-ins with the Czech authorities and even with the Zlin factory, who incidentally turned down his application to join them as a test pilot. In 1959, although flying a machine which was especially reserved for his use, he was prohibited from adopting a clipped-wing modification until it had had wind-tunnel tests; four years later he was able to incorporate the clipped wings in time for the WAC in Spain, and eight years later the modification emerged as a feature of the Z-526 series! In the later sixties he managed with his Lockheed prize-money and the proceeds of activities such as coaching and airshows to construct his own Zlin, the first privately-owned series aircraft in post-war Czechoslovakia.

To execute his lomcováks, and in particular to perform his planned programme of 25 high-scoring manoeuvres in the 1964 World Championship in Bilbao, he had a 168 hp motor installed in his Zlin 226 Akrobat Special and lightened the airframe by doing away with everything that was not strictly necessary: battery, starter, several instruments (including rpm indicator!), flaps, carburettor heat, brakes, and also the cockpit floor (removed in order to instal the first ever clearview panel for aerobatics in the fuselage underside). Along with other changes, to the fuel and oil tanks, tailwheel, etc., he had a special wood propeller fitted, with an Avia constant-speed unit which permitted him to fly a programme 20 per cent more difficult. The aircraft weighed 519 kg (1144 lb), as against some 565 kg (1243 lb) for the production Z-226AS.

Ladi eventually became a state test pilot, as well as instructor, judge, federal inspector and airline pilot. He was closely associated with research into the stresses caused by his lomcovák manoeuvre (gyroscopic and g forces and velocity of angular rotation), and was instrumental in placing severe restrictions on its use by pilots with unsuitable experience and equipment – but not until after six instances of propellers being lost, in Czechoslovakia, England, Poland and Germany. As a pioneer aircraft owner he always had hopes of liberalizing the Communist attitude towards private enterprise, but in the end his efforts caused him nothing but trouble.

Meanwhile six Czech contestants had flown in the 1963 Lockheed, and three of them had come away with the first three places: Jaromír Hůlka first (Z-226AS) with a display described as beautifully integrated and elegant, Ladi Bezák second and Ladislav Trebatický third, both flying the Z-226T. This trio had also battled it out for the Czech national title in 1963, in which Bezák emerged the winner.

Jaromír Hůlka, Lockheed Trophy winner 1963. (Jan F Šára)

It was the greatest era for the Czech pilots internationally, one in which their brilliant performances revolutionized the aerobatic world. New standards of technical proficiency were set, more demanding manoeuvres such as the vertical roll and knife-edge flicks made their way into competition programmes. Above all, figure sequences became faster and snappier, more closely integrated instead of allowing pauses to regain altitude, peppered with flicks in every conceivable attitude and combination.

Bezák and Trebatický returned again for the 1964 Lockheed, along with Stoklasa, Šouc and Eva Kaprasová, a student of Bezák's who had been a Czech national female champion and had tried her hand in both the WAC and the previous Lockheed competition. It was another triumph for the Czechs and their Zlin 226s, who as if by unspoken agreement seemed now to take it in turns to carry off the Trophy! This year's winner was Juraj Šouc, with Bezák third and Stoklasa fourth. All flew the new Z-226AS, which astounded observers with the way it could, from a low airspeed, perform a roll-off-the-top, pause for three seconds, and then execute another. With its wonderful vertical penetration the machine was ideal for vertical rolls of all kinds, which by now had become the key to success in international competition; and by proliferating

Juraj Šouc, Lockheed Trophy winner 1964.

(via Lynn Williams)

these vertical manoeuvres its pilots were able to centre their display in a drill-square of sky positioned right in front of the judges.

The 1964 World Championships are covered in detail when we reach Chapter 14, so we will confine ourselves here to following the fortunes of the Czechs once more. Bezák and Trebatický, both with the Z-226AS, followed behind the Spanish winner Tomas Castaño into second and third place respectively, but only four out of their six pilots made it through to the final. The fourth of these was a new young adherent of the dynamic school, Jiří Kobrle.

Followers of the sport will recognize this name as one of our most distinguished jury-members today and a Vice-President of CIVA who works tirelessly in the interests of aerobatics. He had been competing since 1960, was Czech Champion in 1969, and in 1970 began a long career as a test

Jiří Kobrle, an up-and-coming pilot in the 1960s, became Czech National Champion in 1969 and was twice bronze medallist in the Socialist Countries Championships of 1971 and 1972.

(Jan F Šára)

pilot for the Aviation Research and Development Institute in Prague, test-flying practically all aircraft produced in Czechoslovakia, from ultralights to jets! He still enjoys flying aerobatics, though for pleasure nowadays, not competition; and in his air displays he loves to perform fluid and classical manoeuvres to the accompaniment of music. Back in 1964, however, Jiří Kobrle was a rather junior team member in his first World Championship, though he finished a creditable twelfth in the overall results; František Skácelík came tenth.

Bezák, Stoklasa and Kaprasová were back again in 1965, together with 1963 winner Jaromír Hůlka, in what was sadly to be the last of the Lockheed Trophies. Gynaecologist Jiří Stoklasa had already drawn appreciative comment the year before with his well positioned and tightly-drawn performance, and now in 1965 it was his turn to emerge the winner. He started a beautiful sequence at 700 ft (210 m) with a spectacular pull-up to the vertical, half-roll left, half-roll right

Jiří Stoklasa, winner of the last Lockheed Trophy competition in 1965. *(Jan F Šára)*

and stall turn, right in front of the judges. Bezák was the other Czech finalist and managed third place overall, but his programme appeared restrained compared with Stoklasa's which was liberally sprinkled with lomcováks.

During some typical British weather on the previous day, which had postponed competition flights, Ladi Bezák went up to entertain the spectators with a demonstration of the new Z-526 Trener which was being seen for the first time outside Czechoslovakia. At the end of his demonstration a British Tiger Moth pilot started up to do the same thing, and as he climbed away suddenly had the sensation that he had company.... Bezák had spotted the Tiger, caught it up and quickly half-rolled to inverted overhead, whereupon he spent the next few moments in mirror formation with the British aeroplane! Mirror-flying was yet another aerobatic speciality of Ladi Bezák's.

Another triumph for Bezák was to follow when later that year he won the newly established Biancotto Trophy competition in France, commemorating the memory of the late Léon Biancotto, which became the unofficial 'European Championship'.

1966 brought another FAI World Aerobatic Championship,

Ladi Bezák and his family wave happily, but clearly show signs of strain after their terrifying flight across the border to Germany, December 1971. *(via IAC)*

held in Moscow. Czechoslovakia sent a full team of five men – Bezák, Šouc, Kobrle, Skácelík and Stoklasa – plus three women. Nobody stood much of a chance against the Soviets on their home territory, however, equipped as they were with a more powerful version of the Yak military trainer and a highly trained team. Ladi Bezák was still on top form and ended up in fifth position as highest placed non-Soviet contestant, flying the Z-526T. By now, such was the phenomenal success of the Zlin machines that they were flown by no fewer than 35 of the 63 participants, and 12 out of the 18 finalists.

The events of 1968 are a sad memory to the Czech people, and are vividly remembered in conjunction with the World Championship that year because the Soviet invasion of their homeland coincided with the event held in Magdeburg, East Germany.

The Czechs fielded the same team as in Moscow, with the exception of Ladi Bezák, who by now was having troubles with the authorities and had fallen into disfavour. He was not to appear as a team member again. With things getting ever more difficult at home, he eventually made the agonizing decision to seek a new life in West Germany. On 19 December 1971, he made a spectacular flight over the border near Bayreuth, with all his family squeezed into his Zlin 226 OK-MUA. The whole episode was like something out of a James Bond movie, with Ladi in his hopelessly overloaded machine evading an intercepting MiG with some desperate aerobatics. On one pass a sudden steep turn pulled him away from his pursuer; on the next pass, a quarter roll to knife-edge deluded the fighter into thinking that he was repeating the same evasive action, and the MiG – ready this time – sailed off into a high speed turn while Ladi neatly rolled out again and continued straight on course. His escape was helped – though navigation without instruments was greatly hindered – by thick cloud cover.

Eventually he landed safely in Nuremburg, and afterwards became something of a globetrotter; but the life of a refugee is not conducive to the furtherance of an aerobatic career – as Ladi says, taking your aeroplane with you to the West is not quite the same as taking your violin or your tennis racquet! He did, however, fetch up at last in Canada where he again became happily involved with aerobatic training.

Bezák's place in the 1968 team was taken by the remarkably talented Ivan Tuček, who was destined to become World Champion ten years later. They were flying three brand-new Z-526 Akrobat Specials which had been strengthened and lightened to their particular requirements and equipped with a sliding canopy. Things looked good for the Czechs, although with weather and organizational problems there was a threat that the final programme might fall by the wayside; until, as the competition progressed from Programme 2 to Programme 3, they realized that the invasion had happened and of course became desperately worried about homes and loved ones. A few managed to get in some flights, but the team as a whole retired at that point and the feelings of all those present went out to them.

The contest at Magdeburg could not be finished, and the results were accordingly declared on the basis of two programmes only, the home pilots Erwin Bläske and Peter Kahle taking the first two places. At the prizegiving ceremony, however, the biggest cheer of the evening went up as the name of Czechoslovakian pilot Juraj Šouc was announced in third place. As in 1964 and 1966, it was a Czech who had succeeded in scoring the highest marks after the winning pilots of the home teams.

We end this chapter on Czechoslovakian aerobatics with the last two internationals in which they flew the old-style Zlin, which were the 1970 and 1972 World Championships. In England in 1970 they were represented by a smaller team than usual – only four men and no female pilots – but Ivan Tuček and Jiří Kobrle were both in the magic top ten (eighth and tenth respectively) with the single-seat Z-526AF model which sported a new engine and constant-speed propeller. There were new aircraft appearing, however, to challenge the Zlin's superiority: although 35 of the 58 contestants flew Zlins, only three of the top ten pilots used them. The American Pitts Specials and the Swiss Acrostars had arrived on the scene and were stealing their thunder.

In 1972 in France, Kobrle was the highest placed Czech in seventh position and Tuček followed him in eleventh place, both flying the ultimate Z-526AFS model. This time the Zlin pilots had reduced to 25 out of 59 contestants, with the new French CAP 20s gaining ground internationally as well as the Pitts Specials. It was evident that now was the time for a new design concept on the part of the factory which had started out of a shoe-box in Moravia forty years before, and devotees of the fine Czech machines such as the British pilot Neil Williams, now a force to be reckoned with in international aerobatics, speculated as to whether the new model would perhaps hark back to the great days of the 160 hp Z-226. Nothing could have been farther from the ideas of the forward-looking Zlin design team, however, and when the new Zlin 50 aircraft emerged in 1975 it was a radically different design – different size, different shape, different undercarriage, different motor, and above all, a very different aeroplane to fly.

13

Britain and the Lockheed Trophy

In post-war Britain, still afflicted with shortages, rationing, bomb damage, disruption and austerity, one would be tempted to think it the unlikeliest of places to foster a rebirth of competition aerobatics. Indeed, 'rebirth' is scarcely the correct word, since the sport had scarcely ever featured in the British aviation arena.

Yet there had grown up in pre-war Britain a spirit of aviation pioneering out of all proportion to the general mood of the times: British pilots were first to fly the Atlantic, first to fly to Australia, first to fly to the Cape, and had set world records in height, long distance and speed. With scant government backing, even the speed record – achieved with the Schneider Trophy Supermarine S.6B in 1931 at 407 mph (655 km/h) – was only possible with the financial support of a private individual, Lady Houston.

Despite Sir Alan Cobham's travelling 'Aerial Circus' and i's aerobatic entertainments, the only real interest in precision aerobatics lay with the Royal Air Force, where great store was set on a proper mastery of aerobatic skills by every serving pilot. And it is to the RAF's pre-war choice of standard trainer for the acquisition of such skills that post-war British aerobatics owes an incalculable debt. I am, of course, referring to the Tiger Moth.

The firm of de Havilland had already captured the lion's share of the world's light aeroplane market during the years before the war, when it decided to bring out a trainer version of the popular DH60 Gipsy Moth biplane, challenging the virtual monopoly which the Avro trainers seemed to enjoy with the RAF. Born in 1931 as a somewhat rough and ready modification of the DH60T design, the Tiger Moth was given staggered wings to allow better access (and egress) for an instructor in the front cockpit encumbered with full kit and parachute, and was then given a few degrees of sweep-back on both upper and lower wings to restore the centre of

gravity. When equipped with the excellent 130 hp Gipsy Major inverted engine from 1934 onwards, the celebrated DH82a Tiger Moth was created in the form in which it still continues to fly over 50 years later.

Immediately scoring points on the grounds of economy over its larger and heavier Avro rival the 215–240 hp Tutor, the DH Tiger also proved far more difficult to fly than the RAF's other trainer, the sweet-natured Hawker Tomtit, and for this reason was again preferred. And when it came to ease of maintenance, the Tiger Moth came out tops every time. With the threat of war looming imminently, soon Tigers were equipping the RAF Volunteer Reserve, the Civil Air Guard, the Grading Schools, the Empire Training Scheme and the Fleet Air Arm, with orders coming from all over the world and subsidiary production set up as far afield as Australia and New Zealand.

Civilian orders had not been lacking, either, for clubs, flying schools and the like – with Alan Cobham getting in on the ground floor by acquiring two of the very earliest models, modified, like several of the RAF machines, to run while inverted – and thus by the time hostilities started and the Air Services needed to draw on supplies of reserve pilots, nearly all of them, civilian or military, had received basic training on the same type of machine.

Altogether something in the region of 9,000 Tiger Moths of one kind or another were produced, and with the arrival of peace there was a fair number of war surplus models available and a queue of willing buyers; indeed, in the absence of any better fully aerobatic trainer, Tigers even continued in uniform with the RAFVR as late as 1950, being supplanted only when the DH Chipmunk appeared on the scene. The last Tiger was withdrawn from RAF service in 1955.

Meanwhile, the ubiquitous little biplanes set off on a

Flight Fantastic

second career in the late forties and early fifties as glider tugs, crop dusters and banner-towing craft, as well as being snapped up for civil flying training and sport aviation. Many ex-wartime pilots now enjoyed the new feeling of freedom to fly as they wished, just for the fun of it, and the Tiger Moth was the foremost choice for anyone aerobatically inclined.

It must be admitted, first of all, that the Tiger Moth's ailerons are dreadful, and a slow roll is extremely hard work. They say if you can roll a Tiger, you can roll Tower Bridge! But loops, stall turns and barrel rolls are great fun, and the aeroplane is strong enough to withstand quite hefty amounts of *g*. Charles Turner-Hughes, during the course of one year's flying with the Cobham Circus, kept a log of his total aerobatics which added up to 2,328 loops, 2,190 rolls, 567 bunts, 522 upward rolls, 40 inverted falling leaves and five inverted loops (negative or outside loops). In one season he spent 170 hours in inverted flight! His successor, Geoffrey Tyson, used to loop a Tiger around a ribbon attached between two posts. To say that he judged this performance

Tiger Club display team of two Super Tigers and a Stampe tied together in formation. *(Mike Hooks)*

to a nicety is almost an understatement: standing the aeroplane on the ground between the posts, there would be no more than 4 ft (1.2 m) clearance between each wingtip and its neighbouring post, and 6 ft (1.8 m) between the upper mainplane and the ribbon!

Turner-Hughes and Tyson went on to become test pilots, and many of the ex-World War II pilots, especially those who had been involved in test flying machines for the RAF, were also attracted by this career after the war; one such was Squadron Leader Neville Duke. Duke had had his first taste of flight as a ten-year-old in one of Alan Cobham's joyriding Avro 504s, and had learned to fly in 1940 with the RAF – on Tiger Moths, of course! After flying Spitfires and the American Tomahawks and Kittyhawks, he was attached for a year to the Hawker firm for production testing of Typhoons and Tempests – successors to the Hurricane – emerging in 1946 with a permanent commission in the RAF. But test-piloting had appealed to him so much that he enrolled with the newly founded Empire Test Pilots' School to learn the job thoroughly, and in 1948 Duke returned to Hawker's full time.

Every year the Society of British Aircraft Constructors mounted a huge trade fair and air display at Farnborough

which constituted their shop window, the forerunner of today's biennial events; and from 1948 onwards, with the admission of the general public, the air display at Farnborough became more and more of an entertainment for the crowd. Neville Duke soon showed his talent as a display pilot, especially in the early fifties with the Hawker Hunter. His performances were a byword for grace and beauty of manoeuvre, symmetry and accuracy. As a sideline, Duke bought himself a little blue Tomtit trainer which he took around the airshows in 1949/50 giving displays of crazy flying. For a while he also performed mock dogfights with fellow Hawker pilot Doc Morrell, who flew an orange and silver Tiger Moth.

Contemporary with Duke was de Havilland test pilot John Derry, first British pilot to 'break the sound barrier', as the popular press would have it, on 6 September 1948 in the DH108 experimental jet (US Air Force pilot Chuck Yeager had been first to fly faster than sound in level flight, in the Bell XS-1, on 14 October 1947). The new jet age was an exciting time for aviation achievements, and Derry soon became a popular hero and a favourite at Farnborough. Reputable sources say that he slow rolled the DH Venom on its very first

Squadron Leader Neville Duke, DSO, DFC (left), seen here as a member of the RAF High Speed Flight in 1946 with Meteor in the background. With him are Squadron Leader W A Waterton, AFC (centre), and Group Captain E M Donaldson, DSO, DFC (right). *(Chaz Bowyer)*

John Derry. Derry was the twenty-first British test pilot to be killed during the seven years since the end of the war.
(British Aerospace)

flight; and only two or three days later he took it to the 1949 Farnborough show, giving a display of such polish and accuracy that you would never have thought he had only a few hours on type.

In the 1950 SBAC demonstration he introduced a new display figure which he called the 'reverse roll', but which soon afterwards became known as the 'Derry Turn': flying fast in front of the crowd line at about 300 ft (90 m), he would snake along in a series of high g 180 degree turns, switching from a vertical bank in one turn to a vertical bank in the next (knife-edge to knife-edge) by half-rolling through the

inverted position. But he was not, in fact, the inventor of this manoeuvre: Flight Lieutenant Pat Maxwell had thought of it many years before, while he was at the Fighter School at Wittering before the war, and taught it as an evasion tactic in combat!

Derry gave much thought to the art and purpose of display flying, and wrote about it in the magazine *Flight* in 1951. It was especially tragic, therefore, that he was killed while flying his Farnborough display that year, when the prototype DH110

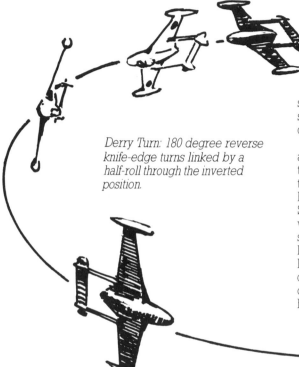

Derry Turn: 180 degree reverse knife-edge turns linked by a half-roll through the inverted position.

shut down the other engine, and ended the cartwheel with a spin which he stopped nicely lined up for the next man-oeuvre.

This achievement would never have been possible without a painstaking study of the masses and forces involved with the heavy Meteor-type fighter, which was fully loaded with twenty-four 90 lb rockets and two 100-gallon tip tanks. On being questioned after the event by his erstwhile Empire School instructor H P 'Sandy' Powell, Zurakowski countered with a comprehensive technical explanation of the absolute safety of the manoeuvre; he had calculated that in view of the low airspeed at which the yaw was performed, there was little or no stress on the fin of the machine. Zurakowski went on to become a test pilot for Avro Canada, where he often caused the boffins a headache by calculating and reducing his own test results!

fighter suffered a structural collapse and disintegrated in mid-air. Twenty-eight members of the crowd were killed by pieces of the fractured aircraft, the worst ever accident at a British display. In its aftermath a new set of safety regulations was adopted for display flying.

Before we leave the jet fighter displays at Farnborough, which properly do not fall within the scope of this aerobatic history, one more outstanding aerobatic achievement must nevertheless be recorded: the Zura Cartwheel (sometimes known as the 'fin sling'!).

Jan Zurakowski was a Polish test pilot with the firm of Gloster who had flown with the RAF during the war and trained at the Empire Test Pilots' School. He was a brilliant technician as well as pilot, and in his 1951 Farnborough display of the twin jet Gloster G.44 Reaper performed an entirely new manoeuvre of his own devising, which was a unique version of the stall turn. It could only be done with a twin-engined machine, since it involved cutting one engine as the speed fell away at the top of the vertical climb to about 4,000 ft (1,200 m), whereupon the aircraft was yawed into a pivot of not merely 180 degrees but fully 540 degrees – 1½ complete rotations! – under the asymmetric thrust of full power on one engine. After three-quarters of the rotation he

Gloster test pilot Jan Zurakowski.   *(John Underwood)*

The Zurabatic Cartwheel.

Farnborough continued to be a source of new and interesting display aerobatics, and not only by the fast and powerful jet fighters. In 1949 Ranald Porteous, chief test pilot for Auster Aircraft Ltd and a long-time instructor and airshow pilot on light aircraft since before the war, enchanted the crowd with a mild and gentle aerobatic display in a silver Auster Aiglet trainer (145 hp Gipsy Major 1), in which he performed for the first time in Britain a flick roll at the top of a complete loop, which he named the **avalanche**. Unknown to him, of course, it had featured in American aerobatics since the 1920s, when

Ranald Porteous pulls up into the start of an Avalanche with the Auster Aiglet. (Ranald Porteous)

stunt pilot Earl Daugherty had made it a speciality in his Curtiss 'Jenny', though Daugherty only succeeded in doing it by the skin of his teeth (page 71). It was also developed in France at about the same time as Porteous performed it in England, by the pilots of Saint-Yan with their Stampes.

Porteous wrote amusingly about his early attempts at the avalanche while working on his display routine shortly before Farnborough. Having proved to himself that the aeroplane would flick reliably from inverted to inverted at the top of a loop, he took the Aiglet up one day at Rearsby Airfield and tried it out in view of a number of people including his Managing Director, Frank Bates. Feeling modestly pleased with the result, Porteous then landed and approached Bates for a first-hand reaction: did he think the strange new manoeuvre would look effective at Farnborough? Bates regarded him quizzically for a moment, then replied: "Are you trying to tell me that was *intentional*?"

This new breed of test pilot, cast in the mould of the great pre-war test pilots like Détroyat, Doret and Colombo, now yielded the only exponents of top level aerobatics in Britain. Yet however innovative and however meticulous their demonstrations, there was no common denominator of excellence, no school of proficiency, no whetstone of competition on which to hone and perfect their technique. Aerobatics had reached a crossroads; with the specialists – test pilots and RAF – going in their own directions, while the non-professional pilots lacked any cohesion or sense of purpose.

Wing Commander 'Sandy' Powell, one-time instructor at the Empire Test Pilots' School where so many of the outstanding test pilots were trained, was a tireless advocate of

Flight Fantastic

aerobatics as a training technique and regretted its decline in Great Britain. Knowing that the art was flourishing overseas, in France in particular, he formulated the idea of an annual aerobatic competition on a truly international scale, to which the best foreign pilots would be attracted; and he persuaded the Lockheed Hydraulic Brake Company, of which he was Aircraft Sales Manager, to present the winner's trophy. The event was to take place in conjunction with the annual Air Pageant and National Air Races which were held at Coventry Civic Aerodrome, Baginton.

Fellow-enthusiast Major Oliver Stewart, ex-World War I Camelbatics exponent and editor of the magazine *Aeronautics*, had gone into print several times deploring the neglect of what he called 'the higher aerobatics' in Great Britain, and pointing out that contests were regularly being held in several continental countries. In 1954 he proposed to the Royal Aero Club that an annual aerobatic competition be held.

Sandy Powell found a willing cohort in Oliver Stewart, who accepted Powell's invitation to become Chairman of the Judges when the Lockheed Trophy idea was taken up by the Royal Aero Club in 1955; and thus began the first 'world series' of competition aerobatics, 21 years after the first

£100 prize for the highest points in each. The first, second and third placed pilots would receive prizes of £500, £300 and £200 respectively (NB: these prizes, as well as several of the finer points in the rules, underwent changes from year to year).

The competition was organized by the Royal Aero Club under the regulations of the FAI, and the rules were really very simple: a freestyle programme of five minutes duration was required, which during the initial three years had to include at least one slow roll, one loop, and one roll-off-the-top. From 1958 onwards this compulsory requirement was dropped. After a practice day, the first day's competition flights consisted of Eliminating Trials between all the competitors, and on the second day the Finals took place between a shortlist of six to eight of the previous day's competitors. The marking system awarded points for five different aspects of performance, which together totalled a maximum possible 100 marks:

Scope (range of aerobatic manoeuvres)	20
Pilotage (getting the best out of the aeroplane)	20
Accuracy (in execution of the manoeuvres)	25
Artistry and **Positioning** (sequence of manoeuvres, etc.)	25
Originality	10

*The Lockheed Trophy.
(Automotive Products)*

Tiger Club insignia.

World Championship in Paris which had been won by Gerhard Fieseler.

The Trophy itself was a handsome 60 cm sterling silver design symbolizing 'movement and manoeuvrability at speed', these qualities being represented by six swifts encircling a globe in fluid curves, the globe itself held in a compass ring supported on a stand. Surmounting this there rose a spire engraved with stars, and at the top a victor's crown and laurel.

The competition was open to any and all types of aeroplane, flown solo by any suitably qualified pilot from anywhere in the world. The only distinction made was to categorize the aircraft into two weight groups, with an extra

From the pilot's total score, points would be deducted 'severely' for exceeding the time limit and for bad airmanship, including flying over the crowd or below 100 m (330 ft). By 1960, however, the lower height limit had been reduced to a minimum 30 m (98 ft) in the finals.

Sandy Powell was Secretary to the Judges and ensured that the judging panel of test pilots was highly qualified for the task. The 1955 judges were Captain Hubert Broad, former chief test pilot for de Havilland; Jeffrey Quill, Supermarine's test pilot on the Spitfire; Geoffrey Tyson, chief test pilot for Saunders-Roe; and Air Commodore Allen Wheeler, one time Commander of Experimental Flying at Farnborough. In subsequent years this panel was joined by Squadron Leader Charles Turner-Hughes (of Armstrong Whitworth), Bill Bedford (Hawker's) and for the final two contests David Morgan (Vickers).

Sandy Powell's programme notes for the event set the

scene graphically, and illustrated the philosophy underlying the whole contest:

> … A more aesthetic aspect of flying is the art of aerobatics. Here the aeroplane is a medium for the true art of flying, the pilot becomes an artist, the sky his canvas, and the aeroplane his means of enacting the picture. In all countries where flying has flourished, aerobatics still represent the ultimate artistry in the air…. The purpose of the trophy which Lockheed's have presented is to encourage and perpetuate the art of aerobatic flying amongst pilots of all nations. Today's is therefore an event of great importance and precedence.

Judges' Chairman Oliver Stewart kept his own marks as well as the other judges, but they would only be used in the event of a casting vote being needed. In his briefings he told the contestants that the judges would be looking for a pattern traced in the sky which must hold the spectator's interest and at the same time extend the virtuosity of the pilot to the ultimate limit of his powers.

Beyond the marking out of 20, 25, etc., under the headings already mentioned, there was no compulsion on the judges to use any particular marking system – unlike the pre-war European contests, where individual figures were accorded difficulty values and the total was multiplied by the judge's marks. Some judges marked on overall impression of the flight, while others kept detailed notes under the various headings of Scope, Pilotage, and so on; Air Commodore Wheeler's system was rather more meticulous, allocating marks stage by stage through each performance. He later observed, tellingly, that it was necessary to award the first pilot a maximum of no more than about 60 per cent, in order to leave room for manoeuvring later. This, of course, is a sure sign of an imperfect system, and when the FAI World Aerobatic Championships commenced five years afterwards a great deal of thought and effort went into the attempt to find a really efficient method of judging.

Nevertheless, the Lockheed Aerobatic Competitions were fairly run and greatly enjoyed by ever increasing numbers of competitors, running annually from 1955 until 1965 inclusive. As the years went on various changes were made to the list of judging criteria and their attendant marks, the first being the elimination of the **Pilotage** criterion leaving four headings each worth 25 points.

Later each of the four headings subtly changed in emphasis, but the one constant and unaltered criterion was **Accuracy**. The final run-down of headings as adopted from 1961 onwards was:

Scope	25
Accuracy	25
Originality	25
Presentation (timing, artistry and positioning)	25

1955 Lockheed Trophy

1.	Léon Biancotto (Stampe SV.4A)	French
2.	Alain Hisler (SIPA Minijet)	French
3.	François d'Huc Dressler (Stampe SV.4A)	French
4.	Ranald Porteous (Auster J5L Aiglet)	British

The 1955 contest served more or less to test the water where most entrants were concerned, for the reputations were already known of the expert French pilots Biancotto, d'Huc Dressler and Hisler, and their success seemed inevitable (see Chapter 11). Of the nine others who completed the Eliminators, one was the seasoned Spanish pilot José Aresti (Jungmeister), seven were British pilots pretty well unused to competition of this sort, and the last, Santiago Germano, was the proprietor of an Argentinian flying school, who came with a Focke-Wulf Stieglitz which he managed to assemble only just in time to fly.

Jet entries included a British Vampire and Meteor 7/8, but the scope of their performance was limited by the inability to perform the flick manoeuvres which graced the remainder of the displays; similarly the lack of inverted engine systems prevented other British entrants from performing the bunts and negative tail-slides, figures-of-eight, etc., featured by the French and German machines. One of the hits of the meeting was Alain Hisler's diminutive Minijet, whose sparkling performances were done at the minimum altitude; its highly effective ailerons enabled it to perform the most spectacular and

Sipa Minijet, one of the 1955 Lockheed entrants (flown by French pilot Alain Hisler). *(Maurice Marsh)*

Aircraft line up at an early Lockheed competition (1956), while two Canberras perform a crossover flypast.
From foreground: Zlin 226T (OK-JEB) of Jiří Bláha, Stampe SV.4C (F-BCXK) of d'Huc Dressler, SR.7B Monitor (OO-SRZ) of Léon Biancotto, Morane 230E (F-BGJV) of Alain Hisler, two Tiger Moths of British entrants, Percival Provost of Richard Wheldon, and (just visible) tail of Meteor PV 7/8 flown by Geoffrey Worrall. *(Flight)*

accurate rolls of various kinds, all of which made up for the aircraft's deficiencies as compared with the elegant Stampe of the other Frenchmen, equipped with a Renault 4PO5 with full inverted fuel and oil systems.

The winner in this first Lockheed Competition was Léon Biancotto with an absolutely immaculate performance, followed by Alain Hisler and François d'Huc Dressler, with Ranald Porteous in fourth place with the Aiglet trainer (having included his speciality the avalanche in a beautifully precise routine). José Aresti and Geoff Worrall (Meteor) were the other two finalists; but Worrall's large, fast aircraft, though impressive, was not really competitive, and Aresti lost marks on an uneven rolling circle and on emerging from some figures off-axis.

Most pilots included a four-point hesitation roll, and Hisler with the Minijet included a neat eight-pointer; Biancotto also included his own version of the avalanche plus figures-of-eight, both positive and negative. *The Aeroplane* magazine added a graceful note of appreciation to the several foreign visitors who had come from far afield to a country where they could but imperfectly understand the rules and the language,

and noted that in doing so they gave tremendous pleasure to the watching thousands. The event had proved a great success, and it was hoped that it would stir up enough enthusiasm within Britain for a supply of competitive aircraft to be available for the following year.

At this point in our story we must digress a little from the theme of the Lockheed Competitions and take note of a phenomenon which came into being at about this time, and which was to have an effect on British aerobatics which lasts to this day: the Tiger Club.

It was in early 1956, during the brandy-and-cigars stage of a Royal Aero Club Racing Dinner, that a group of members hit on the idea of a club especially for Tiger Moths. Naturally enough it was racing they had in mind, and one of their number, Norman Jones, furnished the five Tiger Moths with which their first race meeting was held the following September at Elstree Aerodrome. Jones, who became President of the Tiger Club, was a well-heeled businessman who had been an Auxiliary Air Force pilot between the wars; in 1945 he resumed flying for fun, taking up racing with war-surplus Tiger Moths in 1954.

When the Rollason aircraft maintenance company at Croydon went broke in 1956, Norman Jones took it over and dedicated its efforts for the next year or so to refurbishing Tiger Moths for civil use. He produced no less than eighty, some of them donated to the Club – whose stated aim was 'to provide members with good sporting flying at the lowest possible cost'. It was decided that, unlike other flying clubs, no training would be available and indeed the only people eligible would be those who had 100 hours in their logbooks as pilot in charge of a light aircraft. The Club's base of operations was Redhill Aerodrome, near Gatwick in Surrey.

Within its first year of existence, formation flying and aerobatics became prominent features of the Club's activities and a 'Tiger Club Circus' air display was inaugurated, following the time-honoured format of the pre-war Alan Cobham Circuses. Though thirty years have passed, the keenness on racing, formation, precision and aerobatic flying continues unabated, and Tiger Club airshows are still a much-loved part of the British scene.

1956 Lockheed Trophy

1. Léon Biancotto (SR.7B Monitor)   French
2. Jiří Bláha (Zlin 226T)   Czech
3. Alain Hisler (MS 230)   French

Although the Tiger Moth had made an appearance in the previous year's event, with the same machine returning again this year with its pilot Francis Fisher, 1956 marked the first entry of a Tiger Club pilot into the world of aerobatic competition. This was C A Nepean Bishop, Secretary and later CFI of the Club, who entered with G-ANSH.

But at this contest only the Tiger Moth G-AHRC belonging to Northamptonshire farmer J W Tomkins featured an inverted fuel system – installed by Brooklands Aviation Ltd – together with an ingenious alteration to the aerofoil which entailed adding a symmetrical metal-covered portion ahead of the front spar along the leading edge of the lower wing, and between the fuel tanks and slats of the upper wing. With

Members of the Tiger Club watch Stampe aerobatting at Redhill. In the foreground is the Rollason Beta prototype.
(Lewis Benjamin)

this improvement the aircraft was said to handle as well inverted as erect. His flying, however, did not demonstrate the high degree of artistry required of a Lockheed finalist, and indeed was described by one reporter as 'rock 'n' roll flying'!

Bishop included a falling leaf in his routine, together with a succession of loops at five different points of the compass, and thereby took a Tiger Moth into the Lockheed finals. Fisher, sharing his aircraft this year with John Pothecary, fared less well although managing two creditable flick rolls; Pothecary also featured an inverted falling leaf (which entailed an 800 ft [245 m] height loss) and a four-point roll: all quite remarkable achievements in a Tiger Moth, though it was later found that the inverted falling leaf could lead to structural damage!

Among the French pilots, François d'Huc Dressler flew a delightful programme but contravened the minimum height limit and was accordingly disqualified. Sadly, it was to be his last Lockheed performance: in May the following year he lost the wing of a Turbulent and was killed. Biancotto and Hisler, although on markedly different aircraft from those they had flown the previous year, both achieved the same superlative form. Biancotto's low-wing Stampe et Renard Monitor IV was unique in competition aerobatics, Belgian registered, powered by a 180 hp Cirrus Bombardier engine with fuel injection and inverted oil supply – not beautiful but immensely strong and handled superbly by its pilot – and with it he again won the Trophy with an off-the-cuff display in the finals to suit the low cloudbase and poor visibility of the English weather.

It was during this competition that the French pilots were first seen to perform the 'M', consisting of two stall turns linked by a short passage in the middle with the aircraft on its

Flight Fantastic

back. Though not actually introducing anything new to aerobatics, the figure was nonetheless an original combination of existing manoeuvres which produced a pleasing effect.

Jiří Bláha, the first of a long succession of distinguished Czech competitors at Coventry, introduced the Zlin Trener to an enraptured audience and achieved second place, making a great impression with the extraordinary precision of his flying, a feature especially evident in an immaculate eight-point roll and in his stopping of flick manoeuvres.

Hisler meanwhile had won many hearts with the 27-year-old Morane trainer with spoked wheels and an uncowled

| 5. Miroslav Přikryl (Zlin 226A) | Czech |
| 6. José Aresti (Jungmeister) | Spanish |

By 1957, with the assistance of de Havilland, Nepean Bishop's Tiger Moth sported a pressurized auxiliary tank which permitted inverted flying for a limited period. No less than three other Tiger Club members shared the machine, with yet more Tigers being flown by Charles Boddington and Frederick Symondson. A valiant show of Tiger Moths indeed, but none of the British contingent, unfortunately, qualified for the finals. With the Zlins and Jungmeisters out in force, and with the additional disadvantage of a blustery wind, it was all too

1956 Lockheed Trophy entrant was this 1930s Morane-Saulnier 230 flown by Alain Hisler. (Flight)

250 hp Salmson radial engine, which he had brought over from Saint-Yan, the foremost French school of aerobatic instruction, and in which he nonchalantly half-rolled to await the starting signal from an upside-down position. As if to prove that the venerable machine was still competitive, Hisler's programme contained no less than 18 manoeuvres, including a negative spin, outside (negative) loops and superbly judged upward flick rolls. The last two finalists, with Bishop, were British test pilots Dick Wheldon (piston Provost T.1) and Geoff Worrall (Meteor P.V.7/8).

1957 Lockheed Trophy

1. Vilém Krysta (Zlin 226A)   Czech
2. Léon Biancotto (SR.7B Monitor)   French
3. Jean d'Orgeix (Stampe SV.4)   French
4. Jiří Bláha (Zlin 226A)   Czech

The Lockheed Judges at the 1956 contest: (left to right) Group Capt H A 'Bruin' Purvis, DFC, AFC; Major Oliver Stewart, MC, AFC (Chairman of the Judges); Capt Hubert Broad, MBE, AFC; Jeffrey K Quill, OBE, AFC; Air Commodore Allen H Wheeler, CBE, MA; Geoffrey Tyson, OBE; Wing Commander A H 'Sandy' Powell, AFC (Secretary of the Judges). (The Aeroplane)

evident that the Tiger Moths were thoroughly outclassed.

This year there were four Czechs, a German, a Belgian, and a special treat by way of a Spitfire entry flown by Israeli pilot Hugo Marom. Although his performance was hampered by drizzle and a ceiling of less than 1,000 ft (300 m), judge Jeffrey Quill congratulated Marom on handling the Spit to its limits. José Aresti was back once more, and Francis Liardon from Switzerland, both flying Jungmeisters. And from France came Léon Biancotto again and Jean d'Orgeix.

Biancotto's performance was once more characterized by a smooth, flowing quality and effortless positioning within a very small performance area; but the new spectacular, whirling brilliance of the Czechs presented a serious challenge and resulted in a win for Vilém Krysta with a programme packed with non-stop action. Bláha again brought forth comments for his extreme precision, and greatly impressed observers with a profusion of flick rolls, in particular with his new speciality of flick rolling from knife-edge to knife-edge.

The Chevalier d'Orgeix made his first appearance in this contest and continued to delight Lockheed audiences for several years more, often accompanied by an entourage of starlets from his Paris theatre; flying the Stampe SV.4 he was considerably more affected by the strong wind than most, but displayed exceptional artistry. His eight-point roll and ultra-slow slow roll earned much praise.

Worth noting as well was the performance of José Aresti, again featuring an abundance of flick rolls including a downward flick after a tail-slide, but he unfortunately positioned himself too high and probably lost marks because of the diminutive size of his aircraft. In the airshow following the contest he stunned all onlookers with his superbly judged low-level inverted flying, and landed off a flick roll in true Cantacuzino style (see Chapter 14).

1958 Lockheed Trophy

1.	Léon Biancotto (Zlin 226T)	French
2.	Zdeněk Beseda (Zlin 226T)	Czech
3.	Jean D'Orgeix (Stampe SV.4A)	French
4.	Vilém Krysta (Zlin 226A)	Czech
5.	Francis Liardon (Jungmeister)	Swiss
6.	Jaromír Hůlka (Zlin 226T)	Czech
	Gérard Verette (Stampe SV.4C)	French

Prior to the 1957 event the Royal Aero Club had held a British Competition at White Waltham on June 10 which was won by Captain D W Phillips. Now a year later the Tiger Club mounted a competition in June of 1958 at Sywell, with Geoffrey Hancock emerging as the winner. This was an invaluable preparation for the Lockheed competition the following month, and it set a precedent which resulted in the De Havilland Trophy competition being established, which from 1960 decided the annual British Aerobatic Champion.

Hancock appeared at the July Lockheed competition flying the Tiger Club's G-APDZ, which had been christened *The Bishop* in honour of the Club's CFI, Nepean Bishop. This machine had the advantage of a new and improved fuel system fitted by Rollasons, whereby mechanical fuel pumps driven off the camshaft fed petrol to an additional jet in the carburettor, which was brought into operation in the inverted position by moving the mixture control to a particular setting in the 'weak' position. Thereafter the mixture and throttle controls were both moved together. Other modifications included cleaning up the top wing by moving the fuel tank to

the faired-over front cockpit, and the addition of the more powerful 145 hp Gipsy Major 1c engine driving a metal propeller. The lightened aircraft weighed some 1,120 lb (509 kg) as against the normal 1,250 lb (568 kg), and take-off and climb performance were accordingly greatly improved; top speed was over 120 mph. G-APDZ was the first in a series of such Tiger Club conversions which appeared one by one in subsequent Lockheeds, all bearing suitably ecclesiastical names.

In all, seven out of the eight British pilots flew Tiger Moths, most of them *The Bishop*. Competitor number eight, Hunting's test pilot Barry Radley, entered this and the following year in a Chipmunk, the new RAF monoplane trainer which had replaced the Tiger (see page 250). None, however, made a place in the finals, although Léon Biancotto's impromptu display in a Super Tiger showed the potential of the revamped machine and made it clear that with enough talent at the controls it might well stand up to foreign competition. Nevertheless it lacked the power of the Zlin, the fast roll of the Jungmeister, or even the effective ailerons of the Stampe (ailerons in the Tiger being fitted only to the lower wings).

Beseda, Krysta and Hůlka appeared with Zlin 226s – fewer than expected from Czechoslovakia because another engagement in Moscow clashed with the dates. True to form, they achieved 'top six' places, the positions being determined this year for the first time by the eliminating round only, due to adverse weather. By now the delights of the Zlin Trener had lured Biancotto away from his Stampes of previous years, and he showed yet again his mastery of the art by capturing the Lockheed Trophy for the third time; some observers remarked, however, that he seemed noticeably less at home in the Zlin and that it was less manoeuvrable than the SR.7B Monitor. Notable in Biancotto's performance was the use of vertical rolls, both climbing and diving, and use also of the 'y axis' with a number of figures flown at 90 degrees to the judging line for better positioning and variety of effect.

Jean d'Orgeix's programme, started with an impressive 1½ flick rolls, closely resembled his routine of the previous year in which he gained third place: he had evidently found a winning formula, for he was placed third again in 1958.

New to this year's group of winners was the Swiss military pilot Major Francis Liardon, already widely known as a superb Jungmeister exponent and, like d'Orgeix, destined soon to win the victor's laurels himself. His mastery of the knife-edge to knife-edge flick produced a *double* flick roll in this attitude, no less, and he also scored highly with three continuous flick rolls across the field.

1959 Lockheed Trophy

1.	Francis Liardon (Jungmeister)	Swiss
2.	Jean d'Orgeix (Stampe SV.4A)	French
3.	Gérard Verette (Stampe SV.4A)	French
4.	Léon Biancotto (Super Tiger)	French
5.	Gerhard Pawolka (Jungmann)	German
6.	Marcel Charollais (Stampe SV.4C)	French
	Colin Labouchere (Super Tiger)	British

The 1959 Lockheed Competition was the 145 hp Super Tiger's finest hour, with a second Rollason conversion, G-ANZZ (*The Archbishop*), joining *The Bishop* and serving the needs of no less than nine Lockheed entrants between them. The surprise of the meeting was to see Léon Biancotto competing at the controls of *The Archbishop* when he could so easily have taken his pick of other mounts, but it was a measure of the

Flight Fantastic

greatness of the man that he came fourth even so.

Twenty-year-old Colin Labouchere, an RAF technical officer, was the first UK finalist in the Lockheed for three years, flying *The Bishop* (although again the disappointing weather prevented an actual 'finals' from taking place); and it was evident that the week-long practice camp for Tiger Club pilots held at Sywell the previous April had repaid the considerable effort that such arrangements always entail.

Sadly, *The Bishop* was destined not to be seen in competition again, as it was written off the following May by Tiger Club pilot Elwyn McAully in a crash in which he lost his life. Nevertheless, two more Super Tigers emerged from Norman Jones's company the following year, *The Deacon* (G-AOAA) and *The Canon* (G-ANMZ), which joined *The Archbishop* in a long and varied life of aerobatics, air racing and glider towing. *The Archbishop*, by the way, was flown inverted across the Channel on 27 June 1959 to mark the 50th anniversary of Blériot's crossing (and the 25th anniversary of Geoffrey Tyson's first inverted Tiger Moth crossing!).

The Aeroplane reported that in general the overall standard was reckoned to be much higher in 1959 than in previous years. "There were no new manoeuvres as such, but the combinations were, perhaps, more thoughtfully chosen to give a coherent pattern rather than a disconnected series of different movements". This was particularly true of the winner, Swiss pilot Francis Liardon: "Liardon flew his Jungmeister through a beautiful series of manoeuvres, with no significant pauses between them. He also showed a nice balance of contrast by following a slower movement with a rapid one – for example, a series of five slow rolls to starboard was followed by a sudden flick roll to port."

Liardon's entry to the competition scene marked the beginning of a long line of outstanding post-war Swiss pilots to challenge the French domination of the sport. For a sport it now most certainly was, and thanks to the Lockheed Trophy a truly international one on a regular basis, with

1959 Lockheed winner Francis Liardon of Switzerland.
(Mike Jerram)

scrupulous rules and safety standards: too scrupulous for some commentators, who would have preferred to see something rather lower and more sensational! But most people considered that it struck the right note, performed as it was within the context of an Air Display, and the contestants always had the chance to put on their spectacular airshow acts in a separate display after the contest had finished.

It is difficult at this distance in time to visualize the kind of performance one could expect to see at a Lockheed contest. A sequence of 18 or so figures in five minutes – perhaps more in such as the agile Jungmeister, perhaps fewer in those aeroplanes which needed to reposition themselves after altitude losses – would suggest a well-integrated programme moving along at an average pace not so very much slower than a 'compulsory' programme in one of today's international competitions, where a horizontal line is demanded between each figure; but the manoeuvres it contained would be more simple in terms of both difficulty and complexity.

Today, with modern high-performance machines, much greater vertical penetration is possible, as is also the juxtaposition of a range of taxing manoeuvres which in machines of 1950s performance would be downright dangerous to attempt. Few of today's highly-decorated combination figures would be seen. Multiple flick rolls were rather more popular then, and less emphasis was placed on drawing accurate lines than on action and interest. But artistry was important, too, and there were plenty of the slow-moving figures – rolling circles, Horizontal and Vertical 8s, etc. If one were so unkind as to compare it, however, with today's unlimited Freestyle programme, which is its nearest counterpart, the standard of the Lockheed would certainly seem very tame.

1960 Lockheed Trophy

1. Jean d'Orgeix (Stampe SV.4A)   French
2. Juraj Šouc (Zlin 226T)   Czech
3. Léon Biancotto (Nord 3202)   French
4. Zdeněk Beseda (Zlin 226A)   Czech
5. Eva Krenčová (Zlin 226A)   Czech
6. Gérard Verette (Stampe SV.4A)   French
7. Jiřina Lockerová (Zlin 226A)   Czech

With François d'Huc Dressler's death in 1957 still fresh in their memory, lovers of aerobatics now sadly mourned the loss of Lockheed Trophy winner Vilém Krysta in a flying accident in 1959. And although they were not to know it at the time, the great Biancotto himself was also about to be taken from them, only a few short weeks after the 1960 Lockheed, as he practised for the first World Aerobatic Championship in Czechoslovakia.

But no such thoughts troubled the sixteen contestants as they prepared to do battle for the 6th Lockheed Competition in Coventry at the beginning of July. The British – four flying Super Tigers and one a 65 hp Currie Wot – included John Ayers, Charles Boddington and Peter Phillips who were to be Britain's World Championship team; but they didn't stand a chance now that the Czechs were back in force (bringing two women pilots with them) and four Czech pilots out of five reached the finals.

Liardon was absent due to illness, but Swiss flying instructor Albert Rüesch, later to become a regular World Championship contender, put up a good show with his Jungmeister which included negative flick rolls – still an unusual figure in those days. From France d'Orgeix, Charollais and Verette were back again with their Stampes, and Biancotto, ringing the changes yet again, flew an ex-French Air Force Nord 3202, painted yellow with a red chequered fin. This was also to be his mount for the World Championship, but the cumbersome machine could never be called really suitable for top-level aerobatics although it remained a standard French military trainer for several years. After an uncharacteristically shaky start in the Lockheed eliminators, the touch of the supreme master showed through eventually and Biancotto reached the finals and third place overall, though the Nord seemed to labour its way through the programme. Léon himself was in fine form, having tuned three of the cooling fins of his Potez engine to play *Au clair de la lune* when struck in the correct sequence!

But 1960 was his compatriot Jean d'Orgeix's turn to win the Trophy with his familiar yellow-and-black Stampe. Opening

variety of content, and as usual the French pilot scored highly for his well-nigh perfect positioning. Such a display of artistry from start to finish well deserved to win.

1961 Lockheed Trophy

1. Jiří Bláha (Zlin 226A) — Czech
2. Gérard Verette (MS 350) — French
3. Ladislav Trebatický (Zlin 226T) — Czech
4. Francis Liardon (Jungmeister) — Swiss
5. Jean d'Orgeix (Stampe SV.4A) — French
6. Jaromír Hůlka (Zlin 226A) — Czech
7. Marcel Charollais (Stampe SV.4C) — French

The 1961 Lockheed proceedings endured some prticularly unfriendly weather even for an English summer, and at one point the judges' caravan was blown right over in a whirlwind

Chevalier Jean-Marie-François de Thonel d'Orgeix, consummate artist with the graceful Stampe was the Lockheed winner in 1960. A delightful reminder of his equestrian background was his characteristic flourish at the end of a competition programme – a flick roll topped off by dipping the nose in an elegant bow to the judges. (Mike Jerram)

with an inverted spin and inverted exit, his performance interlaced the slower manoeuvres with the faster, snappier ones, including a varied mixture of lazy vertical rolls, crisp flicks, bunts and negative stall turns, and featured a beautiful rolling circle turning to the left while he rolled to the right. Great store was set on smoothness and fluency as well as

which threatened no good to the aeroplanes either. However, no significant damage was suffered, and the event got under way on the Thursday and Friday preceding the Coventry Pageant in order to avoid clashes with the airshow displays. Three Super Tiger pilots from Britain competed against a strong foreign contingent once more, and enjoyed the thorough trouncing which had by now become traditional! From a large French presence of five pilots, three made the finals together with all three Czechs and Liardon again from Switzerland. Albert Rüesch accompanied his fellowcountryman Liardon, again flying a Jungmeister, but did not manage a good showing until he switched in following years to the 'Super Jungmann' Lycoming conversion.

Specifications for the standard DH 82 Tiger Moth (145 hp Gipsy Major):

Span	29 ft 4 in (8.95 m)
Length	23 ft 11 in (7.29 m)
Height	8 ft 9½ in (2.68 m)
Empty weight	1,190 lb (495 kg)
Max speed	109 mph (175 km/h)
Rate of climb	673 fpm (13.4 m/sec)

Tiger Club Super Tiger 'The Deacon' was flown in the 1961 Lockheed competition by Flight Lieutenant John Ayers.
(Lewis Benjamin)

Gerhard Pawolka with KZ-8 in 1962.   *(Mike Hooks)*

Swiss Jungmeister HB-MID was entered in the 1955 Lockheed by German pilot Albert Falderbaum.   *(Maurice Marsh)*

Albert Rüesch entered in 1963 in the 170hp Lycoming-engined Bücker Jungmann, HB-UTH.   *(Peter Phillips)*

Flight Fantastic

This year, five years after his first attempt in the contest, Czech MiG-15 pilot Jiří Bláha at last won the Trophy flying a Zlin 226 single-seat Akrobat; his display, crisp and full of interest, included the seldom seen sixteen-point hesitation roll and was afterwards described in the judges' report as one of the great aerobatic performances of all time.

1962 Lockheed Trophy

1. Jean d'Orgeix (Stampe SV.4A)   French
2. Albert Rüesch (Bücker R-170)   Swiss
3. Peter Phillips (Stampe SV.4B)   British
4. Gérard Verette (Stampe SV.4C)   French
5. Albert Guillou (Stampe SV.4C)   French
6. Marcel Charollais (Stampe SV.4C)   French

With the Czechs staying at home to practise for the forthcoming World Aerobatic Championships, the strongest team at the 1962 event was undoubtedly that of the five French pilots, all of them old hands at the Lockheed. German National Champion Gerhard Pawolka appeared for the third time, having switched from his Jungmann of previous years to the interesting Swedish designed/Danish-constructed KZ-8 of which only two were built; more will be heard of this machine in Chapter 15, which deals with its later modification by the outstanding Swiss pilot Arnold Wagner. In this contest Pawolka suffered from the diminutive size of the attractive little monoplane, a disadvantage which was not helped by his display being performed at too great a distance from the judges.

This was something of a Lockheed syndrome: pilots were allowed a specified amount of time to climb to 2,000 ft (600 m), but – ready or not – were compelled to start when the time was up. If you got caught out of position, you just had to start your programme anyway.

Albert Rüesch from Switzerland also brought a change of machine, and caused quite a stir with his up-rated Bücker Jungmann modified to take a 170 hp Lycoming engine. Crisp accuracy was the hallmark of his performance, and he achieved a well-deserved second place. His fellow-countryman Eugen Hasler also flew a Jungmann, but it was the old 105 hp Czech-built version.

The UK, represented by five pilots, had the pleasure of seeing Peter Phillips placed higher in the final results than any previous British contestant. The Tiger Club had recently obtained a French Stampe, now registered G-AROZ, and named it *Léon Biancotto* after the unforgettable Frenchman who was so loved and revered in England. Three Tiger Club pilots flew the Stampe, including lone 1962 WAC entrant Nick Pocock; while of the two others who flew Super Tigers, one was a young RAF pilot from the Royal Aircraft Establishment, Farnborough, by the name of Neil Williams. He was unplaced in this contest, but was soon to make a name for himself as Britain's best ever aerobatic pilot.

As in the previous year, stiff winds dogged the finals and spoiled the flow of several performances. Marcel Charollais suffered the mortification of a failure in his inverted fuel system half way through, and by the time he was able to refly

Peter Phillips, in the Tiger Club Stampe 'Léon Biancotto', placed 3rd in the 1962 Lockheed Trophy.   (Peter Phillips) Fellow club member Nick Pocock (inset) flew G-AROZ as sole British entrant in the 1962 World Aerobatic Championships. (Nick Pocock)

the programme fell victim to the deteriorating weather, as did fellow Frenchmen Gérard Verette who constantly had to interrupt his flight to reposition himself. The urbane Parisian Jean d'Orgeix was in inimitable form, however, and gave a lively but relaxed display, full of artistry and beautifully positioned. It was the second win for this most popular and talented Frenchman.

1963 Lockheed Trophy

1.	Jaromír Hůlka (Zlin 226AS)	Czech
2.	Ladislav Bezák (Zlin 226T)	Czech
3.	Ladislav Trebatický (Zlin 226T)	Czech
4.	Hansruedi Rüesch (Bücker R-170)	Swiss
5.	Jean d'Orgeix (Stampe SV.4A)	French
6.	Albert Rüesch (Bücker R-170)	Swiss
	József Tóth (Zlin 226T)	Hungarian

A record number of contestants – 29 in all – flocked to Coventry in August 1963 for the Lockheed Competition: eight from the UK, seven from France, six from Czechoslovakia, four from Switzerland and two from Hungary, with Gerhard Pawolka in the KZ-8 from Germany again and a new entrant, Colonel Salvi, flying a Zlin 226 from Italy.

With the Czechs out in such force, including 1960 World Champion Ladi Bezák, their incredible brilliance swept the board of the first three places and even relegated 1962 World Champion József Tóth to joint sixth position. This was a period when the Czech pilots were at the absolute zenith of their form, constantly breaking new ground, and no-one could touch their special brand of wizardry. The Lockheed atmosphere was electric with two World Champions pitted against each other; but the Hungarians were newcomers to a genre that was very different from a World Championship, and the Czechs were by now past masters.

The Rüesch father and son from Switzerland made a strong and confident team with their powerful Lycoming Jungmann, a modification so successful that further versions (some with improved wing section) continued to be used by Swiss World Championship pilots right up to 1970. The Chevalier d'Orgeix, however, now found himself at a disadvantage against the new breed of Zlin and Bücker machines and though presenting a stylish display, had gone about as far as it was possible to go with the faithful Stampe. The judges remarked that he had 'just about wrung the Stampe dry'!

Meanwhile the Tiger Club, maintaining faith in the graceful and responsive Stampe, had added a second model to their embryo aerobatic fleet. G-ASHS was flown in the Lockheed by the young James Gilbert, a staunch devotee of aerobatics who is these days more well known as editor of the popular British magazine *Pilot*. Neil Williams was in the 'Biancotto' Stampe this time, and Peter Phillips shared Zlin 326 G-ASIM with veteran aerobatic pilot Neville Browning. At the age of 62, Browning was the Lockheed's oldest competitor, and had been flying since 1918 when he won a £5 bet from a friend by looping on his first solo. He held one of the earliest commercial licences dated 1926, flew with the RAF in World War II and involved himself with student pilot and night-fighter training, later running an eccentric and highly individual photographic unit. At one time he had a private Spitfire, and when he imported the Z-326 T in 1963 it was the most up-to-date aerobatic craft on the British register. But it was all to no avail when the final selections were made: the Czechs and Swiss had the contest virtually sewn up. There was, however, a new Pearl Hyde Trophy inaugurated to encourage the

British pilots, and its first winner in this contest was Nick Pocock, sole representative of the UK in the 1962 World Aerobatic Championships.

1964 Lockheed Trophy

1.	Juraj Šouc (Zlin 226AS)	Czech
2.	Albert Rüesch (Bücker R-170)	Swiss
3.	Ladislav Bezák (Zlin 226AS)	Czech
4.	Jiři Stoklasa (Zlin 226AS)	Czech
5.	Ladislav Trebtický (Zlin 226AS)	Czech
6.	Marcel Charollais (Stampe SV.4A)	French
7.	Gérard Verette (Zlin 226T)	French

The year 1964 brought a change of venue for the competition, due to increased traffic congestion at Baginton, and for its final two years it was run at Sywell in Northamptonshire. This resulted in a more relaxed timetable for the event, without the pressures of the Coventry Pageant and Races.

Again the more numerous contestants came from Britain (seven), Czechoslovakia (five) and France (four), with Albert and Hansruedi Rüesch appearing once more from Switzerland. It was father Albert this time who put up the better showing, aided by the excellent qualities of his 'Super Jungmann' plus a stiff brandy at the starting line!

Jean d'Orgeix was feeling off-colour and even his supreme artistry and showmanship could not gain him a place in the finals this year; indeed, the criterion of artistry which had counted for so much in previous years was now no longer able to tip the balance, and the more technical attributes of scope (versatility), originality, accuracy and timing were those which assured the top placings.

This, of course, was where the Czech pilots scored heavily. The vertical roll, a demanding figure for both technique and aircraft performance, had become the determining factor *par excellence* in top-level aerobatics: the Hungarian József Tóth had practised for hours on this manoeuvre alone prior to winning the World Championship. Now the Czech aerobatics seemed confined almost entirely to rolls in the vertical plane, with only the occasional rolling circle, figure-of-eight or spin interspersed between aileron and flick rolls forever going up and down.

One of the Zlin Akrobat's many virtues was its ability to conserve height and, indeed, to perform height-gaining manoeuvres from a low airspeed when other machines ran out of breath. Bunts both downwards and upwards (this latter a new application of the term) were effortless, and quarter, half, three-quarter and complete vertical rolls were punctuated with hesitations and reversals of direction. Normal loops had become a rarity, but six- or eight-sided hesitation loops had been added to the repertoire; and flicks, both positive and negative, might be executed at virtually any stage in a manoeuvre.

Lomcováks were by now much in evidence (see page 170), with Stoklasa performing two in succession in his display. But just to prove that the Czechs did not have the monopoly, Marcel Charollais showed the first lomcovák ever seen in competition in a Stampe, and qualified for the finals for the fourth time in seven Lockheeds. Charollais was an instructor and ex-wartime flyer with 7,000 hours in his logbook, 2,000 of them aerobatics!

Britain was well represented, with its WAC team for 1964 (Peter Phillips, Robert Winter and Neil Williams) all flying the Tiger Club 'Biancotto' Stampe. Young Neil Williams, who had put in a phenomenal amount of practice, gave a performance that was much appreciated by the French; some even thought that he might just squeeze into the finals. But the most successful UK performance of the day turned out to be that by Barry Tempest in *The Archbishop*, who really sold himself to the judges in what was described as the best aerobatic display ever performed with the Super Tiger.

In the end it was flying instructor Juraj Šouc who won the Trophy with a 22-figure sequence executed without pause

1964 Lockheed Trophy winner Juraj Šouc. (Jan F Šára)

and all the time maintaining his positioning with parade-ground precision in front of the judges. Looking at his programme, one could see how far aerobatics had progressed even in only the past five years.

1965 Lockheed Trophy

1.	Jiří Stoklasa (Zlin 226AS)	Czech
2.	Neil Williams (Stampe SV.4B)	British
3.	Ladislav Bezák (Zlin 526)	Czech
4.	Charles Boddington (Stampe SV.4B)	British
5.	André Delcroix (Zlin 326)	French
6.	Herbert Greb (Zlin 226T)	German
7.	Roland Longchambon (Stampe SV.4A)	French
	Gérard Verette (Zlin 326)	French

A somewhat depleted field of fifteen contestants for the last of the Lockheed competitions spoke of much aircraft unserviceability, with only four pilots each from Britain, Czechoslovakia and France. Lone entries from Italy, Belgium and Germany made up the total, among whom the 1965 German champion Herbert Greb did well to make the finals at his first attempt. Germany had enthusiastically returned to top-level aerobatics in the sixties and resumed their National Championships from 1960 onwards, and the fact that their pilots were sparsely represented at Lockheed contests was not for want of trying: time and again they were prevented by aircraft problems or adverse weather.

All the British and Czech pilots were Lockheed veterans, but among the French there were plenty of first-timers: Roland Longchambon, who piloted his Stampe into the finals, and father and daughter team André and Madelyne Delcroix,

whose chances at first seemed ruined when Delcroix senior landed the family Zlin wheels-up. However, they were generously loaned a replacement machine by the Czechs who then proceeded to work overnight in order to get the French aeroplane flying again the next day. József Tóth had given similar assistance to a fellow-competitor a couple of years previously.

It was a gesture typical of the deep-rooted cameraderie that prevails between opposing pilots in such circumstances, and which often mystifies the onlooker who fails to detect the dividing line. There exists a genuine fellow-feeling among pilots when an opponent is beset with technical trouble, which generally over-rides competitive rivalry and sometimes even the more deadly rivalry of combat. Normally a pilot will go out of his way to lend aid when an opponent is having problems with his machine: while on the other hand no quarter will be given in a straightforward fight, whether fairly or unfairly matched.

Nineteen-year-old Madelyne was destined herself to win the women's world aerobatic competition three years later; but in the 1965 Lockheed she was not yet displaying that top form, although she drew congratulations by putting up a good performance in an unfamiliar aircraft. At one point in her programme some anxious Czech faces were observed as she performed a tail-slide – intentionally – which apparently in the Z-226 Akrobat Special could cause the constant-speed prop to feather for good!

Eight pilots went forward to the finals, and the sensation of the meeting was the selection of two British pilots, both flying the Tiger Club Stampe G-ASHS: Charles Boddington and Neil Williams.

Although the Czechs put up their usual sparkling show, only two featured in the list of winners, with Bezák seeming rather more restrained in comparison with Stoklasa, well known for his fondness for lomcováks, whose sequence started with a pull-up to the vertical from 700 ft (200 m), half-roll left, half-roll right and stall turn.

Neil Williams's thorough preparation and hard work paid

Neil Williams at the 1965 Lockheed competition.

(Nick Pocock)

Another victorious Czech – Jiří Stoklasa wins the last Lockheed Trophy in 1965. *(John Underwood)*

off by displaying everything that the Stampe was capable of, while at the same time maintaining that precise as well as artistic presentation so necessary for good marks in the Lockheed. His dedicated competitiveness, later a hallmark of his success, extended even to the extent of performing his preliminary practice flights well out of sight of the airfield to avoid giving anything away.

In a Lockheed final which was of the very highest standard, it was remarkable how many pilots were caught unawares by the Very light signalling their time to finish; only the two British pilots were the exception. The programme which took Neil Williams into a well deserved second place was timed to the last split-second, with the end of his final manoeuvre – a quarter clover pull-up and half flick roll – pointing the aircraft neatly head-on to the judges when the closing signal was fired an instant later.

The Lockheed Competitions were a landmark in aerobatics in that they started a truly international series of world-class competitions, which led directly to today's World Championships. New aircraft types and modifications were engendered by the exchange of ideas in the seminal post-war years, and no less so new aerobatic manoeuvres and figure-combinations. After the 'French M' in 1956, for example, came another stall turn variation: pivot around 90 degrees at the top, stop in knife-edge, push through 180 degrees horizontally, and then continue the last half of the stall turn. The Derry Turn and the straightforward stall are both manoeuvres which are now lost to aerobatics, along with the slow roll changing direction through 180 degrees which is seldom seen. And developments of figures which were not new, but which became greatly refined, included the rolling circle with alternating rolls inward and outward (first performed in Germany in the 1930s), and the very difficult complete outside loop with two negative flick rolls at the top (a double-negative-avalanche!).

Lockheed competitor Peter Phillips has commented on the uniqueness of the competition because, "the aerobatics were judged as an art as well as an exercise". Originality – the inclusion of new manoeuvres as well as new applications of old manoeuvres – counted highly, but the variety of different types of figure was also important: it was no use concentrating on all the showy, attention-getting fireworks without demonstrating that you could perform the flowing, classical manoeuvres which perhaps demanded a higher degree of co-ordination and control to execute perfectly. Accuracy and timing appeared as criteria, but counted for no more than 25 per cent of the available marks; and it was here that the great difference lay between Lockheed Competitions and the FAI World Aerobatic Championships which superseded them.

Rightly or wrongly, when the firm of Lockheed decided they could no longer continue their involvement, the event was allowed to die in favour of the WACs which started in 1960. Here every tiny individual manoeuvre was marked for accuracy, with that mark being multiplied by the manoeuvre's predetermined difficulty value, and a separate overall mark was awarded for positioning. This mathematical quantification of each pilot's performance was supposed to lead to objectivity, but it took a long while for all the countries of the world to agree on the exact criteria for how each particular figure must be flown to obtain top scores; and even so, sometimes a judge's visual acuity was somewhat hampered by the national flag in front of his eyes. . . .

Though the Lockheed judging may have been primitive by comparison, there were nevertheless in all its eleven years never any accusations of unfairness or bias, even if critics disagreed with the rules or with the emphasis placed on that elusive quality, artistry. Although the Lockheed criteria fell into disfavour when the new mathematical formulae came in, we shall see that a time was to come when the ideas and ideals of the Lockheed were to be introduced once more to international aerobatics.

14

New influences

The post-war period ushered in a new lease of life for the Jungmeister, which many considered the definitive top-level aerobatic mount. Its popularity grew even more when both Spain and Switzerland made some of their military machines available on the civilian market. One of the most colourful figures of the 1950s, Romanian Prince Constantin Cantacuzino*, had been flying Jungmeisters since the 1930s, when he had registered as an entrant in the 1936 Berlin Olympics Celebration Contest, although aircraft unserviceability prevented him from appearing. His family had a strong aviation history, his father having taken lessons in 1912 at Brooklands, England, and his uncle being the air pioneer Prince George-Valentine Bibesco.

He flew Bf 109s for the Romanian Air Force during World War II, and afterwards, when it became a Marxist republic, fled his homeland to Spain. Being a captain with the Romanian State Airline at the time, he simply flew his DC-3 over the border to Milan, sending a telegram on arrival which stated that 'in view of the circumstances' he considered himself dismissed. . . .

He remained to live in exile in Spain for many years, where the Jungmeister was already the undisputed king of aerobatic machines, and he soon became legendary on the European circuit for his extraordinary airshow performances – which he was equally happy to give in a Spanish bull-ring or on an English aerodrome.

Cantacuzino managed to acquire the fifteenth German production Bü 133C from the Spanish Air Force (160 hp Siemens), which he registered in Spain as EC-AEX. After several years service with the Prince, it was bought by Spanish pilot J L Aresti who sold it to American Jungmeister fanatic Frank Price, in whose hands it first became N87P and subsequently, in 1980, N178P. Price later acquired a second Jungmeister from Aresti, and still treasures them both to this

day. Cantacuzino's next mount was a Spanish-built CASA Cl 133 Jungmeister, EC-AMO, originally powered by a 160 hp Hirth, but which appeared in England in June 1957 with a 275 hp Lycoming engine, making it probably the most powerful Jungmeister ever to fly!

There was something about the Jungmeister's sparkle and brio that appealed to the Latin temperament, and it was a tremendous favourite in Spain. Its forte was a sensationally fast and controllable flick roll, which was utterly reliable and could be stopped with split-second precision. All its exponents used this to maximum effect, but Cantacuzino took it to the absolute limits. Ranald Porteous remembers watching him perform a negative flick from inverted to inverted at a height of something like 5 metres, and still recalls feeling the whoosh of the machine's turbulence as it passed right in front of his nose. One of the highlights of his act was to complete his routine, approach, touch down innocently, then with an unexpected burst of power drag the Bücker into the air again for a final full flick roll and then land in a perfect three-pointer!

His art was always to keep a surprise up his sleeve, to half-roll inverted within seconds of take-off and climb away inverted, to perform a deceptively languid super-slow stall turn and then suddenly, when it was least expected, explode into a 1½ flick roll; and always his flicks were performed at grass-clipping altitude. Oliver Stewart was more than once irresistibly reminded of the superb Camel performances that used to be given, over thirty years previously, by the never-forgotten Captain DV Armstrong.

Known by the nickname 'Buzz', Prince Cantacuzino was a superb showman who would leap from the cockpit to kiss the hand of a pretty girl in the crowd, or feign an engine cut-out (by switching off the magnetos) whilst running up the Jungmeister on the ground, glowering at his mechanic in a fit of mock pique. During a triumphant tour of England, Spain,

*Many different spellings exist of the Prince's name, which underwent various transformations depending on which country he was in at the time! He came from an ancient Byzantine family which produced a seventeenth century ruler of the Romanian states, Serban Cantacuzino, who led them in their struggles against Turkish domination. The original Romanian spelling is preferred here.

Prince Constantin Cantacuzino, master of audacious low-level aerobatics. Against all probability, he died a peaceful death in his own bed. (via Musée de l'Air)

Cantacuzino's Jungmeister EC-AEX flies a typically hair-raising inverted pass preparatory to the famous flick-roll landing. Note enlarged rudder area, tiny wheels. (Tony Bianchi)

France and South America in the mid-1950s, he fitted up his aeroplane with spotlights and performed a ten-minute *tour de force* of night aerobatics, all below a maximum 175 m (570 ft), with loops started at 50 m (165 ft).

Those who saw his airshows never forgot them. Journalist and aerobatic pilot James Gilbert, writing twenty years later, described a typical Cantacuzino exhibition in his book *The Great Planes* (Grosset & Dunlap, 1970):

It was the amazing precision and almost impossible audacity of his flying that made it so enthralling to watch. For no more than an infinitesimal instant was he ever in level flight. Mad, insane maneuvers followed each other with effortless ease. At no time was he ever more than five hundred feet above us, and every maneuver seemed to finish with the little biplane inverted, its cat's feet stretching up to the clouds, its hanging rudder almost parting the daisies.

We were quite unprepared for his finale. We thought he had finished and was coming in to land. Motor throttled back, he glided down in front of the crowd till his wheels lightly but firmly touched the grass. Then, without warning, we heard the throttle advanced and saw the nose rear up into the summer sky; everything let loose as he entered the wildest snap roll, and we gasped in shock, for he was only twenty feet above the grass. As suddenly as it had started, as soon as the Jungmeister was right way up, the roll stopped. The throttle closed and he landed, for all the world as though that crazy gyration had never happened.

In competition aerobatics the Bücker Jungmeister continuously earned laurels in the hands of masters such as Albert Rüesch and Francis Liardon from Switzrland, Gerhard Pawolka, Walter Wolfrum and Herbert Greb from Germany, and José Luis Aresti from Spain. In 1956 at Epinal, a French-held 'European Championship' had Liardon second and Aresti third. The Lockheed Competitions, as we have seen, were also graced by regular attendances of Jungmeister pilots including Aresti, Liardon, Rüesch, and the German pilot Ederer.

But an era was passing. Perhaps it was inevitable that the relaxed, freestyle Lockheed Trophy, so redolent of Englishness and amateurism, should soon be overtaken by a highly-organized and regimented international championship. One of the attractions of the early Lockheeds had been the wide variety of aircraft types that could compete on their own terms, and it was always a delight to see the Jungmeister among them. As a sporting occasion, the Lockheed had always represented a pleasant sojourn among flying friends with the added spice of a trophy awarded at the end of the weekend, and in general it was reckoned that the judges got it pretty well right each year.

But the demands of the Lockheed were not really rigorous, and the method of judging was subjective. Mathematical systems of evaluation already existed, and had done since Fieseler started them for the German Championships in 1928. Not only was that system still in use in Germany, the Saint-Yan aerobatics centre in France also had its sophisticated structure for competitions described in Chapter 11, which utilized a catalogue of 85 coefficients ranging from 1 to 8 in difficulty value. Each individual manoeuvre performed in a sequence was graded 1 to 5 for accuracy of execution.

When the first FAI World Aerobatic Championships came into being in 1960, what was really needed was some general agreement about a truly international judging method.

We have already seen how the French pilot François d'Huc Dressler brought out a notation system which he published in 1955, and which was tried out for writing the contestants' Free Programmes in the 1960 World Championships. Sadly, he had died in 1957 before he could develop his system any further, but the sport of competition aerobatics was very fortunate in that a successor to d'Huc Dressler appeared shortly afterwards on the scene, who took on the mammoth task of creating a dictionary out of the symbols and their combinations.

Colonel José Luis de Aresti Aguirre, a Spanish grandee from an old and distinguished family, was born in Bilbao and became a flyer in the 1930s in time to get involved in the horror of the Civil War – which cut short his studies as a medical student. Becoming a pilot for the republican government, he was assigned the manoeuvrable Polikarpov I-16 Rata low-wing monoplane and within six months found himself flying demonstrations for his military chiefs; it was the most modern fighter in service in the world until the Bf 109 made its début in 1937, and a very tricky one as well, which suffered from severe instability at low speeds and high altitudes. It took a skilled pilot to handle the I-16 successfully.

He gave his first public airshow at Palma de Mallorca in 1939 at the age of 20. Then, precluded from military service by his former republican allegiance, he joined the Jerez Pilot Training School as an instructor. Here there already existed

José Luis Aresti with Jungmeister EC-ALP. Aresti also favoured an enlarged rudder area for more positive control.
(John Underwood)

an enthusiastic aerobatic group, and Aresti's responsibilities included training several hundreds of pupils who were to be tested for progression to fighters. For these tests he used a system of aerobatic notation and held judging sessions. He had a flair for organization, and drew up a training rulebook as well as an 'Aerobatic Flight Manual' for the Spanish Air Force in 1944.

After the war, Aresti became a test pilot for the Air Ministry Flight Test Centre in Madrid, and founded several civilian pilot training schools in Spain, while flying airshows around Europe in his ex-military Jungmeister. With typically Latin verve and dash he soon had an international reputation for exciting, low-level displays for which the agile and responsive Bücker was the ideal mount. In competition he seldom managed to get the better of his great rival Cantacuzino, but he excelled at the airshow aspect of aerobatics, and in the 1957 Lockheed programme he was seen to perform that extraordinary landing from a flick roll which Cantacuzino had made his own. He also did a series of superbly judged inverted runs just a few feet above the grass. When Aresti gave a display, it was always something to look forward to.

After the experiences of the first World Championships, the International Aerobatics Commission of the FAI (CIVA) got together in 1961 to make recommendations for the next event, and Aresti attended as the representative from Spain. Louis Notteghem represented France, Mike Murphy and Bevo Howard the USA. On the agenda were several recommendations, from Aresti, Notteghem, and Oliver Stewart of Britain, concerning the regulations and the attribution of marks. Vice-President Notteghem was delegated to investigate these recommendations and formulate a list of difficulty coefficients on behalf of the Commission. Aresti volunteered to help him.

Meanwhile, by the end of 1961 J L Aresti had published his own *Sistema Aresti*, which was already in use in Spain. It was a comprehensive dictionary of all possible aerobatic manoeuvres, and the Spanish Aero Club urged its adoption internationally. Some of the symbols themselves were new, in particular the sign for the tail-slide and the triangular symbols for flick rolls and spins; but in general the notation was quite familiar to any pilot who had been around the aerobatic scene for any length of time, and as a catalogue it was not too difficult to use. Contestants in 1962 were again asked to draw a sketch of their free sequence to give to the judges, but no

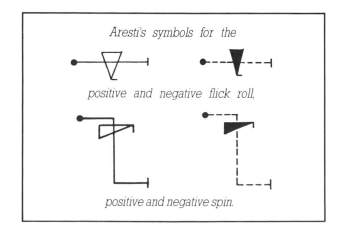

Aresti's symbols for the

positive and negative flick roll,

positive and negative spin.

agreement had been reached about the *Sistema Aresti*, and the universal language was still d'Huc Dressler's. By now, Gerhard Fieseler had joined the International Commission, and it was far from unanimous in its views on the subject.

With Spain as the host of the 1964 World Championships, a decision was eventually made in 1963 to go ahead with the Spanish system. The Aresti Dictionary has remained in use ever since, growing from an initial 3,000 or so manoeuvres to a maximum of some 15,000, all with their own symbols and difficulty coefficients. François d'Huc Dressler was not forgotten, by the way, when the vote was taken by CIVA: a touching note was made in the Minutes paying tribute to 'the late aerobatic pilot d'Huc Dressler, who was the originator of Aerocryptography'.

Aresti himself received many awards for his work, including Gold and Bronze Medals from the FAI, and he served as President of CIVA in 1968–69. He was largely instrumental in bringing about the strong government involvement in Spanish aerobatics, whose competition pilots until 1972 came chiefly from the Air Force, and which until 1977 continued to receive military support for its equipment. At that point, of course, with the great changes after the death of Franco, a Spanish Civil Aeronautical Federation (FENDA) took over the sporting side of aviation, in conjunction with the Royal Spanish Aero Club. This meant that a new look could be taken at the outmoded Zlin 526s, 726s and Acrostars in use at the time, with which it had not been possible to compete seriously in World Championships since 1972; and at last it was decided to bring the Spanish international pilots right up to date with a brand new fleet of Zlin 50s. The machines were delivered in 1980 – too late, unfortunately, for the World Championships at Oshkosh – but from 1981 onwards a new young team of Spanish pilots began making their mark internationally. The lead taken by Aresti in 1964 was even then strongly in evidence.

The Spanish team fielded at the 1964 World Championships comprised five Air Force flight instructors, each with some 2,000 hours apiece, and they lacked for nothing in the way of support. National prestige was very much at stake. Spain had a proud tradition of military aerobatics, dating back to the much-loved war hero Captain Joaquín García Morato and his two companions of the 'Blue Flight', Julio Salvador and Bermúdez de Castro. All had been famous exhibition pilots in the 1930s, and Morato had been sent as an instructor to the Military School of Aerobatics, when the Civil War broke out and they found themselves members of the same squadron. From then onwards they were inseparable. Flying the Fiat CR-32 Chirri, their most memorable exploit was in February 1937 when the three of them attacked a group of 36 I-16 Ratas, bringing down eight of their opponents. Morato received the highest military decorations for this and other brave feats, but his death came as a tragic shock, three days after the war

ended, when his faithful Chirri collapsed from a structural failure in a power dive. He had brought down a total of 40 enemy aircraft and survived the entire Civil War, only to die filming a mock dog-fight.

No doubt the memory of García Morato was very much alive in 1964 when preparations started for the World Championships, and the Spanish Air Force team was provided with a fleet of the latest Zlins – the 326 models – for the occasion. All five were moved with their wives and families to the Bilbao area, where they practised over the field full-time for months. Both the Czech and Soviet teams had also been thoroughly prepared and trained, and it was not surprising that pilots from these three nationalities walked away with nine of the top ten placings.

One of the biggest advantages that any pilot could have was an acquaintance with the new coefficient system, since in the Free Programme he was able to choose any 25 manoeuvres for his sequence, and the more valuable they were, the better he would score. The Spanish, naturally, had a head start with this, and members of Frank Price's little Tiger Club aerobatics group in America also benefitted from Frank's long dialogue with Aresti on the subject (see Chapter 18) which had been going on since 1960. Even so, one of the Americans drew his sequence diagram wrongly on the sheet he handed to the judges, and lost thousands of marks for this discrepancy. Many foreign teams stayed up until all hours, drawing and redrawing their programmes.

Another innovation brought in for the World Championship in Bilbao, as well as the Aresti Dictionary, was an Unknown Compulsory programme which comprised one manoeuvre each selected by the individual teams competing. The judges put them together into a sequence, adding a few figures where necessary to make the combination work, and the pilots had to fly them straight off, without practice. In effect it was a stroke of genius, and one of the best innovations ever introduced to competition aerobatics, testing the fundamental skill of the pilot with tricky manoeuvres that he and his own opponents had chosen.

A home win had been predicted, and Tomas Castaño from Spain lived up to expectations, winning two out of the six programmes and coming in first overall. As the new World Champion his prize was the newly established Aresti Cup, a huge and ornate affair made of silver with gold embellishments, surmounted with a golden globe. Aresti had donated this trophy himself, to be awarded to each overall World Champion. He wanted it to be truly international in nature, so

Joaquín García Morato, famed pre-war Spanish aerobatic pilot whose intrada a Morato *has been described as an early form of* lomcovák. *He flew the Italian CR 32 Chirri, arguably the most manoeuvrable biplane fighter of the 1930s.*

(via Sebastian Almagro)

1964 World Champion Tomas Castaño (centre) with previous World Champions Ladislav Bezák (left) and József Tóth (right).

(via Gabor Fekecs)

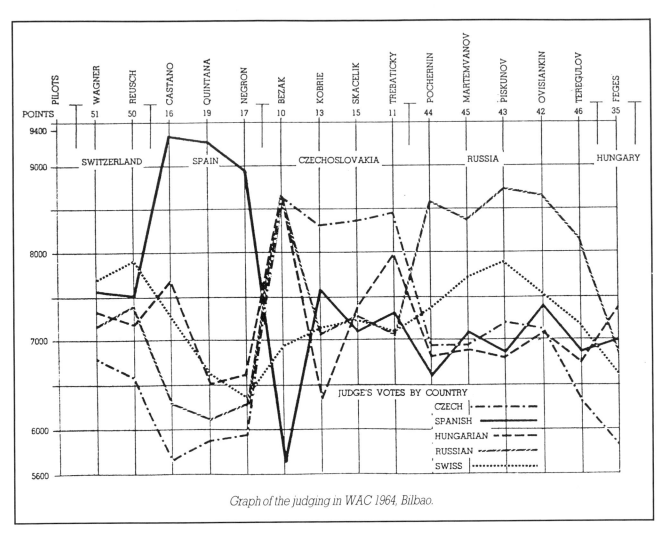

PILOTS	WAGNER	REUSCH	CASTANO	QUINTANA	NEGRON	BEZAK	KOBRIE	SKACELIK	TREBATICKY	POCHERNIN	MARTEMVANOV	PISKUNOV	OVISIANKIN	TEREGULOV	FEGES
POINTS	51	50	16	19	17	10	13	15	11	44	45	43	42	46	35

SWITZERLAND   SPAIN   CZECHOSLOVAKIA   RUSSIA   HUNGARY

JUDGE'S VOTES BY COUNTRY

CZECH · — · — · —
SPANISH ————
HUNGARIAN — — — —
RUSSIAN ⁓⁓⁓⁓
SWISS ·············

Graph of the judging in WAC 1964, Bilbao.

he invited all the members of the FAI to furnish a large gold coin and a gold emblem of their National Aero Club to decorate the body of the trophy. On top of all was a little silver model of a Bücker Jungmeister, Aresti's much loved aeroplane.

Top honours for the other programmes were equally distributed between USSR and Czech pilots. Most agreed that the event was well organized and the Spanish were hospitable and friendly, but many pilots went down with stomach upsets due to a combination of the unaccustomed food (delicacies such as octopus cooked in its own ink) and the unbearable heat, which also had its effect on engine performance. It was obviously an advantage, as everyone knew already, to be the host nation and have unlimited practice in local conditions. It was also a disadvantage to come from a western democracy where aerobatic teams had to fund themselves and train as a spare-time activity!

Two of the 'old hands' at aerobatic competition, Gerhard Fieseler and Mike Murphy, had more serious complaints to make. Both were worried about the judging difficulties, from two standpoints which remain as valid today as they were then.

Fieseler was primarily concerned about the workload placed on the judging panel, who had to assess 45 pilots flying three programmes each, followed by 16 pilots flying the final three programmes, which amounted to a total of 183 flights. And all were carried out in different weather conditions and with the judges in different stages of health and humour, at different times of the day, trying all the way

through any one programme to match the performance of the present competitor against that of the first pilot he saw fly that morning.

In modern world contests, with a field of nearer 80 contestants, the total of flights to be watched can reach as many as 260–270 over a period of eight to ten days, and of course there is also the special difficulty in aerobatics that competitors fly a great assortment of different aircraft types, which it requires great expertise to compare and appraise objectively.

Fieseler also had some sharp words to say about the partisanship of the judging, and this was the main criticism levelled by Mike Murphy, veteran airshow pilot and US International Judge. As a judge in Hungary in 1962, Murphy had been dissatisfied with the scoring as it affected his team pilots, and considered that bias was the main reason that the US had lost the individual championship. Protests for the same reason had been lodged by the Czech and USSR teams at the time, although they were disallowed.

Now, with improved and simplified grading systems adopted by CIVA, it had been hoped that the Spanish contest would produce fairer and more objective marking; but this, according to Murphy, was not so. To illustrate his point, he produced a graph of a selection of judges' marks as they affected the top pilots who went into the finals. Five of the seven judges were shown, with the French judge and Murphy himself unfortunately missing from the graph. Although the highest and lowest judges' scores were thrown out before the eventual totals were computed, it was evident that the wide disparity between the various marks, based on what appeared to be national bias, was sufficient to produce a severe distortion of the results.

It was for reasons such as these that a statistical method of 'normalizing' judges' scores was later introduced by Soviet judge Yuri Tarasov, and modifications to the computer-based system over the years have constantly improved its ability to smooth out inaccurate scores and prevent them unduly influencing the results of the contest; but the problem still remains of unskilled and partisan judging in aerobatics.

On a happier note, the occasion of the 3rd World Championships in 1964 brought one particular competitor sharply into focus on the international scene, and that was the British pilot Neil Williams.

A member of the Tiger Club in Britain since 1961, he had taken up competition aerobatics the following year and flew in the Lockheeds from 1962 to 1965, coming second in the last contest. It was obvious that Neil's was a great talent, but there was always the perennial British problem of what aircraft to fly. The Tiger Moth was outdated before it even started to compete, the Stampe had had its day by the time the British took to acquiring them for competition aerobatics, and the only truly appropriate machine to take to Bilbao as a competitor was probably the Czechoslovakian Zlin.

But Zlins were scarce as hen's teeth in England, and as Williams prepared to enter his first World Aerobatic Championship in 1964, a fantastic idea began to form in his mind: she was called *Ballerina*, and she was an air racer.

Again the name of Tony LeVier crops up in our story, for this veteran American racing ace, now Lockheed's chief pilot, had been invited by the Cleveland Air Race organizers in 1946 to help re-establish the races in the midget class. The class had started out as the Goodyear Trophy formula, and soon became known as Formula One for air racers; since the engines were so tiny – no more than 190 cubic inch (3.1 litre) displacement – the aeroplanes were tiny as well, and designed with the best aerodynamic streamlining possible.

The idea appealed, and Tony LeVier formed LeVier and Associates, all Lockheed staff, but working in their spare time as a private venture, and pledged to build a series of Formula One aircraft during 1946–7. LeVier designed the wing himself; five engineers did the rest. The result was to become a legendary aircraft in its day, and still is forty years later: the Cosmic Wind.

The first two completed were *Little Toni* (named for LeVier's daughter Toniann) and *Minnow*, which won third place in the 1947 Goodyear race piloted by 'Fish' Salmon. The following year, after modification, it came in first. Next and last to be finished was *Ballerina*, and this was the machine which found its way, in the fullness of time, to the Tiger Club in England.

Being a club that went in for aerobatics as well as racing, it was not long before its members found out that *Ballerina* had the most incredibly responsive handling combined with enormous strength. She had a 360 degree per second roll rate, and had the ability to do a dead-stick outside (negative) loop at the top of a positive half loop pull-up, which was a favourite way of starting a display. She had beautifully balanced, full-span ailerons, which were light but strong; aerodynamic/mass balances gave her superb handling in

roll, with scarcely any adverse yaw, and her rolls could be started and stopped almost instantaneously.

One major drawback was the absence of an inverted system, although a rather Heath Robinson fuel feed was devised; but worst of all there was the frequent problem of a cut-out when the mixture became too rich in certain attitudes when flying aerobatics. The pilot had to anticipate this before it happened, and select fuel 'off' momentarily to avoid a cut. Neil Williams, in his book *Airborne* (Airlife, 1977), recalled ruefully, "it shows the attitude of near-desperation in which we competed in those days, since I had to turn the fuel off 16 times during one free sequence in order to keep the engine running".

Ballerina exhibited other embarrassing features as well, when it came to aerobatics, such as her lightning speed which would take her from one end of the box to the other in a flash. And of course the *g* loads in such a fast and clean machine could be quite punishing. One foreign pilot, trying her out for fun, took the speed up to 250 mph (400 km/h), rolled inverted and pushed into an outside loop, without realizing that the stick pressure needed in the little racer was much less than he had energetically applied. He had reached −7*g* by the time he gave up and landed with eyes – literally – blood red.

With a maximum dive speed of 300 mph (480 km/h), she handled "more like a Hunter than a piston-engined aeroplane", according to Neil Williams, who obviously loved her with a great passion. "If she had any faults, they were overshadowed by her virtues."

It was an enormous gamble to take such a craft to the World Championships, but Williams was never deterred by long odds against him. If anything, they increased his resolution. "Had there been a prize for sheer courage against apparently overwhelming odds," commented one reporter, "the unanimous choice would have been Neil Williams." "Neil Wiliams renewed our faith in the British character," said another, "the scoreboard figures could not reflect the tremendous determination and airmanship offered by this RAF pilot."

In the end, it was the aircraft that kept him out of the finals; defects haunted the inverted system, which meant that not only did he have to keep air-starting the engine, he even had to break off his first sequence and land dead-stick when it quit cold in an outside loop (fortunately he was allowed to re-fly, and ended that programme in thirteenth place). But with no inverted performance, Neil could not choose the top-value negative manoeuvres that would have earned him high marks in the Free Programme, and his total possible – around 580 – compared badly with some of the top men who were recording possibles of 850. By the end of the eliminators he had achieved thirty-first place.

Ballerina herself caused a sensation at the Championships, and earned herself the nickname *Ranita* – 'Little Frog' – partly due to her colour and partly because of her habit of bouncing and porpoising along when landed on grass; commentator John Blake described her progress down the runway as "a series of grunting hops".

There were, however, advantages to flying a totally strange machine in a contest, according to Neil Williams:

… not the least of which was the fact that nobody knew what manoeuvres such as flick-rolls were supposed to look like. During the unknown compulsory programme which included several manoeuvres I had not flown before, I was demoralised to watch world-

Stampe formation of Rothmans Aerobatic Team. Original members were Neil Williams, Manx Kelly, Iain Weston and Raymond Hoggarth. (courtesy of Rothmans)

Span	18 ft 11$\frac{1}{4}$ in (5.77 m)
Length	16 ft 8$\frac{1}{2}$ in (6.7 m)
Height	4 ft 3$\frac{1}{2}$ in (1.3 m)
Empty weight	600 lb (273 kg)
Max speed	200 mph (322 km/h)
Rate of climb	2,500 fpm (12.7 m/sec)
Limit load	+9, −4.5 g

LeVier Cosmic Wind 'Ballerina' (present engine 100 hp Continental 0-200A). Flown here by her latest owner, British Aerobatic Champion Peter Kynsey, she is painted in her original green. (Peter Kynsey)

J L Aresti with the Aresti Cup first awarded to the World Aerobatic Champion in 1964. The two epaulettes hanging at either side are pure gold and at the time were valued at $22,000. (via FAI)

Flight Fantastic

famous pilots falling out of control from them. One such figure was an inverted flick-roll with an inverted climb of 45 degrees. I determined to use *Ballerina*'s novelty to my advantage: at the appropriate moment I gave the rudder a nudge, pushed forward a little on the stick, and slammed on full aileron. In a flash she was around the roll, and still hurtling upwards at 45 degrees! I would not have dared to flick-roll at that speed! It was one of the very few times that I achieved the maximum score of ten points – and I had not even stalled the aircraft! (*Airborne*, Airlife Publications, 1977)

This bravura performance on Neil William's part sent his estimation rocketing upwards in the eyes of international observers. The 30-year-old Canadian-born Welshman, who had been flying since the age of 16, emerged from his first World Championships something of a celebrity, if not a hero. Added to his aerobatic skills, he soon discovered a great desire and ability to communicate via the written word, and though his output was small – just two books and a handful of articles – his impact was considerable.

Neil had always been crazy about aviation, and took his PPL on Tiger Moths as a teenager with an Air Training Corps Flying Scholarship. After an engineering training he joined the RAF at the age of 21, by which time he had begun systematically, and unofficially, to teach himself aerobatics. Even more remarkable was the fact that he was able to conceal from the medical examiners a recurrent asthmatic condition which would certainly have disqualified his entry. This condition he kept in check by sheer will power and by training himself – as an extremely powerful swimmer – in breath control. Neil took his training with the RCAF, winning the Course Trophy, and in 1962 graduated from the Empire Test Pilot's School at Farnborough, where he remained as a test pilot until he left the RAF in 1967 to join Handley Page.

He came from a Welsh mining background, interwoven with a strong, much-decorated military strain, and Neil's achievements were nearly all accomplished by dint of press-on determination and hard work; certainly he had none of the advantages of education and personal wealth that smooth the path so effectively in aviation.

His flying activities outside the competition arena are too numerous to list, but two are especially worthy of mention: first, his Spitfire demonstrations, which were hailed as 'definitive'; and second, his co-founding, with Manx Kelly, of the famous Rothmans Aerobatic Team, which started up in 1970 with a formation of four Stampes. Later he rejoined them when they acquired their new fleet of Pitts S-2As.

He was a 'compleat pilot' if ever that could be said of anyone: he had a sympathetic rapport with any type of flying machine, from Avro Triplane to D H Vampire, and was often called upon to test-fly or display the most precious of aircraft – perhaps the unique survivor of a certain type, or an antique that might have been several years in restoration – regardless of whether he had had experience on the type before. It was just simply known that Neil Williams was the man you could trust with your aeroplane. For the same reason, he was constantly in demand for film work.

His book *Airborne*, already quoted, is a collection of classic adventures and love-affairs with aircraft which this author, for one, has read and reread endlessly; and his other more famous book, *Aerobatics* (also published by Airlife, 1974), has been pivotal in the world of competition aerobatics since the day it was published. Not only was it the most authoritative and readable aerobatics primer of its day, it also had a world-wide popularity which introduced pilots of all

creeds and tongues to a sport which had, until then, had no apologists. Manoeuvres and techniques were explained and beautifully illustrated, sequences were constructed, the contest format set out understandably, even the merits of different aerobatic aircraft were compared. It would be difficult to overstate the importance of this book and its influence on the growth of aerobatics. Now, more than ten years later, it still has plenty to offer the student and enthusiast.

From thirty-first place in the 1964 World Championships Neil Williams rose to fifteenth in 1966, and then fifth – twice over – in 1968 and 1970. In 1967 he won the prestigious Biancotto Trophy, the 'European Championship' of its day, and in 1974–75 the Coupe Champion, France's other international-class contest. Neil was a brilliant pilot but inconsistent in his brilliance, and sometimes made mistakes that ruined his gold medal chances. In Salon de Provence, 1972, he pushed when he should have pulled in his Free Programme and sacrificed 500 points as a result.

But the time that most people agreed he deserved a gold medal, though he did not receive one, was in the 1976 World Championships in Kiev. Some said he was morally the overall victor, and but for biassed judging should have been named World Champion; be that as it may, nearly all sportsmen who were present at the time agreed that he easily excelled in the Unknown Programme, and for this performance at least should have won first place.

But competition aerobatics is full of might-have-beens, and Neil's placing in this his last World Championship was a very honourable fourth, with a silver medal in the final Freestyle. The following year, in a routine ferry-flight from Spain in a Heinkel 111, he ran into weather problems and crashed in the mountains. His second wife, who had also made a name for herself in aerobatics, was among the victims of the accident. But for this tragedy, who knows where Neil might have been placed in 1978 or 1980?

The most famous escapade in Neil Williams's flying career, and one that earned him the Queen's Commendation for Valuable Service in the Air, has now become aerobatic folklore. Practising in 1970 for the World Championships that were shortly to be held in Britain, he had reached the fifth figure in his practice sequence when suddenly there was a loud bang from the left and he was thrown sideways as a severe jolt shook the machine. Looking at the port wing, he saw no sign of trouble; until, checking in the other direction, he saw the rest of the aircraft rolling inexorably upwards while the port wing remained horizontal! The wing had failed at the root.

Losing height fast, his mind was forced to think quickly, and he remembered a report he had heard several years before of a Bulgarian pilot in a Zlin machine, not unlike his own Z-526 Akrobat, who had had a top wing-bolt fail whilst inverted: the aircraft had involuntarily flicked erect, and the wing had held sufficiently for him to land in one piece. By now quite badly frightened, Williams opted for taking some positive action, and bearing in mind the Bulgarian story, he half-rolled left and at the same time pushed. The wing snapped back into place immediately. With eight minutes of inverted flight available to him, he must now make a decision about attempting to land.

The only sensible choice appeared to be an inverted approach with a last minute roll-out, in the hope of making a wheels-up belly landing on the grass. Gingerly he must try whether a left- or a right-hand roll would be better, and at his

Zlin Akrobat G-AWAR flown by Neil Williams.
(Peter Hewitt, via Tony Bianchi)

Neil Williams Challenge Trophy.
(Peter D Blake, via Lynn Williams)

Neil Williams, fourteen times British Aerobatic Champion.
(Mike Jerram)

left-handed attempt the wing started to fold again. He had his answer. Now he had to try the real thing. Neil Williams continues the story in his own words (*Airborne*, ibid):

I crossed the boundary of the aerodrome slightly high, at 200 feet, at 180 km/h with the throttle closed. I slowly levelled the aeroplane as low as I dared, at 140 km/h I rolled hard to the right, opening up to full power at the same time, and holding just enough negative *g* in a slight outside barrel roll to keep the wing in place. The axis of the roll was the left wing tip, which left a furrow through the grass for 36 feet, without breaking the plastic cover on the navigation light. By a combination of good judgement, and incredible luck, I had got it right!

When the aircraft had careered to a stop, it was a total wreck – but Neil Wiliams was unhurt. The fault was not, as he had thought, a wing bolt failure, but a fatigue failure in the centre section lower spar boom, inboard of the undercarriage leg. A little later a telegram arrived from the Zlin manufacturers in Czechoslovakia with just three words: "Sorry – congratulations – thanks".

Neil won the British National Championship altogether a phenomenal fourteen times, and it was fitting that, after his death, a new trophy for the nationals was commissioned by the *Sunday Telegraph Magazine*. Designed and largely made by his brother Lynn, who provided the drawings that illustrate both of Neil's books and also this one, it depicts the Zlin Akrobat during the penultimate quarter of its outside (negative) barrel roll, as the wing-tip brushes the grass at Hullavington.

It must not be imagined, however, that Neil Wiliams had it all his own way during those 16 years of competition in England. Neck and neck with the Welshman for much of the time in the fight for the British title was Manx Kelly, co-founder of the Rothmans Team, and Peter Phillips, who had himself spent many hours aerobatting the Cosmic Wind. Indeed, Peter generally used *Ballerina* to a much greater extent than Neil for airshows and the like, and had developed some outstanding manoeuvres with the machine. In 1964 he was planning also to fly the Cosmic Wind in Bilbao, but switched to the Stampe at the eleventh hour, unwilling to trust the rudimentary inverted system which left him going through most of the competition with the propeller stopped!

Peter Phillips was a brilliant young RAF pilot who excelled at aerobatics and had been the Central Flying School's Vampire display pilot in 1957/58. It was during his spell there as an instructor that Peter developed the first **four-point vertical roll**, as part of a competition routine that he helped put together for one of his particularly gifted students, Flight Lieutenant Bert Cann. Hesitation rolls had always been his speciality, including a four-point Derry Turn, so it was fairly natural to extend it to the vertical plane. The manoeuvre itself was extremely difficult to place accurately and perform precisely, and of course it had not hitherto been possible until an aeroplane came along with sufficient performance: with the CFS Vampire it was possible, and having perfected it on this machine, Peter afterwards included the four-point vertical roll in his Hunter display routine as the Fighter Command demonstration pilot. He was also regularly doing outside loops with the Vampire, during which he kept the relight button pressed all the time.

Vertical hesitation rolls became his *pièce de résistance*, and he later developed the **eight-point vertical roll** in displays with the Cosmic Wind, and a twelve-pointer in the Bjørn Andreasson BA4B biplane, exceeding the Vne (velocity never to be exceeded) in order to do it – with permission from the designer!

Both being Tiger Club members, he and Neil saw a great deal of each other's aerobatic displays; but generally a tacit respect for the other pilot's speciality manoeuvres tends to deter competition pilots from baldly imitating them, and it was not until 1964, when they were practising together for Bilbao, that Neil asked Peter to teach him the eight-point vertical roll in the Cosmic Wind, which he then used to great effect in his free programme. Though developed initially in the fast jet fighters, it had very soon found its way into the repertoire of aerobatic competition.

Finally, the most persistent threat among Neil Wiliam's British contemporaries and friendly rivals was another Celt, a Scotsman by the name of James Black, who went on to a very distinguished aerobatic career of a rather different kind.

James was introduced to aerobatics when he joined the University Air Squadron at Oxford, where he was reading for a law degree; he had previously learned to fly on Chipmunks, but it was not until his RAF training at Oxford that he started to savour the enjoyments of doing things upside down.

Peter Phillips, here pictured as Fighter Command Hunter display pilot (54 Squadron), performed first vertical hesitation rolls in 1957/8. *(Peter Phillips)*

British 'Aerobatics International' team in the 1970s were all competition pilots: (Left to right) Brian Smith, Philip Meeson, James Black, Neil Williams. *(James Black)*

On leaving Oxford he joined Shell-Mex & BP, as it then was, which offered the side-benefit of an enlightened private flying scheme for employees; since then he has remained with the same company over the ensuing twenty years, rising just about as high as one can possibly rise, to his present position of Chief Executive – BP Hong Kong. A similar rise to the highest pinnacle in international aerobatics took him by way of CIVA Delegate to CIVA Secretary and finally CIVA President, a position he has held since 1980.

As an aerobatic pilot, James Black has never stopped being competitive since 1965 when he first joined the Tiger Club, winning the Esso Voltige and McAully Trophies the following year, later winning the Icicle Trophy and the De Havilland Trophy in 1969 which designated him British Champion.

He still retains a lasting impression of his first World Championship in 1966, flying a Tiger Club Stampe to Moscow as one of the first western light aircraft to cross the iron curtain since before the war. He loved the graceful, sweet-natured Stampe and found the sport of aerobatics fascinating, especially the intricacies of designing Free Programmes to conform to the governing rules about maximum point values for a permitted number of figures. With his legal background it was inevitable that he should gravitate towards the official bodies that govern the sport, and in 1970, already representing aerobatics within the Royal Aero Club, he was one of the organizing committee of the 1970 World Championships. By then he was also British Delegate to CIVA, and the work he did drawing up the regulations for Hullavington went a long way to form the basic framework from which today's regulations derive.

But James was not merely a theorist about the sport, he was a competing pilot who for ten years attended every World Championship, reaching his highest placing of tenth in 1972 in France. Moving with the times, he changed first to the Zlin and later, with greater success, to the Pitts S-1S (importing the first competition Pitts to Europe from America in 1972). With this machine he felt, as did Williams, that the British pilots could really be competitive in 1976, and indeed as a team they won the bronze medal; but unfortunately this second visit to the USSR was not so happy as the first, and the bad impression left by the goings-on in Kiev (see Chapter 16) nearly discouraged him from competing again.

For some years past he had been doing more and more judging at contests, an activity which he took up in 1967 when a training accident left him temporarily unfit to fly. He had gone from a Vertical S to a 1½-turn spin in a Zlin 226TS, and the spin went flat: unable to recover, he had spun in and crashed – but miraculously survived – and then spent the next six months in hospital with, among other injuries, two broken legs. Judging was interesting, but he was attracted more by the work of the International Jury, the adjudicating body set up to see fair play at FAI Championships: this, therefore, became his main interest after 1972, the year in which his election as Secretary of CIVA qualified him to serve.

The year 1974 was very active, and one in which he came third in the Biancotto Trophy, out of the largest number of competitors that had ever competed. In the same year he and Manx Kelly, both keen competitors, founded the British Aerobatic Association with the aim of getting British aerobatics efficiently organized, running an annual National Championship, and sending a team each year to the various internationals.

When he took over Presidency of CIVA in 1980, James Black had done his fair share of judging, culminating in the job of Chief Judge at the 1980 World Championships in Oshkosh, Wisconsin. The full story of Oshkosh is told in Chapter 19, so we will not elaborate here, save perhaps to reflect on the enormous effort such a job always demands in terms of time, energy, patience and diplomacy mixed with firm control, not to mention the perpetual war of attrition waged with mosquitoes, dust, wind and every possible extreme of weather, against none of which can the poor judge defend himself as he concentrates his gaze fixedly at the sky above!

But from being judge and jury-member for so many years, the yen returned in 1983 to enjoy the fun of competing again, and James reappeared in the European Championships that year in Italy with his Pitts in place of his rule-book. Mid-field placings of twenty-third and twenty-fourth in the early programmes heralded a shaky start, but confidence was restored in the Unknown Compulsory, the programme where experience and piloting skills really count, and here he scored with a rank of ninth. This contest represented a span of seventeen years in international aerobatics, surely a record for any pilot to remain not only active in the sport, but competitive, too.

We have covered a wide range of influences in this chapter, each leaving a strongly individual mark on aerobatics: the Bücker Jungmeister, starting point and inspiration for the 'Sistema Aresti'; J L Aresti himself, and James Black, both Presidents of CIVA, and recipients of FAI awards for their contributions to the sport; Neil Williams, who with his books – not to mention his flying – helped bring the charisma of aerobatics to a wider appreciation than ever before.

The Aresti system proved a neat and elegant solution to the need for an international language of aerobatics, and with modifications here and there the Aresti Dictionary served well for over twenty years; though with such an over-abundance of material, much has fallen into disuse. Nothing pleases everybody, however, and a major cause of dissatisfaction with the system has been its regimentation into a fairly restrictive choice of available figures – only those figures, and in those forms, that were envisaged back in the 1950s; hence it lacks flexibility. As this book goes to press there are movements afoot to bring out a new type of catalogue for the 1980s, and this author has been involved with some of the work preparing it: I can only say that it is a very, very complicated task!

One of the unconscious ironies brought about by Aresti and his dictionary was that it sadly proved the undoing of the Jungmeister. At one time the ultimate in aerobatic aircraft, its handling and harmonization were unrivalled, but its vertical rolling and negative looping qualities were poor. Aresti accordingly gave low values to those manoeuvres at which the Jungmeister excelled – such as single and multiple flick rolls – and high values to those at which it was not so adept. Thus a premium was placed on vertical penetration which led to aerobatics of the 'yo-yo' variety, sometimes described as 'aerial gymnastics'; and later aircraft designs took the concept ever further in terms of power and performance. Eventually much of the charm and character of machines like the Jungmeister were lost to aerobatics for good.

15

Swiss, German and Swiss~German

Small, fiercely independent, diversified, influential; these few words characterize both Switzerland and her not inconsiderable aviation tradition. The first Swiss air meeting took place in 1910, heralding a long series of international aviation events which were held regularly at the Dübendorf (Zurich) airfield. As early as September 1911 aeroplanes were used in Swiss Army manoeuvres, and military aviation was officially established with No. 1 (biplane) and No. 2 (monoplane) squadrons in August 1914. Famous for precision engineering, the Swiss gave the world the outstanding Hispano-Suiza aero engine which was developed by Marc Birkigt in the year 1915.

Living cheek by jowl with Germany, Switzerland's links with the germanic nations go back more than 700 years. Indeed, the great Hapsburg dynasty originated as a family from the Swiss Jura, though the people of Switzerland later spent centuries fighting off their unwelcome attentions. Yet half the nation is *Suisse Romande* – French speaking – and the country boasts no less than four distinct languages and an untold number of incomprehensible dialects. When thinking of the Swiss as a people, therefore, a coherent national image is impossible; and not surprisingly so, since they are themselves at pains to emphasize their regional differences.

Though the Everlasting League between the first few valley-cantons was founded in 1291, in truth there is little in the way of unity between this loose confederation of states, and the Swiss take a perverse delight in the fact. The people of one town may be characterized as 'mischievous and malevolent' by those of another only 90 km distant; others will be considered 'impertinent and mean'; others 'unreliable', 'lazy' or 'slow-witted', depending on what town or canton they hail from. Though today such epithets are used more in jest than in earnest, their roots go deep nevertheless.

Blessed with some of the most beautiful yet inhospitable terrain on earth, the Swiss have taken meticulous stock of what assets they have and used them with resounding success. For protection they practise an aggressive neutrality in which every adult citizen is an armed, fully-trained member of the militia: pacifists they are not! Buttressed behind this neutrality, they rest secure as the world's bankers – an eminently respectable profession, to be sure, though one in which you can find a strange assortment of bedfellows.... Again, a wary knife-edge path is trod. But the game is worth the effort, for it provides along with its obvious advantages another not so obvious: a further assurance of neutrality. After all, what country of the world would stand by and see its own bank pillaged?

From this vantage point, making use of their *petit-bourgeois* virtues of thrift, conservatism and obedience to regulations, an impregnable economy has been built. Switzerland has become the nerve centre of Western capitalism and the quiet leader of industrialized Europe. The spirit of competition is ingrained; but not for them the nationalistic ardour which in a country like Germany manifested itself in three minor wars and two world conflagrations. In Switzerland, nothing is excessive: they have a winning formula.

Although little in the way of original aircraft design emerged from Switzerland before the 1940s, they were avid consumers of the best available aviation hardware, and in the 1920s–1930s equipped their military pilots with Fokker D-VIIs, Bücker 131s and 133s, and Messerschmitt 109s, all from neighbouring Germany.

They organized the famous five-yearly International Aviation Meetings at Zurich where aerobatic competitions were held in addition to air rallies, races and formation team displays; and they were the first European nation to invite the

Germans as participants after World War I (though with equivocal results, as Gerhard Fieseler experienced to his cost – see page 84).

Francis Liardon, a military pilot who joined the Swiss Air Service in 1933, must be one of the few living pilots who can make an off-the-cuff comparison, from personal experience, between the D-VII and his own favourite mount the Jungmeister, whose flying characteristics he says greatly resemble those of the Fokker machine but with the advantage of greater finesse and, of course, technological development.

An instructor and regular competitor in pre-war Swiss championships (which for military pilots had been taking place since the 1920s), Liardon flew Bf 109s on home defence duties as a squadron leader, claiming a victory in June of 1940 when he forced down an intruding aircraft in a fight in the Jura mountains.

Returning to aerobatics for more peaceful purposes, he won the title of Swiss (military) champion three times in succession after the war, in 1948, 1949 and 1950, and also contested many of the other competitions which sprang up in France and Italy (second in Modena in 1953, second again in Epinal in 1956). When the British Lockheed competitions started they were an irresistible attraction to this avid competitor, and he entered for the five successive contests from 1957 to 1961, though engine trouble kept him from actually competing in 1960.

Liardon had by then a considerable reputation as a Jungmeister pilot, and reigned as the veritable 'pope' of Swiss aerobatics. He was much in demand for airshows all over Europe and as far away as Dallas, Texas. Three times in all he was a Lockheed finalist, and in 1959 brought Switzerland her first resounding victory in a world-class event by winning the Trophy itself, in a competition whose overall standard was rated as much higher that year than previously. Liardon flew

Francis Liardon giving his Bücker an airing at Basel, 1958.
(Francis Liardon)

his Jungmeister through a beautiful series of figures, which he put together without disruptive pauses and with a fine sense of balance, contrasting the slower movements with the more abrupt and rapid manoeuvres to achieve a cohesive whole.

Hot on Liardon's heels came Albert Rüesch, another Jungmeister exponent. Three times national champion and the foremost civilian Swiss aerobat of the day, he too became a regular Lockheed participant, joining Liardon in 1960 and continuing every year thereafter until 1964. On three of these five occasions he was a finalist, and twice he achieved second place overall (1962 and 1964).

Introduced to aviation in 1930 at the age of 21, his one goal immediately became that of learning to fly, and ultimately of becoming an instructor. But he was hampered by lack of funds, being one of eleven children who were used to going barefoot from the spring to the first snowfalls, and it was not until 1937 that he gained his licence after enduring many privations. He achieved his second ambition in 1949 when he became a flight instructor, and from that moment on, Rüesch's output of successful students became one of the most prolific in Switzerland, if not in Europe. By 1955 his reputation reached the ears of Swissair and he was recruited as an instructor in their basic training programme, where he remained for six years. But his first love was always aerobatics, so in 1962 he left his secure position with the airline to open his own aerobatics centre at Yverdon on Lake Neuchâtel.

Things seemed to go well at first, but the little project finally folded through opposition from his competitors in nearby Lausanne. Rüesch was forced to move on, but eventually he took up residence at Porrentruy, where he turned the charming, scenic little airfield into a veritable Promised Land for devotees of aerobatics, which it remained for the next 16 years. Students came from all over Europe and as far away as America to fly his Bücker trainers and glean knowledge from the master, for whom competition in aerobatics was always the highest manifestation of the art.

Liardon's ex-military Jungmeister HB-MIC.   (Francis Liardon)

Of Albert Rüesch's three sons – all pilots – it was the middle son Hansruedi who at the age of 26 joined his 54-year-old father in England for the 1963 and 1964 Lockheed contests. By then both had flown in the first World Aerobatic Championship in 1960, and after a break in 1962, both returned again in 1964 to compete in the third World Championship in Spain. Hansruedi gradually overtook his father in these later events, having scored a fourth place at Coventry in 1963, and reaching fifteenth in Bilbao the following year.

Dissatisfied with the performance of available machines, it was the Rüeschs who first began an innovative trend in aerobatic aircraft which eventually had a profound influence on later events in Switzerland and Germany: by 1962 Albert had exchanged the once-traditional Jungmeister for a version of the Bü 131 Jungmann, HB-UTH, which Flug- und Fahrzeugwerke AG (successor to the manufacturers Dornier-Werke) had modified to operate on a 170 hp Lycoming engine.

This 'Super Jungmann', or Bücker R-170, greatly impressed observers in England on its first appearance and gave the venerable Jungmann a totally new lease of life. Fellow-competitor Peter Phillips commented, "I would give my back teeth for that aeroplane!", and indeed the sturdy little two-seater suddenly became a desirable aerobatic mount all over again after a career of nearly thirty years. An even better modification was the later substitution of a 180 hp Lycoming together with a wing of improved section for inverted flight, designed by Swiss engineer Fritz Dubs, and this version – fitted to the Pilatus-modified Jungmann HB-URN – was the famous Bücker Lerche (Lark) brought out by Max Datwyler & Co. It made its international debut at the 1966 World Cham-

Albert Rüesch (right) and son Hansruedi, pictured with their Bücker Jungmann HB-UTH with 170 hp Lycoming engine, forerunner of the 'Lerche'.   (Lynn Williams)

Bücker 'Lerche': Swiss-modified Jungmann with 180 hp Lycoming and improved aerofoil. It is seen here at the 1975 European Championships at Esbjerg.   (John Blake)

pionships, and continued its competition career until as late as 1970, far longer than that of its more glamorous single-seater stablemate the Bücker Jungmeister.

From these early beginnings a new concept in aerobatic aircraft was to emerge to challenge the dominance of the Eastern European Zlins, and would soon equip a formidable array of Swiss and German aerobatic pilots.

Gerhard Pawolka with Jungmann at Coventry for the 1959 Lockheed Trophy. (Mike Hooks)

Albert Falderbaum (with Jungmeister) in the 1930s. (Musée de l'Air)

To catch up with events in Germany meanwhile, the sport of aerobatics had been revitalized in the late 1950s, as soon as power-flying was freely permitted after the war, under the renewed guidance of Gerhard Fieseler. Starting in 1960, the *Deutsche Aero Club* now organized a new series of German Championships.

The last championships, in 1938 and 1939, had been won by a young Luftwaffe officer named Albert Falderbaum, a great Jungmeister specialist who became the airshow pilot *par excellence* in post-war Germany. Anxious to get back into competitions as soon as ever they started again, he had entered the first Lockheed Trophy in 1955 with a Swiss Jungmeister but was prevented at the last minute from attending. He did, however, attend the revived German Championship in 1960, and made aerobatic history by winning the title not only three times in succession but over a time-span of 22 years!

The mount he was to have used in 1955 was HB-MID, one of nine Jungmeisters which the Swiss Air Force had sold off as surplus in 1954 and which were bought by the Swiss Aero Club. Two of these machines appeared later in the Lockheed competitions, flown by Swiss pilots Francis Liardon and Albert Rüesch, the latter machine eventually making its way to Germany to be flown by Walter Wolfrum (see below).

It was not until 1955 that power flying became permissible in Germany after the war, and some pilots, like Falderbaum, too impatient to wait ten years for their wings, had obtained or renewed their licences in nearby Switzerland. With Bücker Jungmann and Jungmeister training aircraft common to both countries, and with a thriving aviation movement in Switzerland, just over the border and speaking the same language, it was natural for the keen German flyers to gravitate to the Swiss airfields. Hence a significant interchange of techniques and influences took place between the two nations, and often in the early 1950s Swiss pilots would place their machines at

the disposal of German friends who had none of their own.

Another who had benefitted from the proximity of Switzerland was Gerhard Pawolka, a pre-war flying instructor who flew jet fighters including Me 262s in the Luftwaffe. Pawolka started out competing in the Lockheeds with a Jungmann, an immaculate machine which bore the distinctive Bavarian blue-and-white diamond checkerboard pattern on its rudder. Later he changed to the KZ-8, a Danish-built aircraft designed by Swedish engineer Bjørn Andreasson (who was responsible also for the all-metal BA4-B aerobatic biplane), constructed in Denmark by V Kramme and K G Zeuthen. Registered D-EBIZ, it was one of only two that were ever built, and its sister ship, HB-EPB, found fame in the hands of a Swiss pilot whom we shall shortly meet.

Pawolka had succeeded Falderbaum as German Champion in 1961 and then again in 1964, and as soon as the FAI World Championships were started he made a regular member of the German team.

Often it seems to happen in aerobatics that a trio of pilots of similar excellence will tend to dominate the scene in their country for a while; just as Fieseler, Achgelis and Stör had been the greatest talents of the 1930s, now Gerhard Pawolka was joined by Walter Wolfrum and Herbert Greb at the forefront of German aerobatics in the 1960s. All three were much the same age (born respectively in 1921, 1923 and 1927), and the two first mentioned were ex-military pilots. Herbert Greb, however, was just too young for war service and did not start power-flying until 1955, though he had already taken up gliding in 1942 as soon as he was old enough.

When Greb had his first flight in a Tiger Moth he was captivated by the idea of aerobatics, took his rating in 1958 and started flying a pre-war aircraft, the Klemm Kl 35, which was still a favourite machine with excellent performance. Earning his living as a sales representative, Greb started doing airshows at the weekend in order to cover his outgoings, and this brought him regularly before the public. He became a tremendously popular air display performer of

the 1960s with Klemm, Jungmeister and Zlin 226, and took the German national title four times between 1963 and 1967. Greb flew in two World Championships, the second in 1964 at Bilbao where he was the lone representative from his country: without financial support or encouragement of any kind, he was so conspicuous as the solitary West German, in contrast to the five-strong fully equipped team from East Germany, that the Federal German government was shamed into placing funds at the disposal of the Aero Club for aerobatic training from 1965 onwards.

A likeable man with strong views on aerobatics both as pilot and as judge, Herbert Greb presently lives in the USA but keeps in close touch with aerobatics in Europe and still flies for his own enjoyment.

The last member of our trio, Walter Wolfrum, won the third post-war German Championship in 1962 and came second in four others (to either Pawolka or Greb). Wolfrum was destined to become a major influence in German aerobatics and later in international and world-class aerobatics, where he still enjoys a high reputation today as an FAI judge.

He was an outstanding World War II ace with 137 victories, and served as a front-line fighter pilot with JG/52, rising to the rank of *Staffelkapitän* (squadron leader). During his initial training with the Luftwaffe in 1940–42, he remembers getting into trouble more than once with the authorities for performing 'prohibited aerobatics'! Nothing could keep a good man down, however, and as a Messerschmitt 109 pilot he indulged in his favourite pastime as often as possible, even though the types he flew – G2, G4, G6, G14 and K4 – were not in his opinion tremendously good aerobatic machines. But any excuse was good enough to put on an airshow to liven things up a little, especially when the occasion was a visiting troupe of entertainers with pretty girls to impress!

At the end of the war Wolfrum shared the frustration of all other German sport-pilots having to await official permission to fly in Germany. But he was more fortunate than most, because in 1951 he found himself domiciled for three months in London – sent by his firm to learn English – and at the little

Walter Wolfrum (centre) winner of the 1962 German Championship with Herbert Greb (left) and Gerhard Pawolka (right). (Walter Wolfrum)

Walter Wolfrum with Messerschmitt 109G6 in March 1944. (Walter Wolfrum)

flying field of Fairoaks in Surrey he found sympathetic fellow-pilots who soon arranged to clear him for aerobatics with the Tiger Moths and Miles Magisters that equipped their club. Then in 1953 like many others before him he renewed his power-flying licence in Switzerland, continuing on to take aerobatic training with famed Swiss instructor Albert Rüesch who immediately recognized his talent and advised him to go in for serious competition.

Nothing in the way of competition aerobatics existed in Germany at the time, however, nor much in the way of suitable equipment. As soon as powered flying was allowed again, Walter Wolfrum bent his energies to building his own little two-seater Jodel D-11, importing the plans from France, and during the years 1956–1959 he enjoyed the pleasure of many touring flights to such places as Sicily, Spain, Morocco, Sweden and England.

With the competition scene starting to reappear in about 1957, his first opportunity to lay hands on a suitable machine came in 1959 with the earliest Zlin trainer, the Z-126. Other machines in use at the time included Swiss-built Jungmanns and Jungmeisters and a Czech Aero Z-131, with the Zlin 126 and 226 appearing in Germany in 1958/9. Encouraged at reaching third place in the 1960 German Championships with a machine of only moderate performance, Wolfrum now entered fully into the zest for competition and in 1962 bought for himself a Bücker Jungmeister which had originally belonged to Albert Rüesch, and with it won the national title. In both 1962 and 1963 he entered for the Lockheed contest but was mortified on being kept away on both occasions, the first by adverse weather and the second by aircraft unserviceability.

Actively concerned with improving aerobatic standards in Germany, he knew that one of the basic hurdles was getting the right equipment. He was greatly attracted by the 180 hp Lycoming-engined Bücker Lerche produced in Switzerland, with its improved wing aerofoil for aerobatics, so in 1966 he acquired a Jungmann in this way and flew it to second place in the German Championships. He also flew the Lerche when he joined Gerhard Pawolka for the first time to contest the World Championships, which took place in Moscow that year; but the German standings in these competitions continued steadily declining and Wolfrum knew now that it was not merely the equipment that was to blame.

Gerhard Fieseler had been a vigorous fighter for aerobatics and had done wonders in his time, but by the mid-1960s the new FAI Championships had their own language, judging methods and criteria which it was essential to master if one was to be at all competitive. Unfortunately, under Fieseler's control the Germans were still using their time-honoured methods which dated back to the 1930s. For example, while in FAI contests the scoring system was to assign a mark from 0 to 10 for a manoeuvre, which was then multiplied by the difficulty coefficient given in the catalogue – in other words one assessed it on a percentage basis – under the Fieseler system, if the difficulty coefficient of the manoeuvre was, say, 18, the judge was required to mark the performance out of 18. If 12, he marked out of 12.

Although this may not seem on the face of it to be crucial to aerobatics – after all, a loop is a loop, you may say – nevertheless, both pilots and judges must be completely at home with the language and notation of a system if they are to make it work, and cannot be forever changing techniques between one method at home and a different one abroad. A

pilot to whom the complete infrastructure of international competition is not second nature is at a severe disadvantage.

The compulsory adoption of the Aresti system by the FAI in 1964 had been a revelation, if not a nightmare, to pilots at the World Championship, and Wolfrum saw in 1966 that his little team was very definitely out of its depth. The only solution was to make representations to the German Aero Club for total adoption at home of the new international system. This, of course, was heresy. But it was the only way forward, and on Walter Wolfrum now devolved the job of representing the interests of aerobatics within the Aero Club in place of Gerhard Fieseler.

The first thing he did was to arrange pilot training camps and get some cohesion into the general understanding and outlook on the sport. No such training had been organized before, it had always been every man for himself, and progress in isolation is very slow in aerobatics. Every pilot needs a ground observer to critique his performance and point out faults from the judge's point of view, which is very different from the pilot's point of view up in the sky! At the same time, such training encourages and develops new talent, and Wolfrum was pleased to see that a group of new young pilots was now emerging to take the place of the long-established Pawolka-Wolfrum-Greb trio, who now moved over to make room for their successors.

New on the scene now were Richard Hecht, a student of Greb, engineer Josef Hoessl from Straubing, and Norbert Holzberger – another top-flight trio which augured well for future international success until the sad loss of Holzberger in a flying accident in 1972. These were the up-and-coming pilots who battled for top honours in the German championships (now taking place only in alternate years when the World Championships did not occur), and in international

Josef Hoessl (winner) and Norbert Holzberger (second) in Biancotto Trophy at Carcasonne, 1971. (Walter Wolfrum)

Flight Fantastic

A young mechanical engineering graduate from the ETH*, Zurich, he was selected for pilot training under the Swiss government scheme at the age of 18 in 1959 and obtained his licence and aerobatic rating (on the Bücker Jungmann) the following year. In 1961 he became a full-time pilot in the Swiss military service, passing from Bücker trainers to Pilatus P-3s and thence to DH115, Vampire and Venom jet fighters, but at the same time having an interest in aerobatics that tempted him to try his hand at the beginners' level of competition. High in the aerobatic firmament of the time was Lockheed-winner Francis Liardon, and the great aircraft of the day was the Bücker Jungmeister.

Always something of an iconoclast, Wagner was unimpressed by everybody else's favourite machine and, while continuing to fly aerobatics with the Jungmann, started casting his eye around for some alternative to the ubiquitous Bückers and Zlins. By 1963 he had moved up to become winner of the intermediate (B-class) Swiss championship and started to get bookings for air displays, while in the same year he left military service and joined Swissair as an airline pilot; he has stayed with them ever since, and presently flies Boeing 747s in the left-hand seat.

It was in 1965 that Wagner espied a long-forgotten KZ-8 under a dust sheet in an old hangar and bought the little Danish-built aircraft with its 145 hp Gipsy engine. He had already given proof of his mettle the previous year in the World Aerobatic Championships in Spain, being selected as reserve team member and finishing ahead of all the others in a remarkable eighth place. His mount for the 1964 event had been the Bücker Lerche which was enjoying great popularity at the time; but Wagner's taste favoured the monoplane rather than the biplane, and in his new machine he swept away the Swiss National Championship of 1965 in the unlimited class.

Wagner was convinced that airframe design for aerobatic machines was lagging behind the progress made in engine/propeller technology, which now featured powerful, lightweight power units with full inverted capability (like the American Lycoming) driving efficient, variable pitch or constant-speed propellers. Quietly he set about modifying the KZ-8 so that the control surfaces of elevators and flaps could be interconnected in a special way, enabling the pilot to have at his command an unusually wide range of control surface variations. Hitherto, extreme changes in the angle of attack of the wings to achieve aerobatic manoeuvres had necessitated extreme aircraft attitudes, which were both inefficient and inimical to the fundamental goal of precision aerobatics – perfection of line.

The variation of wing camber is an efficient way of changing the effect of airflow over the wing, and comes into play every time an aileron, flap or leading-edge slat changes position in flight, thereby producing a different configuration over the mainplane as a whole without moving the mainplane itself. By the same token, Wagner's new system – which was already an established technique in control-line models – relied on major changes in the control surfaces of both mainplane and tailplane, to produce the same effect that would otherwise have necessitated major changes in aircraft attitude. The logical extension of this idea was to add aileron deflection to the other interconnecting control surfaces as well, but this had to wait until a totally new design could be built.

The KZ-8 was the test-bed for this new control system, and

German Championship 1975: first Manfred Strössenreuther (centre), second Richard Hecht (left), third Hermann Liese (right). (Walter Wolfrum)

competitions such as the Biancotto Trophy in France, where in 1972 Josef Hoessl was the winner from Holzberger in second place.

But now, in the cross-pollination between Germany and Switzerland, a new and vital influence entered the scene whose name was Arnold Wagner.

Swiss Champion and Acrostar designer Arnold Wagner. (Arnold Wagner)

* *Eidgenössische Technische Hochschule* = Swiss Institute of Technology.

Wagner's modified KZ-8 with interconnecting elevator-flap deflections (145 hp Gipsy 8). (Arnold Wagner)

its potential was quickly recognized by German pilots like Walter Wolfrum and Josef Hoessl, as Arnold Wagner proceeded to win top placings in the Swiss and German national competitions with his modified machine. Soon they had started putting their heads together to design a revolutionary new aircraft, especially built for aerobatics, which would incorporate these and many other sophisticated design ideas; and by 1969 the Acrostar concept was born.

Of course there had been stiff resistance from the conservative Swiss Federal Aviation Authority to the KZ-8 modifications, and Wagner had overcome bureaucratic opposition during the winter of 1967/8 only by dint of bombarding the civil servant concerned with daily deliveries of registered mail! He knew there was little hope of getting Swiss certification for his new experimental aeroplane, so the result was that 'Project Acrostar' was moved to Germany, and when it saw realization in 1970 it was a prototype machine built for Wagner, Wolfrum and Hoessl by the firm of Wolf Hirth at Nabern/Teck. It was partly funded by the sale of the KZ-8 to British pilot Bob Mitchell. together with further considerable investment on Wagner's part, but he found great satisfaction in leading the design team that was transforming his sketches to reality, and in the pleasure of eventually taking D-EMKB to the air on 16 April 1970, for its first flight.

As was to be expected, there were plenty of glitches to be ironed out in testing the prototype such as flutter, oil-pressure drops, etc. Arnold Wagner still has a vivid memory of the initial flat spinning characteristics of the prototype, and of a particular episode when it took 22 turns and more to come out of one!

At last he had realized his dream of a machine built exclusively for competition aerobatics, just like a Formula One racing car, with no concessions and no compromises. The wing was absolutely symmetrical with zero angle of incidence and zero dihedral, the all-flying elevator was again linked to the flaps, and the flaps themselves were interconnected to the ailerons ('flapperons') so that with appropriate stick inputs they would deflect along with the ailerons, but to twice their extent, for rolling manoeuvres. In Wagner's own words, the aerobatic confraternity was not (and still is not) ready for such radical thinking. Complete symmetry of wing design with integrated control surfaces and neutral roll response are still, he contends, alien to machines of the

1980s. But although he was ahead of his time, perhaps Wagner's unorthodox ideas were not altogether lost on the aerobatic community: fifteen years later, two excellent aerobatic machines presently incorporate linked elevator and flap movement. First came a 1985 modification to the Soviet Union's Yak 55 mid-wing monoplane, then later the same year the Ultimate 10 Dash 100 design of Canadian pilot Gordon Price (see page 266), which includes a 'Macro Flap' system linking 5 degrees of flap movement with each 30 degrees of elevator.

Test-flying of the Acrostar was completed in time for Wagner and Hoessl to win a double victory at the Swiss championships of 1970, taking first and second places respectively, and for Wagner then to fly the aircraft over to England for the World Aerobatic Championships held at Hullavington,

Integrated control system of the Acrostar: ailerons follow flaps half way.
(top) Stick pushed completely,
(bottom) Stick fully pulled. (Lewis Shaw, courtesy of IAC)

Flight Fantastic

Wiltshire. For him the championship results provided the culmination of his competitive career, with an overall fourth place in the still-unfamiliar machine, together with the highest score in the final Free Programme flights; but unfortunately weather prevented this section of the contest from being completed by all contestants, and therefore it did not feature in the eventual results.

Nevertheless, Arnold Wagner felt that he had achieved all he could hope to achieve in the sport, with an outstanding championship result to his credit and a near-perfect flight in the fourth programme; and he resolved there and then to retire from competition flying. It is remarkable now to reflect that he achieved all this as a mere 29-year-old, and of course he subsequently received many invitations to return to aerobatics. But Wagner is indeed an extraordinary man, and was quite content at the time to concentrate on flight-testing, modifying and gaining certification for the Acrostar in Germany, later initiating a series production from which eight more machines were built and sold. Sadly, with the combination of the fuel crisis of 1974, the difficulties of the Hirth firm, and the bankruptcy of the Franklin engine company, the Acrostar venture came to an end and Wagner's plans for an improved Mk3 version were never realized.

Before we leave the Arnold Wagner story, one more achievement of his must be mentioned, and that is his *Handbook on Aerobatics* written in 1971.

Still flying as a Swiss Army reserve, with the rank of first lieutenant, Wagner annually attended his obligatory military training but proved a little hard to keep under control at times. One day, having wagered his squadron leader that he could hit a ground pistol target from an airborne P-3, Wagner went up and proved he was right by the simplest possible means – by doing it. But the authorities found out about the escapade and clapped him in military detention for ten days.

This gave him a startling idea how to use the time profitably, and, requesting paper and writing materials, he set to work to write an excellent 80-page aerobatic primer which he completed within the allotted timespan and published shortly afterwards. In his Foreword to the book, datelined Emmen Barracks, 25 September 1971, Wagner included among his acknowledgements a typically tongue-in-cheek word of thanks to the Swiss military authorities for affording him the free time in which to do the work!

Meanwhile, in 1968 Arnold Wagner had organized a training camp for Swiss competition pilots and had 'imported' one-time Czech national champion Vladimir Pohořelý to become the official team trainer. This man was a first-class aerobatic pilot who had been an instructor of World Champion Ladi Bezák. He had a high reputation as a trainer in Czechoslovakia and had invented his own systems of tracking and notating aerobatic sequences. When he came to Switzerland, Pohořelý introduced a method of training which made an indelible mark and is still in use today.

Trainers tend perhaps to be somewhat overlooked in sports where the successful competitors themselves receive all the limelight, but Vladimir Pohořelý – like Kasum Nazhmudinov, trainer of the Soviet team in more recent years – possessed a touch of magic which communicated itself to his protégés. Appointing him as trainer was indeed a stroke of genius, for the result was that three of his early students – Eric Müller, Christian Schweizer and Michel Brandt – received the best of instruction and encouragement to go on to achieve great things. All three have vied with each other for the best

Vladimir Pohořelý, trainer of the Swiss team.
(via Arnold Wagner)

part of 15 years for top honours in the national championship of Switzerland, while Brandt has been a World Championship silver medallist and Müller and Schweizer have each won top European titles.

In 1971 the Swiss Aerobatic Association was founded with the aim of providing a firm base for the Swiss Team in international events and in order to obtain the best aerobatic aircraft of the day – the Acrostar – for the pilots to fly. Eric Müller, an architect by profession who had come to top-level aerobatics quite late in life at the age of 34, eventually continued flying the Acrostar for longer than any other pilot, a total of ten years in all, becoming the acknowledged master of the aircraft throughout Europe. With it he invented a new figure in 1974 which he called the **Zwirbelturm** ('Spiralling Tower'), which to some extent resembled a lomcovák by virtue of its manner of entry from an ascending autorotation, and hence acquired among its many alternative names the title 'Müllercovák'!

Known in America as the 'helicopter spin', it starts with a vertical roll to which negative flick inputs are slowly added until a negative ascending spin is achieved with a very flat attitude to the horizon. At the top of the figure, if performed well, the aircraft is whirling around almost horizontally with no forward speed, and the pilot has a sensation of zero *g* until he starts to descend again in a positive flat spin. Müller featured this in his winning programme in 1974 at the Biancotto Trophy competition, and the event was recorded in an excellent 45-minute film entitled *Zoom*, still one of the best films ever made about aerobatics.

Ten years later, after earning a world-wide reputation as a theorist and instructor – as well as medal-winning competitor – Eric Müller made a major contribution to the small store of literature on the subject. *Flight Unlimited*, written in collaboration with this author, gave not only the basic techniques and how to master them, it also revealed many of the secrets that go to win competitions: such as how to check orientation in every type of manoeuvre, and how to effect wind-correction in a way that is undetectable from the judge's point of view.

The sensational Acrostar displays its classic lines in a vertical climb. *(Alain Ernoult)*

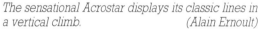

Zwirbelturm or 'helicopter spin', invented on the Acrostar.

Swiss team at the World Championships, Hullavington. (Left to right) Front row: Christian Schweizer, Michel Brandt, Denis Hugli. Back row: Vladimir Pohořelý, Arnold Wagner, Eric Müller, Alex Leitner, Jean-Pierre Freiburghaus.
(Arnold Wagner)

The book rapidly became essential reading for every aspiring aerobat.

Christian Schweizer, a young licensed engineer who joined the training group originally as a mechanic but was then invited to fly, took on complete responsibility for aircraft maintenance with the SAA as well as competing and flying airshows to raise funds. As soon as the Acrostar was acquired his form increased dramatically, and in his second World

Manfred Strössenreuther, undefeated German National Champion from 1979 to 1986.
(Carl Lang)

Christian Schweizer, Swiss Champion in both powered and glider aerobatics. *(Don Berliner)*

Another Swiss National Champion: Michel Brandt with his special Pitts BS-1S. *(Michel Brandt)*

Championship, in 1972, he came away with a magnificent fourth place! Then, following on Josef Hoessl's triumph with the Acrostar in the Biancotto Trophy, the major European championship of 1971, Schweizer flew the Swiss Acrostar to victory in the next major European event in 1973, the Scandinavian Cup at Roskilde, where he first performed a figure now known as the 'Schweizer-Acht' (Swiss 8). In this figure he performs one-and-a-quarter flick rolls as he pulls up in each of the looping sections of the figure of eight, going over the top in knife-edge and rolling back to erect with one-and-a-quarter slow rolls as he completes each 45 degree line.

Schweizer flew the Acrostar from 1972 to 1975, and still considers it to be one of the finest machines ever built for aerobatics. Although it suffered from some instability problems and from being simply too heavy, he believes that these faults were curable, and that with an engine of around the 260 hp mark the Acrostar could still be competitive today. Certainly many agree that it is one of the most exciting and impressive visual designs ever built. When Schweizer changed in 1976 to an American aircraft, the Pitts Special, this did not in fact indicate dissatisfaction with the Swiss machine, but was a decision dictated by the fact that maintenance work on the SAA's Acrostar was taken over by somebody new; as a qualified engineer himself, Christian Schweizer understandably prefers to fly only those aeroplanes on which he personally does his own maintenance.

At the same point in time he took up glider aerobatics, helping to found what is now a flourishing association for the sport in Switzerland, where he has won the Swiss Nationals four times in the glider as well as the powered category. He is also a ski expert and has won a number of medals in the slalom and giant slalom events of his regional championships.

Christian holds ATPL and instructor's licences and is a professional pilot these days with the Swiss Air-Ambulance Service, flying Learjets and Canadair Challengers on mercy missions to repatriate sick and injured travellers abroad. With so many interests and such a demanding work schedule, unfortunately he tends to find less and less time now for aerobatics; but one can almost certainly rely on his fiercely competitive Swiss instincts to keep him working hard at his art, keeping him at the forefront of competition aerobatics for many a long year yet.

The third member of our Swiss trio from the 1970s is French-speaking Michel Brandt, small, dark and gallic, with the same consummate skill as the other two plus a flash of latin temperament in addition. A graduate in aeronautics of the famed Zurich Institute of Technology, he is brilliant in his field and presently works for Airbus Industrie as Deputy Director of Engineering Operations. Before that, he was Chief Engineer and Test Pilot at Avions Robin for 12 years, until the company hit financial problems.

Yet you would never believe that this quiet, boyish figure was such an intellectual powerhouse. Born in 1944 at La Chaux-de-Fonds, near the beautiful lake of Neuchâtel, he graduated from gliders to power flying, and at the age of eighteen started teaching himself aerobatics on a Bücker 131 Jungmann. Even before taking any training, he won the Swiss championship in the less advanced ('Espoir') class; but on joining the 1969 training camp organized by Wagner, with Pohořelý as trainer, Michel Brandt soon qualified for the 1970 team that was going to the World Championships in Hullavington, England.

Sharing a Bücker Lerche with Eric Müller, Brandt came twenty-sixth and Müller thirty-fifth in their first world contest. But while Müller and Schweizer then forged ahead with the Acrostar, Brandt – living and working for Robin in France – found himself too far from Swiss activities and once more was thrown back on his own resources. It was not until he built his own Pitts Special, certificated under its own special designation Pitts BS-1S in France, that he found an aircraft on which he could really excel. With this machine in Kiev in 1976 he was the highest placed member of the Swiss team in eighth position, and won a silver medal in the Known Compulsory programme. He followed this excellent result with tenth place in 1978 and seventh in 1980. But at this point we will leave the fortunes of our Swiss trio, for Chapter 19 picks up the threads during the 1980 World Championships in Oshkosh, USA, and then brings us up to the present day.

16

Rise of the Soviet Union

This extraordinary confederation of fifteen separate republics, stretching from the Pacific to the Baltic, is a land on which the sun never sets: when dusk falls in the west it is already dawn in the east. The largest country in the world, it occupies one-sixth of the total land surface of our planet, with extremes of climate ranging from the warm, subtropical Transcaucasia in the south to the eternal snows of the Arctic in the north.

When the story of aviation began it was Imperial Russia, ruled by the Tsars, with a massive peasant population literally a hundred years behind the developed western nations. For a privileged few the luxury of aviation was possible, and several early flying machines were constructed in the first decade of the 1900s. The first Russian to distinguish himself as an outstanding pilot was Michael Efimoff, who learned to fly on Voisins in France and took part in the 1910 aviation meeting at Nice; there he won several prizes and created quite a furore with his daringly banked turns.

The Russian military forces took to aviation early on, and Efimoff was appointed chief instructor at the School of Military Aviation organized under the patronage of Grand Duke Alexander Michaelovich. The Imperial Russian Air Service soon became well established, and in 1912 a Gnôme-powered design by Igor Sikorsky won the international military trials at St Petersburg against ten other entrants. However, it was eventually decided to equip chiefly with aircraft of French design which proved more reliable.

Petr Nikolaevich Nesterov, famous as the first pilot to 'loop-the-loop', was one of Russia's 200 pre-war military airmen. He was an energetic pioneer in many areas of aviation, not only in aerobatics but also in night flying, artillery fire direction and record-breaking long distance flights.

He was also an inventive young man with ideas of his own

about many things including the design of aeroplanes. Having repeatedly tried his hand at constructing and modifying various types, on taking command of the XI Corps Air Squadron at Kiev he then bent his mind to devising means whereby enemy aircraft might be destroyed by ramming in flight. His celebrated mid-air attack on an Austrian machine not only made him Russia's first air war hero, but also placed him at the beginning of a long line of fellow-countrymen who went on to employ similar ramming (taran) tactics right up to World War II.

His aerobatics were soon emulated by military colleagues, and in December 1913, just a few months after Nesterov's loop, a Russian naval lieutenant by the name of Iliya Ilyich Kulnev inverted his S-10 seaplane and flew in that position for more than a minute. Then in the autumn of 1914, Nesterov's great admirer Evgraf Nikolaevich Kruten took up a French Farman 16 biplane whilst undergoing his aviation training at Gatchina, and looped it twice to the great astonishment of all observers, who had been given no inkling that he intended to try the manoeuvre.

Kruten was a brilliant and courageous pilot and a great innovator of aerial combat manoeuvres during World War I, developing and codifying his ideas for the benefit of his fellow pilots. He was among the earliest to employ and recommend the stall turn as an attacking manoeuvre, pulling up under an opponent's blind spot and diving away again after delivering a crippling burst of fire. As commander of the Second Fighter Group based at Brodi he was tireless in training the pilots under his command at a time when there was no such thing as preparation for aerial combat. Credited with 15 victories, he eventually met his death in 1917 in a stall/spin accident with his Nieuport 23 whilst making a gliding turn at low altitude, having run out of fuel during a fighter escort patrol. He was much loved by all his men, and many of his

Flight Fantastic

combat instructions remained valid for decades more, until superseded by the jet fighter age.

An important contribution to spin recovery technique was made by Russian pilot Konstantin Artseulov, who on 24 September 1916 deliberately spun and recovered his Nieuport 21 to test the ideas which he had been working out theoretically. Although the spin by now was in general use at

fairly and squarely as they occur. In general, however, our concern is purely with the development and progress of aerobatics; and so we continue our narrative with a great Soviet pioneer, Valeri Pavlovich Chkalov, remembered in the Soviet Union as the foremost aerobatic exponent of the inter-war years and as a significant force in aviation as a whole.

Konstantin Artseulov.　　　　*(via Kasum Nazhmudinov)*

Valeri Chkalov. The Chkalov Cup, in his memory, was awarded to the Soviet Champion until 1974; then from 1975 onwards the award was transferred to the overall winner of the Socialist Countries Championships.

(via Kasum Nazhmudinov)

the Front, and indeed Artseulov's fellow-countryman Dybovski had demonstrated it more than a year earlier (see Chapter 6), the significance of Artseulov's contribution was that having perfected his recovery technique, he was able to teach it to trainee pilots when he went on to become an instructor at the Kachinski School of Aviation. From then onwards aerobatics were used as a vital tool in pilot training, just as at the military schools of Gosport in England and Pau in France.

Under the new Communist regime introduced as a result of the 1917 revolution, the Union of Soviet Socialist Republics was born and probably the greatest ever experiment in organized society began. More than sixty years later we in our orderly western world find it hard to comprehend the magnitude of that undertaking, and the enormity of the obstacles that had to be overcome. Many grave mistakes have been made by the Soviet Union in its path to economic development and self-realization, and many have been made by the west; but they are not the subject of this book. In a chronicle that deals with what has become an international sport we cannot afford to ignore political differences when they arise, and so far as is possible they will be confronted

Valeri Chkalov was born in 1904 in a town called Vasilevo in the Gorki district, now renamed Chkalovsk in his honour. In 1919 he volunteered for the Fourth Aviation Regiment of the Red Army and served as an aircraft engineer and fitter, then from 1921 to 1923 he underwent flying instruction at the Egorevski and Borisoglebski Aviation Schools in the Moscow area: here he was recognized as an exceptional pilot and was sent on to take advanced training at the Moscow Military Aviation School of Aerobatics. After further instruction in gunnery and aerial combat, Chkalov served as a fighter pilot and became a flight commander with the Bryansk Air Brigade.

Aerobatics were his particular love, and he was the first Soviet pilot to work out for himself and execute the slow roll, as well as many other complex new figures, though the details of these have unfortunately not survived. He was a prolific inventor of tactics in aerial combat, low-level flying and bombing, and after his military service he went on to

become a pilot-instructor at the Leningrad Aviation Club; then from 1930 onwards he took up a career as a professional test pilot.

By 1935 Chkalov had become outstanding in the aviation world and was awarded the Order of Lenin in recognition of his research and experimental work. The following year he set out on a different kind of aviation adventure, making the first of his two epic long-distance flights, non-stop from Moscow via the Arctic Ocean to Petropavlovsk (Kamchatka), just about the furthermost point you can reach in the Soviet Union east of Moscow on the same latitude. In 1937 he took his single engined Antonov ANT-25 an even longer distance, three days without refuelling across the North Pole to Vancouver, another destination on roughly the same latitude as his starting point in Moscow, but even further East!

Decorated and honoured repeatedly – his latest award being the Order of the Red Banner – Chkalov by now had become a public figure, and in December of 1937 found himself elected Deputy of the Supreme Soviet. But although involved in ever greater amounts of government work as well as test flying and research, he still found time for painting and music which he loved. Of the myriad aircraft types flown, tested and certificated by him, it is interesting for us to note that one was the Polikarpov I-16 Rata monoplane, a machine which Col José Luis Aresti flew during his time as a pilot in the Spanish Civil War.

The story of Chkalov's death sets a fitting seal on the career of this very great man. During his first test flight of the new Polikarpov I-180 fighter in December 1938, he was presented with the agonizing predicament of an engine failure over a built-up area: to bale out would have meant a crash costing the lives of many people all unsuspecting in the houses below. Instead, he chose to sacrifice himself by staying with the aircraft and gliding with it to a more distant – but for him fatal – forced landing. In tribute, the Central Aero Club of the USSR was named after him.

A contemporary of Chkalov's but with a special interest in design as well as piloting was Victor Pisarenko, who in the early 1920s, without any technological training whatsoever, accomplished the remarkable feat of building two original and extremely successful light aeroplanes.

Pisarenko had the idea of building the first machine while he was an instructor at the Sevastopol Flying School, and he and his pupils made use of whatever materials they could lay their hands on, including used spare parts, to put the aircraft together in the school workshop. The VOP-1 was a single-seat low wing cantilever monoplane – the first such monoplane in the Soviet Union – of wood construction, wire braced, and powered by a 35 hp Anzani of the type used by Louis Blériot in his channel-crossing Blériot XI. It first flew in November 1923, and proved to be an excellent design.

His second project, the Pisarenko-T trainer, was a much more powerful machine with a 150 hp Hispano-Suiza engine. It was a parasol monoplane and featured a most unusual aerofoil shape which seems to have been more or less symmetrical, entirely flat on both under and upper surfaces, with a rounded leading edge. The manner of its construction was exactly the same as that of the VOP-1, being put together in the workshop of the school at which Pisarenko happened to be an instructor at the time. He flew the aircraft in 1925 (entirely without permission, since no calculations had ever been made!) and on his first flight took it to Moscow where he performed a highly skilled aerobatic routine that included

slow rolls and barrel rolls. After this he was asked to collaborate on developing a trainer – officially this time – but the project never got off the ground and Pisarenko sadly died in a flying accident in 1931 before he could turn his talents to any more aerobatic aircraft.

Sport aviation competitions in the Soviet Union started in the 1930s, with a long-distance circuit race in 1935 of some 5,500 kilometres beginning and ending in Moscow. Winner of the event was the UT-2 two-seat monoplane trainer of a certain young constructor by the name of Alexander Yakovlev, of whom the reader will shortly hear much more.

In 1938 the first national championships were held for the training wings of aeroclubs which were allied to the air force, using UT-2s. Then from 1949 annual competitions began to be held specifically for sport flying, to cater for the growing network of civilian flying clubs; the nature of these contests was very varied and interesting, and each year would include some or all of the following tests:

1. Performing 4 complete turns against the clock
2. Dead-stick spot landing from 1,000 metres
3. A sequence of aerobatics performed within a strict time limit
4. Accurate navigation and landing from 300 metres
5. Accurate navigation and engine-off landing from 500 metres
6. Instrument flying on courses of 50 and 100 kilometres
7. Climb to maximum height against the clock
8. Accurate night-flying navigation and landing
9. Night flight of 150 kilometres
10. Aerobatics in erect and inverted flight
11. Aerobatics in inverted flight only

Teams from the various Soviet Republics took part in these nation-wide sporting contests, and members of the USSR National Aerobatic Team would participate in the individual aerobatic championship events. Over the succeeding years, aircraft in use for these competitions included Po-2, UT-2, Zlin 226 and 326, and the famous Yak-11, Yak-18, Yak 50 and Yak 52 designs of Alexander Sergeivich Yakovlev.

Born in Moscow in 1906, Alexander Yakovlev was insatiably curious as a child about all things mechanical, and at school he even built himself a wireless receiver that worked. Attracted by the idea of constructing a glider, he sought help from his contemporary Sergei Ilyushin, then an engineering student; and at the age of eighteen Yakovlev produced his first original design, the Pegasus, which immediately won a prize of 200 rubles in a national glider competition.

Burning to work in aviation, he obtained a job in the engineering workshop of the Soviet Air Force Academy, and while there started to design a little two-seat biplane, the Air-1, which was completed and first flown in May 1927. Powered by a 60 hp engine, it flew non-stop from Sevastopol to Moscow, a distance of more than 1,200 kilometres, in 15½ hours. This success earned him a coveted place as a student at the Academy, and on graduating he joined the Polikarpov design office, later setting up on his own in a one-time bed factory in Moscow. From these humble beginnings the famous UT-2, the first modern Soviet trainer, emerged in 1935 and won the official trials as well as the Moscow Aviation Day air race. The UT-1 advanced aerobatic trainer followed, a single-seat version which gained a world record in its class by flying at 160 mph, one mph for each of its 160 horsepower.

With the clouds of war gathering in the late 1930s, Yakovlev was invited to enter – and won – a design contest for a new fighter aircraft; his I-26 design, which became the Yak-1, earned him a prize of 100,000 rubles together with the Order

Yakovlev UT-1 advanced aerobatic trainer of the 1930s.
(Lynn Williams)

of Lenin award. This was only the first of many awards to come, including an honorary Doctorate of Technical Science.

Production was hastily set up on the far side of the Urals out of the way of Hitler's invading troops, and Yakovlev went on to produce a multiplicity of fighter and trainer designs which amounted in total to some 30,000 aircraft by the end of the war. Though the lightweight Yak-3 was his great masterpiece of speed and agility, all of Yakovlev's fighters were considered delightful to handle, stable and controllable even in extreme combat manoeuvring, from the Yak-1 capable of 584 km/h (363 mph) to the last piston-engined Yak-9U and -9P at some 675 km/h (420 mph), rated as comparable to the North American P-51 Mustang in performance.

But we are more interested here in Alexander Yakovlev's postwar aerobatic trainers, which proudly carry the Yak name after more than fifty years of continuous aircraft production. Perhaps we in the west nowadays associate Soviet aviation more with fighters such as the MiGs; but the Yak designs are still going strong, and they still carry an emotive aura derived from their illustrious past. The name

'Yak' means to the Soviet people very much what the name 'Spitfire' means to the British. Not surprisingly, there is a very real sense of national pride in the Soviet fleets of Yak 50s and 55s, latest in the Yak line of competition machines with which their young pilots defend the Red Flag in the league table of aerobatic achievement.

The line originated in the prototype Yak-18 of 1946, an all-metal trainer whose geometry closely resembled the UT-2 mixed with elements of the Yak piston-engined fighters. Equipped with a close-cowled 5-cylinder M-11FR radial engine of 160 hp, with variable pitch propeller, it was a tailwheel aeroplane with retractable undercarriage. A simple, rugged and reliable trainer, the Yak-18 easily outstripped its predecessors in performance; it sold in large numbers throughout the Eastern bloc and was also produced in China. At one time or another virtually all military flying personnel in the USSR received their initial training on the Yak-18, including pioneer cosmonaut Yuri Gagarin. From the beginning of the 1960s it became the basic aerobatic machine of the civilian flying clubs.

Later modifications to this two-seater design produced two

Yak-18 two-seat trainer (160 hp M-11FR).   *(Jean Alexander)*

Span	10.6 m (34 ft 9 in)
Length	8.35 m (27 ft 5 in)
Height	3.35 m (11 ft)
Empty weight	825 kg (1,819 lb)
Max speed	315 km/h (196 mph)
Rate of climb	10 m/sec (1,968 fpm)
Limit load	$+9, -6 g$

Yak-18PM, with more power (300 hp AI-14FR), lightened airframe and new flat wing design. (John Blake)

versions with tricycle gear, the 160 hp Yak-18U and then the Yak-18A, the latter with its more powerful (260 hp) engine introducing the circular cowl shape so distinctive in all subsequent models. But it was the range of single-seaters – the Yak-18P seen in 1960 at the World Championships in Bratislava, followed by the Yak-18PM in 1966 at Kiev and Yak-18PS in 1970 at Hullavington – which gained international fame for the Soviet Union in World Championships; and over a thirty-year development period they led directly to the high performance Yak 50 design of 1975, and the Yak 55 of 1982, purpose built for international aerobatic competition.

The 18P design kept the same upswept wings, tricycle undercarriage and 260 hp engine as the 18A, but was the first single-seat design and was tried with a variety of cockpit positions before the eventual forward placement over the wing was adopted in production. There was a substantial saving in weight over the two-seater, and the extra thrust gave a much healthier climb and speed performance.

Following the 18P came the 18PM with similar fuselage and gear, but featuring a new wing with very little dihedral and also an improved, rearward cockpit position for better field of vision. An increased rate and smaller radius of roll were achieved, but lack of rudder authority made good slow rolls and rolling circles extremely difficult. All the Yak-18s were heavily built and carried heavy power plants, retractable gear, etc., and continuous efforts were made to achieve weight savings. The 18PM model was lightened and at the same time equipped with the more powerful (300 hp) AI-14FR engine, giving a vertical performance so outstanding when seen at the World Championships in Kiev that it was rumoured the engine was giving a 400 hp output! In fact an air-brake was provided under the centre section which was necessary for vertically diving manoeuvres. The lighter construction was fabric covered (both wings and fuselage) over a steel tubing frame, with metal spars and metal covered wing leading edges. As in many other European designs, toe straps were incorporated to help anchor the feet to the rudder pedals in inverted flight.

Last in the Yak-18P series came the 18PS in 1970, uncompromisingly designed for international level competition.

Along with the existing 300 hp engine and clean lines of the 18PM came the improvement of a tailwheel undercarriage and cockpit position at the wing trailing-edge, plus refinements to reduce weight such as the extremely small fuel tank with capacity for only 25 minutes endurance – plenty for the short duration of a competition flight! The advantages of tailwheel gear were well known, both for reduction in drag and for general lightness of assembly compared with tricycle gear; and, of course, there was also the advantage that with this configuration the machine's inverted performance did not suffer from an excessive outcrop of appendages on what became the main lifting surfaces when it was upside down.

Better vertical penetration and a higher rate of roll were among the improvements, although even so it was still essentially a fighter trainer design and tended to be heavy on the controls and to have a poor flick-roll performance. Pilots who tried the Yak for the first time always came away with new respect for the Soviet pilots.

Like all the Yak aeroplanes, the Yak-18PS was a large, graceful monoplane that was easy to see and judge in the competition box. Neil Williams in his book _Aerobatics_ (Airlife, 1974) had the following comments to make:

A beautiful and graceful aeroplane to watch in flight is the Yak-18PS. Quiet and powerful, it purrs through the sequences, seemingly without effort, and it is not until one flies the Yak and notes its very high directional stability which in conjunction with its standard wing makes the positive flick roll a little awkward, that one can appreciate the very high skill and training of the Yak pilots. On the other hand, the standard wing stalls sharply in inverted flight and gives the Yak a startling outside [negative] flick roll performance for such a big aeroplane. It ... is not very good in the rolling circle as it will not fly properly on its side, and it relies on a large energy content for its performance: if it loses speed at low altitude it takes a long time to build it up again.

Williams quite rightly commented that larger aircraft had many advantages in competition, not only that they had a greater visual density, but that they also appeared to fly more slowly, thereby giving an impression of ease and grace. This is as true today as it was ten years ago, and even the very latest Soviet designs still adhere to the pattern of the powerful radial engine set in a long, sleek monoplane airframe, and with devastating effect!

In the first World Championships of 1960 the Soviet Union fielded a team of which only one pilot, Boris Vasenko, flew a Yak-18P, the other four using the Zlin 326. It was evident that they were not in the same league as the Czechoslovakian hosts of the contest, as indeed nor was any other competing nation, so it was greatly to Vasenko's credit that he made the finals and achieved fifth place with the big Yak against so many agile and manoeuvrable Zlins. As the sole USSR finalist among eight Czechs, you may be sure that his performance was closely watched, especially by those who were on the look-out for political bias; but Oliver Stewart reported that apart from a doubtful 1½ flick roll in the first programme and some inaccurate timing, Vasenko was obviously on top of his form and handled his big heavy aircraft with finesse.

In the 1962 and 1964 Championships, though still handicapped by the Yak-18P with its 260 hp engine and non-aerobatic wing, the Soviet Union produced excellent pilots in the shape of Vladislav Loichikov (winner of two programmes and second overall in Budapest) and Vladimir Piskunov (winner of programme 3 and overall fourth in Bilbao). Taking their cue from the World Championship format, they decided

Yak-18P single-seater with tricycle gear (260hp AI-14R), a
rare colour picture taken at the 1964 World Championships in
Bilbao.   (Peter Phillips)

Span	10.6 m (34 ft 9 in)
Length	8.35 m (27 ft 5 in)
Height	3.35 m (11 ft)
Empty weight	818 kg (1,803 lb)
Max speed	275 km/h (171 mph)
Rate of climb	8.6 m/sec (1,693 fpm)
Limit load	+9, −6 g

to host an international contest themselves at Moscow in
1963, where Loichikov was again the winner, and this set the
pattern for a regular series of Socialist Countries' Championships which started being held at irregular intervals until,
from 1971 onwards, they became an annual event.

Meanwhile, the USSR had already put in a bid to mount the
World contest in 1964, but a prior claim on the part of Spain
deferred the Soviet event until 1966. By now the better
organized of the National Aero Clubs had set up team
selection and training procedures (Czechoslovakia, Hungary,
Spain, the USA, etc.) and many had furnished their pilots with
the best aerobatic aircraft that money could buy. The Spanish
in 1964 had acquired six new Zlin Akrobats and spent months
practising at the Bilbao location; while the Czechs had
brought out a constant-speed prop modification for their
Zlins, which they refused to sell abroad.

Yak-18PS, 1970 tailwheel version of the 18PM, special
modification for top-level competition.   (John Blake)

Span	10.6 m (34 ft 9 in)
Length	8.35 m (27 ft 5 in)
Height	2.93 m (9 ft 7 in)
Empty weight	825 kg (1,819 lb)
Max speed	320 km/h (200 mph)
Rate of climb	12 m/sec (2,362 fpm)
Limit load	+9, −6 g

The Soviet selection system was to hold numerous contests, wherein civilian Aero Clubs participated from all over the USSR; of these there existed around 100, almost all of them sponsored by trade unions, where competition was keen to gain a place for flight instruction. After team selections, months of disciplined training ensued for the pilots. Their four crimson Yak-18Ps were overhauled to new condition, especially instrumented for aerobatics, and air lifted to Spain in two large Aeroflot Antonov AN-12 turboprop transports.

Although Soviet pilots did not win a place in the top three, in James Gilbert's opinion everybody at Bilbao was enormously impressed by the sheer quality of their flying – "most precise and relaxed in its style". American Nick D'Apuzzo reported: "Russia has claimed the team championship because of the superb performances of Vladimir Piskunov, Vadim Ovsyankin, Vitold Pochernin and Vladimir Martemianov who finished 4th, 5th, 6th and 7th respectively." In fact it was a particular joy for them to win this prize, since it was the very fine Nesterov Trophy which the Soviet Union had itself inaugurated in 1962.

A full team of three female pilots had also been sent in

The Nesterov Cup, awarded to the overall Team Champions.
(Kasum Nazhmudinov)

Soviet team aircraft lined up in Bilbao, 1964 World Championships. *(John Blake)*

hopes of competing for a Women's World Championship, but in the absence of the required minimum of ten contenders there was no separate result. Setting a standard of excellence that has continued ever since, however, two of the Soviet girls outscored more than half of all the men. Rosalia Zanozina, the USSR Women's Champion, placed fourteenth in the eliminators and would have flown in the finals had she been a man; but since there was no women's championship, there were no finals for the women. This anomaly left her in overall seventeenth place, after 16 men had flown in the final round, and Liudmila Vasiljeva followed her closely into eighteenth position.

A particularly valuable innovation at the 1964 World Championships was the inclusion of an Unknown Compulsory programme, originated by the Soviet Union who had first tried it out in the 1963 Moscow contest. This required each pilot to fly at sight, with no previous practice, a sequence

Victorious Soviet team in 1966 (left to right): Dimitri Teregulov, Vladimir Piskunov, Vladimir Shumilov (trainer), Vitold Pochernin, Vasili Pisetsky (manager), Vladimir Martemianov, Vadim Ovsyankin. *(Kasum Nazhmudinov)*

Flight Fantastic

made up of one individual manoeuvre suggested by each team. Naturally, the art was to suggest a manoeuvre that one had practised well and hoped the others had not! As a test of skill it has since been universally recognized as the clincher in world-class competition, and there are many who recommend substituting a second Unknown Compulsory for the present Free Programme which takes up so much time and effort for so very little purpose....

Having brought home an excellent result from Spain, the Soviet Union now set about preparing to host the 1966 World Championships at the grass airfield of Tushino set beside the Moscow River. In fact they probably benefitted from being delayed two years, for by that time the new Yak-18PM had been developed and its superior performance, allied to the thorough preparation of its pilots – some of whom had put in over 400 hours practice – undoubtedly helped win them the championship.

This time there were exactly ten female pilots to allow a first ever Women's Championship to be awarded, which was won by Galina Korchuganova, a graduate engineer of the Moscow Aviation Institute who was a keen parachutist, glider and speed racing pilot; she had already established a world speed record over a 100 km closed circuit in a Yakovlev sporting jet, and went on to become a test pilot.

At the head of the male team, changed by only one member from that fielded in Spain, came 30-year-old Vladimir Martemianov from Siberia where he had flown in the Kemerovsky National Team for over ten years; his wife, Liubov, was a pilot-instructor there. Several times champion of the USSR, Martemianov was a good-looking, amusing and

Vladimir Martemianov, 1966 World Aerobatic Champion.
(Kasum Nazhmudinov)

interesting man of some depth, an amateur landscape painter and author of a book *Sky, I Love You.* He was always ready to enjoy a joke, yet capable of forming close ties with his fellow team-members. As the Soviet Union's first World Champion he scored a convincing victory by a clear margin of some 260 points, at the same time winning five out of the six individual programmes of the contest. In the Free Programme of the eliminators, in which the total available points amounted to 7,000, Martemianov racked up an amazing 6,842.1.

By the end, the USSR team had swept the board of the top four places: "a landslide for the Soviets, honestly earned" was the verdict of US judge Mike Murphy, who reported "we were treated and cared for in a friendly atmosphere and with all care and courtesies that could be expected". He and other commentators remarked on the transformation that the top Soviet engineers had worked on the Yak-18P to produce the new 18PM version, with more horsepower, dihedral removed from the wings to give more manoeuvrability, and all electrics such as starters and generators removed in the interests of weight reduction. The precision with which the Yak pilots flew their lines and angles had the appearance of a programmed autopilot, and according to Joe Christy the new model had, "the wing loading of a condor, the agility of a hummingbird and the vertical flight characteristics of a yo-yo"!

The exemplary organization and conduct of the championships were highlighted all the more by contrast with what had happened in Bilbao last time (see Chapter 14), and in analyzing the final results of the judging it was considered altogether very fair. It was evident, as usual, that each judge favoured the contestants from his own country, but this time the tolerances of the marks awarded were generally acceptable, and the panel was ruled with a firm though magnanimous hand by Chief Judge Vladimir Shumilov, who decreed a mid-morning Cognac Break and mid-afternoon Vodka Break each day, accompanied by caviar and other welcome refreshments.

In the meantime, with the series of Socialist Countries' Championships held from 1963 onwards, several of the other Eastern bloc nations had entered international aerobatics. The Poles with their Zlins contested most WACs, and hosted the Socialist Countries' event at Lodz in 1965, though without conspicuous success for their own pilots.

Where they did contribute substantially, however, was in the area of international judging of the sport, and two of their very top pilots who excelled in this specialist area were Andrzej Abłamowicz and Helmut Stas – of whom Andrzej has already been mentioned in Chapter 8.

Helmut Stas became Polish National Champion in 1971 and in the same year came fifth in the Socialist Countries' Championships, the best place achieved by a Polish pilot. He won two bronze medals in the individual programmes as well. From the age of 18 he had been flying aerobatics with every aircraft he could lay his hands on, and had entered the Polish Championships ("very cheeky of me!") as early as 1962. His first World Championships were in 1968, when he was placed nineteenth, and he competed each year afterwards until in 1974 a tragic accident cut short his flying career.

As a flying instructor and distinguished aerobatic pilot he often took part in airshows, and on this occasion just before of Zlin 126 and 226 aircraft began to arrive, and soon a series of local GDR contests were set up. In the years leading up to 1966 Kurt Rusch, Günther Börner and Heinz Richter generally vied with each other as leaders of the field, until the two newcomers Peter Kahle and Erwin Bläske moved into the lead from 1965 and were joined by Dieter Kapphahn for the team in Moscow. The placings in this championship of their

Helmut Stas, Polish Aerobatic Champion 1971 and noted International Judge.   *(Author's collection)*

the 1974 Nationals he was giving a mirror-formation display with fellow team member Pawel Pawlak, in two Zlin 526AFSs. With Helmut underneath and Pawel on top, they pulled up into a loop that was just a little too close, and the aeroplanes touched: Helmut lost his left arm in the collision.

Readjustment was particularly hard since he was left-handed, and it cost him nine years away from flying. But he regained his licence in 1984, thanks to the support of staunch friends, and with it the determination to resume aerobatics – not in the big internationals, but in the smaller contests. Helmut's personal loss as a pilot was to be the gain of aerobatics as a sport, for he took up judging in 1976 and has since become Poland's foremost International Judge. And he is enthusiastic to continue this work that he has done so well over the years, particularly since he has that extra dimension of knowledge and past experience in the techniques and problems faced by the pilot in the competition box. All too often the vital rôle of the judge is overlooked in aerobatics, but without good judges the sport would surely die.

The Romanians were also frequent competitors during the 1960s, but had less luck with their equipment and were obliged in 1966, along with the Bulgarian and Yugoslav entries, to do their best with Yak-18P types borrowed from the USSR. In 1978, however, they arrived with a new fleet of Zlin 50s, and thereafter proceeded to compete with them regularly. Their neighbours in Hungary had of course quickly swept into the forefront of the sport with the 1962 World Championships, and their ups and downs over the years are covered separately in one of the later chapters in this book dealing with WAC 1984, at which the Hungarians played World Championship hosts for the second time (Chapter 20).

The newly created German Democratic Republic, rebuilding itself out of the rubble of a world war, had had Yak-18s for military training since 1956 when their first post-war flight instructors' course was established, and in the following year six flying centres were set up where aerobatics began to be possible with the Soviet-built trainers. Then in 1959 a number

GDR Team in Magdeburg: Erwin Bläske (centre), Peter Kahle (right), Dieter Kapphahn (left).   *(via Werner Garitz)*

top four pilots – Börner 6th, Bläske 10th, Kahle 12th and Kapphahn 16th – showed them to be strong contenders in their own right, and this encouraged the East Germans to make a bid for the 1968 World Championship to be held in Magdeburg, a town which lies on the Elbe some 40 kilometres inside the East-West border.

They were by now, in fact, well seasoned in international aerobatics. In 1963, 1964 and from 1966 onwards they regularly hosted championships open to pilots from abroad, and in addition to competing in the 1962 and 1964 WACs, had sent pilots to the Biancotto Trophy contests in France. Here the popular Erwin Bläske, a calm and patient flying instructor from Cottbus, had come second in 1965, and young Peter Kahle came second in 1967. Later they were to make a clean sweep of the first three places, Kahle – Bläske – Börner, in the 1969 Biancotto.

Newly equipped with a fleet of Zlin 526 Akrobats, the GDR pilots practised their hearts out to prepare for the 1968 World Championships, and in fact flew superbly well all the way

Flight Fantastic

through. The event, however, was dogged by problems from the world go. In an attempt to apply the rules strictly and fairly, mechanical devices were set up by the organizers to measure positioning in the box (which carried a potential 13 per cent or so of the maximum available marks, and could quite easily tip the balance from a good flight to a medal-winning one), and also to measure height infringements, which carried penalties capable of decisively influencing results in the opposite direction.

Rather than leave the matter to human fallibility, an electro mechanical tracking system was set up which utilized two sighting aids and purported to determine aircraft positioning exactly in relation to the contest axes: maximum scores were to be obtained, of course, by a symmetrical placement of the programme around the centre of the performance zone. Unfortunately, everyone's faith in this arrangement was considerably shaken when an observant Spanish pilot announced that he had discovered an alignment error in the apparatus, and then proceeded to earn himself an exceedingly high positioning score by flying deliberately off-centre.

Neither was the height-measuring system free from trouble, for severe discrepancies were noticed in the readings taken from barographs installed in the competition aircraft. The barograph system had been perpetuated even though it was well known that such aneroid devices were susceptible to differences in cockpit geometry and aircraft speed and attitude. British test pilot Neil Williams made an official protest and offered his aeroplane for testing, but his plea was refused even though a West German pilot made an impromptu flight with two barographs placed in different positions inside his cockpit and found a difference of 250 feet (76 metres) between them!

Over the years there had been much dithering about the dimensions of the performance zone, and in the Compulsory Programmes a maximum height limit of 800 metres (2,600 ft) was supposed to apply, with a 1,000 metre (3,300 ft) limit in the Free Programmes – though the rule never had been operated strictly. Now that the organizers had their mechanical devices, however, infringements were penalized for top as well as bottom height limits, and for excursions beyond the sides of the 1,000 metre × 800 metre aerobatic zone (or box). It was truly pitiful to see the Soviet pilots in their magnificent Yaks falling out of even the most basic of manoeuvres in order to avoid the crippling 200-point penalties. The problem was particularly bad in the first, Known Compulsory programme, which had been drawn up months before without heed to height problems for the Yaks, and which had not been challenged at the time for the simple reason that the penalty rule had never been strictly applied before. Quite legitimate remonstrations that the compulsory sequence was not Yak-able within the confines of the box fell on deaf ears, and at the end of this programme the highest placed Soviet pilot was twenty-first.

Protests about these and other problems abounded, but the International Jury, whose job it was to oversee the proper running of the contest, proved singularly inflexible and came up with what was generally regarded as 'some curious decision-making', which did not improve the sour note that had begun to pervade the competition. To cap it all, news suddenly came through that the USSR had sent tanks into Czechoslovakia to quell the growing movement towards liberalization, and the unfortunate Czech contestants then could think of nothing else but to return to their families at

once. This, together with delays and bad weather, combined to prevent the third programme of flights from being completed, and a result had to be declared after only two programmes.

It is easy to look back after the event and seek to apportion blame: if the rules had not been applied so inflexibly . . . if the contest had been moved along at a slicker rate . . . if technical matters had been dealt with in a more businesslike fashion . . . and so on. Some acccused others of deliberately employing delaying tactics, though it is difficult to see who would have benefitted: the German Democratic Republic by delaying matters would merely invite a washed-out contest and the attendant loss of prestige, which is more or less what happened; the Soviet Union would have lost their crack at the only programmes with a 1,000 metre height limit in which their Yaks could score well (their top pilot Igor Egorov already had a clear lead in programme 3 when the flights were stopped); and the British and Americans also needed these last two flights to recover from a shaky start. Perhaps the most unfortunate aspect of the whole event was that international goodwill began to founder, and where allowances would have been made in the past, suspicion and accusation now began to creep in.

According to the prevailing rules there was no World Aerobatic Champion in 1968, although there was a team championship which was won by the GDR with the USSR second and the USA third. Erwin Bläske emerged as overall male winner after two programmes, and the 22-year-old French girl Madelyne Delcroix, who was already a veteran of World Championship and Lockheed events, placed top in

Erwin Bläske, overall winner in WAC 1968: born in 1930, his first interest was in gliding until in 1957 he took up power flying and in 1961 aerobatics. Qualified as an instructor in both, he is presently chief of the Cottbus training centre for aviation and parachute sports. *(via Werner Garitz)*

Madelyne Delcroix, winner in the Women's World Championship, 1968, pictured here with Neil Williams.
(Lynn Williams)

Werner Garitz, leading light of aerobatics in East Germany for 20 years, International Judge and Jury member.
(Author's collection)

Svetlana Savitskaya, female World Champion in 1970.
(via Kasum Nazhmudinov)

Igor Egorov had already shown great talent at his first World Championship in Magdeburg when, from thirty-second place in the first programme, he rose to third place in the second, and finally earned the highest score of the men who had completed the third programme (all but three flew). He now proceeded to walk away with all three of the programmes that were flown at Hullavington – weather unfortunately put a stop to the fourth – and emerged a convincing World Champion in 1970, with fellow-countrywoman Svetlana Savitskaya as Female Champion.

Savitskaya's subsequent career as a cosmonaut has somewhat eclipsed her 1970 championship title, but she was an outstanding pilot even at the age of 20 when she took up aerobatics in 1967 after being a keen parachutist. Daughter of an air marshal and World War II fighter ace, aviation was undoubtedly in her blood. She was a graduate of the Moscow Aviation Institute, and in 1974–5 turned to supersonic jets, establishing a number of world records for speed and rate of climb to add to her tally of national and world records – about twenty in all. After a career as a test pilot, Svetlana became a cosmonaut and made space flights in 1980 and 1984, in the second of which, as a Flight Engineer on Salyut 7, she made history as the first woman to walk in space. Effecting a repair to a leaking fuel pipe, she managed to cure a problem that had afflicted Salyut 7 for almost a year.

Igor Egorov, World Champion at his second attempt, was a small, slight and rather enigmatic young man. Aged 31 in 1970, he was a qualified engineer and a gifted pilot who loved both the sport of aerobatics and the people involved in it; in fact he had a lot of time for people, though he was discriminating in the friendships he made, valuing integrity and honesty above all things. He also had a passion for music and loved to play the guitar, at which he was very talented. One thing particularly noticeable was how he struck up a rapport with pilots of other nationalities, and here he was surely aided by music which transcends the barriers of language.

the female league. If you request information from the FAI today, however, you will receive a document that lists both a male and a female World Champion for that year; and such is the cameraderie among flyers that nobody nowadays begrudges Bläske and Delcroix their semi-official titles, earned in a year when just about everything that could go wrong with a championship did go wrong.

A note of calm returned to proceedings in 1970 when Britain took on the job of running the World Championships, and much interest centred around the new Yak-18PS which the Soviet team had brought in addition to their now-familiar 18PMs, to be flown by their two best pilots Egorov and Ponomaryov. 1966 champion Vladimir Martemianov was sadly mourned, having been killed in a training accident only three months previously.

Flight Fantastic

1970 World Champion Igor Egorov, never far from his guitar.
(Madelyne Delcroix)

He had a genuinely creative flair and was always working out new ideas, a trait which helped him to stay competitive for many years: even after being dropped from the Soviet team after 1976, he still picked up an astounding two bronze medals in 1978 on being hastily pressed into service, with virtually no preparation, to fly in the World Championships at ten days' notice.

Egorov has been described, by those who watched him and were in competition with him, as an almost perfect pilot. Seldom is that said of anybody, and even more rarely in aerobatics. The 1972 World Champion, Charlie Hillard, called him one of the all-time greats, and 1980 Champion Leo Loudenslager remembered him more personally:

He had a love for music, and you didn't have to be a Russian to see why the team loved him. He would sit and play his guitar, and you would never know he was a world champion pilot.

From the 1972 WAC in Salon de Provence, France, the members of the American team still retain a vivid memory of how the bonds of friendship were cemented by the power of music in the hands of the young pilot from east of the Urals. In Mel R Jones's recent book*, Tom Poberezny recounts how the Americans heard distant strains of music echoing from the Soviet team's quarters, and tracked down the source to the bathroom area of the French military barracks where they were quartered.

There, sitting on and under sinks and lining the wall, were more than 30 pilots from … many countries. Astride one of the basins sat Igor Egorov strumming a guitar. The defending World Aerobatic Champion from Russia was accompanied by Polish and French guitarists.

'God, I wish I could share this with somebody,' Tom remembered saying to himself. 'All these people from all these countries jammed into a big long bathroom, singing, exchanging stories, and having a good time. The next day we were all going to be out there competing hard against one another.'

During the 1972 competition the Soviet pilot made a serious timing error which lost him all chance of a second win, and the victor, Charlie Hillard, removed his own wristwatch and presented it to Egorov in wry tribute. He and the other Americans from Salon, as well as the aerobatic community all over the world, were shocked and saddened in 1981 when Igor Egorov met his death during his work as a test pilot: he crashed in the test flight of a light aircraft which had been designed by students.

Above and Beyond: Eight Great American Aerobatic Champions, Tab Books 1984.

17

The new monoplanes

In the French camp during the mid 1960s the standard of aerobatics had visibly slipped since the day of the much-loved Stampe had passed. Military pilots still resolutely attempted the international competitions in their Nord 3202s, and the private entrants did as well as they could with various Zlin models, until in 1968 the French participation in Magdeburg dwindled to just two individuals: father and daughter André and Madelyne Delcroix. Such was the enthusiasm and determination of young Mady that she had undergone intensive instruction with Czech aerobatic star Ladislav Bezák, and while coming in with highest marks of the female pilots, actually ranked fifteenth – one quarter of the way down – when compared with the overall male and female scores.

Meanwhile, the French National Centres for aviation training were becoming more and more oriented towards touring rather than advanced flying techniques, and in 1966 those who were interested in promoting aerobatics in France got together to form the AFVA, the French Aerobatic Association. Among its founder members, and still in the forefront of French aerobatics today, were Annie and Pierre Violet. With one of its main aims being to encourage the development of aerobatics, gradually a number of competitions at various levels of expertise were introduced, from beginners to advanced to unlimited.

In the international class there was the Biancotto Trophy in each year when there was no World Championship, although, like the Lockheed Trophy, it was never won by a pilot from the host nation. A list of results will be found in Appendix II. At national level, second only to the National Championships in longevity, was the Coupe Marcel Doret, introduced in 1957 after the great ace's death and won on that first occasion by Léon Biancotto. A new regulation in 1963 reserved the Doret Cup for non-professionals only, and shows that the military pilots were clearly ahead of the

civilians in the sport. This situation was made possible because in France they continued to use piston-engined trainers of a type suitable for the full range of aerobatics, and were encouraged – as indeed they are today – to take part in competitions. In Britain the world of top-level competition aerobatics has been closed to RAF aircraft since negative and flick manoeuvres were banned on service machines in the 1930s.

For their own part, the military pilots from Salon de Provence inaugurated a new annual Coupe Champion in 1969, which soon attracted a fair sprinkling of foreign participants; this together with the National Championship was used to determine the French Team.

Coinciding with the founding of the AFVA, a new French trainer, aimed primarily for military use, also made its début in the summer of 1966. The two-seat CP 100 was a promising design right from the start, although it suffered a tragic setback when in a test flight the following January it crashed and killed aerobatic pilot Gérard Verette, remembered fondly from the Centre National de Carcasonne and for his long and distinguished competition career. The machine was based on the CP 301 Super Emeraude of Claude Piel, a light sporting aircraft whose elliptical wing was modelled on the famous Spitfire wing; this new aerobatic development was conceived by a team headed by Auguste Mudry, a man who was to have a profound influence on the future of French aerobatics. After tests it emerged in August 1968 as the CAP 10B. It proved an immediate hit with civil as well as military customers, and the Armée de l'Air placed orders which amounted to 32 in the first ten years (CAP 10s are still in military use today).

While working on the side-by-side two-seat trainer, Mudry had already begun to nurture the idea of a single-seater for aerobatic competition, an aircraft with which the French

Mudry CAP 10B (180 hp Lycoming).   *(via IAC)*

could enter the lists on equal terms with the rest of the world. An original idea for a CP 200, a single-seat version of the Emeraude, was discarded as a result of calculations by the Yugoslav engineer Hrisafovic, and in 1967 the first plans for an entirely new model were started, using the wings of the CAP 10 but with a new ovoid fuselage. In 1969 the prototype CAP 20 had its maiden flight.

Once again the major customer was the Armée de l'Air, and the aircraft was built with this in mind. From 1970 the Stampes of its *Equipe de Voltige Aérienne* (aerobatic team) based at Salon de Provence were replaced by the new monoplanes. Their chief duties were aerobatic instruction and demonstration and, of course, competition.

In 1970 the first CAP 20 was seen in Hullavington at the World Championships, though to no great effect since it was still very new and relatively untried. By 1972 the French team had the aircraft much better in hand, and had done well in the intervening year in European contests; but in the World Championship held in their own country at Salon de Provence their placings were between thirteenth and eighteenth with the new machine, which was obviousy outclassed by the foreign competition.

It was not long before the EVA was asking for a more powerful motor than the 200 hp Lycoming with which it was equipped, and in one machine Mudry accordingly tried out a 260 hp Lycoming with the very efficient Christen oil system designed for inverted flight. But no matter what the improvement in power, nothing would alter the fact that the design of the aeroplane just was not comparable with other leaders of the international field – and, moreover, the complicated construction method put the price of the machine out of reach of private owners. In performance there were faults which needed attention such as the heavy elevator response and weak ailerons in inverted flight, the excessive amount of muscle required to achieve a fairly modest rate of roll, and the very laborious positive flick characteristics.

Already the military pilots had tried clipped wings to improve the roll rate, and various angles of dihedral less than the original 5 degrees were also tried; but series production incorporating these modifications was prohibitive. As to the 260 hp version, although better in performance, it was found to be heavier to fly. A total rethink was clearly necessary, and in 1975 the Mudry team came up with a revised version, called the CAP 20L (*Léger* = light), which was in fact a completely new machine: only the wing section remained the same. In the hands of test pilot Louis Peña, ex-EVA member

and one of the foremost French pilots today, the machine started its flight testing on 15 January 1976.

This model featured a CAP 10-type plywood fuselage, cheaper and simpler to build, replacing the complicated wood structure of the standard CAP 20. It had a redesigned wing, shorter and with almost no dihedral (1.5 degrees), aided by enlarged and more effective ailerons. Of the tail group the vertical surfaces were also enlarged, only the horizontal stabilizer remaining from the previous CAP 20.

It was a race against time to get the machine ready for the next World Championships which would take place in the USSR in 1976, and now Mudry could look for little of the offical support and encouragement which had so helped his first two military-oriented designs. The test programme was still under way when the prototype was released to go to Kiev that summer, where pilot Jean-René Bourgeois achieved nineteenth place. But the 180 hp motor with fixed pitch propeller clearly lacked punch, and from the end of 1976 the new production model became the CAP 20L equipped with a 200 hp Lycoming and constant-speed unit.

In flight the new version was delightful, light (as its name promised), and with positive, quick control response. Its rate of roll was livelier than its predecessor, and faster even than its great rival the Swiss Acrostar – 360 degrees of roll in 2.3 seconds compared with the Acrostar's 2.5 seconds. The elevator was nicely balanced and a great improvement over the CAP 10 and standard 20. From the pilot's point of view the aeroplane was considerably less fatiguing to fly, a major consideration in the physically punishing competition arena. Only the flick roll characteristics left something to be desired in the new monoplane, but with practice a clean flick without too much barrelling could be achieved. Working within the available framework, Mudry had produced an affordable production-line aircraft for top level competition. Since the demise of the Acrostar no other West European country had such a machine.

The years 1973–5 were falllow years, for the fuel crisis restricted activities in all motor sports – of which aerobatics perhaps seemed the most exotic and impractical of the lot – and although many air shows and contests did take place, it proved very difficult to make advance plans for anything as complicated as a World Aerobatic Championship.

Both Poland and the German Federal Republic had spoken of hosting the 1974 event, but neither was able to make a formal proposal to CIVA due to the prevailing fuel problems;

and with every country in the same boat, it soon appeared that no 1974 proposal at all would be forthcoming. The year of 1974 therefore goes down in history as the one in which no World Championship was held. People stayed at home and bent their thoughts to new and better aeroplanes.

Whereas, once upon a time, competitions had been an integral part of the public spectacle of an air display – right up to Lockheed times, in fact – international championships had now become quite regimented affairs. Trained and groomed national teams marched under national flags and wore national uniforms; national anthems were played as the winners received their medals; and in many cases national prestige hinged on the outcome, especially if the aeroplane you flew was your own national product.

Rules and regulations became paramount, standardized methods of judging and scoring were adopted, and teams began to feel the need to have their own judge on the judging panel in order to counteract the 'national bias' that was perceived to be holding sway in the results. Such bias is, of course, only human, and likely to be rife if a sport does not take care to establish a central, international cadre of unexceptionable judges to uphold judging standards.

It would serve no good purpose, in retrospect, to accuse any one nation's judges *vis à vis* any other. Time does not stand still, and judges do change, very often for the better. But though a bad judge one year might improve or give way to a good judge the next, a malaise had set in which was hard to shake off. Politics had begun to enter aerobatics, it is true – but thankfully only on the ground. The pilots continued to be there simply to fly, to measure themselves and their machines against each other, and to enjoy the company of fellow-specialists from around the globe.

Many and long were the meetings of CIVA, the international aerobatics commission of the FAI, to try to sort out the knotty problem of poor judging, whether from national bias, ineptitude, or partiality to certain styles of performance. Yuri Tarasov of the USSR, a professor of aircraft structures at the Kuibyshev Aviation Institute, introduced in the early 1970s a statistical system of computer scoring to replace the previous method of deleting the highest and lowest scores and averaging the rest. This had been used successfully in the USSR and the Socialist Countries' Championships.

It was carefully studied by member nations of CIVA, and in 1974 a refinement was introduced by a brilliant young German computer specialist named Hans Bauer. This not only 'smoothed out' the wide variations in judges' marking styles, but also showed up those scores which fell outside acceptable tolerances or 'confidence intervals': they were then discarded. It was admitted that even such a sophisticated system might perhaps be manipulated, but in the main any outright bias in marking would tend to have an opposite effect to that intended. The Tarasov-Bauer system was first used in the 1978 World Championships.

Attempting to revive something of the Lockheed spirit of freedom and artistry, the British had recommended to CIVA that the second Free Programme, instead of being a repetition of the programme flown once already, should comprise a Five-minute Freestyle*, untrammelled by the codified manoeuvres of the Aresti Dictionary from which all other programmes, including the so-called 'Free', had to be composed. Indeed, inventiveness and the introduction of new figures should form part of the requirement for the new Freestyle. To their disappointment the idea was foiled so far

Hans Bauer, creator of the Bauerization system of computing scores – the 'Tarasov-Bauer' method. Bauer flew a Zlin 526 in the 1972 World Aerobatic Championships.

(Author's collection)

as the 1970 competition in Britain was concerned, but it eventually saw light in 1972.

For progress in the art of aerobatics the concept is a good one, some would even say vital, to offset the stultifying effect of flying everything from a catalogue. Judging criteria were later introduced which reflected the criteria of the Lockheed competitions, and this move was an aid to proper judging of the flights: harmony and rhythm, versatility and originality were added to the more obvious demands of accuracy and good positioning. It soon became known as the five-minute 'airshow', and it called for a combination of talents rather different from those required in the other programmes, stretching the pilot and demanding a sense of artistry and invention. Of course, when a pilot puts on an aerobatic show to entertain the public he doesn't use the Aresti Dictionary; and were there not judges to consider in competition, there would be no need for a catalogue in the first place. The idea was really one which attempted to return to the grass-roots of aerobatics.

Of its first operation in Salon de Provence, when American Charlie Hillard won the championship, the story is told in Chapter 18. For this competition Charlie flew what had become by then almost standard equipment among the American pilots, the little Pitts Special biplane, whose development we shall trace also in that same chapter. On that side of the Atlantic, thanks to the spirit of free enterprise epitomized by the Experimental Aircraft Association, pilots did not have to rely solely on manufacturers to come up with new aerobatic designs. Whether for competition or for fun, they could build and modify their own aircraft at home, and later have them certified in an 'experimental' category.

But in Europe things were different. Now the world of international competition tended to dominate the aerobatic scene; those aircraft designers who catered for the small and

Span	8.06 m (26 ft 5 in)	Empty weight	620 kg (1,364 lb)
modified to	7.44 m (24 ft 5 in)	Max speed	376 km/h (234 mph)
Length	7.21 m (23 ft 8 in)	Rate of climb	10 m/sec (1,970 fpm)
Height	1.40 m (4 ft 7 in)	Limit load	+ 8, − 4 g

Mudry CAP 20 Standard (200 hp Lycoming). (John Blake)

CAP 20 LS (200 hp Lycoming). G-BIPO is here flown by British aerobatic pilot Tony Bianchi near Booker, High Wycombe. (Arthur Gibson, via Tony Bianchi)

specialized market recognized this, saw where their customers' requirements lay, and came up with more powerful and more manoeuvrable machines.

The 200 hp CAP 20 and 220 hp Acrostar were the principal designs produced in Western Europe, where market demands dictated the limits to which experiment – and engine power – could be pushed. In the Eastern bloc it was a different story, and in the year 1975 both the Soviet Union and Czechoslovakia came up with their new wonderbirds, dedicated to the performance of unlimited aerobatics, and both of them potential world-beaters.

The USSR's Yak 50 was seen for the first time by western eyes in the 1976 World Aerobatic Championships at Kiev. After the trials and disappointments of 1974, the Americans had attempted to set up a 1976 WAC at Sherman, Texas, but when the chips were down nobody could guarantee the full international participation on which it depended: the distances and travelling costs were just too great. At that point the Soviet Union heroically stepped in and volunteered to take on the 1976 event at short notice. Unfortunately, by then there had arisen such an entrenched mistrust between East and West that few people expected the event to be fair and above board, and few were disappointed.

Line-up of brand new Soviet Yak 50s ready for the 1966 World Championships, Moscow. (John Blake)

One of the greatest mistakes on the part of the organizers was to conduct the contest paperwork, including forms and notices, using the Cyrillic alphabet. None of the visitors had expected this and nobody was therefore prepared for wading through laborious translations and transliterations. A shroud of mystery and incomprehension enveloped the normal day-to-day running of the event, and for a lot of the time people simply did not understand what was going on. This engendered confusion over even the most straightforward of matters.

The computer operation, judge's panel and International Jury were all headed by Soviet personnel, in whom confidence was soon lost. Mistakes in computer inputs proved difficult to rectify, the judging was characterized by unbridled partiality, and the line judges – whose job it was to call the penalties when aeroplanes made excursions out of the box – were simply making up their own rules as they went along. It was felt that the Jury, who were there, after all, to see fair play, were totally ineffectual.

The above tales of woe were gleaned by the writer from many who were there to experience the problems of Kiev at first hand, and it is particularly painful to have to catalogue them since the Soviet pilots themselves were – and are – so obviously excellent sportsmen, as are their team trainers,

Start your
Job Search with Job & Career Accelerator™

Access from your library or home computer—free of charge—with your library card.

Go to your library's website or visit:

User:

Password:

Start your Job Search with

Job & Career
Accelerator™

> **Explore over 1,000 occupations and match those that fit your interests**

> **Search available jobs from over 5 million job postings**

> **Create professional resumes and cover letters**

> **Master interviewing skills**

> **Get tips and advice on how to improve your search each step of the way**

> **Organize and track your job search progress**

LEARNINGEXPRESS

2 Rector Street, 26th fl. · New York, NY · 10006
www.learningexpressllc.com

G-BIPO
Lovell
Lovell

th	7.57 m	(24 ft 10 in)
nt	6.46 m	(21 ft 2 in)
y weight	1.80 m	(5 ft 9 in)
speed	485 kg	(1,067 lb)
of climb	372 km/h	(231 mph)
load	14 m/sec	(2,755 fpm)
	+8, −6 g	

Flight Fantastic

engineers and other technicians whose only interest is in sporting achievement. It would be fair to say that none of the resentment felt by visiting teams was directed at the home pilots, and it was hoped that none rubbed off on them. Indeed most observers felt that the eventual victors – Victor Letsko for the men and Lidia Leonova for the women – would have carried off top honours anyway, without help (or hindrance!) from those with motives unconnected with sportsmanship.

Nor were the Eastern bloc judges by any means the only ones manipulating the system. While it was observed that Igor Egorov's three gold medals were much too good to be true, and that British pilot Neil Wiliams should really have won the Unknown Compulsory programme with his quite brilliant flight, it was also noted that Victor Letsko himself was cheated out of the high score he deserved in programme 4, when he emerged only tenth in position.

Twenty-five year old prodigy Letsko had been selected for the Soviet Team at the age of nineteen, and in the years 1974,

Lidia Leonova, Women's World Champion in 1966.
(via Kasum Nazhmudinov)

1966 World Champion Victor Letsko.
(via Kasum Nazhmudinov)

75 and 76 had won a first and two seconds in the Socialist Countries' championships, together with second place in the 1974 international Biancotto Trophy, the unofficial European Championship. He was, in fact, tipped as favourite in 1976 over the former champion Egorov, but managed to win the title only on his aggregate scores, rather than coming first in any of the individual programmes: a rare occurrence in competition aerobatics.

Lidia Leonova, on the other hand, not only won programmes 1 and 4 in the women's class, she actually beat the

score in programme 1 of Manfred Strössenreuther, who won the men's gold medal, by nearly 60 points. Her eventual score in the championships placed her next after the first two men, Letsko and Egorov.

Lidia had been a factory worker until at the age of 23 she took up flying at the Tula Aeroclub, and was talent-spotted for her aerobatic skills. Of all the Soviet Union's women pilots she has been the most regular team member over the years, from 1970 right up to 1984, since when she has retired from international sport and now concentrates on training young up-and-coming pilots at Tula. Her simple, home-loving interests (including the oh-so-Russian pastime of picking mushrooms!) contrast strongly with her top-level career in such a highly cerebral and technological sport; a career in which she has amassed a formidable number of medals and awards, including six World Championship gold medals in individual programmes. In Lidia the USSR had the chance in 1976 of a real 'first' in aerobatics, that of a FEMALE overall World Champion and recipient of the Aresti Cup, an opportunity which they missed by a mere whisker. And a whisker of their own devising, perhaps. . . .

Praise for Leonova's flying in Kiev was unstinted, as indeed it was for the whole superb team of Soviet women pilots (Yaikova, Nemkova, Mochalina, Savitskaya). All have at some time or other carried off gold, silver and bronze World Championship medals, and many of them today still fly equally as well as – if not better than – their male counterparts.

A word of credit must here go to trainer Kasum Nazhmudinov from Dagestan in the warm Caucasus, himself a national* champion of his region of the USSR between 1962 and 1969. Although Kasum himself had the chance of being in the 1963 Soviet Team, he had by then been a flight instructor for some while, coach of his national team, and head of his local flying

*With the Soviet Union comprising a number of separate Republics, each has its own team and its own annual championship; for convenience the translation used here is 'national' team and 'national' champion.

Kasum Nazhmudinov, Soviet team trainer since 1969.
(Author's collection)

two-blade propeller was an aid to counteracting this, and produced the characteristic throaty growl which we have come to associate with the magnificent Soviet engines.

With an improved power/weight ratio the aircraft had very good vertical penetration, and its extreme stability allowed beautifully precise vertical rolls; stability is not one of the qualities most looked for in aerobatics, however, and figures such as stall turns and rolling circles suffered badly in the Yak. It was still felt to have the Yak-18's heavy response in positive flick rolls, although the negative flick was rapid and very potent, as exemplified by the ease and grace of the Yak 50 lomcovák.

One thing that was rumoured from the outset was that the new Yak had a very short airframe life, and soon histories of misfortunes began to reach western ears. That rumour often belies facts (especially *American* rumour about *Russian* facts!) may be seen by the statistics that out of 250 Yak 50s built, only two crashed through airframe failure, though several others came to grief thanks to over-energetic pulling and pushing by the Soviet pilots.

Ten days before the World Championships in 1978 the tragic news broke that a wing had folded on young Victor Letsko in flight: death in such cases is instantaneous, as the folding wing almost inevitably collapses on top of the cockpit. Hastily brought in to replace his missing team mate, the one-time World Champion Igor Egorov was scarcely expected to perform miracles at such short notice; but somehow, after an unpromising start, he managed to find his old form and came in third in both of the final two programmes.

In the Unknown Compulsory flight Igor was scheduled to fly immediately after American Leo Loudenslager, on a day when low cloud had necessitated that the earlier contestants break their programme at a prearranged point in order to climb and regain height. For an hour before Leo's flight the weather had been clear, but no word came through to change the arrangement until, just as the American was preparing to taxi, an official suddenly came over and announced 'No break'. Under the stress of the Unknown programme, where pilots have to fly a tricky sequence with no prior practice, Leo now felt some anxiety about the height-consuming downward half vertical flick and push-up, before which everyone else had had the opportunity to reposition. Fortunately, with his light, nimble Laser monoplane (see Chapter 19) he was able to carry it off, even though he pushed down into the flick from no more than an estimated 900 ft (275 m). Igor Egorov, following him, had a similar problem of readjusting his plans to take account of the change, but he was flying the bigger and more powerful Yak 50 whose massive inertia could get him into severe trouble if too much height was lost before and during the figure.

As Leo was unbuckling his harness he suddenly heard a gasp go up from the crowd, and swinging round he caught sight of Igor entering the downward push at something like 1,300 ft (400 m). Then it seemed as if he somehow miscalculated the half flick, failed to get it to break, half-rolled instead and disappeared inverted behind a hill, before reappearing in view again after – thankfully – completing the push-up to vertical. In the process he had violated the lower height limit and given everybody a severe fright. Such was the contrast in performance between the lightweight American homebuilt and the heavier Soviet Yak.

club: thus it was not hard to decide that his strengths lay more in training others. He had the knack of getting the best out of his charges, which did not go unnoticed. Eventually in 1969 he was invited to take on the job of trainer for the USSR Aerobatic Team, which already included some excellent pilots, of course, both male and female; but especially remarkable is how the WAC scores of the girls immediately took an upward trend in the early 1970s to rank alongside the very best of the men. He was the first to realize the full potential of the female Soviet team, which has deservedly held number one position in the world ever since.

Kasum still speaks admiringly of the enthusiasm and dedication of those young people for whose progress he has been responsible; and no-one can be in any doubt whose gentle genius underpins their outstanding success.

But gold medals in aerobatics cannot be won without the right equipment, and the new Yak 50 was the right aircraft at the right time. A direct descendant of the Yak-18s which dated back to the 1940s, it incorporated a tried and tested formula – but with more power, and brought right up to the minute technically. Its designers were Alexander Yakovlev's talented son, Sergei, together with Yuri Yankevich.

The airframe was smaller and lighter, and the flat underside of the old wing was now replaced by a cambered lower surface more suitable for the dual purpose of erect and inverted flight, for which an absolutely symmetrical aerofoil shape is the ideal choice. The semi-monocoque construction was of metal, with fabric-covered rear fuselage and control surfaces. The prototype, built in 1975, was equipped with fixed undercarriage, but in the production versions it was retractable, as in the Yak-18; and with this gear and an even more powerful engine – the 360 hp Vedeneyev M-14P radial – it carried quite a hefty amount of weight. The geared-down

Span	9.5 m (31 ft 2 in)
Length	7.68 m (25 ft 2 in)
Height	3 m (9 ft 10 in)
Empty weight	765 kg (1,686 lb)
Max speed	320 km/h (200 mph)
Rate of climb	16 m/sec (3,150 fpm)
Limit load	+9, −6 g

Soviet Yak 50, descendant of the Yak-18 and still in competition use in 1986 (360 hp Vedeneyev M-14P). Note engine vents for variable cooling, operated like venetian blinds, which can completely blank out the engine when closed.
(Don Berliner)

(left) Leo Loudenslager at České Budějovice and
(right) Igor Egorov in Yak 50 after a gruelling competition flight.
(Don Berliner)

An altogether different kind of animal was the sensational new Czech design which also appeared in 1975. Just about the only resemblance which the Zlin 50 bore to the traditional Zlin designs was that it was a monoplane – all else about it was entirely brand, spanking new.

Using state-of-the-art technology (sprung titanium landing gear, 260 hp Lycoming with Christen oil system and three-blade Hoffmann constant-speed prop), the Czechs had enlisted design ideas from the West to enhance their own

The new monoplanes

Zlin Z-50 L (260 hp Lycoming).   (Omnipol)

Span	8.58 m (28 ft 2 in)
Length	6.62 m (21 ft 9 in)
Height	1.985 m (6 ft 6 in)
Empty weight	570 kg (1,254 lb)
Max speed	290 km/h (180 mph)
Rate of climb	12 m/sec (2,362 fpm)
Limit load	$+9, -6\,g$

superb all-metal construction techniques and aerobatic know-how. Five of the first machines appeared in Kiev in 1976, equipping the Czech and Polish teams.

Immediately noticeable was the resemblance of the wing to that of the Acrostar: trapeziform for best flick-roll characteristics, thick, symmetrical and with virtually no diheral. Its span of 8.5 metres (28 ft) was somewhat wider than that of the Swiss machine, but this did not detract from the rate of roll which was the most amazing thing about it: 1 second for 360 degrees of roll! Compare this with the rate of some 6 seconds per 360 degrees in the Bücker Jungmann. The new Zlin could aileron-roll as fast as the American Pitts could flick.

All control surfaces were huge and carried balance tabs; the roll rate being achieved with the help of $2.8\,m^2$ of full-span ailerons, an installation rivalled only by the full-span 'flapperons' of the Arnold Wagner design. In contrast to the snappy aileron roll, the flick roll and spin characteristics were gentle and docile, with the negative flick even sluggish. The vertical roll performance, crucial in cmpetition aerobatics for the past 15 years, permitted four full rolls where the Acrostar and CAP 20LS could manage perhaps two or three. Like the Acrostar it was a strong aeroplane: its limit loads were +9 and −6, but word was that it had been taken to 12.5 g positive and 6.5 g negative without harm.

Some reservations were expressed about the aesthetics of the aircraft, with such square-cut lines and a starkly functional vertical tail jutting up at the end of a slender fuselage; but the one surprising problem that was universally felt (apart from the price!) was the length of time it took to become accustomed to the Zlin 50.

German champion Manfred Strössenreuther acquired his first Z-50L in 1979 and, although continuing to excel in all competitions he entered, found it hard work adapting to the unusual 'feel' of the unconventional machine. Most difficult of all to master were the ailerons, extraordinarily powerful yet surprisingly delicate thanks to the balance tabs; the elevators were extremely light at small deflections, yet heavy as the deflections grew larger; and the rudder was heaviest of all, requiring considerable effort for any movement of the control surface. Evidently a perceived need for more feel to be built into the rudder had resulted in a good deal of overkill!

Altogether 21 models with the 260 hp Lycoming were built, before the ever-present need for better performance was felt, and the decision was made to upgrade to a 300 hp engine – the Z-50LS. For a sacrifice of 30 kg in weight, the rate of climb was increased from 12 to 14 m/sec (2,362 to 2,756 fpm) and the maximum speed (level) from 290 to 308 km/h (180 to 191 mph). Naturally, with so much extra power and quick control response one found the aerobatic box an extremely small area to work in, and with the positive maximum load factor now reduced to 8 g the Zlin 50LS pilot was constantly flying close to the limits. In the dive, however, with the constant-speed prop going automatically to fully fine and its three blades acting as an effective airbrake, single or multiple rolls could be performed on the diving line without excessive speed build-up.

It was easy to see that this feature held advantages for any high-powered aerobatic machine, and one fine day Hoffmann Propellers GmbH received an order for one of their three-blade propellers, with full and detailed specifications (but with no indication of the aircraft it was intended for) bearing an address in the Soviet Union. Soon afterwards it was seen gracing the nose of a Soviet Team Yak 50! They had found the

Ivan Tuček in 1985, with the latest Czech Zlin 50LS (300 hp Lycoming). *(Fomo photograph)*

performance of the M-14P radial consistently less than its rated 360 hp, and with the Hoffmann they estimated an upgrading, from the previous 300 or so, to around 320–330 hp. The experiment had worked well, but there was still room for improvement.

Quick to recognize the benefits of additional power in the Zlin 50, in 1982 Manfred Strössenreuther had his 260 hp Lycoming tuned to a 300 hp output by BMW; then in 1984 he appeared with a brand new 300 hp Zlin 50LS fresh from the Moravan factory.

The first Zlin 50 to be seen in international competition sporting a 300 hp engine was OK-IRG, at the 1982 World Championships in Austria. This aircraft had originally been a Z-50L, but had suffered damage due to structural failure in a landing accident the previous year, in which top Czech pilot Petr Jirmus happily escaped injury. In this his first World Championship attempt, Jirmus flew the upgraded machine in 1982 to a remarkable fourth place. Flying it again in 1984, at his second attempt, he won the title of overall World Champion.

By that time, on every occasion that Yak and Zlin 50 aircraft had competed in a World or European Championship, the overall winner had flown one or other of these types.

The events of the 1976 championship in Kiev have already been described, so let us end this chapter with an account of the 1978 World Aerobatic Championships which took place at České Budějovice, near the western border of Czechoslovakia.

Fortunately for the sport, which had taken some severe knocks in its recent past, the Czechs bent over backwards to ensure an utterly fair and above-board contest. The Tarasov-Bauer statistical system had now been adopted by the FAI's International Aerobatics Commission and was put to good use. The line judges observing the limits of the box were irreproachable, the organization was orderly and businesslike, and the International Jury gave firm rulings which further

Valentina Yaikova, 1978 women's World Champion.
(Kasum Nazhmudinov)

Czechoslovakia, the home team, were therefore favourites for the male competition, with the USA also looking a strong contender although three of their number were newcomers to a world-class event. In the female stakes the obvious leaders were the girls from the USSR, of whom four out of the five were seasoned campaigners with nine previous World Championships between them. True to form, they took the first five places and all the available gold medals; World Champion Valentina Yaikova amassed enough points to place her score eleventh highest in the overall competition, and third of the Soviet pilots.

Valentina had been a team member since the World Championships in France, where she competed under her maiden name of Goldobina, and had come sixth in 1972 and second in 1976. One of eight children born of peasant stock, she graduated as an engineer in 1966, but by then had had her first taste of flight and immediately bent her energies to qualifying as a pilot. In 1969 she became a pilot/instructor at the Minsk Aeroclub, and since then has been trainer of the Byelorussian National Team. Out of more than 100 medals won for aviation sport, Valentina has won 3 golds, 3 silvers and a bronze in World Championships, and has been Women's European Champion no fewer than three times. A quiet but delightful personality, she has won hearts as well as medals in her international career, and as a pilot is held in esteem equally as high as any of her male counterparts.

Manfred Strössenreuther, with his newly acquired Zlin 50, equalled his previous best result by carrying off a gold medal in programme 2 of the contest, and came in fourth overall. But it was two US pilots who presented the greatest challenge to the home team: they were the new young contender Kermit Weeks, who picked up a bronze and a silver in the individual programmes and placed second in the overall results, together with team-mate Leo Loudenslager with two golds and a silver in the individual programmes.

A convincing winner, in the end, was Czech pilot Ivan Tuček whose placings were 2nd, 4th, 1st and 2nd in the four competition flights. A veteran of four previous World Championships, in which he had gradually moved up from thirteenth to third place, he was now the first World Champion on the Zlin 50 aircraft.

reinforced confidence in the event as a whole. It seemed that a corner had been turned.

One or two circumstances marred the full enjoyment of the Championships, however, and the first was the tragic loss of Victor Letsko ten days before, as already recounted. Although the outcome of this was a reinstatement of Igor Egorov in the team, whose presence was greeted with much pleasure, nevertheless it was obviously a depleted male contingent from the Soviet Union that competed in České, and no sportsman likes to meet a respected opponent on unequal terms. The British team had suffered a tragedy of even greater magnitude with the death of its leading pilot Neil Williams in 1977, and with the non-appearance of his two closest cohorts, Philip Meeson and James Black, fielded three first-timers who understandably ranked in the lower half of the results.

1978 was also marked by the absence of the team from the German Democratic Republic, whose Yak 50s had arrived a mere two weeks beforehand and who had therefore insufficient practice to put in an appearance. It would be several years before they were in a position to compete again in an FAI Championship, partly for technical reasons and partly for lack of suitable aircraft. The word as this book goes to press, however, is that they are ready to assemble a team as soon as they have the necessary complement of Zlin 50s.

Three more new monoplanes of the 1970s are pictured below and overpage.
The Spinks Akromaster, an American design which we shall meet in Chapter 18 (200 hp Lycoming). Only one was built, and it flew in the 1970 World Championships. (EAA)

The superb Acrostar, already described in Chapter 15 (220 hp Franklin), of which nine were produced.

(John Blake)

Span	8.28 m (27 ft 2 in)
Length	6.11 m (20 ft)
Height	1.78 m (5 ft 10 in)
Empty weight	485 kg (1,067 lb)
Max speed	310 km/h (193 mph)
Rate of climb	15 m/sec (2,953 fpm)
Limit load	+8, −8 g

The Cranfield A1 (210 hp Continental IO-360D), built by the Cranfield College of Technology to specifications drawn up by Neil Williams; the prototype still occasionally flies in competition.

(Lynn Williams)

Span	33 ft (10.05 m)
Length	26 ft 2 in (7.975 m)
Height	7 ft 2 in (2.18 m)
Empty weight	1,280 lb (545.5 kg)
Max speed	170 mph (106 km/h)
Rate of climb	2,590 fpm (13 m/sec)
Limit load	+9, −6 g

18

Meanwhile, in America...

America had ended the 1930s with a vigorous and popular aviation movement. Air racing had promoted giant strides in aerodynamic engineering; aerofoil theory had been studied exhaustively; the constant-speed propeller and 100-octane fuel had been pioneered.

Now, after four years of war, it was time to pick up the pieces and start over again; but sadly, many of the great names from the past were missing – and so were suitable aeroplanes.

The first prevalent machine in 1945–6 was the ex-military Stearman PT-17 two-seat biplane trainer, a majestic and sedate performer with its original 220 hp Continental engine, but powerful and impressive when twice as much power was substituted with the 450 hp Pratt and Whitney. Some were also rebuilt with 300 hp Lycomings.

With the Cleveland Air Races starting up again in 1946, Bill Sweet's National Air Shows, who had made the first 450 hp Stearman conversion, took over the entertainment at the races very much in the style of the old Gates Flying Circus. Down in Miama, Florida, the All-American Air Maneuvers were also resurrected after the war, and a new aerobatic competition inaugurated under the sponsorship of Gulf Oil. The contest was originally entitled the Miami All-American Air Maneuvers National Aerobatic Championship, but later in time it acquired the title of 'International' Championship. It ran annually from 1947 to 1952, with the winners being as follows:

Gulf Trophy. Miami

1947 Beverly (Bevo) Howard, Clipped-wing Piper J-3 Cub
(85 hp Continental)
1948 W W (Woody) Edmundson, Monocoupe (185 hp Warner)
1949 Bevo Howard, Jungmeister (145 hp Warner)
1950 Rod Jocelyn, Great Lakes (165 hp Kinner)
1951 Rod Jocelyn, Great Lakes (185 hp Warner)
1952 Marion Cole, Stearman (450 hp Pratt and Whitney)

In an attempt to organise it properly, a fairly difficult known compulsory sequence was later introduced for the contest which everybody had to fly. Though there was a grading system for difficulty with coefficients ranging from 1 to 20, judging was still as subjective as it had been in the pre-war days, and this led to dissatisfaction with the arrangement. When Gulf Oil pulled out of the sponsorship in 1952, the event came to an end.

Twice winner of the trophy, and second on two other occasions, Beverly 'Bevo' Howard had been competing in precision aerobatics since the 1930s. As a forerunner to the Gulf Trophy wins, he had won the Betty Carstairs Aerobatic Trophy in 1946 and was named International Aerobatic Champion. During his long career he was one of the best-loved aerobatic pilots in the whole of America, on a personal as well as a professional level.

Born in South Carolina and raised in Georgia, he was a true Southern gentleman, a first-rate businessman, and a consummate pilot. He first got interested in aerobatics in his twenties, graduating from a Waco 10 to a Travel Air to a Taperwing Waco, and presenting skilled precision aerobatics in airshows while at the same time running his successful flight training business. But his real fame began when in the late 1930s he turned to low-power lightplanes for aerobatics. With his 37 hp red and white Piper Cub, he won the National Lightplane Aerobatic Championship in 1939–40–41 – having been the first to perform an outside loop in a lightplane in 1938.

Leaving junior college at the age of eighteen, Bevo had joined the newly established company Hawthorne Aviation at Charleston, S C, and within the span of four years from 1932 and 1936 had risen from line boy to president. By the time war arrived his leadership of the company placed it as one of the top US flight training schools for military pilots. Under his

Woody Edmundson, 1948 Gulf Trophy winner, was renowned for performing his aerobatic routines dressed up in a business suit. During 1940–42 he was an instructor at a British Fighter Training School. (via Woody Edmundson)

control several other training establishments were opened for the Army Air Force, and many thousands of students received training both during the war and after. It soon became a ritual that for each graduating class, Bevo Howard would put on a superb demonstration of aerobatics, culminating in an inverted pass, stick held between his knees, with both hands waving outside the cockpit.

Although Bevo was successful in competition, he was more famous as an airshow pilot and in particular for his airshows with the Bücker Jungmeister. It was in 1948 that Mike Murphy sold Bevo his prized Jungmeister, NC15696, which had once belonged to Alex Papana and which he had lovingly rebuilt from a heap of wreckage mainly by computing dimensions from photographs. Howard had fallen in love with the machine when Murphy first let him try it in 1941. "I knew I just had to own that airplane," he said. "The control pressures were perfect, and its ability to execute any routine I asked of

Bevo Howard and the Jungmeister that was once Alex Papana's (185hp Warner Super-Scarab). The restored machine is now on view at the National Air and Space Museum's Silver Hill facility, Washington, DC. (Smithsonian Institution)

it was like something out of a dream. In my judgment it has proved the best aircraft of its type ever flown."

Soon Bevo and the red and white Bücker became synonymous, the precision and artistry of the man complemented by the agility and responsiveness of the machine. Famous for his inverted ribbon-cuts, he often fixed two ribbons between his 18 ft (5.5 m) poles, 40 ft (12 m) apart, and cut the lower one in an inverted pass. Once he added a third ribbon underneath, and still snipped it cleanly without touching the other two! He acquired an unassailable reputation both in America and abroad in Europe, where he was regarded as the foremost American aerobatic pilot.

In keeping with his responsibilities in the training rôle, Bevo was safety-conscious in the extreme and meticulous in his pre-planning. Thus the news was almost impossible to believe when it was heard that he had crashed and died, in October 1971, during one of his inverted passes. The accident investigation findings were that he had run out of fuel during his performance – which, typically, was given for charity – and that the engine had quit while he was inverted. During his half-roll erect for a landing, they said, Howard had misjudged the roll and crashed into a nearby tree. "Calculation of probable point-to-point fuel consumption for Mr Howard's known flights before the air show indicated there would have been less than 6 gallons remaining," said the report. On arrival he had declined fuel, and when the crash occurred he had already performed 16 minutes of aerobatics.

There are those today, however, who still say that Bevo Howard would never have made a mistake over fuel, that he knew exactly the fuel capacity and consumption of his Bücker, and always had it planned down to the last drop. "Bevo's checklists were the most thorough in existence," says 1972 World Champion Charlie Hillard. The common view is that he simply failed to notice the tree on his blind side as he made his inverted run.

After the demise of the Gulf Trophy, competition aerobatics in the United States virtually ceased existence. There were still some airshow pilots who flew precision aerobatics in their routine – maybe fifteen in all – but there was no challenge by way of a contest, no matter how subjectively judged, to match their skills against each other.

For a certain South Texas crop-duster pilot named Frank David Price the situation was unbearable. Burning to revive the spirit of competition, he had heard about the new series of Lockheed Trophy contests being held in the UK, and started corresponding with the organizers in the hope of taking part – even though it meant crossing the Atlantic to do so.

Frank had bought a 185 hp Warner-engined Great Lakes from Gulf Trophy winner Rod Jocelyn, a high-performance aerobatic machine with ailerons installed on both top and bottom wings. Though he had not yet managed to get to England, Frank heard in 1960 that the first World Aerobatic Championships had been announced to take place in Bratislava, Czechoslovakia, and now determined to take his Great Lakes over by air freight to participate. There seemed to be no interest in aerobatics on the part of the National Aeronautic Association of America, whether nationally or internationally, so Frank's only recourse was to make the whole trip at his own expense. He was the only representative from the USA.

At the end of the competition he had to leave his aircraft behind in Europe while he crop-dusted for a full seven

Frank Price (standing behind flag-bearer), lone representative of the USA in the 1960 World Aerobatic Championships. *(Frank Price, via IAC)*

months to earn the cost of bringing it home again. But he had made a host of friends, among them the Soviet team members who were impressed and intrigued by his smoke-system, shown off to great effect during the opening air display. The ice had soon been broken when he took off, half-rolled inverted, and immediately sprinkled all his personal belongings and spare parts all over the field!

Frank remembers his Czech hosts as warm, friendly, lovely people, the Czech pilots as simply outstanding: they were light-years ahead of what was going on in America at the time. And the experience of being there, regardless of any success in the contest itself, was beyond value. From that one trip Frank Price brought back home with him the lomcovák, which he learned from Jaromír Hůlka and later reproduced in his Great Lakes and Bückers; the Aresti system, which José Aresti himself explained in Czechoslovakia and in years of subsequent correspondence; and most important of all, the idea of forming in America a Tiger Club under the auspices of the British Tiger Club whose members he had met and befriended on the way to Bratislava.

Hearing Frank's problems about the lack of competition at home, Norman Jones had come up with the idea of an American branch of the famous club; but knowing that he could not reproduce the same set-up as in England, Frank's plan was to confine his little group's activities strictly to aerobatics, both competition and training. It heralded the true revival of sport aerobatics in the USA, and in 1985 the club celebrated its twenty-fifth year of operation.

Frank Price in 1962 with Jungmeister N87P, previously EC-AEX belonging to Prince Cantacuzino. *(Frank Price)*

The year 1962 marked the first officially-sanctioned National Aerobatic Championship in America for ten long years. In 1958 Frank Price and Harold Krier (see below) had tried to set up a championship in conjunction with the Antique Airplane Association's fly-in at Ottumwa, Iowa, but official NAA sanction was not forthcoming: contests were held anyway, in 1958–59–60, and Price came second to Krier on the first two occasions.

But 1962 was different, and Duane Cole, of the famous Cole brothers airshow team, organized a truly National Championship to be flown in January of that year at Phoenix, Arizona, in conjunction with the Experimental Aircraft Association.

This interest on the part of the EAA marked the beginning of what has become in later years the most significant movement in American aerobatics. Founded in the early 1950s by enthusiast Paul Poberezny, working out of the basement of his own home, the Association had fought to represent and safeguard the interests of America's many homebuilders in their interaction with local and federal authority. It is mainly thanks to this organization, and this one man, that American aircraft owners today have a freedom to experiment with new designs and modifications that is unrivalled anywhere else in the world.

The twelve-strong entry list included Harold Krier, Lindsey Parsons, youngster Charlie Hillard, and of course Frank Price, to whom Hillard had come requesting instruction only a few years earlier. Each contestant was allowed five minutes for his performance. The title of first National Champion fittingly went to Duane Cole, who had organized it all.

At this time in the early 1960s there was not only a shortage of aerobatic pilots, there was also an acute shortage of

suitable aeroplanes. Vintage types had to be modified with more powerful engines for the job, or new types needed to be built.

Of the aircraft from the 1930s that were now being pressed into service, Frank Price again pioneered the way by importing two Bücker Jungmeisters from Europe in 1960–61 by way of J L Aresti. During his travels for the first World Championships in Bratislava, he had talked Aresti into letting him have a 25-minute flight with his Jungmeister, and the experience was a revelation. Frank knew immediately that this was the machine to have. In fact he made elaborate plans with Aresti to share his Jungmeister at forthcoming Lockheed competitions, to save his importing an aeroplane all the way from America, but unfortunately weather and other problems prevented this from happening; try as he may, Frank never did fly in the Lockheeds.

EC-AEX, Prince Cantacuzino's Jungmeister which Price bought via Aresti, arrived in 1960 as the second such aeroplane to come to America and stay. It was fitted with a 185 hp Warner Super Scarab and registered N87P. The following year Aresti's own machine arrived, EC-AME, and received a similar engine and the registration N178P. To clarify the position for any who have found these registrations confusing, it should be explained that Frank Price later asked the FAA to change the registrations around on these two Jungmeisters, and they have been carrying their exchanged numbers since August of 1980.

With these machines, and with his American Tiger Club, Frank Price by his own marathon efforts helped keep precision aerobatics alive in the United States with little more than enthusiasm and a few good friends to help him. He eventually retired from flying low-level aerobatics in 1980, after fulfilling daily airshow engagements during the course of the World Aerobatic Championships held at Oshkosh. A long-time Bücker enthusiast, he initially began selling plans for the Jungmeister, and met with such success that he has since started up a company, the American Tiger Club Inc., which is marketing Jungmann and Jungmeister kits for home-builders. And he still trains aerobatic students on the Chipmunk, and once a year flies a special show for his Tiger Club Air Day.

Duane Cole has already been mentioned as winner of the first US Championships, and he was to win the title again in 1964. Duane flew one of the first clipped-wing Taylorcraft ever used in airshows and contests, which he took to the World Championships in Budapest in 1962 as a member of the US team. After that he retired from competition aerobatics, though he still flies airshows to this day. He was one of the five flying Cole brothers who formed the original Cole Brothers Air Show, of whom Marion was the youngest and the keenest on competition aerobatics.

Marion was the first brother to go in for a contest, which was the Miami Gulf Trophy in 1949 (Duane and Lester followed him in 1950). He went on to compete for the next three years as well, and won the trophy himself in 1952. Marion soloed at the age of sixteen and started airshows and aerobatics in 1946, flying a 450 hp Stearman modified so as to

Marion Cole is seen here performing a car-top landing in brother Duane's Piper J-3 Cub 'Little Bit'. (Author's collection)

be as competitive as anything that was available at the time. Later he recounted that, although red line on a 450 Pratt and Whitney was around the 2200/2350 rpm mark, replacement engines were available at the time for no more than a couple of hundred dollars, so they regularly ran it to 3500/3700 rpm!

In later competitions he flew a 200 hp Jungmann, and managed to stay competitive even with the great changes and advances that suddenly started being made in the mid-1960s. Marion's last international was the World Championship event in 1968 in Magdeburg, after which he decided to retire from competition; his last contest was in 1969 at Oak Grove. Like all the Coles he made flying his living, and when the Cole Brothers split up he became a member of the first 'Red Devils' formation team with Bob Heuer and Gene Soucy.

Harold Krier was perhaps the leading solo aerobatic performer on the 1950s airshow circuit, and went on to become a key international competitor. He was operator of the Garden City Airport at Kansas, but from 1959 spent much of his time on tour with the National Air Shows run by promoter Bill Sweet, who was himself a keen devotee of precision aerobatics. Krier was another of the many pilots to start out on a clipped-wing Piper Cub, which he built himself; later he changed it for a rebuilt and modified Great Lakes 2T-1A, dating from 1932, in which he installed a 185 hp Warner engine and Aeromatic propeller. He was a gifted flyer, but never underestimated the importance of practice and study,

Flight Fantastic

to which he modestly attributed his success in aerobatics. Every day he practised an hour in the morning and an hour in the evening.

When Krier first went into aerobatics in the 1950s, he naturally turned to Frank Price for a lead and often went down to stay with him in Texas during the winter months, learning and exchanging ideas. He had been an Army Air Corps crew chief with Flying Fortress and Liberator bombers during the war, and did not learn to fly until 1945. Krier had that instinctive 'nose' for good design which told him immediately what was right and wrong about an aircraft and what it needed to improve it. He loved constantly to work on and modify his machines, and would immediately share his design ideas or offer help to anyone, quite freely, no matter how busy he was.

From his friendship with Frank Price grew up an inevitable

interest in competition, and Harold was one of the instigators of the Antique Airplane Association contests at Ottumwa, Iowa, which have already been mentioned. In fact, he won the event in each of the first three years that it was held – 1958, 59 and 60 – thus retiring the trophy and putting a stop to the contests!

Unsatisfied with the competitiveness of the modified 'Great Lakes Special', Harold Krier decided in 1962 to design and build his own aircraft, and it turned out to be one of the all-time great machines. The Krier Kraft was constructed by Harold and his brother Larry in nine months total, and was designed to be really strong. It incorporated the best features of both the Jungmeister and the Great Lakes, at the same time reproducing the light wing-loading of Ernst Udet's Flamingo which had made such an impression in the 1930s. The engine was a 185 hp Warner: Harold liked the Warner

Harold Krier's 'Great Lakes Special' (185 hp Warner).
(Author's collection)

(Inset) Harold Krier at the controls of his Super Chipmunk (200 hp Ranger).
(EAA)

Span: (lower)	24 ft 6 in (7.47 m)
(upper)	26 ft 8 in (8.13 m)
Length	18 ft 6 in (5.64 m)
Empty weight	1,120 lb (509 kg)
Cruise speed	110–115 mph
	(177–185 km/h)

Span: (lower)	24 ft 6 in (7.47 m)
(upper)	26 ft 8 in (8.13 m)
Length	18 ft 6 in (5.64 m)
Height	6 ft 5 in (1.95 m)
Empty weight	1,120 lb (509 kg)
Max speed	135 mph (217 km/h)
Rate of climb	1,800 fpm (9 m/sec)
Limit load	$+9, -6\,g$

Krier Kraft (185 hp Warner). Harold Krier sold the machine to Charlie Hillard, and it later passed to the ownership of H E 'Pappy' Spinks of Fort Worth, Texas. (Charlie Hillard)

and the torque it produced. The aerofoil on both upper and lower wings was the same as that of the Cessna 172, and featured a good amount of sweepback like the Bücker. It was rated the best American-produced aerobatic aircraft up to that time.

Although it was to be strong, the Krier Kraft was also designed to be ultra-light. "That thing was so light it was unbelievable," said Frank Price, "if a gust hit it you could see it move." Krier himself said "I didn't know you could build an airplane *too* light, but I did!"

The big advantage over the Great Lakes was that it had vertical penetration and the capability to stay in the box; it could fly down to the bottom line and then come back up with a four-point vertical roll, where the Great Lakes had to break and climb. Pulling up for a full vertical roll, from the beginning to the ending altitude, probably used up 1,100–1,200 ft (335–365 m).

Selected for the US team to fly in Spain along with Frank Price and Bob Nance, Harold Krier took the machine over with him for that contest; but he soon realized that yet another change of aircraft was needed if he was to move with the times. Reluctantly – for the machine had become almost a part of him – he sold it to Charlie Hillard who flew it to second place in the 1964, 1965 and 1966 Nationals, then flew it in the World Championships in Moscow in 1966. The following year, Charlie and the Krier Kraft won the National Championship.

Charlie Hillard from Fort Worth, Texas, was something of a 'boy wonder' at the time, having learned to fly in 1954 at the age of sixteen, and in his enthusiasm for aerobatics turned to Frank Price and Bevo Howard for tuition. Bevo was particularly delighted since young Charlie had bought his old clipped-wing Piper Cub N38333 (85 hp Continental). After meeting Charlie at the 1959 Ottumwa competition, Harold Krier was sufficiently impressed to invite him to join the National Air Shows team, and a great friendship was struck between them despite the ten years or so difference in their

Flight Fantastic

ages. Still flying the Cub, Charlie joined the outfit in 1960 and stayed with them a total of eleven years. The Cole Brothers were their chief rivals on the circuit.

From 1962 onwards the Americans regularly sent a full team to the World Championships, though without conspicuous success at the outset except for Lindsey Parsons's excellent fifth place in Hungary: generally the problem was a lack of really competitive machines for the job, and an absence of organized training. They were tending to fly more in the airshow mould, whereas international competition, especially after the advent of the Aresti system, placed less emphasis on the more dramatic flick-rolling manoeuvres and more on the highly-valued vertical figures.

Krier remained in the team until 1968, and Hillard joined him in 1966 with the Krier Kraft. By that time, realizing that specialized aircraft were needed, Harold Krier and new team-member Art Scholl had opted for the monoplane format which was so obviously favoured in Europe; both men brought out their own souped-up versions of the DH Chipmunk, a two-seat trainer designed by W J Jakimiuk of de Havilland Aircraft of Canada, which had been in use with the RAF since 1950.

The machine's handling qualities were excellent, but engine power needed to be increased, so Krier installed a 200 hp Ranger (later a 295 hp geared Lycoming). Modifications to the airframe included clipped wings, extended ailerons, strengthened fuselage, and an enlarged and strengthened tail. Having a canopy proved a definite advantage, and the vertical performance was a marked improvement over the draggy biplane types in use before. Art Scholl produced a similarly modified Chipmunk of his own, then went one stage further with another machine and installed retractable gear (from a Bellanca) together with an extended rudder and 260 hp Lycoming engine. Known as the 'American Yak', its performance proved an enormous success and Art continued to use it in his spectacular airshows, to the accompaniment of smoke and fireworks, right up to his much

Art Scholl and Super Chipmunk (260 hp Lycoming). 1974 US National Champion, Scholl came 9th in the 1972 World Championships. He was a college professor, and a much loved airshow pilot and instructor at weekends. He died in a filming accident in September 1985. (Mike Jerram)

regretted death which occurred during filming in 1985.

The 1968 World Championship was Harold Krier's last major contest, and he retired from competition afterwards. He continued to work hard for the cause of American aerobatics, coaching the team pilots and helping with design ideas, and making a study of the Aresti system so that his team-mates would have a more perfect understanding of this essential tool. He was a respected and revered father-figure of the sport, and was bitterly missed when he met his death in 1971 while test-flying a cabin version Spinks Akromaster for type certification. He had flat spun it down from over 12,000 feet (3,650 m) when it failed to recover and he had to bale out. Harold had plenty of altitude for the jump, but the parachute streamed instead of opening.

The 200 hp Akromaster monoplane was the brainchild of

DH Chipmunk (145 hp Gipsy Major 8). Designer Wsiewołod Jakimiuk was a leading designer with PZL before the war and later became one of the key men on the Concorde supersonic airliner. (Dick Stouffer, via IAC)

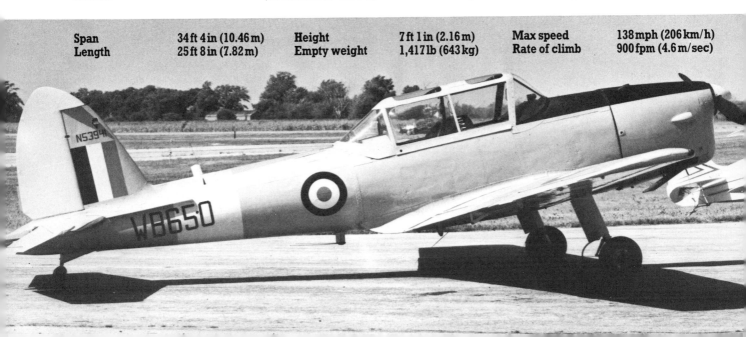

| Span | 34 ft 4 in (10.46 m) | Height | 7 ft 1 in (2.16 m) | Max speed | 138 mph (206 km/h) |
| Length | 25 ft 8 in (7.82 m) | Empty weight | 1,417 lb (643 kg) | Rate of climb | 900 fpm (4.6 m/sec) |

Charlie Hillard and a design team working in 1967–8 with M H 'Pappy' Spinks, a generous and long time supporter of US aerobatics. It was a logical development of the then-prevalent monoplane concept, with symmetrical aerofoil and wing planform similar to the Chipmunk. Charlie flew it to third place overall in the 1970 World Championships; but this spoke more for the attributes of the pilot than the aeroplane itself which, though elegant and a delight to handle, revealed no extra edge of performance to challenge the latest European machines. In particular the negative flick roll was mediocre, since the wing was reluctant to stall inverted.

Harold Krier had a great influence in the 1960s, when, thanks to his leadership and that of a few other enthusiasts, aerobatics in the USA had begun to get organized. After the second (1963) National Championship, won by Krier, at last the NAA had come up with official sanctioning of the event from 1964 onwards, when the contests began to be held under the auspices of Bill Stead at Stead Airport, Reno, in conjunction with the Reno Air Races.

As early as 1962, a group of pilots, judges and promoters (Harold Krier, Charlie Hillard, Nick d'Apuzzo, Rod Jocelyn, Frank Price, Mike Murphy, Bill Sweet) had begun calling itself the Aerobatic Club of America, and soon this became an official organization which was incorporated in 1964. Lindsey Parsons and Harold Krier were its first two presidents. Its main concern, of course, was the running of National Championships and the costly business of sending teams to international events abroad; so it was not surprising that a grass-roots movement also started to develop, with more of an interest in aerobatics for those who were not so advanced along the path. This movement eventually became the International Aerobatic Club, the body nowadays responsible for aerobatics in the USA.

During that time, many homebuilders were building aerobatic aircraft and wanting to fly aerobatics for fun, which meant that the EAA, primarily concerned with safety, began to consider an aerobatics division. It was logical to look to the possibility of the ACA becoming an affiliate – with all the attendant advantages of the parent body's financial and organizational structure.

It was the failure of this attempt at a partnership that led a group of EAA members, spearheaded by Bob Heuer and Don Taylor, to start up a separate group in 1970 under the name of International Aerobatic Club, as a division of EAA. The rest is history. With a present membership of some 4,000 world wide, the IAC manages to combine the efficient running of domestic aerobatics – including contests, judging, training and safety – with a truly international outlook which keeps the US abreast and at the forefront of world-wide activities. In 1982, inevitably, it took over from the ACA; but the result has actually had more the appearance of a friendly merger, with former ACA officers now respected colleagues in the larger alliance.

At this point in the story a small and very forceful character appears, one that has had an untold effect on aerobatics throughout the western world: the Pitts Special.

Conceived in 1942 as an airshow mount for its designer, Curtis Pitts, it was born in 1944 as a tiny, low-powered (55 hp) biplane incorporating the best attributes of those two favourite machines, the Jungmeister and Great Lakes. With a 90 hp

Span	16 ft 9 in (5.1 m)
Length	14 ft 8 in (4.47 m)
Weight	644 lb (292.7 kg)

Red-haired Betty Skelton with N22E 'Little Stinker', smallest Pitts Special in existence (note black and white skunk motif on tail). (Smithsonian Institution)

Franklin and inverted system it started to look like something really promising, and interest began to stir. But an attempt at a production run in 1946 ended in failure, and only the first model in the series ever came off the line: this achieved fame on both sides of the Atlantic as *Little Stinker*. The owner of the diminutive red and white aeroplane was diminutive herself, but an extremely competent aerobatic pilot, by the name of Betty Skelton. She captured the US Women's Aerobatic Championship in 1948–49–50, flying the Pitts in the latter two contests. Its 5-metre wingspan made it just about the smallest aircraft at any airshow, and the public loved it.

"The first time I flew the first little airplane," said 'Pa' Pitts, "was the biggest thrill for me. It was like a ride in a skyrocket after flying those other airplanes." Small, compact and stubby, the design was also immensely strong, and allowed you to extract maximum performance from your power plant. This combination of agility and performance soon became a world-beater.

Another young woman flyer came along in 1950 to request a third Pitts Special with rather more power, and this 125 hp Lycoming engined machine went the rounds of the air displays in the hands of Caro Bayley. Taking over where Betty Skelton left off, she won the Woman's Aerobatic Championships from 1951 to 1954. Aside from these models, and a specially-built big brother version known as *Samson* (450 hp Pratt and Whitney), the only Pitts Specials that emerged in the 1950s and early 1960s were homebuilt from plans (S-1E designation). *Joy's Toy* was one which Dean Case built for his daughter Joyce, another young woman who carried away top female honours in the aerobatic competitions of the late fifties.

With the regeneration of interest in competition aerobatics in the 1960s, Curtis Pitts came up with a new version to take power plants of up to 180 hp (Pitts S-1C). The midget biplane with the nippy performance now began to be very popular with homebuilders. But Curtis's most important development of all was a new set of wings in 1966. The original, relatively flat-bottomed wing (N-6 aerofoil) was fine for erect flight, but for efficient inverted flight one needs a biconvex aerofoil shape that will develop nearly the same amount of lift when upside down, and this was what Curtis Pitts produced in the winter of 1965: a set of symmetrical-section wings with two sets of ailerons. The result was the S-1S model with improved inverted performance and faster roll rate – 180 degrees a second. Flicks and multiple flicks went by in a flash, and up to six consecutive flick rolls could be performed in the horizontal. In fact, two flicks were easier than one: so rapid was the autorotation that it was difficult to catch and stop on axis.

Thanks to a high horsepower to weight ratio, its acceleration and rate of climb were nothing short of phenomenal. In fact, according to Neil Williams the aeroplane was rather overpowered, 'sheer brute force' being one of its main characteristics! But you couldn't quarrel with attributes like the climbing power of a lark, and acceleration which allowed you to finish a climbing half outside loop just on the 1 g stall and within 5–7 seconds to start a full vertical roll upwards without any need to dive for speed. It was this tiny powerhouse that took US team members Bob Herendeen, Charlie Hillard, Gene Soucy and Mary Gaffaney to medal-winning places in the 1970–72 World Championships.

A later two-seat Pitts model for training purposes started factory production in 1971: the standard S-2A featured a 200 hp Lycoming with constant-speed prop, and the larger airframe commended itself for better visual density from the ground. Taking advantage of this, a single-seater version with 260 hp engine appeared in 1978 (S-2S). Last in the list of larger-sized Pitts Specials was the S-2B model, new in 1983, with two seats and full capability as an unlimited class competitor. Meanwhile the ultimate high-performance version of the S-1S appeared in 1981, a 200 hp constant-speed version designated the S-1T. This had a noticeably enhanced roll rate in aileron and flick rolls.

Back in 1964, however, the only Pitts available to aspiring US champion Bob Herendeen was a homebuilt S-1C with 180 hp Lycoming. The 36-year-old Herendeen had learned to fly at the age of 16 during the war, and had always loved aerobatics – he had looped and spun on his first solo. After a spell as an instructor, he went on to fly Mustangs in the Korean war. Bob's first machine when he started taking aerobatics seriously was the Piper Cub *Little Bit*, N33584, which had belonged to Frank Price and before him to Duane Cole; but you could only get so far with a Cub, and Herendeen had his sights set on unlimited competition. The little Pitts biplane was not a widely used mount at the time, but he had recognized its strong potential and in 1964 had found a model for sale in Kennett, Missouri, which he fixed up with an inverted system. Shortly afterwards, Bob witnessed a breathtaking performance in a Pitts by Don Pittman at the 1964 US Nationals, who included a lomcovák in his routine: he knew then that it was the right choice for him. "I thought that was the wildest thing I ever saw," said Herendeen. Having once taken the decision to buy N66Y, he never afterwards wavered from his allegiance to the Pitts machines.

Still a novice in competition aerobatics, Bob entered the 1965 US Nationals at Reno and had to get some quick on-the-spot coaching from the ever helpful Harold Krier on how to use the Aresti notation. With Krier winning first place and Hillard second, Herendeen amazed himself by coming in third and at the same time qualifying for a place in the US team for the 1966 World Championships in Moscow. It was the first time that a Pitts had ever been seen in international competition, and great interest was centred around the little biplane, so quick and snazzy compared with the majestic Yaks and graceful Zlins.

"Obviously too fast for this kind of contest," said the report in the German magazine *Aerokurier*, and others agreed that it was either too small or too rapid – or both – and therefore difficult to judge. But many were the pilots at Moscow who took note of the little American homebuilt, which could perform the entire range of aerobatic figures with ease, and which did not suffer from the usual biplane problems of excessive drag to sap away performance.

Back home in September at the National Championships, after a scant two years experience in competition Bob Herendeen beat all the veterans to become US Champion of 1966. In 1967 he qualified for the team again, but this time he got Curtis Pitts to build him a new S-1S model (N266Y) with the symmetrical wings that had just been brought out. Bob's performance in East Germany in 1968 made even more of an impression on the international scene, as at the end of the first two programmes he lay in seventh place and seemed a real contender for the top three. But then the weather conditions

Today's standard single-seater Pitts specifications are:

	S-1S (180 hp, fixed pitch)	S-1T (200 hp, CS propeller)
Span	17 ft 4 in (5.3 m)	17 ft 4 in (5.3 m)
Length	15 ft 5 in (4.7 m)	15 ft 6 in (4.75 m)
Height	6 ft 3 in (1.9 m)	6 ft 3 in (1.9 m)
Empty weight	720 lb (327 kg)	830 lb (377 kg)
Max speed	176 mph (283 km/h)	185 mph (298 km/h)
Rate of climb	2600 fpm (13 m/sec)	2800 fpm (14 m/sec)
Designed limit load in excess of + 6, − 3 g		
Ultimate load factor tested to + 9, − 4.5 g		

and the retirement of the Czech team prevented programme 3 from being completed – in which he was lying second to Igor Egorov when flying was stopped – and Herendeen's chances of a medal-winning score in Magdeburg were dashed.

Many Americans will quote him as third overall in the 1968 World Championship, and that is indeed the position you reach if the marks are added for all the flights actually flown so far. Nevertheless, with two of the star Czech pilots (Šouc

and Tuček) among those still to fly when programme 3 was abandoned, I am sure Herendeen himself would agree that, national enthusiasm aside, that third place was by no means unassailable. The only results that could officially be announced after a meagre two programmes were the team positions, and here the Americans emerged in third place, bringing home the first set of medals they had ever won in a World Championship.

Bob Herendeen went on to win the National title again in 1969, and qualified for the World Championship team for England in 1970. Here he encountered another piece of bad luck when his engine quit during a spin in programme 2, the Unknown Compulsory, and by strict reading of the regulations he was deprived of a score for that manoeuvre when his

Gene Soucy, three times US Champion, third overall in the 1972 World Championships. Gene is presently an airline pilot and aerobatic instructor in Texas. (Lee Fray, via Gene Soucy)

Flight Fantastic

sequence was reflown. Once more he yielded first place to the brilliant Soviet pilot Igor Egorov, coming in as overall second with a difference of only 125 or so points behind Egorov's 12,800. This was a real vindication of the excellence of Herendeen's flying, and the highest pinnacle a US pilot had ever reached in World Championships. With Charlie Hillard third and Gene Soucy sixth, their combined scores brought them the Nesterov Cup as team champions in 1970; and female pilot Mary Gaffaney brought home the bronze medal for third overall and a gold medal as winner of programme 1 in the women's championship. Four of the six-strong team flew Pitts S-1Ss: the day of the Pitts had well and truly arrived internationally.

Charlie Hillard soon latched on to the potential of the Pitts. At the end of 1971 he bought the bright red S-1S (N442X) belonging to Bob Heuer of the 'Red Devils' formation team, and set about preparing for the next World Championship due to take place in Salon de Provence, France. With over 16 years of aerobatics experience behind him – and still only 33 years old – he was the mainstay of the US team and its principal contender for the world crown. As usual, the Americans aimed for nothing short of top honours; they had come so close in 1970 that once more a superhuman effort was put into fund-raising, training and preparation.

Charlie's two team-mates Gene Soucy and Tom Poberezny (son of EAA founder Paul) had already been Pitts pilots for some years. Ten years his junior, Gene had been a true professional and a competition winner since 1967, and since 1969 had been a member of the 'Red Devils' team with Bob Heuer and Marion Cole. The young Kansan had only recently risen to the very top in American aerobatics, and was the first ever three-times National Champion in 1970–71–72.

After the original 'Red Devils' came to an end in 1971, Gene teamed up with 25-year-old Tom Poberezny whom he had encouraged and trained in aerobatics for the past two years; in that short space of time Tom had achieved fifth place in the 1971 Nationals, and later moved up to second in 1972 and National Champion in 1973. These two gifted youngsters, working together with Charlie Hillard as a trio to promote and raise funds for the 1972 World contest, almost inevitably found themselves dubbed the 'Red Devils' as successors to the original team. Soon they decided to form a regular three-man partnership, which is still going strong today after more than 13 years – though nowadays they fly as the 'Eagles' formation team in Christen Eagle I biplanes.

Back in 1972, the three had trained long and hard, both in America and at their practice site in France prior to the championship. A new formula for the finals had been brought in this year: instead of a repetition of the contestant's earlier Free Programme, this time it would be a Five-minute Free-style along the Lockheed Trophy lines, with no Aresti, no individual coefficients for manoeuvres, and – as yet – no clear notion of how it would be marked! Later, criteria were introduced (at Charlie Hillard's suggestion) such as harmony and rhythm, originality, versatility, accuracy of execution*;

The Eagles Aerobatic Team: (left to right) Charlie Hillard, Tom Poberezny, Gene Soucy. (Christen Industries)

*Readers will recognize many of these criteria from the recent and not-so-recent past!

but at its first introduction the judging was bound to be totally subjective. This might prove an advantage or a disadvantage: nobody yet knew. But in theory at least, it ought to favour the American airshow performers.

At the end of the first two programmes, Gene had won gold medals in both and led the field; but Charlie was close behind, and after moving up to take the gold in programme 3 with a very good score, he entered the final fourth round just a whisker ahead of Gene's aggregate marks. The title of World Champion now depended on the untried Freestyle, and when they drew lots for the starting order, Charlie found himself number one to fly.

Known as the 'wind dummy' position, number one can be a handicap in any contest programme because the first pilot has to find out the meteorological conditions at competition height, and especially how strong are the effects of the wind. In programmes such as the Unknown Compulsory the disadvantages are even greater, as may be imagined, and a tradition has grown up in aerobatics that the pilot drawing number one always gets a roisterous round of applause, catcalls and whistles to cheer him on his way.

From the marking point of view, position number one is not so great either. For Charlie Hillard it meant that his Freestyle flight was the anchor point around which all the judges' marks would be centred, and, moreover, this was a new style of judging which had not been tried before. It would be virtually impossible for him to get top marks, for that would mean that the judges' scores could then only go downwards for the remainder of the flights. However, he had to put such thoughts to the back of his mind. He had worked up a good airshow routine, including a new manoeuvre which he called the **torque roll**, and all he could hope for was a high enough position to keep his narrow lead and stay ahead on aggregate.

The torque roll had been pioneered in the US by Pitts pilot Don Pittman during the 1960s, and Charlie had first seen it performed by Bob Schnuerle, his former team-mate from WAC 1970. The figure is best described as a rolling tail-slide, in which the roll is initiated in that direction in which the torque of the power plant helps the rotation – for the right-turning Lycoming engine, the direction of the torque will therefore be to the left. Climbing in a furious series of vertical rolls at full power, Charlie held the throttle setting and (left) aileron input until the machine had lost all forward movement and was actually sliding *backwards* again; then with the aircraft's attitude held steady by means of rudder, the engine torque took over and perpetuated the left-hand rotation as it rolled downwards for as many as five or six turns.

It was the first truly new manoeuvre* in competition aerobatics since the lomcovák, and it impressed the judges sufficiently to overcome the disadvantages of flying as number one. He was awarded sixth place in the finals, and kept his overall lead to become the first American World Champion. With Gene third and Tom sixth, the team trophy also returned again to the USA; and to Mary Gaffaney went the women's championship title, with an excellent score that ranked fifth in the overall male/female calculations.

Having bagged all three top trophies, the team could not have asked for more. Requested to fly the traditional winner's slot in the closing airshow, Charlie suggested instead that he, Gene and Tom should perform a formation display, and they scored yet another hit as the 'Red Devils' team delighted and thrilled the French crowds. Though Pitts formation acts were

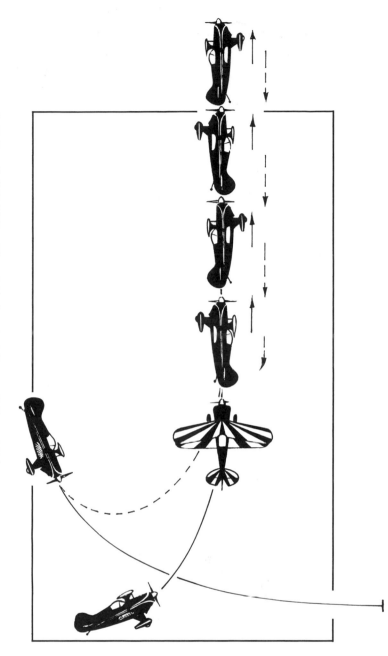

The torque roll, demonstrated by Charlie Hillard at Salon de Provence in 1972.

Mary Gaffaney, 1972 Women's World Champion.
(Author's collection)

*A vrille sur la queue, or 'tail-sliding spin' had been listed as a manoeuvre in the 1934 World Championship catalogue, though not performed in the competition (see Chapter 8). See also 'spinning tail-slide' (Chapter 5) and 'corkscrew tail-slide' (Chapter 4).

(a) Henry Haigh and (b) Kermit Weeks, both US Champions and both placed second in World Championships.
((a) Dan Mackie, via IAC)
((b) Dick Stouffer, via IAC)

Span	16 ft (4.88 m)
Length	16 ft 6 in (5.03 m)
Empty weight	770 lb (350 kg)
Max speed	190 mph (306 km/h)
Rate of climb	3000 fpm (15 m/sec)
Limit load	± 12 g

Weeks Special (200 hp Lycoming), flown in competition by Kermit Weeks and (as here) by fellow team pilot Linda Meyers.
(Dave Gustafson, via IAC)

Flight Fantastic

later to become firm favourites in Europe, this was the first that had ever been seen on this side of the Atlantic.

⊹⊹⊹⊹⊹⊹⊹⊹⊹⊹⊹

Thereafter, the attraction of the impudent little Pitts biplanes became irresistible. In the United States, and soon all over the world, they were being homebuilt from plans, put together from kits, or bought off the shelf from the now thriving Pitts factory. At the following World Championships in Kiev, no fewer than 21 pilots from eight different countries flew Pitts Specials.

True, they still suffered the disadvantage of being very tiny and very fast in competition, so judging them accurately was not easy. But they were rewarding – and fun – to fly, they were affordable, and they were always a terrific hit with airshow audiences who loved to see the incredible gyrations of the pocket-sized biplane with the buzzing, snarling motor.

The immensely strong airframe also lent itself to modifications for improved performance. Among the US team members in succeeding years there appeared many who were true successors to the Harold Krier spirit of innovation and creativity in aircraft design, and foremost among these in the dimension of biplane modification were Henry Haigh and Kermit Weeks.

Henry and Kermit could scarcely be more different from each other, although they share the same irreverent sense of fun as a foil to their dedicated competitiveness. Henry came to aerobatics late, and was over forty when he got involved in competitions in the late 1960s and started racking up an impressive list of wins: among his 36 first placings he lists the 1979 US Nationals, and among his 17 second places he can claim the distinction of being runner-up (by 5 points!) to the World Champion in 1982. Always a craftsman with his hands, one of his first innovations was an entirely original tailwheel design, lightweight and durable and at the same time in keeping with the neat shape of the little modern taildraggers. Two driving forces are apparent in Henry Haigh, and the first is a genuine love of the beauty of aeroplanes, an appreciation of their design and a desire to produce something aesthetically satisfying. The second is work, work and then more work. There's no satisfaction, he says, unless the competitive edge is there to hone and improve your proficiency. "The more I work, and the better I get at it, the more I enjoy it. To go up and fly sloppy aerobatics is really no fun at all."

Henry was the first to bring out a lightened, streamlined Super Pitts in 1974 with spring gear and a 200 hp engine,

giving at least 20 per cent improvement in performance over the standard 180 hp Pitts. Kermit Weeks by then had been competing for barely a year. Born in Salt Lake City in 1953, he was brought up – and now lives – in Florida with its ideal climate for flyers. Although he has since inherited considerable wealth through his grandfather's dealings in the oil business, Kermit started out in life having to struggle for his flying just like anyone else, and now that he has the means, he uses it to support and encourage aviation and, incidentally, to maintain an aircraft museum.

Even while he was still in high school he was building aeroplanes, and throughout a varied list of college courses he learned the practical as well as the theoretical skills of aircraft engineering. After seeing Henry Haigh's clean-up job on his Pitts and the extra performance it gave, especially in vertical penetration, Kermit borrowed some of his ideas and came up with a dramatically altered Pitts of his own. He swept both wings, added spring gear and symmetrical ailerons, moved the cockpit aft, lightened the whole machine, and installed a Hoffmann constant-speed prop to go with the 200 hp Lycoming. The aircraft was christened the Weeks Special.

Kermit flew the Special from 1977 to 1980, placing second in both the 1977 and 1979 US Nationals. More importantly, he also qualified for the 1978 and 1980 World Championships, and placed second and third respectively: an astonishing achievement for one who had only been flying competitions since 1973.

Not content with second-best, he turned his thoughts to a new machine of entirely his own design, a potential world-beater. It appeared in 1981 under the name Weeks Solution, and we shall meet it in the next chapter. Kermit is not one to shirk going out on a limb with his own ideas, and has not lost that sense of wonder and delight in the sheer performance of aeroplanes. For most people, his new 300 hp powerhouse represents just about as far as you can go in biplane design, though Henry Haigh has long had thoughts of a superbipe of his own, with 260–290 hp and retractable gear. Both are irrepressible innovators, and both take the view that whereas a manufacturer cannot afford the risk of speculative new ideas, a few individuals with creative flair can contribute a lot to aircraft design progress.

But nothing in aerobatics stands still for long, and the biplane could not hold sway forever. Already in 1971 a young contender had arrived on the American scene with a monoplane design for unlimited competition. Developed and improved over the years, the Laser 200 was to become the Pitts's greatest rival.

19

1980 ~ The Oshkosh experience

Anyone who has been to the EAA's annual week-long convention, or who has even heard about it, knows that the name Oshkosh carries a certain magic. Here every year in the Wisconsin summertime thousands of aircraft, and hundreds of thousands of visitors, gather together to watch, plan, talk, think, breathe and dream one thing only: flying.

In August 1980, the Americans hosted the World Aerobatic Championships in conjunction with the EAA fly-in: it made a unique occasion, and the organizers tried hard to maintain a carnival atmosphere, with airshows and audience attractions, despite the effects of quite dreadful weather.

With so many nations sending teams a far greater distance than they had ever had to attempt before, elaborate arrangements were made for practice sites and even aircraft to be available to visiting teams. American generosity was at its greatest, and foreign competitors were welcomed into homes in many neighbouring communities. Even so, the Germans reckoned that the cost of the trip worked out to some $6,000 per head, and for the Australians it was more like $15,000 each!

One or two setbacks began to be felt early: first the Czechs, Poles and East Germans stated they were unable to participate, due to financial considerations. Next the Soviet Union declined to come. Technical problems were given as the reason, which some linked to the reports that had been filtering through over a period of time of Yak 50 wing failures (or perhaps more accurately wing overstressing by their more energetic pilots). But it was also known that America had very recently severed its sporting links with the USSR by boycotting the Moscow Olympics after the Soviet invasion of Afghanistan. Maybe this was retaliation? If so, its effects were felt only by a handful of disappointed sportsmen – scant

likelihood of breast-beating in the Pentagon on account of an aerobatics contest.

With no Hungarians or Romanians either, there was thus a total absence of any Eastern European nation at the World Championships, which meant that the American pilots' chief adversaries, the Soviet and Czech teams, were not there to challenge their lead. These three nations were by now solidly entrenched at the forefront of the sport, their only serious rivals being the three Swiss – Brandt, Schweizer and Müller – and the German Strössenreuther. The Championship was inevitably downgraded as a result of their absence, though it was far from being the 'waste of time' that some observers would claim. Ten individual nations were represented by 51 pilots and among their number were several of the world's élite.

Along with the excellent organization of facilities for the competition, including a huge electronic scoreboard flashing up the results, was an innovation in computing the positioning of the contestants' flights. Since a separate coefficient of either 50 or 70 was assigned to the positioning or 'framing' of the performance – its symmetrical placement about the centre axis of the box – obviously a good positioning score could make a significant difference to the end result. The Americans introduced a first-rate radar/computer device for this purpose, using a Balloon Tracking and Windfinding Radar System donated by the National Oceanographic and Atmospheric Administration, and this was linked to a microcomputer and printer to give both an on-screen and hard copy read-out of the pattern of each flight. Not only the framing was recorded, but also any excursions out of the box for which penalties were applicable.

The accuracy, it was claimed, was phenomenal: it was capable of tracking a target the size of a Christmas-tree

The flying field at Oshkosh for the 1980 World Championships.
(Don Berliner)

ornament at a distance of 185 kilometres. The impressive set-up was assumed to be infallible until, in fact, its very range let it down in a flight by Kermit Weeks, when it locked on to grain silos several miles from the airfield and gave him a low-flying penalty! The problem was rectified, but faith in the system was somewhat shaken.

Later, faith was shaken in a different way when the competition rules were overturned in favour of the top US female pilot, Betty Stewart (Pitts S-1S), for a flight which she performed in the wrong direction. This should have carried a zero score for the whole programme, but the Americans protested that a clerical error had been made in the drawing of her sequence diagram. To many observers the protest grounds seemed flimsy, since Betty had been seen to fly the

Betty Stewart, Women's World Champion 1980.

(Betty Stewart)

official results had even been posted. Requests to see the scoresheets were refused, and, contrary to normal practice, they never were released for checking. It was a sad end to the competition, and the final farewell party was boycotted by many.

Betty Stewart, a fine pilot who had always held the sporting ambition to be 'World Champion' rather than 'Women's World Champion', had been flying well in the first two programmes; her scores in both flights beat some of her male fellow team-members, as well as the females. She had a substantial lead when the incident happened, and retained that lead afterwards to win the Women's World Championship of 1980.

A more convincing victory in the following Women's Championship in Austria placed Betty in the top ten pilots of the world, even with Soviet and Czech teams present. And she will always be remembered for a particularly warm-hearted gesture during that contest, when she generously shared her Pitts with Australian pilot Chris Sperou, whose machine had been damaged in transit.

With this 1982 win Betty Stewart became the first competitor, male or female, ever to hold a World Championship title twice. In her own words, the after effect was a real emotional let-down: "Where else am I going to go, after two World Championships?" Where to go proved not such a difficult question after all, since she soon found life as a professional airshow pilot far more attractive than her previous work as a pharmacist: from 1983 onwards she gave up competitions and concentrated on air displays instead. Nevertheless, just like Bob Herendeen – previous owner of N266Y which she flew in both World Championships – that basic upbringing on competition aerobatics could never be ignored. Betty says her airshows include "a lot of competition style flying"; and you may be sure that when the enthusiasts go to watch her, they see a World Champion in action.

Those other two stars Kermit Weeks and Henry Haigh also produced top form in 1980, Kermit with the Weeks Special gaining a gold medal in the Unknown Compulsory programme, and finishing in third position overall. Beating him as runner-up to the World Champion, Henry Haigh won first place in the Known Compulsory and second in the Free. Something like 163 marks separated them.

But we have not yet met the young man who captured the 1980 title by a margin of nearly 400 marks, with two golds and two silvers in the qualifying programmes, and in an aeroplane which he called the Laser 200.

Aviation writer Don Berliner tells a story of the 1980 World Championships when an enthusiastic member of the public rushed up to him and asked, "Can you tell me who's in the lead right now?" "Leo Loudenslager", said Don. "Oh," said his inquirer, somewhat crestfallen, "I'd rather hoped it was an American."

Leo, of course, *is* an American, born in Columbus, Ohio, in 1944. His love of things mechanical was at the root of his Air Force stint as an aircraft mechanic, and even as a teenager he began homebuilding – his first project being a beautiful Corvette-powered Austin-Healey sports car.

Single-mindedness seems to characterize Leo's entire career; it was mostly by sheer dedication and willpower that he covered the mountains of work necessary to obtain the PPL, commercial, instructor and instrument ratings that would lead him to an airline pilot's job. Except for a short spell of ground school, he was mostly self-taught from books. In 1966 he

sequence starting the opposite way to the other pilots (vis à vis the prevailing wind), which would indicate an error in the cockpit rather than in the paperwork! However, for reasons variously quoted as gallantry, petitioning among the other women pilots, and giving the benefit of the doubt, the International Jury allowed the flight to stand. In some cases, judges had ceased marking her flight when it became obvious that it merited a zero, so where marks were missing for this reason, a score was averaged out from among the other judges.

This decision unfortunately caused a great furore, fuelled by the fact that the Jury's leniency had been applied to one of the home team. Weather-related delays had already shortened tempers, and computer breakdowns and errors also contributed to the general aggravation: the computerized scoring system required rather more sophisticated equipment than was on hand, and 'Bauerization' of the results (see page 233) took an unconscionable time. Indeed at the end of the fourth competition programme, a prizegiving ceremony was held for the benefit of television cameras before the realized his ambition and joined American Airlines: from that moment onwards he was free to indulge his growing passion for aerobatics.

Already he cherished the dream of becoming World Champion. But his first priority, before even considering entering a contest, was to build the ideal aerobatic aircraft.

In 1967 Margaret Ritchie, winner of the US Women's Championships the previous year, had decided that she wanted a monoplane especially built for competition aerobatics. To this end, she and her husband collaborated with engineers Clayton Stephens and Eddie Allenbaugh to produce plans for an original design. Allenbaugh was the designer of Art Scholl's famous racer *Miss San Bernardino*, of which the new aircraft would include many features, including the mid-wing configuration – which was entirely new to aerobatics, though quite standard in air-racing ever since the 1930s. But Allenbaugh died during the early stages of the project, and the machine was named after Clayton Stephens: the Stephens Akro.

Six or seven sets of plans had been sold to interested homebuilders, including a set to Leo Loudenslager, when Margaret Ritchie tragically met her death in a training accident with the prototype. This prompted Leo to re-examine his ideas somewhat. But the accident investigation vindicated the integrity of the structure, so he pressed on with the building project and completed it in 1971 after three years of unflagging effort.

With only one prior contest at Intermediate level to his credit, Leo went straight for the US Nationals at Unlimited level and placed tenth at his first attempt. Only the Nationals interested him, as a prelude to world class competition, and he remained true to that philosophy for the next twelve years. Meanwhile, modifications and improvements were constantly made to the Stephens Akro, registered N10LL, until in 1975 the need to build a new wing inspired a thorough reworking of the design. It emerged in the form that it essentially takes today, and Leo christened it the Laser 200.

Stephens Akro (180 hp Lycoming) – now G-RIDE – owned by British aerobatic pilot Bob Mitchell.

(Air Portraits via Bob Mitchell)

In addition to the different wing and aerofoil, changes included a raised turtledeck and faired-in canopy replacing the bubble canopy of the original; the rudder was cleaned up and the tailplane enlarged; and the whole frame was considerably lightened. This configuration was arrived at after trying no less than three changes of spinner, five propellers, three cowlings, two forward fuselages, three turtledecks, two new wings and two tails.

Leo's new machine had an impressive power/weight ratio that rivalled even the Pitts, giving even better vertical penetration. Its generous control surfaces gave a faster roll rate, and it could also out-turn a Pitts – all of which gave it that slight but appreciable edge in performance. Being the only serious competitor currently using the Stephens-type design, he had shouldered the entire workload of development and testing, but at last he was satisfied with the result.

As if to prove that he had found the winning formula, at his fifth try he won the US National Championship in 1975, at the same time qualifying for the forthcoming World Championships in the USSR. But all hopes of a top placing in 1976 were soon dashed, of course, by the goings-on at Kiev that have already been described in Chapter 17, in which the US team felt itself to be a major target. Disillusioned, as many international contestants were on their return, Leo nevertheless tried again for a place in the following Championships, winning his third consecutive national title in the process. WAC 1978 was to be hosted by the Czechs.

No-one was more surprised than the Americans when the World Championship at České Budějovice turned out to be friendly, well-run and absolutely fair. Leo was in great shape for the first two programmes, for which he won a gold and a silver, but in programme 3 his orientation in the rolling circle somehow went adrift and he came out after 270 degrees instead of 360 degrees. Naturally this zeroed a number of figures until he was back on heading again, but by that time he had lost more than 1,000 points and it was impossible to salvage the flight. He finished thirty-fifth in that programme.

With so much riding on the result, this disaster dealt Leo a body-blow from which many lesser men would never have recovered. But he had managed to secure a place in the fourth, Final Freestyle programme that was flown by one-

Span	24 ft 4 in (7.42 m)
Length	19 ft 1 in (5.82 m)
Height	5 ft 9 in (1.75 m)
Empty weight	830 lb (377 kg)
Max speed	165 mph (265 km/h)
Rate of climb	4000 fpm (20 m/sec)
Limit load	$\pm 12\,g$

third of the men, and – incredibly – bounced back to the top again to win another gold. He finished in twelfth place overall. Such was the great talent and obvious courage of the young American, that top pilots from both the Soviet and Czech teams sought him out after the contest to compliment him on his flying and offer condolences on his bad luck.

Winning the World Championship title at Oshkosh in 1980 brought, in his own words, a sense of relief. An ambition conceived over 15 years before had been realized, and the pilot/aircraft combination totally vindicated. Leo continued to win US National titles to a total of seven in all, and flew again in the world series in 1982, but never again did he reach his 1980 pinnacle. To claim that topmost position in aerobatics requires not only a flawless performance from both man and machine, it also requires an extra something in out-and-out superhuman endeavour that is seldom capable of repetition twice in a row, and in time Leo moved over to make room for those jostling for position from below. With ever increasing demands for air displays the length and breadth of the United States, he eventually decided to give the frenetic world of competition aerobatics a rest, and enjoy the less punishing routine of airshow flying – a decision which was precipitated by his missing the 1984 World Championships due to a technical disqualification* at the team selections.

Already in Czechoslovakia in 1978 two other Stephens Akro types were being flown internationally, one being a standard Clayton Stephens machine built from plans, registered G-RIDE, and belonging to British pilot Bob Mitchell. The other was the Super Star of former Pitts devotee Henry Haigh.

Henry had also built his machine from plans, but had introduced modifications according to his own design ideas which were somewhat different from Leo's. In one area they were significantly divergent, and that was in the tail feathers, where Henry's version modified out all the complications of the original Stephens structure. His present elevator/stabilizer configuration is the fifth he has tried. Retaining the same wing section and span, he redesigned the wing structure several times before coming up with a solution that satisfied his ideas in every way, including the safety aspect. In contrast to Leo's cool blue-and-gold colour scheme with white stars, Henry painted his machine a brilliant red with the wing undersides dark navy blue for clear distinction. In 1982 in Spitzerberg, Austria, it was Henry Haigh's Super Star that eclipsed the Pitts, Zlin and French CAP aircraft, as well as the other Stephens derivatives ranged against him; in the final analysis he was beaten to the world title with a margin of only 5 points by Victor Smolin in the Yak 50.

Why should the Americans turn to the monoplane after such a successful formula had been found in the Pitts, a powerful, high-performance aircraft that was proven and readily available?

To answer this question one must place oneself in the judge's position, for at the end of the day, the winners in competition aerobatics must always be determined by a panel of observers seated on the ground.

The biplane configuration has a lot going for it, and although it may have been viewed with misgivings when it first appeared 1966, its many good qualities far outweighed its faults: convenient to obtain, strong and robust, better in knife-edge flight due to the channelling effect of its wings, light and responsive to handle. But the Pitts simply is not easy on the eye in flight.

The comparative advantages of the monoplane are perhaps slight: better all-round vision without the obstruction of the upper wing, better ability to 'turn a corner' and better vertical penetration with less inherent drag in the structure. Yet the all-important visual presentation is clean, graceful, and far easier to read when judges are assessing accuracy of manoeuvres to within 2.5 degrees and the aircraft is performing at a distance of anything up to 1,500 m (5,000 ft) away. Viewed at an angle – which it usually is – the biplane gives the appearance of a little ball without clearly delineated features; whereas the monoplane's cruciform shape shows up strikingly at most angles and distances.

What tips the balance, perhaps, is the evident disinclination of judges in aerobatics to give top marks to a Pitts where they will to a Laser. Somehow the judge tends to the feeling that he may have missed something, some minute fault, that was hidden amid the struts and wings and bracing wires. It has often been said that a 10 is seldom awarded to a biplane, simply because the judge is unsure of what he has seen. The clarity of the monoplane is, of course, a two-edged sword, as Leo Loudenslager readily admits: if you fly anything less than perfectly, the monoplane is more likely to tell on you. But when you do fly well, your chances of a top score are greater.

One who still holds out hope for the biplane configuration is Kermit Weeks, who has faced all the criticisms and has come up with his own design – the Weeks Solution – which is intended to avoid the worst of them, while still taking advantage of the biplane's many merits. In the first place it is strong and powerful, with a 300 hp Lycoming and three-blade, constant-speed Hoffmann propeller. The cockpit location is noticeably well aft of the wings. Perhaps even more important, Kermit has designed the machine to be visually distinct to the ground observer in a way that the average biplane is not, with modification following modification until he was properly satisfied. Even the solid black paint-scheme, picked out with gold and orange, is designed for stark clarity against the surrounding sky.

Since initially airing the machine in 1981, Kermit has taken a first in the US Nationals and two consecutive gold medals in World Championships, for the four-minute Freestyle programme in each case, in which the power and presence of his aircraft are undoubtedly a great asset. His 1984 World Championship result equalled that achieved in 1980, ending in third position overall; but since 1980 in programmes other than the Freestyle he has still not managed to hit those medal-winning places and has yet to equal – or beat – his best result of overall runner-up to the World Champion in the 1978 contest in Czechoslovakia. But Kermit is still a youngster in aerobatic terms, and a determined and resourceful competitor. Perhaps in his hands the biplane may yet beat the odds and prove the monoplane-fanciers wrong!

Let us now take a look at the foreign teams who went to make up the 1980 World Championships in Oshkosh, where the entire gamut of visiting nations who managed to make the trip – and they numbered nine in all – turned out to be those

---

*US aerobatic contests are so densely attended that often the next competitor is actually kept holding, airborne and without radio, pending the finish of the current competitor's flight. Disqualification is the penalty for mistakenly entering the box before the previous pilot has finished, and this was Leo's error in 1983.

Leo Loudenslager's Laser 200 N10LL (200 hp Lycoming) in its present livery. (Leo Loudenslager)

Henry Haigh's Super Star (200 hp Lycoming).
(Dave Gustafson, via IAC)

Span	24 ft (7.3 m)
Length	19 ft (5.8 m)
Empty weight	875 lb (398 kg)
Max speed	220 mph (354 km/h)
Rate of climb	3000 fpm (15 m/sec)
Limit load	$\pm 12\,g$

Kermit Weeks's Weeks Solution (300 hp Lycoming).
(Dave Gustafson, via IAC)

Span	17 ft 4 in (5.28 m)
Length	18 ft 6 in (5.64 m)
Empty weight	960 lb (436 kg)
Max speed	215 mph (346 km/h)
Rate of climb	3800 fpm (19 m/sec)
Limit load	$\pm 9\,g$

Flight Fantastic

whose aerobatics were totally self-financed by individual and concerted effort: no state subsidy in sight!

First, the Americans' next-door neighbours, the Canadians, who had the shortest distance to travel.

It was in 1972 that Unlimited aerobatics started getting really organized in Canada, as a result of close links with the American-based International Aerobatic Club. Serious team training was started, with the aim of participating in the next world-class championships; selections being made at the Canadian Nationals, which were now run at the Unlimited level. Canada's foremost pilot, Gerry Younger, took the title five years in succession.

As it happened, the next World Championships were not until 1976; but Canada was ready, with Gerry Younger and Jay Hunt making the expensive and difficult journey to the Soviet Union to participate and gain valuable experience. They returned realizing that the Pitts was rapidly becoming a back number compared with the trend in Europe towards mono-planes like the Zlin 50, which had astounded all observers with its lightning-fast rate of roll.

Jay started to form the germ of an idea for a Canadian-designed and built monoplane, available as a kit, that would be within the reach of homebuilders but would compete on equal terms, without extra modifications, at the Unlimited level. He drew up a tough list of criteria for the machine, but he found award-winning designer Chris Heintz of Zenair, formerly of Avions Robin in France, willing to take on the challenge. In 1982 the 'J-Bird' emerged, officially christened the Super Acro Zenith, and gradually established a niche for itself in the highly-specialized aerobatic market. With stubby

Canadian Super Acro Zenith (200hp Lycoming). It comes as a 200hp custom-built aircraft or as a kit that can be 'built in a single winter requiring no special skills'. (via Jay Hunt)

wings and full-span symmetrical ailerons with squared-off trialing edges, it is reported to roll faster than a Pitts (270 degrees per second at cruise), climb higher (15 metres/sec, 3,000 fpm), and land easier (thanks to excellent forward visibility).

Gerry Younger's crown as long-standing Canadian Champion passed in 1979 to 37-year-old Gordon Price, a DC-9 Captain for Air Canada. As an Air Cadet he had learned to fly at age 17, later joining the Air Force where he flew Chipmunks, Harvards and T-33s before moving on to Sabres and Starfighters. Always an active homebuilder, Gordon built and flew his own aerobatic aeroplanes to win several Canadian titles before becoming National Champion 1979 to 1981. In his first attempt at the World Championships, at Oshkosh 1980, he flew his own modified Pitts S-1S and reached fifteenth position overall, narrowly missing a place in the finals.

Gordon's thoughts had also turned to bringing out an aircraft to rival the top-performing monoplanes, but his approach was centred around the well-tried Pitts, concentrating on improvements in wing design. In 1980 he brought out the 'Ultimate Wing' for the S-1S, a radical redesign of wing and aileron which allowed a rate of roll up to 360 degrees per second ... and five vertical rolls on take-off! As a do-it-yourself kit or ready assembled, it appealed to many top-line competitors and added a new dimension of performance to the faithful Pitts.

Finally, in 1985 a new Gordon Price design arrived, again aimed at the homebuilder who preferred the biplane format. Called the 10 DASH 100 (or 180, or 200, or 300) it was a small, 16-ft span (4.88 m) aerobatic machine with the capability of taking a power plant of the owner's choice, from 100 hp upwards. Stressed to ±8.5g, and featuring the 'Ultimate' wings with four full-span ailerons, a very interesting aspect of the design was an interconnected elevator-aileron system

Gordon Price with his Ultimate Pitts.　　　　　*(Gordon Price)*

whereby the ailerons acted as flaps with pitch input: 5 degrees of flap with 10 degrees of elevator. Shades of Arnold Wagner's KZ-8 were manifested once more. . . .

And what of the redoubtable Swiss, Wagner's one-time protégés who had risen to lead the aerobatic movement in Switzerland and capture many of the top honours in European competition? As if to underline their astonishing versatility and sheer airmanship, the three pilots Brandt,

'Ultimate' 10 DASH 100 (100 hp Lycoming).　　　*(Gordon Price)*

Schweizer and Müller not only switched in short order to aircraft types for WAC 1980 that were totally new to them – at Oshkosh they actually introduced between them two entirely new types to international aerobatics!

Chris Schweizer and Michel Brandt were both confirmed Pitts pilots of some years standing by the time 1980 arrived, but the cost of transporting their aeroplanes all the way across the Atlantic was prohibitive. At home the Swiss Aerobatic Association had only a tiny membership of a few dozen pilots, and even for practice they were forced to train over the border in neighbouring France, due to the noise problem in congested Switzerland.

Christen Eagle II (200 hp Lycoming).   *(Christen Industries)*

Span	19 ft 11 in (6 m)	**Height**	6 ft 6 in (1.98 m)
Length	18 ft 6 in (5.6 m)	**Empty weight**	1,025 lb (466 kg)
		Max speed	184 mph (296 km/h)
		Rate of climb	2,100 fpm (10.7 m/sec)
		Limit load	$+7, -5\,g$

The Eagles Aerobatic Team, flying the Christen Eagle I
(260 hp Lycoming).   (Christen Industries)

Flight Fantastic

But being ranked among the world's best pilots, and a threat even to the home team, Chris and Michel found a ready listener when they talked to a certain Mr Frank Christensen about acquiring the use of one of his aeroplanes for the competition.

Frank was the originator of an aerobatic biplane which he had brought out in America some three years previously to challenge the supremacy of the ubiquitous Pitts. An aerobatic pilot himself, he had collaborated with Curtis Pitts a while back in the design of an excellent oil system for inverted flight, which he had been marketing along with other aerobatic aircraft accessories under the umbrella of Christen Industries. Liking the Pitts design but, along with so many others, seeing room for much improvement, Frank took an enormous gamble in 1977 and put on the market a new aircraft type of his own, the Christen Eagle.

It was a kit-built, two-place biplane of very similar configuration to the Pitts S-2A – which by then had full certification and could be bought off the shelf – but it was a perfectionist homebuilder's dream. Everything about it, right down to the paint design of the finished machine, spelled beauty and quality. Perhaps the only obviously visible changes were the Eagle's streamlined cowling, canopy and state-of-the-art one-piece spring gear; but the design clean-up extended to many more subtle areas than these, and a respectable improvement in performance over the equivalent Pitts was gained with the Eagle's greater conservation of energy, together with a cleaner, neater flick roll. Even for a two-seater it had an excellent rate of climb and a roll rate of 187 degrees per second. It also had a price tag of $30,000*: more than the cost per seat of many factory built aircraft!

The inevitable spin-off from the original Eagle was a single-seat version, maintaining the larger size of the airframe but adding a 260 hp engine for top performance. Former US Champion Gene Soucy had persuaded Frank Christensen to put the Eagle I single-seat version together in 1978, for his

*Now nearer to $50,000 complete with prop and engine.

return to competition flying, and with it he took third place in the US Nationals after a five year lay-off. Still flying airshows with Charlie Hillard and Tom Poberezny under the banner of the 'Red Devils', Gene was mightily impressed by the aircraft and so were his partners: soon a brand new idea had taken shape, and the 'Eagles Aerobatic Flight Team' was born, campaigning the Eagle I across America. Composed of three individual US Champions, and led by the World Aerobatic Champion of 1972, they have proved an unbeatable American airshow formation.

It was a Christen Eagle I model that Brandt and Schweizer shared during WAC 1980, its début on the international scene. The aeroplane was a lot bigger and more powerful than the Pitts S-1s they normally flew, and they had only a few short but precious hours on type, maybe twelve in all, gleaned during practice sessions in America before the competition started. But the calibre of the two men was amply shown by their World Championship results with the unfamiliar machine: Michel finished seventh and Christian eighth.

The third Swiss pilot, Eric Müller, flew an even newer design of aircraft – a prototype in fact – which had only had its maiden flight on 23 June 1980, a mere 56 days before the start of the Championships.

Although he still kept the magnificent Acrostar for air displays, Müller had realized for some little while that it was no longer in the running with the latest machines which had appeared in the late 1970s; with the 1980 event being held in America, he also knew that he could not afford to ship his own aircraft across the Atlantic.

He had always been impressed with the CAP 20L, and when he heard of Auguste Mudry's plans for a new unlimited machine, the CAP 21, he immediately started a campaign of besieging the French constructor with telephone calls enquiring about the aircraft's progress and availability. Only the prototype existed, however, and eventually a deal was

Mudry CAP 21 prototype in inverted flight (200 hp Lycoming). (Author's collection)

struck whereby M. Mudry generously freighted the aeroplane over to America for its competition début, with Eric Müller sharing it in the World Championships with its test pilot, French Champion Louis Peña.

The big innovation with this machine was the wing. Thick, angular and symmetrical, it was longer in span but considerably less in area than the CAP 20L, with an aerofoil section especially designed for aerobatics by the computers of the great French Aérospatiale conglomerate. Overall the effect was a significant reduction in drag, which was aided by the lightweight glass fibre spring undercarriage. Flick-roll performance in its predecessors had always been found wanting, and this new wing was outstandingly successful in rectifying that fault. With powerful ailerons spanning 86 per cent of the wing, the rate of roll was also appreciably better.

Eric Müller compared its performance with his own 220 hp Acrostar, finding that most manoeuvres needed a far lower entry speed, especially vertical climbs, and that the CAP 21 had a much greater reserve of power, mainly thanks to reduced drag. Comparing rates of roll, he reckoned that for 360 degrees the CAP 21 took 1.8 seconds, the CAP 20L 2.3 seconds, the Acrostar 2.5 seconds.

With an unrefined prototype, and having only had the period 23 June to 15 July to try it out before it was crated up for departure, Eric Müller and Louis Peña flew the CAP 21 to ninth and tenth places respectively in the 1980 Championships: a remarkable achievement. The machine, a top-performance monoplane that was to be manufactured in series production, had at last posed a serious challenge to the only other comparable production monoplane available, which was the Czechoslovakian Zlin 50.

No need, of course, to point out that there was a sad dearth of Zlins at Oshkosh. But the solitary Zlin 50 pilot who transported his exotic bird all the way across the Atlantic, from Germany to America, easily made up for the absence of the rest. Manfred Strössenreuther, Germany's greatest post-war champion, had aerobatics in his blood ever since childhood

Manfred Strössenreuther.   *(Author's collection)*

days when his father took him to see the great pilots like Wolfrum, Greb and Pawolka. Blessed with the hands of an artist and the good looks of a film star, he appeared (according to one Oshkosh commentator) like "a star soccer forward amid a bunch of weekending airline pilots".

Manfred started aerobatics at 21, in 1969, under the tutelage of his flying-instructor father. From 9th place in the 1969 German Championships he gained 1st place in 1975, winning his first international contest in the Yugoslavian Zadar Cup in 1973. From 1979 onwards he became the unassailable German champion, exchanging his Pitts for the Zlin 50 which had become the ultimate aerobatic craft of the day. He soon became legendary for his own spectacular brand of airshow, specializing in flick rolls on take-off and long, low inverted passes just a few metres above the ground. At Oshkosh he quickly earned the nickname 'The Red Baron', and the crowd took him to their hearts. His brilliant flying resulted in 4th place overall in the championships.

Though flying was both profession and hobby, he vowed he would never tire of World Championships: he loved the camaraderie and friendship as well as the constant challenge. During the 1970s he moved up from 6th overall in 1976 to 4th in 1978; later, in 1984 he reached the magnificent position of 2nd in the world. But tragically for aerobatics, and for those who knew and loved him, Manfred was killed in a midair collision in March of 1986. He would never win that elusive title of World Champion which many thought would one day be his.

Next highest scorers among the Europeans were the French, with a full five-strong male team and female team. Though the Eastern Europeans were indefatigable in producing top-class women pilots, it was the French and Americans virtually alone among the Western nations who regularly fielded a competitive female team to challenge them. The French could not, however, shake the domination of the American girls in 1980.

Another new French aircraft also made its way to Oshkosh in addition to the CAP 21, and this was the ASA 200 of Noël Jourdan and Gérard Feugray, who placed thirteenth and twenty-second respectively. It was not dissimilar to the CAP 21 in concept, being an attempt to create an 'improved CAP 20' by substituting a better wing and a lighter undercarriage; but the method of realization was entirely different, and an extremely good aeroplane was the result. First of all, the wing chosen was that of the highly successful Stephens Akro – but redesigned by Noël Jourdan and mounted as a low wing in this instance. Next, an all-out effort was made to reduce weight by doing away with everything that was not *absolutely essential* (including starter), which achieved a very modest empty weight indeed of 420 kg (924 lb), and thus a healthy rate of climb. The rate of roll, aided by the short-span Stephens wing, was more than 240 degrees per second.

Significant for future development also was the design team's idea to mount the spring undercarriage on the fuselage underside, instead of the wings, with a view to permitting removal of the wings for road transportation: again the object was achieved admirably, with a dismantling time for one person of no more than an hour.

Louis Peña, test pilot of the CAP 21, was later to be inspired in part by the success of the ASA 200 project to venture forth on his own with a little CAP 21 derivative called the CAP-PEÑA.

Three times French Champion, he had learned to fly at 18 and immediately knew that to be a pilot was the only career for him, which is why he entered the French military service

Flight Fantastic

Louis Peña.   *(Author's collection)*

at the earliest opportunity. During his instructor training course in 1963 he would snatch every available moment to fly aerobatics, and soon he was good enough to be selected for the ALAT demonstration team which flew the Nord 3202.

There are always two threads running through French aerobatics, those of the civilian pilots and the military, and there have been times when the two have not seen eye to eye. Since the early 1970s, however, with the CAP aeroplanes becoming almost the universal mount in France, distinctions between the two have diminished and mutual liking and respect have grown; present-day Armée de l'Air pilots such as Claude Bessière and Patrick Paris – both recent French Champions – are extremely popular and vital members of the French Team.

This rapprochement was greatly aided in 1972 when the World Championships were held at the military base of Salon de Provence, and the Salon aerobatic team loaned a CAP 20 aircraft to the French Aerobatic Association for the championships. Louis Peña was one of the military pilots invited to fly the CAP, and thus WAC 1972 was his first World Championship.

The training and selection methods in France gradually firmed up into a selection process at the end of the season after the French Championship results, whereupon the team would go in spring to a training camp for either one week or two, depending on whether a World Championship was in the offing, and then a further two weeks of training would be arranged immediately prior to that year's Championship, World or European. During these practice camps all pilots would live, eat and work together, and in time a good spirit of cameraderie grew up quite easily.

After cementing a good relationship with Auguste Mudry while flying the CAPs, Lous Peña was delighted at the opportunity to join Avions Mudry as test and demonstration pilot on leaving military service in 1975, and although he later moved to the Dax Aero Club as CFI, he still went back to fly the prototype CAP 20L and CAP 21 as chief test pilot. It was this excellent relationship with his former employer that greatly helped Louis in his CAP–PEÑA design project, started in 1983 (though conceived much earlier), for which he used the CAP 21 fuselage as a basis and then added a wing of his own, designed by Michel Dozières, using the wing section of Loudenslager's Laser 200. With few resources and little

technical expertise himself, Louis rather timorously rang up M. Mudry one day and asked if he would object if he based his design on a smaller version of the CAP 21.

"Object?" said Mudry, "Of course not! Any help you want, just ask. My design bureau is at your disposal for the calculations, and I shall be most interested to see the result."

Needless to say, it was not only the calculations that were produced at Avions Mudry; and the help received by Peña in both advice and building materials was beyond price. In recognition, when the little bird first flew in July 1984, Louis combined both CAP and PEÑA in its name.

The British contingent at Oshkosh featured three experienced pilots and two very new to international championships, of whom the outstanding team member was ex-RAF pilot Philip Meeson. Aided by the generosity of Freddie Laker, and by dint of marathon fund-raising efforts, they managed to transport their own Pitts aeroplanes to America for the competition. The loss of Neil Williams was still keenly felt, for he had been a source of inspiration and enthusiasm for the team effort as a whole, as well as its star pilot; and James Black was now no longer flying but had taken on the responsibility of Chief Judge for the Championships. Nevertheless, Meeson proved well able to carry the banner for the British and earned himself a place in the finals, reaching a very respectable twelfth position overall.

It was only his second World Championship, and it promised well for the future: but although he was to win the British National title four times in all, hence qualifying for the team, the pressures of starting up his own freight airline shortly afterwards put a stop to his competition activities. Aerobatics still remained a part of his life, however, and in 1982 he founded the Marlboro Aerobatic Team, a trio flying Pitts Specials in an excellent and very popular airshow routine. With his two partners Nigel Lamb and Ian Peacocke, he ensured that the Marlboro show always featured more solo display fireworks than the average run of formation performances, and Philip never lost that edge of precision which hallmarks the competition pilot.

Before leaving the British scene, mention should be made of Richard Goode, who started competing as a Pitts pilot and in turn, like so many others, changed to a monoplane design. In 1981 he bought from Michel Brandt an unfinished Stephens Akro project for which Michel had designed a special CAP 21 type aerofoil. This Richard proceeded to modify, as he does all his aeroplanes, bringing it to the 1982 World Championships as the 'Pace Spirit'. Misfortune struck, however, before the machine could fulfil its promise, for Richard was ill during the 1982 Championships and was later involved in a crash which completely wrote off the aircraft. But the performance of that particular Stephens Akro variant was impressive, and a similar fuselage-wing combination was later to prove extraordinarily successful as the Extra 230.

Since 1980, newer campaigners under the British colours include three times National Champion Peter Kynsey and fellow Pitts pilot John Harper, both dedicated members of the celebrated Tiger Club where aerobatics at all levels are still practised enthusiastically; and on the monoplane side the very talented Tony Bianchi, CAP 20 and 21 pilot, whose normal line of business has him flying anything from Blériots to Spitfires for air displays and the film industry.

Mention should be made, too, of a gifted young British pilot who only once appeared in an international competition, and that was in the European Championships of 1981.

Philip Meeson leads the Marlboro aerobatic formation team.
(courtesy of Marlboro)

David Perrin, crazy to fly since boyhood and a professional pilot almost as soon as he obtained his licence, was a member of the fabulous Rothmans Aerobatic Team and ended up as their solo (Pitts S-2S) pilot after the full team itself

David Perrin, Rothmans Solo Display pilot 1980–81.
(courtesy of Rothmans)

disbanded in 1980. Few people at so young an age could have made such a deep impression both as a pilot and as a person; as a formation flyer he was nothing short of phenomenal, and his promise as a competitor was borne out by reaching the finals of that first competition he entered in 1981. But in the spring of 1982 he met his death in a helicopter accident during the filming of *High Road to China*, and that promise was never to be fulfilled in the greater arena of World Championships.

Apart from those participants already mentioned, the 1980 World Championships also included strong teams from Australia and South Africa, showing sure signs of a healthy growth of the sport of aerobatics in those countries. Indeed, Australia came from virtually nowhere to take the third team place in America. But both these countries will be examined in detail when we get to Chapter 21 – Masters of Aerobatics.

Not to be overlooked was the appearance of a staunch pilot from New Zealand, who had been a World Championship contender since Kiev in 1976, and this was Pam Collings. In that earlier contest she had appeared under her maiden name of Pamela Lock, accompanied by fellow New Zealander David Owen in a borrowed Zlin 526, though both were very new to international aerobatics and finished at the bottom of the list. Pam in fact had put up a good performance in her Pitts after spending some months in America taking serious instruction, subsequently importing the first Pitts S-1S into New Zealand. Due to the enormous expense of travelling to Europe she missed the 1978 WAC, when Pitts pilot Allen Hogan fared rather better and finished thirty-seventh out of 48 men, having trained and travelled with the Australian team.

Determined to try her luck again in 1980, Pam was fortunate to be able to train with the American team and use one of their aircraft: such, again, is the generosity of fellow aerobatic competitors. In between times she had had no Unlimited level experience whatsoever, for there were no competitions at that level at home in New Zealand! Aerobatics certainly were practised, and contests had been run for many years at the less advanced levels, the longest established dating back to 1949. But the lack of competitive machines inevitably meant a lack of top-level pilots, and Pamela found herself virtually alone in her keenness to participate internationally.

Her present interests are channelled into a different form of competition, precision flying, which still offers the challenge she seeks though in a different discipline. But she promises not to stay away from world aerobatics too long.

Now, having surveyed the more seasoned campaigners at Oshkosh, let us end this section with a look at the newcomers who made their very first World Championship appearance in 1980: the Italians.

Though they had not previously been at WACs, Italian pilots had been contesting European events since 1965 when one of their most colourful characters, Antonio Costanzo, had competed in the Lockheed Trophy. Famed as the proprietor of a glass eye with which he delighted in performing antics of a stomach-turning variety, Costanzo was a military pilot who flew a Zlin 326 appropriately registered I-COST.

One very excellent Italian pilot, Guido Zuccoli, had emigrated to Australia in the mid-1970s and flew in Kiev in 1976 representing his newly adopted country. He is still an extremely good aerobatic pilot, but tends to spend more time these days in the cockpit of his personal Sea Fury (as indeed who would not?). He will be encountered again in Chapter 21. Zuccoli, together with fellow Italians Sergio Dallan and Pino Valenti, took part in the European Championship at Chateauroux in 1977 which was won by Soviet champion Victor Letsko.

By this time a regular series of Italian contests had started in 1976 with the first Trofeo Crippa. This trophy commemorated artist and pilot Roberto Crippa, the founding father of organized aerobatics in Italy, who by sheer enthusiasm had started up the first aerobatic group at the Milan Aero Club flying Zlins and Jungmanns. He had died in a spin accident in 1972. Sergio Dallan, the outstanding Italian pilot ever since those days, started as a member of the Crippa group.

Sergio was born in 1944 and started flying at the age of 21, with aerobatics immediately capturing his main interest. Like Swiss pilot Christian Schweizer, Sergio is a hands-on genius in the mechanical side of aviation and started out with the Milan aerobatic group as an engineer, soon afterwards being enlisted as a pilot. He still works as Chief Engineer with the Milan Aero Club to this day.

Although Sergio was keen to try his luck at the 1978 World Championships, his only available mount was a Zlin 526 and the Italian Aero Club pronounced it too old for the job. They followed up this disappointing decision, however, by purchasing two CAP 20Ls for the team, and arranged for a

serious programme of training in preparation for the 1980 Oshkosh Championships. His fellow team-mates were Nicola Colangelo, Aldo Locatelli, Diego Nardi and Massimo Lucia. Dallan had started a project with Lucia, constructing a modified Steen Skybolt for competition, until Lucia sadly met his death shortly after Oshkosh in a training accident.

Finishing in twenty-first place, Sergio Dallan easily outranked the other Italians who ended up clustered in the last half-dozen men. But it was only their first World Championship, and from among their number Nicola Colangelo at least would begin to be heard of with ever more promising results.

These two leading Italians, Dallan and Colangelo, soon afterwards made their mark in aerobatics in similar yet very different ways, when Italy hosted the European Aerobatic Championships in Ravenna in 1983. Both came up with sensational top-performance aeroplanes for the occasion, which were destined to set new standards in monoplane design for the other western nations.

Sergio Dallan's aircraft was his own reworking of the Mudry CAP 21 with all the vital improvements that knowledgeable commentators had recommended right from the start: a more powerful engine (260 hp), aerodynamic clean-up on cowling and canopy, wing-root fairings, and fuselage-mounted landing gear to permit wing dismantling. In typically fun-poking Dallan style, the machine emerged calling itself *The Silver Chicken*. But Papa Mudry back at the factory took due note of these excellent modifications to his 1980 design, and soon a CAP 230 was to appear with an even bigger

Italian Champion Sergio Dallan and CAP 21 DS 'The Silver Chicken'. (Tony Lloyd)

power plant – 300 hp – together with many other of the Dallan features. Sergio and his CAP 21 DS won an outstanding fifth place overall in the 1983 European Championships, together with a bronze medal in the Unknown Compulsory programme.

Competing with him for top honours, Nicola Colangelo appeared at the same contest with a brand-new Stephens

Nicola Colangelo in cockpit of the prototype EA230. Sadly he was not to compete again after the 1984 World Championships, having lost his life in an accident to a (non-aerobatic) light aircraft in which he was a passenger.
(Sergio Dallan)

Akro derivative which was the prototype of an exciting new design. This machine was the brainchild of the very gifted German pilot/engineer Walter Extra, and was as fundamental a redesign of the basic Stephens mid-wing configuration as were the Loudenslager and Haigh versions before it. There was a difference, moreover, which made the project very interesting to the ring of admirers that quickly gathered to inspect the gleaming blue monoplane: the Extra 230 was intended to be custom-built to order.

Twenty-nine years old and already a seasoned aircraft builder endowed with a perfectionism that would do credit to Frank Christensen, Walter Extra had started competitions almost as soon as he qualified in both glider and powered aerobatics. He had been producing modified Pitts aircraft for 2½ years in between his studies as a mechanical engineer, but now he had decided to bring out an aeroplane entirely his own, top to bottom – not only the fuselage, cockpit and tail, but more importantly, the wing.

Inspired by the already proven aerofoil of the CAP 21, Extra designed a similar wing section by slimming down the thickness, graduating it from 15 per cent at the root to 12 per cent at the tip; in the full-span ailerons he featured the square-cut trailing edge which was a very old idea brought right up to date. As a result the all-important roll performance in aileron and flick rolls was delightfully responsive; and with the 230 hp engine you could sail round a climbing quadruple vertical roll, and still have penetration enough to draw a neat climbing line at the top before kicking over into a stall turn. Perhaps the most impressive quality of the machine was the power reserve you never had to use: with its very low minimum speed regime, entry speeds for most aerobatic figures were significantly less than you would expect, and you found yourself working much of the time with about 75 per cent power instead of roaring through a sequence at full throttle!

By the 1984 World Championships three pilots were flying the EA 230, including Walter Extra himself who achieved eighteenth place in the competition, his best WAC result ever. The following year in the European Championships, no fewer than seven pilots were using the new machine, with a total of eight built so far – and that seven included the whole of the pace-setting Swiss team of Müller, Schweizer, Hagander, united for the first time ever in its choice of the same aircraft type in any one contest.

EA 230 owned by Christian Schweizer and the Hagander brothers. (Inset) Talented young Swiss pilots Nils (in cockpit) and Erik Hagander.   (Fred Podolak, via Erik Hagander)

20

Spotlight on Eastern Europe

Back in action again for the European (1981) and World (1982) Championships, the Soviet and Czech pilots quickly demonstrated that they had not lost their fabulous form. And with so many new developments in the way of aircraft design from the West, all eyes were now turned curiously in their direction to see what innovations their manufacturers might have devised.

With the Zlin 50, of course, there was no need for second thoughts about the design: once mastered by its pilots it performed superlatively, and, equipped with engines of 300 hp from 1982 onwards, it remained outstandingly competitive.

But with the Yak 50 the story was a different one. It derived from a long and honourable lineage, but this did not necessarily commend it as an aerobatic aircraft of the 1980s. Moreover, though it was still capable of getting round the ever more complex and taxing figures that were becoming *de rigueur* in World Championships, it was a heavy machine and laborious to fly, which attributes served it badly as regards the life of the airframe.

For some time it had been rumoured that a new Yak was on its way, and sure enough, at Spitzerberg in August 1982 the USSR team arrived with the first example of the all-metal Yak 55.

Once again the machine had been built around the engine – the Vedenyev 360 hp M-14P radial – whose size and weight determined so many of the design parameters. But, apart from the inevitable similarity at first glance of fuselage and cowling shape, the new model was in fact startlingly different. Shorter in length and span, more slender and with an angular fin and rudder, it featured that ubiquitous one-piece landing gear together with the mid-wing configuration which the Stephens Akro devotees had established as the state-of-the-art formula. The 'Laser-Yak', the Americans called it, but,

although it invited comparison, the Yak 55 suffered side-by-side with its light and compact American cousin: its massive, thick, symmetrical section wing and wide, straddling under-carriage gave it a ponderous look which was accentuated by the blunt nose.... But, as always with the Yak, it was quite a different proposition in flight: here, to the accompaniment of that wonderful engine note, an excellent visual impact was presented and a healthy performance, thanks to an improved power/weight ratio compared to the Yak 50.

It was, however, reportedly difficult to fly. Only one Soviet pilot flew the machine in Spitzerberg, Michael Molchaniuk, the Yak test pilot, whose previous championship placings had been around the sixth and seventh mark. But he unfortunately went down with an illness after his first flight, and consequently – though he soldiered on through the rest of the contest – the machine was not shown off to its best advantage. It was, in fact, still completing its test programme, and if it seemed awkward to handle it was doubtless still suffering from teething troubles. Though finishing in 16th place overall, this score belied Molchaniuk's particularly good performance in the Final Freestyle, where he regained his form and used the Yak's full performance envelope to good effect.

The 33-year-old Victor Smolin now appeared as the USSR's top contender, having won the European Championship title in 1981. Curiously enough, in the Socialist Countries Championships – which had, of course, continued being held annually – Smolin repeatedly found himself in third place behind his fellow team-members Nikolai Nikitiuk and Yurgis Kairis; but in the 1982 World Championships, though Kairis and Nikitiuk made an excellent start, winning the gold and silver medals in the first programme, Smolin eventually emerged head and shoulders above them. There was quite a strong tussle between Smolin and the three top Americans;

Spitzerberg, scene of the 1982 World Championships.(via IAC)

but two Zlin 50 exponents – Manfred Strössenreuther and Petr Jirmus – eventually outranked both Loudenslager and Weeks of the US team, leaving only Henry Haigh to challenge Smolin's supremacy. Thanks to a better consistency than his team-mates throughout all four programmes, Haigh finished in second place; he was pipped by a mere 5 points.

Victor Smolin, an unassuming, gentle giant of few words, attested to the highly efficient Soviet team training system. Under Nazhmudinov's guidance the pilots would fly upwards of 100 aerobatic hours a year, many of them in their local clubs and competitions, though often the 'first team' members were too busy with international activities to challenge the USSR National Championship! Team practice sessions of 2–3 weeks each would take place at strategic periods: in January to get back into condition after the winter rest, in April/May to start the season in earnest, and then an intensive preparation in July shortly before the World Championships.

An instructor in his home aero club at Leningrad, Victor had started flying in 1967 and was a seasoned campaigner of over ten years experience in home and international contests. He was already eminent in aviation at home, and had been leader of the Soviet National Aviation Sports Team since 1979. When he came to Spitzerberg in 1982 he had already won the 1981 European Championships, so when he won the World title, followed shortly by the USSR National Championship in September, it proved to be a crowning two years in his career.

As a long-time Yak 50 pilot, he was one of those who naturally wanted a better mount for modern competition but at the same time had doubts about the 'unfinished' new Yak model, which did not yet seem to strike the right note. With several wing configurations having been tried – one of quite considerably longer span which was never seen in competition – the Yak 55 presented at Spitzerberg was the third prototype made so far. Along with the thick leading edge and zero dihedral/zero incidence pioneered in such machines as the Acrostar, the wing was extraordinarily strong as well, and in tests had been taken to 16g before suffering permanent deformation! Its full-span ailerons gave it a splendid roll rate, but contributed to its awkward handling with extreme lightness at low speeds and heaviness at high speeds.

By 1984 the wing had undergone a complete and felicitous change, with sweep-back and a reduction in surface area, and with its profile considerably slimmed down. It flicked better and rolled faster this year, and the new wing now clearly satisfied the right criteria. But improvements did not stop there: yet one more very interesting change was to be seen in the summer of 1985, and that was a linked elevator-

Yak 55 with new wing, photographed in 1984.   (Tony Bianchi)

Yak 55 (360 hp 9-cylinder Vedeneyev M-14P). (Aviaexport)

(Inset) Victor Smolin lands his Yak 50 after winning the World Championship at Spitzerbeg (note three-blade Hoffmann propeller). (Carl Lang)

aileron system (again harking back to the Acrostar) for better longitudinal response at lower angles of attack. And with more time on the machine, the Soviet pilots were flying it much better.

The Yak 55 was not, however, the only new bird in the collection. In 1983 it became known that for the first time a manufacturer other than Yakovlev had taken a hand in aerobatic design for the Soviet Team. The result was expected, with great anticipation and interest, in 1984.

At this stage in our story, it is time to spotlight one more Eastern European country – or rather, Central European – which has had a long-standing aviation tradition and a close involvement with World Championship aerobatics since the

early days. In 1962 Hungary hosted the 2nd WAC at Budapest, and now in 1984 it was host again, this time in south-eastern Békéscsaba.

This small land-locked country, not much bigger than Ireland or Indiana, is sandwiched between Austria on the west and the Soviet Union on the east, and forms a true meeting point between the two vastly differing ways of life. Although the Magyar nation has existed independently since before the year 900 AD, for the past 4½ centuries the territory itself has been either extended, divided or decimated, depending on the fortunes of the great powers into whose hands it fell. Subjugation by the Turks for 150 years followed by 200 years of annexation by the Austrian Hapsburgs added their richly varied overlay to a nation with already strong traditions of good humour, superb horsemanship, fiery food and wine, and an independence of spirit which has led them continually to rebel – sometimes at great and horrific cost – against their various overlords.

In the early years of mechanical flight, the dual monarchy of Austro-Hungary encompassed a vast territory which included Czechoslovakia and parts of present-day Poland, Romania, Yugoslavia, the Ukraine and Italy. After World War

Span	8.2 m (26 ft 11 in)
Length	7.5 m (24 ft 7 in)
Empty weight	640 kg (1,408 lb)
Max speed	320 km/h (200 mph)
Rate of climb	16 m/sec (3,150 fpm)
Limit load	± 9 *g*

Antal Bánhidi.   *(via Gabor Fekecs)*

l, Hungary was prised free of this not always happy alliance, but lost at the same time two-thirds of her former territories and 50 per cent of her population. When we speak of modern Hungary, therefore, we speak of a small nucleus wrenched from the heart of a lost empire.

The Budapest of 1914, where 30,000 Hungarians saw their first looping exhibition performed on a Blériot by the French Baron Pasquier, was one of the glittering capitals of nineteenth century European culture; among Pasquier's audience were the Archduchess Augusta, Archduke Joseph, and Prince Louis of Bavaria.

Under the constraints of the Versailles Treaty aviation in post-1918 Hungary was severely limited, but nonetheless popular, with gliders much in evidence. Power flying was given its earliest impetus in 1921 by the Sport Flying Club of the Institute of Technology in Budapest, where in 1926 Árpád Lampich designed and built the little 35 hp L-4 Bohóc (Clown). During the years 1927–30 this aircraft was widely displayed by Károly Kaszala, but naturally didn't lend itself to anything spectacular in the way of aerobatics!

Hungary's great aerobatic innovator of the 1930s was Antal Bánhidi, a graduate of the Institute of Technology, who had

his first encounter with state-of-the-art aerobatics on a trip to Sweden in 1929. He returned afire with enthusiasm to build a first-rate Hungarian aerobatic machine, and the result was the BL-5, a two-seat biplane trainer, which he designed in collaboration with Lampich. Bánhidi was a student pilot at the time and had only just soloed, so in order to get the machine certified for aerobatics a test pilot had to be hired for the official demonstration. To his disgust, however, when he arrived at the airfield the test pilot refused to fly without additional bracing wires being installed, and try as he may, Bánhidi was unable to convince him otherwise. With the party of Aviation Authority officials about to depart, our hero saw nothing for it but to duck quickly out of sight, climb stealthily into the cockpit himself, and illicitly fly his own demonstration sequence – which was a series of loops.

The BL-5 duly got its aerobatic rating, but Bánhidi awaited his punishment in trepidation. Eventually it arrived: a stern letter from the authorities and a painful fine for what amounted to a whole list of crimes – taking off without permission, flying solo without an instructor present, in charge of an aeroplane without a licence, performing aerobatics without a rating.... But at the same time they awarded him his full pilot's licence! His machine soon became the principal aerobatic trainer in Hungary throughout the early thirties.

Bánhidi's next aeroplane, in 1930, was the 100 hp Gerle

Flight Fantastic

(Turtle dove), with which he acquired a growing international reputation. He was entirely self taught: although he knew of the advanced manoeuvres being flown by such as the great Fieseler, he had no idea of the techniques involved, and indeed he only discovered for himself how to fly the slow roll (in the BL-5) whilst trying unsuccessfully to master the flick roll!

He had seen fellow-pilot Benno Fiala perform a bunt in 1928 in a foreign registered Ju 47, and managed to reproduce this successfully in his own machine; but despite repeated attempts the full outside loop eluded him. He had actually given it up as impossible for the Gerle when in 1932 he was invited to give a demonstration in Berlin, so he decided to have another try in honour of the occasion. This time he achieved success by means of starting the loop with the push upwards after half-rolling to the inverted position. A glance at his programme for the 1932 Berlin display shows that he was performing slow rolls, outside (negative) loops, Vertical and Horizontal 8s, a rolling eight* and a push up into two vertical rolls from inverted. Not bad for a 100 hp Genet Major!

Apart from a lone entry by János Majoros at the Zurich meeting of 1937, coming ninth in Category A with a Klemm 35, Hungarian pilots rarely tried their hands at competition aerobatics during the prolific inter-war years, no doubt due to a lack of competitive aeroplanes able to take on the 400–600 hp monsters of the French and German professional pilots. Caught up in the orbit of Mussolini's Italy and Hitler's Germany, Hungary began to receive supplies of Bücker Jungmanns as military trainers in the late 1930s, but with these – together with the later Bestmanns – her young lads were taught the essential skills of flying for an altogether different purpose: that of war.

World War II brought unprecedented suffering and devastation to Hungary, with virtually all aircraft being destroyed when the Germans retreated, and with yet another ban on flying as the aftermath. But with Hungarian ingenuity (remember the Rubik cube?) they managed by dint of salvaging bits and pieces, and building new wings, to reconstruct no less than 42 Jungmann aircraft by the year 1947 when the post-war flying ban was lifted. These continued operating until spares ran out in 1953.

The Hungarian Aeronautic Association organized regular air displays during the immediate post-war period, when the outstanding pilots included Antal Hepper (Jungmann), Endre Karsai (Klemm 35) and Lászlo Kalmár. With supplies arriving in the early fifties of the Czechoslovakian Bestmann-type Zlin 381 trainer, a new three-ship aerobatic formation team was founded under the leadership of Ferenc Páloczi who already had a considerable reputation as a solo display pilot. Páloczi exemplified the prevalent style of gentle, harmonious aerobatics so appropriate to the graceful monoplane, and the team became famous for precision displays while tied together with cables 5 m (16 ft) in length.

This tradition of formation aerobatics has featured strongly ever since, always with the country's top solo pilots in the team, the aircraft changing over the years from Yak-11 to Zlin 50.

With new developments in aerobatic aircraft came changes in flying style in the late fifties, precipitated by the prodigious successes of the Czechs. Visits by a Czech team of Z-226s and by the Lockheed Trophy winner Vilém Krysta in 1956/7 convinced Hungarian pilots and instructors that the key to international success lay in re-equipping with Z-226 and 326 types in place of their old fleet of Z-381s. Gradually they became more competitive, and in the very first World Aerobatic Championships of 1960 Hungary was able to send two good contestants equipped with Z-226 Trener 6s.

Undoubtedly the high spot in Hungarian aerobatics was the year 1962, when from 17 to 29 July the ancient city of Budapest played host to the second World Aerobatic Championships at Budaörs airport.

The very first of the biennial FAI Championships, as we have seen, took place in Bratislava (a city which was itself once part of Hungary), where the home team set the pattern for future championships by carrying off all the honours. The top Hungarian pilot of the time was Endre Karsai, an outstanding powered aircraft and glider pilot of considerable experience; he and the younger Zoltán Pál returned from Czechoslovakia with fifteenth and twentieth places respectively, from a field of 29 contestants.

To tackle the 1962 event they set up a training squad of eight up-and-coming pilots under the expert coaching of Ernö Mandl, with two training camps and a series of selection contests to decide the eventual team of five. The three Trener formation pilots successfully made the team – Sándor Katona, Péter Fejes and Miklós Fejér, who placed 6th, 8th and 12th respectively in the World Championship – together with Zoltán Pál who improved his previous position by one place to come in nineteenth.

Péter Fejes won programme 1 of the finals, and Sándor Katona won the last Free Programme. But the dark horse of the team was fifth man József Tóth, a glider aerobatics pilot with very little power aerobatics experience, who now managed to beat the Czechs at their own game and with their own aircraft by winning the World Championship title with a Zlin 326A.

Despite the conflict of prevalent styles – the elegantly harmonious classical style and the Czech 'dynamic' style (described in Chapter 12) – by an adroit combination of the two the Hungarians came away not only with the Aresti Cup won by József Tóth as overall champion, but with the Nesterov Cup for the top-scoring team of pilots. It was their finest hour in international aerobatics.

Tóth was an aircraft engineer for the Hungarian airline Malév, and was already well known for his glider aerobatic displays. At the time of the 1962 championships he had only just taken his PPL and was by far the newest power pilot of the whole team, with virtually no competition experience. Nevertheless, displaying the calm nerve of a veteran in the face of so many well-seasoned opponents from nine different countries, he managed a victory by 19 points over his nearest rival, Soviet pilot Vladislav Loichikov. He had practised unremittingly to prepare for the great event, and Neil Williams later averred that Tóth had spent over 70 hours working on vertical rolls alone! His reward was a handsome one: he was offered training as an airline pilot, and served as a Malév captain for about ten years until he left the country in the early 1970s. He is living now in Canada.

József Tóth's was the last successful challenge to the new 'dynamic' aerobatics. The Bezák-inspired style represented progress, and progress is inexorable. Although he went over to compete for the British Lockheed Trophy the following year – where he tied in sixth place – Tóth never again managed an outstanding World Championship rating, and in the next World Championship of 1964 he unfortunately fell sick and managed no better than twenty-seventh.

*Rolling eight = a horizontal figure-of-eight consisting of two rolling circles, one with rolls to the inside and one with rolls to the outside.

Opening Ceremony at WAC 62, Budaörs Airport, Budapest: Czechoslovakian Zlins in foreground, USSR Yak-18Ps in right background with KZ-8 visible to their left. (Imre Z Nagy)

Gold, Silver and Bronze Medallists in WAC 62: (left to right) József Tóth, Vladislav Loichikov, Ladi Bezák. (Imre Z Nagy)

1963 was a particularly busy year, with no less than two international championships organized within the Socialist countries, both of which were attended by Hungarian pilots. They also held their own first Hungarian National Championships, where Tóth won the title from a field of 19 participants. And in addition, they took part in the British Lockheed contest where Tóth came sixth and Péter Fejes eighth. From a pre-1962 situation where the World Championships represented a rare opportunity to fly competitively, suddenly aerobatics were all the rage!

In 1964 the Hungarians took part with equal enthusiasm in the World Championship in Spain, Tóth flying a Z-326 modified to his own specifications with an M 337 engine and variable pitch propeller. But here Péter Fejes was the only Hungarian finalist: he achieved fourteenth place. This was a disappointment after their previous record, and in the 1966 World Championship in Moscow things were no better, with none of their pilots reaching the finals.

From now onward there was a lull in Hungarian aerobatics which kept them out of the world's top ranking pilots for a ten year period. To make matters worse, Péter Fejes, a very experienced team member, instructor and airline pilot, died in the left-hand seat when his Hungarian Airlines TU-134 crashed in 1977.

In the mid-1970s, they took a long hard look at the state of the sport and realized that something must be done. The Home Defence Association, which is the organizing body behind all sport flying in Hungary, joined forces with the Agplane Service – once a government agency, now a firm in

At the 1983 Hungarian National Championships: 1st László Tóth, 2nd András Molnár, 3rd Tibor Pászti. (Gyula Rozman)

Flight Fantastic

its own right – and new resources were injected into aerobatics. A new national competition was organized, known as the Nyirség Cup, to take place annually on Nyiregyhaza airfield in eastern Hungary where agpilots are trained. The first Nyirség Cup was won in 1977 by András Molnár, a new young pilot who has won the cup twice and has continued in the forefront of Hungarian aerobatics ever since. Molnár, together with fellow Agplane Service Instructors Lászlo Tóth, a five-times Nyirség Cup winner, and Tibor Pászti (who sports a beard of epic proportions), became the backbone of the Hungarian international team from then onwards.

Tragically, the team was again hard hit by another air disaster shortly before the World Championships in 1982, which cost the lives of two of their best pilots, Lászlo Simon and Péter Witek, together with the gifted female pilot Katalin Hollóyné Tóth and three other male pilots from the pool. Katalin, together with Eva Tóth, had gone to Kiev as Hungary's first two female World Championship pilots back in 1976. The team's AN-2 hit a hillside near Budapest and altogether nine squad members were killed, including their trainer and three engineers. The blow immediately destroyed any hopes of a good placing in the Spitzerberg contest, even though for the first time in many years they now had a fleet of the latest Zlin 50 aircraft.

Many of the team's earlier problems had revolved around their lack of competitive aeroplanes for the sport: while the Americans and Western Europeans had forged ahead with Pitts, Acrostar, CAP20/21 and Stephens Akro types, and the Soviets and Czechs had their Yak 50 and Zlin 50 variants, Hungarian pilots were still soldiering on right up to 1981 with the graceful but elderly Zlin 526, a design originally dating back to the year 1965.

It was with much rejoicing, therefore, that instructors at the Agplane Service's flying school took delivery in 1982 of three brand spanking new Zlin 50LAs which as team members they were able to use in training and in competition. This brought them right back into the running with some of the most sophisticated equipment available.

Two more Zlin 50s purchased by the Home Defence Association arrived in 1983, with a third delivered in late 1984. With two years of training on the new aircraft the Hungarians were in peak form when they came to stage the World Aerobatic Championships for the second time, in August 1984 at Békéscsaba.

This was an airfield with strong historical connections. It was here in September 1911 that aviation pioneer András Kvasz demonstrated powered flight to an enraptured audience in an aircraft of his own construction, and after returning there from the 1914–18 war his devoted work helped make it a great centre for sport aviation. On this field, too, Hungarian astronaut Bertalan Farkas was trained; and Békéscsaba also hosted two of the Socialist Countries championships, in 1974 and 1979. The inhabitants of Békés County were now ready again to give a warm Hungarian welcome to the 65 competitors who arrived to take over the airfield in August 1984.

The start of the contest was not a propitious one from the point of view of weather, with most of western Europe socked in for days on end. Teams were delayed crossing over from as near as Austria next door, and the Spanish formation almost started an international incident when they detoured from their flightplanned route to avoid thunderstorms, and found themselves being buzzed by Hungarian MiGs!

Peter Besenyei, top scoring Hungarian pilot at Békéscsaba.
(Foma photograph)

USA team aircraft being loaded into C5A Galaxy for transport to Frankfurt and Hungary.

(USAF photo by Georg Wegemann, via IAC)

All was carried off with characteristic good humour, however, and later the weather smiled on Békéscsaba and all championship flights were completed well ahead of schedule.

From overseas there was the usual strong entry from the USA, who sent five men and four women pilots, their nine aircraft having been airlifted intact in an Air Force C5A Galaxy all the way to Frankfurt. Without Leo Loudenslager this time, their top contenders were Kermit Weeks and Henry Haigh, who finished in third and fourth places respectively, along with new WAC competitors Harold Chappell, Alan Bush and Gene Beggs. Three of the four girls were first-timers, with 1982 'veteran' Brigitte de Saint Phalle joined by Debby Rihn, who won the women's overall bronze medal at her first attempt, plus Julie Pfile, who finished ninth, and Linda Meyers, gold medallist in programme 1.

There was also a very professional turn-out from the Australians who had earlier that year staged a lavish World Aerobatic Super-Challenge in Melbourne and Sydney (see Chapter 21) and were obviously well on form. Their top scorer, Frank Fry, finished eighth overall and won a bronze in programme 1, which put him well up with the top pilots of the world.

Among the usual World Championship 'regulars' there were the Romanians with their two 260 hp Zlin 50s and the Spanish who had been similarly equipped with Zlin 50s by their Central Aeronautical Federation in 1980; the French, West Germans, Italians, Swiss and British; and of course the USSR, Czechoslovakia and Hungary. But no sign of the Polish team, whose aircraft were being worked on at the factory, nor of the German Democratic Republic, though it was known that the GDR was still waiting and planning for a fleet of Zlins to bring them back into the competition arena.

A newcomer to World competition in 1984, and a very welcome one, was 37-year-old Austrian pilot Walter Egger with his Pitts S-1S.

Austria had always had her aerobatics exponents – military pilots in the main – and the Bücker Jungmann had reigned as the top favourite machine both before and after World War II. But it was not until the late 1960s that domestic competitions started, under the leadership of Herbert Thonhauser and Peter Lambert, and then they were always dogged by the problem of obtaining suitable machines. Lambert, however, took part in the Zadar Cup in Yugoslavia in 1973 and came tenth out of 20 contestants, an encouraging result; and four Austrian pilots also flew in the first FAI European Championship in Esbjerg, in 1975, though they finished well down at the bottom of the list.

The first giant stride towards competitiveness on an international level was made in the late 1970s, when the first Pitts Specials came to Austria. Leader of the field at that time was architect Erich Stiasny, who took the sport seriously enough to attend special training courses with the Hungarian and

283

The magnificent Sukhoi Su-26 at Békéscsaba, 1984, with original wing.
(Inset) Cockpit view showing clear-vision panel.

(Tony Bianchi)

Su-26M in 1985 with new wing, lightened and strengthened.

(Foma photograph)

Petr Jirmus, World Aerobatic
Champion 1984, European
Champion 1983 and 1985.
(Author's collection)

(Su-26M)
Span   7.8 m (25 ft 7 in)
Length   6.82 m (22 ft 5 in)
Empty weight   805 kg (1,771 lb)
Max speed   330 km/h (205 mph)
Limit load   +12, −10 *g*

Flight Fantastic

A helping hand for Austrian Champion Walter Egger, from his two little boys.   *(via Walter Egger)*

without hesitation and reposition at a safer height, which earned him much respect. After one particularly unfortunate flight he was next seen being driven around the airfield on a lap of honour, in a motorcycle sidecar, laughing and brandishing the Austrian flag!

Manfred Strössenreuther arrived with his new 300 hp Zlin 50LS, his previous mount being now the property of South African pilot Peter Celliers. Peter himself, despite an attempt to cross over to participate in the event, was regrettably refused a visa and had to return to Austria; it transpired that the Hungarian organizers, so exemplary in all other respects, had failed to issue invitations to South Africa – quite contrary to the non-political rules of the FAI. Meanwhile Manfred's new Zlin confusingly carried the same registration as his old one, D-EMUJ – perhaps for sentimental reasons? – or maybe for good luck?

Whatever the reason, he had scant need of luck to help him on his way to three silver medals in the individual programmes and an overall second place in the Championships. His fine flying spoke for itself.

The Soviet Union as usual fielded full teams of five men and five women, and once more the women swept the board of medals. Moscow-born Khalide Makagonova, who had

Khalide Makagonova, 1984 Women's World Champion.
    (via Kasum Nazhmudinov)

Czech team trainers. He had a particularly good reason for wanting to reach a high standard, for the forthcoming European Championships of 1981 were due to be held in Punitz, Austria.

The Championships themselves were an enormous success, as were the World Championships held by Austria at Spitzerberg the following year: well organized and thoroughly enjoyable. Stiasny himself had not the skill or experience to make a good showing so early in his career, but he was working hard and building a basis for the future which showed promise. Tragically, that promise was cut short when he died in a training accident with his Pitts in July 1983.

So Walter Egger's presence at Békéscsaba was all the more gratifying since it showed that Austria was back on the international scene again, albeit with another brave newcomer who was there more to gain valuable experience than to challenge the top medal-winners.

He was, however, an athlete of considerable standing already, and his sporting accomplishments would fill at least two pages; they included parachute jumping (bronze medallist with the Austrian National Team); ski racing (twice Regional Champion); windsurfing (Regional Champion); sailing (bronze medallist in Soling category, Austrian Championship); and para-skiing (gold and bronze medallist in World Cup contests between 1964 and 1972). Not forgetting his kayak, cycle and mountain-climbing activities, plus gliding and glider aerobatics!

With his ready smile and sense of fun, Walter was unanimously voted a great asset to aerobatics, especially when it was noted that he was a responsible pilot with an over-riding concern for safety: if he found any section of a programme caused him difficulties, he would interrupt his performance

entered her first WAC in 1978, won the Women's World Championship from Liubov Nemkova, who could count a full fourteen years of World Championships to her credit!

Khalide was trained as an engineer, specializing in physical metallurgy and the heat-treatment of metals, and was a graduate of the aircraft construction faculty of the famous Moscow Aviation Institute. After some years spent on research projects, she returned to work at the Aviation Institute as a laboratory assistant/engineer; but after learning to fly and excelling in aerobatics, she followed the usual route of becoming a pilot-instructor at her local Aero Club to allow full dedication of her time to this activity.

But the major interest of the meeting centred around the new aircraft brought by the Soviet team and flown, on this occasion, only by three of the male pilots: the Sukhoi 26.

This radically new machine had been designed within the space of a year, largely by the Sukhoi Experimental Design Bureau with the aid of students of the Moscow Aviation Institute. It had flown for the first time at the end of June 1984, in the hands of test pilot Evgeni Frolov, a past USSR aerobatic team member; and in a rush test-programme the factory trials were completed within two weeks, allowing the Soviet team members to start training with the machine in mid-July. At the same time the remaining tests and finishing touches were carried out.

Equipped with the trusty 360 hp M-14P, but sporting a three-blade Hoffmann prop, the Su-26 was significantly smaller overall than the Yak 55 and lighter, with a higher wing loading. It certainly had the edge on performance over the Yak as well, both in speed and rate of roll, and in the final four-minute Freestyle, Yurgis Kairis was seen to coax five vertical rolls out of the machine – challenging the multiple rolling performance of Kermit Weeks's powerful Weeks Solution!

Many aspects of the aircraft were unusual, such as its mixed construction of steel-tube fuselage and fibreglass wing with carbon fibre spar. The construction of wings and control surfaces was classified 'experimental', comprising three-ply GRP panels filled with plastic foam, without employing conventional wing ribs. A major advantage of the steel-tube construction was that plexiglass panels could now be inserted in the lower fuselage sides for downward visibility, an aid to orientation which the Soviet pilots had not been able to employ before. Yet another innovation was the 45 degree rake to the pilot's seat-back, allowing him to fly in an almost reclining posture with feet practically at shoulder height: an optimum position for withstanding heavy *g*-forces.

With the unfamiliarity of the design and the short space of time available for acclimatization, it was not surprising that the Sukhoi pilots did not have the mastery of the machine in Békéscsaba. It was a speedy and powerful beast with performance characteristics that they were not used to, and many times it acted like a mettlesome horse with an excess of energy which needed to be kept in check! Nevertheless there was much comfort in its designed limit loads of +11 and −9 *g*, 'with reserve', as the pilots expressed it. Though they might have difficulty, for the moment, in staying inside the confines of the box, at least they knew that an over-energetic pull to turn a swift corner would not result in what is sometimes called the 'ultimate prayer' – when the wings meet palm to palm above the cockpit!

So with the Soviet pilots working hard at mastery of their new fleet, with Strössenreuther second, and the two Americans third and fourth, we now come to the winner of the 1984 championships – a pilot who took not only first place overall, but gold medals in three out of the four competition programmes and a bronze in the fourth: Petr Jirmus, the new World Champion.

Born in České Budějovice, Czechoslovakia, Petr was taught to fly by his father in 1973 and soon started enjoying aerobatics. He had started international competitions only as recently as 1979, in the Socialist Countries' annual contests, and gradually rose to topmost positions in succeeding years: in the 1981 Europeans and in the 1982 World Championships he was fourth. But it was the year 1983 that marked his breakthrough, when he won the title of European Champion at the 'Eurobatics' held in Ravenna, Italy. Building on his modest but growing experience, he now displayed not only impressive skill but artistry of performance as well.

Following in Victor Smolin's footsteps, Petr now repeated the formula of progressing from European Champion in 1983 to World Champion in 1984; and no-one who saw him at Békéscsaba, not even the most dyed-in-the-wool nationalist supporter, would deny his absolute mastery of the art. A mere 27 years old, Petr Jirmus displayed accomplishments well beyond his years: he had a certain fluidity of style with the otherwise rather angular Zlin 50, a certain poise and balance which lent an almost balletic feel to his performance and made him a delight to watch. Here was a true World Champion in action.

21

Masters of aerobatics

Right from the 1930s, when ultra-refinement of technique started to take shape – *la haute école aérienne* as Détroyat called it – precision aerobatics showed signs of parting company with the popular kinds of air display which so delighted the public.

One or two aerobatic exponents regretted this growing disparity (Marcel Doret for example); but in the main the outstanding virtuosi of the air, from that day to this, came simply to accept the precept that aerobatics of the competition variety was an esoteric art form sadly beyond the appreciation of ordinary aviation enthusiasts. . . .

But is this really so? One has only to look at the final four-minute Freestyle competition programme of a big international to appreciate what an extraordinary combination of ingenuity, artistry, excitement and technical wizardry goes into the sport. Often compared to figure-skating in its blending of technique with fluid choreography, aerobatics of the highest level is always a joy and a revelation to watch, and spell-binding to the informed observer.

Yet it has become very much the Cinderella of aviation. Once a source of pride and wonder to audiences in their tens of thousands (remember the World Cup at Vincennes and the Berlin Olympics of 1936), competition aerobatics, especially over the past 25 years, has over-regulated itself into a backwater. Writing of the World Championships at Oshkosh, *Pilot* magazine's reporter opened with the statement: "As a spectator sport, aerobatics ranks right up there with watching grass grow." And it has become fashionable to agree with him, even among the aerobatic fraternity itself.

True, he ended his article with a retraction. "Did I say a world aerobatic meet was boring? I take it back." But in this he was recalling not so much the competition itself as some of the irresistible side-show aspects of the occasion. Such as that ritual which has become known as 'the dance':

The impression of having wandered by mistake into a choreographer's convention ... walking through their Aresti sequences on the ground – shouting, grimacing, leaping arabesques and pas de deux with camera shutters clicking all around like transistorized applause.

And, quite naturally, the brilliant Air Show displays given by the international line-up of champions – a traditional accompaniment to such events – had impressed our reporter immoderately. But not the World Championship itself.

There are two main reasons for this state of affairs, and the first of these is safety. Championship aerobatics imposes the most punishing of set routines on its pilots. Plus 8 *g* (eight times normal bodyweight) and minus 4 *g* (five times normal bodyweight in the wrong direction) are quite usual conditions experienced in competition, often following swiftly one upon the other in a 'switchback' effect. The effort of moving limbs and neck against these high *g* loadings is a continual muscular strain; head movement is restricted, where vision is affected to the point where it may become severely limited. And all these phenomena combine to aggravate the inevitable disorientation that comes from flying-upside-down or rotating at dizzy speeds. Many ground spectators feel nauseous just imagining what goes on up there in the cockpit!

The manoeuvres themselves require fierce concentration and split-second accuracy while the pilot undergoes these debilitating effects; moreover, there is an overlay of stress – competition nerves – which accentuates the difficulty factor and introduces an element of apprehension during the flight. Pilots who have pulled +8 *g* in training may easily pull 8½ or 9 in performance.

In this radio-controlled, computer-assisted, *g*-suited generation, the demands of top level competition aerobatics comprise arguably the most taxing and complicated tasks that exist for any unaided man-machine combination.

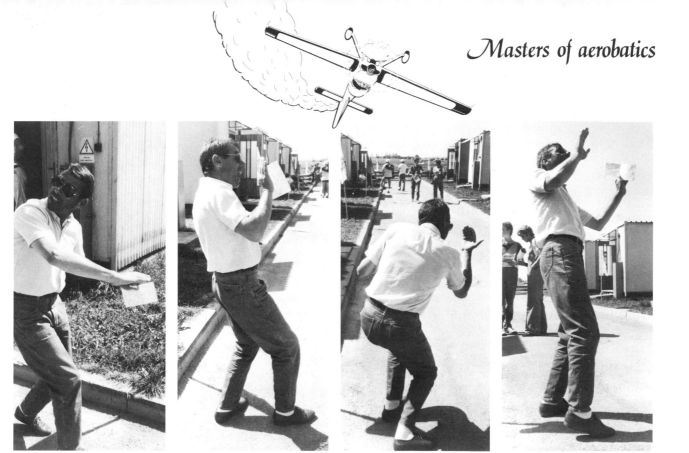

'The dance': French champion Claude ('Co-Co') Bessière goes through his routine before a championship flight.
(Author's collection)

The sensation of severe negative *g*, when the blood-flow rushes into the head in 'outside' manoeuvres, in the words of one world-class pilot "feels as though you've stuck your head in to infra-red oven". He describes the sensations experienced in a vertical negative flick roll as probably the most unpleasant of all:

I pull maybe eight *g* positive going up, and all the blood is on the way down. Then, bang! The plane goes into its roll, and suddenly it feels as if my head is going to come off. The pressure is beyond description. I'm looking out at the wingtip when I do the maneuver, so my inner ear and neck muscles are 90 degrees to my body. For a second, as everything is flashing past, my throat is being filled with lungs and stomach. It would be easy for me to lose orientation. If I do, I won't have the slightest idea where to stop the maneuver.

Considerations of safety demand that this sort of routine be carried out at a safe height. Airshow aerobatics may be performed right down on the desk, where a seasoned display pilot can make even the simplest manoeuvres look impressive because of their proximity to eye level. But competition manoeuvres take place in a mid-range between 100 and 1,000 metres above the airfield: a necessary reassurance for the pilot in case things should begin to go wrong, but not very exciting for the casual spectator, as our *Pilot* reporter at WAC 1980 was quick to point out!

Should they be brought lower? Well, it never has been a blood-sport like motor racing, where enormous rewards may perhaps tempt a competitor to gamble with his life. In spite of occasional airshow, filming and training disasters, which always achieve lurid publicity, aerobatic competitions themselves have an enviably accident-free record, and on the whole the pilots prefer it that way.

The second reason for lack of spectator appeal in aerobatics can be put down to the matter of judging. In *Flight*

Unlimited, the book on aerobatic technique written by Eric Müller and myself, we described contest flying as a game played between two groups of people: on the one hand the pilots, the illusionists who must create a satisfactory effect when viewed from below; and on the other hand the ground observers, whose function is to award marks for the illusion. Judging is an arduous job that requires skill, impartiality, tenacity, and a vast storehouse of knowledge. Even so, the best of judges may still be fooled by a master of illusion, or be unconsciously swayed by the 'halo factor' attaching to a particular pilot or aeroplane.

To avoid these pitfalls, modern international competitions are hedged around with a multiplicity of judging instructions, criteria and rules, and performances are minutely examined not as a whole, but manoeuvre by tiny manoeuvre. The top handful of winners in a modern World Championship – the best aerobatic pilots in the world – are unlikely to reach as high as 85 per cent of available marks, so stringent are the standards. And in order to compare like with like as much as possible, the same aerobatic manoeuvres are repeated time after time, with (to the untutored eye) almost equal perfection, by anything up to eighty-odd pilots.

To anyone who has not had the rules of the game explained, or who has not taken the trouble to find them out, the analogy with watching grass grow may perhaps have a certain relevance. But once understood, there are endless vistas of fascination to be found in competition aerobatics. And in recent years, a few people with vision enough to see and appreciate this fact have started to pioneer new types of contest, aimed at that ideal medium which can really bring the intricacies of the sport, and its unique visual impact, to a mass audience: television.

There has always been a sprinkling of invitation or 'Masters' events in the aerobatics calendar, and one way in which they

View from the cockpit as Frank Christensen enters a left-hand spin in the Christen Eagle II.   (courtesy of Christen Industries)

always score with spectators is in the limited numbers of competitors taking part. No national teams are involved, and they all compete as individuals. With fewer contestants comes greater ability to recognize and identify with one or other of the pilots; there are fewer repetitive programmes to watch and judge, the contest is shorter and snappier, the performances easier to recall and compare.

And who better to realize the mass-media potential of a Masters of Aerobatics competition than Don Taylor, American television producer, top level aerobatic pilot and judge, and Contestant Director of the World Championships at Oshkosh?

The idea of featuring aerobatics on television was one originally shared by Don and Frank Christensen (of Christen Eagle fame) in the late 1960s. But it was not until the 1980 World Championships that Don got together with director Russ Mayberry, another competition pilot, and successfully sold the event as a television special to CBS TV. It went well, and a new deal was struck for an aerobatics programme in 1981, with options for further coverage in the future.

Now it was up to Don and his team to devise an attractive formula for the 1981 competition, and the notion of a small invitation event with a maximum twelve or so participants was very appealing. Sponsorship was a fundamental requirement, to provide handsome prizes and to subsidize the cost of travel, hotel and other expenses. But with guaranteed television coverage, sponsorship was not too difficult to find.

At the time of the 1976 World Championships in Kiev, one of the Hilton Hotels Vice-Presidents (Advertising), Art Thompson by name, had been over there as a spectator. Don approached him in the hope that Barron Hilton – himself a keen pilot – might be interested: and indeed he was. With the major sponsor fixed, and with subsidiary sponsorship from the Avco Lycoming engine firm, Hartzell propellers and Beckett aviation fuel, Don Taylor was able to offer an expenses-paid two weeks for all contestants in the Hilton Masters of Aerobatics Competition. The overseas pilots need only pay their fare over to the USA: from the moment they set foot on American soil, all else was covered. Nor did they need to go to the expense of bringing their own aeroplanes, for a deal with the famous Pitts factory resulted in three brand-new Pitts S-1T aircraft being placed at their disposal for the duration, with a week's practice to get accustomed to them beforehand. What more could a pilot ask?

For a competition of this calibre, those on the invitation list had to be the best in the world, but at the same time must be a good cross-section of many different nationalities. So the qualification for entry was eventually decided as being either a Gold, Silver or Bronze Medallist in the overall FAI World Championships, or a National Champion of the entrant's own country within the past fifteen years.

Initial invitations went out to a selection of the world's élite pilots, including representatives from the Soviet Union and Czechoslovakia, but America's strained relations with the Warsaw Pact countries somehow seemed a barrier to their coming. The organizers were fortunate, however, in that the National Champion of Poland, Jerzy Makula – an international champion also in glider aerobatics – was able to accept in

October 1981 for the first event, and indeed later returned for the second. With him came the much loved and respected Polish judge Andrzej Ablamowicz.

The other foreign participants who made their way to the Hilton Masters in Phoenix, Arizona, were Otakar Josefčák from Germany, Christian Schweizer and Eric Müller from Switzerland, and Bill Waterton from Australia. From the USA came Henry Haigh, Kermit Weeks and, making a welcome return to competition aerobatics, 1970–72 US Champion Gene Soucy.

The two keynotes of Don Taylor's philosophy, based on sixteen years of competition experience, were to make the event (a) scrupulously fair and (b) attractive to watch.

In the interests of fairness, he and his wife Gail put together a tightly-knit organization on a more human scale than the vast World Championship structures, and anonymity was strictly preserved not only by concealing the identity of the contestants while they flew, but even by the precaution of writing the numbers on each pilot's sequence diagram *by typewriter*, lest the judges should recognize a tell-tale trait of handwriting! With everybody flying the same type of machine no pilot had the extra advantage of a better aeroplane than any other; and to eliminate the disadvantage of being 'wind dummy' in the Unknown Programme, all pilots were kept sequestered while the others flew. Even the Known Compulsory programme was changed, to ensure that no pilot had longer practice than any other; and for the same reason there were new rules for the Free Programme which necessitated everyone drawing up a fresh sequence for the occasion.

The most radical innovation of all was airshow smoke, strictly forbidden in FAI Championships: in the still Arizona air the long, snaking trails of white against the intense blue sky made a vivid picture. Though the judges found it disconcerting at first, they soon managed to disregard it and concentrate on the aircraft instead. For the television audience, in-flight camera mounts enabled viewers to experience aerobatics from the pilot's point of view; and clever graphics explained how the contest worked and what the judges were looking for.

CBS were delighted, the weather was perfect, the contest organization superlative, and the experience, especially for the visiting pilots, was glorious. In the first Hilton Masters of Aerobatics the results ran as follows:

Hilton Masters of Aerobatics, 1981

1.	Kermit Weeks	US	16,731.2
2.	Gene Soucy	US	16,465.8
3.	Henry Haigh	US	16,176.9
4.	Eric Müller	Swiss	16,065.0
5.	Bill Waterton	Australian	16,019.1
6.	Chris Schweizer	Swiss	15,789.4
7.	Otto Josefčák	German	14,927.9
8.	Jerzy Makula	Polish	13,358.4

When 1983 arrived another top-line list of champions was invited, with the addition of Gordon Price from Canada, Australian Frank Fry in place of Bill Waterton, and from Switzerland the third member of the top aerobatic trio, Michel Brandt, came to join his two compatriots. The top three Americans from 1981 appeared once again to defend their hold on the top places.

The extremely attractive prize money remained the same as before, thanks to the generosity of Hilton Hotels: 1st place $10,000, 2nd place $5,000, 3rd place $3,000, 4th place $1,500,

and from 5th to 10th $1,000 each. Hilton by now had extended their interest in aerobatics to sponsorship of the US World Championship Team that went to Austria in 1982, and now, obviously happy with their investment, returned again to support the 1983 Masters both financially and with luxury accommodation at the Phoenix Hilton throughout the event. Avco Lycoming, the world's leading manufacturers of engines for aerobatics, were back to underpin the contest as well.

Once again three brand-new Pitts aircraft were provided – two-seater 260 hp S-2Bs this time – courtesy of Frank Christensen who had newly acquired the Pitts aircraft company. They were fed, watered and generally maintained by factory engineers, rolled out for the pilots fresh and bright each morning, and placed under the seat of their pants.

The same arrangements applied, and the same practice airfield was used, situated on the edge of the Arizona desert where rattlesnakes, scorpions and road-runners were silent observers of the aerial gymnastics above. Thanks in large part to the attentive care of host Gail Taylor, a relaxed and carefree atmosphere prevailed on the airfield – further aided by the wry humour of Gord Price and Frank Fry and the outgoing friendliness of the three Americans. Particularly noticeable was the spirit of camaraderie among 'opposing' pilots, even with substantial prize-money at stake, every contestant critiquing the others whenever it was needed. American pilot Linda Meyers, on this occasion a helper rather than a contestant, even learned a few words of pidgin Polish to critique Jerzy Makula whose English was not quite up to everyone else's.

Strangely – in view of previous successes – CBS declined to take up the 1983 option on the event, which gave Don Taylor's company Cumulus Productions the opportunity to make a quite stunning television programme as an independent venture. Not only did it receive the 'Monitor' Award given by Video Production Associates of New York for Best Photographed Sporting Event of the year, but its director Glenn Giere was also one of the four finalists nominated for Best Director. Action-packed, entertaining and amusing, some of its most memorable sequences are images showing the flattened and distorted features of the (otherwise quite human-looking) pilots under the effects of *g*!

At the end of the contest, Weeks and Soucy had repeated their previous success and come out again in the top two places, but Swiss champion Christ Schweizer now captured third place, with $3,000 to take home with him. Michel Brandt's position at the bottom of the field belied his fine flying – he had come second in the extremely difficult Unknown Programme – and was the result of a technical disqualification in programme 2 for (sin of sins!) forgetting to switch on his smoke system and then failing to recognize the recall signal instructing him to land and start again.

Hilton Masters of Aerobatics, 1983

1.	Kermit Weeks	US	14657.5
2.	Gene Soucy	US	14650.8
3.	Chris Schweizer	Swiss	14314.0
4.	Henry Haigh	US	14265.0
5.	Frank Fry	Australian	14113.7
6.	Gordon Price	Canadian	13970.6
7.	Eric Müller	Swiss	13625.9
8.	Jerzy Makula	Polish	12740.0
9.	Michel Brandt	Swiss	9567.9

Flight Fantastic

With the advantage of lessons learned in these first two events, Don Taylor's unstinting search for the best possible contest format has led him to inaugurate a subtle change in the 1985 event, about to be held at Homestead, Florida, as this chapter is written. Aware of the necessity for an international group of judges, he has invited each overseas contestant to bring his own trainer/judge with him, who will help the pilot during practice but will then form the judging panel for the competition itself.

So how will anonymity be preserved in such circumstances? Simply by replacing the Free programme with a second Unknown Programme (an idea already widely advocated by many people in the sport), and by setting the Four-Minute Final Freestyle apart from the overall competition marking, deciding the winner on the first three programmes only. No-one wants to lose the Freestyle from the competition, of course, with its exciting and inventive flavour; so a

In 1983 the three competition aircraft were Pitts S-2Bs.
(Don Taylor)

special first prize of $1,000 has been set aside for its winner, with $500 going to the winners of the other individual programmes.

When Frank Fry returned home after the 1983 Hilton Masters contest, he was already talking of holding a similar event in Australia which he was sure would make equally attractive television viewing.

Again the whole venture depended upon a healthy injection of sponsorship funds, since the Australian Channel Seven TV company favoured importing not only exotic pilots but exotic aeroplanes, too, and the payment of transportation costs in addition to the usual on-the-spot expenses started to look like a very great many dollars indeed.

The day was saved in this instance by Philips Industries, the consumer electrics and electronics people, who packaged the whole event as a giant sponsored television special, hoping to recoup something of the vast outlay by combining

Line-up of pilots for the 1983 Hilton Masters contest. Left to right (back row): Henry Haigh, Frank Fry, Gene Soucy, Michel Brandt, (front row) Gordon Price, Kermit Weeks, Chris Schweizer, Jerzy Makula, Eric Müller. (Don Taylor)

Frank Fry, Australian National Champion, came 5th in the 1983 Hilton Masters. He returned home determined to mount a Masters Competition in Australia. (Author's collection)

the two-stage competition (Melbourne and Sydney) with large scale air displays on successive Sunday afternoons.

Undoubtedly Frank's greatest coup was his success in enticing Soviet ace and World Aerobatic Champion Victor Smolin over to Australia, accompanied by genial trainer Kasum Nazhmudinov – on this occasion performing the duties of judge – and an immaculate Yak 50 was shipped from Vladivostok and almost lost on arrival, being deposited in a corner of the Melbourne dockyard reserved for scrap containers!

Female World Champion Betty Stewart was also lured to Australia, despite her avowed preference for the life of an airshow pilot, together with her two indispensable fellow-countrymen Kermit Weeks and Henry Haigh. Two other veterans from the Hilton Masters – Gordon Price and Eric Müller – were also invited, and the final tally of European talent was completed by Italian Champion Sergio Dallan and Richard Goode from Great Britain.

The Australian line-up was headed by Australian champion Frank Fry himself, acting as organizer, chief engineer and smoke-system doctor, television liaison man, father-confessor and, when time allowed, competition pilot as well; Mal Beard, Australian number two pilot; Chris Sperou, eleven times Australian Champion and three times World Cham-

293

Victor Smolin's Yak 50 being assembled in Melbourne.
(Richard Goode)

pionship Team member; and Geoff Selvey, 20 years old and already a World Championship contender with the Australian Team in 1982.

Competition aerobatics had really started to get organized in Australia only since the end of 1970, when a group of enthusiasts who flew mostly D H Chipmunks formed the Australian Aerobatic Club and arranged competitions of a fairly basic level. When the 1972 World Championships were

Yak 50 in formation with Frank Fry's Stephens Akro-Z over the Australian countryside. *(Richard Goode)*

fixed for Salon de Provence, France, six of their number got together and, without much knowledge of what it was all about, decided to enter a team. Two of their number were to fly in the competition with a locally hired Zlin.

Unfortunately for their hopes, a restriction was suddenly placed on Zlin aircraft by the French authorities, in the wake of a training accident, and two weeks before the competition was due to start the Australians found themselves without an aeroplane of any kind. They went along anyway and, according to Gordon Lee, one of their number at the time,

It was probably the best thing that ever happened to us, because we went there and were absolutely astounded at what we saw. At that stage none of us had ever seen a Pitts fly, and I can always remember getting to Salon late one night, and next morning, when I woke up, I

heard this terrific roar.... I rushed outside and there was this little red aircraft zotting along inverted at about 300 feet and it just pushed up from inverted, over the top, snapped down again and crossed the airfield inverted at 300 feet again, and I'd *never* seen anything like that in my life! We just stood there amazed, thinking, 'My God, what's this? It's a new world!'

When they got back home again there was one thought uppermost in their minds, and that was to get hold of one of these fantastic new Pitts Specials. Losing no time, three of their number immediately ordered a Pitts S-2A from America, but it did not arrive until the end of 1973, which was essentially the start of a new movement towards serious aerobatics in Australia.

More imports followed, and by 1976 there were enough single-seat Pitts pilots for a team of four to make their way to Kiev in the USSR, with Chris Sperou achieving best placing of forty-second and Italian-Australian Guido Zuccoli placed fiftieth. By 1978 Guido had moved up to thirty-first, leading Rob Poynton and Hilton Selvey, father of competition pilot Geoff; and in 1980 a full team of five was fielded, their highest scorers being Bill Waterton and Frank Fry who both flew in the finals, finishing eleventh and fourteenth respectively. In great triumph they brought back the bronze medal in the team competition that year.

A superhuman effort in 1982 managed to afford a four-man team in Austria, but only by such expedients as purchasing a local aircraft with the intention of selling it again after the competition, as they had done in America in 1980. Indeed Chris Sperou was obliged at the last moment to use a borrowed machine in Spitzerberg, which Betty Stewart generously loaned to him.

The tiny aerobatics community in Australia continually found itself beset by problems, not least being the highly conservative attitude of the Australian Aviation Authority (their Department of Transport). Minimum height restrictions have always been extremely tight, and even now in the 1980s a special low-level waiver is still necessary for Unlimited pilots to fly aerobatics at 500 ft (152 m). To practise for World Championships down to the 100 m (328 ft) level, yet another special dispensation has to be applied for.

Another big problem for the Australians was distance, not only from the rest of the world's centres of aviation, but also the vast distances, measurable in thousands of kilometres, between individual members of their own tiny aerobatic community. Although they received a modest injection of government aid to help with World Championships, by the time 1982 arrived the expense of participation had escalated so tremendously that the end of the line had been reached, and they saw no way forward unless a marathon effort was made to find commercial sponsorship. So there was a great deal riding on the success or failure of the Philips World Aerobatic Challenge in March of 1984.

Thanks to the eager participation of the international pilots, who crated and shipped treasured aircraft half way across the world in support of what had started out as one man's dream, Frank Fry was able to present his line-up of star sportsmen and aircraft from seven different countries.

Though most of his fellow-countrymen still used the faithful Pitts Special, Frank himself had moved on to the monoplane format and since 1982 had a splendid 200 hp Stephens Akro-Z which was beautifully finished in blue on the upper surfaces and fuselage, and bright yellow underneath. An airline pilot by profession, he had flown fighters in the RAAF (Vampire,

Sabre, Mirage and Macchi jets) and saw service in the Vietnam War on an exchange posting to the US Air Force. On leaving the Air Force as an advanced flying training instructor in 1974, he joined TAA, the domestic Australian airline, and graduated to First Officer on Boeing 727s. A keen home-builder, Frank first built his own Pitts in 1978 and took up aerobatic competition a year later. The Akro project was also home-built from plans, and completed in under twelve months altogether.

Another Stephens-type monoplane owner in Australia was Guido Zuccoli, who had twice flown for Australia in World Championship teams and still actively flew aerobatics for enjoyment, but had recently found his successful civil engineering concern in Darwin too demanding to allow sufficient free time for competitions. Also his few available flying hours over the winter of 1983/4 had somehow found him more frequently in the cockpit of his newly restored Sea Fury than in his Akro, so for the World Aerobatic Challenge he did not feel ready to fly as a contestant.

Philips World Aerobatic Challenge: nine of the international contestants pictured together (left to right) back row: Victor Smolin, Kermit Weeks, Geoff Selvey, Henry Haigh, Gordon Price; front row: Eric Müller, Sergio Dallan, Richard Goode, Frank Fry. (Richard Goode)

Instead, he generously offered the use of his aeroplane for the contest to Sergio Dallan, who was an old and dear friend from his native Italy, and to Eric Müller from Switzerland who was to share the same machine. Italian speakers all three, they were soon known as the 'Spaghetti Team'; they retaliated in kind by dubbing host Frank Fry with the name 'Francesco Fritto'!

Many of the visiting pilots found flying in Australia sadly restrictive (you had to file a flight plan to fly almost *anywhere* except over the Outback); in addition to a strict 500 ft minimum, there was an absolute embargo on aerobatics over

Flight Fantastic

British pilot Richard Goode in 'Pace Spirit', another Stephens Akro-based type, originally designed by Michel Brandt of Switzerland.   (Richard Goode)

(Inset left) Gene Beggs in Pitts S-2B, (Inset right) Manfred Strössenreuther in Zlin 50, two favourite machines at the 1985 World Aerobatic Masters Tournament, South Africa.
(Peter Celliers)

The ritual of prop-swinging: Sergio Dallan in the 'Spaghetti Team' Akro gets a start. Many aerobatic aircraft dispense with self-starters in order to reduce weight. (Richard Goode)

an airfield, and a positive paranoia, as Richard Goode remarked, about flying regulations. Small wonder, then, that the entire aerobatic community took Victor Smolin to their hearts when he performed a thoroughgoing one man beat-up of Melbourne's Essendon Airport by way of test-flying his newly arrived Yak 50! The machine had just been assembled after its ocean crossing, and elaborate arrangements had been made to shepherd him safely by radio, via an interpreter, out of controlled airspace and on his way to the contest site at Ballerat. Imagine the consternation among officialdom, therefore, when Victor took off, roared back over the runway, pulled up into a vertical roll, and went into an impromptu aerobatic work-out culminating with a series of low slow-rolls which, according to Richard, really *were* quite low.

By next morning, some local wag had decorated Victor's machine with a sticker saying 'I LOVE ESSENDON AIRPORT', which it sported for the duration of the contest.

Tailoring the competition format to suit both television and airshow audiences, the Philips World Aerobatic Challenge presented the most radical departures from normal Championship procedures yet attempted anywhere in the world, and they were very valuable as working experiments for the future.

With one round at Melbourne and another at Sydney, contestants were asked to fly only two programmes on each occasion, the second of which was the individual's own World Championship Four-minute Freestyle. This was preceded by a novel kind of Unknown Programme, which was constructed from figures dreamed up not by the contestants themselves but by the organizers. They were free to practise the rather unusual assortment of 29 figures (including a lomcovak and a torque roll), but were told that only ten would eventually be selected after practice was over. Of these, five would be flown at Melbourne and the remaining five at Sydney, with each contestant drawing his first five out

of a hat – thus ensuring that every programme would be interesting and different, though containing the same nucleus of ten manoeuvres.

All ten were assigned the same difficulty coefficient of 50, and only the ten would be marked. There was no sequence to be built with manoeuvres linking one to the next, rather the pilots were asked to place each figure centrally for the benefit of the television cameras, simply performing a turn-around in between to re-position. It was extraordinary, but it worked well for both airshow and television audiences: they received a running commentary analysing the previous figure, with marks flashed up on the TV screens, while the contestant was actually lining up to perform the next.

It was a great pity that Smolin was not on top form and did not show the standard one had come to expect: possibly the fact that the powerful Yak was required to perform within the confines of a much smaller box than the usual $1,000 \times 1,000$ metres may have had something to do with it.

All the international 'Masters' veterans predictably appeared in the top five, with Kermit Weeks once again taking top honours in his Weeks Solution, and Frank Fry scoring a personal triumph by taking third place after having so little opportunity to concentrate properly on training. In addition to his other chores, he had agreed to be the guinea-pig for an in-flight relay transmission (a technique perfected by the Australians for the Americas Cup) from a small camera mounted in the rear baggage locker, which photographed the action through a periscope. It made for very exciting television while the actual flight was in progress.

Given the full blockbuster treatment, the Philips World Aerobatic Challenge was sold impressively in all the media, and undoubtedly gave its sponsors their money's worth. Like Hilton before them, Philips decided to go the whole way with aerobatics and support the Australian Team in its World Championship efforts, so the month of August 1984 saw a professionally turned-out group of Aussies in Békéscsaba, Hungary, where 'Francesco Fritto' happily carried off the bronze medal in the Known Compulsory.

Philips World Aerobatic Challenge

1.	Kermit Weeks	US	7,755
2.	Eric Müller	Swiss	7,542
3.	Frank Fry	Australian	7,511

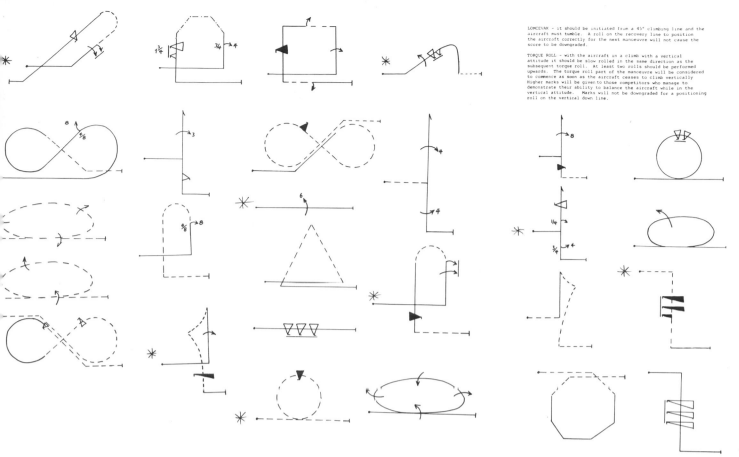

LOMCEVAK - it should be initiated from a 45° climbing line and the aircraft must tumble. A roll on the recovery line to position the aircraft correctly for the next manoeuvre will not cause the score to be downgraded.

TORQUE ROLL - with the aircraft in a climb with a vertical attitude it should be slow rolled in the same direction as the subsequent torque roll. At least two rolls should be performed upwards. The torque roll part of the manoeuvre will be considered to commence as soon as the aircraft ceases to climb vertically Higher marks will be given to those competitors who manage to demonstrate their ability to balance the aircraft while in the vertical attitude. Marks will not be downgraded for a positioning roll on the vertical down line.

The list of 'unknown' figures from which ten (marked with an asterisk) were eventually selected for the pilots to fly. The Lomcovák and torque roll were not chosen!

4.	Henry Haigh	US	7,459
5.	Gordon Price	Canadian	7,362
6.	Geoff Selvey	Australian	7,267
7.	Victor Smolin	USSR	7,144
8.	Richard Goode	British	6,929
9.	Chris Sperou	Australian	6,913
10.	Sergio Dallan	Italian	6,611
11.	Mal Beard	Australian	6,431
12.	Betty Stewart	US	6,222

To bring this final chapter right up to date in the chronicle of world aerobatics, we move now to our last location and to the most recent of all 'Masters of Aerobatics' contests: the World Aerobatic Masters Tournament in South Africa, October 1985. And once again this event was the brainchild of one man with a dream.

Peter Celliers was reigning South African National Champion in 1983–4 when the World Aerobatic Championships were announced in Békéscsaba, Hungary, and having participated in the 1982 event in Spitzerberg he wanted to take part in 1984 as well. South Africa's position in the world at large was plummeting to an all-time low at the time, due to its reluctance to abandon the hated apartheid system, and international feeling was such that in some countries of the world South African citizens simply would not be allowed an entry visa; Hungary was one of them.

Whatever the rights and wrongs of the larger issue, it is a fact that the FAI has always been a totally non-political body, which is one of the great virtues of sporting aviation today. May it always remain so. In the Sporting Code governing aeronautical contests the precept is clear that all member Aero Clubs of the FAI have the right to be invited to an international championship, and if they are not invited the Code is broken. South Africa was not invited in 1984.

One has every sympathy with the Hungarian hosts, of course, placed in the intolerable position of having to obey government edicts which cut across the spirit of sportsmanship; and at the same time one has even more sympathy with a keen pilot like Peter Celliers, who came all the way to Europe on the outside chance of gaining a visa to take part in the contest. Predictably, he was turned back and refused permission to land in Hungary; which left him disappointed on the Austrian side of the border while his fellow sportsmen continued on to Békéscsaba and the World Championships.

It was at that moment that Peter Celliers formulated his great idea: if aerobatics were to be barred to South Africans

South African Champion Peter Celliers, the man behind it all.
(Peter Celliers)

outside their own country, then perhaps they could bring aerobatics to South Africa instead.

He set to work immediately to frame the outline of the event: it must be more relaxed and less formal than a World Championship; it must contain the largest possible cross-section of nationalities and a wide range of abilities, from the seasoned medal-winners to the up-and-coming pilots who maybe had not even yet tried competing at World Class level. Above all, it must introduce the wonderful country of

Flight Fantastic

South Africa to people who had perhaps never experienced it; and it must promote friendship and understanding among sportsmen, encourage them to talk together and get to know each other. Aware that improvements were needed within the sport of aerobatics itself, Peter was sure that the way forward lay in communication and exchange of ideas.

The usual search for sponsorship was duly launched, to cope with a twenty- to thirty-strong list of entries and an ambitious programme of competition, touring, sightseeing and airshow flying. In the by-now established mould of Masters events, travel and accommodation was to be provided, together with a selection of aircraft from which the pilots would choose their own mounts.

But as preparations got under way the world situation worsened, and international sanctions against South Africa whipped up to fever pitch. All at once pressure started to be put on would-be entrants by those government departments who had the power to influence sporting activities, and in some cases by employers who took it upon themselves to determine what their employees would and would not be allowed to do with their leisure time. Invitation lists were drawn up and re-drawn, names were scratched and replaced, and people started losing confidence that the Masters Tournament would ever happen at all.

At the eleventh hour – the worst possible time for a withdrawal of support – the promised commercial sponsorship fell through. Peter and his little group were left to finance the whole operation themselves, and everything had to be staked on the gate money from two large-scale airshows at which the international pilots (if they came) would provide the main attraction. Meanwhile the organizers had commitments for airline tickets, travel arrangements and accommodation; but thanks to the generous support of South African Airways and the Republic's Tourist Board, who alone remained to underpin the event, at least this side of things went ahead without a hitch.

As the first week of October arrived, pilots, judges and international representatives from all over the world started to trickle into Johannesburg for the Tournament. The trickle became a stream, and eventually a total of twenty-four pilots assembled to compete from thirteen different nations, accompanied by an international throng of aviation enthusiasts who were there to help, support and participate as occasion warranted. The organizers need not have worried. Indeed, by the time everyone had arrived the international gathering totalled something like sixty in all, sharing the spirit of friendliness and sportsmanship that Peter Celliers had been so anxious to promote.

Getting the competition under way, each pilot had the choice of a range of Pitts aircraft to fly – S-1S, S-1T, S-2S or S-2B – or Peter's own recently acquired Zlin 50 with a 330 hp Lycoming and more than a passing resemblance to Manfred Strössenreuther's old machine. A couple of practice flights usually settled the matter of choice, except in the case of Kermit Weeks, who decided at last to fly every competition programme with a different aeroplane!

A similarly sporting view was taken by Pitts veteran Henry Haigh, who was sorely tempted to fly the Zlin, but knew that he would probably sacrifice the chance of coming out in the top three if he did so. In the end the unique opportunity of competing with the new machine won and he opted for the Zlin.

Patrick Paris from France was presented with a similarly agonizing dilemma, and likewise chose the Czechoslovakian Zlin though he had never laid hands on one before. An Armée de l'Air pilot who normally flew Cap 10s, 20s and 21s, Patrick impressed all onlookers with some immaculate flying

Patrick Paris, French Champion 1984, came sixth flying the Zlin 50 for the first time. (Author's collection)

in the difficult machine, finishing in sixth place after a grand total of two 15-minute training flights!

All the other pilots opted for machines with which they had some familiarity: the Spaniards Luis Cabre and Fernando Adrados for the Zlin 50, along with Manfred Strössenreuther from Germany; the remaining American, Canadian and European pilots for the trusty Pitts Specials.

Apart from Peter Celliers himself, who finished tenth, there were two other South African contestants: ex-National Champion Brian Zeederberg (fourteenth) and newcomer André van Kryenburg, who acquitted himself extremely well to finish in seventh place.

A brief look at the early days of aerobatics in South Africa shows that the leading light of the sport when it started there in the early sixties was undoubtedly Nick Turvey, who had

Nick Turvey, eight times South African Champion.

learned to fly on Tiger Moths and Harvards in the 1950s with the SAAF Active Citizen Force and who later became a civilian flying instructor. Eight times South African Champion, Nick made his first expedition to a World Championship in 1964, to Bilbao in Spain, and later captained the South African team in Magdeburg in 1968.

Contemporaneous with Nick, and fellow-members of the 1968 team, were Twisty Winternitz and Ewald Wessels, all three flying a borrowed Zlin Z-226T for the occasion. This was when Twisty made an unforgettable mark on the international scene, as during the first compulsory programme he managed to get ever lower and lower, until horrified observers saw him enter an inverted spin from which a negative exit was prescribed. By now he should have stopped the programme and climbed for height. But one of the very fundamental disciplines that a beginner has to learn in aerobatics is to continue on and finish the flight to the end when he would really prefer, for whatever reason, to break off and try afresh; this should never, of course, over-ride safety considerations, but Twisty was now obviously locked into the 'press-on' syndrome and was psychologically unable to make the break even though he was about to hit the ground.

When he pushed out from the spin his rudder had less than 2 metres (7 feet) clearance, and at that moment he literally disappeared from view, in the inverted position, while everyone on the airfield waited for the sickening crash. But mercifully none came. He had pushed out at just the spot where there was a slight hollow in the surface of the field, and had got away with it. Realizing at last what had happened, he broke off and landed. Fellow contestants still remember that moment to this day, and one pilot swears that Twisty's barograph had a reading of 1 metre when it was checked after the flight!

By 1969 Nick had been joined on the scene by a brilliant and headstrong young ex-military pilot named Selwyn 'Scully'

The Reid Rooivalk, first and only South African-designed aeroplane.   *(John Blake)*

Levin, who proceeded to capture the National title in 1970. Shortly afterwards, he and Nick were presented with the intriguing offer of a purpose-built aerobatic machine of South African origin, designed by a certain Professor Maitland Reid of the Department of Mechanical Engineering at Natal University, and named the Rooivalk (Red Hawk). Described by its inventor as a world-beating aerobatic aircraft, it was used in the trials to select who would represent South Africa in the 1972 World Championships, and is remembered now with fond amusement by those who had the singular experience of flying the machine.

In general it was an exceedingly strong biplane, about the size of a Steen Skybolt and very heavy – impossibly heavy to fly. It was powered by a 230 hp Continental and equipped with a constant-speed unit featuring a reversible-pitch propeller, which had the unfortunate tendency to go into reverse mode without warning, immediately depriving the unlucky pilot of all elevator authority. Some recall a few nice characteristics of the Rooivalk such as its very docile behaviour and its ability to perform a majestic Vertical S, but it was generally acknowledged to have the rolling capacity of a DC-3 and was soon abandoned as an aerobatic mount; but not until after a 'national rush of blood to the head' had sent Nick and the Rooivalk to Salon in 1972, courtesy of transportation by South African Airways, where he only just managed to execute the sequences and finished last in a field of 47.

Meanwhile dissatisfaction had set in at home with the organization of aerobatics by the Aero Club of South Africa, and Scully Levin took a hand in establishing the new Sport Aerobatic Club to handle their own affairs, for which he worked from 1972 to 1976 formulating the rules, running judging seminars and coaching aerobatic pilots. Having won the National Championship three times, he then concentrated on running his own part-time aviation school and left competition flying to the others – though he continued to enjoy airshow work and in 1984 aerobatted a Pitts S-2A on the circuit in *Playboy* colours. Many still speak of Scully's hilarious airshow routines, such as the 'remote-controlled aeroplane', bristling with dummy aerials and wires, which he flew

Flight Fantastic

undetected from the covered-in rear seat while a henchman on the ground ostentatiously operated a mock 'control box' complete with control stick, antennas and flashing lights.

At the 1985 Masters Tournament airshows he was much in evidence leading his new three-ship formation team of Pitts S-2Bs in tight precision; demonstrating the SAA Junkers 52 with a zest almost reminiscent of the 1930s Trimotor kings; performing a truck-top landing with elegant accuracy in his Piper J3 Cub; and giving a crazy-flying act (the 'old man in a

The shortest runway in the world! Scully Levin's truck-top landing with the Piper J3 Cub.   (Frank Versteegh)

licence back, including his CPL, and continues to run his own aviation company.

To conclude the report of the South African Tournament, and indeed to conclude this survey of the past eighty years of aerobatics, let us look at some of the new and rising young pilots whose names have not been featured before, as well as mentioning the well-established 'Masters' like Swiss pilot Eric Müller who on this occasion emerged the winner of the competition. With his usual consistency and accuracy of

runaway aeroplane') which had you doubled-up with laughter from beginning to end. For air displays there is patently no-one to touch him.

At about the same time that Scully moved away from the scene, Nick Turvey flew his last World Championship in 1980 at Oshkosh. This was because the following year he had his celebrated prang with a Pitts at the end of a long, inverted flat spin during which the engine suddenly became intermittent and the aircraft started unaccountably rocking and pitching. The incident happened at an airshow, and by the time he had pulled out of the spin his only option was to land among the cars in the parking area rather than put the machine down in the crowd; Nick's ensuing injuries kept him away from flying for more than a year, and his four broken vertebrae cost him $4\frac{1}{2}$ cm in height! Fortunately he now has his health and his

performance, Müller overtook German star Manfred Strössenreuther after Manfred made a bad error in the third (Unknown) programme, which lost him the clear lead he had held up till then.

The perennial Kermit Weeks came second, demonstrating sportsmanship as well as airmanship in his decision to fly a different aircraft type in each programme, and after Manfred in third position came a young lady to watch out for, American pilot Linda Meyers who finished fourth ahead of all her fellow-countrymen except Kermit. In her recent appearance in the 1984 World Championships Linda took the gold medal for the Known Compulsory programme, and she is undoubtedly a name to watch in the women's events of the future.

Patrick Paris's phenomenal performance in the tricky

One of America's star pilots, Linda Meyers, (above) in the cockpit and (below) on a lap of honour after her sensational 4th placing in the South African Masters. *(Peter Celliers)*

from Belgium, Albert Hage and Philippe Wolff, upheld the new Belgian presence which has begun to be noticeable in European internationals.

At the bottom of the league, in the ultra-new newcomers section, were two first-time-ever representatives of their respective countries in a Category 1 event: André Fusdahl from Norway and Frank Versteegh from Holland. Though they are yet to prove themselves serious contenders in the international aerobatics arena, both are already popular visitors to the larger American aerobatic competitions, and both score highly in the 'nice guy' stakes.

Do these names include among them a World Aerobatic Champion of the future? Only time will tell.

World Aerobatic Masters Tournament, South Africa

1.	Eric Müller	Swiss	13329.1
2.	Kermit Weeks	US	13284.3
3.	Manfred Strössenreuther	German	13100.6
4.	Linda Meyers	US	12756.1
5.	Gene Beggs	US	12706.3
6.	Patrick Paris	French	12677.6
7.	André van Kryenburg	RSA	12662.9
8.	Fernando Adrados	Spain	12590.3
9.	Harold Chappell	US	12440.3
10.	Peter Celliers	RSA	12284.7
11.	Henry Haigh	US	12262.8
12.	Guido Lepore	Canadian	12081.5
13.	Luis Cabre	Spanish	11854.6
14.	Brian Zeederberg	RSA	11621.2
15.	Sergio Dallan	Italian	10967.9
16.	Peter Anderson	US	10934.1
17.	Brian Lecomber	British	10821.1
18.	Albert Hage	Belgian	9579.7
19.	André Fusdahl	Norwegian	9491.2
20	Walter Egger	Austrian	8461.3
21.	Philippe Wolff	Belgian	7894.9
22.	Sebastian Grassl	German	7556.9
23.	Frank Versteegh	Dutch	5068.6

The four winners. Left to right: Linda Meyers (4th), Manfred Strössenreuther (3rd), Kermit Weeks (2nd), Eric Müller (1st).
(Klaus Habermann)

Zlin 50 which took him to sixth place has already been mentioned, and next on the list of lesser known pilots should be mentioned the two Spaniards, Fernando Adrados, who finished eighth, and Luis Cabre (thirteenth), airline pilot and part-time bullfighter, an explosive and lovable personality who always led the night-time revels until the early hours with songs to his own enthusiastic guitar accompaniment. Luis and Fernando showed that Spain still has material of high quality to offer, if only the authorities would allow them more than the present ridiculously limited access to their Zlin 50s for training.

In a very creditable twelfth position in his first big international came Canadian pilot Guido Lepore, a quiet young man and an athlete whose interests encompass water sports such as wind-surfing, as well as aviation. A new and popular contestant from Germany, hailing from the 'Strössenreuther country' of Bavaria, was Sebastian Grassl; while two pilots

Appendix

1

World aerobatic championships

1960 – BRATISLAVA, CZECHOSLOVAKIA

					Eliminators	Finals
1.	Bezák, Ladislav (5,6)*	Czech	Z-226 T	677.66	700.67
2.	Bláha, Jiří (1,2,3,4)*	Czech	Z-226 A	711.62	693.66
3.	Skácelík, František	Czech	Z-226 A	669.31	687.40
4.	Hůlka, Jaromír	Czech	Z-226 A	668.99	676.09
5.	Vasenko, Boris	USSR	Yak-18P	654.73	647.35
6.	Beseda, Zdeněk	Czech	Z-226 A	656.67	641.48
7.	Stoklasa, Jiří	Czech	Z-226 T	623.99	638.38
8.	Trebatický, Ladislav	Czech	Z-226 T	656.04	630.68
9.	Šouc, Juraj	Czech	Z-226 T	637.35	624.32
10.	Studyonov, Anatoli	USSR	Z-326 A	619.27	
11.	Voloven, Vladimir	USSR	Z-326 A	618.66	
12.	Kovsirko, Arkadi	USSR	Z-326 A	605.39	
13.	Kasperek, Stanislaw	Polish	Z-226 T	597.68	
14.	Pawolka, Gerhard	FRG	Bü 133	586.31	
15.	Karsai, Endre	Hungarian	Z-226 T	581.01	
16.	Krenčová, Eva†	Czech	Z-226 A	578.53	
17.	Verette, Gérard	French	Stampe SV.4A	559.34	
18.	Rüesch, Albert	Swiss	Bü 133	557.57	
19.	Studencki, Stefan	Polish	Z-226 T	547.56	
20.	Pál, Zoltán	Hungarian	Z-226 T	512.01	
21.	Ackerman, Stanislaw	Polish	Z-226 T	500.12	
22.	Zhuchkov, Semion	USSR	Z-326 A	477.91	
23.	Lockerová, Jiřina†	Czech	Z-226 A	470.14	
24.	Price, Frank	USA	Great Lakes	462.62	
25.	Charollais, Marcel	French	Stampe SV.4C	457.24	
26.	Rüesch, Hansruedi	Swiss	Bü 133	452.93	
27.	Phillips, Peter	British	Tiger Moth	446.90	
28.	Ayers, John	British	Tiger Moth	421.74	
29.	Boddington, Charles	British	Tiger Moth	355.29	

*Denotes winner of individual programmes shown in brackets
†Denotes female competitor

1962 – BUDAPEST, HUNGARY

1.	Tóth, József	Hungarian	Z-226 T	6207.1
2.	Loichikov, Vladislav (2,5)*	USSR	Yak-18P	6188.3
3.	Hůlka, Jaromír (3)*	Czech	Z-226 A	6172.5
4.	Bezák, Ladislav	Czech	Z-226 T	6102.2
5.	Parsons, Lindsey	USA	Great Lakes	6091.3
6.	Katona, Sándor (6)*	Hungarian	Z-226 T	5955.4
7.	Piskunov, Vladimir	USSR	Yak-18P	5952.0
8.	Fejes, Péter (4)*	Hungarian	Z-226 A	5938.6
9.	Vasenko, Boris	USSR	Yak-18P	5648.3
10.	Ovsyankin, Vadim	USSR	Yak-18P	5478.7
11.	Orlov, Boris (1)*	USSR	Yak-18P	2810.7
12.	Fejér, Miklós	Hungarian	Z-226 T	2799.9
13.	Jocelyn, Rod	USA	Great Lakes	2797.9
14.	Pawolka, Gerhard	FRG	KZ-8	2747.6
15.	Rusch, Kurt	GDR	Z-226 A	2577.5
16.	Stoklasa, Jiří	Czech	Z-226 T	2573.3
17.	Trebatický, Ladislav	Czech	Z-226 T	2541.9
18.	Richter, Heinz	GDR	Z-226 A	2401.5
19.	Pál, Zoltán	Hungarian	Z-226 T	2397.4
20.	Ackerman, Stanislaw	Polish	Z-226	2368.5
21.	Skácelík, František	Czech	Z-226 A	2323.6
22.	Wiland, Michał	Polish	Z-126	2252.9
23.	Kasperek, Stanislaw	Polish	Z-126	2202.9
24.	Wikto, Jerzy	Polish	Z-126	2191.6
25.	Bläske, Erwin	GDR	Z-226 A	2159.3
26.	Zschocke, Günther	GDR	Z-226 A	2137.7
27.	Calota, S	Romanian	Z-226	1959.8
28.	Studencki, Stefan	Polish	Z-126	1919.2
29.	Cole, Duane	USA	Taylorcraft BC40	1880.5
30.	Pocock, Nicholas	British	Stampe SV.4B	1701.2
31.	Greb, Herbert	FRG	Bü 133	1433.4
32.	Crismaru, Ioan	Romanian	Z-226	1332.0

*Denotes winner of individual programme(s) shown in brackets

1964 – BILBAO, SPAIN

1.	Castaño, Tomas (1,5)*	Spanish	Z-326 TM	30,431
2.	Bezák, Ladislav (6)*	Czech	Z-226 AS	30,138
3.	Trebatický, Ladislav (4)*	Czech	Z-226 AS	29,645
4.	Piskunov, Vladimir (3)*	USSR	Yak-18P	29,575
5.	Ovsyankin, Vadim	USSR	Yak-18P	29,525
6.	Pochernin, Vitold (2)*	USSR	Yak-18P	29,266
7.	Martemianov, Vladimir	USSR	Yak-18P	29,222
8.	Wagner, Arnold	Swiss	Bü 131 R-170	29,050
9.	Negron, Angel	Spanish	Z-326 TM	28,898
10.	Skácelík, František	Czech	Z-226 AS	28,864
11.	Rüesch, Hansruedi	Swiss	Bü 131 R-170	28,786
12.	Kobrle, Jiří	Czech	Z-226 AS	28,503
13.	Teregulov, Dinet	USSR	Yak-18P	28,356
14.	Fejes, Péter	Hungarian	Z-226 T	28,288
15.	Quintana, Ignacio	Spanish	Z-236 TM	28,181
16.	Ugarte, Manuel	Spanish	Z-326 TM	25,370
17.	Zanozina, Rosalia†	USSR	Yak-18P	13,961
18	Vasiljeva, Liudmila†	USSR	Yak-18P	13,735
19.	Börner, Günther	GDR	Z-326 A	13,545
20.	d'Orgeix, Jean	French	Stampe SV.4A	13,451
21.	Kaprasová, Eva†	Czech	Z-226 AS	13,431
22.	Richter, Heinz	GDR	Z-326 A	13,263
23.	Bläske, Erwin	GDR	Z-326 A	13,114
24.	Verette, Gérard	French	Stampe SV.4A	13,094
25.	Baurin, Michel	French	Stampe SV.4A	12,952
26.	Kirsanova, Margarita†	USSR	Yak-18P	12,742
27.	Tóth, József	Hungarian	Z-326 Special	12,733
28.	Kahle, Peter	GDR	Z-326 A	12,729
29.	Fejér, Miklós	Hungarian	Z-226 T	12,729
30.	Bogdandi, Tibor	Hungarian	Z-226 T	12,634
31.	Williams, Neil	British	Cosmic Wind	12,576
32.	Šouc, Juraj	Czech	Z-226 AS	12,559
33.	Katona, Sándor	Hungarian	Z-226 T	12,294
34.	Rusch, Kurt	GDR	Z-326 A	12,242
35.	Price, Frank	USA	Bü 133 (Lycoming)	11,997
36.	Charollais, Marcel	French	Stampe SV.4A	11,940
37.	Krier, Harold	USA	Krier Kraft	11,230
38.	Greb, Herbert	FRG	Z-226	11,229
39.	Lacour, Reine†	French	Stampe SV.4A	10,388
40.	Turvey, Nick	S. African	Stampe SV.4B	9,828
41.	Winter, Robert	British	Stampe SV.4B	9,698
42.	Rüesch, Albert	Swiss	Bü 131 R-170	8,629
43.	Bois, Daniel	Swiss	Bü 131 R-170	8,595
44.	Phillips, Peter	British	Stampe SV.4B	8,410
45.	Nance, Robert	USA	Great Lakes	5,478

*Denotes winner of individual programme(s) shown in brackets
†Denotes female competitor. No female title awarded since there were fewer than 10 contestants (otherwise Zanozina, 14th in the eliminators, would have flown in the finals)

1966 – MOSCOW, USSR
Men's Championship

1.	Martemianov, Vladimir (1,3,4,5,6)*	USSR	Yak-18PM	26,289.5
2.	Ovsyankin, Vadim (2)*	USSR	Yak-18PM	26,028.6
3.	Piskunov, Vladimir	USSR	Yak-18PM	25,323.5
4.	Pimenov, Alexei	USSR	Yak-18PM	24,988.1
5.	Bezák, Ladislav	Czech	Z-526 T	24,844.1
6.	Börner, Günther	GDR	Z-326 A	24,775.0
7.	Pochernin, Vitold	USSR	Yak-18PM	24,695.2
8.	Šouc, Juraj	Czech	Z-226 AS	24,680.3
9.	Pascal, Michel	French	Nord 3202	24,586.8
10.	Bläske, Erwin	GDR	Z-326 A	24,532.4
11.	Castaño, Tomas	Spanish	Z-326 A	24,486.7
12.	Kahle, Peter	GDR	Z-326 A	24,400.8
13.	Ugarte, Manuel	Spanish	Z-326 A	24,384.0
14.	Gomez-Carretero, Francisco	Spanish	Z-326 A	24,381.7
15.	Williams, Neil	British	Z-226 S	24,285.4
16.	Kapphahn, Dieter	GDR	Z-326 A	24,246.1

17.	Kobrle, Jiří	Czech	Z-226 AS	24,201.8
18.	Skácelík, František	Czech	Z-226 AS	24,109.1
19.	Stoklasa, Jiří	Czech	Z-226 AS	13,990.6
20.	Farkas, Sándor	Hungarian	Z-226 T	13,934.3
21.	Hübler, Heinz	GDR	Z-326 A	13,916.5
22.	Kasperek, Stanislaw	Polish	Z-26 SKA†	13,909.6
23.	Gil de Montes, Augustin	Spanish	Z-326 A	13,897.9
24.	Verette, Gérard	French	Z-326 A	13,816.8
25.	Quintana, Ignacio	Spanish	Z-326 A	13,794.9
26.	Herendeen, Bob	USA	Pitts S-1C	13,782.5
27.	Wagner, Arnold	Swiss	KZ-8	13,728.3
28.	Tóth, József	Hungarian	Z-226 T	13,614.7
29.	Hillard, Charlie	USA	Krier Kraft	13,593.8
30.	Krier, Harold	USA	Super Chipmunk	13,530.2
31.	Haig-Thomas, Tony	British	Z-226 S	13,494.0
32.	Kasperek, Ryszard	Polish	Z-26 SKA†	13,441.3
33.	Ackerman, Stanislaw	Polish	Z-26 SKA†	13,379.2
34.	Baurin, Michel	French	Nord 3202	13,344.0
35.	Roger, Denis	French	Z-326 A	13,310.2
36.	Mikołajczyk, Edmund	Polish	Z-26 SKA†	13,305.4
37.	Scholl, Art	USA	Super Chipmunk	13,259.1
38.	Amen, Robert	French	Nord 3202	13,218.4
39.	Rozman, Gyula	Hungarian	Z-226 T	13,214.4
40.	Bogdandi, Tibor	Hungarian	Z-226 T	13,185.8
41.	Heit, Gaspar	Hungarian	Z 226 T	13,100.7
42.	Studencki, Stefan	Polish	Z-26 SKA†	13,025.6
43.	Calota, S	Romanian	Yak-18P	12,851.0
44.	Pawolka, Gerhard	FRG	Z-526	12,823.4
45.	Wolfrum, Walter	FRG	Bü 131 Lerche R	12,683.1
46.	Orgis, S	Yugoslav	Yak-18P	12,564.5
47.	Stoyanov, M	Bulgarian	Yak-18P	12,359.3
48.	Black, James	British	Stampe SV.4B	12,205.0
49.	Georgiev, Angel	Bulgarian	Yak-18P	11,426.9
50.	d'Erlanger, Robin	British	Stampe SV.4B	11,071.6
51.	Allan, David	Australian	Stampe SV.4B	10,833.8
52.	Pukl, S	Yugoslav	Yak-18P	10,517.2
53.	Hasler, Eugen	Swiss	Z-326	9,241.8

*Denotes gold medallist in individual progamme(s) shown in brackets
†SKA = Super Kasper Akrobat (160 hp two-seater modified to single-seater)

Women's Championship

1.	Korchuganova, Galina (2)*	USSR	Yak-18PM	14,394.2
2.	Peresekina, Taisya (30)	USSR	Yak-18PM	14,356.4
3.	Kirsanova, Margarita	USSR	Yak-18PM	14,148.3
4.	Vasilieva, Liudmila (1)*	USSR	Yak-18PM	14,036.4
5.	Delcroix, Madelyne	French	Z-526 A	13,809.8
6.	Kaprasová, Eva	Czech	Z-226 AS	13,648.7
7.	Turkina, Evgeniya	USSR	Yak-18PM	13,302.4
8.	Lockerová, Jiřina	Czech	Z-226 AS	13,185.4
9.	Solovieva, Galina	USSR	Yak-18PM	12,664.4
10.	Kapustová, Alžběta	Czech	Z-226 AS	10,998.3

*Denotes gold medallist in individual programme shown in brackets

1968 – MAGDEBURG, GERMAN DEMOCRATIC REPUBLIC
Men's Championship

				Progs I–II	(Prog III)
1.	Bläske, Erwin (2)*	GDR	Z-526 A	6581.2	(5859.7)
2.	Kahle, Peter (1)*	GDR	Z-526 A	6502.6	(6059.7)
3.	Šouc, Juraj	Czech	Z-526 AS	6317.1	(Retired)
4.	Kapphahn, Dieter	GDR	Z-526 A	6241.4	(6022.2)
5.	Williams, Neil	British	Z-526 A	6199.9	(5070.0)
6.	Wagner, Arnold	Swiss	KZ-8	6189.3	(5672.1)
7.	Herendeen, Bob	USA	Pitts S-1S	6178.8	(6214.8)
8.	Schofield, Carl	British	Z-526 A	6157.1	(5492.7)
9.	Scholl, Art	USA	Super Chipmunk	6105.6	(5921.3)
10.	Pimenov, Alexei	USSR	Yak-18PM	6075.6	(5992.5)
11.	Egorov, Igor	USSR	Yak-18PM	6065.0	(6253.6)
12.	Börner, Günther	GDR	Z-526 A	6050.2	(5723.2)

13.	Tuček, Ivan	Czech	Z-526 AS	6047.7	(Retired)
14.	Ponomaryov, Valentin	USSR	Yak-18PM	5989.8	(5963.5)
15.	Skácelik, František	Czech	Z-526 AS	5908.7	(5197.8)
16.	Ugarte, Manuel	Spanish	Z-526 F	5902.6	(5473.5)
17.	Mikołajczyk, Edmund	Polish	Z-326 A	5885.0	(5394.3)
18.	Hoessl, Josef	FRG	Super K1 35D 160	5877.3	(5633.5)
19.	Stas, Helmut	Polish	Z-326 A	5842.4	(206.0)
20.	Kasperek, Ryszard	Polish	Z-326 A	5834.3	(5183.1)
21.	Quintana, Ignacio	Spanish	Z-526 F	5824.6	(5883.2)
22.	Kawala, Felicjan	Polish	Z-326 A	5824.3	(5246.0)
23.	Romanchikov, Boris	USSR	Yak-18PM	5819.4	(4141.1)
24.	Cole, Marion	USA	Bü 131 (200 hp)	5812.2	(5377.4)
25.	Hecht, Richard	FRG	Z-526	5796.8	(4237.5)
26.	Hillard, Charlie	USA	Super Chipmunk	5793.4	(5974.3)
27.	Delcroix, André	French	Z-526 A	5777.4	(4692.2)
28.	Farkas, Sándor	Hungarian	Z-526 A	5749.9	(5429.0)
29.	Krier, Harold	USA	Super Chipmunk	5743.4	(5906.0)
30.	Kovacs, Pal	Hungarian	Z-526 A	5735.9	(3110.0)
31.	Stoklasa, Jiří	Czech	Z-526 AS	5714.9	(5779.1)
32.	Erdös, Mihaly	Hungarian	Z-526 A	5713.7	(5392.5)
33.	Durucz, Jenö	Hungarian	Z-526 A	5686.8	(5494.4)
34.	Turvey, Nick	S. African	Z-226	5529.6	(3540.0)
35.	Farkas, Gyula	Hungarian	Z-526 A	5487.6	(5688.1)
36.	Balcells, José-Luis	Spanish	Z-526 F	5328.5	(4637.1)
37.	Martemianov, Vladimir	USSR	Yak-18PM	5289.9	(6010.7)
38.	Jurk, Manfred	GDR	Z-526 A	5266.6	(5441.2)
39.	Alos, Carlos	Spanish	Z-526 F	5197.2	(5784.2)
40.	Kobrle, Jiří	Czech	Z-526 AS	5077.3	(Retired)
41.	Kasperek, Stanislaw	Polish	Z-326 A	4871.4	(5807.4)
42.	Patzig, Kurt	FRG	Z-526 A	4862.7	(4921.6)
43.	Holzberger, Norbert	FRG	Z-326	4843.4	(5193.1)
44.	Gomez-Carretero, Francisco	Spanish	Z-526 F	4767.0	(5716.3)
45.	Wessels, Ewald	S. African	Z-226	4757.7	(2888.8)
46.	Lukasek, Josip	Yugoslav	Z-526	3864.0	(1867.4)
47.	Black, James	British	Z-526 A	3533.2	(5747.5)
48.	Pintar, Janez	Yugoslav	Z-526	3431.5	(2986.5)
	Winternitz, Thomas	S. African	Z-226	Disqualified	

*Denotes gold medallist in individual programme shown in brackets

Women's Championship

				Progs I–II	(Prog III)
1.	Delcroix, Madelyne	French	Z-526 A	5969.5	(5094.5)
2.	Fleck, Monika	GDR	Z-526 A	5920.2	(5820.1)
3.	Korchuganova, Galina (2)*	USSR	Yak-18PM	5892.1	(2155.8)
4.	Uhlig, Margit (1)*	GDR	Z-526 A	5763.5	(5476.3)
5.	Lockerová, Jiřina	Czech	Z-526 AS	5624.5	(Retired)
6.	Oschmann, Angelika	GDR	Z-526 A	5604.3	(5378.5)
7.	Kapustová, Alžběta	Czech	Z-526 AS	5509.0	(Retired)
8.	Solovieva, Galina	USSR	Yak-18PM	5505.8	(5011.3)
9.	Kirsanova, Margarita	USSR	Yak-18PM	5445.0	(5099.5)
10.	Gaffaney, Mary	USA	Pitts S-1S	5434.4	(5456.6)
11.	Wallentin, Jutta	GDR	Z-526 A	5165.6	(5446.2)
12.	Krenčová, Eva	Czech	Z-526 AS	5101.2	(Retired)
13.	Kaprasová, Eva	Czech	Z-526 AS	2825.0	(Retired)
14.	Macrae, Frances	British	Stampe SV.4	2415.5	(3723.8)

*Denotes gold medallist in individual programme shown in brackets

---

1970 – HULLAVINGTON, ENGLAND
Men's Championship (three programmes flown)

1.	Egorov, Igor (1,2,3)*	USSR	Yak-18PS	12801.875
2.	Herendeen, Bob	USA	Pitts S-1S	12678.375
3.	Hillard, Charlie	USA	Spinks Akromaster	12418.875
4.	Wagner, Arnold	Swiss	Acrostar Mk II	12222.5
5.	Williams, Neil	British	Z-526 F	12205.625
6.	Soucy, Gene	USA	Pitts S-1S	12192.75
7.	Schnuerle, Bob	USA	Pitts S-1S	12170.125
8.	Tuček, Ivan	Czech	Z-526 AF	12049.0
9.	Ponomaryov, Valentin	USSR	Yak-18PS	11991.125

10.	Kobrle, Jiří	Czech	Z-526 AF	11978.625
11.	Kahle, Peter	GDR	Z-526 A	11898.25
12.	Bläske, Erwin	GDR	Z-526 A	11848.625
13.	Pimenov, Alexei	USSR	Yak-18PS	11845.25
14.	Kainov, Evgeni	USSR	Yak-18PM	11844.75
15.	Arnhold, Jürgen	GDR	Z-526 A	11706.0
16.	Mikołajczyk, Edmund	Polish	Z-526 F	11612.0
17.	Ordoux, Jean-Claude	French	Z-526	11511.875
18.	Gomez-Carretero, Francisco	Spanish	Z-526 F	11511.625
19.	Kasperek, Stanislaw	Polish	Z-526 F	11471.75
20.	Kawala, Felicjan	Polish	Z-526 F	11468.0
21.	Jindra, Josef	Czech	Z-526 AF	11446.875
22.	Hecht, Richard	FRG	Z-226	11394.625
23.	Jurk, Manfred	GDR	Z-526 A	11359.0
24.	Paar, Robert	French	Nord 3202	11343.875
25.	Kasperek, Ryszard	Polish	Z-526 F	11340.0
26.	Brandt, Michel	Swiss	Bü 131 Lerche	11334.6
27.	Samoylov, Victor	USSR	Yak-18PM	11307.5
28.	Börner, Günther	GDR	Z-526 A	11238.625
29.	Hoessl, Josef	FRG	Acrostar Mk II	11203.0
30.	Black, James	British	Z-526 F	11200.0
31.	Kovacs, Pal	Hungarian	Z-526 A	11182.4
32.	Alos, Carlos	Spanish	Z-526 F	11175.375
33.	Erdös, Mihaly	Hungarian	Z-526 A	11097.0
34.	Stas, Helmut	Polish	Z-526 F	11076.5
35.	Müller, Eric	Swiss	Bü 131 Lerche	11057.5
36.	Schofield, Carl	British	Z-526 F	11039.5
37.	Scholl, Art	USA	Super Chipmunk	11024.75
38.	Gil de Montes, Augustin	Spanish	Z-526 F	10990.375
39.	Inclan, Enrique	Spanish	Z-526 F	10961.875
40.	Orlita, Radomír	Czech	Z-526 AF	10943.5
41.	Holzberger, Norbert	FRG	Z-326	10920.375
42.	Farkas, Gyula	Hungarian	Z-526 A	10880.3
43.	Baudoin, Robert	French	CAP 20	10726.375
44.	Schweizer, Christian	Swiss	Z-526 A	10524.4
45.	Hugli, Denis	Swiss	Z-526 A	10494.9
46.	Patzig, Kurt	FRG	Super K1 35D 160	10219.375
47.	Héligoin, Daniel	French	Z-526	9900.25
48.	Jarvis, Peter	British	Z-526 T	9463.875
49.	Féliot, Yvon	French	Z-526	8692.25
	Gaster, David	British	Z-526 T	Retired through illness

*Denotes gold medallist in individual programmes shown in brackets

Women's Championship (four programmes flown)

1.	Savitskaya, Svetlana (3)*	USSR	Yak-18PM	17278.25
2.	Lizunova, Zinaida (2)*	USSR	Yak-18PM	17110.75
3.	Gaffaney, Mary (1)*	USA	Pitts S-1S	16988.625
4.	Schösser, Monika	GDR	Z-526 A	16520.75
5.	Leonova, Lidia (4)*	USSR	Yak-18PM	16483.75
6.	Uhlig, Margit	GDR	Z-526 A	15413.875
7.	Podolyak, Svetlana	USSR	Yak-18PM	15241.75
8.	Morokhova, Liubov†	USSR	Yak-18PM	10225.875
9.	Paul, Angelika	GDR	Z-526 A	9874.125

*Denotes gold medallist in individual programme shown in brackets
†Later married name Nemkova

1972 – SALON DE PROVENCE, FRANCE
Men's Championship

1.	Hillard, Charlie (3)*	USA	Pitts S-1S	17631.9
2.	Pimenov, Alexei (4)*	USSR	Yak-18PS	17609.4
3.	Soucy, Gene (1,2)*	USA	Pitts S-1S	17561.2
4.	Schweizer, Christian	Swiss	Acrostar	17203.9
5.	Egorov, Igor	USSR	Yak-18PS	17157.2
6.	Poberezny, Tom	USA	Pitts S-1S	17136.2
7.	Kobrle, Jiří	Czech	Z-526 AFS	17093.4
8.	Müller, Eric	Swiss	Acrostar	17092.6

9.	Scholl, Art	USA	Pitts S-2A	17050.6
10.	Black, James	British	Pitts S-1S	16994.5
11.	Tuček, Ivan	Czech	Z-526 AFS	16921.6
12.	Kahle, Peter	GDR	Z-526 AFS	16902.9
13.	Peña, Louis	French	CAP 20	16837.2
14.	Dousson, Robert	French	CAP 20	16745.9
15.	Letsko, Victor	USSR	Yak-18PS	16714.0
16.	Jindra, Josef	Czech	Z-526 AFS	16108.5
17.	Williams, Neil	British	Pitts S-1S	14021.8
18.	Baudoin, Robert	French	CAP 20	14014.8
19.	Šmíd, Václav	Czech	Z-526 AFS	14014.4
20.	Bläske, Erwin	GDR	Z-526 AFS	13999.0
21.	Jurk, Manfred	GDR	Z-526 AFS	13974.0
22.	Hoessl, Josef	FRG	Acrostar	13951.0
23.	Gomez-Carretero, Francisco	Spanish	Z-526 FS	13919.4
24.	Ordoux, Jean-Claude	French	Acrostar	13915.8
25.	Gil de Montes, Augustin	Spanish	Z-526 FS	13886.3
26.	Stas, Helmut	Polish	Z-526 AFS	13778.6
27.	Polonec, Daniel	Czech	Z-526 AFS	13763.4
28.	Arnhold, Jürgen	GDR	Z-526 AFS	13752.3
29.	Hugli, Denis	Swiss	Acrostar	13742.3
30.	Thomas, Bill	USA	Pitts S-1S	13738.5
31.	Kasperek, Ryszard	Polish	Z-526 AFS	13700.8
32.	Alos, Carlos	Spanish	Z-526 FS	13670.2
33.	Pawlak, Pawel	Polish	Z-526 AFS	13647.5
34.	Ponomaryov, Valentin	USSR	Yak-18PS	13624.6
35.	Kawala, Felicjan	Polish	Z-526 AFS	13582.4
36.	Brandt, Michel	Swiss	CAP 20	13407.5
37.	Riley, Mike	British	Z-526	13380.6
38.	Ehrle, Eberhard	FRG	Acrostar	13325.4
39.	Hecht, Richard	FRG	Acrostar	13260.5
40.	Bauer, Hans	GDR	Z-526 AFS	13047.3
41.	Farkas, Sandor	FRG	Acrostar	13011.1
42.	Kuzma, Jerzy	Polish	Z-526 AFS	12988.8
43.	Castaño, Tomas	Spanish	Z-526 FS	12949.1
44.	Paar, Robert	French	Acrostar	12505.5
45.	Strössenreuther, Manfred	FRG	K1 35-D 160	12408.1
46.	Mitchell, Bob	British	KZ-8	12193.4
47.	Turvey, Nick	S. African	Reid Rooivalk	11423.0

*Denotes gold medallist in programme(s) shown in brackets

Women's Championship

1.	Gaffaney, Mary (1,2)*	USA	Pitts S-1S	17197.8
2.	Morokhova, Liubov[1]	USSR	Yak-18PS	17123.5
3.	Leonova, Lidia (4)*	USSR	Yak-18PS	16780.1
4.	Savitskaya, Svetlana	USSR	Yak-18PS	16669.9
5.	Lizunova, Zinaida (3)*	USSR	Yak-18PS	16622.9
6.	Goldobina, Valentina[2]	USSR	Yak-18PS	16193.3
7.	Uhlig, Margit	GDR	Z-526 AFS	13196.3
8.	Schösser, Monika	GDR	Z-526 AFS	13018.8
9.	Krenčová, Eva	Czech	Z-526 AFS	12942.6
10.	Salisbury, Carolyn	USA	Pitts S-2A	12644.9
11.	Angerhöfer, Gerlinde	GDR	Z-526 AFS	12509.2
12.	Bulka, Halina	Polish	Z-526 AFS	11736.1

*Denotes gold medallist in programme(s) shown in brackets
[1]Later married name Nemkova
[2]Later married name Yaikova

1976 – KIEV, USSR
Men's Championship

1.	Letsko, Victor	USSR	Yak 50	17864.2
2.	Egorov, Igor (2,3,4)*	USSR	Yak 50	17771.7
3.	Tuček, Ivan	Czech	Z-50 L	17707.4
4.	Williams, Neil	British	Pitts S-1S	17645.6
5.	Pimenov, Alexei	USSR	Yak 50	17388.9
6.	Strössenreuther, Manfred (1)*	FRG	Pitts S-1S	17366.3
7.	Molchaniuk, Michael	USSR	Yak 50	17356.5
8.	Brandt, Michel	Swiss	Pits BS-1S	17151.0
9.	Frolov, Evgeni	USSR	Yak 50	16985.1
10.	Jurk, Manfred	GDR	Z-526 AFS	16982.8
11.	Müller, Eric	Swiss	Acrostar	16969.8
12.	Josefčák, Otakar	Czech	Z-50 L	16962.4
13.	Haigh, Henry	USA	Pitts S-1S	16897.8
14.	McHenry, Clint	USA	Pitts S-1T	16832.3
15.	Mikołajczyk, Edmund	Polish	Z-50 L	16808.5
16.	Meeson, Philip	British	Pitts S-1S	16737.9
17.	Šupák, Petr	Czech	Z-50 L	16729.2
18.	Black, James	British	Pitts S-1S	16669.1
19.	Bourgeois, Jean-René	French	CAP 20 L	16635.2
20.	Čičo, Pavel	Czech	Z-50 L	16352.1
21.	Pawlak, Pawel	Polish	Z-50 L	13726.3
22.	Gideon, Jochen	GDR	Z-526 AFS	13709.4
23.	Loudenslager, Leo	USA	Laser 200	13630.7
24.	Hecht, Richard	FRG	Pitts S-1S	13602.6
25.	Riley, Mike	British	Pitts S-1S	13596.5
26.	Feltès, Jean-Louis	French	CAP 20	13563.6
27.	Pospíšil, Jiří	Czech	Z-50 L	13563.1
28.	Lindner, Wolfgang	GDR	Z-526 AFS	13556.6
29.	Varga, Zoltán	Hungarian	Z-526 AFS	13528.3
30.	Sbihi, Jean-Louis	French	CAP 20	13483.4
31.	Thomas, Bill	USA	Pitts S-1T	13417.0
32.	Wettig, Valk	GDR	Z-526 AFS	13391.9
33.	Kalinovski, Krzysztof	Polish	Z-50 L	13382.6
34.	Tschierpke, Hans-Jürgen	GDR	Z-526 AFS	13381.4
35.	Liese, Hermann	FRG	Tornado	13368.1
36.	Simon, László	Hungarian	Z-526 AFS	13135.2
37.	Bottome, Peter	Venezuelan	Pitts S-1S	13088.7
38.	Tóth, László	Hungarian	Z-526 AFS	12987.2
39.	Treder, Zdislav	Polish	Z-526 AFS	12819.0
40.	Le Berre, Jean-Pierre	French	CAP 20	12709.7
41.	Davis, Bob	USA	Pitts S-1S	12570.6
42.	Sperou, Chris	Australian	Pitts S-1S	12563.8
43.	Hernik, Marek	Polish	Z-526 AFS	12434.3
44.	Younger, Gerry	Canadian	Pitts S-1S	11857.0
45.	Scott, Jim	Australian	Pitts S-1S	11831.5
46.	Smith, Brian	British	Pitts S-1S	11797.7
47.	Flachsmann, Urs	Swiss	Acrostar	11175.5
48.	Albu, Mihai	Romanian	Z-526 AFS	11104.2
49.	Patterson, John	Australian	Pitts S-1S	10951.5
50.	Zuccoli, Guido	Australian	Pitts S-1S	10920.8
51.	Hunt, Jay	Canadian	Pitts S-1S	10519.0
52.	Rusu, Cesar	Romanian	Z-526 AFS	9070.6
53.	Zimmerman, Franz-Josef	FRG	Acrostar	8551.6
54.	Lafille, Jean-Pierre	French	CAP 20 L	7197.0
55.	Trucmel, Ioan	Romanian	Z-526 AFS	7051.6
56.	Owen, David	NZ	Z-526 AFS	2085.2

*Denotes gold medallist in programme(s) shown in brackets

Women's Championship

1.	Leonova, Lidia (1,4)*	USSR	Yak 50	17708.3
2.	Yaikova, Valentina (2)*	USSR	Yak 50	17298.4
3.	Nemkova, Liubov	USSR	Yak 50	17188.5
4.	Mochalina, Liudmila (3)*	USSR	Yak 50	17114.6
5.	Savitskaya, Svetlana	USSR	Yak 50	16838.7
6.	Everest, Betty[1]	USA	Pitts S-1S	15551.5
7.	Kovačičová, Olga	Czech	Z-526 AFS	12780.1
8.	Geminel, Françoise	French	CAP 20	12437.9
9.	Hallóyné, Gabora	Hungarian	Z-526 AFS	12041.7
10.	Tóth, Eva	Hungarian	Z-526 AFS	11617.5
11.	Lack, Monika	Swiss	Acrostar	11527.4
12.	Lock, Pamela[2]	NZ	Pitts S-1S	10316.3

*Denotes gold medallist in individual programme(s) shown in brackets
[1]Later married name Stewart
[2]Later married name Collings

Flight Fantastic

1978 – ČESKÉ BUDĚJOVICE, CZECHOSLOVAKIA
Men's Championship

1.	Tuček, Ivan (3)*	Czech	Z-50 L	17636.6
2.	Weeks, Kermit	USA	Weeks Special	17325.6
3.	Pospíšil, Jiří	Czech	Z-50 L	17066.4
4.	Strössenreuther, Manfred (2)*	FRG	Z-50 L	16800.6
5.	Smolin, Victor	USSR	Yak 50	16728.3
6.	Molchaniuk, Michael	USSR	Yak 50	16699.1
7.	Carmichael, Bob	USA	Pitts S-1S	16688.2
8.	Haigh, Henry	USA	Super Star	16683.6
9.	Melton, Chipper	USA	Pitts S-1S	16671.2
10.	Brandt, Michel	Swiss	Pitts BS-1S	16625.8
11.	Frolov, Evgeni	USSR	Yak 50	16578.7
12.	Loudenslager, Leo (1,4)*	USA	Laser 200	16509.6
13.	Egorov, Igor	USSR	Yak 50	16445.1
14.	Polonec, Daniel	Czech	Z-50 L	16391.7
15.	Josefčák, Otakar	Czech	Z-50 L	16325.6
16.	Schweizer, Christian	Swiss	Pitts S-1S	16227.0
17.	Saller, Jiří	Czech	Z-50 L	13052.6
18.	Bourgeois, Jean-René	French	CAP 20 LS	13009.5
19.	Peña, Louis	French	CAP 20 LS	12841.5
20.	Champseix, Pierre	French	CAP 20 LS	12827.2
21.	Pawlak, Pawel	Polish	Z-50 L	12771.3
22.	Dallach, Wolfgang	FRG	Pitts S-1S	12754.1
23.	Nikitiuk, Nikolai	USSR	Yak 50	12658.8
24.	Godbille, Jacques	French	CAP 20 LS	12607.7
25.	Farkas, Sándor	FRG	Tornado	12516.4
26.	Collière, Bernard	French	CAP 20 LS	12260.7
27.	Szufa, Marek	Polish	Z-50 L	12008.1
28.	Szybalski, Bogdan	Polish	Z-50 L	11975.6
29.	Albu, Mikai	Romanian	Z-50 L	11851.2
30.	Padden, Ian	British	Pitts S-1S	11743.7
31.	Zuccoli, Guido	Australian	Pitts S-1S	11688.4
32.	Rusu, Cesar	Romanian	Z-50 L	11614.9
33.	Witek, Péter	Hungarian	Z-526 AFS	11600.6
34.	Simon, Lászlo	Hungarian	Z-526 AFS	11586.2
35.	Molnár, András	Hungarian	Z-526 AFS	11265.5
36.	Trucmel, Ioan	Romanian	Z-50 L	11045.6
37.	Hogan, Allen	NZ	Pitts S-1S	10859.9
38.	Selvey, Hilton	Australian	Pitts S-1S	10808.4
39.	Poynton, Rob	Australian	Pitts S-1S	10714.5
40.	Mitchell, Bob	British	Stephens Akro	10672.0
41.	Goode, Richard	British	Pitts S-1S	10519.8
42.	Jedrysek, Krzysztof	Polish	Z-50 L	10467.6
43.	Brocard, Georges	Swiss	Acrostar	10421.9
44.	Wroblewski, Janusz	Polish	Z-526 AFS	10228.8
45.	Burdet, Pierre Alain	Swiss	Acrostar	10086.6
46.	Guraly, Béla	Hungarian	Z-526 AFS	9819.3
47.	Pászti, Tibor	Hungarian	Z-526 AFS	9817.5
48.	Schiller, Werner	Swiss	CAP 20 LS	5451.8

*Denotes gold medallist in programme(s) shown in brackets

Women's Championship

1.	Yaikova, Valentina (4)*	USSR	Yak 50	16581.3
2.	Leonova, Lidia (1,2)*	USSR	Yak 50	16517.9
3.	Nemkova, Liubov (3)*	USSR	Yak 50	16355.0
4.	Mochalina, Liudmila	USSR	Yak 50	16160.4
5.	Ajnetdinova, Khalide[1]	USSR	Yak 50	15544.3
6.	Kovačičová, Olga	Czech	Z-50 L	15402.6
7.	Geminel, Françoise	French	CAP 20 LS	15254.2
8.	Lacour, Hélène	French	CAP 20 LS	12254.1
9.	Roux, Marianne[2]	French	CAP 20 LS	12247.0
10.	Marion, Catherine[3]	French	CAP 20 LS	11828.7
11.	Novotná, Emilie	Czech	Z-50 L	11124.4
12.	Collière, Rose-Marie	French	CAP 20 LS	11084.4
13.	Chromcová, Sona	Czech	Z-50 L	10090.7

*Denotes gold medallist in programme(s) shown in brackets
[1] Later married name Makagonova
[2] Later married name Maire
[3] Later married name Manoury

1980 – OSHKOSH, USA
Men's Championship

1.	Loudenslager, Leo (3,4)*	USA	Laser 200	17826.9
2.	Haigh, Henry (1)*	USA	Pitts S-1S	17442.8
3.	Weeks, Kermit (2)*	USA	Weeks Special	17280.0
4.	Strössenreuther, Manfred	FRG	Z-50 L	17222.7
5.	Melton, Chipper	USA	Pitts S-1S	17111.9
6.	Collier, Tom	USA	Pitts S-2S	16844.6
7.	Brandt, Michel	Swiss	Christen E-1	16828.8
8.	Schweizer, Christian	Swiss	Christen E-1	16367.9
9.	Müller, Eric	Swiss	CAP 21	16328.3
10.	Peña, Louis	French	CAP 21	16060.0
11.	Waterton, Bill	Australian	Pitts S-1S	15920.4
12.	Meeson, Philip	British	Pitts S-1S	15541.3
13.	Jourdan, Noël	French	ASA 200	15177.4
14.	Fry, Frank	Australian	Pitts S-1S	15139.5
15.	Price, Gordon	Canadian	Ultimate Pitts	12980.1
16.	Liese, Hermann	FRG	Z-50 L	12977.4
17.	Goode, Richard	British	Pitts S-1S	12870.3
18.	Poynton, Rob	Australian	Pitts S-2S	12831.5
19.	Padden, Ian	British	Pitts S-2S	12811.6
20.	Collière, Bernard	French	CAP 20 L	12760.3
21.	Dallan, Sergio	Italian	CAP 20 L	12752.0
22.	Feugray, Gérard	French	ASA 200	12673.9
23.	Selvey, Hilton	Australian	Pitts S-2S	12510.5
24.	Senior, Ian	British	Pitts S-1S	12430.4
25.	Harper, John	British	Pitts S-1S	12341.0
26.	Jaegle, Wolfgang	FRG	Pitts S-1S	11960.3
27.	Sperou, Chris	Australian	Pitts S-1S	11919.6
28.	Younger, Gerry	Canadian	Pitts S-1S	11737.0
29.	Turvey, Nick	S. African	Pitts S-1S	11628.8
30.	Lafille, Jean-Pierre	French	CAP 20 L	11484.9
31.	Wurster, Hermann	FRG	Pitts S-1S	11366.9
32.	Hay, Bob	S. African	Pitts S-1S	11128.6
33.	Extra, Walter	FRG	Pitts Extra	11127.4
34.	Otten, Noel	S. African	Pitts S-1S	10978.5
35.	Percy, Warren	S. African	Pitts S-1S	10884.9
36.	Jenkinson, Frank	Canadian	Pitts S-1S	10803.9
37.	Lucia, Massimo	Italian	CAP 20 L	10501.0
38.	Locatelli, Aldo	Italian	CAP 20 L	9723.0
39.	Nardi, Diego	Italian	CAP 20 L	9575.5
40.	Colangelo, Nicola	Italian	CAP 20 L	9534.6
41.	Zeederberg, Brian	S. African	Pitts S-1S	9082.2
42.	Kennedy, Bill	Canadian	Pitts S-1S	8258.7

*Denotes gold medallist in programme(s) shown in brackets

Women's Championship

1.	Stewart, Betty (1,2,3)*	USA	Pitts S-1S	16042.5
2.	Johnson, Patti (4)*	USA	Pitts S-2S	15431.2
3.	Moore, Paula	USA	Pitts S-1S	15230.4
4.	Marion, Catherine†	French	ASA 200	14333.7
5.	Geminel, Françoise	French	CAP 20 L	13082.2
6.	Collière, Rose-Marie	French	CAP 20 L	13000.7
7.	Roux-Maire, Marianne	French	CAP 20 L	11140.6
8.	Collings, Pam	NZ	Pitts S-1S	10763.3
9.	Perronet, Sylvie	French	CAP 20 L	9354.5

*Denotes gold medallist in programme(s) shown in brackets
†Later married name Manoury

1982 – SPITZERBERG, AUSTRIA
Men's Championship

1.	Smolin, Victor (3)*	USSR	Yak 50	16404.4
2.	Haigh, Henry	USA	Super Star	16399.4
3.	Strössenreuther, Manfred	FRG	Z-50 L	16310.8
4.	Jirmus, Petr	Czech	Z-50 LS	16194.5
5.	Loudenslager, Leo (2)*	USA	Laser 200	16182.9

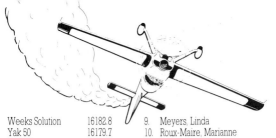

6.	Weeks, Kermit (4)*	USA	Weeks Solution	16182.8
7.	Nikitiuk, Nikolai	USSR	Yak 50	16179.7
8.	Saller, Jiří	Czech	Z-50 LS	15763.7
9.	Brandt, Michel	Swiss	Pitts BS-1S	15549.0
10.	Schweizer, Christian	Swiss	Pitts S-1S	15448.2
11.	Kairis, Yurgis (1)*	USSR	Yak 50	15405.6
12.	Peña, Louis	French	CAP 21	15335.1
13.	Dallach, Wolfgang	FRG	Diabolo	15330.5
14.	Müller, Eric	Swiss	CAP 21	15281.6
15.	Paksas, Rolandas	USSR	Yak 50	15256.4
16.	Molchaniuk, Michael	USSR	Yak 55	15255.4
17.	Roberts, Jim	USA	Laser 200	15185.9
18.	Feltès, Jean-Louis	French	CAP 20/260	15154.6
19.	Witt, Bill	USA	Pitts S-1S	14995.7
20	Čičo, Pavel	Czech	Z-50 LA	14987.7
21.	Bessière, Claude	French	CAP 20/260	14901.1
22.	Fry, Frank	Australian	Stephens Alro-Z	14784.3
23.	Harper, John	British	Pitts S-1S	13207.8
24.	Sperou, Chris	Australian	Pitts S-1S	13187.1
25.	Jaegle, Wolfgang	FRG	Pitts S-1S	13147.6
26.	Kynsey, Peter	British	Pitts S-1S	12944.8
27.	Price, Gordon	Canadian	Ultimate Pitts	12887.7
28.	Pászti, Tibor	Hungarian	Z-50 LA	12837.4
29.	Selvey, Geoff	Australian	Pitts S 2SE	12689.5
30.	Burda, Petr	Czech	Z-50 LA	12671.2
31.	Extra, Walter	FRG	Pitts Extra	12663.4
32.	Albu, Mihai	Romanian	Z-50 LA	12641.8
33.	Lavigne, Bob	Canadian	Pitts S-1S	12639.4
34.	Dallan, Sergio	Italian	CAP 20 L	12625.7
35.	Courtonne, Patrick	French	CAP 21	12625.3
36.	Marzetti, Tomaso	Italian	CAP 20 L	12594.4
37.	Mitu, Marcel	Romanian	Z-50 LA	12550.1
38.	Selvey, Hilton	Australian	Pitts S-2SE	12511.1
39.	Feteanu, Mielu	Romanian	Z-50 LA	12478.2
40.	Joudan, Noël	French	ASA 200	12435.6
41.	Adrados, Fernando	Spanish	Z-50 LA	12423.7
42.	Hagander, Erik	Swiss	Pitts S-1S	12382.5
43.	Peroutka, Vladimír	Czech	Z-50 LA	12362.2
44.	Botes, Johan	S. African	Pitts S-2S	12304.5
45.	Balcells, José Luis	Spanish	Z-50 LA	12224.4
46.	Cabre, Luis	Spanish	Z-50 LA	12191.2
47.	Chmiel, Marek	Polish	Z-50 L	12148.3
48.	Makula, Jerzy	Polish	Z-50 L	12051.7
49.	Ucelay, Ciro	Spanish	Z-50 LA	11942.5
50.	Balatoni, József	Hungarian	Z-50 LA	11763.6
51.	Locatelli, Aldo	Italian	Acroduster	11686.3
52.	Hay, Bob	S. African	Pitts S-1S	11651.2
53.	Colangelo, Nicola	Italian	CAP 20 L	11383.2
54.	Jenkinson, Frank	Canadian	F J Special	11376.5
55.	Kasperek, Janusz	Polish	Z-50 L	11358.0
56.	Iana, Aurel	Romanian	Z-50 LA	11316.5
57.	Tóth, Lászlo	Hungarian	Z-50 LA	11196.3
58.	Molnár, András	Hungarian	Z-50 LA	11171.5
59.	Valle, Carlos	Spanish	Z-50 LA	11057.6
60.	Diaconu, Ioan	Romanian	Z-50 LA	10414.9
61.	Zeederberg, Brian	S. African	Pitts S-1S	10311.8
62.	Celliers, Peter	S. African	Pitts S-2S	9692.8
63.	Nardi, Diego	Italian	CAP 20 L	9087.2
64.	Goode, Richard†	British	Pace Spirit	9018.8
65.	Stiasny, Erich	Austrian	Pitts Extra	6589.8

*Denotes gold medallist in programme shown in brackets
†Retired through illness

Women's Championship

1.	Stewart, Betty (1,3,4)*	USA	Pitts S-1S	15482.4
2.	Nemkova, Liubov	USSR	Yak 50	15243.9
3.	Makagonova, Khalide (2)*	USSR	Yak 50	15139.3
4.	Leonova, Lidia	USSR	Yak 50	15096.5
5.	Johnson-Nelson, Patti	USA	Laser 200	15007.6
6.	Yaikova, Valentina	USSR	Yak 50	14764.1
7.	Manoury, Catherine	French	CAP 21	14217.1
8.	Mochalina, Liudmila	USSR	Yak 50	14200.8

9.	Meyers, Linda	USA	Weeks Special	12917.5
10.	Roux-Maire, Marianne	French	CAP 21	12817.4
11.	Ionitza, Ana Nina	Romanian	Z-50 LA	12371.1
12.	de Saint Phalle, Brigitte	USA	Pitts S-1S	12209.1
13.	Sulean, Maria	Romanian	Z-50 LA	11849.1
14.	Sábliková, Jana	Czech	Z-50 LA	11695.1
15.	Avramescu, Ludmila	Romanian	Z-50 LA	11313.5
16.	Lacour, Hélène	French	CAP 21	10683.9

*Denotes gold medallist in programme(s) shown in brackets

1984 – BÉKÉSCSABA, HUNGARY
Men's Championship

1.	Jirmus, Petr (1,2,3)*	Czech	Z-50 LS	16602.7
2.	Strössenreuther, Manfred	FRG	Z-50 LS	10288.1
3.	Weeks, Kermit (4)*	USA	Weeks Solution	16168.0
4.	Haigh, Henry	USA	Super Star	16000.1
5.	Smolin, Victor	USSR	Yak 55	15939.7
6.	Müller, Eric	Swiss	EA 230	15887.2
7.	Nikitiuk, Nikolai	USSR	Yak 55	15642.1
8.	Fry, Frank	Australian	Stephens Akro-Z	15639.2
9.	Bush, Alan	USA	Pitts S-1S	15554.2
10.	Chappell, Harold	USA	Pitts S-1S	15505.6
11.	Peña, Louis	French	CAP 21	15490.0
12.	Besenyei, Péter	Hungarian	Z-50 LA	15297.7
13.	Tóth, Lászlo	Hungarian	Z-50 LA	15266.1
14.	Paris, Patrick	French	CAP 21	15247.5
15.	Molnár, András	Hungarian	Z-50 LA	15232.5
16.	Čičo, Pavel	Czech	Z-50 LS	15097.1
17.	Saller, Jiří	Czech	Z-50 LS	15092.4
18.	Extra, Walter	FRG	EA 230	14967.5
19.	Srnec, Miroslav	Czech	Z-50 LS	14924.5
20.	Dallan, Sergio	Italian	CAP 21 DS	14895.5
21.	Selvey, Geoff	Australian	Pitts S-1E	14867.6
22.	Beggs, Gene	USA	Pitts S-1T	14766.6
23.	Muzergues, Georges	French	CAP 21	14704.0
24.	Kairis, Yurgis	USSR	Su 26	14694.8
25.	Sperou, Chris	Australian	Pitts S-1S	12819.2
26.	Kynscy, Peter	British	Pitts S-1T	12599.5
27.	Adrados, Fernando	Spanish	Z-50 LA	12578.1
28.	Marzetti, Tomaso	Italian	CAP 21	12479.4
29.	Bessière, Claude	French	CAP 21	12444.1
30.	Balatoni, József	Hungarian	Z-50 LA	12392.9
31.	Mitu, Marcel	Romanian	Z-50 LA	12370.8
32.	Zamfir, Valeriu	Romanian	Z-50 LA	12319.2
33.	Lesage, Christian	French	ASA 200	12303.9
34.	Shpigovsky, Alexandr	USSR	Su 26	12221.6
35.	Feteanu, Mielu	Romanian	Z-50 LA	12160.4
36.	Valle, Carlos	Spanish	Z-50 LA	12034.8
37.	Beard, Mal	Australian	Pitts S-1S	11963.4
38.	Diaconu, Ioan	Romanian	Z-50 LA	11946.9
39.	Pászti, Tibor	Hungarian	Z-50 LA	11767.6
40.	Paksas, Rolandas	USSR	Su 26	11695.0
41.	Cabre, Luis	Spanish	Z-50 LA	11432.2
42.	Harper, John	British	Pitts S-1T	11411.0
43.	Bianchi, Tony	British	CAP 20 LS	11137.9
44.	Colangelo, Nicola	Italian	EA 230	11006.0
45.	Graham, Roger	British	Pitts S-1D	10489.5
46.	Rossetti, Giorgio	Italian	CAP 21	9450.7
47.	Egger, Walter	Austrian	Pitts S-1S	4598.0
48.	Peroutka, Vladimír†	Czech	Z-50 LS	3471.2

*Denotes gold medallist in programme(s) shown in brackets
†Retired through illness

Flight Fantastic

Women's Championship

1.	Makagonova, Khalide (2,4)*	USSR	Yak 55	15001.9
2.	Nemkova, Liubov (3)*	USSR	Yak 55	14567.7
3.	Rihn, Debby	USA	Pitts S-1S	14508.9
4.	Jonita, Nina	Romanian	Z-50 LA	14148.9
5.	Manoury, Catherine	French	CAP 21	14140.2
6.	Meyers, Linda (1)*	USA	Weeks Special	13983.3
7.	Maire, Marianne	French	CAP 21	13929.0
8.	Yaikova, Valentina	USSR	Yak 55	13549.5
9.	Pfile, Julie	USA	Pitts S-1S	12056.9
10.	Sáblíková, Jana	Czech	Z-50 LA	11999.8
11.	Leonova, Lidia	USSR	Yak 55	11917.4
12.	de Saint Phalle, Brigitte	USA	Pitts S-1S	11521.0
13.	Adabash, Irina	USSR	Yak 55	11508.2
14.	Sulean, Maria	Romanian	Z-50 LA	11268.6
15.	Franckel-Lacour, Hélène	French	ASA 200	10924.3
16.	Coca, Elisaveta	Romanian	Z-50 LA	10300.1

*Denotes gold medallist in programme(s) shown in brackets

Appendix

2

Principal European aerobatic championships

1965 Biancotto Trophy, Dax, France
1. L. Bezák CSSR   2. E. Bläske GDR   3. G. Verette FRA
1967 Biancotto Trophy, Dax, France
1. N. Williams UK   2. P. Kahle GDR   3. I. Quintana SPA
1969 Biancotto Trophy, Dax, France
1. P. Kahle GDR   2. E. Bläske GDR   3. G. Börner GDR
1971 Biancotto Trophy, Carcasonne, France
1. J. Hoessl FRG   2. N. Holzberger FRG   3. C. Schweizer SWI
1973 Scandinavian Cup, Roskilde (Copenhagen), Denmark
1. C. Schweizer SWI   2. M. Jurk GDR   3. E. Müller SWI
1974 Biancotto Trophy, Rochefort, France
1. E. Müller SWI   2. V. Letsko USSR   3. J. Black UK
1975 1st European Championship, Esbjerg, Denmark
1. M. Strössenreuther FRG   2. C. Schweizer SWI   3. M. Brandt SWI
1977 2nd European Championship, Châteauroux, France
1. V. Letsko USSR   2. I. Tuček CSSR   3. E. Müller SWI
1981 3rd European Championship, Punitz, Austria
Men:
1. V. Smolin USSR   2. M. Strössenreuther FRG   3. J. Saller CSSR
Women:
1. V. Yaikova USSR   2. K. Makagonova USSR   3. L. Leonova USSR
1983 4th European Championship, Ravenna, Italy
Men:
1. P. Jirmus CSSR   2. M. Strössenreuther FRG   3. V. Smolin USSR
Women:
1. V. Yaikova USSR   2. K. Makagonova USSR   3. L. Leonova USSR
1985 5th European Championship, České Budějovice, CSSR
Men:
1. P. Jirmus CSSR   2. M. Strössenreuther FRG   3. E. Müller SWI
Women:
1. V. Yaikova USSR   2. K. Makagonova USSR   3. M. Maire FRA

Appendix

3

Socialist countries aerobatic championships

1963 USSR, Moscow (7 countries, 27 men and 3 women)
  1. V. Loichikov USSR   2. B. Chernov USSR   3. V. Pochernin USSR
1965 Poland, Łodz (5 countries, 27 contestants)
  1. V. Ovsyankin USSR   2. J. Tóth HU   3. S. Kasperek HU
1971 USSR, Orel
  1. V. Ponomaryov USSR   2. I. Egorov USSR   3. A. Pimenov USSR
1972 Czechoslovakia, Nyitra
  1. I. Tuček CSSR   2. A. Pimenov USSR   3. J. Kobrle CSSR
1973 GDR, Karl-Marx-Stadt
  1. E. Bläske GDR   2. I. Egorov USSR   3. J. Kobrle CSSR
1974 Hungary, Békéscsaba (5 countries, 22 men and 8 women)
  1. V. Letsko USSR   2. S. Kruglikov USSR   3. I. Tuček CSSR
1975 USSR, Kiev (5 countries, 27 men and 14 women)
  1. E. Frolov USSR   2. V. Letsko USSR   3. S. Kruglikov USSR
1976 Czechoslovakia, Mlada Boleslav (4 countries, 23 men and 6 women)
  1. I. Tuček CSSR   2. V. Letsko USSR   3. M. Molchaniuk USSR
1977 USSR, Kiev (5 countries, 24 men and 6 women)
  1. I. Egorov USSR   2. I. Tuček CSSR   3. V. Smolin USSR
1978 Poland, Radom (6 countries, 29 men and 4 women)
  1. I. Tuček CSSR   2. V. Letsko USSR   3. Y. Kairis USSR
1979 Hungary, Békéscsaba (7 countries, 32 men and 8 women)
  1. J. Pospíšil CSSR   2. E. Frolov USSR   3. Y. Kairis USSR
1980 GDR, Karl-Marx-Stadt (5 countries, 22 men and 7 women)
  1. S. Artishkyavichius USSR   2. Y. Kairis USSR   3. V. Smolin USSR
1981 CSSR, České Budějovice (6 countries, 31 men and 12 women)
  1. E. Frolov USSR   2. N. Nikitiuk USSR   3. V. Smolin USSR
1983 USSR, Vilnius (6 countries, 19 men and 7 women)
  1. N. Nikitiuk USSR   2. V. Smolin USSR   3. P. Jirmus CSSR
1985 USSR, Kiev (5 countries, 25 men and 12 women)
  1. P. Jirmus CSSR   2. V. Smolin USSR   3. Y. Kairis USSR

Index and Bibliography

Flight Fantastic

Berriman, A H – **Aviation** (Methuen 1913)
Bingham, Hiram – **An Explorer in the Air Service** (Yale University Press 1920)
Bishop, W A – **Winged Warfare** (Hodder & Stoughton 1918)
Blanc, Edmond – **L'Aviation des Temps Modernes** (Larousse 1953)
Bonnefon, M P – **Le Premier As Pégoud** (Berger-Levrault, Paris 1918)
Bowyer, Chaz – **Sopwith Camel – King of Combat** (Glasney Press 1978)
Bramson, Alan & Birch, Neville – **The Tiger Moth Story** (Airlife 1964/1982)
Brandley, Ray – **Taperwing Wacos** (National Waco Club)
Casey, Lewis S – **Curtiss: The Hammondsport Era** (Crown Publishers 1981)
Cobham, Alan – **A Time to Fly** (Shepheard-Walwyn 1978)
Courtney, Frank T – **Flight Path** (William Kimber 1973)
Cynk, Jerzy – **Polish Aircraft 1893–1939** (Putnam 1971)
Deighton, Len – **Fighter** (Jonathan Cape 1977)
Détroyat, Michel – **Pilote d'Acrobatie** (Hachette 1957)
Doret, Marcel – **Trait d'Union avec le Ciel** (France-Empire 1954)
Dorman, Geoffrey – **British Test Pilots** (Forbes Robertson 1950)
Duke, Neville – **Test Pilot** (Allan Wingate 1953)
Duncan, Richard – **Stunt Flying** (Crosby, Lockwood & Son 1930)
Dunn, William R – **Fighter Pilot** (University Press of Kentucky 1982)
Dwiggins, Don – **The Barnstormers** (Tab Books 1981)
Ethell, Jeffrey – **Mustang** (Jane's Publishing Company 1981)
Fieseler, Gerhard – **Meine Bahn am Himmel** (Bertelsmann Verlag 1979)
Fokker, A H G – **Flying Dutchman** (Routledge 1931)
Garros, Roland – **Guide de l'aviateur** (Pierre Lafitte 1913)
Gilbert, James – **The Great Planes** (Grosset & Dunlap 1970)
Glines, C V – **Jimmy Doolittle** (Macmillan 1972)
Grahame-White, Claude & Harper, Harry – **The Aeroplane** (Michael Joseph)
Grahame-White, Claude & Harper, Harry – **Heroes of the Air** (H Frowde 1911)
Grahame-White, Claude & Harper, Harry – **With the Airmen** (Milford, OUP)
Hadingham, Evan – **The Fighting Triplanes** (Hamish Hamilton 1968)
Hamel, Gustav & Turner, C C – **Flying: Some Practical Experiences** (Longmans, Green
    & Co 1914)
Harper, Harry – **Lords of the Air** (Lutterworth Press 1940)
Harper, Harry – **My Fifty Years of Flying** (Associated Newspapers 1956)
de Havilland, Geoffrey – **Sky Fever** (Airlife 1979)
Hawker, Muriel – **H G Hawker: Airman** (Hutchinson 1922)

Henshaw, Alex – **Sigh for a Merlin** (John Murray 1979)
Herlin, Hans – **Udet: A Man's Life** (Macdonald 1960)
Immelmann, Franz – **Immelmann: The Eagle of Lille** (Greenhill Books 1984)
van Ishoven, Armand – **The Fall of an Eagle** (William Kimber, 1979)
Jerram, Mike – **The World's Classic Aircraft** (Frederick Muller 1981)
Johns, W E – **Biggles: The White Fokker**, etc. (Dean & Son)
Johnson, Howard – **Wings Over Brooklands** (Whittet Books 1981)
Jones, Mel R – **Above and Beyond: Eight Great American Aerobatic Champions**
    (Tab Books 1984)
Jouhaud, Reginald – **Stampe SV4** (Editions Ouest-France 1981)
Krier, Harold – **Modern Aerobatics & Precision Flying** (Tab Books 1963)
Lewis, Cecil – **Sagittarius Rising** (P Davies 1936)
Liardon, Francis – **Technique de vol** (Office Federal d'Aviation Civile, Berne, 1983)
Lloyd, Tony – **The Lockheed Aerobatic Trophy** (Midland Counties 1976)
McCudden, James – **Five Years in the RFC** (Aeroplane & General 1918)
McMinnies, W G – **Practical Flying** (Temple Press 1918)
Miller, H C – **Early Birds** (Angus & Robertson 1968)
Moore, W G – **Early Bird** (Putnam 1963)
Müller, Eric and Carson, Annette – **Flight Unlimited** (Müller/Carson 1983)
Penrose, Harald – **British Aviation, The Pioneer Years** (Putnam 1967)
Pixton, C Howard – **The Brooklands Story** (A V Roe & Co 1955)
Pletschacher, Peter – **Deutsche Sport Flugzeuge** (Motorbook Verlag 1977)
Pudney, John – **A Pride of Unicorns** (Oldbourne 1960)
Quellennec, Jacques – **Memoires de Roland Garros** (Hachette 1966)
Quill, Jeffrey – **Spitfire: A Test Pilot's Story** (John Murray 1983)
RAF Museum Series – **Fighting in the Air** (Arms & Armour Press 1978)
Rhode, Bill – **Baling Wire, Chewing Gum and Guts** (Kennikat Press 1970)
Robertson, Bruce – **Air Aces of the 1914–18 War** (Letchworth 1959)
Robertson, Bruce – **Fighter Aircraft of the 1914–18 War** (Letchworth 1959)
Rocchi, R – **La Meravigliosa Avventura** (Edizioni Bizzarri 1976)
Schmid, S H and Weaver, T C – **The Golden Age of Air Racing** (EAA Aviation
    Foundation 1983)
Shamburger, Page and Christy, Joe – **Curtiss Hawks** (Wolverine Press 1972)
Sims, Edward H – **Fighter Pilots and Strategy 1914/1970** (Cassell 1972)
Smith, Constance Babington – **Testing Time** (Cassell 1961)
Spick, Mike – **Fighter Pilot Tactics** (Patrick Stephens 1983)

Flight Fantastic

Springs, Elliott White – **Diary of an Unknown Aviator** (Hamilton 1927)
Stewart, Oliver – **Aerobatics** (Faber 1928)
Stewart, Oliver – **First Flights** (Routledge & Kegan Paul 1957)
Stewart, Oliver – **Words and Music for a Mechanical Man** (Faber 1967)
Sweet, Bill – **They Call Me Mr Airshow** (Ken Cook Transnational 1972)
Taylor, J W R – **C F S: Birthplace of Air Power** (Putnam 1958)
Townsend, Peter – **Duel of Eagles** (Weidenfeld & Nicolson 1970)
Udet, Ernst – **Ein Fliegerleben** (Motorbuch Velag 1954)
Underwood, John – **Acrobats in the Sky** (Heritage Press 1972)
Underwood, John – **The Stinsons** (Heritage Press 1969)
Verdon-Roe, Alliott – **The World of Wings and Things** (Hurst & Blackett 1939)
Wagner, Arnold – **Handbuch des Kunstflugs** (Walter Zuerl 1973)
Weyl, A R – **Fokker: The Creative Years** (Putnam 1965)
Whitehouse, Arch – **The Early Birds** (Thomas Nelson 1965)

Williams, Neil – **Aerobatics** (Airlife 1975)
Williams, Neil – **Airborne** (Airlife 1977)
Wheeler, Allen – **Building Aeroplanes for 'Those Magnificent Men'** (G T Foulis & Co 1965)
Wheeler, Allen – **Flying Between The Wars** (G T Foulis & Co 1972)
Yakovlev, Alexander – **Notes of an Aircraft Designer** (Arno Press 1972)

Magazines, journals etc.:

L'Aéro, Aéro France, Aeronautics, L'Aérophile, The Aeroplane, Aerokurier, Aéro Revue, Les Ailes, Air-Britain Digest, Air International, Air Progress, Air Trails, Aviasport, British Aerobatic Association Newsletter, Car Illustrated, Deutsche Luftwacht, Flight, Flying, Icare, Letectvi & Kosmonautika, National Aeronautcis, Pilot, Le Pionnier, Popular Aviation, Royal Aeronautical Society Journal, Repüles, Sport Aerobatics, Sport Aviation, Tiger Rag, Le Trait d'Union.

This painting, by Lynn Williams, was specially commissioned to appear on the cover of Flight Fantastic. In it are depicted thirty individual aircraft which, together with their pilots, have a special place in the history of aerobatics.

1. Sukhoi Su 26 (USSR)
2. Stephens Akro (USA)
3. Yak 50 (USSR)
4. Zlin 50 (Czech)
5. Southern Martlet (UK)
6. Blackburn Lincock (UK)
7. Sopwith F-1 Camel (UK)
8. Liesel Bach's Raka 26 Tigerschwalbe (Ger)
9. Tex Rankin's Great Lakes 2T-1A (USA)
10. Fiat CR 32 (Ital)
11. Gerhard Fieseler's Raab-Katzenstein KL 1b Schwalbe (Ger)
12. Józef Orłowski's PWS Special (Pol)
13. British Team Zlin 526A (Czech)
14. Ilsa Festenrath's Fieseler F5 (Ger)
15. Willy Stor's Messerschmitt M35 (Ger)
16. Bücker Bü 131A Jungmann (Ger)
17. Bücker Bü 133V-1 Jungmeister prototype (Ger)
18. Graf von Hagenburg's Bücker Bü 133 (Ger)
19. Finnish Focke-Wulf Fw44 Stieglitz (Ger)
20. Belgian Fokker D-VII (Ger)
21. Fieseler's F2 Tiger (Ger)
22. Frantisek Malkowsky's Avia BH 21 (Czech)
23. Blériot-Spad 25 (Fr)
24. Morane-Saulnier 225 C 1 (Fr)
25. Marcel Doret's Dewoitine 530 (Fr)
26. Pitts S-2A (USA)
27. Harold Krier's Great Lakes 2T-1A Special (USA)
28. Freddie Lund's Waco CTO Taperwing (USA)
29. Udet's U12 Flamingo (Ger)
30. Tiger Club Stampe SV4b (Belg)

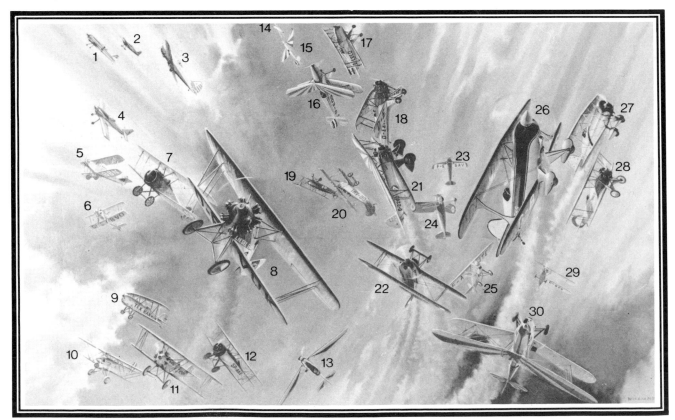